DATE DUE

DEMCO 38-296

The Ambassadors and America's Soviet Policy

The
Ambassadors
and America's
Soviet Policy

David Mayers

New York   Oxford

OXFORD UNIVERSITY PRESS

1995

Oxford University Press

Oxford   New York
Athens   Auckland   Bangkok   Bombay
Calcutta   Cape Town   Dar es Salaam   Delhi
Florence   Hong Kong   Istanbul   Karachi
Kuala Lumpur   Madras   Madria   Melbourne
Mexico City   Nairobi   Paris   Singapore
Taipei   Tokyo   Toronto

and associated companies in
Berlin   Ibadan

Copyright © 1995 by Oxford University Press, Inc.

Published by Oxford University Press, Inc.,
200 Madison Avenue, New York, New York 10016

Oxford is a registered trademark of Oxford University Press

Library of Congress Cataloging-in-Publication Data
Mayers, David Allan
The ambassadors and America's Soviet policy/David Mayers.
p. cm.   Includes bibliographical references and index.
ISBN 0-19-506802-5
1. United States—Foreign relations—Soviet Union.
2. Soviet Union—Foreign relations—United States.
3. Ambassadors—United States—History—20th century.
4. Ambassadors—Soviet Union—History—20th century.
I. Title.   E183.8.S65M373   1995
327.73047—dc20   94-30032

1 3 5 7 9 8 6 4 2

Printed in the United States of America
on acid-free paper

The Ambassadors and America's Soviet Policy

David Mayers

New York   Oxford

OXFORD UNIVERSITY PRESS

1995

Oxford University Press

Oxford   New York
Athens   Auckland   Bangkok   Bombay
Calcutta   Cape Town   Dar es Salaam   Delhi
Florence   Hong Kong   Istanbul   Karachi
Kuala Lumpur   Madras   Madria   Melbourne
Mexico City   Nairobi   Paris   Singapore
Taipei   Tokyo   Toronto

and associated companies in
Berlin   Ibadan

Library of Congress Cataloging-in-Publication Data
Mayers, David Allan
The ambassadors and America's Soviet policy/David Mayers.
p. cm.   Includes bibliographical references and index.
ISBN 0-19-506802-5
1. United States—Foreign relations—Soviet Union.
2. Soviet Union—Foreign relations—United States.
3. Ambassadors—United States—History—20th century.
4. Ambassadors—Soviet Union—History—20th century.
I. Title.   E183.8.S65M373   1995
327.73047—dc20   94-30032

1 3 5 7 9 8 6 4 2

Printed in the United States of America
on acid-free paper

To my son, Peter

PREFACE

Whether or no he had a grand idea of the lucid, he held that nothing ever was in fact . . . explained. One went through the vain motions, but it was mostly a waste of life.

Henry James, *The Ambassadors*

This book occupies a point of intersection for several analytical concerns. First and rather narrowly, this study belongs to the category of bureaucratic history. As such, it tells the story of those U.S officials most intimately involved with the Soviet Union: ambassadors in Moscow. Their appointments, place in the foreign policy hierarchy, and reporting are scrutinized here. Second, this book is concerned with the American response to life in the USSR as it evolved during seven and a half decades. Literature on this subject has emphasized the impact of the Soviet Union on the imagination and experience of disaffected Americans drawn to the promise of socialist justice. Comparatively little, however, has been written on the reaction of U.S. envoys during successive stages of Soviet history from Lenin and Stalin to Gorbachev. Finally and most important, the book examines Soviet–U.S. relations and Cold War diplomacy from an angle that has received insubstantial scholarly attention—the embassy in Moscow.

Each of the book's sections is assembled in a distinctive way that indicates something about its objectives and comprehensiveness. The first part, dealing with pre-1933, amounts to an extended introduction and depends largely on materials of a secondary nature: memoir literature, other scholars' research, published government documents such as the estimable *Foreign Relations of the United States* series, and a moderate number of primary documents. The second part, corresponding with Stalin in power, constitutes the core of the book. It depends on the same type of materials mentioned, but the proportions of mix are changed in favor of primary sources from such repositories as the Library of Congress, National Archives, Hoover Institution, and presidential libraries. The third section, on the post-Stalin era, is handicapped by problems familiar to writers of contemporary history: a lack of perspective and inadequate access to major collections. The vagaries of the federal government's declassification procedure are surpassed only by that confusion reigning in many archives of the former Soviet Union. The third part necessarily hinges on sources of an uneven and elusive type: memoir litera-ture, newspaper and journal articles, oral histories, and interviews.

Not everyone whom I approached for an interview granted one. I say this without rancor but to emphasize my gratitude to those people who let me impose upon their time and patience. These men and women are named in the interview and correspondence section of the bibliography.

Three institutions generously supported me in the course of writing. Fellow-ships enabling me to take academic leaves and to travel to archival collections came from Boston University, Hoover Institution at Stanford University, and the John M. Olin Foundation. My stay as a visiting scholar at Hoover was exception-ally pleasant.

Professional associations allowed me to make presentations of my work in progress. I gladly acknowledge the help I received from Brown University's Wat-son Institute for International Studies, the European International Studies Confer-ence in Heidelberg, Harvard University's Russian Research Center, the Society for Historians of American Foreign Relations (SHAFR), the University of Southern California's Center for International Studies, and the U.S. Naval War College. Portions of chapters were originally published in slightly different form. Much of Chapter 4 appeared as "Preparing for Moscow: Training U.S. Diplomats and the Dilemmas of Recognition," *Brown Foreign Affairs Journal* (Winter 1992); part of Chapter 5 as "Ambassador Joseph Davies Reconsidered," *SHAFR Newsletter* (September 1992); Chapter 8 as "After Stalin: The Ambassadors and America's Soviet Policy, 1953–1962," *Diplomacy and Statecraft* (July 1994).

Again, it was a pleasure to work with the editorial staff at Oxford University Press. I want to thank Valerie Aubry and David Roll, in particular, for their courtesy and encouragement.

I do not want to implicate any of the following people in this book's shortcom-ings, either interpretative or factual. Still, the criticism and advice of these friends and colleagues were crucial: George Baer, Philip Bayer, Vladimir Brovkin, Walter Clemens, Stephanie Fawcett, Irene Gendzier, Norman Graebner, William Green, Wendy Hazard, Stephen Jones, William Keylor, Murray Levin, Igor Lukes, Ste-ven Lyne, Richard Melanson, Charles Neu, Arnold Offner, Lucian Pye, Christine Rossell, Mauki Satzger, Robert Schulzinger, the late Paul Seabury, Mark Silver-stein, Michael Joseph Smith. Special thanks to Walter Connor and Hermann Eilts.

While on a memorable faculty exchange in St. Petersburg (then Leningrad) and Moscow, I conceived the idea of writing this book in conversations with Peter Kenez. Since then, he has read every chapter, saved me from egregious errors, and urged me to reflect on views that he found untenable.

Once more, despite demands from her professional career, my wife, Elizabeth, has provided invaluable assistance as editor par excellence.

Our son, Peter, did not contribute directly to this took. But he added joy to the years of its writing.

Newton, Mass.   D. M.
April 1994

CONTENTS

United States Chiefs of Mission in St. Petersburg and Moscow, xi
Introduction, 3

I   Before Moscow

1. St. Petersburg and the U.S. Diplomatic Tradition, 11
2. From Comity to Estrangement, 35
3. War and Revolution, 67

I I   In Stalin's Time

4. Preparing for Moscow, 93
5. Purges and the Failure of Collective Security, 108
6. Fragile Coalition, 136
7. Neither War Nor Peace, 164

I I I   Great Power Rivalry

8. After Stalin, 191
9. Controlled Rivalry, 212
10. Collapse and the Art of Diplomacy, 239

Notes, 261
Bibliography, 307
Index, 323

United States Chiefs of Mission in St. Petersburg and Moscow, 1780–1992[1]

Name	Res.	Career	Title	Appointment	Pres. of Cred.	Term. of Mission
Francis Dana[2]	Mass.		Min	19 Dec. 1780		
William Short[3]	Va.		MP	8 Sept. 1808[r]		
John Quincy Adams[4]	Mass.		MP	27 June 1809	5 Nov. 1809	Left post, 28 Apr. 1814
James A. Bayard[5]	Del.		EE/MP	28 Feb. 1815		Left post on or soon after 14 Feb. 1818
William Pinkney	Md.		EE/MP	7 Mar. 1816	13 Jan. 1817	
George Washington Campbell	Tenn.		EE/MP	16 Apr. 1818	7 Feb. 1819	Left post, 8 July 1820
Henry Middleton	S.C.		EE/MP	6 Apr. 1820	17 June 1821	Left post on or soon after 3 Aug. 1830
John Randolph[6]	Va.		EE/MP	26 May 1830	11 June 1832	Presented recall, 5 Aug. 1833
James Buchanan	Pa.		EE/MP	4 Jan. 1832		
Mahlon Dickerson[7]	N.J.		EE/MP	28 May 1834		
William Wilkins	Pa.		EE/MP	30 June 1834	14 Dec. 1834	Left post, 24 Dec. 1835
John Randolph Clay	Pa.		CdA	29 June 1836	2 Sept. 1836	Left post, 5 Aug. 1837
George M. Dallas	Pa.		EE/MP	7 Mar. 1837	6 Aug. 1837	Left Russia, 29 July 1839
Churchill C. Cambreleng	N.Y.		EE/MP	[25 May 1840[8]]	21 Sept. 1840	Presented recall, 13 July 1841
Charles S. Todd	Ky.		EE/MP	27 Aug. 1841	28 Nov. 1841	Presented recall, 27 Jan. 1846
Ralph I. Ingersoll	Conn.		EE/MP	8 Aug. 1846	30 May 1847	Left post, 1 July 1848
Arthur P. Bagby	Ala.		EE/MP	15 June 1848	14 Jan. 1849	Transmitted recall by note soon after 14 May 1849
Neill S. Brown	Tenn.		EE/MP	2 May 1850	13 Aug. 1850	Presented recall, 23 June 1853
Thomas H. Seymour	Conn.		EE/MP	24 May 1853[r]		Recommissioned after confirmation
				6 Dec. 1853	2 Apr. 1854	Presented recall, 17 July 1858
Francis W. Pickens	S.C.		EE/MP	11 Jan. 1858	18 July 1858	Presented recall, 9 Sept. 1860
John Appleton	Me.		EE/MP	8 June 1860	9 Sept. 1860	Left post, 8 June 1861
Cassius M. Clay	Ky.		EE/MP	28 Mar. 1861	14 July 1861	Presented recall, 25 June 1862
Simon Cameron	Pa.		EE/MP	17 Jan. 1862	25 June 1862	Left post on or soon after 18 Sept. 1862
Cassius M. Clay	Ky.		EE/MP	11 Mar. 1863	7 May 1863	Relinquished charge, 1 Oct. 1869
John L. Dawson[9]	Pa.		EE/MP			

Name	State		Rank			Notes
Henry A. Smythe [10]	N.Y.		EE/MP	16 Apr. 1869	28 Oct. 1869	Presented recall on or shortly before 1 July 1872
Andrew G. Curtin	Pa.		EE/MP			
James L. Orr	S.C.		EE/MP	12 Dec. 1872	18 Mar. 1873	Died at post, 6 May 1873
Marshall Jewell	Conn.		EE/MP	29 May 1873^r 10 Dec. 1873	9 Dec. 1873	Recommissioned after confirmation Left post, 19 July 1874
George H. Boker	Pa.		EE/MP	13 Jan. 1875	24 July 1875	Superseded, 14 Jan. 1878
Edwin W. Stoughton	N.Y.		EE/MP	30 Oct. 1877	14 Jan. 1878	Left post, 2 Mar. 1879
John W. Foster	Ind.		EE/MP	26 Jan. 1880	11 June 1880	Relinquished charge, 1 Aug. 1881
William H. Hunt	La.		EE/MP	12 Apr. 1882	23 Aug. 1882	Died at post, 27 Feb. 1884
Aaron H. Sargent [11]	Cal.		EE/MP			
Alphonso Taft	O.		EE/MP	4 July 1884	3 Sept. 1884	Presented recall, 31 July 1885
Alexander R. Lawton [12]	Ga.		EE/MP			Recommissioned after confirmation
George V. N. Lothrop	Mich.		EE/MP	7 May 1885^r 13 Jan. 1886	31 July 1885	Presented recall, 1 Aug. 1888
Lambert Tree	Ill.		EE/MP	25 Sept. 1888	4 Jan. 1889	Left post, 2 Feb. 1889
Allen Thorndike Rice [13]	N.Y.		EE/MP	30 Mar. 1889		
Charles Emory Smith	Pa.		EE/MP	14 Feb. 1890	14 May 1890	Left post, 17 Apr. 1892
Andrew D. White	N.Y.		EE/MP	22 July 1892	7 Nov. 1892	Relinquished charge, 1 Oct. 1894
Clifton R. Breckinridge	Ark.		EE/MP	20 July 1894	[1 Nov. 1894^14]	Probably presented recall about 10 Dec. 1897
Ethan A. Hitchcock	Mo.		EE/MP	16 Aug. 1897^r 18 Dec. 1897	16 Dec. 1897	Recommissioned after confirmation Promoted to AE/P
Charlemagne Tower	Pa.		AE/P	11 Feb. 1898	21 Mar. 1898	Presented recall, 28 Jan. 1899
Robert S. McCormick	Ill		AE/P	12 Jan. 1899 26 Sept. 1902^r 8 Dec. 1902	19 Mar. 1899	Presented recall, 19 Nov. 1902 Recommissioned after confirmation
George v.L. Meyer	Mass.		AE/P	8 Mar. 1905	12 Jan. 1903	Presented recall, 27 Mar. 1905
John W. Riddle	Minn.		AE/P	19 Dec. 1906	12 Apr. 1905	Presented recall, 26 Jan. 1907
William Woodville Rockhill	D.C.		AE/P	17 May 1909	8 Feb. 1907	Left post, 8 Sept. 1909
Curtis Guild	Mass.		AE/P	24 Apr. 1911	11 Jan. 1910	Presented recall, 17 June 1911
Henry M. Pindell [15]	Ill.		AE/P	27 Jan. 1914	17 Aug. 1911	Left post, 24 Apr. 1913
George T. Marye	Cal.	NC	AE/P	9 July 1914	30 Oct. 1914	Left post, 29 Mar. 1916

United States Chiefs of Mission in St. Petersburg and Moscow, 1780–1992[1] (*Continued*)

Name	Res.	Career	Title	Appointment	Pres. of Cred.	Term. of Mission
David R. Francis	Mo.	NC	AE/P	6 Mar. 1916	5 May 1916	Normal relations interrupted, 7 Nov. 1917; new Govt. of Russia still unrecognized by the U.S. when Francis left Russia, 7 Nov. 1918[16]
William Christian Bullitt	Pa.	NC	AE/P	21 Nov. 1933ᶠ / 15 Jan. 1934	13 Dec. 1933	Recommissioned after confirmation / Left Soviet Union, 16 May 1936
Joseph E. Davies	D.C.	NC	AE/P	16 Nov. 1936ᶠ / 23 Jan. 1937	25 Jan. 1937	Recommissioned after confirmation
Laurence A. Steinhardt	N.Y.	NC	AE/P	23 Mar. 1939	11 Aug. 1939	Left post, 11 June 1938
William H. Standley	Cal.	NC	AE/P	14 Feb. 1942	14 Apr. 1942	Left post, 12 Nov. 1941
W. Averell Harriman	N.Y.	NC	AE/P	7 Oct. 1943	23 Oct. 1943	Left post, 19 Sept. 1943
Walter Bedell Smith		NC	AE/P	22 Mar. 1946	3 Apr. 1946	Left post, 24 Jan. 1946
Alan G. Kirk		NC	AE/P	21 May 1949	4 July 1949	Left post, 25 Dec. 1948
George F. Kennan	Pa.	C	AE/P	14 Mar. 1952	14 May 1952	Left post, 6 Oct. 1951
Charles E. Bohlen	D.C.	C	AE/P	27 Mar. 1953	20 Apr. 1953	Left post, 19 Sept. 1952[17]
Llewellyn E. Thompson	Colo.	C	AE/P	3 June 1957	16 July 1957	Left post, 18 Apr. 1957
Foy D. Kohler	O.	C	AE/P	20 Aug. 1962	27 Sept. 1962	Left post, 27 July 1962
Llewellyn E. Thompson	Colo.	C	AE/P	13 Oct. 1966	23 Jan. 1967	Left post, 14 Nov. 1966
Jacob D. Beam	N.J.	C	AE/P	14 Mar. 1969	18 Apr. 1969	Left post, 14 Jan. 1969
Walter J. Stoessel, Jr.	Cal.	C	AE/P	19 Dec. 1973	4 Mar. 1974	Left post, 24 Jan. 1973[18]
Malcolm Toon	N.Y.	C	AE/P	24 Nov. 1976ᶠ / 8 June 1977	18 Jan. 1977	Left post, 13 Sept. 1976
Thomas J. Watson, Jr.	Conn.	NC	AE/P	10 Oct. 1979	29 Oct. 1979	Recommissioned after confirmation / Left post, 16 Oct. 1979
Arthur Adair Hartman	Md.	C	AE/P	28 Sept. 1981	26 Oct. 1981	Left post, 15 Jan. 1981
Jack F. Matlock	Fla.	C	AE/P	12 Mar. 1987	6 Apr. 1987	Left post, 20 Feb. 1987
Robert S. Strauss	Tex.	NC	AE/P	2 Aug. 1991	24 Aug. 1991	Left post, 11 Aug. 1991
						Left post, 19 Nov. 1992

[1]Representatives from Dana to Francis were commissioned to Russia; those from Bullitt to Strauss have been commissioned to the Union of Soviet Socialist Republics.
[2]Proceeded to post, but was not officially received at court; left post, Sept. 1783.
[3]Did not proceed to post, his nomination having been rejected by the Senate while he was en route.

[4] Nomination of 6 Mar 1809 rejected by the Senate; nomination of 26 June 1809 confirmed.

[5] Did not proceed to post.

[6] Proceeded to post, but did not present credentials; left post, 19 Sept. 1830.

[7] Declined appointment.

[8] Commission not of record; letter of credence issued on this date.

[9] Not commissioned; nomination rejected by the Senate.

[10] Not commissioned; nomination tabled by the Senate.

[11] Not commissioned although nomination was confirmed by the Senate.

[12] Not commissioned; nomination withdrawn before the Senate acted upon it.

[13] Took oath of office, but died in the U.S. before proceeding to post.

[14] Officially recognized on this date.

[15] Declined appointment.

[16] Felix Cole was serving as Chargé d'Affaires ad interim when the Embassy in Russia was closed, 14 Sept. 1919.

[17] The Govt. of the Soviet Union declared Kennan persona non grata 3 Oct. 1952, and he did not return to his post.

[18] Adolph Dubs served as Chargé d'Affaires ad interim, Jan. 1973-Mar. 1974.

Key: Min, Minister; MP, Minister Plenipotentiary; EE/MP, Envoy Extraordinary and Minister Plenipotentiary; CdA, Chargé d'Affaires; AE/P, Ambassador Extraordinary and Plenipotentiary; NC, Noncareer Appointee; C, Career Foreign Service Officer

Source: United States Department of State, Principal Officers of the Department of State and Chiefs of Mission 1778–1988 (Washington, D.C., 1988).

The Ambassadors and America's Soviet Policy

INTRODUCTION

I

This book has two overarching aims. The first is to make a contribution to understanding the formation and execution of U.S. policy toward the Soviet Union. The book takes as its point of reference the diplomatic mission in Moscow and tells the history of official Americans residing there. These included distinguished interpreters of the Soviet scene, some of whom played vital roles in policymaking, particularly Charles Bohlen, W. Averell Harriman, George Kennan, Jack Matlock, and Llewellyn Thompson. In their different ways, figures such as William Bullitt and Joseph Davies were also significant.

Second, this book argues for the primacy of diplomacy—as an attitude toward international life and as the organizing principle for effective policy. In this connection, two types of diplomacy must be contrasted at the outset. The first is high diplomacy. It involves the most elevated levels of government in the nonviolent settlement of conflicts between powers. Kings, presidents, other potentates, and foreign ministers seek national advantage through negotiation with allies and adversaries. Above these encounters hover the stubborn facts of international life: the distribution of military power, the strength of national economies, and the cohesion of competing societies. In this arena of high diplomacy, statecraft can produce triumph, as in Bismarck's 1878 Berlin Congress, whose main lines of settlement lasted for thirty years. In this same arena, weak leadership presides over failure, as in Woodrow Wilson and the unsustainable Versailles peace of 1919. It was high diplomacy that Winston Churchill had in mind in 1948 when he uttered this hope for ending the Cold War: "With all consideration of the facts, I believe it right to say . . . that the best chance of avoiding war is . . . to bring matters to a head with the Soviet Government, and, by formal diplomatic processes, with all their privacy and gravity, to arrive at a lasting settlement."[1]

The second type of diplomacy exists at a less exalted level. It involves ambassadors and professional staffs, who represent the views of their government to their hosts and otherwise concentrate on political reporting. In recent years, ambassadorial diplomacy has been neglected by scholars who have been impressed by the envoy's declining importance. As foreign ministries and even heads of state communicate directly with one another, the routines of the ambassadorial office have come to seem ancillary, if not superfluous. However, this has not always been the case. To assume it in America's Soviet policy would lead to faulty historical understanding and, by extension, to misleading prescriptions for the post–Cold War world.

Ambassadorial diplomacy was crucial in determining national success during the four most important moments in Soviet–U.S. history: the Grand Alliance corresponding with Harriman; the early Cold War corresponding with Kennan's Long Telegram; the 1962 Cuban missile crisis and Thompson's participation in Kennedy's deliberations; and the collapse of Soviet power during Matlock's tenure in Moscow. Conversely, mediocre (or worse) ambassadorial diplomacy was injurious to the United States. At the birth of Soviet power, a bewildered David Francis groped to make sense of Bolshevism and the October revolution. He remained as unenlightened as Wilson's government, which looked in vain to him for some guidance on the subject. Nor was it an idle curiosity or an indifferent episode when Davies helped confuse the American public about the nature of the Soviet regime during World War II. Notwithstanding Kennan's distinguished services (of which the Long Telegram was but an instance), his bungling as ambassador in 1952 complicated Soviet–U.S. relations at a time when Dean Acheson was trying to gain Moscow's cooperation in ending the Korean War. American interpretation of the Soviet invasion of Afghanistan in December 1979 was not materially aided by Thomas Watson. Only intervention by his professional staff saved matters, thereby helping to restore ambassadorial diplomacy to its proper place—an ingredient essential to the success of international policy.

II

An engaging literature examines the perceptions and experience of unofficial Americans in the Soviet Union. Paul Hollander's *Political Pilgrims* is a fine example of this genre. But with the exception of Hugh De Santis's *The Diplomacy of Silence* (which covers only the years 1933 to 1947), scholarship about U.S. diplomats—the quality of their political reporting, their adjustment to Soviet life, their contact with other missions in Moscow, their influence on Washington's foreign policy—has been sparse and not always especially good.[2] In *The Ambassadors,* I hope to fill a gap in the history of U.S. policymaking and to assess its merits and flaws applied to the Soviet case. At the same time, this study allows for an overall evaluation of diplomacy and its place in national life.

As an element in America's policy establishment and practice, ambassadorial diplomacy has not enjoyed universal appreciation. To many observers, both within the United States and without, ambassadorial diplomacy has been hobbled by amateurism and a lack of sturdy standards. These defects are exemplified by the presidential practice of appointing favorites from outside the professional corps to distant capitals. British observer Harold Nicolson has given this acid, but by no means untypical, critique:

> Amateur diplomatists [as frequently in the U.S. case] are prone to prove unreliable. It is not merely that their lack of knowledge and experience may be of disadvantage to their governments, it is that the amateur diplomatist is apt out of vanity and owing to the shortness of his tenure to seek for rapid successes; that he tends, owing to diffidence, to be oversuspicious; that he is inclined to be far too zealous and to have bright ideas; that he has not acquired the humane and tolerant disbelief which is the product of a long diplomatic career and is often assailed by convictions, sympathies, even impulses; that he may arrive with a righteous contempt for the formalities of diplomacy and with some impatience of its conventions; that he may cause offense when he wishes only to inspire geniality; and that in his reports and dispatches he may seek rather to display his own acumen and literary brilliance than to provide his government with a careful and sensible balance-sheet of facts.[3]

Moreover, as various analysts have decried, the U.S. diplomat is rarely esteemed by his compatriots. They question his political loyalty, attribute all manner of foreign (that is to say, effete and obnoxious) tastes and habits to him, and are likely to charge him with harboring elitist, antidemocratic sentiments. Not only is he a recurrent object of caricature in popular American culture, depicted as a "cookie pusher" in pinstripes, but diplomacy itself is often disparaged by extension. This trend has been reinforced as diplomacy has been superseded in the twentieth century by eruptions of vast international violence and tension (i.e., World Wars I and II, the Cold War) and as national leaders have bypassed classical diplomacy's forms in favor of more dramatic and direct negotiations with other heads of state.

Notwithstanding pressures generated by mass democratic politics and the emergence of negotiating habits made possible by advances in transportation and communication, ambassadorial diplomacy (including the U.S. variant) has remained a distinctive feature of international life. In the context of Soviet–U.S. relations, the embassy in Moscow, to varying degrees over time, shaped official views in Washington about the nature of communist society, economy, and external policy. As the following chapters attest, the United States benefited when high and ambassadorial diplomacies were closely combined. This combination fostered a realism that functioned as the organizing principle for a balanced mix of political, economic, and security interests. Conversely, when overly influenced by ideological and domestic politics or offset by military preoccupations, U.S. policy stumbled from one mishap to another.

III

The first part of this book examines the mission in Russia before Bolshevism. The main point here is to stress, in a synoptic fashion, the continuities between the U.S. experience in czarist Russia and in Soviet Moscow. The following commentary from Neill Brown, a mid-nineteenth-century minister to St. Petersburg, might as easily have been penned by a Bohlen or a Kennan.

> During the last year it has been evident that the policy of Russia toward foreigners and their entrance into the empire was becoming more and more stringent. . . . This arises mainly from political considerations and a fear of foreign influence upon the popular mind.
>
> The position of a minister here is far from being pleasant. The opinion prevails that no communication, at least of a public nature, is safe in the post office but is opened and inspected as a matter of course. . . . The opinion also prevails that ministers are constantly subjected to a system of espionage and that even their servants are made to disclose what passed in their households, their conversations, associations, etc.

Similarly, the observations of C. M. Ingersoll (secretary of legation, 1847–1848) about Nicholas I's Russia would ring true for many post-1917 diplomats: "I look about me—see the world, the people—and I ask myself, are these men, women and children, anything more than a part of a great machine? Can they talk? Or is it Nicholas who is talking, and they simply automatons?" Not without sympathy for people living under a police regime and for whom the conditions of life were grueling, Ingersoll concluded, "The only time a poor Russian looks and acts happy, is when he is drunk!"[4]

The most impressive person to represent U.S. interests in prerevolutionary Russia was John Quincy Adams. Traceable to his term in St. Petersburg (1809–1814), are deeper patterns in the history of Russian–U.S. diplomacy—including an appreciation by both sides that a functioning balance of power in Europe was in their mutual interest. As the nineteenth century unfolded, though, issues arising from czarist mistreatment of political dissidents and persecution of Jews strained the Russian–U.S. connection.

The book is next concerned with the character of U.S. representation during World War I, the Bolshevik coup d'état in Petrograd, and foreign intervention in the Russian civil war. Also explored is the part played by Bullitt and Raymond Robins in aborted attempts to establish a Soviet–U.S. understanding during the early Bolshevik period.[5]

In the second section, attention shifts to those Western idealists, humanitarians, and businessmen who worked in the USSR during the period before Soviet–U.S. relations were established. What drove these people to lend their support to the violent Marxist experiment? When they lost their zeal, what was the cause? Why did others retain their enthusiasm? Concurrent with this informal American presence in Russia was the "listening post" in Riga, Washington's principal source of information on Moscow during the years of nonrecognition. This listening post analyzed the first five-year plan and the impacts of collectivization and famine in the Ukraine. Yet the sober analyses of Soviet reality produced by diplomats in Riga exerted little influence on Franklin Roosevelt's decision in 1933 to recognize Stalin's regime.

This section next covers the events of 1933 to 1941—that is, the Great Purges, isolationism, and the Hitler–Stalin nonaggression pact—from the standpoint of Americans in Moscow. Against this background, a comparison of Ambassadors Davies and Bullitt is instructive. The former has long been held to represent the nadir of U.S. diplomacy; the latter, a study in frustration. The reality of both ambassadorships was more complicated, however.

The second section also concerns the political dynamics of the Soviet–U.S. alliance in World War II and examines the mission's reporting and effect on Washington policymakers. How did the embassy respond to meetings among the "Big Three," and what was its influence on FDR? As for the peak period of Cold War (1946–1953), judgments are offered about the interpretation and advice emanating from the embassy during crises: the Berlin blockade and airlift, Czechoslovakia 1948, Korea. The social and intellectual atmosphere of Embassy Moscow as it sought to lead a "normal life" during the waning days of Stalin is also treated.

The third section covers Soviet–U.S. history since Stalin's death in 1953. His demise coincided with a change of leadership in the United States, when the Republican party assumed control of the executive branch for the first time in two decades. The archival record shows that the Eisenhower–Dulles line on the USSR was more pragmatic and efficacious than conceded by earlier liberal pundits. Yet the administration failed to make proper use of two remarkable men in Moscow: Bohlen and Thompson. Their analyses of the deteriorating Sino-Soviet alliance and of Khrushchev's erratic career would have repaid careful study.

By the early 1970s, emergent Soviet–U.S. détente seemed to have broken the Cold War impasse—in spite of unresolved controversies on human rights and arms control. To make progress in these and other areas, Henry Kissinger sought to free himself of bureaucratic constraints, with the effect of his discarding conventional diplomatic institutions. His mode of operation was immensely demoralizing to Embassy Moscow. Still, it eked out a role in America's Soviet policy, especially in efforts to improve bilateral economic and security relations—resulting in a long-term grain agreement and the threshold test ban.

Despite a dearth of documentation from Jimmy Carter onward, it is possible to evaluate (tentatively) the embassy's view of the post-Brezhnev USSR and Gorbachev's innovations. It will be up to future historians to make confident determinations. Perforce, the last chapter (a cross between sketch and epilogue) merely highlights events from the final decade of Soviet–U.S. rivalry. Those years corresponded with what Matlock has aptly called a hinge of history, "a time when history moves on a pivot from one position to another."[6] Until a new order of things is established, the previous one's full dimension will remain blurred.

I

BEFORE MOSCOW

Whatever we may think of Russia in its character of a despotic power, here is a government which has been uniformly friendly to that of the [United] States, and we can continue our trade with her and improve it if we please, without either endorsing her policy or compromising our republican values.

Thomas Seymour, U.S. Minister to Russia, 1853–1858

1

St. Petersburg and the U.S. Diplomatic Tradition

From the standpoint of power politics, relations between the Russian empire and the American republic were of secondary importance before World War I. Separated by land and sea, their populations, commerce, cultures, and governments seldom came into contact. When there was a crisis involving the two states, it was of brief duration, as were moments of cooperation. Occasionally, the vanity of one party or the other was flattered or injured, but their vital interests were never engaged.

Nevertheless, over the period between 1780—when the Continental Congress sent Francis Dana to St. Petersburg—and the cataclysms of 1914 to 1918, habits of mind developed that influenced the future shape of U.S. attitude toward the Soviet Union. Echoes of a precommunist Russian reality and an earlier diplomatic experience resonated with that of ambassadors in postczarist Moscow. The purpose of this chapter, the first of two devoted to pre-1914, is to show how U.S. envoys between the reign of Catherine II ("the Great") and that of Nicholas I evaluated Russia and coped with its peculiarities.

To St. Petersburg

From the founder of modern Russian *belles lettres* Alexander Pushkin, to Andrei Biely and Boris Pasternak and beyond, writers have sought to capture for their readers the essence of St. Petersburg, a city rarely matched for its beauty or heroic and tragic history. Unabashed in his admiration for the creation of Peter I, Pushkin celebrated it in verse and prose but nowhere more exultantly than in his *Bronze Horseman* (1833):

> Now huge harmonious palaces and towers crowd on the bustling banks; ships in their throngs speed from all ends of the earth to the rich quays; bridges hang

poised over her waters; her islands are covered with dark-green gardens, and before the young capital, ancient Moscow grown pale, like a dowager in purple before a new empress.

Yet to Biely, writing on the eve of World War I, St. Petersburg (in his novel by the same name) constituted a frightening urban landscape. Its jammed streets and mist were laden with menace and the pressure of claustrophobia. However, for Pasternak, living in the dark age of Stalin, the very name St. Petersburg evoked a world of tenderness, a mental refuge for romantic imagination.

Since the city's founding (1703), foreigners in Russia have also paid it homage, recognizing its importance for good and evil. Early U.S. representatives were usually appalled by the physical misery endured by the city's lower orders, to say nothing of conditions suffered by peasants in the countryside. Also evident in the capital were pervasive state secrecy, antidemocratic instincts, and signs of international ambition. No American has rendered St. Petersburg (Leningrad, 1924–1991) with finer feeling than George Kennan, who published these lines in 1956:

> The city . . . is one of the strangest, loveliest, most terrible, and most dramatic of the world's great urban centers. The high northern latitude, the extreme slant of the sun's rays, the flatness of the terrain, the frequent breaking of the land-scape, by wide, shimmering expanses of water: all these combine to accent the horizontal at the expense of the vertical and to create everywhere the sense of immense space, distance, and power. The heaven is vast, the skyline remote and extended. Cleaving the city down the center, the cold waters of the Neva move silently and swiftly, like a slab of smooth grey metal, past the granite embankments and the ponderous palaces, bringing with them the tang of the lonely wastes of forests and swamp from which they have emerged. At every hand one feels the proximity of the great wilderness of the Russian north—silent, sombre, infinitely patient. . . .
>
> In [this] city the attention of man is forced inward upon himself and his own kind. Human relationships attain a strange vividness and intensity, with a touch of premonition.[1]

Hardly an auspicious start to U.S.–Russian relations, the record of the first American at the czarist seat of power contained failures familiar to his successors. Viewed from a perspective of more than two centuries, Dana's tale, indeed, seems full of auguries of future misfortune. For example, like him, Kennan during his ambassadorship was not allowed to meet with the resident potentate. Like Dana, William Bullitt (the first U.S. ambassador to Stalin's Moscow) concluded that he was a useless instrument of policy. Dejected and uncertain about the appropriateness of maintaining lines to the government, all three men quit Russia with remarkably little to show for their exertions.

Dana was one of a handful of Americans sent abroad during the War of Independence to acquire diplomatic and matériel support for the colonial rebellion. With the exception of himself, these were eminent men who assumed leading roles in the early history of the United States. John Adams went to the Netherlands, John Jay to Spain, and Benjamin Franklin to France, where he was hugely successful. On first appearance, there was reason for members of the Continental

Congress to believe that an approach to Catherine would be sympathetically received. Although protesting sisterly feelings for his person, in autumn 1775 she had refused the petition made by George III to send twenty thousand Russian troops to North America to help suppress the insurrection.[2] Three years later, Russia began taking those steps that led to formation of the League of Armed Neutrality (1780), with which the Danes, Swedes, Dutch, Prussians, and Austrians associated themselves. In America, the Armed Neutrality was widely seen as a coalition of maritime powers that threatened war against Great Britain if the Royal Navy persisted in interfering with neutral states still trading with the colonists. In fact, the league was aimed against privateering by all belligerents, including that conducted by the emergent U.S. Navy and its French and Spanish allies. Promulgation of the Armed Neutrality was nevertheless appreciated by Americans as additional evidence of Russian endorsement of their cause. After declaring itself in accord with the principles of neutrals' rights, Congress sought to determine whether Russia might be even more forthcoming. Specifically, Dana was instructed by Samuel Huntington, president of the Continental Congress, to win recognition of American sovereignty, to secure a treaty of friendship and commerce, and, of particular importance, to gain America's admission to the convention of neutral powers.[3] On every count, Dana failed.

Part of the explanation for his failure must be attributed to the limitations of his personality: a narrowness of intellectual imagination, a paucity of poise. An ordinary product of provincial Massachusetts, he had gained nothing from his background or his vocational experience (as a lawyer) to prepare him for the intricacies of court life in Europe. He neither spoke nor read French but relied on the unsteady translating ability of his private secretary, the precocious John Quincy Adams, just fourteen when he arrived in Catherine's empire. Enforced frugality and his Puritan preferences meant that, in comparison with other envoys in Russia, Dana's quarters and wardrobe were drab. He could not compete for the court's attention, social or otherwise. Although the diplomatic corps in St. Petersburg was a mediocre lot, Dana was outshone by most and completely outclassed by the dashing British minister, Sir James Harris.

Dana's disposition was not improved by the severe winters, of which he ceaselessly complained. He was further demoralized by bouts of influenza, displays of favoritism at court, and episodes of blackmail. He was also the first in a long line of Americans to be discomfited by the routine of police surveillance. Making matters worse, Dana was not conversant with European geography or with the history of European international relations.

He blamed the French envoy to St. Petersburg, the Marquis de Verac, for most of his defeats. Too often, brooded Dana, Verac had counseled caution to him in pressing the Americans' cause and did little on his own to promote their interest among Catherine's advisers; he was perfidious. But in fact the Frenchman had tried to tutor his ungrateful colleague in the protocol and complexities of diplomacy, as well as to encourage a Russian–American alliance against Britain. The major reasons for Dana's poor performance were simply beyond his or Verac's ability to control.

To begin with, Dana's purpose had been hampered before he even embarked for St. Petersburg. A certain Stephen Sayre, a flamboyant figure of deficient judgment, had earlier claimed to have authority to represent the Continental Congress in Russia. In reality, self-appointed and little more than an adventurer and fortune seeker, Sayre became involved in a disorganized, ultimately unsuccessful, shipbuilding scheme centered in St. Petersburg. Previously in and out of British confinement (he had been in debtors' prison and was once charged with treason), he sought ridiculously to advance the American, and his own, cause.[4]

In addition to Sayre, Dana was handicapped by another disadvantage. He was ordered by Congress to comport himself as a private person in Russia. He was to reveal the true nature of his mission only if he had sufficient reason to think that an American would win an audience in court. In other words, his status was ambiguous, in ways uncomfortably close to Sayre's. Dana was a quasi-official at best, who (lest he was embarrassed by the Russian government) had to rely on a line of plausible deniability to protect the dignity of the United States. Unfortunately, this ruse was detected at the outset by the vigilant Harris and the Russians and did nothing to enhance Dana's standing in political circles.

To Catherine and her advisers Nikita Panin and Gregory Potemkin, the ultimate fate of the struggling colonies was a matter of indifference. Contrary to analyses produced by naive Americans, premised on misplaced notions about Catherine's desire to expand the free zone, her policy toward the rebellion was based on a conventional understanding of Russian interest. Her soldiers were not sent to North America because they were required to maintain order in the still-uncertain countryside following Emelian Pugachev's peasant uprising (1773–1775). Moreover, in anticipation of imminent hostilities against the Ottoman Empire (possibly Sweden too), it made no sense to send portions of the army to the western edge of the Atlantic. As for the Armed Neutrality, enthusiastically hailed by Americans, it was later dismissed by Catherine as the "Armed Nullity." In any case, it sprang solely from Russian impatience with British depredations on the high seas and was meant to discourage them. It had nothing to do with a commitment to the United States—a point lost on Dana and his patron John Adams, who thought that Catherine was instinctively drawn to the colonists' noble cause. The Russians also regarded as impudent the idea of admitting America, one of the belligerents, to the company of neutrals. Catherine concluded that economic relations between America and Russia were, and would remain, of marginal importance; there was no basis on which to enter into a codified amity. Like the French and Spanish monarchs, the empress was satisfied to see British power and prestige reduced by the Yankee rabble. She was not, however, about to antagonize British naval power for frivolous reasons or so arouse George III that he would from vengeance join Turkey in checking Russia on the Black Sea.

Given these circumstances, there was little room for diplomatic maneuver, and it is hard to imagine what Dana could have achieved.[5] Perhaps a man like Franklin, who was better known to the Russians, could have accomplished something; he had previously corresponded with the gifted scientist Mikhail Lomonosov and later (1789) was made an honorary member of the Imperial Academy of Sciences. As it was, Franklin's talents were better used in France, a country more inclined than Catherine's to challenge Britain to exact compensation for recent injury.[6]

Thus, Dana miscarried with Catherine and languished for two years in St. Petersburg as an unwelcome figure connected with a faraway revolution. He also failed to introduce himself to any of the more alert or sympathetic individuals in Russia. It was actually part of his charge from Huntington to engage in what a later generation would call people-to-people diplomacy: "to lay a foundation for good understanding and friendly intercourse between the subjects of Her Imperial Majesty and the citizens of these states."[7] One of the Russians whose acquaintance might have benefited Dana was Alexander Radishchev (1749–1802), philosopher, social critic, spiritual father of the nineteenth-century radical intelligentsia. Radishchev eventually concluded that the examined life was not necessarily worth living and committed suicide. But before then, he thought reason could persuade passion and dissolve tradition. He assailed the barbarities of serfdom and hoped for the autocracy's abolition.

He also idolized the American experiment in self-government despite his repugnance for plantation slavery and pity for the Indians. Written in 1781 to 1783, his "Ode to Freedom" rhapsodized on George Washington and triumphant liberty:

Gaze on this boundless field.
The armies of evil lie crushed,
Crushed by a mighty foe.
Not mercenaries, nor redcoats
But by an army of freemen,
Leaders all and unafraid.
O Washington, invincible warrior,
Thou art and was unconquerable,
Thy guide being freedom.

Radishchev elaborated upon similar themes in his famous *Journey from St. Petersburg to Moscow* (begun 1780, published 1790). This work chronicled the calamities inherent in serfdom and argued for rights then being affirmed in the United States. By 1790, Catherine's so-called liberal period had ended, and the self-professed devotee of Montesquieu and Voltaire was incensed by the *Journey*. She wanted Radishchev executed. Instead, he was exiled to Siberia and allowed to retire to European Russia after the empress's death in 1796.[8]

Dana's acquaintance with the disaffected Radishchev in the early 1780s would presumably not have advanced his cause in court. Yet it is astonishing, given the latter's outlook, that the two men never met and that Dana was unaware of the philosopher's existence. They overlapped in St. Petersburg. At least once, they were present at the same event: the dedication in 1782 of Etienne Falconet's equestrian statue of Peter in Senate Square. But Dana, linguistically isolated and unsettled by his lack of public recognition, could not or was too peevish to extend himself.

As a personality, he made only the faintest impression on St. Petersburg. It was an abundant relief to him when he left the capital in 1783, convinced that the United States should abandon ideas of cooperating with Russia. Upon learning of his plans to decamp, Sir James Harris chortled, "Mr. Dana, after having made many unsuccessful attempts to be acknowledged here in a public capacity, is now going to return to Boston, and it will be probably many years before any other American will be desirous of being employed as minister at this court."[9]

After Dana

From the signing of the Treaty of Paris, confirming U.S. independence (1783), and John Quincy Adams's return to St. Petersburg as official minister (1809), little of importance occurred between the two governments.[10] The few Russians interested in America were those involved with maritime commerce, excited by the exploits of the fur trade in Alaska, or occasionally sojourning in the United States. One of these was Lieutenant Yuri Lisiansky of the Imperial Navy, who visited cities along the eastern seaboard in 1795 and 1796. His diary contains glimpses into late-eighteenth-century life: plague in New York, impoverished immigrants waiting for something to happen, a notable academy in Cambridge, Massachusetts. The diary shows, too, that Lisiansky was taken by U.S. political practices and potential economic wealth—very like the later Decembrists. In this same spirit was the prophecy made by Baron Friedrich von Grimm, Catherine's agent in France. He wrote her in 1790:

> Two empires will . . . divide between themselves all privileges of civilization and of intellectual, scientific, military, and industrial power: Russia in the east, and in the west America, so recently freed; and we other peoples in the present center of the world will be too degraded and humiliated to remember what we once were, except through a vague and stupid tradition.[11]

Yet the main point stands. Official Russia was not much interested in the United States and considered it unnecessary to send consuls to Philadelphia and Boston until 1808.

Similarly, politically literate Americans agreed with Thomas Paine when he observed that as a non-Atlantic power Russia could not be significant for the life of the United States. To the small degree, it affected U.S. fortunes at all, Russia had been benign in the past and would continue so in the future. Publications like the *New York Magazine* continued to comment favorably about Russian character and reflected the positive experience of American adventurers abroad. The most celebrated of these was John Paul Jones, who by Catherine's invitation served as a rear admiral in her navy (1788–1789). He saw action in the second war against Turkey and played a conspicuous part in destroying the Ottoman fleet in the Dnieper–Liman campaign (June 1788). He admired the fortitude of the officers and sailors under his command and was on personal terms with the Russian military titan of the day, Alexander Suvorov. Jones subsequently concocted an extravagant scheme that he urged upon Thomas Jefferson (who had succeeded Franklin as envoy to France): Russia and the United States should form an alliance for joint naval action against Turkey and Algiers. The two states ought also to enter into broad economic and political agreements (going beyond any concept entertained by the original Continental Congress). Jones's idea made little progress in the councils of either government (discarded as unrealistic), but U.S. opinion remained approving of Russia. Although the mischievous impact of this opinion on citizens' understanding has been exaggerated by scholars, there were elements in post-revolutionary America that uncritically lauded Russia's purported support of the colonies and referred to Catherine as the "Mother of Independence."[12] Jones himself esteemed the empress and presented her with a copy of the U.S. Constitution. She politely accepted this token, but prudently kept its content sequestered from public view.[13]

Beginning in the late 1790s, American ideas on Russia gradually turned ambivalent. Sentimental notions concerning its conduct during the recent war and affection for Catherine coexisted with reservations about its institutions, international policy, and low level of economic development. Inveterate explorer John Ledyard (1754–1789), who tried to reach North America from St. Petersburg by traversing Siberia (he was expelled by authorities as a spy), blamed the degraded condition of the peasantry on the empire's repressive civil and ecclesiastical codes. Another American visitor, Robert Walsh (1784–1859), condemned Russian methods of agriculture as inhumane and inefficient. He was shocked by the serfs' lack of skill and the primitiveness of their farming tools, and concluded—not unreasonably—that their initiative was stifled by superstition and servitude. Even though popular enthusiasm for the French Revolution and regret for the plight of partitioned Poland (it disappeared from the map in 1795) waxed and waned, these were inimical to the strengthening of U.S.–Russian ties. When the Polish patriot Thaddeus Kosciuszko toured the United States in 1797, he was mobbed by well-wishers. Their support of Polish freedom gave rise to a hitherto unknown antipathy for Prussia, Austria, and, above all, Russia.

First Official Mission

While in Dana's employ, John Quincy Adams had formed critical opinions of Russian society. In letters to his mother, the searching teenager scored the tyrannical properties of Catherine, the lamentable condition of her subjects, the court's crude recreations. In one missive, he observed (1783):

> The Government of Russia is entirely despotical. The Sovereign is absolute in all the extent of the word. The persons, the estates, the fortunes of the nobility depend entirely upon his caprice, and the nobility have the same power over the people that the Sovereign has over them. The nation is wholly composed of nobles and serfs, or in other words, of masters and slaves.

He went on to catalog those intrigues and bloody deeds that had rocked political life since Peter the Great.[14] To conduct himself effectively as minister in St. Petersburg, Adams had to rise above his earlier feelings of revulsion.

There were several reasons for Russia and the United States to establish ties in 1809. Commerce was expanding and profitable to each, particularly for America, whose merchant ships carried most of the sugar, rice, indigo, hemp, sailcloth, and iron exchanged between the two sides. The sheer volume of economic activity was overextending the resources of Levett Harris, the ingratiating consul (since 1803) in St. Petersburg. More importantly, after Alexander I and Napoleon agreed to a future design for Europe (Treaty of Tilsit, 1807), the United States and Russia suddenly found themselves jointly concerned about British naval power and the vulnerability of their maritime trade. Previously dependent upon British shipping, Alexander viewed the United States as a potential substitute carrier nation; over the long term, it should be cultivated as a friendly naval power.[15] To the United States, victim of Napoleon's Continental System and British harassment (impressment of sailors, seizure of ships and cargo without restitution), an understanding with Russia was desirable. It would be a "salutary measure," in President Jefferson's phrase, "to engage the powerful patronage of Alexander at conferences for peace." Jefferson reasoned that Russia under the reform-minded czar remained the power most friendly toward America, the one whose long-range interests were most compatible.[16] Paving the way for formal relations, Jefferson had earlier struck up a mutually flattering correspondence with Alexander that touched on practical matters and the virtue of constitutional regimes.

Jefferson's nominee for minister to Russia, William Short, was rejected by the Senate, fearful of overentanglement in European affairs and annoyed by the president's high-handedness in conducting foreign policy. Taking advantage of a shift in the Senate's makeup, Jefferson's successor, James Madison, was able to act quickly on coming to office and won approval of Adams as minister plenipotentiary.

Coinciding with the defeat of Napoleon's ambitions, the years of Adams's residence in St. Petersburg were among the most turbulent in European history. They also marked a fatefulness in the affairs of Russia and the United States. In 1812, France turned on its erstwhile ally and invaded Russia. On the outcome of this and on the dramas of Borodino and Moscow ablaze hung the political composition of Europe and Russia's ability to play an independent role. That same year, the Americans, taking advantage of British preoccupation with France and still vexed by British provocations on the seas, attacked Canada and plunged into a war from which they narrowly escaped national destruction. Alexander's offer as would-be mediator and Adams's diplomatic skill at Ghent helped lead to a settlement and a salvaging of American fortunes.

Adams and his entourage (which included a couple of his Harvard students) arrived in St. Petersburg in October 1809. He and his counterpart in Washington, Count Fedor Pahlen, can be credited with contributing to the agreeable tone in early-nineteenth-century Russian–U.S. history. Adams promptly went to work to promote U.S. interests in neutrals' rights and was politely welcomed during his first interviews with Alexander and chancellor of state Nikolai Rumiantsev.

At the same time, like Dana, Adams and his subordinates suffered from insufficient funds. The official allowance for entertainment and wardrobe was so inadequate that only by dint of extreme frugality did Adams get by. Others in the mission went into personal debt. Adams also loathed the pomp and lavish displays of Russian court life. He soon became bored by the noctural entertainments and fretted that they distracted from serious pursuits: the dignified representation of his country and systematic study to improve his mind. Whereas Pahlen found the quaint ceremony of Washington endearing, Adams reproved the congenital "dissipation" of St. Petersburg. He feared that his steadiness of purpose would disintegrate.[17]

That Adams did not flourish in this or any glittering society was apparent to his underlings; he was plodding in the repartee of fashionable Russian circles. According to John Spear Smith, a youthful member of the legation, his chief was a social liability who badly served his country. "He is an unfortunate appointment for this court," Smith reported to his father in the Senate.

> He has no manners, is gauche, never was intended for a foreign minister, and is only fit to turn over musty law authorities. You would blush to see him in any society, and particularly at Court circles, walking about perfectly listless, speaking to no one, and absolutely looking as if he were in a dream. . . . Dry sense alone does not do at European Courts. Something more is necessary, which something Mr. A. does not possess.[18]

Unknown to the supercilious Smith, Adams had already established excellent working relations with Rumiantsev and was respected by Alexander. In fact, Adams remained on consistently cordial terms with his St. Petersburg hosts. In their meetings along the Neva's embankment—themselves the stuff of legend—diplomat and emperor conversed on diverse topics: the construction and upkeep of the city's quays, the multiethnic quality of American society, U.S. designs on Florida, Russian preparations for war against France. Expecting eventually improved Anglo-U.S. relations even though the two countries were at war, Adams also made a point of staying on decent terms with Britain's ambassador, Lord Cathcart.

Insofar as he was able, Adams sought to make sense of Russian reality. Architectural masterpieces in St. Petersburg and its environs, such as the sumptuous Peterhof palace, impressed him. He was equally appreciative of the art collection housed in the Imperial Palace of the Hermitage. He became acquainted with the Academy of Science, and he studied the punctilio and elaborate liturgy of the Orthodox Church. His curiosity in invention led him to examine Russian techniques for insulating buildings; he noted with approval how they provided equable warmth during the winters. His understanding was less astute, however, when it came to such intangible subjects as Russian mores or psychological traits. And there is no evidence to suggest that he was aware of the fragility (increasingly visible after 1812) of the emperor's personality. Neither unduly generous nor intuitive, Adams lacked the art of empathy. Consequently, he was apt to remark upon the facial hair of an older Russian woman and to generalize foolishly about this supposed feature of the "Slavonian breed." More oddly, in view of his republican commitments, he showed little interest in those attempts by Alexander, Count Mikhail Speransky, and others to reform Russian politics.

A lawyer by training, Adams may have regretted his decision to refuse Madison's offer (1811) to appoint him to the Supreme Court. There were certainly times when he thought himself consigned to exile in Russia. By the end of his tenure, he felt wholly superfluous and doubted that he was adding to his country's well-being. He had little respect for the foreign diplomats in St. Petersburg and, as time wore on, became suspicious of Levett Harris's conduct. This liberally mixed business ventures with diplomacy and raised doubts about conflicts between

private gain and duty. Years later, it became a matter of public record and litiga-
tion that Harris had amassed a small fortune while consul. He was involved in a
number of shady transactions that included certifying as U.S. the ships and car-
goes of other countries (specifically Britain's) in defiance of Russian adherence to
the Continental System.[19]

Despite his unprepossessing manner and anxieties about his mental decline
and Harris's venality, Adams acquitted himself with distinction. As champion of
American shipping rights, he persuaded Alexander to pressure Denmark (member
of the Continental System) into releasing fifty-two U.S. merchant ships captured
by Danish privateers. He outmaneuvered France's ambassadors to St. Petersburg
(the Duc de Vicence and later Count Lauriston) and in 1811 prevailed upon the
Russians to release twenty-three American ships detained in Riga, Kronstadt, and
other ports of the empire.[20] By these actions, the Russians quickened their distance from France. Adams thus contributed, albeit modestly, to the approaching
Franco-Russian crisis that culminated in Napoleon's invasion and Anglo-Russian
rapprochement. Adams also played a credible part in the American effort (aborted)
to sign a commercial treaty with Russia and another one that would have fixed
conflicting Russian and U.S. claims in the Pacific Northwest. These initiatives to
ensure mutually beneficial arrangements were alas undermined in 1811, as the
prospect of Anglo-U.S. war indicated a diminution of Russia–U.S. trade and (possibly) concord.

As for the conflagration that consumed eastern Europe, Adams enjoyed a
unique vantage point for an American from which to view events. He did not
fully share the opinion common among foreign military officers and diplomats in
St. Petersburg that the French would again strike blows against Russia, comparable to Austerlitz (1805) or Friedland (1807), or that Napoleon could easily enroll
the czar in his corps of puppet governors. Even so, Adams was unprepared for
the ferocity of Russian resistance or the totality of French disaster. To Secretary
of State James Monroe, he reported admiringly that every class, serfs no less than
others, had cooperated to annihilate the invading host.[21] In his exultation over the
spectacle of peasant endurance and Alexander at the head of a victorious army,
Adams stood with those for whom French defeat was deliverance. He entered in
his diary on December 3, 1812, "Within the compress of ten days the Russian
armies have taken between forty and fifty thousand prisoners, with cannons, bag-
gage, and ammunition in proportion. There is nothing like it in history since the
days of Xerxes."[22] Adams also divined the significance of French rout for the
prestige and power of Alexander, dubbed by him "the delight of Humankind." To
his mother, Adams explained: "In all human probability the career of Napoleon's
conquests is at an end. France can no longer give the law to the continent. . . .
A new era is dawning upon Europe." Henceforth, he prophesied, Russia would
arbitrate the international order.[23]

To any dispassionate observer at the time, it was unclear what place, if any,
the United States would occupy in the post-Napoleonic world. With the exception
of some scattered naval engagements, the Americans were suffering consecutive
defeats by British forces. Washington, D.C., was captured, and the executive

mansion burned. The invasion of Canada was an unmitigated fiasco. Estranged though he was from the Federalists, Adams shared their criticism of Madison for not foreseeing how U.S. hostilities against Britain added to French advantage. Consequently, and in light of U.S. reverses on land, Adams decided to make a demarche to the Russians to encourage their mediation of an Anglo-American armistice. (Madison later congratulated him for exercising this initiative.) For its part, Alexander's government was anxious to contain or, better yet, end the British–U.S. war. Prolonged strife between its English-speaking associates was undesirable, for it diverted British attention from single-minded concentration against France; continuation of the war might result in America's aligning itself with France, thereby endangering the safety of Russian holdings in the New World. Ultimate concern centered on the possibility that the United States would be severely damaged or, worst of all, reincorporated into the British Empire. In that event, Russia's merchant marine and naval vitality would be compromised, as America was the only foreseeable check against British supremacy on the seas.

Despite attempts by Rumiantsev to arbitrate between the belligerents, the British refused all such arrangements and insisted on direct talks with the upstart Yankees. These were achieved but not until the Crown was satisfied that the United States was punished for its treachery—striking Britain when it was fighting for its very existence against Napoleon. Russian diplomats in any case were excluded from the talks and played no role in negotiating the Treaty of Ghent (December 1814). Yet many Americans believed that for the sake of Anglo-Russian collaboration, Lord Liverpool and Castlereagh were willing to placate Alexander by signing a moderate peace. American representatives at Ghent (Adams, most of all) were pleased to acknowledge that the treaty ending hostilities was signed on Alexander's birthday. This happy coincidence served as a symbol honoring Alexander's offer of mediation and his part in "the conclusion of a peace that is becoming universal."[24]

By the end of the Napoleonic wars and the Treaty of Vienna, Russian–U.S. relations were perfectly correct. Problems related to the occasional misconduct of individuals, as in the case of Harris, were minor. The flap in 1815 about Russian consul Kozlov's alleged rape in Philadelphia of a twelve-year-old servant girl caused a brief diplomatic crisis. But it was resolved by the czar's personal intervention. The chief challenge in the long run to harmonious relations between the two states stemmed from the fact that they belonged to separate political worlds. Therefore, despite a potentially symbiotic maritime relationship and the absence of geopolitical rivalry, no basis for intimacy existed. Russian diplomats in Washington were as a rule not enamored of U.S. institutions or the qualities of citizenship they engendered. Pahlen's successor in Washington, Andrei Dashkov, was repelled by the rudeness and "avaricious nature of the Americans." And though he felt the country had import for the future, he pronounced it flawed in fundamental ways: the level of intellectual attainment and morality in the pioneer society was disgustingly low. He was also contemptuous of the cravenness of those forces charged with protecting the capital against British invaders. He was dismayed by the divisions that weakened Madison's cabinet and thought the president mentally dull. Against U.S. democracy, he leveled the conservative critique: it was rule by the mob and inefficient. He wrote to Rumiantsev in 1814:

> Every artisan and freeholder reads the newspaper, deliberates on politics in his own way and considers himself fit for any post in the government. Artisans, innkeepers, and even butchers demand to be deputies, generals, colonels, and so on, and their wishes are more or less granted, depending on their influence upon the votes of their neighbors. In the hands of people of this kind, who account for the indisputable majority of the votes of American citizens, are the foundations upon which the President is raised. He must constantly flatter them and blind their judgment with strategies of every kind. Jacobin principles, abundantly diffused in this country, draw [the president] into the party of the demagogues. He will be the first victim of the inconstancy innate in every band of rabble.[25]

Dashkov thought Americans so base that he urged Rumiantsev to send presents to Mrs. Madison and pay the expenses of the legation in St. Petersburg. Why not use their conceit and venality to Russian advantage?

No less withering than Dashkov, U.S. diplomats, from Adams onward, were seldom drawn to the Romanov autocracy. In this respect, they held in common with two contemporary European observers of Russia: the socialist Karl Marx and the French aristocrat the Marquis de Custine.

Russia Under Nicholas I

To nineteenth-century liberals and radicals, Russia since the time of Catherine was a lesson in disappointment. Her rule (1762–1796) had enjoyed a tolerant period when she undertook a series of reforms that promised political privileges for the gentry. She not only had been acquainted with various French philosophes, but also had toyed with the idea of introducing into Russia improvements associated with them. Yet as her reign wore on, Catherine became unrelentingly hostile to the liberal credo. She was responsible for the consolidation of serfdom and for the persecution of bold thinkers in her realm, not the least of whom was Radishchev. The short reign of Paul I (1796–1801) was accompanied by feeble measures to lighten the serfs' burden. But Paul's capricious cruelty and deepening lunacy led to a palace plot, and he was strangled to death—with the complicity, or at least knowledge, of his son Alexander. Soon afterward, he inaugurated a period of modest reform. But he ended his life as a religious mystic, and his Holy Alliance exemplified European reaction, which assumed its most virulent shape in Russia. Even more to the point, Alexander was followed by Nicholas I's thirty years of draconian rule, featuring redoubled police activity and stringent censorship.

Like all progressives of his day, Marx condemned Nicholas's Russia as the repository of injustice and semi-Asiatic backwardness. Of Nicholas, he was scornful. Whereas the czar pictured himself a bold leader, Marx perceived an imbecile who mismanaged military affairs and bore responsibility for Russian catastrophes in the Crimean War (1854–1856). A parade-ground "martinet," he surrounded himself with similar men who, in Marx's view, compounded their original sin of stupidity with obsequiousness.

Despite these weaknesses of leadership, Marx believed that Russia's international aims were limitless. It was not simply that Russia regarded itself as the gendarme of Europe and in that capacity had crushed national uprisings in Poland (1830–1831) and Hungary (1849). Marx also attributed appetite for territory and the need for deflecting internal discontent outward as the determinants of czarist foreign policy. At immediate risk were Prussia, Austria, and the European provinces of the decrepit Turkish empire. A century before Winston Churchill sounded a similar alarm in his "iron curtain" speech, Marx warned, "It would appear that the natural frontier of Russia runs from Dantzic, or perhaps Stettin, to Trieste." [26]

He believed that Nicholas's regime would use all available means to further its goals. And there is a congruence between the methods Marx warned against and those used from time to time by the Soviets during the Cold War: shrewd propaganda, appeals to pan-Slavism and transcendent ideologies, diplomatic bluster. [27] Against an uncertain or weak Europe, Russia could do anything, wrote Marx. No Cold Warrior would dispute his admonition: "There is only one way to deal with a power like Russia, and that is the fearless way." [28]

Unlike Marx, Custine had firsthand experience of Russia. He traveled through its European section, later publishing his renown *Russia in 1839* (1843). Similar to his compatriot Alexis de Tocqueville—whose *Democracy in America* served as a model for his own travelogue-treatise—Custine went to examine an area on the periphery of the European world in the expectation that it possessed lessons for France. [29] Tocqueville's exposure to U.S. institutions and Jacksonian politics had been a sobering one. Combined with his reflections on the prospects of French liberty, his travels resulted in acute understanding of the hazards endemic in egalitarian society. Yet nothing in Tocqueville's New World odyssey destroyed his faith in America's future or the inexorability of democratic progress. The contrast with Custine's experience could not have been greater. His journey to Russia unsettled his convictions. In this way, Custine was a forerunner of those twentieth-century Western pilgrims who looked to Russia for inspiration but were disillusioned by its reality. [30]

Custine's family had suffered grievously during the French Revolution. His paternal grandfather and father were guillotined; his mother was imprisoned. He was therefore opposed to republicanism and passionately preferred aristocratic regimes. He assumed that in Russia he would find expression of these principles and would return to France stocked with fresh arguments against democracy. [31] Instead, he was dumbfounded by the enormity of czarist despotism. It was a revelation to him that a type of slavery had been imposed on all ranks of society, even upon the aristocracy, which he had supposed to be a cherished partner of the sovereign. He was unprepared for the extent of police authority in Russia, horrified by the regime's spendthrift attitude toward human life, and depressed by the medieval torpor of rural society. Finally, like countless foreign travelers before and since, he was struck by Russian feelings of inferiority toward the West. Thus, it was not surprising that he agreed with the verdict in Peter Chaadaev's *Philo-*

sophical Letters. Russia's past and future were worthy of despair as the czar's dominion existed in opposition to the moral sphere.[32]

Custine was as adamant as Marx on Europe's need to resist Russian intrusion, and he became an advocate of rule by law and a proponent (however grudgingly) of representative democracy. He ended his *Russia in 1839* with this unforgettable statement, addressed to both his generation and subsequent French idealists:

> If ever your sons should be discontented with France, try my recipe: tell them to go to Russia. It is a useful journey for every foreigner: whoever has well examined that country will be content to live anywhere else. It is always well to know that a society exists where no happiness is possible. . . . [M]an cannot be happy unless he is free.[33]

Although a commercial success, Custine's book did not enjoy universal acclaim. The preponderance of critical opinion was negative, not only in Russia but also in Britain and France; reviewers faulted Custine for factual errors and misjudgments. From a late-twentieth-century standpoint, however, what is striking about him is not his occasional erroneous reporting of events, which understandably bothered contemporaries. Rather, what stands out is his grasp of Nicholas's Russia and the modern police state. As such, the book *was* admired by some of its original readers, such as Alexander Herzen, who judged Custine's treatment the best one ever written of Russia. And Nicholas's chief of secret police, General Alexander Benckendorf, paid him this cynical tribute: "Custine has only put into words those thoughts about us which everyone (including ourselves) has long had."[34]

The impact made by Custine's book on Americans in St. Petersburg cannot precisely be determined. Probably it was minor. Although translated into English and the object of attention in Britain, no review of it appeared in the United States until 1855.[35] With few exceptions, its distribution in Russia was prohibited; the czar occasionally read passages of Custine aloud to members of his family for their collective amusement. Yet his commentary on the oppressiveness of Russia's political system and the penetration of military mentality into everyday life would have seemed fair to most U.S. ministers and their staffs. One American who definitely did read Custine (in the original French) was C. M. Ingersoll, briefly secretary to the legation in the late 1840s. He understood why Nicholas should ban the book: it told unpalatable truths.[36]

Although Custine colored the opinions of Ingersoll and the handful of other Americans who read it, he would not have have persuaded everyone. This category of disbelievers included Henry Middleton, the U.S. envoy with the longest record of residence in Russia, either before 1917 or since. He was appointed in 1820 by James Monroe and served in St. Petersburg for nearly a decade. Formerly a congressman and governor of South Carolina, Middleton belonged to the planter class of southern society. Aristocratic by birth and bearing, this fifty-year-old adapted easily to society in St. Petersburg. Contrary to his New England predecessors, he enjoyed it thoroughly. His gentry attitudes corresponded with those of Russian estate owners, for whom agricultural economy also depended on forced labor. Entirely loyal to U.S. interests, Middleton did develop strong sympathies for Alexander over the course of years and, later, Nicholas. In another age, Middleton might have been accused of "going native." He certainly would have dismissed Custine's and Marx's complaints as uninformed, their proposed reforms as nonsense. To him, no regime, save one that concentrated power in an individual and a small council of advisers, could have succeeded in Russia.

Middleton's attitude was plainly apparent in the crisis of December 1825, when confusion over Nicholas's succession to Alexander led to the daring but bungled attempt by army officers to seize power and establish a liberal polity. Middleton did hope that individual Decembrists would be leniently treated, for they "were not bloodyminded men but enthusiasts who sought after an ideal perfection." Still, he held that Nikita Muraviev, Paul Pestel, and the other conspirators were misguided in trying to topple (or limit) the monarchy. Middleton conceded that innovations might be useful, but their introduction should be gradual. Mindful of French revolutionary excesses and a staunch anti-abolitionist, he never doubted the Decembrists' waywardness. He informed Secretary of State Henry Clay that the "great body of the nobility should incline to bear with the autocracy placed above it, in order to enjoy the benefits of the *savage* beneath it."[37] According to this analysis, without an austere central authority, the primitive population could not be controlled. Violent anarchy would predominate: "The [Russian] mass, or 19/20th of the whole, is really little more than . . . *'La Bête à face humaine.'* Indeed, it enjoys no other but a physical existence and cannot therefore be ripe for the apportion or maintenance of its . . . rights."[38] Undoubtedly, the irony that the minister from the most self-consciously democratic state had denied the Decembrists' validity would not have been lost on Custine.

None of Middleton's successors ever made the case for autocracy so baldly as he. Many of them thought that Russia would gain by the selective introduction of reforms. In the main, however, they agreed with him about the futility of any attempt to adopt a full-scale liberal system. Nor were they indifferent to the presumed advantages found in an autocratic regime. The wisdom among these diplomats held that local circumstances were inhospitable to processes that dignified the individual citizen. Future president James Buchanan, for example (minister in St. Petersburg, 1831–1833), thought that Russians were too backward intellectually and socially to participate in government. It should be noted parenthetically that, unlike Middleton, Buchanan was not a slaveholder and deemed the institution immoral. To President Andrew Jackson, that embodiment of democratic man in the New World, he declared, "The most ardent republican, after having resided here for one year, would be clearly convinced that the mass of this people, composed as it is of ignorant and superstitious barbarians, who are also slaves, is not fit for political freedom."[39] As for the aristocrats, whom Custine would have invested with enhanced authority, Buchanan found them enervated. Given the absence of a political class, he judged Russian despotism legitimate. It seemed to him that the czar's subjects were content to live under his protective paternalism and regarded Nicholas as a version of divinity.[40]

Like Buchanan, fellow Pennsylvanian and future vice president George Dallas admired Nicholas and reported favorably on him. Dallas professed that Nicholas was superior to Peter the Great and deserved praise for his justice, industry, and personal rectitude.[41] But no less than Custine, Dallas despised the Russian social system. He evidenced compassion for the serfs and recognized that there was little to buffer them against the hardness of their masters. About the police, his reporting was also perceptive, as applicable to twentieth-century tyrannies as to Nicholas's realm: "In despotic governments, fears of conspiracy and change are always more or less afloat. The agents of the police keep these alive, as necessary to their own importance."[42] Yet at no time was Dallas sanguine about prospects for democratic innovation in Russia. Instead, he would have agreed with the pronouncement of Charles Todd (minister, 1841–1845) that Russia enjoyed certain advantages by having its "vast energies concentrated by the genius of one mind."[43] In a similar vein, Neill Brown (minister, 1850–1853) likened Nicholas's administration to the smooth running of a fine watch, though he was critical of the rigor of the police, whose presence affected every aspect of life and made St. Petersburg appear to be under a state of siege.[44]

Diplomacy

Middleton was an obvious exception. But most U.S. ministers and their staffs (usually numbering two or three functionaries) disliked their assignments in St. Petersburg. They invariably respected Nicholas as a personality and were grateful for whatever courtesies officialdom bestowed on them. They nevertheless suffered from numerous physical and emotional ailments. Party men with ambitions to elected office, such as Buchanan and Dallas, were impatient with what they regarded as an exile that removed them from the swirl of U.S. debates and decisions. The correspondence and diaries of these two men were inordinately burdened with discussion about partisan affairs, showing that they were as preoccupied with events at home as they were concerned to report accurately on Russia.[45] Men with literary or intellectual interests, such as the historian John Lothrop Motley, who served briefly (1841–1842) as secretary to the legation, felt marooned from the world of ideas. Andrew Dickson White, later of Michigan and Cornell universities, was positively gleeful on leaving (1855) his post (unsalaried attaché) in St. Petersburg and arriving in "cheerful," intellectually unfettered Germany.[46]

Contributing to this sense of isolation was the delay in communication between Russia and the United States. News from Washington and instructions from the secretary of state were agonizingly slow. Eleven, twelve, or more months might elapse between deliveries of mail. Unacknowledged for long intervals of time, envoys typically became snappish. After having been neglected for fourteen months by the State Department, Neill Brown sent this testy reminder to Secretary of State Edward Everett:

> I have had no acknowledgment for (my despatches), from No. 10 to No. 19 inclusive. I do not suppose they have been very important. It is . . . gratifying to a public officer, when far from his country, in the midst of disconsolations

such as exist in Russia, to receive occasional recognitions from the department under whose auspices he is acting, and to know that his course is not disapproved.[47]

The unappreciated Brown was delighted when the time came to relinquish his post.

Existence for U.S. diplomats in St. Petersburg involved the same inconveniences and hazard as experienced by representatives from other countries. Surveillance by secret agents was constant; even household servants were employed as spies. Unless delivered by special courier, mail was opened as a matter of course by postal inspectors. Constraints on travel and information made reliable reporting difficult in the extreme. The winter and material conditions of life were also taxing and made Russia, in Brown's view, "unfitted for the abodes of man." Health was uncertain, and the toll on wives and children could be disastrous. Adams's wife, often lonely and morose, saw her infant daughter die. George Washington Campbell, minister in 1819 and 1820, lost three children from typhus within a single week in St. Petersburg.[48] Naturally, in such a setting, strains developed in and between families. Equilibrium was also disrupted when, for no apparent reason, a Russian friend fell foul of the authorities or disappeared without trace into the Siberian mines. Young Ingersoll's anguish in this regard was intensified by having seen a party of chained prisoners in transport.

In addition, men in the consular and diplomatic services were saddled with uniquely American problems. They usually possessed no, or only a halting, command of French and so were left out and embarrassed. Self-consciously republican in their outlook, they were more apt than European diplomats, drawn from the aristocratic class, to find the conventions of court life fatiguing. This unfamiliarity with—indeed, distaste for—etiquette and protocol could lead to amusing episodes. Once, for example, Dallas was refused admission to a dinner given in his honor by Nicholas because the American was wearing mufti instead of the military-style uniform of an accredited minister.[49] On presenting his credentials to Nicholas, John Randolph of Virginia addressed the august personage in the familiar *tu* form. Randolph later caused the czarina to laugh at his eccentricities. She and officialdom concluded, quite rightly, that the poor man was half-insane. The diplomats' pride as Americans was also wounded when they learned that Russians of breeding knew little about their country and were seldom curious. One female acquaintance of Buchanan's expressed surprise on learning that the United States was independent of Great Britain. She also wondered whether Americans spoke English. Not surprisingly, Buchanan referred to himself as "a stranger in a strange land," while Dallas thought himself a "fish out of water." These two ministers returned to the United States with alacrity as soon as circumstances permitted. Randolph stayed at his post for a record-breaking ten days.[50]

Added to those pressures driving the high rate of turnover was the continuing issue of inadequate salary. Requests for additional funding were routinely refused by Washington. Numerous operational expenses were paid out of pocket by the legation in St. Petersburg. Many of the lesser officers served without salary and lived on the sufferance of their families. Consequently, some would-be ministers were not tempted to accept a position that, though generously compensated by U.S. standards of the 1830s and 1840s ($9,000 salary, $9,000 outfit for travel and related expenses), purchased relatively little in the most expensive European city.[51]

Sympathy in the United States for diplomats in Russia, or elsewhere for that matter, was utterly lacking. To begin with (in line with ancient tradition), the president was not above sending rivals or potential troublemakers to faraway Russia, as when Jackson sent Buchanan and Martin Van Buren dispatched Dallas. James Monroe must have been privately elated to discharge his administration of further liability by sending Randolph packing. Moreover, on returning home, the diplomats were greeted with suspicion as recipients of presidential favor who performed negligible service at taxpayers' expense. One mordant Whig, Philip Hone, vented these feelings in 1839:

> This is an arrangement of the government to pay the stipulated price of duty work performed by some unscrupulous partisan by the office of short duration, long pay and no service. . . . The Minister to Russia makes the *tour d'Europe en Prince,* arriving at length at his post, puts on his diplomatic uniform (exercising all caution to keep the sword from getting between his legs), makes the round of dinners and balls, talks French (if he can) with the Emperor, and has the run of the Palace, and then when the weather is pleasant and the traveling good, receives recall . . . and after all this pleasant marching and counter marching at Uncle Sam's expense, the first thing we hear about him since his appointment is the arrival of his excellency so-and-so, who it is understood makes place for some other patriot who desires to make the tour of Europe.[52]

The amount of business conducted between Russia and the United States during the period of Nicholas was undeniably trifling compared with that transacted with third parties, especially France and Britain. Yet there were ministers who performed competently and added to the fund of amicability between the two countries.

Middleton proved useful to Secretary John Quincy Adams in conveying a sense of the Imperial government's attitude toward territorial claims advanced by the Russian-American Company in Alaska. So too was he able to interpret with confidence and place in perspective Russian aims (never very serious) through the Holy Alliance to squelch revolutions in Spanish America.[53] Following enunciation of the Monroe Doctrine (1823), he was helpful in calming Russian fears of Anglo-American collusion and in soothing the anti-Russian sting that Foreign Minister Count Karl von Nesselrode read into the president's statement. As a negotiator, Middleton was tactful and successful. In 1820 to 1822, when Alexander served as arbitrator between the United States and Britain over the question of compensation for slaves freed by English forces in 1812, Middleton played skillfully on Russian desires to build up America as a naval counterpoise. The czar conceded the force of Middleton's case and judged in his favor. In 1824, Middleton helped negotiate the Russia–U.S. convention that for more than a decade froze problems arising from competing Russian and U.S. land claims in northwestern America. No less than Adams before him, he was a feisty champion of U.S. maritime rights. On at least three occasions, he won indemnification for shipowners who had suffered Russian violations. He also played a helpful supporting role in preparing the way for the U.S.–Turkish treaty of 1830 that allowed American ships to ply the Black Sea for the first time.[54]

During his brief but productive tour, Buchanan almost single-handedly engineered czarist agreement to a commercial treaty (1832) with the United States, whose longevity reached into the twentieth century. He was also unflagging in his reassurances to Nesselrode that despite manifestations of popular feeling for Poland, President Jackson was committed to mutually beneficial relations with Russia. Choleric editorials in U.S. newspapers, including the semiofficial *Globe,* should not be taken as a reflection of administration views. On this last point, czarist officials were incredulous: How could newspapers operate independently? It was inconceivable that editorial writers in Russia would publish opinions incompatible with national policy. Was Jackson, the hero of New Orleans, so impotent that he could not discipline journalists when they slandered a friendly government? Buchanan tried to explain the first amendment and provisions for an uncensored press but without success. Meanwhile, he sought to persuade Secretary of State Edward Livingston that he explore means of restraining the *Globe*'s outbursts. Otherwise, no commercial treaty could be guaranteed, and bilateral relations would suffer. Besides, argued Buchanan, Russia's repression of Polish nationalists was the product of an ancient antipathy between those Slavic nations; to ascribe all fault to one while exonerating the other meant ignoring a history in which both sides bore blame.

Two decades later, Neill Brown expended energy to convince the Foreign Office of his government's continuing warm regard for Nicholas. This was no small task. In 1851, the Hungarian leader, Lajos Kossuth, toured the United States and unleashed another surge of spontaneous demonstration for a captive people resisting Russia. Nevertheless, Brown persisted, and despite frostiness from czarist officials, he managed to renew their confidence in U.S. policy. Thus, an unsentimental diplomacy, premised on the need for economic cooperation and keeping open the channels of communication, dictated the conduct of envoys in St. Petersburg. Private Americans in Russia, like those employed in building telegraph and railway facilities, and Nicholas's ministers in Washington added to the balance in favor of cordial relations. The latter included Alexander Bodisco, who served as minister in Washington from 1837 to 1854. He became dean of the diplomatic corps and was respected for his urbanity. He was also in full accord with his government's aim: the United States should remain friendly and grow in power so that in case of European war the Americans could lend assistance (military or other) to the czarist cause.[55] This proposition was not entirely farfetched, as both countries remained suspicious of Britain and were willing within limits to cooperate against its naval pretensions.

When at the end of Nicholas's reign Russia became engaged against Britain (Crimea), President Franklin Pierce declared the United States neutral. Despite this explicit policy, he tilted ostentatiously toward Russia. Already at odds with London over issues related to Cuba, Central America, fishing rights, and the Oregon Territory, Pierce made it known that another instance of British interference with U.S. shipping would provoke a military response, as in 1812. (The Americans were not put to the test this time as Britain allowed that "the neutral flag shall protect the cargo.") Pierce was also quick to prohibit British recruiters from enlisting U.S. volunteers in Her Majesty's army. Secretary of State William Marcy went out of his way to warn Russian diplomats that Britain had plans to strike Alaska, and the U.S. consul in Hawaii alerted czarist agents to a Franco-British naval offensive near the Siberian coast. The results in this second case were impressive—the Russian fleet was warned in time and won a victory.[56] Through his pro-Russian minister in St. Petersburg, Thomas Seymour, Pierce later offered to mediate between the belligerents, thereby relieving Russia from a hopeless contest.

Individual Americans were prepared, actually eager, to take riskier steps. Senator William Gwin, a proslavery advocate from California, told Russian officials that his state could supply the fast ships and able sailors necessary to sweep Britain's navy from the Pacific. Three hundred Kentucky riflemen hoped to resume their feud with the redcoats and join czarist forces at Sevastopol or anywhere else they were needed. Offers also came from citizens willing to organize a volunteer army to drive the British Hudson's Bay Company from Vancouver Island. And a shadowy figure named "Amicus," about whom little is known, claimed he could kindle an all-European revolution along the lines of 1848 that would cripple the Anglo-French war effort. To this end, he said he would employ Giuseppe Mazzini and Kossuth.[57]

Despite anti-British feeling in the United States and wishful thinking in Russia, chances were slender that the Americans would enter hostilities on the czar's side or offer more than moral aid. Pierce, and belatedly Seymour, recognized that U.S. security and prosperity would be untouched no matter the war's outcome. Why, then, depart from the tradition of noninvolvement in European matters? Neill Brown gave this concise expression of majority opinion when he wrote from St. Petersburg shortly before the war began: "I sincerely hope that nothing may tempt us to intervene in the affairs of Europe in any way. To do so would be to enter upon an indifferent career of difficulties. Europe is not our battlefield nor our destiny."[58] Only through the superior example of its own institutions and its serene way of life should the United States presume to influence. Brown's preference for neutrality was also reinforced by his assessment of Russian military competence. Like Dallas before him, he believed that Nicholas's legions looked imposing from a distance; viewed from closer quarters, the army was paltry—supplied with antiquated equipment, poorly led, unable to sustain an offensive campaign. In this respect and as the record of defeat in Crimea confirmed, Custine and Marx had exaggerated the threat to Europe posed by Russia.

*   *   *   *

Competing claims in the Pacific Northwest and U.S. anxiety over Russian meddling in Latin America did not prevent the two states from establishing good relations by the end of Nicholas's life. Differences in ideology and practice meant that the regimes were "political antipodes" (Buchanan's phrase). Yet this condition was not allowed by either side to upset mutually convenient arrangements. In the meantime, each country continued to expand at the expense of weaker neighbors. While U.S. territorial acquisitiveness was directed against Mexicans and Indians, Russia's imperial drive victimized Turks, Persians, and Circassian tribes on the eastern shore of the Black Sea. Officials in St. Petersburg and Washington had no cause to dispute Todd's verdict: the two countries were "the best neighbors" and fated to remain so for they possessed "no conflicting points of interest."[59]

Based on the record of early U.S. officials in Russia, a few general points emerge: the diplomats were disappointingly uninformed on the cultural vitality and subterranean discontent alive below the veneer of autocratic conformity. Middleton's attitude toward the Decembrists and the peasantry was complemented by that of other U.S. diplomats, who tended to repeat the European line about Russia: at best, its culture was derivative; essentially, it was barbarous. Ingersoll, for one, was convinced that if the Russian state were deprived of the services rendered by its German and Baltic administrators, the economy, army, and political apparatus would instantly collapse. Far more scholarly than most Americans assigned to St. Petersburg, Motley wrote of Nicholas's Russia, "The present Emperor is unquestionably a man of great energy; but how can one man uphold this mass, even in the state of crepuscular civilization to which they have reached?"[60] In vain does one look in the despatches or reminiscences of Middleton, Motley, Dallas, Buchanan, and Brown for signs of comprehension of those social and intellectual forces that were to explode with ferocity in the remaining decades of the nineteenth century. Similarly, the creative energies that made possible Russia's contribution to world literature went undetected by the diplomats. By the time of Nicholas's death in 1855, Pushkin had transformed Russian language and literature. Dostoevsky, Belinsky, Gogol, Tolstoy, and Turgenev had already made their mark or were beginning to.

Why were the Americans so oblivious? Why did they not probe deeper? Part of the answer rests on the simple fact that with few exceptions they did not stay long enough in Russia to acquaint themselves with local conditions. There was often the barrier of language. Owing to undependable roads and other obstacles to travel, the envoys seldom ventured outside the vicinity of St. Petersburg. Only once in his ten years did Middleton leave the capital, and that shortly before he returned to the United States.[61] Additionally, social circumstances rarely allowed for the Americans to meet with original thinkers and writers. Frequently out of official favor, they did not belong to those circles in which diplomats circulated. At one time or another, it should be recalled, Pushkin, Dostoevsky, and Belinsky suffered some combination of banishment, prison, or sentence of death.

Even if service in St. Petersburg failed to quicken their understanding of Russian rumblings, it heightened the regard of Americans for their own country. Appreciative statements by diplomats after their postings were especially poignant as U.S. events were being overtaken by the crises of disunity and approaching civil war. Perhaps the most telling words came from Brown of Tennessee. Like Custine, he saw in a Russian sojourn a useful lesson in patriotism. He wrote his

superiors in 1853: "[Russia] is the best school in which to Americanize our countrymen. . . . They are enabled to view their own Government by the law of
contrast, and inspect it from new points of observation; and I envy not him who
can do so, and return without an increased attachment to our institutions." Motley
of New England testified that seen from St. Petersburg the "simple and just proportions" of the republic presented themselves unambiguously.[62] Still, civil war
came, and when it did the loyalties of men who had been in Russia were as
divided as those of any group previously employed in public service. Popular in
St. Petersburg during his ministerial term (1858–1860), Francis Pickens was governor of South Carolina when Confederate artillery in Charleston opened fire on
Fort Sumter.[63]

As practitioners of their art, the diplomats were clearly a varied lot. The ineptitude of men like Dana and Randolph was balanced by the relative achievements
of Adams, Middleton, and Buchanan. If the overall record was not glowing, neither was it disgraceful. It could have been a great deal worse, given the shal-
lowness of U.S. diplomatic tradition at the time. The ministers were rarely outmaneuvered by adversaries, and they performed their tasks with reasonable
proficiency. The most egregious problem from a systemic standpoint was that
policy was loosely coordinated between Washington and St. Petersburg. Even this
problem must be kept in perspective, however. Except for brief spells, U.S.–
Russian relations were not crucial to either side. Successive presidents concluded
that they could afford the idiosyncrasies of individual envoys.

The experience of diplomats in Nicholas's empire touched the institutional memory of the twentieth-century State Department and Foreign Service.[64] Neill
Brown's reportage struck Kennan (in the 1930s) and Walter Bedell Smith (in the
late 1940s) as penetrating and helped explain the circumstances of life in Stalinist
Moscow. To underscore the continuities between nineteenth- and twentieth-
century Russian ambitions, Kennan in a 1935 analysis quoted lengthily from
Brown's despatches. The import of these was that Russian foreign aims were
grandiose, impelled by a national sense of mission. On another occasion, he drew
up for Bullitt's signature a despatch composed, without initial attribution, exclusively of passages from Brown's reports. Bullitt signed this, only adding at the
bottom a statement to the effect that the above observations, while as true on that
day as the day they were written, were not his own but those of his eminent
predecessor.[65] While reviewing his tenure as ambassador in 1946 to 1948, Smith
invoked Brown's authority to justify his own judgment on aspects of Soviet life:
tyranny of censorship, sullen poverty, nervous secrecy. The scholar and occasional State Department consultant Hans Morgenthau, in his primer on international affairs, *Politics Among Nations,* used long quotations from Brown to illustrate his argument: the immutable Russian soul had survived the Bolshevik
upheaval.[66]

Future generations of diplomats were also influenced by the interpretations of
nineteenth-century Europeans, especially Custine. Along with other colleagues,
Bohlen and Kennan first read his *Russia in 1839* while assigned to Moscow in the

1930s. In combination with daily experience, the effect of this reading was to shape their understanding of the resilience of traditions. The vanity of Lenin's effort to begin the world anew and the inability of "scientific socialism" to free Russia from the weight of its past were propositions at first dimly perceived by Bohlen and Kennan. With the aid of Custine, these became articles of conviction and were broadly shared subsequently by other officers in the embassy: Russia had transformed Marxism, not vice versa. Walter Bedell Smith felt confident in dismissing altogether the importance of the 1917 revolution. He in fact asserted that it was the Soviet Union's irreducible Russian core that made the country an intractable problem for the United States.[67]

Smith also reckoned that if he substituted present-day names and dates to whole sections of Custine and sent them verbatim to Washington as his own, his superiors would have found them in harmony with his previous communications. On the authority of Custine, Smith went on to distinguish Russia from the West and emphasized that unfortunate conditions had perverted the course of Russian civilization.

Apart from Marx's admonition that the West must stand firm against Russia, nineteenth-century writers were less helpful to U.S. officials in determining an appropriate policy. Still, Custine might have exercised a subtle influence on Kennan and his version of containment. There is an unmistakable, if unacknowledged, trace of Custine in his thinking about the Cold War. Both men were convinced that Russia lacked meaningful answers to the social-economic difficulties afflicting the West. Both held that the major threats to Western society were of an internal nature; if these were surmounted, Russia could not pose too grave a danger. Specifically, the West had to satisfy its standards of conscience and control the excesses of self-gratification common to open societies. The following words of Custine were familiar to Kennan and might as easily have been delivered by him in one of his Cassandra-like pronouncements: "It appears to me that [Russia] is chiefly determined to chastise the corrupt civilization of Europe. . . . The eternal tyranny of the East menaces us incessantly; and we shall have to bow before it, if our extravagances and iniquities render us worthy of punishment."[68] Like Kennan decades later, Custine also paid attention to the power of example in determining the distribution of prestige among nations and abhorred heavy reliance on military instruments. At the height of the Vietnam War and nuclear arms race, Kennan quoted the marquis:

> It is not by the pride of conquest nor by the exercise of a tyrannical power over foreigners that [some states] have won the right to universal recognition; it is by their good example, by their wise laws, by an enlightened and beneficent administration . . . by directing their energy upon themselves and becoming what they can become under the double influence of spiritual and material civilization.[69]

It is plausible too that Kennan's thinking about the Cold War and the importance of example for national standing was buttressed by his reading of Brown's despatches. Along with John Quincy Adams, Brown and Kennan belong to that school of thought that seeks international stature at home, as measured by the quality of domestic cohesion. This statement of Brown's in January 1852 contains themes prominent in Kennan's Long Telegram (1946) and "X" article (1947):

> The steady, silent, but magnificent displays of our example, will accomplish more in liberalizing Europe than all the armies we could send. Our vast growth, physically, morally, and intellectually already amazes all who contemplate it. . . . And let no one suppose that the eye of inquiry will be closed to the cause of . . . our success. That cause [sound laws and industrious habits] is known by all. . . . The example will be contagious so long as it remains a mere example.[70]

Less than a decade after Brown penned these lines, his native republic was no longer a compelling example to anyone. The fratricide of 1861 to 1865 nearly destroyed the nation. Yet through this ordeal, the Russian–U.S. tie held despite Abraham Lincoln's blundering emissaries in St. Petersburg.

2

From Comity to Estrangement

Beginning with the Crimean War, the era of cordial Russian–U.S. relations lasted through the 1860s and intensified during the Civil War. The sale of Alaska to the United States in 1867 marked the high point. Thereafter, continuing to the 1914 European emergency, bilateral relations became ever strained. This decline in mutual confidence was caused by American impatience (on official and popular levels) with anti-Jewish pogroms and other persecutions in the empire. Incipient Russian–U.S. rivalry for influence in the Far East produced additional complications. This second concern in the United States was dissipated by Japan's startling victory over czarist forces in the 1904/1905 war, which incidentally strengthened the disdain felt by many Americans for Russian institutions and backwardness. Yet there was never serious threat of an open breach. Relations between St. Petersburg and Washington remained correct to the end of the Romanov dynasty.

The quality of U.S. diplomats in Russia was uneven during the final decades of the czars. Able men were assigned to St. Petersburg, of whom the best were John Foster, Andrew Dickson White, and George von Lengerke Meyer. On the other hand, incompetents were also sent. Cases in point were the ministers during the crisis of southern rebellion: disreputable Simon Cameron and maladroit Cassius Marcellus Clay.

Civil War Diplomacy

Had the Confederacy waged only a war of erosion and refrained from taking the offensive, for which its manpower and logistical resources were inadequate, it is possible that the Union would have sued for peace and allowed secession. In place of a single republic, two large states would then have competed for dominant influence in North America. In addition, Mexico and British Canada would have been able to play more prominent parts in New World affairs. Something like a balance-of-power system would have replaced U.S. supremacy. Such an outcome to the war was eminently desirable from the standpoint of Europe's major powers in the 1860s, France and Great Britain. That one or both of them would therefore recognize the Confederates and intervene diplomatically, or even militarily, on their behalf was a distinct possibility through the end of 1863.

To Napoleon III, a divided United States would have advanced his ambition of returning the French empire to North America. At their most grandiose, his plans envisioned the seizure of the Gulf Coast from Florida to Louisiana, the establishment of a naval base in Key West, and French preeminence in Mexico. In 1863, he persuaded the reluctant Archduke Maximilian of Austria to accept the Mexican (Catholic Empire) throne and French protection. But despite his marked pro-South sympathies and adventure in Mexico, Napoleon was unwilling to take unilateral action on behalf of the Confederate cause. For a risky undertaking, he needed Britain's cooperation.

Prime Minister Palmerston and Foreign Secretary Russell felt that a broken Union would help safeguard Canada and render North American relations more susceptible to British influence. London's support of the Confederacy not only would serve this desirable end, but also would guarantee the steady and economical supply of southern cotton to British textile manufacturers. By the summer of 1862, the government was sorely tempted to recognize the Confederacy, as it appeared—after a string of Union defeats—that a new nation had been created and was on the verge of breaking an unwanted political association.[1] Preliminary steps were taken by the French and British in September to offer mediation of the conflict on terms favorable to the South. The failure, though, of General Lee's army to destroy federal lines in Maryland (Antietam) and to carry the war north made Palmerston adopt a more cautious policy toward the war and a conciliatory tone toward the Union's representative in London, Charles Francis Adams. Still, the danger that Britain and France would recognize the South or take some type of intervention remained for another year.[2]

On at least one occasion after Antietam, an Anglo-U.S. clash of arms seemed imminent. In the spring of 1863, U.S. warships intercepted the British vessel *Peterhoff* and confiscated Confederate mailbags from among its cargo. Just as in the earlier *Trent* episode (mediated by Alexander II in 1862), there was an uproar in England, which made threats of war to redeem the "insult" to Her Majesty's honor. The Confederate commissioner in London, James Mason (like his colleagues John Slidell in Paris and Dudley Mann in Belgium), meanwhile continued to campaign for recognition and matériel aid. Direct assistance was never forthcoming, but the British did build a number of cruisers for southern purchase—including the dreaded *Alabama*—that took a toll on Union maritime commerce valued at more than $15 million.[3]

Russian interests in the Civil War were exactly opposite to those of the west European powers and took as point of reference British desires for a divided United States. Whereas from the existence of two jealous North American republics Britain would have feared nothing—and through their conflicting ambitions might have dominated them—Russia would have lost a counterbalance to British naval power. Consequently, within the limited means at its disposal, Alexander's government sought the Union's preservation. In the phrase of Foreign Minister Prince Alexander Gorchakov, it was "an element essential to the universal equilibrium."[4]

Czarist officials made it clear that a Confederate envoy to St. Petersburg would be barred from court, like the hapless Dana of yore. As a result, the would-be southern commissioner L.Q.C. Lamar was never admitted to Imperial territory. Only if the United States established diplomatic relations with the Confederacy would the empire follow suit, Baron Edouard de Stoeckl (minister to Washington, 1857–1868) assured Secretary of State William Seward. The Russian government also rejected Anglo-French proposals to join in a mediation effort. Neither did the Russians object to Union efforts to have Confederate privateers declared illegal. At the same time, Russia's press and censorship apparatus were coordinated to emphasize the importance of northern battlefield victories and to play down Union defeats.

In the absence of other great power support, northern publicists embellished the moral significance of Russia's benign neutrality. They eagerly drew comparisons between Alexander II, who in 1861 liberated approximately 20 million serfs, and Lincoln, who issued the Emancipation Proclamation two years later. Northern abolitionists claimed that the complementarity of their cause and Russia's had been obvious ever since 1852, when Harriet Beecher Stowe published *Uncle Tom's Cabin* and Ivan Turgenev produced *Sportsman's Sketches,* depicting serfs as wonderful, fully realized human beings. Throughout the war, Lincoln and Seward used every opportunity to persuade British and French ministers in Washington that the Union enjoyed a powerful ally. This idea was also communicated to the northern civilian population. In the emotional atmosphere of wartime, gratitude in the North for military services rendered by Russian volunteer officers such as Colonel John Turchin (the "mad Cossack") embraced the czar himself. After hostilities ended, the popular poet Oliver Wendell Holmes referred to Alexander as "our friend when the world was our foe."[5]

Never was the Union attitude toward Russia more apparent than in September 1863, when six ships of the Imperial Navy unexpectedly entered New York harbor. A month later, another Russian squadron of six entered San Francisco Bay. The majority of press and public regarded the presence of these warships as betokening Russian sympathy and as timely warning to the British and French that their intervention would have consequences reaching far beyond North America. In fact, the Russian ships (none of them equal to the vessels in the British or French navies) had anchored in U.S. ports for reasons unrelated to the northern cause. A possibility existed in 1863 that Palmerston and Napoleon would press the issue of Polish insurrection, and Russia's squelching of it, to the point of war. To prevent the fleet's being trapped in the Baltic, as had occurred during the Crimean War, Admiral Krabbe (chief of Imperial naval operations) ordered a number of his ships to take refuge in North America. In the event of hostilities, they might prove valuable from there as commerce raiders. (Although not acting under orders from Krabbe, Admiral Popov had relocated his command to California for similar reasons: if war began, his ships should be away from East Asian seas patrolled by French and British flotillas.) In New York and San Francisco, as well as in Boston and Washington, the ships' officers and sailors were feted. Parades, banquets, and balls were held to honor the Union's "true friends." War weary, its morale sapped by antidraft and race riots, the Union attitude was best expressed by Secretary of the Navy Gideon Welles, who exclaimed, "God bless the Russians!" Although he, Lincoln, Seward, and Charles Sumner (chairman of the Senate Foreign Relations Committee) knew the real motivation behind the naval visits, they had no desire to broadcast it.[6]

To retain St. Petersburg's sympathetic neutrality, Lincoln did not register any protest over the Russian crushing of Polish rebellion. Notwithstanding a fierce dispute between Seward and Sumner, the latter predisposed to assist Poland, the government also refused Anglo-French entreaties to help negotiate a peaceful settlement in Poland. The administration held that the United States did not presume to meddle in the internal affairs of sovereign states.

The years 1861 to 1865 produced no stronger U.S.–Russian friendship than had existed in the Crimean conflict; only a direct common threat (i.e., Britain) could have induced close cooperation. Even in that event, Stoeckl would have had qualms about forging strong bonds with the United States. Happily married to an American woman, he nevertheless harbored the reservations of his predecessors about the resilience of U.S. society. The test of civil war added to his doubts. In the aftermath of the Bull Run debacle (1861), he sent a report to Gorchakov describing Washington as a city endangered by roving gangs of deserted soldiers, a collapsed municipal authority, and a babble of opinions coming from selfish interest groups. He thought the capital was tottering on the brink of anarchy; a reign of terror no less horrid than that of the French Revolution might convulse the North. On other occasions, he disparaged the leadership of Lincoln and his cabinet. The president he judged an honest man, but one also vacillating and inept. He lacked the bearing to command. If the president was a nonentity, Stoeckl damned Seward as a scandal: he was ignorant of international realities, and his arrogance made him unsusceptible to advice. These two officials not only demonstrated the weaknesses on the Union side, but also confirmed the liabilities inherent in all democracies. Stoeckl wrote to the Foreign Ministry in 1863:

> The republican form of government so much talked about by the Europeans and so much praised by the Americans is breaking down. Democracy in the United States has become irresponsible, owing to the rising streams of radicalism and universal suffrage at home, to the influx of socialists. . . . What can be expected from a country where men of humble origin are elevated to the highest positions, where honest men refuse to vote and dishonest ones cast their ballots at the bidding of the shameless politicians? This is democracy in practice, the democracy that the European theorists rave about. If they could only see it at work they would cease their agitation and thank God for the Government which they are enjoying.[7]

Stoeckl softened his judgment after Lee's surrender at Appomattox, and he applauded the determination with which Northerners undertook reconstruction. He concluded that the Americans were irrepressible and strangely attractive, despite their many failings as a nation and culture.[8] In any case, he never doubted the wisdom of his government's attitude toward the war or the desirability of northern victory.

Luckily for the Union, its cause in St. Petersburg did not depend solely on its diplomats. Cassius Clay, who represented the United States during most of the Civil War, was an unlikely candidate for overseas assignment. Steady application of intelligence and tact were as alien to him as the other prerequisites for diplomacy: poise, discretion, and Washington's confidence. Born in 1810, the scion of a prominent Kentucky family (Henry Clay was a distant cousin), he was sublimely egotistical and possessed a superabundance of frontier bravado. He was also a determined ladies' man—not unhandsome—as well as a brawler and duelist. Whether in the United States or abroad, he typically sported a bowie knife and pair of pistols. During his long career as a pugilist, he killed a couple of men and maimed with his knife an unspecified number of others.

Before his 1861 appointment to St. Petersburg, Clay had seen military action in the war against Mexico (1846–1848), where he was taken prisoner; had served in the Kentucky legislature; and had earned a reputation as an orator who could concentrate the attention of the most raucous crowd. He was also an abolitionist who disavowed his family's slave-owning legacy; he founded a newspaper, the *True American,* to publish his uncompromising views on the subject. By 1860, he had emerged as a prominent figure in the Republican party, with hopes of winning the presidential nomination. When it became plain at the Chicago convention that this would elude him, he threw his delegate support behind Lincoln and later campaigned for him. He coveted a cabinet post as reward for this service and sought the War portfolio. This position, however, went to a still more influential party man, Simon Cameron of Pennsylvania. Failing to obtain any cabinet seat, Clay (and his supporters) expected his nomination to a prestigious ministerial post in Paris or London. Once again, Clay was disappointed, and he made known his feelings about Lincoln's ingratitude. To avoid offending men whose cooperation was necessary if Kentucky and other border states were to remain loyal, Lincoln finally offered Clay the recently vacated position in Russia. He accepted with magnanimity but also stated that he would like to serve his nation on the battlefield. He preferred a general's commission as soon as it was convenient.

In keeping with his predecessors on their way to St. Petersburg, Clay tarried through western Europe. But unlike them, he also acted the buffoon. In London and Paris, he held forth on various subjects in such a way as to insult his hosts and alarm the diplomatic community, including the U.S. contingent. Already on icy terms with Charles Adams, Clay further aroused his contempt with his antics. Adams labeled him a "noisy jackass." In May 1861, Clay had sent a letter to the London *Times* invoking Britain's tradition of liberalism as a basis of support for the North and predicting an American population that anyway would be twice the size of Britain's in fifty years. This mix of appeal and thinly veiled threat caused comment in Parliament and needlessly complicated Adams's mission. Later, at a public assembly in Paris, Clay explained that France would surely maintain its friendship with the United States and take aim against Britain if the "hereditary foe" joined forces with the Confederacy. From a British standpoint, Clay's run of gratuitous remarks was an example of his—and the Union's—haughtiness.[9]

By his own estimation, Clay was an unrivaled diplomatic success. In his memoirs, self-promoting even by the conventions of that genre, he endowed himself with every conceivable excellence. As ignorant of foreign policy as of French or Russian, he boasted that his "greenness" was a precious asset: courtiers could unburden themselves to this direct American, so unlike the dissemblers kept by other governments in St. Petersburg.[10] He congratulated himself for progress made in the 1860s by Russians and Americans in connecting their countries by telegraphic communication across Siberia and the Pacific. In the end, he took credit for dissuading the czar from joining the British and French in any of their interventionist plots. He was the man whose unsurpassed efforts had preserved the United States: "I carried Russia with us, and thus prevented what would have been the strong alliance of France [and] England . . . against us; and thus was saved the Union!" He also claimed that his ideas on slavery were decisive in destroying that institution, for they had inspired Lincoln to proclaim the emancipation.[11]

To Seward and Lincoln, Clay wrote voluminously about matters unrelated to his mission in St. Petersburg. To their annoyance, he advised them on the proper handling of military operations against the Confederacy and on naval modernization. He preached on the virtues of conscription, the liberation of slaves, and the management of freed men's affairs. Seward eventually became so angry that he ordered Clay to confine his attention strictly to Russian issues.

His political reporting displayed no particular acumen, however. His dispatches showed not the slightest appreciation for the Polish side of the Polish–Russian conflict, for example. Indeed, he was zealous in his support for the liquidation of the Polish insurrection, which he said was led by Catholic reactionaries who had duped their countrymen into rebellion; if that leadership should be successful, it would impose a tyranny over its subjects exceeding anything known under the czars. The Russians, by contrast, were taking strides toward a humane constitutional monarchy and embodied the truest force for progressive civilization in Europe: "No people are making more advances comparatively than the Russians in the fine and useful arts, in science and letters, and in general intelligence. A great destiny lies before her."[12]

Although Lincoln was grateful for Russia's benign neutrality and sensibly impressed by Alexander's policy toward the serfs, there is no evidence that he ever revised his original opinion of the Russian autocracy as the world's leading despotism.[13] In any case, neither he nor Seward took Clay seriously and ignored his policy pronouncements, as when he talked of an improbable Russia–U.S. alliance. Czarist officials, too, kept Clay at a distance. He knew nothing about their sending naval ships to American harbors until after the fact. Gorchakov had earlier grown weary of his insistent protests that the Union would emerge from the war victorious and stronger than before. By every account, he found Clay tedious. Gorchakov and other officials were also irritated when he congratulated them on directing Russia down the path of enlightenment blazed by the United States.[14]

Neither did the internal life of Clay's legation inspire confidence. His nephew, Green Clay, served as secretary but after a brief stint returned to America. Clay then recruited Henry Bergh, a frail dandy and son of a shipbuilding magnate, to

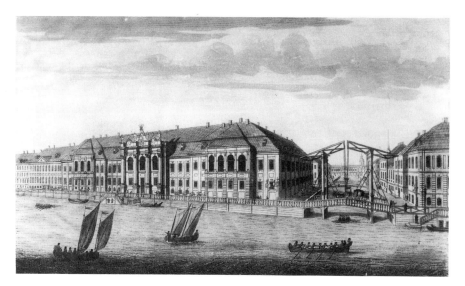

View of the Winter Palace, St. Petersburg (ca. 1794).

Francis Dana.
(National Archives)

John Quincy Adams.
(National Archives)

James Buchanan.
(National Archives)

Cassius M. Clay.
(National Archives)

John W. Foster.
(National Archives)

George von L. Meyer.
(National Archives)

David R. Francis.
(National Archives)

serve as secretary. In Russia, this hypochondriac, exposed to all manner of physical hardship, became so preoccupied with his and his wife's health that his attention to duties waned. He was further diverted by his horror at the brutalities that wagon drivers inflicted on horses in St. Petersburg. He eventually became a one-man rescue operation and would patrol the city streets by carriage. Whenever he spied someone mistreating animals, he would leap from his vehicle and give the miscreant a verbal thrashing. Bergh left Russia in 1864, and once back in the United States helped found the Society for the Prevention of Cruelty to Animals.[15]

Bergh was replaced in the legation by Jeremiah Curtin of Wisconsin. At first, he enjoyed his chief's respect and was valued by many—including Alexander—for his linguistic ability, which included a sure command of Russian.[16] But Clay, the prima donna, became jealous of Curtin's success. He eventually accused him of being a drunk, mountebank, and tool of his arch enemy, the villainous Seward. Curtin, on sounder ground, in turn charged Clay with financial chicanery related to construction (abandoned) of the American–Russian telegraph.[17]

All that can positively be said about Clay's tenure in St. Petersburg is that in his careless way he enjoyed it. Like Middleton and other Southerners before him, he felt at home among the Russian gentry and entertained on a lavish scale. Predictably, he went into debt. He joined a few social clubs and through them fostered decent personal relations with members of the court. He also managed to find friends in the diplomatic community, Britain's Sir Andrew Buchanan among them. From a distance, he admired Prussia's envoy, the young and obviously talented Otto von Bismarck. Clay was enthusiastic about the ballet and ballerinas and became a connoisseur of each. He thought Russian women uncommonly attractive and, though married, pursued flirtations and affairs with wives of noblemen. These adventures led to scrapes and challenges to duel. Rumors of Clay's private conduct reached his wife, who fled the scene of scandal, never to return to St. Petersburg. Although not confirmed, it is likely that he had a son out of wedlock by one of his Russian paramours. (In 1866, he was also charged with the attempted violation of a middle-aged woman and her daughter.) His amorous escapades and persistent questions about his financial transactions led to his recall by Washington in 1869.[18]

The only period of respectable American diplomacy in 1861 to 1865 occurred during Clay's absence from St. Petersburg. For a brief time, in 1862 and 1863, he escaped his diplomatic confinement and had his chance to perform service (without particular distinction) as a major general in the Union army. During this interregnum, Simon Cameron, whose administration of the War Department had been a comedy of incompetence and corruption, was ordered by Lincoln to remove himself to Russia. The overwrought Cameron wept when he learned of his cruel fate: to be an "exile" in St. Petersburg. He stayed briefly after presenting credentials to Alexander and then returned to the United States to salvage his political career.[19] This hasty departure left the legation in the hands of the young writer-traveler Bayard Taylor. He was appointed chargé d'affaires and was by the standard of the day eminently suited for his position. He knew French, learned Russian, was familiar with the country on the basis of previous visits, and regarded service there as worthwhile.

While heading the legation, Taylor had the good luck of intercepting (March 1863) instructions from Confederate secretary of state Judah Benjamin to Lamar. These emphasized the necessity that in any potential agreement with Russia the Confederate government not commit itself to opposing African slave trade. The propaganda value of the Confederate confession was not lost on the Union in the weeks following the emancipation decree. Taylor actually forwarded the wayward Confederate document to Seward on March 3, 1863, two years to the day after Russia's serfs had been freed from servitude. In London, Minister Adams fired:

> The bald pretense that these [Confederates] are struggling with oppression is refuted by the proof given that on the contrary they are fighting only to establish it. . . . What is the effect of such a document as the present but to show the way in which the conspirators cower under the apprehension of a possible application to their case of the opinion of the civilized world? Verily such is the doom of the unrighteous! [20]

Not only did Taylor cause the Confederacy this embarrassment, but he was an able spokesman in representations to Gorchakov. In early autumn 1862, following massive bloodletting at the second battle of Bull Run and Antietam and the capture of twelve thousand federal troops by Stonewall Jackson, Gorchakov expressed anxiety that the war was a disaster; nothing good could come from its continuation. He feared a permanent separation of North and South or, barring that, a nation so exhausted by war that it could not play an active role in world affairs. To this concern, Taylor replied vehemently: come what may, northern resolve to preserve the republic was unshakeable, Russia's support of the Union would be vindicated. Persuaded by Taylor's response, Gorchakov reaffirmed his regard for the United States and pledged once more his hostility to British and French schemes of interference. Shortly after this meeting, the *Journal de St. Petersburg* (mouthpiece for the czar) declared the Imperial position: "We consider that whatever may be the misfortunes of which North America is at present the theater, the foreign powers have no right to impose their mediation upon the country." In subsequent interviews, Taylor argued with renewed verve that the Union would win and would accomplish an unvengeful reconstruction. Convinced by eloquent reassurances and buoyed by Union successes, Gorchakov resisted any temptation he might have felt to support versions of mediation. [21]

Despite his accomplishments and having been led by superiors to expect promotion to minister following Cameron's resignation, Taylor was passed over by Lincoln in 1863. The reason was that Clay had proved himself to be a nuisance even in uniform. Lincoln was eager to dispose of him. It suited both that Clay return to St. Petersburg. Thus competent U.S. diplomacy (not for the last time) was sacrificed to expediency. Taylor had been badly used and was indignant that Clay, whose swaggering in St. Petersburg was already lore, should replace him; livid, he left the legation. For his part, Clay had no use for Taylor, and in his memoirs flung this barb: "As some of Taylor's friends have been desirous of placing him in the attitude of superior service to the Republic, and to crown his brow with laurels which I honestly won, I can say truly that, in all the time I was in St. Petersburg, I never heard his name mentioned in any way." (Of course, it is doubtful that anyone dared refer to Taylor in conversation with the preening Clay.) In any event, nothing stood in the way of his return to a flamboyant career. He enjoyed parading in his general's uniform and continued to keep up with his women, bully his subordinates, and harangue his superiors.[22]

Was the Union cause damaged by Clay's return to St. Petersburg? Probably not. For one thing, Lincoln shared the opinion of most others, including Bismarck, that Gorchakov was sagacious. He therefore wagered that the prince would not deviate from his opinion that the European balance of power (and Russian security) required an intact United States. To attain that end, Gorchakov would even suffer Clay. By mid-1863, with the victory at Gettysburg and the return of European attention to continental matters (over Poland and the Prussian–Danish crisis involving Schleswig-Holstein), the danger of outside intervention disappeared. In other words, the critical time was fast passing, and Clay's ineptitude could not hinder the conclusion of civil war or U.S. policy in Europe.

In Washington, Lincoln continued to show Stoeckl unusual courtesy by meeting with him more often than with other foreigners. He forgave his haphazard effort at mediation in the frantic weeks before the shelling of Fort Sumter and encouraged the Russian's access to high-ranking military officers, who permitted him to obtain blueprints of the ironclad *Monitor*. Stoeckl may never have entirely overcome his original reservations about Lincoln and remained convinced that Jefferson Davis was the most brilliant man in America. Yet in the end, Stoeckl was largely won over and was revolted by the president's assassination and the wounding of Seward in April 1865.[23]

After the War

A year after John Wilkes Booth and his accomplices struck in Washington, a radical university student, Dimitri Karakozov, shot at Alexander in St. Petersburg. Unhappy with the slow progress of Russia's former serfs in obtaining their rights under the new dispensation, Karakozov concluded that the czar had deceived his nation by granting an illusory liberty: emancipation without a fair apportioning of land was meaningless, and the redemption tax was potentially ruinous for millions of peasants. Only the quick reflexes of a former serf, Osip Komissarov, prevented Karakozov's shots from fatally wounding Alexander as he passed a crowd in front of the Letny Gardens. Governments around the world sent their congratulations at the czar's "providential" escape. But the U.S. response was singular and suggested to observers that the western republic and eastern empire were about to enter into formal alliance.

In addition to Seward's conveying regards to Alexander, the administration sent a special delegation to St. Petersburg with instructions to present the autocrat with a joint resolution of Congress. This testified to northern gratitude for Russia's moral support during the recent war:

> The many ties which have long bound together [Russia and America] have been strengthened by the unwavering fidelity of the Imperial government to our own,

throughout its period of convulsion. The words of sympathy and friendship then
addressed to the government at Washington, by command of your Imperial Majesty, are fixed in the eternal remembrance of a grateful country.

The congressional statement also favorably contrasted the czar's abolition of serfdom with the sanguinary American conflict: "The peaceful edict of an enlightened
sovereign has consummated a triumph over an inherited barbarism which our republic has only reached through long years of bloodshed."[24]

This message was carried in the summer of 1866 by Assistant Secretary of the
Navy Gustavus Fox. He and his entourage sailed to St. Petersburg in the modern
ironclad monitor *Miantonomoh,* accompanied by two more conventional warships.
The voyage of this contingent was closely followed by French and British observers, including an edgy Napoleon III. After Fox made his presentation to Alexander
in Peterhof palace, he and the American dignitaries, plus Clay, were treated to a
series of balls and receptions. They met Russia's most important military and
political personalities (and Komissarov, who had been promoted to the nobility).
They made a countrywide tour that included visits to Moscow and the Great Fair
at Nizhni Novgorod. Wherever they went, Russians expressed satisfaction for the
warm reception of their ships in Union ports three years earlier. Pieties of every
description were proposed and reciprocated by guests and hosts. Countless toasts
were drunk to undying U.S.–Russian friendship. Clay enjoyed this love feast as
much as anyone, despite his fretting that irregularities of protocol came at his
expense or that Fox had not immediately acknowledged his incomparable service.
Clay was not ignored—behavior that he would not have allowed—but he betrayed
an uneasy sense that he was an accessory to the main attraction, Secretary Fox.[25]

Nor did Clay play an important part when, in the aftermath of Fox's mission,
the U.S. and czarist governments reached agreement on the sale of Russian–
America. True to fashion, Clay claimed most of the credit for this transaction: "I
was in favor of that purchase . . . from the beginning and I may safely say that
it was owing to the good relations which I have been able to maintain with Russia
that such a purchase was possible."[26] In fact, he was not consulted by Seward
and was surprised to learn that on the evening of March 29, 1867, the secretary
and Stoeckl had agreed that Russia would cede its North American lands (afterward christened Alaska) for a purchase price of $7.2 million.

Not all Russians were in favor of this sale. Gorchakov, for one, was unenthu-
siastic. Yet the prevailing view, represented by Grand Duke Constantine, was that
Russian-America amounted to a long-term liability for the empire. It was vulnerable in time of war to British seapower. The territory was unprofitable for the
Russian-American Company, and the Imperial treasury would soon have to act as
receiver. Furthermore, acquisitive Americans, hungry for gold and fisheries and
animated by notions of Manifest Destiny, were likely to overrun the area sooner
or later as they had Mexican California. The disagreeable choice would then be
either to confront the United States or to stand by idly as Alaska silently slipped
into American hands. An additional incentive was that England's position on the
west coast would be compromised as the Americans acquired land to the north of
British Columbia. Might U.S. pressure eventually expel Britain altogether from

the Pacific? As it was, with the establishment of Vladivostok and the consolidation of Russia's position in East Asia, Alaska's value as a strategic base was diminished. In short, the time had come to relieve Russia of responsibility for a distant province of secondary importance.

As for the Americans, not until after a strenuous campaign led by Seward and Senator Sumner did Congress allow the purchase. Widespread doubts had to be overcome about the wisdom of adding territory not contiguous to the United States, of unproven economic value, and whose acquisition might complicate relations with Britain. Purchase of the territory would also further deplete the Treasury's financial resources, already burdened by the first demands of Reconstruction. Apart from these charges of profligacy and overextension (leveled by the publisher Horace Greeley, among others), there was a suspicion that President Andrew Johnson had orchestrated the Alaskan affair to distract public attention from his controversial southern policy and acrimonious conflict with radical Republicans. Resistance to Alaska was so strong at one point that Sumner advised Stoeckl to withdraw the Russian offer, thereby providing a graceful way out for all parties. Nevertheless, by focusing on Alaska's potential economic and strategic importance, the administration finally persuaded most congressional skeptics that acquisition was in the national interest. In the summer of 1868, the House overwhelmingly approved the necessary funding, and the territory—more that twice the size of Texas—was transferred to the United States.[27]

Contributing to this outcome was Stoeckl's use of hard-driving lobbyists and (very likely) his bribery of some congressmen, including Representatives Thaddeus Stevens of the influential House Ways and Means Committee and N. P. Banks, chairman of the Foreign Relations Committee. Stoeckl himself became so depressed by Congress's dawdling and the spectacle of bitter debate among self-seeking officials that he requested, and received, transfer from his post in ("politically fetid") Washington. Clay meanwhile offered encouragement from the sidelines to Seward and exclaimed that Alaska was worth at least $50 million; in future, the wonder would be that the United States had bargained so shrewdly. On this score, of course, Clay proved correct. Still, the point stands that he was not taken into Seward's confidence—or anyone else's in St. Petersburg or Washington—about Alaska and was relegated to dealing with issues marginal to the real business.

Into this second category fell straightening out the claims of a Boston merchant, Benjamin Perkins, against the Russian government. During the Crimean War, Perkins had entered into an oral agreement with Stoeckl to supply Russia with matériel, including 150 tons of gunpowder. But the war ended before any delivery or payment could be made. Perkins, and later his heirs, argued that the Imperial government should make good on his losses. The Foreign Ministry refused to recognize the validity of the case, however. In their representations to Alexander in the early 1860s, both Seward and Clay periodically raised the question and then dropped it. It was revived in 1867 by congressmen opposed to the Alaska purchase as an outstanding problem; during the most intense period of public debates, the Perkins matter threatened to become an insuperable obstacle to Alaska's sale. As it happened, Clay was not successful in resolving the grievance, but when the crucial moment arrived, no one much cared. Neither Seward nor a majority in Congress was prepared to let a trivial dispute prevent momentous American expansion.[28]

From the standpoint of U.S.–Russian history, the remainder of Clay's ministry after Alaska was uneventful. Following his return to the United States in 1869, he boasted about his expertise in matters Russian and in his discursive way expounded upon leading figures and politics. He commented favorably about Gorchakov, whom he felt would have made a first-rate parliamentarian in a democratic country. He spoke of Alexander as "a man of good common-sense." Of the Russian people, Clay said that there was "no more charitable nation on earth." These utterances fed into that body of postwar opinion impressed by what it regarded as instances of St. Petersburg's generosity (sending elements of the fleet to Union harbors, making a "gift" of Alaska) and that looked forward to a formal entente cordiale. None other than Mark Twain (later critic of czardom) joined the chorus of grateful Americans to laud Alexander as "kind," "affectionate," and "noble." As a troop of pundits were wont to explain, there was also a curious symmetry of experience between the two countries. Both had endured social revolution with the freeing of serfs and slaves; they had overcome regional insurrections (in Poland and the South); they were carving national territories out of their respective continents; they shared an antipathy for British power. In the editorial opinion of the *New York Herald,* the destinies of the two states were intertwined, and they "must ever be friendly" while advancing "hand in hand in their march to empire."[29]

Divergence

Contrary to these hopes, the remainder of the nineteenth century was marked by a hitherto-unknown tension in U.S.–Russian relations. The first cracks to appear in the "traditional friendship" were superficial and unrelated to the basis of power or its international distribution. Yet it was not a light matter when in December 1871 Ulysses Grant requested that Russia withdraw its minister, Constantine Catacazy. Grant charged that Catacazy had made himself personally objectionable and would no longer enjoy access to officialdom.

Apart from the irregularities and adventures of his youth (running away with the beautiful wife of an aged Neapolitan prince), which made him a subject of repressed envy in Washington, Catacazy fervently voiced his opposition to the hoary and once again resurrected Perkins claim. And in private and public statements, he heaped scorn on the administration—Grant in particular—for graft and corruption. The Perkins claim eventually involved Catacazy in a labyrinth of intrigue that featured forged letters, taunts by his official hosts, and threats of libel proceedings. On another and more important matter, he tried to derail sensitive Anglo-American negotiations in Washington. These were aimed at settlement of U.S. grievances arising from damage caused by the *Alabama.* Anything suggesting rapprochement between the English-speaking powers was anathema to

Russia, and Catacazy was under instructions to foil it if possible. However, his stratagems were so clumsy that he only succeeded in drawing additional embarrassing attention to himself. Subsequently, when the Grand Duke Alexis made his 1871/1872 tour of the United States, he received polite notice from Grant but not an invitation to the White House: protocol would have required the presence of Russia's odious minister as well. This official discourtesy marred the czar's son's otherwise pleasant holiday—which included hunting with Buffalo Bill Cody, viewing the Great Fire damage in Chicago, and witnessing a demonstration of modern naval technology. Grant's unusual behavior excited disbelief in St. Petersburg, where for years society had suffered the ridiculous Clay.[30]

Clay's immediate successor in Russia was Andrew Curtin, former governor of Pennsylvania and a career Republican party man. He was mindful of the low repute to which the legation had sunk. In the words of one associate, Curtin's primary goal was "to renew suitable relations with [his hosts] and restore the legation to its proper position and influence."[31] This task he advanced by exhibiting elaborate bonhomie, delivering a version of campaign stump speech on presenting credentials to Alexander, and playing the attentive guest at innumerable gilded ceremonies. Through his efforts, the social position of American officials was rehabilitated. He also managed as tactfully as anyone could the St. Petersburg end of the Catacazy episode.

Besides attending to these responsibilities, there was nothing memorable in Curtin's Russian career. His reporting about czarist attitude toward the Franco-Prussian War (1870–1871) was perfectly matter of fact but not especially perceptive about the war's significance or German unification. There was, incidentally, no misplaced complacency on the Russian side. After the French defeat at Sedan (September 1870), Russian anxiety became palpable. Eugene Schuyler, the legation's conscientious secretary, wrote the State Department, "The late successes of the German army have directed attention [in the czar's circle] to the vulnerable points of Russia in case of the complete victory of Prussia."[32]

Nevertheless, U.S. imagination in St. Petersburg was not engaged by the events unfolding in France and Germany: Bismarck, Napoleon III's capture, the siege of Paris, and the Commune were the appropriate concern of others. By late 1873, the legation's attention was concentrated instead on the amorous exploits of one spirited Hattie Blackford (née Ely), the daughter of a Philadelphia Presbyterian minister. By the time she arrived in the Russian capital, she had been the mistress of several men, including a Texas tycoon and a French nobleman. In St. Petersburg, she captured the favor of Grand Duke Nicholas, nephew of Czar Alexander. After a torrid romance, they scandalized polite society by deciding to marry. Intervention by the duke's father and police put an end to this nonsense; Blackford was briefly detained in jail and pressured to divest herself of the duke's love letters and gifts of family jewelry. She was finally shunted out of harm's way back to Paris.

Safeguarding Blackford's legal rights and forestalling adverse repercussions on Russian–U.S. relations were matters of concern to the new American minister, Marshall Jewell, and to Schuyler (also an admirer of Blackford). The entire diplomatic corps in St. Petersburg followed the escapade with merriment—no doubt to the chagrin of Jewell, for whom the affair consumed depressingly long hours. Russian officials, moreover, were embarrassed by the episode, touching as it did on the dignity of the czar's family, and angry with Jewell, whose actions on Blackford's behalf prolonged the issue.[33]

Possessing as they did elements of comic opera, the Catacazy and Blackford episodes might have been remembered as no more than annoyances in an otherwise unruffled Russian–American friendship. In fact, they helped usher in an era of disquiet. The basic problem was rooted in the U.S. reaction to the accelerating tempo of revolutionary violence and repression in Russia.

Although Alexander's administration willingly promoted reforms beyond the serfs' emancipation—establishment of the *zemstvo* system, renovation of the judiciary, moderation of censorship, improvements in education—critics demanded more. Liberals sought an expanded franchise and the creation of a constitutional monarchy. To establish an egalitarian society, radicals like Peter Tkachev, Serge Nechaev, Michael Bakunin, and their disciples waged war against the autocracy and private property. The violent teachings and deeds of the last, which included the murderous Narodnaia Volia, reinforced the conservatives' argument that change had gone far enough. The momentum of reforms did not completely halt, and measures were adopted in the early 1870s affecting municipal and military life. But the pace became more fitful after the 1866 and 1867 assassination attempts on Alexander. University curriculum, guided by the minister of education, Count Dimitri Tolstoy, was forced to return to traditional, less politically pernicious, subjects (classical history and languages). Stringent Russification was imposed on sullen Poland; pressure on the press was gradually intensified; the authority and prerogative of the *zemstva* were curtailed; even the highly touted new legal system was not immune to official influence, especially in cases involving political crimes. Discriminatory measures and violence against Jews also increased severalfold.

A number of Jewish American citizens (formerly czarist subjects) were themselves victimized when they traveled to Russia to transact business or visit relatives. Consequently, not unlike the Blackford case, U.S. diplomats became involved in ensuring the legal rights of these compatriots. Indeed, this issue became one of the leitmotifs that marked for decades the correspondence between envoys in St. Petersburg and their Washington superiors. Questions concerning visas denied or revoked, a jaundiced disregard by customs officers for American passport holders, instances of forced detention or expulsion, and similar mistreatment were reviewed by U.S. officials, who on occasion then filed protests. Expressions of concern by their coreligionists in the United States, meanwhile, found satisfaction in State Department pronouncements favoring Jewish emigration to America. Other religious minorities were also welcomed, including Mennonites opposed to military service and members of the pacifistic Dukhobors.[34]

Aggravating matters (from a czarist standpoint), in 1873 Schuyler exposed the existence of slave trading in Russian Turkistan. He purchased a Persian slave "openly in the bazaar in the city of Bokhara" and brought another one through Samarkand and Tashkent to freedom in the U.S. legation. For years before this event, Russians had maintained that slavery had been abolished wherever the Imperial writ extended in the east. After Schuyler's demonstration, the responsible authorities applied greater pressure in containing the "shameful traffic."[35]

The cumulative effect of Schuyler's "meddling" in Imperial matters and of U.S. action on behalf of sects outside Russian Orthodoxy was corrosive. In 1875, Alexander made known his disinclination to send a delegation to the centennial celebrations (in Philadelphia) of U.S. independence. But for the proddings and professions of friendship by George Boker, a passable poet and dramatist-turned-diplomat, the Russians would have avoided the festivities.[36]

In the years following, U.S. diplomats watched with fascination as the struggle between czardom and its enemies grew more gruesome. Wickham Hoffman, legation secretary in 1878, was in sympathy with the "singular verdict" of acquittal pronounced on Vera Zasulich after her wounding of the military governor of St. Petersburg, General Fyodor Trepov. Hoffman was aware of Zasulich's history: two years of incarceration and four years of enforced separation from her family, all on the unproven suspicion of having involved herself with a revolutionary propagandist. Hoffman also knew of Trepov's inhumane treatment of prisoners in his custody, including the flogging of a prisoner that had caused Zasulich to act. To the secretary of state, he wrote, "It was not the prisoner who [was] on trial: it [was] General Trepov and the police system of Russia. . . . [T]he verdict of 'not guilty' was in reality a verdict of 'guilty' on . . . the police administration." Nor was Hoffman persuaded by the state's perfunctory trial (and hanging in 1879) of an army lieutenant, Hadimir Dombrovine, for his alleged membership in a "secret Nihilist society."[37] All the same, the appalling "emperor hunt" conducted by Narodnaia Volia, as well as the indifference of the educated class to the terror endured by the Imperial family, was sympathetically followed by the legation. In April 1879, a would-be assassin emptied the chambers of his revolver at Alexander. In December, one of the Imperial trains on which the czar was thought to be riding was blown up. The next February, an explosion of dynamite destroyed the emperor's dining room in the Winter Palace at the hour when the royal family normally took dinner. None of the family was harmed, but sixty soldiers in a nearby guard room were killed or wounded. In Hoffman's view, this last attempt on Alexander's life hastened the demise of the ailing empress; she died in June.[38] At the same time, casualties mounted among officials targeted by revolutionary violence. Among these were Colonel Heyking of the Gendarmerie in Kiev (killed 1878) and General Mezentsev, chief of the secret police (stabbed to death in 1879).

Disaster occurred on March 13, 1881, the day that Alexander was to approve Count Mikhail Loris-Melikov's scheme allowing partial representative government. The remnant of Narodnaia Volia, its numbers reduced by police actions, killed Alexander with hand bombs as his carriage approached the Catherine Canal on its way to the Winter Palace. The U.S. minister at the time, John Foster, did not exaggerate when he later wrote, "The bomb of the conspirators in St. Petersburg, who claimed to be laboring for the freedom of Russia, stayed the work of reform and threw the country into a long period of reaction."[39] The new czar, Alexander III, immediately discarded thoughts that he once apparently had for liberalizing Russia: Loris-Melikov was forced to resign as minister of the interior and was replaced by the duplicitous and reactionary Count Nicholas Ignatiev. As if to symbolize the new age, a spate of anti-Jewish pogroms occurred in the southwestern provinces of the empire, with heavy loss of life and property in Kiev and Elizabethgrad. The fury of the Christian mobs and their atrocities so revolted Foster that he exclaimed, "The acts which have been committed are more worthy of the Dark Ages than of the present century."[40]

Alexander III's reign (1881–1894) was dominated by the miasmatic spirit of Constantine Pobedonostsev, former law professor at Moscow University, one-time tutor to Alexander, and (as of 1880) director general of the Holy Synod. This pallid and pedantic man (see Ilya Repin's *esquisse*) insisted on the inerrancy of the Orthodox Church, from which he had Leo Tolstoy excommunicated. He taught and promoted an aggressive species of Russification that denied the religious rights of national minorities. He encouraged anti-Semitism and inveighed against the West for its rationalism, materialism, and misplaced belief in the innate goodness of human nature. Absolutism, Pobedonostsev believed,was the legacy and destiny of Russia; any democratic impulse was alien and should be destroyed. In his *Moskovskii Sbornik* (1896), he gave this formulation:

> The history of mankind bears witness that the most necessary and fruitful reforms
> . . . emanated from the supreme will of statesmen, or from a minority enlight-
> ened by lofty ideas and deep knowledge, and that, on the contrary, the extension
> of the representative principle is accompanied by an abasement of political ideas
> and the vulgarization of opinions in the mass of the electors.

Redoubled censorship, increased police activity and arrests, and the repeal of earlier reforms were his bequest.[41]

The small U.S. colony in St. Petersburg was not directly affected by the reaction that settled over Russia. The routine of inspecting the mails, spying on households, and interdicting forbidden literature did not become appreciably more onerous. Foster, for one, still found much to enjoy in St. Petersburg. This self-conscious American (proud of his service against slavery; previously a lawyer, newspaper editor, and chairman of the Indiana Republican committee) discovered congenial companions in the corps of diplomats.[42] And though he considered Alexander III lethargic and did not sympathize with Pobedonostsev, he retained fond memories of his reception by Russian officials.[43] None of these sentiments, however, prevented him from protecting American Jews in Russia or from protesting the regime's mistreatment of its own subjects.

He initially followed the example of his predecessors and worked to ameliorate the hardships that befell individual Jews in Russia. On behalf of Henry Pinkos and, later, Marx Wilczynski, Foster and his staff made remonstrations to the Foreign Office: by virtue of their U.S. citizenship, these men should be exempt from decrees that ordered all Jews to leave the capital and other cities. Could a way be found to extend their stays in Russia so they might conclude their business affairs in a just, expeditious way? In both the Pinkos and Wilczynski cases, a compromise was achieved; Russian officials adopted a lenient attitude toward persons euphemistically labeled "meritorious."[44]

In making his case to the Foreign Ministry, Foster also argued along the lines of higher principle. Not only were the rights of Americans at risk in Russia, but discrimination and religious bigotry anywhere were abhorrent to civilized conscience. In presenting this appeal for tolerance, Foster was supported, actually encouraged, by Secretary of State William Evart and his successor, James Blaine. In Evart's phrase, U.S. diplomacy, however practical, must also "be consistent with the theory on which this government was founded." This statement and others like it helped placate the concerns brought forward by the Union of American Hebrew Congregations.[45]

The Russian response to Foster, in the person of Foreign Minister Nicholas de Giers, contained themes that were to reverberate throughout the remainder of the czarist era and beyond. First, not even the most enlightened nations were free of racial and other types of prejudice. For example, did not the mistreatment of Chinese in the United States (blacks were later added to the category of victims) illustrate the delicacy of treating general humanitarian questions? Moreover, one should bear in mind that the czar's Jewish subjects were faithless, and a number had been involved in the explosion at the Winter Palace. (Later, an incredulous Foster was told that Jews had figured conspicuously in the fatal attack on the czar.) It was a prudent measure in the interest of public safety that Jews be removed from St. Petersburg. Finally, Russia did not need instruction in the handling of its internal affairs. But if Foster cared deeply about the "vexatious" Jewish question, he would be edified by reading the twelve hundred pages of Russian law on the subject. In fact, this undigestible volume was delivered to him. But it proved murky and impossible of clear interpretation. Foster's successor, William Hunt, was exactly right when he stated that the regulations governing Jewish life were vague and confusing. They were "arbitrarily interpreted and applied to meet the exigencies of each case."[46]

Variations of the Foster–de Giers exchange were repeated throughout the next two decades; with each recital, the testiness in Russian–U.S. relations increased. Accumulating evidence of fresh pogroms in Warsaw, Odessa, and elsewhere and episodes involving U.S. Jews in Russia were driving a wedge between the two countries (despite goodwill briefly engendered by the 1881 Russian rescue of U.S. survivors from the Arctic-exploring ship *Jeannette*). An additional concern on the American side was that the pogroms were producing a mass migration of Jews to the United States. Indigent, without knowledge of English, unaccustomed to American habits of work, and ignorant of national institutions, these people seemed unassimilable to Protestant nativists. Additional numbers of them (estimates ran as high as a million) would overwhelm charitable organizations. In August 1890, the House of Representatives passed a resolution instructing President Benjamin Harrison to inform Congress of any information he might obtain about forthcoming czarist edicts against the Jews. And Secretary Blaine ordered the legation to advise Alexander that the condition of Russian Jewry was a matter directly bearing on the welfare of the United States, "upon whose shores are cast daily evidences of the suffering and destitution wrought against this unhappy people."[47]

Coinciding with this concern about Russian Jewry, there emerged in Europe and the United States an awareness of the scale of political repression in Alexander's empire. Attention was riveted on the far-flung penal system by such people as the Danish literary critic George Brandes. After a trip to Russia, he wrote in 1889— at the height of his popularity—that placed in every provincial town was the jail, invariably packed to capacity.[48] Slightly earlier, beginning in 1888 and running through 1889, *Century Magazine* published a series of articles about what one can call (with allowable anachronism) the czarist gulag in Siberia. Written by George Kennan, distant relative and namesake of the twentieth-century diplomat, these essays presented with unblinking clarity the degradations inflicted on political prisoners in Russia. Although the enormity and severity of the penal system excoriated by Alexander Solzhenitsyn dwarfed the one depicted by Kennan, his account exercised a similar effect on American minds. Unable to conceive of future regimes that would kill and incarcerate millions of people belonging to a given social or ethnic category, Kennan's first readers thought that he had unearthed *the* supreme form of state savagery. An outraged Mark Twain expressed the view of many when he declared that such evil deserved the "remedy" of dynamite.[49]

A veteran of Russian travel and respected author on the country, Kennan had returned to Siberia in 1885/1886 to examine the penal system and was prepared to write a defense of it. As he had earlier championed Russia and the czar against critics, he was given official assistance to inspect the methods of conveyance, confinement, and treatment administered to the sixteen thousand Siberian exiles. But Kennan was stunned this time by his Russian experience and remained thereafter the autocracy's enemy. His articles (compiled in two volumes and published in 1891 under the title *Siberia and the Exile System*) constituted his first salvo in an unremitting campaign of writing and lecturing, in which he countenanced the use of violence against oppression. At the same time, he developed abiding attachment for the czar's victims. To Kennan, the men and women he encountered in Siberian mines and prisons epitomized courage. In many instances, these people were also personally charming and well educated. To see them and their half-starved children suffering from squalor and brutality was more than he could bear. He once confessed:

> I was stirred . . . to the very bottom of my soul by the wrong and injustices that I witnessed. I am not ashamed of it! On the contrary, I should be ashamed of myself and despise myself if I were *not* capable of being stirred by such things. Many pages of my *Century* articles were written with my eyes so full of tears that I could hardly see the paper on which I was writing.[50]

So affecting were Kennan's testimonials and so palpable their impact on U.S. opinion that Alexander's government sought to counter them. One means chosen was to respond in the popular press, as when Pierre Botkine, secretary of the Russian legation in Washington, published "A Voice for Russia" (1893), also in *Century*. It was a turgid piece of czarist propaganda, typical of such tracts appearing at the time and unpersuasive to the majority of readers. Botkine castigated Kennan for having misrepresented the conditions prevalent in Russian prisons and argued that they were among the most enlightened in the world. As evidence, he cited the delegates to the Fourth International Prison Congress of 1890, convened in St. Petersburg, who "expressed their [admiration for] the extremely humane treatment of convicts on the part of our authorities." The essay was also intended to allay readers' concerns about anti-Semitism, but in defending the czarist record resorted to ugly myths about Jews. Their ingrained habits, claimed Botkine, were "dangerous and prejudicial" to the honest, easygoing Russians.[51]

Whatever the faults of Botkine's essay, he was on firm ground when he reported that the findings of the prison congress were favorable to Russia. In fact, from a propagandist's standpoint, the congress was sensational. The U.S. delegate gushed, for example, that the progress made by Russian penal science was known and respected everywhere. From other American quarters, the Kennan thesis was also challenged, though not successfully refuted. In St. Petersburg, Minister Charles Emory Smith and the vice consul publicly denounced Kennan's reports as malicious. In an article of his own, the irascible Cassius Clay lambasted Kennan for being duped by the "Nihilists." And former ministers George Lothrop and Lambert Tree tried to soften the picture of Russia drawn by Kennan. They reminded their audiences that Russia's friendship for the United States had stood the nation well, above all during the Civil War, and should serve nicely in future years.[52]

Thus, by the end of Alexander's reign, the need felt by U.S. officials for a continued working relationship with Russia was being eroded by popular disapprobation aroused by czarist practices. This state of affairs was never more evident than during the ministry of Andrew Dickson White. By any standard, his public career was exemplary and set him apart from many who had earlier served in St. Petersburg. Sixty years old when he presented credentials to Alexander, White had been a professor of history at the University of Michigan, the first president of the American Historical Association, and the first president of Cornell University. He was a tireless proponent of civil service and educational reform and in 1879 to 1881 had been minister to Germany. Although his political ambitions were mostly frustrated, he had served as a member of the New York Senate. After failing to obtain the Republican nomination for gubernatorial candidate in the New York election, White accepted (1892) from President Harrison the assignment to St. Petersburg.

Like John Quincy Adams, White went to Russia with preconceived ideas based on youthful experience, in his case from his employ (1854–1855) by Minister Thomas Seymour. The empire of Nicholas had originally struck White as "thoroughly barbarous"; its citizens were smothered by despotism and the "standing enemy," vodka; its ruling class was "unscrupulous." A visit to ancient Moscow elicited this response from the young man: "Everywhere were filth, squalor, beggary, and fetishism. Evidences of official stupidity were many." In contrast with most Americans at the time, White had hoped that Russia would lose the Crimean War; then this "most utterly detestable" civilization might begin to implement needed reforms. Even so, he was skeptical that any Russian leadership, no matter how competent, could overcome what he saw as the country's stupefy-ing moral and social backwardness. The charges leveled by Custine were incontro-vertible.[53]

A devout believer in the inevitability of progress in the European and North American worlds, the mature White experienced nothing to dislodge his earlier views on the empire. What depressed him most about Russia after an absence of forty years was the remarkable lack of change. True, a railway system more exten-sive than that of the 1850s connected distant provinces to St. Petersburg and Mos-cow. True, the peasants were no longer constricted by serfdom and were free, at least in theory, to sell their labor and work their own land. Yet these signs of change were more apparent than meaningful. The state-owned railway was ineffi-cient, reported White; in spite of ample expenditures to improve it, the entire network of transportation was barely improved over previous decades. Because of assiduous efforts by reactionaries to thwart Alexander II's purpose, White ob-served "little, if any, practical difference between the condition of the Russian peasant before and since obtaining his freedom." Servile, superstitious, and illiter-ate, he lived as previously in soul-destroying poverty. White concluded that the country remained what it had always been: abnormally retrograde, a place where the hand of repression killed change.[54]

However disheartened by Russian conditions, White bestirred himself more than most diplomats to know the country's leading personalities. He became ac-quainted with the professorate at Moscow and St. Petersburg universities. From one philosopher, he was reassured to learn that a movement was afoot to revive the teaching of Kant in Russia. White also visited Tolstoy, with whom he re-viewed Russia's prospects, assessed the promises and failings of America (Tolstoy was sickened by lynchings in the South), and delved into those philosophical problems central to the writer: the purpose of art, the nature of property, pacifi-cism, the goal of history.[55]

Ironically, given his disapproval of Russian political practice, White also came to admire certain qualities of Pobedonostsev. This architect of reaction, dubbed by critics "the Torquemada" of his era, seemed to the diplomat a person of impec-cable aesthetic tastes and broad education. The two men enjoyed discussions about practical and theological matters. White listened indulgently to the hostile reaction of Pobedonostsev to suggestions favoring religious tolerance or smacking of ecu-menism—a "droll" invention of modernity, scoffed the latter. He was agreeably surprised to learn of Pobedonostsev's knowledge of American literature and aston-ished that he, of all people, had translated Ralph Waldo Emerson into Russian. Moreover, White found that the director general of the Holy Synod was prepared to exempt the United States from his blanket condemnation of Western culture. It was a country remote to him, belonging to the category of dreamland. It was also a state, he assured the minister, with which Russians wanted to preserve good relations.[56] And yet it was Pobedonostsev's policies that were daily damaging U.S. confidence in Russia.

Before proceeding to St. Petersburg, White had stopped in London, where he met Lord Rothschild and Sir Julian Goldschmidt. As had their coreligionists in the United States, they impressed upon him the disabilities suffered by Jews in Russia. These interviews quickened White's already considerable appreciation for the Jewish issue, which in his view was related to the problem of undesirable immigrants flooding U.S. cities. In his *Autobiography,* he asserted—without sensitivity to the inequalities of power and of legal status possessed by the two sides—that the Jewish and Christian leaderships in western Russia were fanatical; they had created an endless cycle of violence and vengeance. From this situation, the United States had become a victim, thereby throwing doubt on Russian professions of goodwill toward the republic. Secretary of State W. Q. Gresham made precisely this same point when he wrote White in 1893:

> The measures adopted by the Imperial government against the Jews, although professedly a domestic policy directly affecting the subjects of the Czar, were calculated to injuriously affect the American people by abruptly forcing upon our shores a numerous class of immigrants destitute of resources and unfitted in many important respects for absorption into our body politic. The continued enforcement of such harsh measures, necessarily forcing upon us large numbers of degraded and undesirable persons, who must, in great measure, be supported, cannot be regarded as consistent with the friendship which the Russian Government has long professed for the United States.[57]

On appropriate occasions, White conveyed his anxiety over the treatment meted to Jewry and its consequences to U.S. life. He was also involved in trying to rescue American Jews from the mishaps that continued to befall them in St. Petersburg and Moscow. Of particular value, he prepared for the State Department a detailed study of the history and condition of Russian Jewry. Commended by his superiors for its thoroughness, the report ended with this reaffirmation of the American position: "The present system of repression toward the Israelites is from every point of view a failure, and . . . it is doing incalculable harm to Russia."[58]

Reflecting both its displeasure with U.S. carping about Jewish "malcontents" and a temporary thaw in the Anglo-Russian cold war, the czarist attitude showed unmistakable signs of reserve. Despite White's lobbying efforts, the Foreign Ministry sided with Great Britain in the arbitration tribunal (in Paris), adjudicating the Anglo-U.S.-Canadian dispute over seal-hunting rights in the Bering Sea. Notwithstanding public statements of gratitude to American charities for food relief from the famine of 1891/1892, there was simultaneously a show of Russian prickliness and hurt pride in accepting outside assistance. For his part, White was dismayed by the indifference of the czarvitch (the future Nicholas II) to the magnitude of the famine and subsequent cholera epidemic. Nicholas, who had been appointed to lead the special committee charged with providing aid to the 11 million people affected, struck White as ignorant of the starving conditions in the countryside and unwilling to meet the crisis energetically. In the meantime, the two countries did complete a treaty of extradition, but only after popular outcry in the United States had forced incorporation of safeguards preventing its use against political offenders. Even so, Kennan and his allies in the Jewish American community

(Jacob Schiff and Oscar Straus) continued to campaign against Senate ratification of the treaty. The debate over the treaty (signed in 1887 but not approved by the Senate until 1893) could not have reassured the Imperial government about future U.S. intentions.[59]

Secretive in its deliberations, distrustful of foreigners, and irresponsible in managing the welfare of its subjects, the czarist regime discouraged White's compatriots. In 1892, Congress considered adopting Representative Dungan's (Ohio) proposal that the United States sever diplomatic relations with "horrific" Russia. White himself believed that the structure of empire would finally collapse under the weight of its own injustices. Given an opportunity, he would have admonished Alexander III, "What a world of harm you are destined to do! . . . You will try by main force to hold back the whole tide of Russian thought; and after you will come the deluge."[60]

Twilight of the Czars

Pogroms and Abrogation of the 1832 Trade Treaty

Nicholas II used the death of his father (1894) as an occasion to reinforce the primacy of autocracy in national life and to remind his subjects to whom they owed their allegiance. Was it a premonition of future catastrophe and a desire to preempt it that prompted Nicholas to commend patriotism and loyalty? "Let us console ourselves," he said on the day of Alexander's passing, "in the consciousness that our grief is also the sorrow of all our much-loved people, who cannot forget that the strength and stability of holy Russia are in their union with us, and in their unqualified devotion to our person."[61]

Contrary to Soviet historiography, there was nothing inevitable about the collapse of the Romanov dynasty. In the first decade of his rule, Nicholas's Russia enjoyed an economic resurgence and demonstrated vitality in foreign affairs. Under the tough-minded Sergei Witte, minister of finance (1892–1903), Russia started to develop the attributes of a modern competitive economy. On his initiative, the tariff was reorganized, and foreign investments (French, chiefly) were obtained. Taxation of liquor increased government coffers. Adoption of the gold standard helped stabilize the exchange value of the ruble. The Trans-Siberian Railroad was built, and the entire railway system doubled in mileage. The Russo-China bank was established, and the settlement and exploitation of Siberia advanced. Although the agricultural sector languished and the foreign debt bulged, manufacturing jumped dramatically. Heavy industry produced record levels in the critical areas of coal, steel, and pig iron. Although Russia's industrial strides and new financial strength did not close the gap between itself and the principal powers of Europe, only the United States exhibited comparable rates of growth. There was nothing false in the assessment of Minister Clifton Breckinridge when he told Washington that Witte was a man of tremendous "ambition and ability." By turn of the century, American representatives in St. Petersburg spoke glowingly of Russia's "extraordinary progress in industrial enterprise" and viewed the country as a market ripe for U.S. manufacturers of sundry machinery and transportation equipment.[62]

Even if Russian motives were far from pure and tied to anxieties about a prohibitively expensive arms race in a period of stringency, the government displayed welcome initiative when it caused to convene the international peace conference at The Hague in 1899. Contrary to Nicholas's wishes and making nonsense of them, events in later decades belied the meeting as "a happy augury for the century about to open." As White, who led the American delegation, had foretold (and as all but the most naive expected), the conference did not lead to universal disarmament or a decrease in global military spending. Yet the results were not negligible: the legal rights of noncombatants and belligerents in warfare were expanded, and the International Court of Justice was founded as a permanent court of arbitration.

Unhappily for Russia, neither economic progress under Witte nor the innovations of czarist diplomacy were able to counteract the debilitating effects of continued political reaction. Had personalities like Alexander II, Loris-Melikov, and Witte (for whom Nicholas had antipathy and dismissed from the Finance Ministry in 1903) led the country, disastrous war in 1904 and revolution might have been averted. Instead, until his death in 1907, Pobedonostsev continued to work his baleful influence on the weak and vacillating mind of Nicholas. The archreactionary Viacheslav Plehve, as minister of the interior, helped oversee additional restrictions against the press, university students, and the rickety *zemstvo* system. Russification was also intensified. Its stormy pace in Finland turned that once-contented province into a zone of mutiny. In 1904, the governor-general of Finland was assassinated. That same year, Plehve was killed by a Socialist Revolutionary, just as his predecessor had been two years before. According to one U.S. diplomat, between 1900 and 1906, nearly two thousand officials and other notables had been killed by revolutionaries. This number included clergymen and manufacturers, as well as the more obvious targets of governor-generals, army officers, and prefects.[63] In Nicholas's presence, Peter Stolypin, president of the Council of Ministers, was assassinated in 1911 by Dimitri Bogrov (one of those baffling prewar figures whose mentality combined equal parts of the police agent and revolutionary). These shootings and bombings were met by a kaleidoscope of measures designed to coopt or crush the opposition: half-hearted agrarian reforms, courts-martial, punitive expeditions, emergency decrees. Thus, state repression and revolutionary terror reinforced each other. They also created a climate of violence that, coinciding with deteriorating conditions in the peasants' economy, exploded in new outrages against Russia's Jews.

Though by no means the worst that occurred during the century's first decade, the Easter 1903 pogrom at Kishinev did more than any other to fan anti-Russian sentiment in the United States. Graphic newspaper accounts of women and children slaughtered and the complicity of local police authorities with the perpetrators confirmed the widespread conviction that Russia was "the barbarian of Europe." There was a flood of financial aid to the victims, enactment of measures to facilitate immigration, public demonstrations, and condemnation from editorial pages, pulpits, and lecterns. According to the most authoritative account, the rampage had produced forty-seven fatalities, four hundred wounded, and ten thousand homeless and had caused property damage valued at $1,250,000.[64] Realistic about the ramifications of trying to contain popular wrath before an upcoming presidential campaign, Theodore Roosevelt hesitated but permitted (against his better judgment) a petition of protest to be presented to the Russian government. Predictably, the Foreign Ministry refused to receive this document, which charged the czar with being derelict in his duty to civilization and enjoined him to combat racial and religious hatred. Yet the point had been made: the normal habits of diplomatic intercourse could not be insulated from an indignant (and outlandish, from a Russian viewpoint) democratic population. The practical effect of the petition was to raise the pitch of defensive declarations from St. Petersburg. These denied official misconduct, deplored outside interference while intimating that the U.S. record of tolerance was spotty, and reproached the ingratitude of a nation whose survival had depended on czarist goodwill.

The situation for Jews in Russia worsened in the ensuing years and produced corresponding complications abroad. Inflamed to greater passion by the anti-Semitic press and revelations in the spurious *Protocols of the Elders of Zion*— appearing for the first time in Russia just months after Kishinev—the pogromists and their allies in government were especially active during the repression following the 1905 revolution. Occasionally quick to blame imagined provocateurs in the Jewish population (socialists, anarchists, or vigilantes) for starting the violence, U.S. diplomats diligently recorded the massacres and pillaging that caused tens of thousands of Jewish casualties and made far more homeless and impecunious. In September 1906, the hardworking chargé, Spencer Eddy, ended a report with this observation: "The Government is trying to make it harder and harder for a Jew to remain in Russia, and are prejudicing the people against the Jews to that end."[65] Those who could escaped to western Europe, Palestine, or, more often, the Americas. By 1910, slightly fewer than 2 million Russian-born Jews resided in the United States.

Continued public unease about the desirability of accommodating everyone who sought asylum and concern about Jewish suffering (sometimes campaign posturing, sometimes genuine) caused Congress to consider an unprecedented measure in 1911. Its signal intention was to foster salutary changes in Russia. In February, Herbert Parsons of New York introduced legislation in the House calling for abrogation of the 1832 Russian–U.S. treaty of commerce on the grounds that czarist officials had repeatedly harassed Jewish holders of American passports (in violation of provisions guaranteeing the rights of U.S. citizens). Hearings followed, and in December, by a vote of three hundred to one, the House passed the proposal. Senate feeling ran equally high and would have produced a comparable resolution. To forestall this and avoid what they saw as gratuitous injury to Russia, President William Taft and Secretary of State Philander Knox advised St. Petersburg that both sides should agree to cancel the existing treaty and negotiate a new one; ideally, the governments would make a joint announcement to this effect. Foreign Minister Sergei Sazanov, however, refused to be party to this idea and warned that Russia would only sign a new treaty that conformed to the original. Ambassador Curtis Guild then answered that the United States would not seek the treaty's annual renewal; as of January 1, 1913, it would cease to be in force. Contrary to Knox's preference and despite his communications with Russian diplomats, no new agreement was concluded before World War I.[66]

Termination of the treaty was endorsed by the broad American public. Both national parties, as well as Roosevelt's Progressives, wrote supportive planks in their 1912 platforms. By late summer 1913, the United States was no longer admitting certain Russian products (e.g., wood pulp, paper) under the minimum tariff provision of the 1832 treaty.

Derision and anger were the Russian response. In an interview with Guild, Sazanov charged that it was incomprehensible that the United States would wantonly sacrifice its Russian market, worth hundred of millions of dollars in the future. Still, he controlled his temper as Guild explained Congress's motives: to induce Russia to abandon restrictions on native and foreign Jews and to learn from the U.S. experience—absolute freedom of speech and movement preempted treason by removing potential grievances. To this declaration of faith in American life, the foreign minister rejoined that what was true in the United States did not automatically apply to Russia. Could the Americans not understand the complexity of the Russian situation, where Jewry constituted a "perpetual menace" to the integrity of the empire, shunning its laws and disrupting its tranquility? He added with a straight face that Nicholas would gladly consider any proposal effecting the transfer of all Russian Jews to the United States. No amicable discussion followed. An exasperated Sazanov condemned the congressional action as unprovoked hostility that pressed demands no self-respecting nation would satisfy.[67]

More fury followed. The official press thundered that through its "controlling influence" on finance and newspapers, U.S. Jewry had stirred American opinion into a "frenzy" against Russia. Jingoist pamphleteers inundated the pavements of St. Petersburg and Moscow with diatribes against the United States. Reactionaries and monarchists in the Duma, such as Count Bobrinski and Bishop Eulogius, pushed for punitive legislation. It would bar all foreign Jews from entering Russia and exact stiff levies on U.S. goods. Cooler voices in the Duma eventually prevailed, and liberal dailies *(Retch* and *Russiia Viedomosti)* had a calming effect on opinion. But Russian–U.S. relations had nevertheless reached a nadir. As for the empire's Jews, Congress's foray into diplomacy did not save them from their tormentors. The embassy in St. Petersburg reported in early 1914 that abrogation of the commercial treaty "instead of helping the position of . . . Jews, had the contrary effect, and spurred the Russian Government to enforce existing regulations against all Jews, both foreign and native, and even to put into force new and more severe ones."[68] Improvement in the Jewish condition had to await radical change in Russia; after the monarchy's abolition, the Provisional Government adopted laws granting civil equality to all citizens.

From the standpoint of conventional diplomatic wisdom, it was predictable that outside pressure proved ineffective in accomplishing its aim with Russia. Guild harbored no enthusiasm for being an instrument of democratic diplomacy and accepted the injunction regarding the importance of confidential government-to-government consultations. Even White, whose hostility to czarism was public knowledge, had felt bound to warn Kennan and like-minded critics against a policy premised on a "holier than thou" attitude.[69] In other words, formal diplomacy, with its deliberation and gravity, was more likely to produce results compatible with U.S. interests than intrusions by an evangelizing Congress and emotional public. For this claim, contemporaries could have cited as evidence the ambassadorship of George von Lengerke Meyer, who had served in St. Petersburg during the tumultuous years just preceding the treaty's abrogation.

The Russo-Japanese War and Revolution

Meyer enjoyed the friendship and full support of President Theodore Roosevelt. They had been undergraduates together at Harvard. Afterward, their attachment to big-game hunting, the sportsman's life, and the Republican party kept them close. Temperament and experience also aided Meyer in his Russian assignment (1905–1907). Like the president, he possessed the casual confidence that comes from inherited wealth and early success. He was also direct and decisive, yet capable of considerable tact; he had acquitted himself well for more than four years as ambassador in Rome. Roosevelt himself did not respect the customs of ordinary diplomacy. After John Hay's death in 1905, he ignored the State Department and assumed the role of his own secretary of external affairs. Still, as the president confided to Meyer, he needed a person on whom he could depend: "The trouble with our ambassadors in stations of real importance is that they totally fail to give us real help and real information, and seem to think that the life-work of an ambassador is a kind of glorified pink tea-party. Now, at St. Petersburg I want some work done, and you are the man to do it."[70] To ensure unimpeded consultations, the two men elected to bypass the State Department and established direct cable communication and weekly exchanges. These proved eminently useful in the president's mediation of the Russo-Japanese conflict.

Roosevelt was the most prominent of the many Americans (Kennan was another) who in 1904/1905 hailed Japanese daring and victories in its war against Russia. His contempt for Nicholas—he called him a "preposterous little creature"—meshed with his belief that in advancing its claims in Manchuria and Korea, Japan was pursuing a policy harmonious with U.S. interests. Competition for political and economic influence in Manchuria had placed a strain on Russo-American relations as early as 1895. Russia's "lease" of Port Arthur and Dalny on the Liaotung Peninsula and dispatch of troops to most of Manchuria (following the Boxer Rebellion) further complicated matters. The belated and lukewarm endorsement by Foreign Minister Muraviev of Hay's Open Door notes—signifying U.S. interest in Chinese markets and territorial integrity—merely highlighted the incipient rivalry between Russia and America in East Asia. Thus, the clash of Russian and Japanese imperialisms and the unexpected defeat of the former confirmed Roosevelt's conviction that Japan had successfully "fought our battle as well as her own." Yet he was not oblivious to the possibility that Japanese naval power, emboldened by its destroying of Russia's fleet in the Tsushima Straits and by the 1902 Anglo-Japanese accord, might one day threaten America's Pacific possessions, Hawaii and the Philippines.[71] Indeed, he viewed with growing apprehension the possibility that Russian influence might be driven entirely from the Pacific; at one point, he thought the Russian retreat would extend to the west of

Lake Baikal. For the sake of an Asian balance of power conducive to U.S. interests in China and security requirements in the Pacific, Roosevelt welcomed the chance to broker a peace between the belligerents. This opportunity arrived in late May 1905 (just days after Tsushima), when Japan's minister in Washington, Takahira, broached to the president the desirability of a diplomatic end to hostilities.[72]

Roosevelt immediately instructed Meyer to see Nicholas and urge him to accept U.S. brokering. The timing could not have been better. Lest protracted war spark full-blown revolution in Russia, the czar's cousin, Kaiser Wilhelm II, had just recommended that he seek Roosevelt's assistance "to bring the Japanese to reasonable proposals." And the shattering of the Russian fleet was causing consternation in St. Petersburg and demands that the bungling bureaucracy—whipping boy of the autocracy—be taken to task for the defeat. Yet the Imperial government betrayed that queer indolence, characteristic of its final years, when it learned that Meyer was to deliver an urgent message from Roosevelt. Meyer was curtly told by the foreign minister that the czar's engagements were booked far in advance. The next day especially was unthinkable: Nicholas and the empress would be celebrating her birthday in private. Saner minds in private counsel evidently prevailed, and Meyer was permitted on the morrow to see Nicholas at the palace in Tsarskoye Selo.

After hearing the president's proposal, Nicholas tried to save face by protesting that until he ascertained what his subjects really wanted, he was uncertain whether to respond to the U.S. offer. Everyday, he said, he received hundreds of letters from people, ordinary and distinguished, encouraging him to continue the war and offering money or services.

Meyer responded with flattery and cajolery: of course, there was no feeling in Russia for peace at any price; if the Japanese made extreme demands, a united Russia would rise as one man in vengeful wrath. And if it was hard to make decisions contrary to one's pride, there was consolation in choosing peace, as it would save countless lives and win the world's respect. No Christian army, including the czar's valiant one, could quell the Japanese soldier, imbued with a fanaticism that glorified death. Timid capital (and foreign lenders) required greater domestic stability in Russia before it could be persuaded to develop Siberia's unbounded resources. In the end, Nicholas consented to the U.S. proposal, adding in understatement that Meyer had come at the "psychological moment"—before Japanese soldiers had set foot on Russian territory. As they could now take Sakhalin island at will, Nicholas expressed hope that meetings could be arranged before such a disaster occurred. On taking leave, Nicholas allowed that Russia and the United States should renew their "old friendship," the innocent victim, he opined, of a scurrilous press.[73]

Despite the initial outburst of Count Cassini, Russian ambassador in Washington, that Meyer must have misunderstood the czar's intention, by mid-June Russia and Japan had agreed to talk. There was haggling over the site of meetings—Paris or The Hague or Washington (in the event, it was Portsmouth, New Hampshire). Additional delays were caused by travel and uncertainty on the Russian side about whom to entrust with negotiating. After considering a couple of other candidates to lead the mission, including the physically infirm and intellectually sluggish

A. I. Nelidov, Nicholas made a personally distasteful selection and chose Witte as chief plenipotentiary.

During the months of negotiations (the treaty was signed on September 5, 1905), Meyer continued to play a critical role, particularly as a steadying influence on Nicholas. Shortly after Japanese and Russian commissioners first convened (August 5) at Roosevelt's home in Oyster Bay, Meyer met with Nicholas. The czar was nervous about Russia's possibly making a dishonorable peace that would include the surrender of territory, specifically Sakhalin, and payment of a substantial indemnity. Contrary to the drift of discussions that had taken place at Oyster Bay, Nicholas argued that division of Sakhalin into Russian northern and Japanese southern halves would be a source of irritation and future strife. As for paying a war indemnity, this was an insulting idea for a nation by no means near capitulation. Nicholas told Meyer that if the issue were forced, he would go to the East and assume personal command of the army. Meyer answered by gently reminding the czar that southern Sakhalin had been so briefly in the empire's possession that it could hardly be considered an authentic part of Imperial territory. As for a contiguous Russo-Japanese presence on the island, it would not necessarily cause problems. Meyer contended disingenuously that a case in counterpoint was the long and peaceful Canadian–U.S. frontier; in any event, a Russian base in northern Sakhalin would be sufficient to protect czarist holding in the Amur area. Nicholas conceded Meyer's points about Sakhalin, which helped make possible the peace of Portsmouth—a moderate agreement that recognized Japanese suzerainty in Korea, surrendered the Liaotung Peninsula to Japan, did divide Sakhalin in half, but included no indemnities. As underscored by the huge demonstrations and anti-American rage in Japan following the announcement of terms, Russia obtained a settlement better than its military performance warranted.

The Imperial government awarded Meyer the Grand Cordon of St. Alexander Nevsky for his efforts in ending the war. A grateful Roosevelt acknowledged him as among the premier world diplomats and one whose service was incomparable.[74] In 1907, Roosevelt promoted Meyer to the cabinet, where he served as postmaster general. He was later (under William Taft) secretary of the navy. Before then, however, Meyer was witness to the revolution of 1905 and the following wave of reaction.

One historian of the Russo-Japanese War faults Meyer for not being fully informed about the revolution and for failing to keep Roosevelt properly apprised of it.[75] This is an unduly harsh evaluation, however. All things considered, Meyer was a keen observer. It is true that he could have been quicker in discerning the depth of disaffection, but by early July 1905 (he had arrived on the scene only in mid-April), he was entirely alert to the fatefulness of events. The opinions he committed to paper also show him to have been a credible judge of personalities, at least on the government side. He saw clearly that Nicholas was the captive of poor counselors (foremost the Empress Alexandra, who watched him "like a cat"), was badly served by the haughty Cassini in Washington, and was undermined at home by a bureaucracy riddled with corruption. The czar himself, Meyer perceived, was without force or breadth of mind. Meyer also criticised his lackadaisical approach to reform and compared Nicholas with Louis XVI: "It is a pity that the Emperor . . . does not study the causes and results of the French Revolution of 1789 and profit by the events which are rapidly being repeated in his own Empire."[76]

Through its neglect of the peasant population, uneducated and "living like animals," and its fighting a needless war, the regime was merely reaping the results of its own misrule, wrote Meyer. The long-term solution, he suggested to Roosevelt, lay in a liberal tonic of U.S. remedies: comprehensive primary education to raise the standard of citizenship, trial by jury, freedom of the press, a permanent representative assembly. The regime would also have to shed its habits of mystery and follow a course of democratic action. The October Manifesto and creation of the Duma were useful to these ends, and Meyer respected the Cadets. But he feared that their lack of experience in practical affairs would incapacitate the Duma's leadership, and the chasm of distrust between democrats and czar would widen. On these points, he was not wrong. He also proved perceptive when he stated that revolutionary violence would provoke a terrific reaction. A Chekovian unreality in the meantime seemed to suffocate St. Petersburg. Meyer was amazed to see that though the hospitals and morgues in the winter of 1905/1906 were filled to capacity with wounded and dead and the country showed every sign of impending dissolution, fashionable society pursued its leisure: parties, hunting, theater, ballet. Paralysis gripped the imagination of the better classes, he concluded, while revolutionaries and policemen plunged the country into a chaos from which it would not recover. In a diary entry (July 15, 1906), Meyer wrote an epitaph for the fading regime:

> There is only one thing impossible in Russia, and that is to understand Russia. The Tsar is stronger in ideals than in achievements. The education of the masses has been shamefully neglected. The Jews have been persecuted and massacred. The bureaucracy is corrupt and unpatriotic. There are no leaders on either side. The revolutionists want capital punishment abolished, but freedom to use the bomb.[77]

Several days later, Nicholas dissolved the First Duma, which in defiance reassembled in Viborg to agitate against the payment of taxes. In August, assassins tried to kill Stolypin. He escaped, but in the attempt bystanders were killed or mutilated. Meyer wrote in his diary with revulsion and a sense of foreboding, "His [Stolypin's] little girl had both her feet blown off and his boy of a few years a leg broken." Yet nothing blinded Meyer to the ineptitude of Nicholas, whom he reviled for granting reforms when they were too late or when it was obvious that they had been forced upon him. In autumn 1914, as a private citizen, Meyer was emphatic in warning against the possible extension of Russian despotism into Germany.[78]

*   *   *   *

Whether in geopolitical competition in northeastern Asia or in the subtler area of human rights, seldom in history has the past so clearly appeared as prologue as in U.S. policy toward Russia from 1861 to 1914. The relationship of Korea, China, and Japan to the international system was an issue well before communist revolutions and civil wars drew American attention or aggravated fears about Soviet ambition. Additionally, there were the parallel cases of concern about persecuted Jewry and congressional attempts to alter Russian behavior. The same spirit that led to abrogation of the 1832 commercial treaty caused another generation of legislators in the 1970s to withhold most-favored-nation status and credits from the czar's successors. In each instance, an informal (and unlikely) alliance opposed to punitive measures formed between Russian officials and the executive branch of the U.S. government. Each time, the president and secretary of state argued that legislation would not help the victims of persecution but would only complicate relations with an admittedly imperfect regime. A stung Russian government on each occasion leveled charges of hypocrisy against U.S. pretensions but did little to redress the problems giving rise to the original concern. In the case of political prisoners, relations between the two countries were complicated long before the Cold War gave emphasis to a human rights policy. Accolades accorded by the 1890 International Prison Congress and pledges made by Brezhnev in the 1970s notwithstanding, the record of Russian legal practice was a point of constant vulnerability in relations with the United States. And however true czarist and Soviet charges of U.S. imperfection in human rights, they failed in the nineteenth and twentieth centuries to make an elementary distinction about the scope of abuses: American administrations never pursued policies that caused hundreds of thousands of citizens to emigrate or silenced millions more through incarceration and intimidation.

Although restrained by their official positions from direct involvement in Russian legal proceedings, U.S. diplomats in St. Petersburg—like their counterparts in communist Moscow—followed events closely when they involved political charges. Foster, for one, attended several trials and was won over by the defendants, especially Sophia Perovskaya, a leading conspirator in Narodnaia Volia. At the same time, the security apparatus in St. Petersburg continued to make its presence felt in the lives of diplomats. Meyer reported that his hosts possessed the cipher to the American cable code and knew the contents of every dispatch. Even more upsetting to him were the petty obstacles he had to overcome in getting *permission* from the Foreign Office to leave the country. These combined with other annoyances: the difficulty in obtaining information about innocent matters, the brusqueness of officials when faced with a sensitive issue, the unpleasantness of continous surveillance. Like many before him, Meyer left St. Petersburg without sympathy for the regime. Personal experience of Russian paranoia, as much as a cooler understanding of where America's interest lay in 1904/1905, caused him (also White and Foster) to hope for Japan's success. He expected it would act as a catalyst to comprehensive reforms in Russia.[79]

As for the more prosaic aspects of living in St. Petersburg, American reactions varied in 1861 to 1914. Two ministers (James Orr and William Hunt) suffered fatally from the climate, and the health of a third (Alphonso Taft) was permanently impaired. Yet others were pleased that the post's relatively light work load made possible the pursuit of avocations. White wrote most of his magnum opus, *A History of the Warfare of Science with Theology in Christendom*, while in St.

Petersburg. George Lothrop became intimately acquainted with private life in Russia and married off a daughter to a Baltic estate owner. Meyer's daily routine was enough insulated from the disturbances of revolution that he found time to hunt bears, play polo, attend performances of the ballet, and stick with a regimen of ice-skating. Nevertheless, like Clay and for better reason, he took the precaution of going into the streets armed with a pistol. The appreciation of U.S. diplomats for Russian high culture was also mixed; even in the same person there was divided opinion. White, for example, recognized Tolstoy for what he was: arguably the greatest writer in any language. Yet White, an unabashed Germanophile, dismissed Russia as existing outside the currents of European civilization—Renaissance, Reformation, Enlightenment—and as such belonging to an inferior category that included Turkey.[80]

The Russian response to individual diplomats naturally varied, ranging from perplexity over the selection of Clay to admiration for the linguistic talents of Jeremiah Curtin and the negotiating skills of Meyer. One can only imagine what czardom would have concluded about U.S. methods from Secretary Seward's admission, "Some persons are sent abroad because they are needed abroad, and some are sent because they are *not* wanted at home." At the same time, Russians were puzzled that the term of ministerial office was usually so short, and the czar joked about the matter on meeting new U.S. diplomats. Part of the reason for the briefness of tenure, as in previous decades, had to do with paying the expenses of household and entertainment in St. Petersburg. Even though all were men of independent means, the ministers often resented having to purchase what the official establishment required from their private accounts. Thus, added to a forbidding property requirement for appointment was the risk of impoverishing oneself. Moreover, the United States did not maintain in St. Petersburg—or in any foreign capital—a permanent building for diplomatic office or residence. It was up to each new incumbent to locate and arrange rental accommodations. Both Foster and White were adamant on the need of Washington to meet official expenses and provide adequate housing. They and Meyer also urged reforms upon the State Department that would open the diplomatic corps to a system of promotion based on intellectual merit (demonstrated in exams covering foreign languages, modern history, international law), professional accomplishment, and personal integrity. As it was, the diplomatic community in St. Petersburg accurately reflected the pre–World War I State Department and Foreign Service: numerically small, socially elite, dependent on the ruling party for appointment and promotion—amateurish. During the 1905 revolution, the embassy in St. Petersburg (apart from stenographers and clerks) consisted of Meyer and three secretaries, all of whom owed their positions to wealth and influence and none of whom regarded diplomacy as more than a brief diversion from business or political pursuits. Not one had been in Russia more than a year before the war and popular discontent erupted. Only a handful of the diplomats ever posted to St. Petersburg were fluent in French or Russian; most did not possess even a reading knowledge of them. These conditions did not necessarily preclude good diplomacy, as the cases of Foster and Meyer demonstrated, but they made unavoidable embarrassments like Clay.[81]

Through no virtue of its own, the system of presidential elections and campaign spoils occasionally produced capable diplomats before 1914.[82] In the case of representation to the Court of St. James, the list was impressive and included James Monroe, John Quincy Adams, George Bancroft, Charles Francis Adams, and John Hay. In Russia, the record was uneven. Any history that included John Randolph, Cassius Clay, and Simon Cameron should have been read as a moral tale of what to avoid in the twentieth century. But the lesson went unlearned. After the position had stayed vacant for more than a year, Woodrow Wilson finally appointed an ambassador in the summer of 1914. Having failed to shuffle the job onto either Henry Pindell, a newspaperman from Joliet, or Charles Crane, a plumbing magnate and Democratic party booster, Wilson recruited George Marye, a California campaign contributor. A bland personality but blessed with the requisite private fortune, Marye was lampooned by an insider (Joseph Grew) as one who "in his pajamas regarding himself in the mirror [would] say to himself in an awed whisper, 'Ambassador, Ambassador!' "[83] Marye himself regarded his appointment in the same spirit as had such glorified place holders as Taft and Robert McCormick: a sinecure awarded for service and donations to the party in power. Marye found it personally inconvenient to reach St. Petersburg until late October 1914. By then, the Russian Second Army had been obliterated at Tannenberg; German forces were advancing along the fronts in Galicia and Poland.

3

War and Revolution

American diplomacy in St. Petersburg seemed to mock the Provisional Government's herculean effort to prosecute military operations against Germany while establishing democracy. Against the background of Bolshevik audaciousness and despite Washington's need for reliable analysis of shifting conditions, U.S. diplomacy was hesitant and uncomprehending. In contrast to compelling Americans on Russian soil, from the romantic John Reed to the Red Cross's exuberant Raymond Robins, Ambassadors George Marye and David Francis stood out because of their naïveté.

Wartime Diplomacy

Nowhere more than in Russia did the Great War prove the wisdom of Clausewitz's injunction against making warfare into "something pointless and devoid of sense." Casualties in 1914 to 1918 were unimaginable to St. Petersburg as it considered the course to take during the weeks following Francis Ferdinand's assassination. Of the 12,000,000 men who were mobilized for military service, approximately 1,700,000 were killed in battle, 4,950,000 wounded, 2,410,000 captured.[1] Additional fatalities from disease, suffering among civilians, and damage to property were equally fearful. Acquisition of the Black Sea Straits, Constantinople, and other Turkish territories could not have justified these costs, let alone the unleashing of destructive revolution and civil war.

Owing to national unpreparedness, 30 percent of the country's frontline troops were without weapons in mid-1915 and were expected to collect for their use the rifles of their fallen comrades. Earlier that year, the Germans took 100,000 Russians prisoner near the Nieman river in east Prussia. Recapture of Przemysl by the Germans in early June marked the collapse of the northern Russian front. By August, after the loss of Warsaw to Austro-German forces, Nicholas's government prepared to evacuate Riga and other Baltic cities. The prediction of Peter Durnovo (conservative adviser to Nicholas) that general European hostilities would be intolerable to Russia was confirmed in the war's first year.[2]

Yet to Marye, neither the conflict nor Russian military prowess was ever in doubt. Contrary to abundant evidence then available, he asserted that Germany's victories were superficial, that Russia was potentially the greatest victor in the war. In December 1915, he exclaimed:

> When the German collapse will come no one can foresee at this time, but it is inevitable. There may be little left of England when it comes, less of France, and still less of Germany. Russia, if the war lasts long enough, will be the dominant power in Europe, she will have received no vital blow and her vast territory, her immense population, her unlimited resources will enable her to recover faster than the countries that were with her or against her.[3]

Marye betrayed a similar want of judgment in other areas. His published reminiscences of Russia are packed with banalities about diplomatic receptions and the elaborate costumes and ceremonies observed in court; he is breathless in describing the aristocrats that allowed him to come near. In Nicholas, he perceived a gifted intelligence and attributed to him beneficent plans for humanity (destroyed by Germany's evil machinations). In explaining czarist setbacks, Marye relied uncritically on the exaggerations of his Russian acquaintances: he placed inordinate blame on German spies and intriguers in St. Petersburg. His understanding of Russian–U.S. history was also shallow. In one conversation with Foreign Minister Sazonov about the circumstances of the fleet's visit during the Civil War and the sale of Alaska, Marye revealed matchless ignorance. Sazonov was briefly struck dumb.[4]

As the strain of war continued, Marye became less oblivious to its debilitations and began (ploddingly) to analyze its significance. He eventually judged that the autocracy was anachronistic and that parliamentary reforms aimed at enhancing the Duma were desirable. He also hoped Nicholas would act to reduce the gulf between his exalted position and that of the peasants and workers. And he recognized that the damage inflicted on the royal family's prestige by Rasputin was huge; the charlatan should be removed from his position of influence.[5] Marye realized that such measures would help the czar to recover his subjects' confidence but never dared to utter his ideas to Nicholas. These could scarcely have been more different from the czar's own. When in January 1917 the less diffident British ambassador, Sir George Buchanan, urged Nicholas "to break down the barrier" separating him from his subjects, he was rebuffed: "Do you mean that I am to regain the confidence of my people, or that they are to regain *my* confidence?"[6]

All the same, Marye persisted in his cheerfulness about the empire and its ability to wage war. This optimism was rooted in his superficial study of Russia and passionate anti-German feeling. Even as President Wilson and pacifistically inclined Secretary of State William Jennings Bryan tried to maintain U.S. neutrality, Marye had already decided that Germany must be crushed, returned to its pre-Bismarckian fragmentation.[7] He was therefore inclined in his dispatches to minimize, at times overlook entirely, the magnitude of Russian disabilities. This pre-disposition also inclined him (and the embassy's equally anti-German First Secretary Charles Wilson) to be dismissive of continuing Russian misdeeds against the local Jewish population.[8]

Apart from filing slanted reports to his superiors, Marye was in other ways a dubious instrument of policy and so perceived by the administration. To begin with, he was unable to advance the president's goal of negotiating a new commercial treaty, despite a sizable boost in bilateral trade (to U.S. advantage) occasioned by Russia's wartime needs. These resulted in purchases of Westinghouse brakes, Baldwin locomotives, steel rails, and Singer sewing machines. Yet from an Imperial standpoint, there was good reason to be wary of entering into another treaty with the Americans so soon after their abrogation of the 1832 agreement. Nevertheless, Marye's inability to make progress in this area was held against him by officers in Wilson's cabinet. Even more damaging to Marye were those charges leveled against him by the German Foreign Ministry. His failure to dispose of them added to the mounting tension in German–U.S. relations and reinforced suspicions in Berlin that American professions of neutrality were a sham.

At the request of the German and Austrian governments, the embassy had accepted in 1914 the obligation of handling their interests in Russia for the duration of hostilities. During the period preceding U.S. intervention, this assignment meant overseeing the welfare of prisoners of war held in Russia. By the time Marye left his post in March 1916, these numbered in the hundreds of thousands (the majority consisting of Slavic elements from the Habsburg Empire), scattered not only in European Russia but also in Central Asia and Siberia. Officials in Vienna and Berlin naturally sought frequent assurance that their nationals were properly fed, sheltered, and otherwise cared for. The embassy was urged to exercise diligence, which was understood as helping distribute subsidies to soldiers, facilitating Red Cross inspections of camps, and conducting investigations of camp hygiene, housing, and overall standards. In fulfilling these humanitarian requirements, the diplomats failed, according to Chancellor Theobald von Bethmann-Hollweg; their patent disinterest in the matter revealed a hostile intent toward Germany. In an instance of wartime hyperbole, the kaiser claimed (early 1916) that more Germans and Austrians were dying in Russian incarceration from maltreatment and neglect than were being lost on the battlefields. In Berlin, President Wilson's confidant and chief aide, Colonel House, was told that Germany might be forced by the logic of this tragedy to take its affairs in Russia out of American hands.[9]

In 1914 to 1916 and later, Marye defended the embassy's record. He produced a respectable correspondence with Russian, German, and U.S. officials testifying to his and his colleagues' conscientiousness. He pleaded that the task was not an easy one, given conditions of scarcity, inadequate transportation across stretches of sparsely inhabited territory, and a small staff whose energies were overtaxed. He also claimed that operation of the embassy was swamped by the influx of unexpectedly high numbers of POWs; 80 percent of its work was devoted to this issue. But never, he complained, did he receive one word of thanks from Germany or Austria.

Although Marye and Charles Wilson did not deliberately neglect their duties, as Bethmann-Hollweg held, there was ample reason for German apprehension. These officials were sluggish in the performance of German-interest tasks and clearly ambivalent about them. Both men not only supported the Allied cause, but, with the advent of U-boat warfare and the sinking of passenger ships, became convinced that the U.S. and German worlds were irreconcilable; they would clash. Fifteen months before Congress declared war, Marye wrote, "My mind always reverts to the question, what would this world be if the spirit which sank the *Lusitania* could become dominant?" Allegations of German espionage in the United States added to Marye's diminishing enthusiasm for safeguarding Germany's concerns in Russia. The neutrality of the ambassador was obviously in doubt when he admitted in his diary (August 1915):

> We at the embassy here are doing what we can to ameliorate the condition of many Germans held at various places in this vast empire. We naturally observe what the Germans are doing elsewhere and we cannot help contrasting our work here with what they are doing to our people, not only on the high seas but in our own country.[10]

Neither Colonel House nor President Wilson ever seem to have been satisfied with Marye and expressed to each other their reservations. As early as December 1914, Wilson sounded misgivings about him and ascribed Marye's failure to negotiate a commercial treaty to intellectual incapacity. A year later, Wilson asserted that both the ambassador and his Russian counterpart in Washington were peerless in their ineptitude. Consequently, he never consulted Marye about Russia; House did not bother to visit him during his diplomatic errands to Europe.

That Marye was unable to manage better a commercial treaty and, more urgently, the German-prisoners question should not have surprised Wilson. The president had only himself to blame in appointing an unsuitable man to a post that, in House's phrase, required "important work to be done." Marye was, in fact, familiar with four European languages (not including Russian) and had a passable knowledge of international business law. But never in his sixty-six years before St. Petersburg (rechristened Petrograd in 1914) had he served in any capacity abroad. His world was confined to the Democratic party, his law practice, and mining and brokerage enterprises in California and Nevada. It is also worth mentioning that though Marye lived in Washington at the time of his appointment, Wilson made not the slightest effort to meet him or to enlighten him about policy. In fact, the two men never became acquainted. Why, then, was he chosen? One reason was that Marye could afford from his private income the extra expenses of living in St. Petersburg, and he had been brought to the president's attention by an important Democrat, Senator Key Pittman of Nevada. Beyond these slender considerations, all else is speculation—though it bears out Wilson's legendary penchant for casually making high-level appointments.[11]

Nor did foreign colleagues regard Marye's ambassadorship with favor. Britain's Buchanan was not sufficiently interested in Marye even to mention him in his published memoirs. Ambassador Maurice Paleologue of France referred to him only in passing. The Frenchman's casualness in this regard has significance, as he was sensitive to those cultural-political differences separating the United States from Russia: "the very antithesis of each other." As for his successor, David Francis damned Marye's term in office as marred by "inefficiency" and "evasion of responsibility."[12]

Nicholas's government was alone in its approval, though it took time to develop. In its first number for January 1914, *Novoe Vremiia* had stated that Russian–U.S. relations "remained in the same state of cold indifference" that had obtained since termination of the commercial treaty. Russian touchiness stemming from this same cause made it impossible to send to St. Petersburg Wilson's preferred candidate, Henry Pindell. And even when Marye had been appointed and was deemed acceptable by the Russians in 1914, they made clear their detachment: the presence of a U.S. envoy was "not at all necessary," but if one appeared, the czar would at some point grant him an audience. Yet by virtue of his pronounced anti-German sentiments and his wife's work in charities for those injured by the war, Marye restored Nicholas's faith in the unpredictable Americans. In recognition of his service in the cause of Russian–U.S. friendship, Marye was awarded the Grand Cordon of the Order of St. Alexander Nevsky, the last such honor bestowed by the czar on a U.S. diplomat. Presentation of it signaled Russian eagerness to cement relations with the United States and encourage its enlistment in the anti-German struggle. As was obvious in Marye's last interview with Nicholas, officialdom was nervous that Washington cared little about Russia and might replace Marye with someone disposed to helping Germany.[13]

Unease in Petrograd about the import of his resignation (bad health) and Francis's appointment took two months to dispel. It was only when the Russian ambassador to Washington, George Bakhmetev, reassured his government that rumors connecting Francis's appointment to pro-German sympathy were laid to rest.[14] Not for the last time had the Russians detected more design in U.S. ambassadorial appointments—and policy generally—than actually existed. In fact, the selection criteria used by Wilson remain as obscure for Francis as they had been for Marye. More than his predecessor, Francis *was* a prominent Democrat. Born in 1850, he had left his native Kentucky for college in St. Louis (Washington University) and after graduation stayed on to become a prosperous businessman. He was named president of the Merchant's Exchange in 1884. A year later, he became mayor of St. Louis and soon afterward was elected governor of Missouri. In 1896, he was appointed secretary of the interior by Grover Cleveland. After a temporary political eclipse (suffered because of his opposition to free silver and Bryan, both popular in Missouri), he recovered his party position and in 1908 was considered by bosses to be worthy of the vice presidency. But Francis did not pursue this possibility. Instead he ran, unsuccessfully, in the 1910 Democratic primary for the Senate. In 1912, he campaigned for Woodrow Wilson and for this service was offered the ambassadorship to Argentina. He declined this post, however. And he had well-founded misgivings in 1916 about accepting Wilson's offer of Petrograd—based on his lack of experience and slight knowledge of Russia. He agreed to go only out of an old-fashioned sense of duty that obliged him to perform in a period of crisis.

Into the novel worlds of Russia and diplomacy, Francis did not take his wife, with whom his relations were distant. His only personal companion was the family's longtime retainer Philip Jordan. Essentially self-taught, he composed a series of letters that remain to this day the only firsthand account by a black American of life in Petrograd during the revolutionary months of 1917.[15] Also accompanying Francis for the Atlantic voyage to Petrograd was a young scholar of Russian language and institutions, Samuel Harper of the University of Chicago. At the behest of the State Department (its solicitude for the office of Russian ambassador heightened by anxiety about sending another neophyte into the field), Harper had been engaged to tutor Francis and to ease the transition and linguistic difficulties during his first weeks in Petrograd. The contrast between the whisky-drinking, cigar-smoking, card-playing Francis and the contemplative Harper could hardly have been sharper. Nevertheless, they enjoyed a rough-and-ready friendship. It was resented by functionaries in the embassy, who regarded Harper as an interloper, but the bluff ambassador did not notice. In any case, he was genuinely interested in learning what he could from his professor. Unfortunately, few ideas—let alone sophistication of concept—were successfully transmitted.[16]

On board the ship conveying the American party (the *Oscar II* out of Sweden), there was also a Russian lady of considerable charm, Matilda deCram, about twenty-five years the ambassador's junior. During the overland leg of the journey (train from Stockholm to Petrograd), she and Francis became friendly, much to the consternation of Harper, who had earlier been warned that she worked for Germany's intelligence service. The concerns that he and other Americans subsequently expressed to the ambassador about deCram's purported purpose were stoutly denied by him as groundless.[17] Still, she was under constant surveillance by Russian counterintelligence and under investigation by the British. As her friendship with Francis blossomed in Petrograd, he inevitably became an object of suspicion in police circles, of gossip in society, and of embarrassment to his underlings. In defiance of this disapprobation, Francis employed deCram in a secretarial capacity in the embassy. Her situation there came to an end only in November 1917, after the department ordered the ambassador to sever relations with this "undesirable person." (Her husband was arrested in 1918 in San Francisco and charged with being a German agent.) Thereafter, Francis did everything within his power to provide for deCram's comfort during months of privation in Petrograd.[18]

There is no conclusive evidence that deCram was a spy or that there existed between her and her solicitous companion anything other than an innocent, friendship. He once said in indignation, "If anyone charges that I have improper relations with Madame Cramm he is a liar and anyone who repeats the rumor after hearing this denial from myself is a liar." Yet the damage done to his standing in Petrograd was immense. It accounts for the blistering evaluation by Edgar Sisson (Petrograd representative of the American Committee on Public Information) that "no fruitful work" could be done by the U.S. government so long as Francis remained at the embassy.[19]

Apart from his ignoring the appearance of things in a capital rife with rumors about spying and espionage, Francis made additional mistakes due to the unfamiliarity of both setting and role. His outlook was shaped by the shibboleths around which he had fashioned careers in business and the Democratic party. They were irrelevant for making sense of a dying empire or the exigencies produced by a cataclysmic war.

His first failure, the one that most rankled him and that he shared with Marye, was his inability to secure a commercial treaty with Russia. In interviews with Sazonov and other officials, he was reminded that *his* government had destroyed the venerable trade arrangement; Russia was not about to make alterations in its domestic life to obtain an American minority's endorsement of a mere trade treaty. Officials repeated their resentment of U.S. attempts ("arrogant") to intervene in their affairs and claimed that Russian Jews were well treated by the czarist administration. Those few barriers against them were trivial and established only to protect the finances and lives of decent peasants. These Russian protests struck a responsive chord in Francis, who evidently lost confidence in his own government's position and adopted the Imperial viewpoint. Although he denied being anti-Semitic, his fulminations against American Jewry as an impassable obstacle to Russian–U.S. friendship had undeniable implications. This statement made in August 1916 by Francis (to Frank Polk, counselor to the department) could have been delivered by an Imperial publicist: "There is no doubt that if the Jews were given absolutely equal rights of residence, profession, etc., in Russia and the right to own land, they would become possessors of the entire Empire within a comparatively short time. . . . The peasant would stand no show whatever with the designing, usurious, and pitiless Jews." He added that every reprehensible "money-making scheme" was traceable to a Jew. Even more deleterious to the Russian state, a "decided majority" of the Jews were traitorous and spied for the enemy. And all the while, he explained, they were contemptuous of the peasants' piety and made fun of Christianity. As for the distorting influence of American Jews on U.S. foreign policy, Francis said that they would rue the day when the business community realized that commerce with Russia had been damaged by their interference. Incensed by the plank in the 1916 Democratic platform concerning Russian Jews, Francis also warned Woodrow Wilson that a "pro-Hebrew" policy precluded any future commercial treaty. Ironically, it was French ambassador Paleologue, an equivocal democrat, who understood better than Francis the sentiments of the public and their effect on international policy. "I can easily image," he wrote in September of that year,

> what a free "Yankee," brought up on the superstition of the democratic ideal and the craze and reverence for individual initiative, must think of the idea of five million human beings being confined, on the sole ground of their religious beliefs, to a small area where their very numbers doom them to misery. What must he think of the facts that they cannot own or cultivate land, are deprived of all public rights, their slightest acts exposed to the arbitrary control of the police and are always living in fear of periodical massacre?[20]

Francis's obtuseness was not restricted to the subject of Jewry. He would have preferred to ignore the military-prisoner issue and was dismayed by the scope of problems in what he called the "uncongenial task" of representing German and Austrian interests. Still, assisted by relief agencies and U.S. consuls throughout Russia, Francis supervised—in a manner more perfunctory than Marye's—the duties that befell the embassy in this sphere. In contravention of norms governing diplomatic life and in blissful ignorance of their existence, Francis meanwhile speculated in the currency of his host country. In addition to purchasing rubles for profit, he bought Russian securities. Knowledge of these irregularities by resident diplomats would have further eroded Francis's standing and given more material to gossips already excited by his connection with deCram.[21]

Even unencumbered by disapproval about his financial dealings, Francis was slow to make friends among the Russians and was alternately ignored and patronized by his British and French colleagues. He seldom entertained and led an unsociable life in the dilapidated embassy. Most assuredly, Francis *was* sensitive to slights. In a hollow boast to an acquaintance, he said that at one diplomatic reception the czar held a longer conversation with him than with anyone else.[22]

Francis's reportage to the new secretary of state, Robert Lansing, also had its pathetic side. As though announcing a discovery, he solemnly told Lansing that he had concluded, based on recently acquired data, that Moscow was a "more truly Russian" city than Petrograd. He gave credence to the preposterous but oft-repeated rumors that Empress Alexandra was unpatriotic and had pro-German allegience. He thought her nervous condition was related to menopause. He also overestimated the quality of supply, strength, and élan of the Russian army, as General Alexis Brusilov concentrated it for the titanic offensive of 1916. "No such army," Francis gleefully told an associate, "was ever assembled before in the history of the world." By autumn, it had suffered another numbing 1 million casualties from which its morale (never mind Bolshevik agitation) could not recover. On this last point, Francis can be excused. He was not alone in 1916 in thinking that the Russians could regain and sustain the offensive. Less difficult to overlook are his explanations for the food shortages suffered in Russian cities during the autumn of 1916. He accepted the fantastical view that food was deliberately made scarce to incite uprisings; these in turn would justify increased police authority under the deranged A. D. Protopopov (minister of the interior) and finally lead to Nicholas's making a separate peace compatible with the outlook of the German element in court. What is even more remarkable than this misunderstanding of the food shortage, actually caused by the collapse of the transportation system and the peasants' reluctance to exchange foodstuffs for worthless currency, was Francis's continued belief in it until well after 1918.[23] The Russian government's denial of food from sections of the population for political ends was an innovation that had to await that more inventive mind, Joseph Stalin.

For all these faults, if it is not making too fine a distinction, Francis was more able than Marye and tried ardently to accomplish something positive in 1916 to 1917. To a Missouri friend, he exclaimed, "It is more than interesting to be in the position which I occupy at this time. This is the most critical period of the world's history in my opinion, and Petrograd is occupying a very prominent place in the theater of affairs—in fact it is second to none."[24] It was with flair that he presented to the Foreign Ministry Wilson's offer (December 1916) to mediate the European war. And he was quick to identify the possible dangers to the United States of the Russo-Japanese alliance (July 1916), aimed against an unspecified third party with designs on East Asia.

To his credit, Francis also studied the Russian language and showed sympathy on numerous occasions for ordinary people. The sight of troops drilling in the street and of women in subzero weather standing in bread lines moved him. When male members of the embassy's servant staff were conscripted, he tried to win their release from military service or sought to alleviate their families' distress. And he claimed that had he been younger and social conditions more stable, he would have liked to stay longer in Russia to help develop the country's natural resources. Such an attitude in tranquil times would have helped make Francis's a balmy ambassadorship.

Francis was also a fair observer of highly placed Russians and earnestly followed the changes in government roster that marked the last months of bewildered czarist rule. It is true that he misjudged Alexandra, but he did not underestimate the malevolent influence exercised over her by Rasputin or the havoc he inflicted on political administration. And though Francis mistook the conservative Sazonov for a liberal, he was right to see in him a man of ability and unswerving loyalty to his country—far superior to his successor, the pompous Boris Sturmer. Francis also shrewdly judged Premier Alexander Trepov as a person of conviction who might have accomplished things in late 1916 had it not been for inexorable events. Of the better qualities of Nicholas Pokrovsky, who succeeded Sturmer in the Foreign Ministry, Francis was also appreciative. Finally, despite the onset of physical infirmities, Francis dutifully attended sessions of the Duma, including some of the stormiest—as when on November 14, 1916, the Cadet leader Paul Miliukov denounced Sturmer in his "Stupidity or Treason" address.[25] His reports on these matters, especially those that his staff helped compose, were lucid in the main and not handicapped by Marye's peculiar myopia. Francis was fully alive to the wretched conditions on the home front and in August 1916 thought that continuing restrictions on the Duma would produce revolution "before the lapse of even a few years."[26] As it happened, only seven months later, rebellion exploded in the wake of acute food shortages and the government's announcement that parliament would be prorogued until mid-April.

Democratic Revolution and the "Great October"

Although contrary to the traditional counsel of statesmen, Congress chose (April 1917) to involve the United States in Europe's military affairs. American intervention in the Great War helped redress an imbalance in the European balance of power, thereby protecting the integrity of the North Atlantic community of states, on which U.S. security and prosperity depended. Debates in the cabinet and elsewhere in the government centered on economic and security categories into which fell specific issues bearing on the distribution of world power: the danger confronting England by a permanent German occupation of Belgian ports, submarine warfare and its challenge to U.S. maritime trade and naval security, threats to the southwestern border and U.S. prestige in Mexico (the Zimmermann telegram), and the likely repercussions on world trade and investment of Anglo-French defeat.

Popular understanding of U.S. war aims, however, was not anchored in the idiom of realpolitik; rather, it reflected the president's inflated rhetoric about making the world safe for democracy and fighting a war to end wars. Wilson's eloquent but misleading language—the elevation of untrue and in the circumstances dangerous principles—was never more evident than in his war message (April 2, 1917). In this speech, he not only excoriated the German autocracy for causing the world war (a concept that would be transmuted two years later by the alchemy of armistice negotiations into "war guilt", but also endorsed the recent revolution in Russia (March 8–14) and declared that the new democracy would be a fit partner in the posthostilities order. Piling one misconception on another about Russia, he failed to remark that the injuries on its army and economy would constrain the country's ability to wage war regardless of the type of governing regime. Wilson asked, "Does not every American feel that assurance has been added to our hope for the future peace of the world by the wonderful and heartening things that have been happening within the last few weeks in Russia?" Little interested in or knowledgeable about it, Wilson went on to invoke imaginary and implausible witnesses when he said, "Russia was known by those who knew it best to have been always in fact democratic at heart, in all the vital habits of her thought, in all the intimate relationships of her people that spoke their natural instinct, their habitual attitude towards life." Now that czardom had been destroyed, "the great, generous Russian people have been added in all their naive majesty and might to the forces that are fighting for freedom in the world, for justice, and for peace."[27]

Russia's cessation as a belligerent in March 1917 might have enabled the coalition of Prince George Lvov (former chairman of the Union of Zemstva) and Alexander Kerensky (of the Socialist Revolutionaries) to overcome its troubles.[28] These were posed by food and fuel shortages; the wholly autonomous and antipathetic soldiers' and workers' soviets, of which the Petrograd was most conspicuous; and enemies on the right who wanted either to rehabilitate the autocracy or, at the minimum, to replace the Provisional Government with something more congenial to national tradition than the vagaries of parliamentary democracy. Soon after Nicholas's abdication, events began to conspire to undermine the fledgling Provisional Government. With the connivance of German authorities, hoping to prolong Russia's political convulsions, Lenin and his comrades stole into Petrograd, where they immediately pitted themselves against what passed for established authority. In compliance with the original czarist pledge (not to enter into a separate peace with Germany), the army under General Brusilov launched a summer offensive in Galicia that after early successes was contained and then rolled back by German–Austrian counterattacks. In July, the government checked a Bolshevik-led uprising of armed workers and soldiers, only to be threatened weeks later by forces under the supreme commander of the Russian army, General Lavr Kornilov.

Francis was eager that the United States recognize the new democracy in March 1917. Despite fighting in the embassy's neighborhood and grisly murders of policemen and army officers by marauding soldiers, he was relieved by the revolution's relative lack of bloodshed. He felt it incumbent on Washington to encourage new Russia's liberal propensities.[29] His insistence on this last point and the encouraging results of his meeting with officials (Michael Rodzyanko president of the Duma, Miliukov, and Alexander Guchkov) to sound them out on their commitments to the war led to Wilson's normalizing relations with the Provisional Government. It remained for years thereafter a source of satisfaction to Francis that he conveyed recognition of the new regime two whole days before his colleagues from Britain, France, and Italy did so; early establishment of relations was instrumental in lengthening the life of the Lvov–Kerensky government and enabled Wilson to persuade his countrymen that all their allies in the war would be truly democratic. Ultimately, Francis believed, recognition made possible the Allied and U.S. victory. Years after the event, he claimed, "If [right- or left-wing] elements had succeeded an armistice with the Central Empires would have followed immediately and consequently Germany would have sent her hundred-odd divisions from the Eastern to the Western front almost a year sooner than they were sent and at a time when the Allied Armies were particularly ill prepared to resist them." Even before the U.S. Army had been deeply committed to any European battlefield, concern about keeping the eastern front active had assumed urgency. Francis gave voice to a common fear in Washington when he observed from Petrograd: "Should [Russia] go out of the war the whole burden of the contest will fall upon the United States and would [take] untold millions of treasure and probably millions of American lives."[30]

Francis stayed in touch with consular officials outside of Petrograd and with military attachés in the field, all of whom expressed skepticism about Russian prospects. Yet he never grasped the degree to which political authority had become fragmented or understood the army's demoralization (quickened by promulgation of the soviet's Order Number 1).[31] This misjudgment climbed up the chain of command and inclined the United States to embrace two mistaken ideas. First, it underestimated the gravitational pull of the Petrograd soviet on the loyalty of soldiers, sailors, and factory workers in the capital. Second, the highest officers in Washington thought that a Russian democracy would (somehow) cause army and society to sustain the war effort. Consequently, Wilson, House, and (to a lesser degree) Lansing expected from March to November 1917 that central authority in Russia would grow in strength; the country would hold up its end of the war.

To bolster Russia, the administration pursued several expedients. It slated $450 million in credits to Russia (of which less than $200 million was expended) and was prepared to allocate more. It authorized a highly visible goodwill mission to Petrograd, led by the elderly former secretary of state Elihu Root. The purpose of this expedition was to investigate the nature of Russian needs and to make practical suggestions for assistance. Drawn from leading men in business, philanthropic organizations, and labor, the Root mission spent more than a month in Russia.[32] But contrary to the spirit in which it was devised, the mission lectured (and threatened) government ministers in a series of bald representations. American aid would be strictly proportionate to Russia's contribution to the war: in Root's felicitous phrase, "no fight, no loans." The ideological chasm separating the mission's members from their hosts—a number of whom, like Kerensky, were socialists—made for mutual incomprehension and additional distrust. Even the labor representatives were conventional, their ideas far from the increasingly social-democratic orientation of the Provisional Government (to say nothing of the principles causing excitement among the soviets). Raymond Robins of the Red Cross, who was in Petrograd at the time, later recalled that Root was as welcome in Russia as smallpox and aroused as much enthusiasm as an Orangeman leading a parade in Dublin. The mission's recommendations to Lansing were meager: the United States should establish informational programs for the benefit of Russian civilians and sponsor recreational programs under YMCA auspices at military facilities to boost soldiers' morale. In the meantime, econiums to liberty and words of welcome to the fraternity of liberated labor were sent by Samuel Gompers, president of the American Federation of Labor, to Russia's "workingmen." Among socialists, this greeting seemed laughably quaint.[33]

During this same summer, the United States arranged for the dispatch of the Advisory Commission of Railway Experts, under John Stevens (formerly chief engineer of the Panama Canal), in the hope of improving Russia's rickety transportation network, especially that portion connecting Vladivostok to European provinces. The American Red Cross, as well as other semiofficial organizations, also sent representatives, all expecting that their assistance would fortify Russian stamina. But none of these programs bore fruit. Infusions of U.S. financial and technical support could not reverse the disintegration of military discipline, public confidence, and political coherence.[34] Toward the end of the Provisional Government's life, as a last-ditch measure, Francis recommended to Lansing that two or three U.S. Army divisions be sent (via Sweden or Vladivostok) to Russia. This unlikely plan, foreshadowing later U.S. thinking, was outpaced by events in November and was not considered seriously by anyone in Washington.[35]

Owing to his position as envoy of Russia's new powerful ally, Francis enjoyed a hitherto elusive prestige in Petrograd social circles during the summer of 1917. His reclusive habits and the taint of his association with deCram were overlooked. He was cordially received by ministers, including Kerensky, whose protestations of fidelity to the Allied cause buoyed Francis whenever he doubted the resolve of the Russians or became unsettled by the chaotic state of their political life.[36]

Francis's relations with the soviets were absolutely remote, however. Neither side made an effort to understand or to be understood. Francis labored under the haziest knowledge of the ideological divisions within the Marxist and non-Marxist socialist parties and was inclined to dismiss the soviets as run by a "bunch of Jews," a group that he thought included Lenin. The head of Britain's special mission to the Soviet government in 1918, R. H. Lockhart, once noted in his diary, "Old Francis doesn't know a Left Social-Revolutionary from a potato."[37] Nothing dissuaded him from his conviction, shared by many foreign residents in Petrograd, that Lenin and his followers were German agents; the Bolsheviks' ultimate success he counted as the kaiser's victory. He concluded that Lenin was a "fanatic" and that Trotsky was motivated solely by personal ambition and vanity. This matter was proven to Francis's satisfaction when in April a mob, stirred by rumors that an American socialist was scheduled for execution in San Francisco, prepared to attack the embassy. Not much came of this threatened action, but before it fizzled a number of police officers were detailed to protect the ambassador; he armed himself with a pistol and was ready to shoot the first trespasser to break into the chancery. This event, along with the July 1917 uprising, caused Francis to wish that Kerensky had acted with greater ruthlessness in stifling the Marxist opposition: "Had the Provisional Government . . . arraigned Lenin and Trotsky and the other Bolshevik leaders, tried them for treason and executed them, Russia probably would not have been compelled to go through another revolution, would have been spared the reign of terror, and the murder of millions of her sons and daughters."[38] Enfeebled by battlefield losses and desertions from the army, outflanked by the rhetorical appeal of the Bolsheviks in the soviets and in the streets, the Provisional Government was not so much overthrown as it collapsed from shear exhaustion.[39]

The November events in Petrograd that inspired idealistic Americans such as Louise Bryant and John Reed to proclaim "the dawn of a new world" filled the diplomatic community with dread. Whereas Reed marveled that the proletariat had begun "building a kingdom more bright than any heaven had to offer, and for which it was a glory to die," Francis and his staff reported that they knew of no place where human life was so squandered as in Bolshevik Russia.[40] From Moscow, Consul General Maddin Summers reported scenes of depravity perpetrated by Red Guardsmen that caused him to liken Russia to a charnel house; he remained deaf to later Bolshevik claims that they were beginning the most humane epoch in history.

Still, a purely practical question remained for U.S. policymakers and diplomats. On the one hand, Lenin's aims of withdrawing Russia from the war and of redistributing wealth in accordance with socialist precepts were antithetical to Allied–American interests. The violent, then openly terroristic, means employed by the Bolsheviks against clerics, members of the *ancien régime,* and any form of resistance were also repulsive. On the other hand, if the United States could establish working relations with the new leadership, might the Bolsheviks be persuaded to keep the eastern theater active? However weak the Russian armies, their emplacement along the front and sporadic actions would pressure Germany and prevent an augmentation in the size of forces confronting the Allies in Flanders. Perhaps relations between the Western allies and the Bolsheviks would even enable the former to restrain the revolution's extreme ambitions.

Scattered along a wide ideological spectrum, there were Western officials who believed that their countries would benefit by prompt understanding with Lenin. On this could be based military cooperation against Germany, as well as a modus vivendi between world socialism and capitalism. Among these men were Robins; the U.S. military attaché, Brigadier General William Judson; Britain's Lockhart; and the socialist Jacques Sadoul (later a communist), then serving as an army captain with the French military mission in Petrograd. To accomplish their ends, they doggedly sought contact with the Bolsheviks.[41] In these objectives, they were not necessarily supported by the resident diplomats, however. Sadoul for one waged a running battle against his ambassador, Joseph Noulens (Paleologue's successor as of May 1917 and himself a socialist), who was skeptical of offering aid or trying to win Lenin's favor. He thought it unlikely—and Francis agreed with him—that the Bolsheviks would last for more than a few months. Francis was personally offended to learn in early December 1917 that General Judson had defied the existing ban on contacts with the Bolsheviks. He had met with Trotsky with the aim of strengthening his fortitude in the Brest-Litovsk negotiations and doing whatever possible to prevent a transfer of German divisions to northern France. The general's conduct and his criticism to Francis of deCram caused a breach between the two men and Judson's recall to Washington. The resourceful Robins eventually did establish a relationship with Trotsky and Lenin; though Francis decided to go along with this channel of communication, he felt uncomfortable and had no idea of how to exploit it. In solving this dilemma, he received scant guidance from Washington, often cut off from cable communication with the embassy for days at a time. During Brest-Litovsk, the Bolsheviks themselves encouraged but did not place much store in the Allied contacts (though they hoped by them to gain leverage against the Central Powers).[42]

Harrowing events related to civil turmoil and Francis's inelasticity forestalled any accord with the revolutionaries. On new occasions, both Francis's own person and the embassy's premises were threatened by mob action. Persecution of American anarchists Emma Goldman and Alexander Berkman (imprisoned for their opposition to conscription and U.S. entry into the war) was a source of rage to their supporters in Petrograd, who were prepared to make the embassy's personnel pay with their lives if anything untoward happened.[43] (Berkman and Goldman were deported to Russia in 1919, where they stayed for two years before becoming disillusioned with Bolshevism and resuming their peripatetic careers.) And Trotsky delivered an emotional speech in December 1917 to a crowd in the Aleksandrovsky Theater in which he linked Francis by name to alleged enemies of the people—the Kalpashnikov affair—and to General Kaledin's anti-Bolshevik forces operating in southern Russia. Trotsky declaimed to the audience that "the heavy hand of the revolution" would know how to deal with the "adventurer" ambassador.[44] Disgruntled U.S. Marines dragooned from courier service and an unprepossessing group of revolutionary soldiers eventually made up the embassy's guard. Unlike the Italian or British (in 1918), the U.S. embassy was never victimized by looting mobs, but the fear felt by diplomats was warranted and did nothing to endear Trostsky to them. Philip Jordan captured the nervous mood in a missive home: "Now for the Bolsheviks. the first thing I must tell you is that we are all seting on a bomb Just waiting for some one to tuch a match to it. if the Ambassador gets out of this Mess with our life we will be awful lucky. here you cant tell at what minute you will be killed. these crazy people are Killing each other Just like we Swat flies at home."[45]

Bolshevik disregard for the conventions of diplomacy—the Decree on Peace, release of the secret treaties, snarls against bourgeois etiquette—convinced Francis that the Marxists could not be reasoned with; the only way to deal with this lot of Jewish malefactors and German agents was to exterminate them.[46] He predicted that otherwise their ideas and practices would seep westward to pollute life in Britain, France, and the United States. To Russian readers of the still-uncensored press and to whatever interlocutors could be found, he stressed America's continuing regard and the necessity of resistance to German aggression. While the Bolsheviks were still promising "Peace, Land, Bread," Francis nattered on about objectives of no concern to a war-weary population. His calls to arms for a democratic crusade against Germany were without effect and (like his certainty that women had been nationalized by Bolshevism) cast doubt on his overall judgment.

Francis's activities in 1918 indicate the isolation and impotence not only of U.S. diplomacy but also that of the whole foreign community in Petrograd. In early January, he tried to persuade his colleagues in the diplomatic corps, of which he was by then dean, to attend the long-awaited meeting of the Constituent Assembly at the Tauride Palace. Objecting that they had not been invited and frightened by the violence swirling around the palace—its grounds bristling with machine guns, its environs strewn with corpses—they declined. Thus no member of this diplomatic body bore witness to the sole session of the Assembly. Later, Francis was certain that his and others' presence would have had a pacifying effect on the proceedings and might have been a boon to Russian democracy. More likely than not, the drunken sailors occupying the galleries and acting under the "supervision" of A. G. Zheleznyakov (an anarcho-communist) would have invented amusements at the expense of any delegation of ambassadors. (Two Cadet deputies were beaten to death by sailors the night after the Assembly dispersed.) Efforts to edify those present in democracy would have drowned in bedlam.

In another episode that occurred shortly after the Assembly was dissolved, Francis met with some at least superficial success. In response to the harassment of revolutionary units of the Russian army in eastern Romania, the Bolsheviks seized Bucharest's legation, including its minister, Count Constantine Diamandi, with the hope of exchanging him for better treatment of their comrades. Francis immediately called the diplomatic corps to his embassy, where it was decided to protest the Bolshevik action. It transpired that the diplomats, none of whose governments yet recognized the Bolsheviks, met with Lenin in the Smolny Institute, the once-fashionable girls' school then functioning as revolutionary headquarters. Francis, Noulens, and the Belgian and Serbian ministers each delivered statements and handed Lenin a joint declaration demanding the release of Diamandi. Lenin suffered these petitions with a show of courtesy, though the "honey-tongued" suppliants also filled him with loathing. In this, Francis's only meeting with Lenin, his initial but fleeting impression was of the Bolshevik's "sincerity."

At the suggestion of Robins and Judson, Francis toyed with the idea of asking his superiors to press Romania to adopt a moderate policy toward Russian forces on its soil. Although he did not authorize any such approach, his apparent willingness to explore ways of influencing Romania was conveyed—by Robins or his lieutenant, Alexander Gumberg—to Smolny. The day after Francis's visit with Lenin (and to his embarrassment), *Pravda* announced that Diamandi would be freed because the U.S. ambassador was going to protest Romanian misbehavior; this, of course, was an action he never meant to attempt and in the event never tried. Freed in mid-January from the St. Peter–St. Paul Fortress, Diamandi was ordered to leave Russian territory. But he barely escaped with his life. His escort, one Svetlitsky, was carrying orders from Trotsky that the local Red officer was to execute Diamandi upon his delivery to Torneo, Finland. As it turned out, by the time Diamandi and his escort reached Torneo, the Whites were in charge, and they cheerfully shot Svetlitsky instead. As Francis later reflected, the episode had a "most extraordinary character." But the ambassador neglected to add that it lacked vindication of his efforts or the principle of diplomatic immunity.[47]

Of the negotiations at Brest-Litovsk (concluded March 3, 1918) that surrendered the empire's Baltic provinces, Finland, Russian Poland, and the Ukraine to a German sphere of influence and permitted the transfer of scores of German divisions to the western front, Francis was an unhappy observer.[48] He did admire Trotsky's daring "neither war nor peace" formula; but like other Allied diplomats, he blamed the Bolsheviks for nearly allowing a German victory in the west and causing additional hundreds of thousands of British, French, and American casualties. To help energize the eastern front, Francis let it be known to Lenin—and here the influence of Robins was crucial—that Russia's continued participation in the war *could* result in U.S. aid and recognition. Unfortunately, as President Wilson admitted in his message (March 11) to the Congress of Soviets, the United States was not in a position to give assistance. He could only issue platitudes about the inviolability of Russian independence and the need to vanquish militarism. To this statement, the Soviet congress, meeting to ratify the treaty with Germany, responded with a slap to Wilson's face (Gregory Zinoviev's imagery). It proclaimed that the time was fast approaching when the world's toiling masses would eliminate capitalist tyranny and erect a socialist order to uphold future peace.[49] Acting on his own initiative, as cable communication with Washington was again severed, Francis responded to the congress with a statement for the Russian press. Issued after the Brest-Litovsk Treaty had been ratified, it reiterated the president's main points:

> My government still considers America an ally of the Russian people, who surely will not reject the proffered assistance which we shall be prompt to render to any power in Russia that will offer sincere and organized resistance to the German invasion. If the Russian people who are brave and patriotic will hold in abeyance for the time being their political differences and be resolute and firm and united they can drive the enemy from their borders and secure before the end of 1918 for themselves and the world an enduring peace.[50]

Infuriated by this appeal, the German foreign minister, Richard von Kuhlmann, insisted that the Bolsheviks evict Francis from Russia, as he was violating the spirit of the country's new neutrality.

By the time Kuhlmann delivered his eviction demand, Francis and his entourage were ensconced in the town of Vologda, located at the junction of the Trans-Siberian and Moscow–Archangel railways. They were joined by members of the French, Italian, and Belgian missions and by the British chargé Francis Lindley. This remote site was chosen by the Americans (with Lenin's cooperation) for its convenience of transportation and telegraphic communications. It was also 350 miles east of the German forces that were threatening Petrograd in late February and that caused the removal of the Bolsheviks to refuge in Moscow. This site in the wilderness was an acceptable compromise to Francis between leaving Russia altogether (thereby losing any chance to influence events) or following the Marxist government (thereby conferring status on it). In this setting safe from German dislodgement, the Allied representatives established (to the delight of municipal authorities) "the diplomatic capital of Russia." But in truth, the ambassadorial occupation of the town (65,000 inhabitants) placed them physically outside the reach of Russian politics and rendered them absolutely marginal to events. Lockhart described Vologda, with characteristic pithiness, as "a sleepy provincial town with almost as many churches as inhabitants. As a connecting link with Moscow it was as useless as the North Pole."[51]

The embassy was installed in an unused clubhouse, and daily life came to resemble a languid idyll satirized in novels. From this confine, Francis managed as best he could the affairs of the United States in Russia. He continued to inveigh against Brest-Litovsk and against the country's dismemberment. Predictably, the Germans protested each one of Francis's tirades but in vain; the Bolsheviks, who regarded the treaty with Germany as invalid and (they hoped) temporary, replied that the ambassador was merely parroting points regularly made by Wilson. Matters came to a crisis on July 6, when Socialist Revolutionaries assassinated Germany's envoy to Russia, Count Mirbach, and anti-Bolshevik uprisings erupted in Moscow and Yaroslavl. In this emergency, said George Chicherin (Trotsky's successor for foreign affairs), the regime could no longer guarantee the safety of ambassadors in Vologda. Would they not come to Moscow to enjoy the protective care of the revolution? For this purpose, Chicherin sent Karl Radek to the diplomatic colony with authority to expedite its transfer to Moscow.

The response of Francis and his colleagues was to seek alternative safety, fearing that Chicherin would interpret "care" as taking the diplomats hostage. They might then be used to inhibit Allied intervention against the Bolsheviks, which by midsummer 1918 seemed only a matter of time. Might they suffer the fate originally intended for Diamandi and recently (July 16) inflicted on Nicholas and his family at Ekaterinburg?[52]

Francis and his number consequently fled in late July to the far north—to Archangel (then to Kandalaksha and back to Archangel). There Francis became enmeshed in the affairs of Nicholas Chaikovsky and the anti-Bolsheviks of the area, whose career involved coup, countercoup, and kidnappings. Into this tortured situation, naval and military forces of the United States, France, and Britain were interjected; from it nothing plausible or in the Allied interest emerged.[53] Francis hoped that Chaikovsky would prove sturdy enough to receive American grants of financial aid and diplomatic recognition. At the same time, he tried to stiffen the sagging morale of the local garrison of U.S. troops, whose numbers and spirits were reduced more by influenza than combat. By autumn, Francis had depleted his own resources of energy and health. An ailing man, he left Russia in early November on the American warship *Olympia*.[54] He was thus spared from seeing the full agony of Russia's civil war or the haphazard Allied intervention, which, after hesitation, he came to support with enthusiasm comparable to that of Winston Churchill.

About Francis and intervention: throughout the Vologda period, he had relied on two individuals—Robins, who stayed in close touch with the highest Kremlin leadership, and Summers, who from his vantage point studied revolutionary actions against church, property, and the organized resistance. Both men were strong personalities (Summers detested and mistrusted Robins) and urged on Francis conflicting American approaches to Russia.[55] Whereas Robins campaigned for U.S. recognition of the Bolsheviks and accommodation, Summers advocated cooperation with any one of several versions of Allied intervention (especially the Japanese) in the civil war. By this means, he hoped the revolution could be extinguished and the eastern front revitalized. Francis vacillated between these positions for months until in late April he adopted the Summers line, which had been reinforced in Vologda by the French and Italian envoys. Thereafter, his dispatches identified a number of reasons for U.S. involvement: the rescue of the Czech legion fighting its way across Siberia to the Pacific, the protection of war matériel in Archangel and Murmansk from the depredations of foul weather and the Germans, the salvation of a prostrate Russian nation. To Wilson, Francis eventually advocated the most extraordinary ideas. These demonstrated no sense about the danger of becoming mired in the civil war or about the hazards of failing to balance military means with political ends. He recommended that a contingent of fifty thousand U.S. troops, fifty thousand British, fifty thousand French, and twenty thousand Italian accompany their ambassadors to Petrograd. This force would allow for national elections to a new constituent assembly and demolish Bolshevism. Francis later said this about Russia and American security interests at the end of the world war:

> I advocate the eradication of Bolshevism in Russia because it is a blot on the civilization of the Twentieth Century, and for the additional reason that it is to our interest to exterminate it in the land of its birth. I say "our interest" from two points of view. First: If Bolshevism is permitted to thrive in Russia it will promote unrest in all countries. Second: It is our duty to the Russian people, who have always been favorable to America, and of whose greatest offense is that they favored the Allies as against Germany in the world war, to relieve their country of the injury and disgrace inflicted upon it by Soviet rule.[56]

Although it played no part in official deliberations on the merits of intervention, an incisive analysis by the American consul in Archangel, Felix Cole, was available during the summer of 1918. Its timely transmission to Washington, delayed by Francis because he objected to its content, might have helped dissuade Wilson and House from adopting their ill-fated course. It is sobering to recall the points of Cole's advice in view of the five hundred fatalities suffered by U.S. troops dispatched to northern Russia and Siberia (1918–1920), the ineffectiveness of nominal allies such as Alexander Kolchak, and the lurid conclusions drawn by the Bolsheviks about U.S. intentions.[57]

Based on five years of living in Russia before entering government service, in which time he studied the society and economy, Cole's understanding belonged to a category well beyond Francis. The consul warned that by the nature of its "inner necessities" intervention in Russia was bound to require ever greater investments of ships, men, money, and matériel. The country's vastness would "swallow up" even the largest foreign army and frustrate the most elaborate logistical arrangements. In addition, the native population should not be taken for granted. Attempts to win its cooperation would fail; it was too hard pressed by hunger and indifferent to the competing pretensions of Allies, Germans, Bolsheviks, Whites, and others vying for power. At the same time, Cole wrote, the Bolsheviks would occupy the moral high ground and could reasonably portray themselves to the Russian people as their best champion against imperial trespassers, whether Anglo-French, Japanese, or American. The United States and all intervening powers would also be assuming an obligation to feed and protect those millions of Russians who fell into the Allied sphere of influence in the course of operations. Finally, intervention might shove Russia into an accommodation with Germany; irrespective of the war's outcome in western Europe, the Allies would then be presented with the long-term problem of containing a German–Russian bloc. Thus in Cole's words,

> We shall have sold our birthright in Russia for a mess of potage. The birthright is the future friendship and economic cooperation with a great [country] controlling untold riches. The potage will be the recovery of a few thousand tons of materials that we once gave to Russia . . . and the thanks of a few discredited politicians without constituents.

Anticipating Herbert Hoover's American Relief Administration and its work against famine in 1921 to 1923, Cole urged food assistance as the way "to make more friends in Russia."[58]

These offers, in conjunction with revived trade, would not have induced the Bolsheviks to adopt the tenets of democracy, as Cole evidently hoped. But some gesture, toward which the regime was open through 1918, might have tempered the estrangement felt by Soviet Russia from Western values and purpose. Even in February 1919, at the time of the Allies' proposal to convene a conference (Prinkipo) dealing with Russia and its warring factions, Chicherin made explicit once again his desire to improve matters with the West.[59] Intervention (and cancellation of Prinkipo) did not lead automatically to Rapallo and later more astounding German–Soviet agreement, but it made easier their consummation and provided tangible support for Lenin's thesis: the long-run coexistence of the Soviet republic with the capitalist-imperialist powers was unthinkable. Meanwhile, human suffering in Russia caused by the civil war and food shortages—aggravated by the Allied blockade—reached horrendous levels. A tough-minded U.S. Army officer in command of the Thirty-first Infantry in Vladivostok, Colonel Fred Bugbee, wrote to his wife in December 1919: "The winter certainly is dark for the poor devils that live in this country. What people are going to do with no food and no fuel, I don't understand." And he was saddened to think that in the broad reaches of starving Siberia, Bolsheviks and Kolchak's forces did "wicked" things to one another. For this calamity, the Americans should avoid even the appearance of responsibility.[60]

*   *   *   *

Mediocre U.S. diplomacy in St. Petersburg, broken by the accidental appearance of able envoys, culminated in the careers of Marye and Francis. Of Marye, enough has been said. Additional evidence in the case against Francis includes his confidence in the so-called Sisson documents, that collection of forged papers purporting to show that Lenin and his comrades were agents of German militarism. Francis also made a quixotic attempt in late 1918 to organize a "Slavic legion" under U.S. financial sponsorship that would fight the Reds.[61] Understandably, he has not been dealt with charitably by scholarship—with one or two exceptions—or by his contemporaries.[62] What is striking about the consensus reached by this second group is that it included people of diverse philosophies and vocations. Sisson was echoing many when he told the State Department that Francis had no policy toward the Bolsheviks other than one of unfocused anger and that he had been rendered incompetent by old age and ravaging disease. Wilson's unofficial emissary to Lenin in 1919, young William Bullitt, concurred. He thought Francis entirely incapable of comprehending the revolution or its goals (for which at the time Bullitt entertained enthusiasm). Fiorello LaGuardia, then a Republican congressman from New York, condemned Francis in 1919 as numbering among those Americans most ignorant of Russia. His inability to work with his French and British colleagues in 1917 and his neglect of discerning reports by Captain Walter Crosley (naval attaché) and North Winship (consul general in Petrograd) meant that Francis denied himself real familiarity with the Russian situation. According to the congressman, Francis's reports had urged support of Kerensky, whereas the United States should have backed Kornilov, the only person determined enough to have crushed the Bolsheviks. Even though their evaluations of U.S. purpose must be considered in the context of their ideological commitments, both Bryant and Reed were expressing commonly held views when they attacked Francis for being "stupid" and a philistine. Finally, despite commending Francis for braving physical danger in Archangel and for opposing Bolshevik representation in the United States (Trotsky had hoped to appoint Reed), Wilson was disturbed by the deCram matter and uninterested in Francis's interpretations of Russia. Even in 1919, when Wilson was eager to make sense of this problem and to adopt appropriate measures, he did not consult (except for one courtesy call) with his ambassador.[63]

The main inadequacies of U.S. policy toward Russia in 1914 to 1918 did not reside in Marye or Francis, however. Structural weaknesses of wartime diplomacy and the upheaval of international life that marked the end of World War I were at the core of U.S. confusion.

Two structural problems were manifest. First, in the U.S. community in Russia, the lines of responsibility and authority were unclear. Neither Russians nor Americans were ever certain where the president's confidence reposed. In peacetime, one would turn as a matter of course to the ambassador as the president's personal representative. But as part of America's wartime collaboration with Russia, Petrograd and other parts of the empire were host to high-level U.S. commissions, delegations, and missions that collectively eclipsed the embassy's significance. The military mission operated independently and at the pleasure of the War Department (even though its director, General Judson, also functioned as military attaché on the ambassador's staff). In his capacity as chief of operations in Russia for the Committee on Public Information, Sisson reported to its head, George

Creel, who ignored Lansing as much as possible in promoting his own interpretation of U.S. aims. Also closely associated with Creel and Sisson in Russia was Arthur Bullard. Like them, he sought to sidestep the State Department's minions, and he enjoyed access to that most influential of all irregular agents, Colonel House. The American Red Cross in Russia also pursued its policies, as much political as they were ameliorative and medical. Under its original leadership, that of William Boyce Thompson, financial disbursements in the hundreds of thousands of dollars were made to Socialist Revolutionaries after the March revolution. By buttressing their position in Petrograd, Thompson hoped to solidify Russia's domestic situation and move the country back to vigorous participation in the anti-German war. Recipients of his largess were later ridiculed as prostitutes by the Bolsheviks, and Wilson was displeased to learn that a semipublic officer was supporting a partisan group in Russia with private funds. Francis himself learned of Thompson's activities late and indirectly. Whether he knew that Kerensky referred to Thompson as the "real" U.S. ambassador is uncertain. Francis was definitely aware in 1918, after Robins's many intimate communications with the Bolsheviks, that Lenin expected Wilson to dispense with him and appoint Robins as the new ambassador.[64]

Given this procedural and bureaucratic muddle, one can appreciate Francis's complaints to Lansing that U.S. organizations and individuals in Russia—Robins and the Red Cross, above all—were failing to consult him on matters directly bearing on foreign policy. Francis virtually accused them of acting in bad faith, notwithstanding Robins's seeming solicitude. (At times, Robins was shameful in his flattery of the ambassador, whom he did not take seriously, and cooed about his "courage and foresight."[65]) Both Wilson and Lansing also reassured Francis of their esteem. These supportive statements were pro forma, though, and motivated by a desire to avoid finding a replacement for Francis during trying times. Thus he was left to contend with rival sources of American authority in Russia. Unexpected sympathy for his predicament later came from one of his severest critics. With the U.S. diplomatic experience of Russia in mind, Sisson observed after the war that as a rule

> ambassadors sent for pleasant duties remained to face the strange equations of war. They did very well, but expansions and functional additions, bringing in new executives subject to headships at Washington other than diplomatic, tended to create a twilight zone of divided authority. These invasions into the diplomatic zone were. necessary—war-trade boards and various specialized commissions— but an ambassador would not be human if he did not feel that he should be in chief command of all the governmental units in the country where he is the titled representative of his Government.

To fix this problem, Sisson offered a solution:

> If another war should come, it would be better to supersede the ambassadors to allied countries with commissioners-general charged with the coordination of every political, economic, and welfare activity of our Government in those zones. If an ambassador to any country happened to be the best man for commissioner-general, he could be appointed.[66]

This plan had merit as it would concentrate and rationalize authority. Yet its ambiguity about whether an ambassador or someone else—a military officer or a management specialist from private enterprise—would be the proper choice for commissioner reflected wartime indifference to the diplomatic instrument. In any case, Sisson's plan was not adopted, and failure to resolve the issue had serious consequences for diplomacy during World War II.

The second structural problem had to do with the absence in Washington of governmental machinery (comparable, say, to Churchill's World War II cabinet) to supervise the multitudinous aspects of war and plan political strategy for the posthostilities era. No single group of responsible people was ever asked by Wilson to think systematically about a realistic and desirable world future or America's place in it. Instead, Wilson took solely upon himself this burden—doing so, one is tempted to say, for the sake of his compulsion for martyrdom. Whereas diplomacy inside Russia was hurt by lack of coordination and clarity about who occupied the seat of authority, the corresponding issue in Washington was precisely the opposite. Indeed, more than any of his predecessors (including Lincoln in the Civil War or Theodore Roosevelt, who was enlivened by international competition), Wilson held tightly to all reins of power connected to foreign relations. Even if at some level he believed what he said about open diplomacy and open covenants, his conduct of policy—whether in dealing with European heads of state in 1919 or with congressional leaders—was marked by his keeping inordinately close counsel. The compliment of consultation was occasionally extended to Lansing and often to House. But as Wilson's behavior in the battle to obtain Senate ratification of the League of Nations and Versailles Treaty indicated, he was prepared to act without the assistance of anyone. More than a few of the president's supporters thought him abnormally hostile to advice and believed that men who advanced views contrary to Wilson's courted his enmity. Well before their own bitter separation, House noted of Wilson: "He does not like to meet people and isolates himself as much as anyone I have ever met."[67]

This habit of Wilson's mind applied to Russia meant that he did not seek or receive much analysis about the country's conditions from anyone, including House, who was well informed by his own network of agents. Wilson ignored not only Francis, which given the circumstances was justifiable, but also Judson, Robins, and others with firsthand experience of the revolution.[68] The president's repudiation of Bullitt after his secret mission to Moscow in March 1919—undertaken to find common ground between the Western powers and Lenin—was another example of willfully ignoring others' plausible ideas.[69] As a conveyer of information and tool of policy, the embassy was as neglected as Bullitt. The logic of Wilson's modus operandi meant that the formal diplomatic mechanism in Russia was allowed to wither to a degree matched only by the Lincoln–Cassius Clay period.

Finally, a word about the assault to which international values and institutions were subjected during the last year of the Great War. Rival claimants to redefine the world—embodied by Wilson, the Fourteen Points, and the League, on the one hand, versus Lenin, socialism, and the Third International, on the other—were equally impatient with the old concepts. Despite other differences between them,

Lenin and Wilson agreed that balance-of-power politics, spheres of influence, secret diplomacy conducted by the few, and similar devices had encouraged war for centuries and should be discarded. This attitude on Wilson's part reinforced his disposition to ignore ambassadorial diplomacy. In his opinion, its stylized world, with its mania for ceremony, prickliness about protocol, conformity, and inability to depart from received wisdom, was inadequate to the moment. To remake the world in the image of democracy and to ensure peace for future generations, bold innovations like the League and intensified regard for international law required the attention of statesmen.[70]

To Wilson, justice would henceforth provide the organizing principle of international relations. Even more than before, U.S. foreign policy would identify itself with universal advancement:

> An evident principle runs through the whole program [Fourteen Points]. It is the principle of justice to all peoples and nationalities, and their right to live on equal terms of liberty and safety with one another, whether they be strong or weak. Unless this principle be made its foundation no part of the structure of international justice can stand. The people of the United States could act upon no other principle.

In this sort of superior universe, there was no place for the obsolete arts of ambassadorial diplomacy, itself mismanaged by Wilson's men in Petrograd. By neglecting Marye and Francis, Wilson was not so much passing judgment on their devotion to duty or efficacy of service. As the chief architect of moral reformation in the lives of nations, he could not afford to be distracted by the remnants of a discredited era.

II

IN STALIN'S TIME

Did I know a single person whose life turned out well? It was as though my father were at the center of a black circle and anyone who ventured inside vanished or perished or was destroyed in one way or another.

Svetlana Alliluyeva, *Twenty Letters to a Friend*

4

Preparing for Moscow

Obsessed by statistical indicators of economic growth and unabashed in its disregard for the legal protections normally accorded people living in modern society, Stalin's dictatorship emerged during the period when the United States withheld recognition from the USSR (1917–1933). These were the years of Soviet phantasmagoria. Cruelties inflicted on the peasantry by White and Red armies, policies of terror practiced by both sides in the civil war, levies on food in the years of War Communism, and epidemics of disease and famine in the early 1920s caused millions of fatalities and crippled the economy. To secure the population a respite and to pump up production (which by 1921 was a fraction of its pre-1914 level), Lenin inaugurated the New Economic Policy (NEP). It allowed for a modest system of private enterprise and spearheaded national recovery by 1926.[1] Communist party control of politics and the destruction to human values and lives caused by Felix Dzerzhinsky's ubiquitous security police did not diminish, however.

In the struggle for succession following Lenin's death in January 1924, Stalin defeated by turns his rivals on the left (Trotsky), within the "new opposition" (Leo Kamenev and Gregory Zinoviev), and on the right (Nicholas Bukharin and Alexis Rykov). Such as it was, the NEP respite was (in effect) repealed by Stalin at the All Union Congress of the Communist party in December 1927. There followed the explosion of the First Five-Year Plan. The rapid industrialization, collectivization of agriculture, and decision to "squeeze" the countryside's wealth to pay for machinery and foreign technology amounted to an attack by Stalin's government on the population. This massive but lopsided contest between coercive state power and its subjects resulted in countless more fatalities and led to the incarceration, exile, and forced labor of millions of men and women.

However reckless the early Soviet experiment, it would not have achieved what modernization it did without making a successful utopian appeal to elements in the party rank and file, the proletariat, and the intelligentsia.[2] For the Marxist believer and his allies, there was something exhilarating in the challenge of creating a modern economy, a literate and "cultured" society, and a presumably humane order from the coarse material of old Russia. The setting of foundations for industrial complexes such as Magnitogorsk in the Urals, electrification of rural areas, and campaigns to raise popular awareness of everything from socialist precepts to personal hygiene impressed sympathetic observers as first evidence that the sacrifices were not in vain. One U.S. engineer explained in 1930 after living in the Soviet Union for three years: "[The worker] has been told—and he still believes—that the hardships which he undergoes now will end in a more glorious Russia, a Russia of plenty for him and his children."[3] In the cause of heroic socialism, the services of painters, playwrights, filmmakers, and poets were enlisted. They extolled the virtues of collective exertion and depicted a "radiant future." Even artists of true sensibility and talent were not immune to the conceptual power of a redemptive project. In "To a Friend" (1931), Boris Pasternak nervously asked,

Does not the Five-Year Plan assess and score us,
And do I with it, too, not rise and fall?

The more insulated one was from the reality of Soviet life—poverty in the cities, squalor on the collective farms, prisons teeming with "enemies of the revolution"—the easier it was to believe in the incantations of Soviet propaganda that a wonderful world was being born. Hence the phenomenon of those tens of thousands of idealists (nondenominational socialists, Marxists, union votaries) in Europe and America who misidentified the Bolshevik revolution as the supreme ethical moment in history rather that just another expression (albeit a dramatic one) of the unchanging human condition. Despite the executions of such people as the poet Nicholas Gumilev (1921) and the vicar-general of the Roman Catholic Church in Russia (1923), the suicide of the futurist Vladimir Mayakovsky (1930), the emigration of Wassily Kandinsky, the silencing of Osip Mandelstam, and so on, numerous intellectuals in the West praised the Soviet judicial system and the freedom allowed artists. These included Sidney and Beatrice Webb, George Bernard Shaw, Louis Fischer, Harold Laski, Theodore Dreiser, Paul Robeson, and H. G. Wells. Many of them, and thousands more less famous, not only hailed the Soviet republic but journeyed there to lend their labor. It was a measure of their own disaffection from Western society, with its crass materialism and cant about equality, that some of these people on returning from the workers' republic felt too reluctant to denounce it.[4] Although not entirely adequate, such an interpretation partly explains such cases as that of the *New York Times*'s Pulitzer Prize–winning (in 1932) reporter Walter Duranty, who became an apologist for Stalin and deliberately omitted information from his articles about the causes and consequences of the 1932/1933 Ukrainian famine.[5]

Others, however, such as American newsman William Henry Chamberlin and Eugene Lyons, changed from supporting the USSR to agreeing with Britain's Bertrand Russell, who had earlier condemned the revolution's "cruelty, poverty, suspicion, persecution." On the basis of their firsthand knowledge of forced-labor practices, shoddy architectural designs, and elephantine building bureaucracies,

American engineers also returned disillusioned. These included the accomplished Zara Witkin, whose romance with a Soviet screen star (Emma Cessarskaya) and commitment to sound construction techniques caused him personal sorrow and professional frustration during the First Five-Year Plan. He was further disabused when his appeal to France's Romain Rolland (novelist, Noble laureate, socialist) to speak out against illegality and violations of workers' rights in the Soviet Union met with mute response.[6]

During the nonrecognition era, various U.S. businessmen organized profitable trade and enterprises in the Soviet Union through the offices of Amtorg, that institutional expression of Moscow's eagerness for American capital and technology. Concessions were granted to Armand and Julius Hammer to mine asbestos and manufacture pencils. A manganese-mining operation was run by Averell Harriman in the Caucasus during the 1920s that began with the promise of development of a vital natural resource (though it ended in a confusion of red tape and inefficiency). Oil companies, including Standard Oil and Sinclair, won contracts to develop Soviet energy reserves. Substantial quantities of American-grown cotton were exported to Soviet textile industries, themselves partly financed with private U.S. capital. In 1925, fully 10 percent of all tractors manufactured by the Ford Motor Company were purchased by Soviet buyers. American-made locomotives were also sold in bulk. Easing of credit restrictions in 1928 permitted the USSR to purchase more than $20 million worth of electrical equipment from the International General Electric Company, and the Cooper Company sold technical assistance useful in building the Dnieprostroy Dam. By 1930, Soviet–U.S. trade had reached a yearly value of about a $100 million—twice that of pre-1914. Despite concern about Soviet dumping of cheap products in American markets, there was growing optimism among entrepreneurs that business with the USSR was lucrative and—after the 1929 stockmarket crash—could play a role in U.S. recovery.

In contrast with those idealists who went to work in the Soviet Union and then turned against it (or at least suffered doubts) pragmatic businessmen were usually not disappointed. True, they had to maneuver through bureaucratic minefields, but they had at their disposal a compliant work force that was in no position to negotiate for higher wages or improved working conditions and to whom the weapon of the strike was denied. Thus the communist John Scott, who helped build the largest steel mill in the world in the Urals, worried that "Russia's battle of ferrous metallurgy" reaped more casualties than the battle of the Marne through freezing cold, deprivation, and police activity. Walter Arnold Rukeyser, however, whose asbestos firm in the USSR (Asbest) employed thirteen thousand people, supplied contrary testimony about the situation of Soviet workers. After a tour of Soviet cities and factories, he wrote in 1931 for the edification of *The Nation*'s readers that Asbest's employees drew generous wages, lived in spacious communal housing, enjoyed a varied and healthful diet, and received first-class medical care. Begging was nowhere in evidence. His following statement is chilling to read when one reflects that by 1931 gangs of orphaned children were becoming a common sight in Kiev and elsewhere in the Ukraine: "One thing which impressed itself strongly upon my mind was the healthy appearance of the children, whether in the cities or in the country. . . . The children are certainly not being neglected in the Soviet Union."[7]

As for the U.S. government, its public position in the 1920s and early 1930s remained what it had been since Lenin consolidated his power: one of dismay for the Soviets and all their works. Their failure to honor financial debts and to abide by the conventions of law and diplomacy and Comintern meddling in American labor organizations were cited as reasons for nonrecognition by the State Department. Moreover, domestic hysteria about Bolshevism in the early 1920s was incompatible with the establishment of diplomatic relations; this attitude was manifest in the deportation of foreign-born communists, senatorial investigations of alleged communist influence in America, Attorney General Palmer's zealotry, and the irregular trial and execution (1927) of Sacco and Vanzetti. Yet none of these concerns caused the government to oppose those businessmen with the financial and other wherewithal to conduct commerce with the USSR. And though presidents Harding, Coolidge, and Hoover resisted overtures from Moscow to recognize the new regime, the United States undertook a few important projects in the Soviet field. First, Harding authorized Herbert Hoover's American Relief Administration (ARA) to provide assistance to the victims of Russian famine in 1921 to 1923. More than $45 million was raised through public and private means, and 700,000 metric tons of food were distributed in Russia. By this program, Hoover hoped both to save the lives of millions of people (in which aim he succeeded admirably) and to weaken the population's attachment to a regime unable to cope with drought and hunger. On this second count, Hoover, vehemently anticommunist, produced no obvious results but won the suspicion—and later vilification—of the Soviet leadership.[8] The U.S. government's other projects involve the main substance of this chapter. Through its listening posts on the Baltic, the State Department monitored events in the Soviet Union during the 1920s and early 1930s. In anticipation of relations with Moscow, the department also trained a cadre of Russian-language and Soviet-area students. Presumably, their expertise would stand the United States well and help prevent blunders associated with earlier representation. Ironically, in the first episode requiring expertise on Soviet matters (negotiations with Maxim Litvinov on recognition), the executive branch paid little attention to the analyses produced by its battery of specialists.

Missions on the Baltic and the New Foreign Service

The year 1922, associated by Americans with the beginning of the Teapot Dome oil scandal, also stands out in the interwar diplomatic histories of the United States and Soviet Union. In Moscow, the debilitation of Lenin by strokes forced the regime to grapple with the problem of the revolution's global, as well as domestic, future. From the eastern zone of Siberia, the Japanese evacuated their forces, thereby ending foreign intervention and allowing for the integration of the Far Eastern Republic with Soviet Russia. That April, George Chicherin and Reich-minister Walter Rathenau signed the wide-ranging Soviet–German economic and diplomatic agreement at Rapallo; delegates from the two pariah states also entered into understandings of military significance. In Washington, the Provisional Government's ambassador terminated his official function and left the financial attaché to conclude matters remaining from the Kerensky period. A year later, S. Pickney Tuck, the consul in Vladivostok, closed his office; with his departure to Japan, the last American diplomat had left Russian soil.[9] Meanwhile, opinion in the United States condemned the continuing Soviet persecution of the Orthodox and Roman Catholic hierarchies. Although the administration realized that it could not (contrary to the hopes of petitioners) effectively intervene on the victims' behalf, both President Harding and Secretary of State Charles Hughes shared the general sense of revulsion and communicated their disapproval to Lenin's government. And following recognition by the Bolsheviks of Estonia, Latvia, and Lithuania, the United States established diplomatic relations with the Baltic republics, despite doubts that they could maintain their independence against a resurgent USSR.[10]

The Latvian capital of Riga was the principal site of U.S. political and intelligence activities in the Baltic from 1922 onward. This handsome seaport served as home to Frederic Coleman, the first U.S. minister (1922–1931), whose responsibilities embraced representation to all three of the little countries. Coleman was an amiable Republican party activist from Minnesota who, though he seldom wrote dispatches himself, carefully read those prepared by his staff before approving transmittal to Washington. Under his benign and detached tutelage, the legation performed the normal diplomatic functions. Its most significant work, though, was conducted by a small subsection (no more than two or three men at a time) that, freed from operational duties, devoted itself to studying events in Soviet Russia.

The chief of the Russian subsection was David Macgowan, who served in Riga from 1922 to 1931. Born in Tennessee in 1870, he had graduated from Washington and Lee University and later studied at German universities in Halle and Berlin. His career for newspaper and press agencies had led him to Germany, the Middle East, and then Russia. After working for the Associated Press in St. Petersburg, he was appointed in 1915 by Secretary of State Bryan to be a consul, and he saw service in Moscow and Vladivostok. Fluent in German and Russian, he maintained professional and social ties with the editors in Riga of Latvian-, German-, and Russian-language newspapers.

Macgowan's major assistant in the legation was Russian-born (1888) John Lehrs, who had been educated in Germany and Moscow. Although his family's business and other property in Russia had been confiscated by the Bolsheviks, he had stayed on in Moscow, where he was employed by Maddin Summers as a noncareer vice-consul. He played a brave part in helping to evacuate U.S. citizens and left Russia with a trainload of them. Before his appointment (1925–1940) to Riga, he acted as an adviser to the American consul general in Copenhagen on Russian matters and was helpful to the ARA in planning its eastern campaign. His command of written and oral Russian, German, and English was flawless.[11]

Macgowan and Lehrs were prodigious workers. Over the years, they produced a voluminous number of dispatches, reports, and translations of Soviet publications for the State Department. Usually written in response to inquiries about specific matters, the Macgowan–Lehrs corpus covered the full range of Soviet topics: foreign and trade relations, Communist party politics, state administration, agricultural and industrial economy, Comintern policies, the labor and legal systems. Their work was primarily based on Russian-language materials (newspapers, journals, smuggled confidential documents) and interviews with Soviet travelers or émigrés. Macgowan and Lehrs occasionally used disparaging phrases in referring to the Soviets and indulged in invective against socialism and Stalin's mendacity. When it came to analyzing Soviet attitude toward the United States, the Riga legation made hasty references to American labor and civil rights groups targeted by the Comintern. Soviet predictions of an Anglo-U.S. conflagration and tirades against Western imperialism and warmongering also annoyed Macgowan and Lehrs; this annoyance was reflected in their reporting. Evidences of pique were the exception, not the rule, however. The legation's compositions mainly amounted to straightforward reporting and were good of their kind. The judgments were cautious, available evidence was marshaled to support defensible theses, and the analytical quality steadily improved. As a source of information and corroboration, the Macgowan–Lehr work can be useful even today to students of early Soviet history.[12]

In addition to its reporting, the Riga legation (and its office in Tallinn) functioned as a training post in the late 1920s for those officers who had been selected by the State Department for careers in the Soviet field. In the cases of George Kennan, Charles Bohlen, and, to a lesser degree, Loy Henderson, the experiences constituted vital apprenticeships.

All three men were representative of the Foreign Service as it existed following Congress's passage of the Rogers Act in 1924. This legislation, the culmination of reform-minded ambassadors and activists of the progressive type, combined the original consular service with the more prestigious diplomatic corps. Organizational machinery (e.g., exams and fitness evaluations) was also created to enhance professionalism against dilettantism. Hardly a perfect meritocracy, the new service clung to an aristocratic ethos and exemplified privilege in American society. It recruited mainly from the sons of upper-middle-class professional and wealthy business families; admitted a disproportionately high percentage of graduates from prep schools and the social clubs of Harvard, Yale, and Princeton; frowned on applications by Catholics and Jews; and was skeptical of the intellectual ability and loyalty of citizens whose origins resided outside the Anglo-Saxon world. Still, the State Department was in earnest about cultivating a corps of well-educated, disinterested diplomats. Financial and other resources were allocated to a number of programs, all of which aimed to foster the knowledge and élan of a professional cadre. In the case of area specialists, this approach meant immersion in the language and culture of their responsibility.[13]

The department's Soviet studies program was overseen by Robert Kelley, the intellectual and mild-mannered director of the East European division from 1926 to 1937. In many ways, he embodied what was best in the breed of professionals. Born in 1894, he had overcome the financial constraints of his working-class family to attend Harvard (on scholarships), from which he graduated magna cum laude, and the University of Paris. His interest in history and the Crimean War led to his work in Russian-language archives and eventually an M.A. from Harvard. Very likely, he would have completed his researches and Ph.D. but for the disruption of the world war. As an army officer, he was assigned occupation duty in Germany and in 1920 was a military observer in Riga and traveled throughout the Baltic provinces. He joined the State Department in 1922 and won the attention of his superiors, who valued his clarity of mind, experience on the fringes of the Russian empire, and linguistic ability; even though only in his early thirties, he was then appointed to lead the Division of East European Affairs. The plan that he devised for Foreign Service officers concentrating on the Soviet Union emphasized language acquisition and familiarity with Russian political history. It also included a probationary period of overseas assignment and study in a European university. During the years of its existence (1927–1934), this educational regimen graduated seven men and instilled in them a sense of camaraderie. Although a number of writers have viewed Kelley's approach as inherently anti-Soviet, his scholarly attitude was esteemed by his subordinates, all of whom could affirm his assessment delivered in 1975: "The program turned out very successfully and . . . was indispensable to the development of our relations with the Soviet Union. . . . Some of these officers spoke as well as any Russian. It enabled them to get a thorough knowledge and understanding of what was going on in the Soviet Union." [14]

Twelve years older than Kennan and Bohlen, Henderson (born 1892) was not, properly speaking, one of Kelley's "bright boys," of whom he was faintly jealous. He had his own experience of western Russia and the Baltic areas before being posted to Riga in 1927. As a member of the American Red Cross, he had worked in 1919 and 1920 to distribute humanitarian aid (the antityphus campaign in Estonia) and witnessed the chaos of civil war and nationalist struggles. Originally attached to the consular service (in 1922), he joined the State Department's Division of East European Affairs in 1924 and served in Washington for three years under Kelley before posting to Riga. During this stint, Henderson concluded that the USSR wanted to keep the west European states from composing their differences and so discourage their making common cause against the workers' republic; to this end, Soviet diplomacy pursued a conciliatory policy toward Germany in the hope of keeping it divided from France and Britain. At the same time, he took seriously what the communists in Moscow said was their ultimate purpose: international revolution and the destruction of capitalism. [15] Henderson's work under Macgowan in Riga during 1927 to 1930 sharpened his understanding of Soviet economics, and he was astute in seeing the first traces of what later became Stalin's cult of personality. Overall, Henderson's attitude toward the USSR was one skeptical of its ideological pretensions and critical of its connection with dissenters in the United States. [16]

Whereas Henderson kept an emotional distance from his study of the Soviet Union (a minor feat in light of his marriage to a Latvian who had suffered during the revolution), Kennan was passionate and romantic. [17] His interest in Russia had been sparked in his youth by the adventures of his distant cousin in Siberia (Chapter 2). After brief assignments in Tallinn and Riga and a two-year study of Russian at the Oriental Seminary in Berlin, Kelley approved Kennan's assignment to Riga in 1931 to 1933. With the atmosphere of prerevolutionary Russia still pervasive, Riga seemed a faithful miniature portrait of vanished St. Petersburg. Years later Kennan recalled:

> In addition to its more serious cultural amenities, Riga had a vigorous night life, much in the Petersburg tradition: vodka, champagne, gypsies, sleighs or drozhki with hugely bundled coachmen waiting at the door, a certain amount of gaiety. . . . The old Petersburg was of course now dead, or largely dead—in any case inaccessible to people from the West. But Riga was still alive. . . . To live in Riga was in many respects to live in Tsarist Russia.[18]

Nostalgic for what he believed was the humanity (and splendors) of an irretrievable past, Kennan was at the same time dogged in examining Soviet reality, particularly the political economy. With Macgowan and Lehrs as guides, he analyzed and debated with colleagues the significance of Stalin's victory over Trotsky, the virtues of capitalism versus socialism, the fate of Russia's peasantry, the purposes of Soviet propaganda.[19]

Far more than Henderson or Kennan, Bohlen embodied the pre-1924 diplomatic corps. Unlike them, he came from an extremely comfortable family. He was familiar since childhood with fashionable leisure in America and Europe, and he had glided through the challenges offered by St. Paul's and Harvard. Poised, irrepressibly good natured, and a deft raconteur, Bohlen also had his serious side: he became as committed as anyone else to an intellectual approach to the Soviet Union. For two and a half years after entering the Foreign Service (in 1929), he was assigned to the Ecole Nationale des Langues Orientales Vivantes in Paris, where he studied Russian and Soviet history, culture, and economics. Like Kennan, he was linguistically gifted and loved the Russian tongue: "It is a beautiful language . . . excellent for music and poetry."[20] As for his apprenticeship on the Baltic littoral, it was less substantial than Henderson's or Kennan's and basically amounted to two summers in Estonia. There he studied language in an all-Russian environment and enjoyed the pleasures of beach and night life.

The experience of budding Soviet specialists in Riga and Tallinn had a distorting effect on their perception of the USSR and inclined them to unalterable hostility toward it, according to some historians. Indoctrinated by older Russian hands who were sympathetic to the previous order, emotionally drawn to the colony of exiles in Latvia, and suspicious of Marxism-Leninism anyway, these diplomats eventually became an influential clique in the State Department apparatus and remained hostile to decent relations with the USSR. In opposition to their hard line, so runs the argument, was the attitude adopted by Roosevelt at Yalta, when he tried to preserve the Grand Alliance for the post–World War II world; this more generous attitude lived on in later proponents of détente. In a sense, one has here in the dispute between Riga and Yalta (to use Daniel Yergin's schema in *Shattered Peace*) a continuation of that debate first begun by Summers and Robins.[21]

There are certain things wrong with this interpretation, however. It exaggerates Roosevelt's illusions about the USSR and the feasibility of cooperating with Stalin after the destruction of Nazi power. It also simplifies the differences in judgment and emphasis among the mature Henderson, Kennan, and Bohle. More so than his junior colleagues, Henderson identified the Soviet Union as an implacable ideological threat to the West—a cause as much as a national power. Kennan and Bohlen, more impressed by the continuities between Russian and Soviet history, were themselves divided at the time of Yalta; the latter endorsed FDR's conciliatory strategy, whereas the former was appalled. As for the actual Baltic experiences of the three men: it is true that they formed strong attachments to individual refugees from the Russian civil war and felt themselves part of a small community of expert opinion on the USSR. Nor were they deceived by Soviet prevarications about the costs involved in collectivization and the "anti-Kulak struggle." But it does not follow that the conclusions drawn by Henderson, Kennan, and Bohlen were ill-conceived. Overall, their evaluations of the USSR at the time were judicious—far more incisive at any rate than those of the Western political pilgrimage in Russia that lent an aura of respectability to Stalinism. In any case, not Henderson or Kennan or Bohlen ever advised against a diplomatic solution to Soviet–U.S. problems. And when their time for Moscow service arrived, each was eager to satisfy firsthand his curiosity about the Marxist experiment, a curiosity that for Kennan and Bohlen bordered on intellectual obsession.[22]

Kelley and the Recognition Debate

As a presidential candidate in 1932 who sought to distinguish his external policy aims from Hoover's, Roosevelt made known his desire to normalize relations with the Soviet Union. For this purpose, he consulted with Walter Duranty in a highly publicized meeting and quizzed him about Soviet gold production and Moscow's ability to maintain its end of any potential trade agreement.[23] Pursuant to this goal, Roosevelt tried to overcome the objections of Catholics, such as Father Edmund Walsh of Georgetown University, and to soothe the suspicions of leaders in the American Federation of Labor during his first months as president. These exertions to win public support succeeded and culminated in mid-November 1933, when Roosevelt and Maxim Litvinov, commissar for foreign affairs, agreed to establish Soviet–U.S. relations on the following terms. Recognition would go forward on the basis of mutual respect and without interference by either country in the internal affairs of the other. The Soviet Union would liquidate some fraction (between $75 and $150 million) of the debt owed by the pre-Bolshevik regime to the United States. The Soviets would not countenance any organization on their territory that worked to overthrow the social-political system in the United States (an oblique reference to the Comintern). And Americans residing in the USSR would be guaranteed freedom of religious worship. With this agreement, the lobbying efforts of Senator William Borah, Raymond Robins, William Bullitt, and other progressive-minded citizens to place Soviet–American relations on a friendlier footing were rewarded.

To Roosevelt, there were compelling reasons for breaking the sixteen-year Soviet–U.S. impasse. As supporters of the initiative had been arguing, the fortunes of the American business community would surely improve; fresh investment opportunities (in Siberia, notably) and increased trade with a nation of 160 million people should follow an exchange of ambassadors. Rapprochement between the two countries also had a critical security dimension for Roosevelt. He hoped that the specter of Soviet–U.S. combination would have a restraining effect on Japanese aggressiveness in the Far East, which included the occupation and organization of Manchuria (Manchukuo) and military skirmishes along the Soviet border. However modest, Soviet–U.S. cooperation might also slow German attempts directed by Hitler (a newcomer to power but demonstrably determined) to alter the Versailles system in Europe. Parenthetically, there is no evidence to suggest that Roosevelt was aware of Stalin's clandestine attempts to cultivate a working relationship with the Third Reich.[24]

As for the Soviets, in addition to the probable benefits to their economy and maneuverability (in the Asian and European balances of power), recognition by Washington conferred status and reaffirmed the regime's legitimacy. As such, trumpeted *Pravda* and *Izvestia,* the establishment of relations with the "mightiest capitalist power" was a stupendous achievement.[25]

Hardly oblivious to the anomaly of not having direct channels to a powerful nation, Kelley and his colleagues in the East European division nevertheless lacked confidence in Roosevelt's negotiations with Litvinov. And they were dissatisfied with the final result. To them, the terms of agreement set an unfortunate precedent in which the United States jeopardized real interests (related to the debts owed American creditors and Soviet meddling in U.S. life) in exchange for which the USSR did nothing tangible. Only a real quid pro quo would provide a durable basis for long-term relations.

These concerns were presented through the summer of 1933 by Kelley to the committee involved in the preparations for recognition. This group comprised, in addition to Kelley himself, Bullitt in his capacity as special assistant to the secretary of state, Assistant Secretary of State R. Walton Moore, Undersecretary of State William Philips, Henry Morgenthau (then with the Farm Credit Administration), and Secretary of State Cordell Hull. In their deliberations, Kelley argued that a sound Soviet–U.S. relationship could be established only if both sides first settled all outstanding problems. Otherwise, increased Soviet–U.S. intercourse would be plagued by friction and rancor. To begin with, he insisted that the Soviets halt their support of subversion in the United States. Similar interference, he reminded his colleagues, had led to ruptures of relations between the USSR and Britain, China, and Mexico.[26] Soviet-supported Communist party activities in France, Germany, and Poland had also degraded the quality of diplomacy between these states and Moscow. He argued that ideally, "the prerequisite to the establishment of harmonious and trustful relations with the Soviet government is the abandonment by the present rulers of Russia of their world revolutionary [goals] and the discontinuance of their activities designed to bring about the realization of such aims."[27] Failing this change, Roosevelt should make plain that any Soviet support for radical organizations in the United States would not be tolerated. On the question of past debts and confiscated property, Kelley contended that unless precise arrangements were made before recognition, subsequent negotiation on these matters would result in unsatisfactory settlement (as the Anglo-Soviet and Franco-Soviet records attested). Finally, he warned that it would be an error to underestimate the gravity of problems likely to confront Americans in the USSR arising from differences in economic-social structure between the two countries. He predicted that businessmen would face constant irritants in dealing with the communist monopoly of foreign trade and that Soviet conceptions of justice were so alien to those in the United States that individual Americans would become ensnared in legal dilemmas beyond their ken. As case in point, Kelley mentioned (as the trial of the British Metropolitan-Vickers engineers proceeded) that the Soviets' definition of economic espionage was elastic; it could embrace as a matter of violation the conduct of practically every resident foreigner. Questions pertaining to the protection of American lives and property in the Soviet republic therefore had to be settled as prerequisite to expanded relations.[28]

In the main, the president's committee adopted Kelley's viewpoint. Moore and Bullitt were particularly supportive. The former was sensitive to the ethical issues involved in recognizing Stalin and expressed the opinion that "unconditional recognition would not be of any special moral or material advantage." And Bullitt advised Hull that the USSR might be relatively amenable before recognition but afterward could be expected to be adamant on matters still outstanding (including Soviet claims for destruction caused by U.S. expeditionary forces in Vladivostok, Archangel, Murmansk).[29]

In the event, Roosevelt did not press Litvinov firmly on the points broached by Kelley, and nothing like the ironclad guarantees that he recommended the Soviets should produce were forthcoming. Instead, as the mild provisions of recognition and record of negotiations reveal, Roosevelt was not diverted from his preferred policy toward the USSR. He and the documents according recognition placated creditors by gestures and paid rhetorical respect to the principles of freedom of conscience, sovereignty, noninterference.

Assessment of the decision to recognize the Soviet Union and Roosevelt's and Kelley's roles is necessarily mixed. First, the president rightly did not fear the influence of the Comintern in the United States, which was even more inept in the New World than in the Old—a point lost on Kelley, who had exaggerated fears about the vulnerability of labor and civil rights groups to the allure of Soviet communism. Additionally, Roosevelt saw accurately that the question of debt repayment was minor in comparison with that of Soviet–U.S. cooperation before the immediate threat posed by Japan and the one beginning to loom in Hitler's Germany.[30] Yet it is also evident that the case does not belong entirely to Roosevelt. He too easily dismissed Kelley's concern about the debts issue, and the two governments failed in the 1930s to resolve the question. This failure eventually led to recriminations and charges of bad faith by each side. Consequently, the Soviets were unable to obtain a credit loan at favorable rates that, if secured, could have been used to purchase still greater quantities of U.S. goods. No boom materialized in trade relations; by 1937, exports to the Soviets were valued at an unexceptional $43 million. Kelley's most crucial point, however, was his attempt to make FDR understand that the differences between Soviet and American societies had profound implications for recognition. In a sense, Kelley was more right than he realized in 1933 to underline this idea. But he was massively wrong in the particulars.

The pressing issue in 1933 was not that Americans in Moscow and Leningrad would have a rough time dealing with Soviet monopolies or legal norms and practices. They had encountered difficulties before 1917 and since and could reasonably expect to face similar problems in the future. The urgent issue that year was that in the Ukraine and other parts of the USSR, Stalin was promoting policies that fostered death by starvation. In the words of Robert Tucker, that most comprehensive student of Stalin, "The toll in death, suffering, and blighted lives resulting from terroristic collectivization and the famine, which constituted both a part and a consequence of it . . . was one of our violent century's most monstrous crimes against humanity." Approximately 6 million people perished by state-inspired famine in the Ukraine and North Caucasus alone. It was with the regime responsible for this desolation that FDR expected to enjoy friendly relations and to cooperate for the preservation of world peace.[31]

Beginning in 1931, U.S. diplomats in Poland and Romania reported an influx into those countries of thousands of refugees from the Ukraine, fleeing mistreatment and hunger. From his reporters in Riga and travelers such as Samuel Harper, Kelley was personally apprised of the food shortage, its causes, and attendant catalog of horrors: cannibalism, suicides, murders, the web of informers, the shooting of officials for "sabotage." Through these same sources and from other diplomats, Roosevelt was also aware of the dimension of suffering. Yet Kelley made only indirect mention of this holocaust in his presentations to Hull and others near the president; Roosevelt made no reference to it in his communications with Litvinov.[32] Had this issue been directly addressed by the executive branch, as some congressmen, news reporters (Gareth Jones and Malcolm Muggeridge), and Ukrainian-Americans hoped, and discussed with Litvinov, matters might have turned out to the administration's greater credit.

Along the lines of Hoover's ARA, Roosevelt or Kelley could have offered to transfer stocks of food and medicine to the afflicted areas. Almost certainly, Litvinov would have reacted with dismay and (in keeping with the official line) denied that a food shortage, let alone famine, existed in the USSR. In 1933, the USSR actually exported 1.7 million metric tons of grain, and aid collected by European organizations was refused at the Soviet border on grounds that it was not needed.[33] In the words of a righteous A. Enoukidze, chairman of the Alliance of Red Cross and Red Crescent Societies of the USSR: "All the statements of the foreign press regarding food difficulties in the Ukrainian Soviet Republic and the North Caucasus region are simply a premeditated campaign of calumny undertaken by hostile bodies—groups of White Russian émigrés."[34]

If Litvinov absolutely refused to cooperate in any form of rescue for his countrymen, the Americans could have postponed recognizing the USSR. Such a postponement might have envisaged six, twelve, or eighteen months. During this period, Soviet authorities might have been persuaded to find some method of relief—with or without U.S. assistance. Assuming that Stalin still denied the existence of a problem, then the Americans could have continued to withhold recognition.

They would thereby have registered a protest in keeping with the spirit of U.S. political values and those duties (to invoke Stanley Hoffmann) that exist beyond borders.[35]

There was not, as Assistant Secretary of State Moore had noted, any reason in 1933 for an unconditional recognition of the USSR. In the opinion of Hull, the Soviets were so eager for recognition that Washington could name any price.[36] However exaggerated this judgment of the secretary's, the point is that he believed it. Acting on it, the government could have tried to exert pressure, rather than ignoring the man-made famine. As for Roosevelt's best reason for recognizing Moscow, conventional realpolitik, the delayed establishment of relations until 1934 or even 1935 would still have constituted a warning to Japan and Germany. In this context, it should be recalled that the dangers posed by Germany and Japan were not of equal weight to the United States and Soviet Union in 1933. Japan then represented an immediate menace to Soviet security in eastern Siberia but only a vague and somewhat distant threat to American holdings in the Pacific. Geography also played a more obvious role in Soviet–German affairs than between Germany and the United States; based on the geostrategic situations of the two countries, America was in a better position to negotiate favorable terms and had latitude in which to exercise greater ethical discretion. As for the success of the New Deal and recovery of the economy, they were never in anyone's imagination (except Marxist propagandists) dependent on an increase in Soviet–U.S. trade. As it was, by concentrating on secondary issues of Comintern meddling, repayment of debts, and the religious rights of Americans, U.S. officialdom came near to being a passive accomplice to Stalin in the Ukraine.[37]

* * * *

One of the objectionable aspects of twentieth-century U.S. foreign policy has been its moralistic strain, entrenched ever since Woodrow Wilson. Among other things, this quality has been a cause of domestic confusion about the purpose of diplomacy and the nature of world politics, itself a contest for security and economic well-being among competitive states. Of the many questionable reflexes of this moralism, its propensity to confer or withhold recognition according to whether foreign governments satisfy U.S. conceptions of propriety has been unfortunate from two standpoints. First, this use of recognition as emblematic of moral judgment has been inconsistent; selectivity in practice has made a travesty of the idea. In the 1930s, Nazi Germany, militaristic Japan, and fascist Italy were all recognized by the United States and by extension passed, at least theoretically, the test of American standards. By contrast, Huerta's revolutionary Mexico in 1913 did not. To indicate U.S. disapproval, Wilson withheld recognition.

In addition to lending itself to such untenable distinctions, this approach to recognition is incompatible with the success of foreign policy. Properly understood, recognition and the existence of a diplomatic mission in another capital are practical devices for conducting business between governments and for analyzing trends in the host country. As instruments of foreign policy, they are morally neutral and indistinguishable from other tools used to promote national advantage.

When the United States denies or dismantles a diplomatic mission in another country with which it is not at war, it removes a valuable asset from its arsenal of policy techniques.

Yet there are rare occasions when the denial of recognition and all that goes with it *is* an appropriate expression in foreign policy. Even in the ethically circumscribed arena of international power, there is such a thing as dereliction of duty to conscience. The Cambodia of Pol Pot and Germany's massacre of European Jewry are cases in point. Like the Ukrainian famine, they throw ancient questions of theodicy into relief—why did the heavens not darken?—and as such exist outside of ordinary time.[38] It is unimaginable that the United States could have normalized relations and exchanged ambassadors with Cambodia or Germany during the years of their infamy. Undeniably, the U.S. government could have done more in 1941 to 1945 to rescue Europe's Jews (bombing the rail tracks servicing Auschwitz) and could have done more in the late 1970s for Cambodians (loosening quota restrictions). Still, in both cases Washington proclaimed its outrage against perpetrators of criminal policies. In neither the German nor the Cambodian case were the victims decisively helped by this lodging of U.S. censure; but it helped smooth the way for other actions whose cumulative impact led, however belatedly, to international rescue.

In the case of the USSR in 1933, the issue is arguably more complex. If one accepts Robert Conquest's view of the Soviet famine (that starving was part of a policy to break the countryside's resistance to collectivization), in keeping with the spirit of its policy toward Hitler and Pol Pot, the United States should have withheld recognition of Moscow. If instead one assumes, as does Peter Kenez, that starvation was a consequence of collectivization but not something sought by the regime, then the charge of intentional murder is mitigated, and the appropriateness of withholding recognition less justifiable.[39] Even under this second set of circumstances, however, U.S. officials should have at least raised as a point of discussion with Litvinov the question of famine and made a gesture to help.

Instead, to citizens who expressed anxiety about the famine, Kelley demurred that despite U.S. sympathy for those who suffered, "there appear to be no effective measures which this Government can appropriately take at the present time for alleviating the conditions."[40] But the truth was different. There was an opportunity to exercise real imagination—combining, let us say, the indignation that led to abrogation of the Russian–U.S. trade treaty in 1911 and the initiative that helped alleviate the famine of 1921 to 1923. The government, including the president and the State Department's chief Soviet specialist, simply failed to exercise it.

Although his internationalist instincts were sound, Roosevelt occasionally exhibited in his career a casualness (*carelessness* is a better word?) in foreign policy, of which the recognition issue was an early example. As the international environment became more ominous, the Soviet Union and the United States would perforce have established relations sooner or later in the 1930s. But FDR was in a rush to recognize Moscow in 1933 and judged certain conversations inexpedient, with the effect that he failed to address an ongoing calamity.[41]

It is not entirely misplaced to draw one parallel in the behavior of diplomat

Kelley and reporter Duranty, despite the difference in their temperaments and political orientations. Even though Duranty admitted in private conversations that a catastrophe was overtaking parts of the USSR, he assured *New York Times* readers that spot shortages of food and hitches in distribution were being corrected by the managerial skill of the Soviet government. The problems were basically ones associated with rapid growth, and the fact was (this was his favorite saying) "you can't make an omelette without breaking eggs."[42] The reason for Kelley's reticence is even now unclear. Was he afraid to oppose a policy to which FDR was committed and would have pushed through irrespective of the objections advanced by a State Department functionary? Had Kelley made a commotion, would this have redounded to his career's detriment (he recently had been considered for appointment to assistant secretary of state) or jeopardized programs that he was promoting in the department, including the education of Soviet experts? These questions, whatever their exact answers, point to a weakness in the Foreign Service in Kelley's time and since: the career diplomat's innate caution and reluctance to press independent views against highest government officers. It was prudent to accept the prevailing line in the presence of power (which determined promotions and set policy directions). Added to this logic of intimidation was the deference that citizens pay to national leadership. In the case of Kelley, it would have been farfetched for this soft-spoken official from a modest Irish-American background to challenge the Brahmin Roosevelt on one of his pet projects.[43]

Despite his faults in the recognition episode, it would be unfair to cast Kelley in a role of villain or place him in the same category of irresponsibility as Duranty. Kelley did try to craft the negotiations with a view to securing worthwhile U.S. interests. An overall evaluation of his achievement in government does not in any case hinge solely on those months in 1933 when he helped shape American intentions toward Moscow. A balanced assessment must also incorporate his contribution to the founding of the Riga research center in Soviet studies. It played a pioneering role in the development of Sovietology in America (where Samuel Harper at the University of Chicago and Samuel Cross at Harvard were directing fledgling programs in Russian studies). The Riga center was superior to anything then existing in the United States, though falling short of the programs in Birmingham (England), in Prague, and in Königsberg (the Osteuropa Institute). Kelley must also be evaluated against the excellent Soviet training program he designed and the quality of its graduates: above all, Kennan and Bohlen, but also Henderson. Unfortunately, this was discontinued in 1934 because of hardships imposed on the Foreign Service by the Depression.[44] Still, during a short time it produced a cadre of intellectual competence that constituted a departure from previous generations of Russian hands. And though Roosevelt tended to dismiss them as encumbrances on policymaking, they were able in the 1930s and beyond to play a constructive role in Soviet–U.S. affairs.[45]

5

Purges and the Failure of Collective Security

The term *totalitarianism* is held in disfavor by many social scientists, who view it as just a Cold War epithet signifying Western disapprobation of the Soviet Union. Its usefulness as a category in the study of political regime types (to be contrasted, say, with democracy, oligarchy, or tyranny) has been confounded further by conflicting definitions. Hannah Arendt, Carl Friedrich, Zbigniew Brzezinski, J. L. Talmon, William Kornhauser, and Leonard Schapiro are among the scholars who have tried but with only partial success to impart analytical rigor to the word since it first gained currency in the 1920s. Still, it has a peculiar staying power in the vulgate lexicon; historians and political scientists still use it in their references to Mao's China, Hitler's Germany, and Stalin's USSR. However imprecise this usage, it indicates a certain wisdom. The quality that distinguished these states and set them apart from others was their ability to succeed in dominating people by asserting their utter superfluity.[1]

Assuming that the term is meaningful, one can next agree that between Bullitt's residence in Moscow and the time Americans and Russians found themselves on the same side in another war, the USSR had undergone a change of drastic dimension (in political science parlance, a transformation of regime). Stalin's dictatorship, entrenched by 1933, had flared into full-blown totalitarianism by the time Ambassador Laurence Steinhardt left his post in November 1941. The purge trials of the 1930s, the anonymous denunciations and mass arrests, and the deification of Stalin in the civic religion were symbol and substance of the totalitarian polity. The problem for U.S. policy and diplomats centered on the management of affairs with this totalitarian state while coping with the ambitions of another similarly constructed regime, Nazi Germany.

Despite the overall poor quality of Soviet–U.S. relations from 1933 to 1941, the record of American diplomacy in Moscow was fairly good—better than most of what had gone before in Russia. William Bullitt's papers, especially his letters to Roosevelt and Assistant Secretary of State R. Walton Moore, reveal much about his quality of mind in Moscow and mercurial personality. Despite the good literature on Bullitt, things can still be learned from the experience of his disillusionment with Stalin's USSR.[2]

As for Joseph Davies, he was a more complicated figure than many people (myself included) have assumed. On the one hand, there is obviously much to disapprove. He was little more than a Democratic party operator without a shred of foreign policy background. He and his social-hound wife, Marjorie Merriweather Post, were too absorbed in Moscow with attending elaborate dinners and with buying icons and other art objects. The ambassador inadvertently offended members of his staff, above all, Kennan (who never forgave him) but also Bohlen and even the tolerant-minded Henderson. Davies played up to reporters like Walter Duranty and tried to be chummy with Stalin. And his book, *Mission to Moscow,* with its defense of the purge trials, remains a horror to read. Partly on the basis of it and exercises in conciliatory diplomacy, Davies was awarded the Order of Lenin in May 1945, the highest Soviet decoration.[3] On the other hand, what he said in private correspondence suggests a person alive to the realities of Stalinism *and* to the danger to Europe and the United States posed by Hitler's Germany. Davies's argument ran something like this: true, the USSR of purges and police terror was odious, but to contain Germany it made sense for America to cooperate with Stalin—at least in this one area of international security. Some of Davies's letters are surprisingly lucid about the need for a functioning balance of power as a means of preventing global war.

Finally, Laurence Steinhardt: he was the most intellectually impressive of the three ambassadors in 1933 to 1941. He was also the most hard-nosed. His letters and analytical memoranda repay reading by anyone interested in the Soviet Union of 1939 to 1941.[4] It should be added (and will be expanded on later) that during Steinhardt's tenure, embassy morale picked up from the low point to which it had sunk under Davies.

In Moscow

The Tretyakov Gallery in Moscow includes in its collection a painting by Yuri Pimenov entitled *New Moscow*. Except for red bunting festooning a distant building (with a hint of socialist emblem), Pimenov's depiction of a bustling urban scene is reminiscent of studies by Impressionist artists of Paris or London. The tall buildings, the pack of cars and buses, and the density of crowds in *New Moscow* also suggest Manhattan's vibrancy. In the foreground, with her back to the viewer, is a fashionable woman at the wheel of an open convertible. Her blonde hair is cut short according to the contemporary mode. The picture conveys a sense of well-being, holiday cheerfulness, and a touch of glamor. It was painted in 1937—the midpoint of the Communist party purges. The great public trial that year of former Bolshevik leaders featured, among others, Karl Radek and Gregory Pyatakov. Marshal Tukhachevsky, the Red Army's innovative chief of staff, was tried in June in camera and executed with seven other senior generals. The year before, Zinoviev and Kamenev had been shot, and in 1938 Rykov and Bukharin

("Lenin's favorite") were among the victims. Not only did hundreds of thousands of lesser party members and military officers fall prey each year to trials, executions, and deportations, but ordinary Soviet citizens were also caught in the maw of Stalinist terror. Of these, Pasternak's Larisa Feodorovna in *Doctor Zhivago* was one. Like the woman painted by Pimenov, Lara lived in Moscow: "One day [she] went out and did not come back. She must have been arrested in the street at that time. She vanished without a trace and probably died somewhere, forgotten as a nameless number on a list that afterwards got mislaid, in one of the innumerable mixed or women's concentration camps in the north."[5]

For the first U.S. diplomats posted to Moscow, the conceptual distance between Pimenov's and Pasternak's renditions of Soviet life was quickly traversed. None crossed this divide with a keener sense of loss than Bullitt.

Only in his early forties, his selection as ambassador was meant to show Stalin the seriousness in which Roosevelt held relations with the USSR. He enjoyed the president's affection and confidence, and his credentials included his trek as secret emissary to the Bolsheviks and longtime advocacy of Soviet recognition.[6] Enthusiastic, still acquainted with party leaders, Bullitt epitomized that segment of U.S. opinion eager for friendship with the Soviets. Although fragmentary, evidence suggests that they were not entirely pleased with Roosevelt's choice, however. Stalin seems to have viewed with misgiving any Westerner who wore in public his pro-Soviet feeling; a businessman or conventional diplomat would be less susceptible to emotional involvement or disappointment.[7]

Ever since his contact with the Bolsheviks in 1919 and their sympathizers like John Reed (to whose widow he was briefly married), Bullitt was persuaded of the need for officials of "deep wisdom" to monitor Soviet events and formulate U.S. policy.[8] This attitude inclined him favorably toward Robert Kelley's Soviet studies program. In consultation with Kelley, Bullitt handpicked his staff for Moscow from the department's newly minted specialists, as well as from more senior ranks. The embassy's counselor, the number-one position after ambassador, was originally filled by John Wiley, a diplomat of wide experience. His background in the Soviet area was admittedly thin, but his intelligence and sangfroid were (in Bohlen's phrase) "a good offset to Bullitt's exuberance and tendency to go to extremes."[9] Loy Henderson was chief of the economic section and, after Bullitt and Wiley, the mission's senior man. The third secretaries were Bohlen, Kennan, and Bertel Kuniholm. This last one, like his better-known colleagues, was also a Russian-language student and product of Kelley's supervision. The military attaché was Major Philip Faymonville, who, unlike the Foreign Service and other uniformed officers, remained tolerant of the Soviets; during World War II, he was reassigned to Moscow, where he played a controversial role in lend-lease. Faymonville was assisted in 1934 by Lieutenant Thomas White of the army air corps. Proficient in Russian (and Chinese), White managed during his ten months in Moscow to make contact with Red Army generals, including Semyen Budenny and the commissar for defense, Clement Voroshilov. Consular functions were filled by a complement of eleven men, led by George Hanson (about whom more later), and included the polyglot Angus Ward and indefatigable Elbridge Durbrow. This original U.S. contingent, numbering about forty, was assisted by an equal number of Soviet employees at the embassy that included messengers, chauffeurs, translators, auto mechanics.[10]

The first months of Bullitt's tenure were an ordeal to establish routine in a country prone to garrulous confusion. His official residence, Spaso House, once the pride of a Moscow merchant, was practically unfurnished through the spring of 1934. Modern kitchen facilities and other amenities thought indispensable to American life were either inadequate or absent. Several of Bullitt's bachelor subordinates, unable to find satisfactory accommodation elsewhere, lived at Spaso during this early period. Less fortunate ones lived a couple of miles away in the ramshackle Hotel Savoy and, later, in slightly more credible premises on the Mokhovaya in central Moscow. The flavor of American life at the time is conveyed in this passage from one of Bullitt's reports (May 1934) to Roosevelt:

> No furniture for my house has yet arrived from the Department so that I have had to give up all idea of entertaining this spring. As the Department has also been unable to deliver any wire screening, we, are, however, entertaining considerable numbers of flies and mosquitoes. I thank God daily that I picked the staff so carefully. The physical discomforts would make life hellish if all the men were not such good pioneers.[11]

There was at first a good-natured association between those Soviet officials assigned to assist them and the harried diplomats. In fumbling collaboration, they arranged for leases and renovations of office space and living quarters. Bullitt hoped that the United States would be able to build an embassy patterned after Jefferson's Monticello on a choice spot (the Sparrow Hills) overlooking the Moscow River. In this idea, supported by Roosevelt, Bullitt also received Stalin's encouragement.

The only meeting between the envoy and general secretary occurred in December 1933 and seemed auspicious from every standpoint. In addition to the obligatory toasts to friendship and peace given at dinner and Soviet praise of Bullitt ("a new ambassador but an old friend"), Stalin confided to him his anxiety that Japan would attack in the spring. But, he added, the Red Army would triumph under Marshal Alexander Yegorov (who was purged in 1938 and disappeared). Would the Americans not make available 250,000 tons of steel rail so that Moscow could solidify its strategic rail link to the army in the Soviet Far East? Of course, answered Bullitt, he would do whatever possible to help the Soviets obtain this material. After this agreeable reply, Stalin averred that at any time, day or night, he would be delighted to receive the American. "This was a somewhat extraordinary gesture on his part," Bullitt informed the secretary of state, "as he has hitherto refused to see any ambassador at any time."[12] This occasion with Stalin, a kindly greeting by President Kalinin on the presentation of credentials, and promising conversations with Litvinov (plus a "tremendous" banquet by him for the ambassadorial party) stirred Bullitt: these were auguries of a mission that would cement understanding between the two peoples. Soon afterward in Washington, in an atmosphere also brimming with confidence, Soviet ambassador Alexander Troyanovsky assured Roosevelt of his intention to do everything to create the "closest bonds of cooperation and friendship between our nations."[13]

The honeymoon lasted throughout 1934. Bullitt and his staff were exhilarated by much of what they discovered in Moscow, including unsurpassed intellectual vitality. People who had devoted their lives to Marxist idealism and had helped Lenin secure the revolution were still alive. Their company compensated for the Americans' lack of creature comforts, as conversation was the one inexhaustible commodity in Moscow. Bukharin and Radek, both verbal virtuosos, were welcome guests at embassy dinners and events. They and others, such as Boris Steiger and George Andreychin, would engage the Americans in debates about socialism, the Soviet future, the impending capitalist apocalypse. Their seriousness of purpose and sheer determination impressed Bullitt, who told Secretary Moore, "There is an intense ferment here and one's contacts are as interesting as any place in the world." [14]

During that hopeful first year, Bullitt made frequent flights (in a flimsy plane piloted by the intrepid Lieutenant White) to Leningrad, Kharkov, Yalta, Odessa, and Kiev. [15] At each stop, he made polite speeches, toured factories and farms, and was warmly received. To foster goodwill with the military command, Bullitt imported polo equipment and tried (with the assistance of Charles Thayer, then a clerk in the chancery) to teach the sport to the Red Army cavalry. Baseball was also introduced by the ambassador with the aim of bringing the embassy into closer relations with the Moscow soviet. These ventures did not meet with overwhelming success, however. Commissars grumbled that polo was unsuitable as recreation in the proletarian republic; besides, their horsemen lacked appreciation for the game's rules and boundaries. On one occasion, a Mongolian soldier carried the ball in a straight line for three miles beyond the playing field before he could be stopped. As for baseball, the Soviets had little interest. After one Russian was knocked out by a fast ball, the game's cachet diminished further. [16]

Embassy officers were no less pleased than Bullitt with their Soviet hosts and other companions, especially in the German, French, and Italian missions. Ice-skating parties; outings to the opera, theater, or museums; and expeditions to historic churches in the countryside were all part of a varied diplomatic life. In no post, Henderson later recalled, was the diplomatic corps so closely bound by ties of friendship and shared experience as the one in Moscow. Kennan wrote wistfully in 1967, "Most of us look back on those days, I suppose, as the high point of life—the high point, at least, in comradeship, in gaiety, in intensity of experience." In connection with his writing a biography of Anton Chekhov, Kennan interviewed the playwright's widow, "an incarnation of what had previously been a world of the imagination"; so also for Kennan was Tolstoy's home Yasnya Polyana, despite its condition of neglect and his security police escort. Together, Bohlen and Kennan advised a troupe of Soviet actors in their production of the American play *The Front Page,* which conformed to socialist-realism formula by depicting despicable capitalists and gallant workers. These occasions made an indelible mark on the diplomats, most of whom could endorse Bohlen's affirmation: "I know of no one who has been in Russia, whatever his attitude toward the regime, who has felt anything but affection for the Russian people as a whole." [17]

But it was not an undifferentiated mass of gregarious Russians with whom the diplomats had daily to contend. Their business of promoting U.S. interests in the

Soviet Union made virtually no headway during Bullitt's ambassadorship. Early in his correspondence with the State Department, a note of unease crept into reports about Soviet intentions and reliability. Although in 1934 he professed that problems concerning the liquidation of indebtedness, the building of an embassy compound, and the arrangement for a loan to the Soviets could be managed, by 1935 he was persuaded of the opposite. He identified several reasons for this failure.

Bullitt believed that the difficulty lay with Litvinov's personal intransigence, which was rooted in the Jewishness of both the commissar and the Foreign Office. The chief of the Foreign Office's press section (and later ambassador to Washington, 1939–1941) was Constantine Oumansky, described by Bullitt as a "wretched little kike," who from spitefulness made life a misery for the U.S. diplomats. His and Litvinov's behavior contrasted unfavorably with that of Russians such as Voroshilov who were unfailingly decent. In one message to Moore, Bullitt explained, "The Foreign Office has been purged recently of all its non-Jewish members, and it is perhaps only natural that we should find the members of that race more difficult to deal with than the Russians themselves. The Moscow Soviet, which is straight Russian, has been altogether friendly and cooperative." [18]

Bullitt hoped that the Foreign Office's unpleasantness might be corrected by the intervention of that former Christian seminarian, Joseph Stalin. In the meantime, his meetings with Litvinov became tussles, with each man spewing expletives and insults. Moore himself agreed that Litvinov was "the worst actor" with whom the Americans had to deal, but the cause did not necessarily lie in his ethnicity. To boost his prestige in Moscow, Litvinov had secured U.S. recognition of the USSR, but his standing would be lowered, Moore thought, if he were to make agreements touching on the Kerensky debt. [19]

Bullitt eventually realized that the real reason behind Litvinov's rigidity had to do with the lessening of Japanese threat in the East. Only if a Japanese attack were imminent or if the United States suddenly improved its understanding with Tokyo would the Soviets make up their mind to solve the debts and claims issue. According to Bullitt, Litvinov was persuaded that though America would not enter into an agreement with the Soviets against Japan, the United States would inevitably be drawn to the Soviet side in the event of war between the two nations:

> It would make no difference whether our relations with the Soviet Union prior to such an event were warm, tepid or cold. [Litvinov's] entire attitude is based on the belief that any real rapprochement between the United States and Japan is impossible. If he were to think for one minute that we might establish good relations with Japan he would be scared to death. [20]

Bullitt's tendency to personalize American disputes with the USSR and to blame Litvinov rather than Stalin for the main thrust of Soviet foreign policy was misplaced (to say nothing of his anti-Jewish defamations). But the ambassador's dawning awareness that Soviet attitude toward the United States depended on its degree of willingness to play an active role in world affairs was exactly right. Had Washington been willing to accept larger responsibility for Asia and to help check Japanese aggrandizement, the Soviets would surely have acted to break the impasse on minor financial issues. Instead, these were allowed to fester and assume an importance beyond their merits. The same lack of American interest applied to Europe, where beginning in 1934 Litvinov undertook his peregrinations to organize a united front against Hitler. The first fruits of this policy were Moscow's joining the League of Nations in September 1934 (a body previously damned by Soviet propaganda as an imperialist hencote) and conclusion or extension of nonaggression pacts with the Baltic republics, Poland, Romania, and Czechoslovakia. A year later, France and the USSR signed a security alliance caused by mutual concern about German rearmament.[21] But apart from preachments on the need to reduce world naval armaments and the inappropriateness of violence to resolve conflicts, the United States concentrated its attention on solving domestic problems created by the Depression. Investigations by Senator Gerald Nye, beginning in 1934, into the alleged influence of munitions makers on Wilson's wartime policy reinforced the Soviet impression that the United States was passing through an introverted period. Why, then, should Stalin treat Washington and its envoy with anything other than reserve? As it was, again from a Soviet point of view, America was basically one hostile capitalist state among many. Slowly but palpably, the Soviet–U.S. relationship became devoid of political content. Bullitt decided in June 1935 that relations between the two governments existed in name only.[22]

Soviet contempt for the Washington connection was shown by officials when they prevented U.S. diplomats from making currency exchanges that would have allowed them to function without the embarrassing necessity of resorting to Moscow's black market for rubles. This mentality was also apparent in a scheme concocted by the Foreign Office in the summer of 1934. Litvinov let it be known to Bullitt, first through a journalist intermediary and then by a messenger directly from Stalin, that elements in the embassy were violently disloyal to the ambassador. According to "evidence" gathered by Soviet intelligence agents, a cabal composed of senior officers in the mission wanted to destroy Bullitt's reputation and career. To these allegations, Bullitt replied (to Stalin's agent) that his personal relations with Wiley, Henderson, Kennan, Kuniholm, and Bohlen were beyond reproach: "every one of them would resent an injury to me as if it were an injury to himself." His refutation of the charges closed the issue and Soviet attempts (for the time being) to sow dissension in the embassy. One can only speculate about what Stalin hoped to achieve by this little intrigue. Perhaps he believed that a dramatic demonstration of Soviet concern for the ambassador's well-being would seal his personal goodwill. This might be translated into his support for Moscow's side of issues (debts, trade, the Far East) then being discussed with Washington. If so, the plot backfired spectacularly, as it spurred Bullitt's deepening distrust of Stalinism.[23]

Apart from the Kremlin's maladroitness, what is fascinating about this incident is its insight into the methods of prosecution and collection of evidence in the USSR during the 1930s. As with the fantastical charges leveled against Stalin's party victims, there was a scintilla of actual event on which was pegged an invented tale of conspiracy. George Hanson drank too much and when sufficiently inebriated vented his frustrations. In this condition, he once struck his chauffeur in the face, knocked him to the ground, and then proceeded to beat his Chinese servant. In addition to his violent streak, Hanson was angry that U.S. consular operations had become subordinated to the diplomatic. He especially resented having to take directions from Bullitt. When drinking with U.S. businessmen, he tried to impress upon them that he was the real man in Moscow and belittled Bullitt. The ambassador was aware of Hanson's misconduct, tried to soothe his vanity, and otherwise dealt with the problem responsibly. On the basis of this unpleasantness, Litvinov and his confederates fabricated their tale. Unlike those Soviet citizens caught in Stalin's web, however, Bullitt had recourse to conventional standards of evidence and due process and thus dismissed the allegations.[24]

Relations between the mission and Soviet officialdom gradually worsened as conflicts over site, desirable materials, and construction crews blocked building of a new embassy. And negotiations between Moscow and Washington over the outstanding economic questions were deadlocked. Roosevelt's unwillingness to accept Litvinov's overtures for a nonaggression pact in the Far East (involving Japan, China, America, and the USSR) reconfirmed to the Soviets the relative unimportance of the United States for security planning. Finally, Comintern support of the American Communist party and anticapitalist pronouncements by the Kremlin were viewed by U.S. officials as interference in national affairs and contrary to the original Roosevelt–Litvinov accords. In Bullitt's view, the worst violation in this regard occurred in July 1935, when the Comintern convened its Seventh Congress in Moscow.

This congress was memorable in connection with the start of the popular-front campaign, whereby the Comintern abandoned its open hostility to Western liberalism and social democracy. International communism henceforth would work with any nonfascist party willing to cooperate in the containment of Germany. The electoral success of Léon Blum in France in 1936 and his organization of a socialist government were examples of the popular front's initial appeal. To Bullitt, though, the Comintern's meeting in Moscow constituted a flagrant violation of Litvinov's pledge: the Soviet Union would block the meeting on its territory of any organization whose aim was to overthrow the U.S. social order. Among the delegates attending the congress were William Foster, chairman of the American Communist party, and Earl Browder, general secretary, both of whom were elected to the congress's presidium. During the congress, they reviewed party achievements, which included gains in U.S. labor membership, lengthy strikes, and organization of unemployed workers and southern blacks. As for the congress's decision to cooperate with nonfascist parties, Bullitt recognized its tactical nature; he predicted that in the long run the communists would destroy their erstwhile allies. "The emotions of the Congress," he told Roosevelt, "in deciding to cooperate with the Socialists and bourgeois Democrats in a fight against Fascism are, of course, on all fours with the emotions of the tiger when he went out for that historic ride with the young lady of Niger. The Communists feel sure they will come back from the ride with the Socialists and Democrats inside."[25]

Bullitt, who had hoped by his conversations with Litvinov and Radek to preempt the Comintern's addressing U.S. topics, believed the administration had cause to sever relations with the Soviets. This was not a line he advocated, however. Instead, he urged Roosevelt to file a protest with the commissar for foreign affairs, withdraw the exequaturs of the Soviet consuls in New York and San Francisco, and reduce the number of visas granted to officials intending to visit the United States. He predicted that the Soviets would retaliate by becoming frosty with Embassy Moscow and would reduce purchase of American goods in the coming year (projected to be around $30 million).[26]

As did the British and Italians, Roosevelt lodged a stiffly worded protest against Moscow's sponsorship of the Seventh Congress; but beyond that he did not act, despite noises from disgruntled senators. From Roosevelt's standpoint, the United States should not take measures that might seriously jeopardize relations with the Soviet Union. He could cite ample evidence in 1935 that Germany, not the USSR, posed the main threat to the international status quo: a few months before the Comintern's Moscow meeting, the Saar was returned to Germany, conscription was reinstituted by the Nazis, and British foreign secretary Sir John Simon was told by a boastful Hitler that Germany's air force had reached parity with the RAF. All the same, Roosevelt signed the Neutrality Act in August. Its adoption only reinforced Stalin's belief that maintenance of the diplomatic channel with Washington was unimportant; by their own declaration, the Americans were unwilling to involve themselves in European affairs or the anti-German cause.

The fear that suffused Soviet life following the murder of Sergei Kirov (December 1934) in Leningrad also contributed to the embassy's isolation.[27] Normal contacts between the diplomats and citizens ceased. People who had been on personal terms with Americans (and other foreigners) disappeared or wound up in the dock of a courtroom on charges of espionage, spying, or other capital offenses. The category of condemned persons included those of every station—high party and state officials with whom the ambassador was friendly, as well as Russian employees of Spaso and the chancery. In view of this situation, Bullitt decided that "the only thing one can do for one's [Soviet] acquaintances is to avoid seeing them." Personally apprised of a number of cases, he became an authority on police methods. "In Moscow," he wrote in 1936,

> the OGPU is now carrying out arrests every night. . . . In each case, at 2 A.M. the secret police appeared, entered the apartment, took all papers, sealed whatever room contained books, and removed the head of a family. Since the disappearances, wives and children have been unable to get any information as to whether fathers or husbands are alive or dead.[28]

The routines of embassy life inevitably became encumbered with the strain of living under intensified surveillance, attempts to involve the Americans in compromising sexual liaisons, and diverse forms of harassment. On one occasion, Bullitt and his daughter were briefly detained by the police in Leningrad for crossing the Nevsky Prospekt at the wrong corner.[29] In this test of their mettle, the diplomats stood up reasonably well, though the psychic toll on private life could be severe.

Hanson's criticisms notwithstanding, Bullitt's subordinates endorsed his conduct in Moscow at the time, even while he failed to improve Soviet–U.S. cooperation or forestall the deterioration in relations. Henderson, Kennan, and Bohlen were also supportive of their chief in subsequent public print. By their testimony, he was a diplomatic asset for the United States. Despite his impatience, shading into impetuousness, he learned the managerial skills needed to run an embassy, discarded his earlier illusions about the USSR, and acquitted himself with dignity in a malevolent environment.[30]

Bullitt reciprocated his staff's respect for the most part. He spoke glowingly in his reports of Henderson, who, though high strung, was conscientious and hard working. Bohlen, Kuniholm, and Kennan he credited with intelligence and work on a superior level. Kennan's diligence and application of mind especially won the ambassador's admiration. Yet difficulties arose in the life of the embassy. Wiley, for one, was a consummate snob and the source of divisiveness. He treated shabbily those men and their families whom he considered beneath his social level; this inferior group included Hanson and the entire consular section of the embassy. Bullitt feared that those Wiley graced with his favor would become corrupted—notably, Bohlen and Thayer, who were class conscious to begin with. Of Bohlen, the ambassador once sighed, "He might develop into a magnificent public servant but the Lord only knows whether or not he will go Etonian."[31] Bohlen's and Wiley's transfers in 1935 (which Bullitt facilitated) alleviated a potentially grave problem. Meanwhile, as relations between the embassy and its Soviet hosts soured, Bullitt recommended a reduction in U.S. representation in Moscow. For this reason, he resisted Kelley's pressure to expand the size of the mission staff or the field experience of Russian-language students.[32]

On resigning his post in May 1936 for new assignment to France, Bullitt held little hope for Soviet society or its contribution to international order. He remained thereafter a staunch, even shrill, critic of the USSR. He warned against its boring into the vitals of American life through communist agents and Soviet personnel in Washington. Worried also by its progress in industrial and agricultural production during the Second Five-Year Plan, he feared that the USSR would soon threaten countries in central Europe. For the moment, he explained to Roosevelt, the Soviets would "continue to emit loud cries about the Japanese and German militarists but in reality they will have little to fear unless some incident changes the international situation."[33] As for the United States, it should stand aloof from the contest between "the fanaticisms" of communism and fascism and lend neither prestige nor matériel strength to either side. To the Soviets, such advice from Bullitt (made public after his arrival in Paris) was treachery. They mounted a campaign to blame him for the stubbornness of U.S. policy and the unsatisfactory manner in which relations between the two states had lately unfolded.[34]

Reporting the Purges

Three months after Bullitt's resignation, Zinoviev and Kamenev were retried (with fourteen others) as Trotskyite–German conspirators and shot. In his capacity as acting head of the embassy, Henderson told Washington that these executions had "made a profound impression, and a wave of fear, almost equal to that following the assassination of Kirov, [was] sweeping over the country."[35] To Henderson, as well as to members of other foreign missions, the trial itself was a puzzle. He was at first reluctant to say whether the defendants were innocent of the crimes to which they admitted or to hazard guesses to explain their confessions. He hypothesized that Zinoviev and Kamenev had discussed between themselves and with others among the accused the advisability of assassinating Stalin and had reviewed courses of action to pursue following his removal. But Henderson was unpersuaded by the evidence purportedly proving that Zinoviev and Kamenev had entered into a detailed plot to assassinate Kirov or Stalin. He also doubted that Trotsky had sent instructions to the accused to commit the crimes or that German intelligence was involved (eleven of the defendants were Jewish).[36]

Henderson's considered judgment, as it evolved in subsequent weeks, was that the trial had been staged for political reasons. These were to correct misimpressions among party members that the newly proposed constitution (adopted in December 1936) would allow debate of Stalin's policies; to destroy the residual influence of former leaders distrusted by him; to attribute failures in the Soviet economy to the machinations of Trotsky and his followers; and to discredit Trotsky and his adherents in international revolutionary groups by branding them as allies of German fascism. As for the defendants' confessions, Henderson felt they were prompted by the desire to escape torture and to save their friends and families from harm. Most of this assessment was confirmed to Henderson's satisfaction by his talks with journalists and foreign diplomats and those few Soviet citizens who dared in furtive conversations to broach honest opinions.[37]

This trial, as well as those that followed, were part of the maelstrom of terror that (more than any other experience) shaped the attitude of diplomats in Moscow. To Kennan, they were one more evidence that the USSR was unfit as a long-term partner of the United States. Returned to Moscow in autumn 1937, Bohlen witnessed the trial of Bukharin and his co-defendants and later gave this account of the sentencing:

> With obvious relish, [the judge] intoned the names of the defendants, followed, in eighteen cases, with the refrain, "To be shot, to be shot, to be shot." It took more than an hour to read all the sentences, and by the time of the last "to be shot," I felt that the top of my head was coming off. I could not go to sleep easily for almost a month after that.

To Charles Thayer, reassigned to Berlin in 1938, the Nazi capital seemed strangely free compared with the nightmare of Moscow, where a number of his acquaintances had perished.[38]

In contrast to testimony about the purge trials supplied by Bullitt, Henderson, Kennan, and Bohlen, Joseph Davies exonerated in public print the fairness of Soviet legal proceedings. In his best-selling *Mission to Moscow,* an account of his 1936 to 1938 ambassadorship, Davies wrote:

> All of these trials, purges, and liquidations, which seemed so violent at the time and shocked the world [were] clearly a part of a vigorous and determined effort of the Stalin government to protect itself from not only revolution from within but from attack from without. They went to work thoroughly to clear up and clean out all treasonable elements within the country. All doubts were resolved in favor of the government.[39]

This statement was offered along with other positive assertions, including one that innocent creatures such as children and pets were attracted to affectionate Stalin. In the movie version of *Mission,* in whose production Davies cooperated, Hollywood succeeded in making the purge victims (especially Bukharin) into monsters worse than those created by the Soviet courts that sentenced them to death; against them all, a wise Stalin prevailed.[40]

Largely as a result of his book (and the movie gave added emphasis), most historians have accepted the charges against Davies leveled by Kennan and Bohlen. According to them, he was ignorant of Soviet realities, filed biased reports to the State Department, was a dupe of Stalinist propaganda and a disgrace to U.S. diplomacy. This critique is also used by scholars hostile to Roosevelt's Soviet policy as evidence of the president's incompetence (or worse) in the international field.[41]

Unqualified condemnation of Roosevelt's second ambassador to the USSR is not entirely fair, however. To begin with, it ignores a body of contrary evidence supplied by non-Soviet diplomats. France's ambassador in Moscow with Davies, Robert Coulondre, later spoke approvingly of him and of his pleas for international understanding and peace. Despite their disagreements over matters related to diplomatic reporting and running of the embassy, Henderson also respected Davies and developed lasting affection for him; in 1958, Henderson served as a pallbearer at his interment in the National Cathedral.[42] Moreover, Davies's critics ignore writings by him that show he was not blindly unrealistic about the USSR. And they do not allow for extenuating circumstances in the matter of *Mission to Moscow.*

Mindful of Bullitt's failures, Davies arrived in Moscow determined to avoid further disagreement with the Soviets and to seek areas of cooperation, meager though they might be. Specifically, he wanted to reinvigorate Soviet–U.S. trade and resolve the lingering debts issue if he could. Of greater significance, he was ordered to evaluate the political resilience, economic progress, and military strength of the USSR. The unimpeded disintegration of European politics (symbolized by Spain, then in the midst of civil war) and East Asia made this evaluation crucial to Roosevelt. Just before leaving for Moscow, Davies received this instruction from FDR, another indication of the president's unsentimental view of the USSR. To quote from the ambassador's diary:

> Outlining his instructions [Roosevelt] again reverted to the necessity of knowing just how strong the Russians were militarily and industrially. Russian bombers, if they had them, could easily cross the Atlantic, drop their bombs, refuel at some secret base in the Tennessee Mountains, and then hop off to Mexico. He wanted me to center on finding out how strong [the Soviets] were . . . and on which side they would be in case of war.[43]

Much of the responsibility for problems in Davies's ambassadorship (and fixing a proper interpretation of it) undeniably rested on him. He should have been more attentive to the concerns and sensitivities of his younger Foreign Service officers. Too often they felt ignored or patronized. Kennan and Bohlen bitterly recalled in later decades, after the passage of time should have diluted such feeling, that the ambassador treated his staff liked hired help; he rarely exhibited an interest in their views. He preferred the company of news reporters, including Duranty, who by then was viewed with suspicion by every officer in the embassy. Kennan once recorded this experience as Davies's translator in the Pyatakov–Radek trial: "During the intermissions I was sent, regularly, to fetch the ambassador his sandwiches, while he exchanged sententious judgments with the gentlemen of the press concerning the guilt of the victims. I cannot recall, therefore, that I ever discussed the matter with him."[44]

On another occasion, when Davies might have commended his staff for its performance in an area touching on embassy security, he exhibited extreme obtuseness. As the following entry from his diary suggests, he caused embarrassment to men (one was Kennan) who thought they were doing responsible work:

> One or two of the younger secretaries were excited over their detective powers. Up in the garret they had found some evidence that a dictaphone had been installed between the ceiling and the floor. From what I learned from the senior staff, there were indications that someone had been up there, some traces of food, etc. So far as concrete indications of dictaphone [components], none were in evidence. I congratulated them over their diligent vigilance, but could not resist "kidding" them a bit over their "international sleuthing."

Whereas his subordinates took an earnest view of their professional function and the embassy's security, Davies's attitude toward Soviet spying struck them as absurdly lighthearted. "[My] position in any event was that if the Soviets had a dictaphone installed, so much the better—the sooner they would find that we were not conspiring against them the better."[45]

Davies's habit of working more hours in his study at Spaso House than in the chancery and his frequent absences from Moscow to visit distant parts of the USSR or to travel abroad led his subordinates to infer that he lacked seriousness. His well-publicized yachting expeditions on his wife's luxurious *Sea Cloud* (four masts, sailed by a crew of fifty men), frenetic acquisition of Russian art, and prodigal entertainments further offended his staff—particularly Kennan, for whom the banality of diplomatic dinners and the collection of souvenirs contrasted sickeningly with the drama of Soviet life. (Members of the Soviet establishment, including Litvinov and the young Andrei Gromyko, were also repelled by Davies's love of luxury; they sneered at his extravagance, his susceptibility to flattery, his appetite for publicity.) At one point early in Davies's tenure, Kennan and others considered resigning en masse, an idea that was squelched by a stern dressing down from Henderson. Yet Davies was not entirely oblivious to the demoralizing effect he sometimes created. On taking leave of the embassy in 1938, he apologized for his periodic rudeness and admitted that he was a difficult boss.[46]

Although his feelings were not apparent to officers on his staff (Henderson was an exception), Davies liked the people over whom he served. When the State Department proposed to reduce the embassy's stenographic pool because of budget constraints and criticized the mission for inefficiency (during the period between Bullitt's departure from Moscow and Davies's arrival), the ambassador forwarded to Washington a spirited defense of his subordinates. To Bullitt, Robert Kelley, and Cordell Hull, and in his diary, Davies unstintingly praised his Foreign Service men. He valued Henderson for his "most sound judgment" and thought his replacement as chargé d'affaires, Alexander Kirk, "steady [and] well-balanced." In the ambassador's view, Bohlen was an exceptionally able person. As for Kennan, once thoughtlessly treated as a sandwich carrier, Davies wrote: "[He] is of the scholarly type, most capable and thorough, and he has done a perfectly splendid job here." Out of concern for Kennan's health—not yet thirty-four, his nervous constitution had already succumbed to duodenal ulcer and shingles—Davies helped arrange for his medical leave from the USSR in 1937. "I am very fond of Kennan . . . and [though] I feel that the loss to us here would be a most serious one and we would be seriously handicapped for a time . . . it is [unfair] to keep this man here; the price he is paying is too high."[47]

Not only was Davies more solicitous for the well-being of his people than most of them guessed, he was also less naive about the Soviet Union than they allowed. His *Mission to Moscow* (ghost written) contained a sanitized compilation of the reports and letters he composed while ambassador. The book's publication in late 1941 and the movie's release in 1943 were part of that massive campaign in wartime America to solidify popular support for the Soviet and Allied effort against Germany. As such, *Mission to Moscow* was a deliberately misleading account of Davies's actual reporting.[48] A less selective reading of his dispatches from the 1930s supports a more generous view of his acumen about the USSR and international affairs. At the same time, however, such a reading raises questions about the Roosevelt administration's willingness to present the U.S. public with hard truths about the Soviet Union. This lack of candor during World War II led to inflated expectations that the Grand Alliance would prosper in the postwar era and concomitantly to those disappointments manipulated by anticommunist fundamentalists in the early 1950s.

Although committed to FDR's idea of preserving a working relationship with the Soviets, Davies was disgusted in 1937 and 1938 by the purges. He doubted the impartiality of Soviet legality and had sympathy for a number of those injured by it. He also tried unsuccessfully but in good faith to intercede with Kalinin on behalf of an arrested *Izvestia* reporter, Vladimir Romm. To A. F. Neymann, a Soviet expert on the United States and one-time first secretary of the embassy in Washington, Davies confessed that he was aghast at Soviet courtroom procedure. (Neymann himself disappeared later.) In his journal, he recorded not only that Valery Mezhlauk, president of Gosplan, and Arkady Rosengolts, commissar for foreign trade, were accomplished individuals with whom he was friendly, but that it was inconceivable that they would plot traitorous acts for which they were purged in 1937. On another occasion, he expressed to Litvinov his dismay over what passed for Soviet justice, and he protested his respect for men falsely accused of treason. At the Bukharin trial, Davies was so moved by the "desperate and hopeless plight" of the accused, many of whom he had dined with months earlier, that he could not look at them "lest our eyes would meet." Had circumstances permitted, Davies, a University of Wisconsin–trained lawyer, would have helped them: "The defendant[s] [have] no rights as against the government. . . . The door is opened wide to coercion, duress, and tyranny. All through the trial I fairly itched to cross-examine and test the credibility of witnesses and possibly break down their testimony through their own contradictions." This trial and others attended by Davies jarred him as they automatically produced the government's desired verdicts. They were, he assured Roosevelt, exercises in "horrifying oriental ruthlessness and cruelty," staged for one overarching reason: to persuade the public of the iniquities of Stalin's opponents. "The Revolution," he concluded, was proceeding like the French in "chewing up its own children."[49]

That Stalin's dictatorship was brutal Davies thus never doubted, a point not credited by his detractors. Even in *Mission to Moscow,* there are gripping passages about the terror that reached "down into and haunts all sections of the community." Moreover, he was aware of being watched by the police, was alarmed by the OGPU's nocturnal activities, and regretted that many of their prisoners included the nation's leading intellectuals. The plight of what he called "misguided" Americans, who had earlier taken Soviet citizenship but then fallen foul of Stalin's laws and sought rescue by the embassy, was also frequently remarked by him. Davies's efforts to help these expatriates, usually to no avail, added to his sober assessment of the regime: "This is no longer a dictatorship *of* the proletariat but a dictatorship *over* the proletariat." In line with Neill Brown's remarks in the 1850s, Davies suggested that those Americans who complained "of tyranny of Government at home ought to come over here for awhile. They would understand what a government can do to freedom." As it was, he solemnly declared, none of the revolution's vaunted achievements justified the denial of people's religious and political liberties. Ultimately, he believed, the Soviet state would fail, a victim of its own oppressiveness: "The greatest vice is that [the communists] refuse to recognize that a police state, no matter how high its purpose, is destructive of the greatest rights which free men cherish and demand, namely spiritual and physical freedoms. That is the rock upon which this experiment will founder." When the time came, Davies was as content as any of his predecessors to leave Russia. To one friend, he admitted, "Conditions here that constantly express authoritarian tyranny and the horror of a police state cramp down upon the mind unconsciously and [are] oppressive."[50]

Despite appreciating the regime's defects, and aware of the impressions created in Western military-diplomatic circles by the purges, Davies thought that Soviet Russia was still a power with which to reckon. Its sheer land mass, natural resources, and industrial base and the determination of its leaders meant that the country would remain a major player in European politics for the foreseeable future. In Davies's opinion, it was unlikely that the United States and other democracies could ever share in a community of values with the USSR. But it was possible and desirable for them to maintain a spirit of cooperation with Moscow. In answer to the president's questions about Soviet power and proclivities, the crux of Davies's message was captured in this January 1939 statement: "In the event of so dire a calamity as an international conflict between the totalitarian and the democratic states, the Soviet Government is, in my opinion, a much more powerful factor than the reactionaries of Europe concede, and might be of the greatest value."[51]

Davies was not a deep or an original thinker. Many of his reports about the Soviet Union were marred with superficial observations that sprang from his cheerful commitment to American-style free enterprise. He mistook, for example, the introduction of modest material incentives to factory workers as proof of the rise of market forces and a phasing in of full-fledged capitalism. He gave easy credence to Soviet claims of unrivaled economic achievements.[52] In addition, his ideas about European international relations were derivative. They depended on his conversations with Coulondre and Britain's ambassador in Moscow, Viscount Chilston, both of whom advocated (against the prevailing wisdom of their governments) an Anglo-French agreement with the Soviets. Yet the point ought to be granted that Davies did develop a lucid line about European matters and the Soviet Union's role—one perfectly compatible with Roosevelt's.

Adopting as his own the vocabulary of Coulondre and Chilston, Davies converted in his early sixties to a sect of realpolitik, and he placed emphasis on the balance of power as the best means of staving off future war. To the chairman of the Senate Foreign Relations Committee, Key Pittman, Davies taught, "We may not like the idea, but in this world for a long time there will be no Peace until the physical security of each of the great powers is assured. . . . Only 'Balance of Power' can do that, unless the millennium arrives and we have a perfect world." A crucial factor in the balance of power, he told Undersecretary Sumner Welles in 1937, was the Red Army, still potent despite damage caused by the purges: "It definitely contributed to the balance of power. The power and strength of Russia and its relations to France and Britain have been of unquestioned value in deterring Hitler." It would therefore be a monumental blunder if France and Britain discounted the Soviets and struck a deal with Hitler—which would lead to a fascist-imposed peace in Europe. Such a peace could not last and would result in a second European war, with Germany the probable victor. Neither did Davies dismiss the possibility that Hitler and Stalin might reconcile their differences and produce an agreement that would place the rest of Europe at risk. By similar reasoning, said Davies, it was important for states concerned with Japanese expansionism to find means of cooperating with the USSR. To this end, Roosevelt instructed Davies to conduct negotiations with the Foreign Ministry to strike an agreement allowing for exchanges of military information regarding the Far East. These talks, begun after Japanese planes sank the U.S. gunboat *Panay* on the Yangtze River, were not closely pursued by the Soviets and ended in failure. Such an agreement with Washington very likely meant little to Stalin, who would have preferred an all-encompassing arrangement with the United States (and Britain and France) aimed against the Japanese. Ironically, when Stalin later expressed interest in the idea to Davies, the Americans backed off. Cordell Hull responded by asking Troyanovsky to curb Soviet involvement with the U.S. Communist party, and the administration recommenced discussions about the debts issue. Despite Davies's efforts, these sputtered out.[53]

The Nonaggression Pact and War

Davies had expected that Roosevelt would reward him with the appointment of ambassador to Berlin after completing his diplomatic apprenticeship in Moscow. Instead, Roosevelt sent a career officer, the estimable Hugh Wilson, to Germany.

In the summer of 1938, Davies consequently went to Brussels, a not unimportant spot from which to monitor European events.[54] By then, the challenge posed by the "have not" nations to the status quo had made a shambles of international stability. Earlier in the year, Hitler had enlarged the Third Reich by annexing Austria. And the antics of Konrad Henlein to provoke unrest among the Sudeten Germans (the Carlsbad Program) helped ignite a German–Czech crisis that was resolved only when Britain and France reluctantly inserted themselves as coguarantors of Prague's security in May. Meanwhile, Hitler's visit to Mussolini in Rome gave renewed impetus to the Rome–Berlin Axis. Continued Italian and German contribution to Franco's forces in Spain raised the specter of a fragile French democracy confronted on three borders by fascist states. And in China, despite Japanese inability to wrest control of the countryside from guerrilla resistance, populous cities were surrendering to Tokyo's forces, which exerted increased control along the Yellow River.

Through this bleak period lasting to March 1939, the embassy operated without benefit of an ambassador. The slowness with which Roosevelt chose a successor to Davies signaled his unhappiness over the impasse in Soviet–U.S. negotiations. Steinhardt did not present his credentials to President Kalinin until August 11—a mere two weeks before Joachim von Ribbentrop and Vyacheslav Molotov (commissar for foreign affairs as of May 3) proclaimed the Soviet–German nonaggression pact. In the months between Davies and Steinhardt, the embassy performed well, a situation cited as evidence by those (such as Kennan) who argued that the governance of a mission should be the exclusive province of the career Foreign Service.[55]

The chargé d'affaires during this interim, Alexander Kirk, was regarded by his colleagues as vastly superior to Davies and, in absolute terms, as among the ablest of professional diplomats. A graduate of Yale University (1909) and Harvard Law School (1914), he had been seasoned by postings in Berlin, The Hague, Paris, Tokyo, Peking, Mexico City, and Rome. Upon his arrival in Moscow, he interrogated every officer in the embassy to learn his views of Soviet domestic life and external policy. In addition to paying them the compliment of consultation, Kirk took it upon himself to instruct his officers in the art of writing concise reports. He was an exacting and pedantic taskmaster. But it was precisely his personal discipline and high standards that compared favorably with the casualness and small-town odor of Davies. "With Kirk in charge," Bohlen later recalled, "embassy working arrangements changed, and we settled down to a more serious routine."[56] The political reporting naturally concentrated on the simmering German–Czech crisis and Soviet attitude toward it. It seemed to Kirk that the Soviets were unprepared to assist Czechoslovakia, irrespective of existing treaty obligations. Except for moral support and token military aid—no troops—the Soviet Union would be unable to take positive action even if it wanted. Preoccupied with its party–army liquidations, the USSR could not cooperate with anyone (no matter what combination of British, French, and Czech) in blocking German expansion.[57]

After the Munich denouement, the embassy studied and compared the hesitant Anglo-French attempt to establish arrangements with Stalin with the purposeful one directed from Berlin. Through Bohlen's secret contact with the second secretary of the German embassy in Moscow, Hans von Herwarth, the mission followed those German–Soviet negotiations that culminated in the nonaggression pact.[58] Although unable to predict the exact timing of the pact's announcement and provisions, Bohlen and Kirk kept the secretary of state briefed; thus the administration was better prepared psychologically than other Western governments for this crowning act "of a low dishonest decade." Seduced into a false sense of security by physical distance from Europe and persuaded by the sloganeering of isolationists, the majority of Americans meanwhile inhibited Congress and FDR from doing much to alter this outcome; the administration was unavailing in coaxing Stalin in a direction toward London and Paris. In 1938, the United States and the USSR did enter into a minor commercial treaty negotiated by Kirk. But Washington steadfastly refused (because of pressure from the Navy Department) Soviet attempts to purchase U.S. warships and matériel that might have improved Moscow's position against Germany.[59]

Steinhardt's ambassadorship coincided not only with the life of the nonaggression pact but also with the first six months of fighting in the German–Soviet war. To the task of representing U.S. interests, he was eminently suited. Although not knowing Russian, he was acquainted with the country on the basis of visits in 1934 and had played a part in the negotiations that led to recognition. Additionally, unlike most political appointees, he was a veteran diplomat and respected as such by Hull and Roosevelt.[60] Originally trained as a lawyer, this scion of a prominent New York Jewish family was an impassioned FDR supporter in 1932. For his Trojan work, he was appointed at the age of forty-one minister to Sweden, where he served in 1933 to 1937. Steinhardt was then named ambassador to Peru (1937–1939), during which time he was effective at the Eighth Pan-American Conference in Lima and presided over the Inter-American Foreign Service Conference. Briefed in Washington in 1939 by Henderson, Bullitt, and Davies, Steinhardt approached his Moscow assignment with deliberate detachment. He decided he would neither ingratiate himself with the Soviets nor indulge in those displays of temper that had dashed Bullitt's relations with Litvinov.

This approach was classical Steinhardt. He was skeptically minded and his hypersensitivity to slights prevented him from currying favor with anyone, including Soviet officials. His intellectual orientation was that of unalloyed realism. Any utopian project, he believed, was based on misconceptions about human nature, a point amply proven by his experience in the USSR. "The Communist Utopia," he once declared to Sumner Welles, "is probably the greatest fraud perpetrated on mankind in all recorded history."[61] In ordinary politics, he believed that anyone lacking aggressiveness would fail. Not without ambitions himself, he saw his Moscow ambassadorship as a competition with other envoys: Joseph Kennedy in London, Bullitt in Paris, and Davies in Brussels. He complained that they did less work than himself but enjoyed wider popularity in the United States. To offset this problem, he employed publicists in his own cause. At the same time, he craved (and usually received) plentiful praise by Roosevelt, Hull, Welles, and the career Foreign Service.[62] As for international relations, Steinhardt lived without illusions. Just days before the German invasion of Poland, he declared, "There is no civilization in Europe today." Whenever war ensued, if the "decent elements" won, so much the better. Yet, as he told a friend in March 1940, "when nations are put to the test there is not much to choose between them, and while there are a few fine people left in every country, the general level in all countries is [low]. All nations seem to be motivated more and more by self-interest." The version of Wilsonian idealism later incorporated into the Atlantic Charter was pure verbiage from Steinhardt's perspective: "The outcome of the present war will [not] bring any great changes. . . . it is difficult to conceive of decency sweeping over the world merely because the present war has come to an end on the basis of a peace which will doubtless be hailed as a 'cure all' and result in little more than laying a foundation for the next disturbance."[63]

Along with his egocentrism and self-pity, Steinhardt possessed appealing traits. He was capable of personal loyalty (to Roosevelt, for example), had a meticulous sense of justice, and was respectful of his subordinates, such as those who served him in Moscow. "Taken as a whole," he reported to Henderson, "[they are] by far the most intelligent, able, cooperative, and personally agreeable staff that I have known in the Service."[64] Indeed, notwithstanding the unpleasantness of life in Soviet Russia in 1939 to 1941 and the restrictions imposed on them, Bohlen, Llewellyn Thompson, Walter Thurston (the embassy's counselor), Charles Thayer, and Angus Ward worked as an excellent unit for Steinhardt.

Their first assignment was to cope with countless human emergencies resulting from the German, and then Soviet, invasions of Poland. Poles in Scandinavia and western Europe and Polish-Americans applied in the tens of thousands to the embassy. They sought word about the fate of relatives and friends in the Soviet zone of occupation, hoped to send them food and medical supplies, and wanted to explore means of delivering them to safety abroad. The embassy was overwhelmed by the volume of such requests. Making matters worse, Kremlin authorities created obstacles to thwart Steinhardt's taking timely action. Not until a few months after their occupation of eastern Poland did the Soviets allow the delivery of mail or telegrams in the area. Telephonic communication with the outside was also forbidden. And no diplomat or military attaché assigned to Moscow was permitted to enter the zone. Consequently, the embassy was unable to provide much assistance to U.S. citizens in Soviet Poland, let alone aid the thousands of nonnationals about whom inquiries were made. After successive delays, the Soviets finally allowed Steinhardt to send Ward in late December to Lvov to survey the scene and provide what help he could to Americans and others. Ward, whose health suffered from the scarcity of food and shelter in the Soviet zone, reported scenes of heart-breaking chaos and the demoralizing effect on the population of GPU activity. Thereafter, the embassy focused its efforts on securing the safety of U.S. nationals and their property (including the possessions of Ambassador Anthony Biddle) and did what it could to locate and assist specific Polish citizens. Steinhardt was not altogether gracious about the crush of requests by members of the Polish aristocracy. He thought they exerted undue pressure; his only responsibility should be for the welfare of his compatriots. And the Jew in him could not help wondering, "Were the situation reversed, just what [would] the Polish aristocracy have done for *me*."[65]

During this period, the Soviets were unhelpful on other matters, of which the most serious concerned U.S. ships on the high seas. In October 1939, the German battleship *Deutschland* intercepted an American merchant vessel, the *City of Flint*. It was impounded by the Germans because a portion of its cargo was contraband, and a prize crew sailed it and the incarcerated sailors to Murmansk. Steinhardt demanded that the Americans be released and the ship allowed to leave port with its cargo intact. The Kremlin not only balked on this matter (in deference to German preferences), but prevented the embassy from establishing contact with the captain or sailors. To Steinhardt, the episode was the plainest illustration that Soviet professions of neutrality were false and that Stalin cared not a whit for the nonbelligerent rights of the United States.[66]

Far more shocking to Washington than the *City of Flint* saga and surpassing even the consternation occasioned by the Soviet invasion of Poland was the USSR's war against Finland (November 1939–March 1940). Stalin's aims were to acquire Finnish territories in the Karelian Isthmus and the use of naval bases on the Gulf of Finland. These acquisitions by conquest were part of a preemptive strategy: to deny Germany of springboards that could be used in an anti-Soviet campaign. Americans had a sentimental attachment for the Finns, who among their virtues had not reneged on World War I debts to the United States; and in the Winter War, the Finns proved themselves to be plucky soldiers, withstanding the numerically superior Red Army for more than three months. These American feelings did not, however, find practical expression. Shortly before the war, Roosevelt did offer through Steinhardt to mediate a resolution of the Soviet–Finnish dispute, but this idea was not pushed; the administration was discouraged by the Soviets' quick refusal and anxious about public approval of any initiative in Europe. At no time was FDR or Congress tempted (as were the French and British) to take military actions on behalf of beleaguered Finland or otherwise forfeit U.S. neutrality. Still, as a show of disapproval following Soviet expulsion from the League of Nations, numerous legislators (among them Senator Arthur Vandenberg, Representative John McCormack) and editorial writers urged Roosevelt to recall the ambassador from Moscow and sever relations with Stalin. In the administration itself, there was divided counsel. Sumner Welles argued in favor of a formal break with the USSR. He was opposed (and overridden) by Hull and, after vacillation, by Roosevelt—who nevertheless wondered out loud whether the Soviets thought it worthwhile to have relations with the United States.

In Steinhardt's opinion, either his recall or a return to nonrecognition would be equally ill-advised. If he should be recalled without a break in diplomatic relations, the Soviets would dismiss the action as an "idle gesture," likely to cause them mere amusement. Should the Americans cause a total breach, it would accomplish nothing unless accompanied by stringent measures whose character, in Steinhardt's view, would be repellent to Roosevelt's government. To him, these would have to include expelling all holders of Soviet passports, excluding Soviet ships from the Panama Canal and U.S. ports, and imposing an embargo on exports destined for the USSR. If such measures were not part of a bundle of penalties, the Americans would accomplish nothing. He also warned that by closing Embassy Moscow, the United States would injure itself. That action would deny Roosevelt from playing any role when the time came for Soviet–Finnish negotiations. He would also be badly positioned should Anglo-French-German talks be convened to end the European war. As to the Soviets' attitude, Steinhardt doubted that they wanted to cut relations with the United States, but in their current frame of mind they would do little to avoid it.[67]

Certainly, their response to FDR's "moral embargo" (public denunciations of the USSR; bans on the export of airplanes, aluminum, oil, technical information, and sundry machinery; provision of nonlethal aid to Finland) seemed to vindicate Steinhardt's interpretation. In Washington, Oumansky (ambassador as of June 1939) defended the nonaggression pact and war against Finland in such a way that his own person became an object of disdain in the U.S. government and press. Secretary Hull once referred to him as "a walking insult," possessed of "an infallible faculty for antagonizing those of us with whom he came in contact."[68] In Moscow, local authorities increased the already heavy pressure on the embassy. It was not simply that the diplomats felt the pinch of food shortage as the war against Finland progressed; or that the state bureaucracy made more difficult the purchase of everything from gasoline to such trivial items as railroad tickets, shoes, and haircuts; or that permission for commonplace travel, including the ambassador's egress from the country, had to be approved in advance by the state authority (George Meyer redux). Ordinary life in all its dimensions was excruciating. Tampering with the mails became blatant, even by the standard of previous practice. A swarm of hidden microphones invaded the embassy and Spaso. Contrary to all conventions, the personal luggage of diplomats coming into and leaving the country was searched with a ruthlessness exceeding the level previously set by customs officials. Plainclothes police became bolder and ruder as they trailed the diplomats, sometimes only steps behind, even into public toilets. At the same time, the work load of the embassy increased severalfold as Soviet authorities took retaliatory measures against private U.S. citizens. American engineers assigned to construction projects and wanting to leave the USSR faced fresh and formidable obstacles in acquiring authorization or transport. Soviet women married to Americans were not allowed to depart with their husbands and frequently were jailed. On arbitrary charges, U.S. citizens were detained or abused by the police.

Steinhardt recommended retaliation against Soviet diplomats in Washington and reciprocity in all dealings with Stalin. Although Roosevelt rejected the idea of a strict quid pro quo, he did accept Steinhardt's suggestion of treating Soviet diplomats in a manner corresponding to that inflicted on the mission in Moscow. Actions against Oumansky and his embassy never become as intrusive as those undertaken in Moscow. But they were stepped up; the Soviet ambassador complained against them.[69]

The grievances that Steinhardt felt toward his Soviet hosts were cumulative. After half a year's stay in Moscow, he wrote this indictment:

> The Russians are not allowed to associate with any foreigner, particularly the
> diplomats, with the result that after a six month's residence here the only Rus-

sians I have met are the four or five men—not their wives—who are at the head of the Foreign Office. Everyone lives under a fear complex—fear of a knock on the door in the middle of the night and transportation to Siberia the next day; imprisonment or execution without a trial of any kind and without an opportunity of saying good-by to the family. The country is governed absolutely by the GPU. Their sole object appears to be to make the life of all foreigners, particularly the diplomats, as difficult, unpleasant, and unbearable as possible, for they regard the diplomats as a necessary evil who are here to spy on the Communist Utopia. The conditions under which the average Soviet citizen lives are worse than the worst slums in New York, for at least in the slums of New York, if an individual can get his hands on a dollar bill, he can buy something; whereas here the denial of food is used as a means of punishment.[70]

These circumstances, combined with the exertions necessary to manage the embassy, provide accurate reporting about Poland and the Finnish war, and avoid a total collapse in relations between the two governments, exhausted the mission. In the case of Steinhardt, they produced acute depression. To one intimate, he wrote in February 1940: "The [events] here have been so unbearable that I became quite discouraged; but . . . I have gotten over these periods of depression; have dug in [and] gone on fighting. This has been all the more essential, as I rather imagine that the worst days are still ahead of us."[71]

The worst days did indeed lie ahead, especially for those nations fighting Germany during the nonaggression pact era. One after another, Denmark, Norway, the Netherlands, Belgium, Luxembourg, France, Yugoslavia, and Greece were defeated. And British forces were ejected from the continent. In the meantime, despite high casualties and a longer war than the seven to ten days originally envisaged by Stalin, the Soviets expanded at the expense of Finland. Later, they absorbed the Baltic republics of Estonia, Latvia, and Lithuania and seized portions of Bessarabia from Romania. In exchange for finished products, the Soviets shipped heaps of foodstuffs and raw resources to Germany and thus were "silent partner" (Steinhardt's term) in German deeds *and* anxious witness to the crumbling of Western armies.

Steinhardt's view at the beginning of the European war was that the provisions of the nonaggression pact did not fully reflect the nature of the Soviet–German relationship. He faulted the Western press for engaging in "wishful thinking" and castigated those who spoke of Soviet "neutrality" or who posited the future dissolution of the pact. Rather, by any conventional understanding, the Soviet Union was an ally of Germany, as the two countries were economically entwined and cooperated in international policy (even if at times competitively). Steinhardt maintained that no wedge could easily be driven between them. In March 1940, he judged (incorrectly but plausibly according to the available evidence) "that Stalin is definitely committed to a German victory and that the Soviets will do everything within their power to aid and abet Germany." This situation, he felt, would lead to Anglo-French hostilities against the Soviets either in the Baltic or, more likely, in the Black Sea.

After the fall of France, Soviet nervousness became more apparent. Thanks partly to his consultations with London's new ambassador, Sir Stafford Cripps,

Steinhardt saw Stalin's continued honoring of the pact as analogous to earlier Western appeasement. In a meeting with Cripps (the substance of which was immediately conveyed to the U.S. embassy), Stalin stated that the USSR was in no position to risk conflict with the German army in summer 1940; such a fight must be delayed for as long as possible, even if that meant Britain's defeat. Presumably, achieving a victory over the British would exact steep costs from Germany, thereby enhancing the Soviets' overall power position. In any case, the overriding question for Stalin was: How long would his armed forces, lackluster in the war against Finland, have before facing the harshest test? His object was to devise means of postponing it.[72]

Irrespective of Steinhardt's initial misreading of Stalin's commitment to German success against the Anglo-French, he never believed that the nonaggression treaty was anything more than unholy and temporary. True, it might survive until after the defeat of Poland's coguarantors. But it would not last past the moment when either Hitler or Stalin concluded that benefit would accrue from its discarding. By September 1940, Steinhardt was fully alert to the evidences of strain in the Soviet–German pact. And he reported with commendable insight on the implications (dire from a Soviet point of view) of critical events: the German–Finnish negotiations in the late summer, which led to Finland's purchase of German arms and the transport of Nazi soldiers through Finland to Norway; Germany's declaration of intention to guarantee Romanian integrity; and the signing in September of the Tripartite Pact by Germany, Italy, and Japan, which (though aimed against the United States) had overtones of the anti-Comintern agreement. Soviet and German competition for influence in Turkey in 1941 and visible Kremlin disappointment over Bulgaria's joining the Tripartite Pact (March) were later signs to Steinhardt that the Ribbentrop–Molotov accord was unraveling. Finally, he saw the German invasion of Yugoslavia in April, just hours after the Soviets had entered into a friendship and nonaggression agreement with Belgrade, for what it was: *the* turning point in German–Soviet relations. At the same time, he recognized that Stalin was prepared to do almost anything to avoid war with Germany and was disturbed by the quantity of Soviet materials still shipped to Germany.[73]

Steinhardt was so indignant about the mistreatment to which he and his staff were subjected and so horrified by Stalinist actions against Poland, Finland, and the Baltic republics that he disapproved of any thawing trend in Soviet–U.S. affairs. After the fall of France, for example, Sumner Welles held talks with Oumansky to determine if the USSR might revise its orientation away from Germany. For this purpose, the undersecretary dangled concessions involving Soviet purchase of U.S. machine tools and naval armaments. Against this demarche, Steinhardt fired off a cable stating that unilateral concessions of any kind would both impair U.S. prestige and fail to nudge Stalin away from Hitler. After Roosevelt lifted the moral embargo (January 1941) without consulting Steinhardt, who at the time was struggling to obtain release of imprisoned Americans, the ambassador flew into a rage. He lectured Hull:

> I cannot stress too emphatically that concessions made in Washington do not in the mind of the Soviet authorities have the slightest bearing on the international

Spaso House, ambassador's residence in Moscow since 1933.

Andrei Gromyko and Joseph Davies at the end of World War II.
(Library of Congress)

William C. Bullitt.
(Library of Congress)

Joseph Stalin and Averell Harriman at 1945 victory parade in Moscow.
(Library of Congress)

Walter Bedell Smith.
(National Archives)

Alan Kirk.
(National Archives)

George Kennan.
(Drawing by Vint Lawrence)

political orientation of the Soviet Government. . . . The Soviet authorities enjoy trading and barter, and attach no value to anything received unless conditions are imposed and if concessions are freely granted do not feel under the slightest obligation to reciprocate. In fact, they see an ulterior reason for the granting of these concessions where nothing is asked in return. Friendly gestures mean nothing.[74]

In this same spirit, Steinhardt also doubted the advisability of warning the Soviets (in March 1941) that intelligence reports indicated Hitler's approval of plans for invading Russia. Very likely, the Soviets would dismiss this information as invented by the British to weaken Soviet–German ties. And if the Soviets did believe the intelligence, it might cause them to move in any one or combination of directions contrary to U.S. interests: hastening a Soviet agreement with Japan (which happened April 13, 1941), dealing with Germany at Turkey's expense, triggering the Red Army's occupation of Finland, sparking renewed demands on the United States to grant concessions to Moscow, accelerating assistance to Germany in an attempt to avoid a Nazi attack. In the event, Welles, not Steinhardt, was the first American to warn the Soviets of German planning. Oumansky, the designated recipient, "turned very white" on learning the news.[75]

Like many observers in the summer of 1941, Steinhardt and his blunt-speaking military attaché, Major Ivan Yeaton, doubted that the Red Army could repel the Wehrmacht. It was apparent to them that the Red Army had been taken unawares. One member of the staff, who hurried back in late June from holiday on the Black Sea, reported that on the day of invasion thousands of army officers were enjoying vacations in Sochi and other resorts. The ambassador told Hull that at best the Red Army might be able to check its headlong retreat, mount a rearguard action, and then continue to fight in the Urals. Four days after the unleashing of Operation Barbarossa—by which time one-sixth of the Soviet air force had been destroyed and Panzer units had established a wide front—Steinhardt sent Washington a copy of his plan for evacuating mission personnel and records. Earlier, in March, he had taken the precaution of placing in the embassy's dacha (near Tarasovka, fifteen miles north of Moscow) a stockpile of tents, bedding, food, and medicine sufficient to last several months. Tipped off beforehand by an informant in the German embassy of the invasion's timing, Steinhardt had also obtained safe passage for his wife and daughter to Stockholm. He felt that within two months of the invasion's start, Moscow would land in German hands. Nevertheless, not until mid-October, when forward units of the German army were in the suburbs and within sight of the Kremlin's towers, did the embassy remove itself. This action was part of an evacuation that embraced all foreign missions and most of the Soviet government (but not Stalin) to Kuibyshev, a provincial city on the Volga five hundred miles southeast of Moscow.[76]

In the months that followed, Steinhardt continued to issue reports and cables on impending Soviet demise. And although he realized the importance of the Soviet effort in draining German strength and alleviating pressure on Britain, he opposed Roosevelt's policy of unrestricted aid to Russia. He argued that huge amounts of U.S. matériel would wind up in German possession after the Red Army's ultimate defeat. To Steinhardt (and he was supported by Henderson), the United States should instead offer aid in exchange for Soviet cooperation in specific matters. At the embassy level, these should include helping the ambassador locate and care for Americans in the USSR and loosening the restrictions on diplomats' lives. Perhaps the Soviets would also allow the mission to send military observers to the front lines. More importantly, pledges of future good behavior should be exacted as a condition of aid (i.e., the renunciation of territories captured by the Red Army during the nonaggression pact period).

All the same, lend-lease assistance was formally extended to the Soviets on November 7, by which time $1 billion worth of military supplies had already been authorized. However mindful of the justice behind Steinhardt's comments, Roosevelt was adamant that ample supplies be delivered to the USSR. Following hostilities, he expected that eastern Europe, by one means or another, could be restored to the pre-September 1939 status quo ante. And the lesser problems involving the embassy could surely sort themselves out. The urgent problem in 1941 was to ensure Germany's defeat. To this end, all allies should be helped and nothing done that might push Stalin to seek another accommodation with Hitler.

This difference in approach between the president and the ambassador resulted in Steinhardt's marginalization. That he was out of step and without influence in making policy was made obvious in late July 1941. FDR sent his special assistant Harry Hopkins, not the ambassador in place, to Stalin to see how best the United States might furnish matériel aid. Steinhardt was allowed to be present with Hopkins in his first conference with Stalin (this being the first time the ambassador met the chairman of ministers). But his role in the talks was negligible; the principals alone reviewed the types of weaponry needed by the Red Army and the logistical problems in their conveyance. Steinhardt was actually excluded from the subsequent meetings between Hopkins and Stalin in which they discussed the balance of power between German and Soviet forces. It must have nettled Steinhardt when he reported to Hull on the lavish press attention, official courtesies, and generous attention given to Hopkins's mission.

Two months later, Harriman (director of lend-lease operations to Britain) and Lord Beaverbrook (Churchill's minister of supply) led high-level delegations to Moscow to meet with Stalin. Again, Steinhardt was relegated to observer status. As provisions were hammered out for the delivery of British and U.S. aircraft, tanks, artillery, trucks, and food, Steinhardt dealt with minor matters related to the entertainment and billeting of the Anglo-U.S. conferees.

During one discussion with Harriman, Stalin launched a sharp attack on Steinhardt, calling him a defeatist, rumormonger, and coward (for his haste in repairing to Tarasovka early in the war). Harriman defended the ambassador against these charges, but he also knew that Steinhardt regarded himself as an interloper, had misgivings about the desirability and modalities of aiding the Soviets, and had frequently annoyed authorities in Moscow. After his Soviet visit, Harriman consequently told Roosevelt that Steinhardt had lost all standing with Stalin and should be replaced. Hopkins agreed, and Roosevelt obtained the ambassador's resignation in early November. He advised him that Soviet–U.S. relations in the near future would consist of matters connected to supplying Stalin with equipment to fight Germany. In these circumstances, "it would be advantageous to have as Ambassador in [Moscow] someone who is fully acquainted with detailed problems of American production and supply." For this purpose, FDR originally had in mind Major General James Burns, at the time temporary head of the Lend-Lease Administration.[77]

Steinhardt remained at his post in Kuibyshev until mid-November before making a harrowing thirteen-day trip to Washington (whence he was sent as ambassador to Turkey in 1942). He was dispirited and felt victimized by the Soviets. It was in this slightly giddy state that he declared on December 2,

> I confess to having had a pretty difficult time of it during the past six months— between the bombing [of Moscow] and the subsequent trip to Kuibyshev, where the Ritz Hotel has not yet been built, and where they have not learned of the existence of toilet paper—perhaps for the reason that there is not enough food to justify giving much thought to the former subject.[78]

In Leningrad, meanwhile, the population was under siege from the Germans and the coldest winter of the century. Starvation stalked. Although the German army had not taken Moscow (and was subject to counterattacks), it was still emplaced before the city and husbanding its strength for a renewed offensive in the spring. Kiev had fallen. The Ukraine and its bounty were under Nazi control.

*   *   *   *

In the final analysis, evaluation of Roosevelt's Soviet policy in 1933 to 1941 does not depend on affixing blame or praise on Bullitt's ebullience or Davies's breeziness or Steinhardt's fussiness or the steady functioning of the embassy staff. Yet, collectively, these people embodied the president's own ambivalence and groping in devising policy toward the USSR—a country whose professed values and ambitions FDR recognized as antipathetic. In February 1940, he not only condemned Soviet aggression against Finland but pronounced Stalin's regime "as absolute as any dictatorship in the world."[79] The problem, though, was that the United States could not simultaneously check Germany and Japan without the cooperation of that same dictatorship.

Better than Bullitt or Steinhardt, Davies appreciated this dilemma early on. His overriding concern by 1944 was that the Soviet–U.S. alliance should prove durable and that State Department "underlings" opposed to it not "poison" the president's mind.[80] Davies was also a more enigmatic, if less circumspect, personality than the other two ambassadors. He possessed a portion of Machiavellian instinct about the practice and mentality of successful diplomacy. He once confided to his journal:

> It is difficult to assess what reliability one can put upon statements of men in this diplomatic game. There is much "dual personality" in this diplomatic life. It is only on that assumption that one can safely proceed when representing one's country. There are too often two personalities in the same man: the man he would like to be, the other the man he has to be as a representative of his Foreign Office.

This statement of Davies's amounts to his version of that adage attributed to Sir Henry Wotton and used (unfairly) to explain envoys: "An ambassador is an honest man sent abroad to lie for the good of his country." In any case, Davies's observation as applied to himself explains in part the disparity between his breathless friendliness toward Soviet officialdom in 1937 and 1938 and his more matter-of-fact reporting to Washington about Stalin's totalitarianism. In a sense, Davies also used an inverted version of his and Wotton's logic in explaining the Soviet Union to his compatriots during World War II. He was willing for their good (as he understood it) to mislead them about another country—one whose multiple defects had to be explained away if the broad populace was to embrace it as an ally and worthy recipient of billions of dollars of lend-lease relief. In other words, Davies was an ambassador sent abroad who, upon returning home, lied to his countrymen for their own benefit.[81] This orientation was also in keeping with Roosevelt, who admitted in 1942, "I am perfectly willing to mislead and tell untruths if it will help win the war."[82]

Roosevelt not only approved of Davies's conduct in Moscow, but afterward used him to stump the U.S. countryside to build support for the Soviet war effort. And the president sent him as a special envoy in 1943 to consult with Stalin and calm his anger about continued Anglo-U.S. delays in opening a second front. Again with ambassadorial rank, Davies acted as an adviser to Harry Truman at the Potsdam Conference in July 1945. By then, however, what remained of the wartime coalition was fast eroding. At Potsdam, Davies and Harriman (a recent convert to anti-Sovietism) clashed. The latter referred to the Soviets as "barbarians," while Davies answered that a way must be found to preserve the alliance.[83]

Steinhardt's disillusionment with the USSR was not so dramatic as Bullitt's and was even less than Harriman's. He was constitutionally immune from high hopes and deaf to the siren call of Soviet propaganda that claimed a humane order was arising in Russia. Instead, his views, restrained from the outset, were intensified by his living in a totalitarian world. In this, the central object of political activity was to awe people with the power, prestige, and leadership genius of the state. On learning of Theodore Dreiser's remark in late 1939 that the Soviets enjoyed the best standard of living in the world, Steinhardt entertained the wicked idea of "kidnaping Dreiser and making him live [in Moscow] thirty days—not under the wing of Intourist but merely as a foreign ambassador." Under such circumstances, what might Dreiser have learned? And what would he have thought of the experience of Kennan, who while driving to Moscow from the countryside one night picked up a man who spoke freely under the cover of darkness? This passenger bemoaned the moral paralysis undercutting productivity on the farms and the party's complicity in illegal activities. At the same time, he excitedly admired the mechanical perfection of Kennan's car; as nothing else could, this man's reaction underscored the elusiveness of Pimenov's *New Moscow*. To Kennan, he said, "[This car is] just like a living thing. You'd think that it did all these things of its own accord. Who'd ever believe that it was just because you push all those gadgets?" Incidentally, as a metaphor for Stalinist modernity, the automobile was also used by Anna Akhmatova, albeit in a way unintended by the rulers. She wrote in her "Requiem":

And Russia, guiltless, beloved, writhed
Under the crunch of bloodstained boots,
Under the wheels of Black Marias.

Bullitt and Steinhardt were right to insist that a chasm existed between the political-economic realities of Soviet life and those imagined by its apologists. They were also correct to challenge Soviet activities (as they affected both high policy and everyday embassy life) that were incompatible with the Roosevelt–Litvinov accords. In this connection, it is fair to say that Stalin's and Molotov's failure to form meaningful relations with the English-speaking powers and France in 1939 reflected the mediocrity of Soviet statesmanship (as much as that of the democracies). This quality of mind was evident in the Soviets' hostility toward Western diplomats in Moscow, where authorities antagonized people well placed to promote policies against the common menace, Germany. In this sense, the Soviets were (in Steinhardt's words) their own worst enemy: "They follow a steady course of truculent arrogance which is annoying to foreign diplomats and which gains nothing for themselves."[84] Yet there was a parochial quality in some of Bullitt's and Steinhardt's views. More than Roosevelt or Davies, they allowed themselves to lose sight of the fact that the USSR had reasons of its own to cooperate with the British and Americans against Hitler. Their jolting experience in Stalin's universe caused them to lose perspective on international politics, which would have indicated where the immediate danger to U.S. security lay. Still, had more of their attitude been adopted in 1939 to 1941, especially Steinhardt's emphasis on reciprocity, Soviet–U.S. relations in the war's early phase would have rested on something sturdy. It would have been less likely to produce mutual suspicions or those recriminations that plagued the Grand Alliance.

6

Fragile Coalition

Like Europe's wars against Napoleonic France, four successive coalitions arose against Hitler's Germany. The original one, led by Britain and France, ended in catastrophe in June 1940 with the fall of Paris and the establishment of a puppet regime at Vichy. The second coalition featured the British Empire and Commonwealth in cooperation with small states (Greece and Yugoslavia) whose ability to contribute to German defeat was negligible; this effort also ended in failure. The third coalition emerged in June 1941, when Hitler's armies invaded Russia. British and Red forces were thereby joined in common cause, consummated May 1942 with the signing of a twenty-year Anglo-Soviet treaty. Neutral in name only before the Japanese attack on Pearl Harbor and subsequent German declaration of war, the United States played the pivotal role in the fourth coalition, with which this chapter is concerned. This partnership, variously labeled the Grand Alliance or (more accurately) the Strange Alliance, was subject to the stresses and ambiguities that have marked collaborative effort by great powers since time immemorial. Its turbulent career confirmed Trotsky's cynical but apt observation: "An ally has to be watched just like an enemy."[1] To think otherwise, Stalin and Churchill would have concurred—Roosevelt, too, in his vague way—required a suspension of prudence.

The official Soviet version (pre-Gorbachev) of struggle against Germany was used by Stalin's and succeeding governments to bolster the regime's legitimacy and gave rise to the affecting cult of the Great Patriotic War. Its icons ranged from Akhmatova's poetic cycle *The Wind of War* and Shostakovich's bombastic *Leningrad Symphony* to such sentimental favorites as Konstantin Simonov's *Wait for Me* and pictures of soldiers defending Sevastopol or storming the Brandenburg Gate. Erected prominently in every Soviet city were monuments attesting to the rigors of the anti-German war and its stunning climax. According to the official interpretation, the Communist party brilliantly led a unified country against a powerful and determined foe. After hardships and sacrifice, the party and Soviet peoples (above all, the Russians) destroyed Nazi imperialism and struck the decisive blow for Japan's defeat. Subject to amendment as early as 1956 in official historiography, the original account overlooked or trivialized Stalin's misunderstanding of German intentions in June 1941, which led to shattering defeats in the first months of warfare. Collaboration, defections, and aid given the invading German armies by hundreds of thousands of Balts, Ukrainians, and Russians (of whom General Vlasov was the most notorious) were also conveniently overlooked or easily explained. Blunders and perfidiousness were attributed exclusively to the Anglo-American side; by implication, the Western allies had to share with Germany some complicity for the suffering and physical damage inflicted on the USSR. Finally, responsibility for the demise of the Grand Alliance was attributed to British and American misdeeds and bad faith during the war: support of anti-Soviet elements in Poland, paltry lend-lease aid, postponements of a second front in France, and unilateral development of the atomic bomb and inadequate consultation with Stalin about its deployment.[2]

British and U.S. measures in 1941 to 1945 to dispel popular apprehensions about the Soviet Union had an effect—hence, the box office success of such films as *Mission to Moscow, Song of Russia, North Star,* and *Battle of Russia.* Public support was also high for meetings of the Big Three at Teheran, Yalta, and Potsdam. Yet both Churchill and Roosevelt were anxious about their Soviet connection. Neither Soviet tenacity at Leningrad nor victory at Stalingrad erased the fact that Molotov's connivance with Ribbentrop in August 1939 had precipitated Germany's invasion of Poland and conquest of most of Europe. On the British side, there was a barely disguised reproach during the life of the fourth coalition that the Soviets had opened nothing like a second front during the period after France's fall and before June 22, 1941. In those months, while Soviet trade flourished with Germany, Britain had waged a lonely fight against Luftwaffe bombers and U-boat wolf packs and lived in fear of a threatened invasion. The dissolution of the Comintern in May 1943 did not in Churchill's view (and that of many Americans) atone for previous years of virulent Soviet rhetoric and acts against Western interests. Churchill and Roosevelt, moreover, were dismayed by the discoveries made at Katyn forest and by Soviet abuse of Poland's government-in-exile. Later, they were incredulous at Soviet refusal to aid General Bor-Komorowski's underground army in Warsaw (August–September 1944) and angered at Soviet efforts that hampered Anglo-U.S. attempts by air to help the resistance.

Soviet faults as an ally notwithstanding, Roosevelt and Churchill appreciated that Europe would remain subservient to Germany without Stalin's military contribution—Anglo-U.S. security would be jeopardized. Both governments were thus unsparing in welcoming the USSR into the war against fascism and in praising Red Army achievements. Churchill, who had advocated two decades earlier that the infant Bolshevik revolution be strangled in its cradle, acknowledged in 1944 that it was the Soviet fighting men who "tore the guts out of the German army."[3] Throughout the war, Western leaders were also eager (within broad limits) to accommodate Stalin. Although a statement open to challenge and a subject of dispute during the war, it seems fair to say that the scale of foodstuffs, weaponry, vehicles, and machinery provided by U.S. lend-lease (valued at $11 billion) helped maintain the Soviet offensive in 1943 to 1945. The quantity and quality of such matériel in the critical categories actually surpassed the total that France possessed in 1940.[4]

Roosevelt's insistence on Germany's unconditional surrender, furthermore, was designed to impress Stalin with America's commitment and stiffen him against any temptation to enter into a separate peace. Stalin toyed with this idea during the long months when German forces, having reverted to atavistic savagery, pummeled the USSR, but the Western allies failed to engage substantial numbers of Wehrmacht troops (by the standard of the eastern front).[5] During his meetings with Stalin at Teheran and Yalta, Roosevelt was particularly solicitous of the Soviet leader. He hoped to persuade him that alliance problems need not cause a breach; with goodwill, all differences could be reconciled. Roosevelt also applied his fabled charm to this end and tried, to Churchill's chagrin, to convince Stalin that he and the president had much in common, including a distaste for British imperialism. As for Polish grievances, the price of their just resolution was not considered in London or Washington to be worth jeopardizing cooperation with Moscow. As a conciliatory gesture to opinion in their countries (and perhaps as a balm to their own consciences), Churchill and Roosevelt expected to satisfy Poland when they assigned portions of Prussia to Warsaw in compensation for moving the Soviet–Polish frontier westward to the Curzon line.

Once it became clear that Germany would be crushed by a two-front war (after the surrender of Field Marshal Friedrich Paulus at Stalingrad and the Western landings at Normandy), Allied leaders were increasingly preoccupied with the postwar political shape of Europe and the conquest of Japan. Concerning this second issue, to lighten their losses and shorten the Pacific war, Roosevelt and Churchill hoped that Red forces would join the campaign against Japan at the earliest possible date. Well before D-Day, at the Teheran Conference (late November 1943), the Anglo-U.S. leaders were heartened by Stalin's statement that his commanders would start operations against Japan following Germany's vanquishment.

Practical issues of a most urgent sort thus impelled the West to undertake a high degree of collaboration with Soviet Russia that obscured, at least superficially, mutual distrust and rivalry. This situation allowed Roosevelt to entertain hopes for Soviet-Anglo-U.S. cooperation after the war, though this attitude did not extend to his decision precluding the Soviets from work on the Manhattan Project. He also hoped at some level—the seriousness of which cannot precisely be determined—that the three major powers, along with a strengthened China and revitalized France, would cooperate in future years as global policemen. They would correct economic and political injustices wherever they threatened to trigger violence, force aggressors into submission, and lead the United Nations. In the best of all possible worlds, according to Roosevelt, this international agency should be endowed with power to play the dominant role in promoting global stability. Spheres of influence, balance-of-power diplomacy, military alliances, and other discredited devices of international politics could then safely be discarded, belatedly fulfilling Woodrow Wilson's vision. Neither Stalin nor Churchill

had much confidence in the efficacy of such a grandiose collective security system, however. Stalin preferred local arrangements in eastern Europe compatible
with Soviet security and defense-in-depth strategy. And Churchill sought to revive
a balance of power on the continent that would prevent Soviet hegemony. Not so
oblivious to these concerns as his critics have charged, Roosevelt nonetheless
emphasized the virtues of a peace-keeping organization and was gratified at Yalta
when Stalin agreed to the American formula for the UN—an institution that, in
theory, would correct any problem of injustice in eastern Europe or elsewhere.

Opinion in Embassy Moscow during the war was skeptical about the long-
term promise of Soviet–U.S. cooperation. Contradictions between this point of
view and the line emanating from Washington partly explain the failure of William
Standley's ambassadorship and his resignation in 1943. His ineffectiveness was
also related to the reemergence of troubles originally associated with American
diplomacy in Russia during World War I: conflicting lines of U.S. diplomatic
authority in the national capital, the administration's indifference to ambassadorial
advice, and the president's refusal to keep the embassy informed of decisions that
bore directly on its part in Soviet–U.S. affairs.

These problems, which ensured a fumbling diplomacy, were resolved with the
appointment of Averell Harriman in October 1943. In contrast to the inattention
suffered by Standley, Harriman enjoyed the support of Roosevelt and respect of
Stalin. This ambassadorship recorded notable successes, and its reportage, specifically George Kennan's Long Telegram, achieved a singular level of distinction.
In one respect, however, Harriman's experience was similar to Standley's. Like
him, he went to Moscow hoping to improve relations with the USSR and of
placing them on a basis that could survive into the posthostilities world. In the
end, Harriman left Moscow as one of the original recruits in the Cold War
against Stalin.

Diplomacy Neglected

There was little in Standley's background that recommended him for a diplomatic
post, let alone envoy to Moscow. A graduate of the U.S. Naval Academy (class
of 1895), his career spanned more than forty years in the service and culminated
with his appointment as Chief of Naval Operations (CNO) in 1933. He accepted
the directorship of foreign participation for the 1939 New York World's Fair upon
his retirement from the navy and served in 1939 to 1941 as a director and consultant for the Electric Boat Company in New London, Connecticut. Except for his
participation as a delegate to the London Disarmament Conference in 1935,
Standley had never worked in a diplomatic capacity. An affable and direct man,
he held the habitual caution of diplomacy in contempt.

His familiarity with things Russian was also slight. It consisted of his boyhood
acquaintance with the Russian communities of his native California (in Fort Ross
and Mendocino County) and a tour of sea duty in 1896 that included a week-long
visit to Vladivostok. In 1899, while attached to the *Yorktown* on the Asiatic station, Standley witnessed the operation of Russian forces involved in suppressing

the Boxer Rebellion. Instances of their unruliness bothered him. The lessons he drew from these early experiences were unexceptional and did not go beyond the platitudinous: "What the Russian doesn't understand, the Russian doesn't like."[6]

While serving at the Naval Academy in World War I, Standley met the assistant secretary of the navy, Franklin Roosevelt. They remained on friendly, if not intimate, terms thereafter. Roosevelt respected the admiral for his candor even when they were not in accord—as when in 1937 their disagreement over personnel assignments to the Atlantic fleet led to Standley's resignation as CNO.[7] On other matters, they did agree, such as the need for aid to Britain with the start of war in 1939 and the desirability of future armed intervention. Standley was invariably outspoken on these subjects and urged as early as August 1940 that the United States declare war on Nazi Germany. Half a year later, he was called to assist with the Planning Board of the Office of Production Management. Roosevelt selected Standley (with the rank of minister) in September 1941 to accompany Harriman to Moscow, where he led the U.S. delegation in meetings on Soviet naval requirements.

The president did not hold Standley's meager diplomatic and Soviet background against him, but believed that his overall record of service qualified him as ambassador. His enthusiasm for war readiness (especially a big navy), advocacy of aid to countries fighting Hitler, and familiarity with industrial-military production in America also commended Standley. Even so, he was not Roosevelt's first choice for the job. General James Burns, as mentioned (Chapter 5), was originally picked to succeed Steinhardt. But on further reflection, he was considered too valuable in his work with lend-lease to be sent abroad. Roosevelt then asked Joseph Davies, who refused because of poor health. After his Soviet expedition with Beaverbrook, Harriman was asked by Harry Hopkins whether he would be willing to return as envoy. He declined emphatically. He later recalled, "I had just seen what a hopelessly restricted life the foreign diplomats led in Moscow, the way they were fenced in. I was also thoroughly enjoying my relationships with Churchill and the British. I felt I was accomplishing a great deal there in connection with the war and I recognized that in Moscow I would be at the end of the line."[8] He recommended Standley instead, as he had performed credibly on the Beaverbrook–Harriman team.

Unsure about his own qualifications, Standley was also aware that he was not Roosevelt's first choice. He believed, in fact, that the embassy's minister counselor, Walter Thurston, a man with years of Foreign Service experience (mostly in Latin America), was better suited to the job than himself. As for the British Foreign Office, it was lukewarm to Standley's appointment and saw no sound reason for it. In the event, Roosevelt made little use of the admiral. Consistent with his bypassing State Department functionaries (from Cordell Hull downward), Roosevelt relied on alternative methods to conduct business with Stalin. This approach meant that the ambassador enjoyed embarrassingly low prestige with the Soviets. Years later, Andrei Gromyko dryly observed of Standley: "[He] was in Moscow little more than a year . . . and left no trace of having been there."[9]

Standley divided his time between the capital (where a skeleton staff was left in charge of Spaso House) and the government's temporary residence in Kuibyshev, where most of the diplomatic corps also resided. The drawbacks to this arrangement were legion. Apart from occupying a typhus-ridden spot on the Volga and confronting a level of hygiene low even by Soviet standards, Kuibyshev was far from the center of political gravity. Stalin, Molotov, and the defense commissariat remained in Moscow. Until January 1943, when Standley transferred the bulk of U.S. operations back to Moscow, he mainly dealt with second-echelon figures: Andrei Vyshinsky, prosecutor in the party purge trials, then serving as assistant commissar for foreign affairs, and his lieutenant, Solomon Lozovsky. Access to top Soviet leadership was thus indirect; the intermediary level of bureaucracy in Kuibyshev provided additional insulation for the Kremlin against the inopportuneness of American (and other) diplomats.

There was a depressing similarity between the experience of Standley, rusticated in Kuibyshev, and that of David Francis in Vologda. They each endured long patches of idleness while questions of military and political moment were decided elsewhere. In 1942, Kuibyshev had swollen to several times its prewar size with the arrival of 500,000 refugees, for whom the supply of food, housing, and drinkable water varied from sparse to nonexistent. Foreign correspondents, accredited diplomats, Soviet officials, and selected young Russian women lived and entertained in the city's Grand Hotel, an establishment that despite its name was barely distinguishable from the muddy (or dusty, depending on the season) squalor that surrounded it. The American residence and office was a dilapidated town house, Sadovia, once the property of a wealthy merchant. Freezing during winter and infested by flies in summer, maintenance of Sadovia and life within it constituted a minor battle of survival for the seventy-year-old ambassador. During the interminable weeks when they were without instruction from Washington and were not conferring with Soviet officialdom, Standley and his staff tended a vegetable plot (which provided dietary supplement) and flower garden. They constructed a driving range that mercifully distracted Standley, an avid golfer, during his bouts with boredom. He was burdened, too, with an excess of time to play bridge and tennis—the latter often with his NKVD escort, of whom he became fond. He watched Disney and other American-made films, attended performances of operatic and ballet productions, and had time to read *War and Peace*. In line with Soviet restrictions, the aim of which was to prevent any foreigner's spontaneous interaction with citizens, Standley was allowed brief visits to local orphanages, farms, and hospitals. As his discouragement rose over enforced inactivity, he wondered why the Soviets accredited a U.S. ambassador or why FDR kept one: "I labored under a feeling of complete frustration, without conviction of accomplishment." [10]

Reflecting the poor state of bilateral relations in 1942 and 1943 and the Soviets' assessment of Standley's standing in Washington, the Foreign Ministry treated him as a minor entity. Stalin kept the ambassador waiting twelve days after his arrival in Moscow before granting him an audience—an insult unjustified by the exigencies of Soviet military operations then under way. When the meeting finally occurred (April 23, 1942), Standley conveyed what he thought was a wholly new initiative from Roosevelt: the president and Soviet leader should soon meet, off either the Alaskan or the Siberian coast. Stalin replied that this idea had already been proposed through other channels, and its feasibility was under review. In discussing the U-boat and other hazards preventing speedy delivery of lend-lease materials, Stalin chided the former naval officer about flaws in the U.S. convoy system. And at no time in this meeting did Stalin mention Molotov's upcoming travel to London and Washington. Presumably, Stalin saw no reason to enlighten the diplomat as his own government and Britain's ambassador, Archibald Clark Kerr, were content to leave him undisturbed on this subject.[11]

Comparable and numerous frustrations irritated Standley in the following months. Only after repeated delays did authorities allow him and his staff to visit an American bomber crew detained on Soviet territory (having made an emergency landing in Siberia after striking Japanese targets). Aware of Stalin's need to avoid incidents with Japan that could be construed as a violation of Moscow's neutrality in East Asia, Standley was still incensed by the shabby treatment given to the crew during its year-long detention. (Eventually, this and other stranded air crews were allowed by the Soviets to "escape" via Ashkabad and Iran and back to the Japanese war.) The uncooperative attitude of officials toward him and his inquiries was contrary to that spirit of amity that he assumed existed between allies. So, too, were the restrictions placed on his travels, as when he was allowed an absurdly circumscribed visit to Tashkent. Standley's pet project for raising Soviet appreciation of the United States through distribution of Hollywood and educational films (in which cause he hoped to enlist Douglas Fairbanks, Jr.) met with thunderous indifference from the Kremlin, which later imposed insuperable bureaucratic hurdles.[12] Of greater import than these annoyances was the Soviets' refusal to share on a regular basis information about German weapons, tactics, and command-and-control techniques. This intelligence, acquired by contact with the enemy on the field, was vital to Standley's military and naval attachés. Their evaluation and transmittal of it to Anglo-U.S. commanders could help as they mapped the invasion of western Europe and devised means to counter German defenses. Despite protests, the Soviets also prohibited U.S. military observers from visiting the front lines, where additional information might be gathered about enemy equipment and method.

Standley's prestige was further diminished when he quarreled with the Foreign Office over its procrastination in granting visas to lend-lease personnel or complained about its interference with the distribution of U.S. matériel. That Standley was at times the bearer of bad news was also held against him, as when he delivered the Western decision to reduce the number of convoys making the Murmansk run (because of crippling actions by U-boats and torpedo bombers). At other times, the Soviets felt that he dissimulated—for example, when he gave the reasoning for Anglo-U.S. delay in opening a western front in 1942.[13] Also grating were Standley's inquiries on behalf of the Polish government about the fate of missing army officers in Soviet incarceration and his requests for decent treatment of Polish relief agents (most of whom were arrested on unverified charges of espionage) working with refugees in the USSR. Finally, Standley's attempts to explain the U.S. view of Poland's future boundaries and political composition disturbed the Soviets. In Molotov's sulphurous phrase, "There is always trouble where Poles are concerned."[14]

The basic problem for Standley was that he, as Western diplomat sui generis, was distrusted by his hosts. And they could alleviate or worsen the lot of any envoy at whim. Nothing occurred during Standley's ambassadorship to disconfirm his testimony of July 1942: "Since my arrival here the Embassy in practically all aspects of its work ha[s] been continually subjected to delays, interference and indifference on the part of subordinate Soviet officials and that it appear[s] to me that almost a studied effort [has been] made to thwart its cooperative spirit."[15] As always in the USSR, the diplomats' access to ordinary news was blocked and microphones infested their work and living quarters. (The British military mission found twelve listening devices on its premises in a single day.)[16]

More disheartening to Standley than his encounter with the Soviets was his neglect by Roosevelt. Misuse of him would have been understandable had he belonged to that breed of inept envoy sent to founder abroad. But he was a conscientious and reasonably talented diplomat. Despite his age, he was energetic. Whatever his propensity to use "salty sailorman" language, he was also dignified and merited respect. He knew how to employ his staff well, above all Edward Page, a product of Robert Kelley's Russian program and clever interpreter of the Soviet scene. In addition, Standley's reporting to Washington was sound, as the following examples show.

After Molotov had obtained what looked like a Western pledge of a cross-Channel invasion in 1942, Standley warned that failure to redeem this promise (for whatever reason) would severely hurt Soviet confidence in Anglo-U.S. power. He wrote to Cordell Hull in June: "I feel convinced that if such a [second] front does not materialize quickly and on a large scale, these [Soviet] people will be so deluded in their belief in our sincerity of purpose and will for concerted action that inestimable harm will be done to the cause of the United Nations."[17] In this connection, he argued that Stalin stood to reap political benefits for however long the second front was delayed: its postponement fueled the idea that cynical leaders in London and Washington were pleased the USSR was bearing the brunt of German fury. In the end, Stalin would control the moral high ground from which to dominate peace arrangements in eastern Europe. Standley was also perceptive when he predicted that following the war the Soviets would establish in areas occupied by the Red Army a reverse cordon sanitaire, designed to shield the Marxist hinterland. He was alert, too, to the intensity of Soviet ire in being excluded from the Allied Control Commission for Italy in 1943. He made a sensible (but ignored) recommendation to the State Department that the USSR be allowed representation on this body, thereby establishing a precedent that Washington could invoke if other Axis states surrendered to Soviet forces. Finally, Standley doubted that the USSR wanted or could afford to make a separate peace with Germany along the lines of Brest-Litovsk. Such an unlikely event should therefore not influence U.S. policymaking. He assured FDR, "The Red Army will push right on across the German border to Berlin, just as fast as it can get there."[18] From this appreciation it followed that unrestricted lend-lease aid and blind commitment to unconditional surrender were unwarranted. The corollary was that the United States should draw immediate benefits from its lend-lease policy: Soviet flexibility on Polish issues, generosity from Moscow in sharing intelligence information, a relaxation of restrictions on U.S. diplomats, and solicitude for the well-being of nondiplomatic Americans in the USSR (downed airmen, stranded sailors, and the long-suffering cleric Father Braun, who ministered to parishioners in Moscow).[19] Standley's preferred "sailorman" solution to these problems did not mesh with Roosevelt's cautious approach, however. The ambassador's potential value as an instrument of policy withered.

He was routinely left uninformed on central matters affecting the Soviet–U.S. coalition. It was not, for example, from direct communication that he learned of Roosevelt's statement (to Molotov during his Washington visit) that the second front would be launched in 1942. Standley learned this astonishing news from a BBC newscast. Neither did the State Department notify him in advance of the January 1943 Casablanca Conference (Roosevelt, Churchill, de Gaulle) or the meeting in Teheran. He was also not told of diversionary operations preceding the full-scale invasion of Europe: BOLERO, SLEDGEHAMMER, GYMNAST. Nor was he consulted about the wisdom of the Anglo-U.S. decision in the summer of 1942 to curtail lend-lease convoys until the U-boat menace was contained (at a time when the supply route through Iran was bogged down in logistical and bureaucratic confusion). So, too, he learned late and indirectly that the Alaska–Siberia air link was in danger: the Japanese objected to it; Stalin was unhappy with having U.S. airplanes traverse wide reaches of Soviet airspace.[20]

The president's reliance on personal emissaries to Stalin, through whom he transmitted his main concerns, was most galling for Standley. The first of those anointed was Harriman, who returned to Moscow with Churchill in August 1942. The purpose of this visit was to explain to Stalin that the second front would not be opened any time before 1943; Anglo-U.S. plans for war in French North Africa and the Pacific situation were also discussed. Although Standley took no part in these meetings, as a courtesy Harriman informed him of their substance. All the same, he resented being cast off as "a sort of Chief of Protocol, Liaison Officer, Aide, and general factotum for the two VIPs."[21] In his memoirs, he expressed ill-temper about Harriman's unapproachability and his corruption by power.

One month after the Churchill–Harriman visit, Wendell Willkie, lately FDR's Republican rival for the presidency, arrived in the USSR to advance understanding between the two states. To the extent possible, he ignored Standley. When circumstances forced them together, he was either patronizing or rude. Exasperated by Standley's insistence on protocol and deference to his official status, Willkie did not hesitate in trying to embarrass him. For example, when the two men were guests of an antiaircraft battery near Moscow, Willkie proposed a vodka-drinking contest to an assembly at the officers' mess. It should feature Standley, whom he touted as a champion, against any one of the young Soviet officers present. The ambassador deftly sidestepped this preposterous challenge ("a champion never risks his title against an amateur"), but for the remainder of Willkie's tour he accorded him minimal civility. Like Harriman, Willkie conferred with Stalin alone. But unlike Harriman, he was cagey about the subject of his meeting (which dealt with FDR's hope that Stalin would observe correct relations with the Polish government in London).

During his Moscow visit, Willkie reiterated the idea that the Soviet and U.S.

political systems were on a conversion course; the two countries constituted the best hope of humanity. He also assured Soviet officials, and lesser citizens with whom he was allowed (on a selective basis) to meet, that on returning to America he would press to open a second front in Europe. For this purpose, he would appeal directly to "the masses" and "prod" FDR in the desired direction.[22] Thus Willkie demonstrated that he was fully supportive of the Soviet cause and devoted to the goal of posthostilities East–West partnership. The cranky U.S. ambassador with his whining about the Soviet Union and its alleged lack of cooperation should not be mistaken for dominant American opinion.

Stung by Willkie's performance and still smarting from Harriman's dismissive attitude, Standley applied for (and in October 1942 received) a leave to the United States for talks with FDR. The admiral voiced his anger over the sending of high-level representatives while a permanent envoy was already in place. He also pried assurances from Roosevelt that he still enjoyed his confidence. Nevertheless, Standley's position in the USSR did not improve but deteriorated upon his return to Moscow. Part of the problem was of his own making. The rest was beyond his control, tied to the haphazard procedures of his government.

He had long thought that Stalin belittled the magnitude of cost borne by the United States in producing, transporting, and underwriting lend-lease aid. And he was infuriated that the Kremlin rarely acknowledged in public the importance of this assistance. To correct the situation, Standley issued a tart statement to startled news reporters in March 1943, just as Congress was considering whether to approve funding for the second lend-lease protocol:

> Ever since I've been here, I've been looking for evidence that the Russians are getting a lot of material help from the British and us—not only Lend-Lease but also Red Cross and Russian Relief—but I've yet to find any evidence of that fact. . . . Since my arrival in the Soviet Union, I have also tried to obtain evidence that our military supplies are in use by the Russians, I haven't succeeded. The authorities seem to want to cover up the fact that they are receiving outside help. Apparently they want their people to believe that the Red Army is fighting this war alone. . . . It's not fair—the American people are giving millions to help the Russian people and yet the Russian people do not know where the supplies are coming from. The American people are giving generously because of their friendship for the Russian people. The Soviet authorities apparently are trying to create the impression at home and abroad that they are fighting the war alone and with their own resources.[23]

Standley later claimed that he timed these remarks to coincide with Congress's deliberations on funding the second protocol. According to this logic, if he could obtain a definitive statement by the Soviets acknowledging the benefits of lend-lease, Congress and public opinion would override the reservations of critics (such as Senators Hugh Butler and Richard Russell) and support the president's policy. For this interpretation, Standley was able to marshal slender evidence in his memoirs.[24] On balance, it appears that he was speaking primarily from resentment and only secondarily from a concern to counter lend-lease opponents.[25]

The initial Soviet reaction to Standley's blast was one of outrage. The USSR was in the middle of mortal combat with fascism, the entire eastern front blazed

with the clash of multimillion-man armies, key cities were on the brink of annihi-
lation, and Western land forces were absent from all continental battles. Yet the
ambassador had issued this churlish complaint. Was there no limit to American
insensitivity? How could any U.S. spokesman fault the USSR as Red Army casualties soared and the civilian population suffered torments? A number of private
U.S. citizens were also perplexed by Standley's remarks, publicly condemned
them, and urged that he be relieved from his post. Abraham Schenck, an activist
in the Beauty Culturist's Union, implored Roosevelt, "When people stand up to
their necks in the blood of their own sons and daughters, in a struggle that is as
much our nation's as theirs, they cannot be expected to jump to high heaven with
lyric joy over the fact, important and appreciated as it is, that we send them some
steel and iron." Joseph Davies thought that however justified Standley's criticisms,
he should have handled the matter discreetly. Sumner Welles regretted Standley's
making an unauthorized pronouncement. The White House was embarrassed that
it had not been consulted beforehand. Of the few people who did approve
Standley's bluster, such as Britain's Clark Kerr, they expressed their agreement
quietly. From London, Harriman related, "Many of my friends here, both British
and American, seniors and juniors, are secretly pleased at the way Standley spoke
out in Moscow even if this was [impolitic]. The feeling is growing here that we
will build trouble for the future if we allow ourselves to be kicked around by
the Russians." [26]

Standley was gratified as Soviet spokesmen began responding to his outburst
by giving coverage in publicity organs to lend-lease plenitude. But his currency
with the Soviets, low to begin with, had sunk to a new nadir. And pundits conceded that his usefulness in Moscow had been demolished. In the United States,
influential people, including General Burns and Davies, advocated his removal.

In April 1943, Burns went to Moscow in his capacity as executive director of
the Lend-Lease Administration, first in the chain of command after Edward Stettinius. A proponent of unconditional aid to the Soviets, Burns reviewed lend-lease
questions with Soviet officials. And he had a chance to examine firsthand the
battle between Standley and Brigadier General Philip Faymonville, the ranking
lend-lease officer in Moscow. The crux of the problem was that Faymonville operated outside of Standley's command structure. As an independent agent, he was
answerable only to his superiors in the lend-lease apparatus and felt no particular
obligation to cooperate with the embassy, especially not on contentious issues.
The chief of these concerned the Soviets' reluctance to share intelligence with the
army attaché, Brigadier General Joseph Michella. In normal circumstances, Soviet
officers might have asked the attaché for information on military matters and in
exchange provided something to him (for example, details about German tank
design or infantry tactics). This unexceptional quid pro quo was undermined by
Faymonville, however. He was under orders from Lend-Lease to provide whatever
military intelligence he could and without qualification. Consequently, Michella
was ignored by Soviet officers in favor of Faymonville, who delivered on a pro
bono basis. This circumstance led to animosity between the two men, with
Standley taking Michella's side. Indeed, it seemed to Standley that on every matter Faymonville backed the Soviets, including their criticism of lend-lease assis-

tance.[27] Like others in the embassy, Standley also viewed Faymonville's political allegiance with suspicion and was concerned that his purported homosexuality was exploited by the Soviets to additional advantage. Despite promises made by Stettinius (during Standley's visit to Washington) that Faymonville would subordinate himself to Standley—and by extension the issue concerning intelligence cooperation with the Soviets would be placed on proper footing—the problem was not satisfactorily resolved. In Moscow, Burns completely bypassed Standley and spent his working hours with Faymonville. They enjoyed the Soviets' confidence while Standley was left to smolder. He told his wife, "General Burns is of the same belief as Faymonville; Russian interests come first, last and all the time; it's hopeless."[28] He wrote a letter of resignation on May 3 and sent it to Roosevelt.

Hardly two weeks had elapsed after Burns's arrival when Joseph Davies, with the personal rank of ambassador, descended on Moscow. In its edition of May 19, *Pravda* cheerfully greeted this "staunch and good friend" of the Soviet peoples. The purpose of his "second mission to Moscow" (as he was wont to call it) was to reassure the Soviet leadership of America's high regard for it and the Red Army and to encourage Stalin to meet with Roosevelt to settle their many problems. At the time, Davies and Roosevelt worried that issues (new and old) were straining Soviet–U.S. relations to the danger point. There was Standley's gaffe that still needed explanation; the Soviets were clamoring more insistently than ever for the second front; they were resentful of being left out of negotiations with the French in North Africa prior to the Anglo–U.S. invasion. Meanwhile, the Soviets continued to withhold military intelligence from embassy personnel and denied them information about economic and agricultural matters. Although not directly related to military operations, the latter was important to branches of the U.S. government trying to coordinate lend-lease.

In the opinion of Cordell Hull, Davies's trip was an outstanding success, as it "broke the ground" for the conferences at Moscow (foreign ministers in October) and Teheran. Dazzled by wartime propaganda depicting the USSR as democratic and Stalin as beneficent (all reinforced by the success of *Mission to Moscow*), Davies had lost whatever critical distance he once had from the Soviet leaders. In a letter written after meeting with Stalin and Molotov, he exclaimed, "Approached with friendship and confidence, I have found that they return it in kind with generosity." He was positively enamored of Stalin's "wisdom and strength." This caliber of character was evidenced to Davies by Stalin's decision (announced during his visit) to dissolve the Comintern, thereby denying Nazi propaganda one of its potent weapons: "the fear of communist aggression by the Soviets in Europe."[29]

The appearance of Davies, a one-time golfing companion of Standley's, was interpreted by the admiral as final confirmation that he was not needed in Moscow or liked in Washington. There was no credible reason why he could not have been trusted to deliver FDR's message on the need of a Big Three meeting. But Roosevelt knew that Standley was practically persona non grata with the Soviets. Therefore, to indicate his seriousness, Roosevelt sent Davies, whom he hoped would replace Standley on a permanent basis. As before, Standley was left out of conversations between Stalin and the current visiting fireman. Tensions were aggravated when the jealous ambassador took obvious delight in the disagreeable time passed by Davies at a Moscow news conference. Reporters Eddie Gilmore (Associated Press) and Quentin Reynolds (*Collier's* magazine) pressed him on the Soviets' withholding of information from U.S. attachés and correspondents. Would Davies be willing to intercede on their behalf with Stalin or Molotov? Would he ask them to remove censorship restrictions? Davies demurred and answered that these questions were outside his bailiwick. He added that such obstructions as did exist to Soviet intelligence were emplaced by local authorities and had nothing to do with decisions made in the Kremlin—a point unpersuasive to his audience. Davies then proceeded to lecture the newsmen. Whenever they reported negative things about the USSR, they were playing into the hands of Hitler and were treasonous against the Allied cause. Could they not muster magnanimity regarding the Soviet ally? They bore, after all, a sacred trust to promote goodwill between the Soviet Union and Western publics. After listening impatiently to these injunctions, the correspondents lost self-control. The conference ended in pandemonium and shouted recriminations.[30] Humiliating to Davies, Standley thereafter forbade any press briefings unless he, the chief diplomatic officer of the United States in Moscow, personally authorized them. The two men had a particularly rough interview after Standley preempted a conference between navy lieutenant Stamm (Davies's nephew and personal secretary) and another batch of U.S. reporters.

Compounding this unpleasantness, Standley reacted violently to Davies's showing the film version of *Mission to Moscow* to Stalin and Soviet and U.S. dignitaries in the Kremlin. The movie repelled him. And he thought Davies was going to extremes to advance a commercial film in whose success he was personally invested. By Standley's code, Davies's hunger for headlines and his ingratiating manner with Soviet officials amounted to abject self-advertisement. If Roosevelt wanted to entrust U.S. diplomacy to such people as Willkie and Davies, Standley snorted to Edward Page, he would gladly yield the field. Shortly after Davies's departure from Moscow, the admiral received FDR's acceptance of his resignation.[31]

He left the USSR in September 1943. During the intervening time, he made a tour to the Urals and Stalingrad. But his interim status was debilitating to U.S. diplomacy. It was impossible for him to pacify the feud between Michella and Faymonville. He was unable to concentrate on any aspect of the worsening situation involving Poles and Soviets, who severed relations in late April following the Katyn revelations. Most ominous of all, ties between Stalin and the English-speaking allies were loosening. Standley was a passive observer when in August Stalin recalled envoys Maisky from London and Litvinov from Washington, ostensibly because he wanted to confer with men personally familiar with the British and U.S. governments. In fact, their recall was a ringing indication of the Soviets' displeasure. (Once returned to Moscow, Maisky and Litvinov were ignored by Stalin.) At the time, rumors abounded in the West that the ambassadors' return was a first step in Soviet–German reconciliation, perhaps presaging a return to the Molotov–Ribbentrop compact.

Following his arrival in America, Standley dutifully campaigned for the Soviet–U.S. alliance, despite his doubts about its long-term prospects. In one stirring address to a Russian War Relief rally in Boston (June 1944), he highlighted both the sweep of Red Army victories and Soviet longing for peace. He concluded with this hopeful assertion: "I say without hesitation that we are on the threshold of postwar collaboration in the fullest sense of the word. The various agreements in the diplomatic field, if they find further implementation during the post-war period, should lay a firm foundation for mutual accord."[32]

Diplomacy Revived

The president's insistence that Davies succeed Standley in Moscow was blunted by Davies's doctors, who argued that a winter in Russia would kill him. Roosevelt thereupon accepted Cordell Hull's recommendation and appointed Harriman.[33] From the president's standpoint, there was much in favor of this second choice, even if Harriman no longer endorsed, as he had in 1941, the policy of "give and give and give" to the USSR. Friends since childhood and neighbors along the scenic Hudson, Harriman and Roosevelt belonged to that patrician element in U.S. politics that liberally mixed notions of noblesse oblige with the progressive mentality. Possessed of vast personal wealth acquired through his and his father's railroad and investment enterprises, Harriman had broken with his family's Republican allegiance; he supported Governor Al Smith in the 1928 presidential election. Harriman worked in the National Recovery Administration during Roosevelt's first term and later was appointed chairman of the Business Advisory Council. Among the most committed of New Dealers, he was also one of the more efficacious.

At ease with those who wielded power, whether economic or political, Harriman was a natural to coordinate lend-lease to Britain in 1941 to 1943. He was on personal terms with Churchill and even during the prime minister's black moods had influence with him. (Clark Kerr in an irate moment labeled Harriman a "champion bumsucker."[34]) During his years in London, he overshadowed the resident U.S. ambassador, John Winant, and was instrumental in forging the Anglo-American alliance. Apart from his two meetings with Stalin (in 1941 with Beaverbrook and 1942 with Churchill), Harriman had known czarist and Soviet leaders since boyhood; he accompanied his father in 1899 on a well-publicized sailing trip that included stops along the Pacific shore of the Russian empire. He met with Soviet officials in subsequent years and in 1926 successfully negotiated terms with Trotsky for a Caucasian mining concession.[35]

Hard working, pragmatic rather than scholarly, and unwilling to engage in the idle banter common to his class, Harriman won the devotion of his staff in Moscow. Kennan, who in principle opposed political appointees occupying ambassadorial positions, once testified:

> His virtues, as I knew him in Moscow, were virtues in the grand manner. He was a towering figure on our Moscow scene, outwardly unassuming but nevertheless commanding in appearance, without petty vanity, intensely serious but never histrionic in his seriousness, imperious only when things or people impeded the performance of his duty. The United States has never had a more faithful public servant.[36]

Appreciative witness was also forthcoming from Bohlen, who briefly worked with Harriman in Moscow; from Major General John Deane, his senior military aide; and from John Melby, at the time new to the Foreign Service.[37]

To the Soviets, Harriman embodied that spirit of capitalism that aroused their profoundest and most contradictory feelings. Ebullient American capital and Harriman were the class enemy. But they were also the agents of modernization and industrial transformation that had earned the grudging admiration of Marx. Harriman's stature as railroad magnate and confidant of Roosevelt assured Soviet officials that they were in direct contact with the "big-business" establishment—which alone, according to their ideological lights, exercised the levers of American power. Reflecting in 1989 on Harriman's decades-long involvement in Soviet–U.S. relations, Gromyko confessed that he was always fair in his dealings with the Kremlin, even when Soviet and U.S. interests diverged.[38]

Harriman believed in 1943 that he could bolster Allied unity and so accepted—somewhat reluctantly—the Moscow assignment. He wondered whether he would become a glorified messenger between Stalin and FDR and cease to play a worthwhile part after leaving London. He was also aware of the continued restrictions and liabilities that frustrated diplomats in Moscow. And he was disturbed by the fragmentation of authority in the embassy (exemplified by the Standley–Faymonville split) and its low morale. As a condition of his acceptance, Harriman demanded that he be given leeway to remodel the mission's organization and that it be understood by all parties that he alone was *the* responsible U.S. diplomat in Russia. He persuaded Roosevelt that one general-grade officer should be placed in charge of the U.S. military contingent. Although he would report to George Marshall in Washington, this officer would be placed firmly under the ambassador's authority. With the army's cooperation, Faymonville, whom Marshall disliked, was reassigned to an ordinance detail in Arkansas. The diligent General John Deane, formerly secretary to the combined chiefs of staff, was put in charge of collaboration with Soviet armed forces and of the military mission, numbering forty-five army, naval, army-air personnel.

For the civilian side of operations, Harriman was adamant that he have the preeminent specialist on the Soviet Union. His investigations led him to Bohlen and Kennan. He would not relent until one or the other of them was assigned to Moscow. Previously acquainted with Bohlen, Harriman would have preferred him. But in the event he was glad to receive Kennan, after his recovery in London from ulcers, and placed him in charge of the embassy's dozen diplomatic officers.[39] Harriman also arranged for his daughter Kathleen (recently graduated from Bennington College) and his personal secretary, Robert Meiklejohn (a reserve naval officer), to assist him in Moscow. Kathleen Harriman worked in the Office of War Information under the direction of Melby. Her irreverent attitude toward diplomacy and sheer zest enlivened mission routine and won her the additional gratitude of her father, whose wife had stayed in America for reasons of health. Once installed in Moscow, Kathleen Harriman and Meiklejohn assumed charge of the embassy's business affairs, which included organizing the ambassador's weekly (and innovative) conference with his Foreign Service and military staff. All of these people, Harriman worked very hard. In Bohlen's judgment, "He is a rather exacting boss and usually keeps his people on duty twenty-four hours a day."[40]

Harriman and Stalin

I

Harriman's attitude toward the Soviet Union shifted gradually during his ambassadorship, nearly imperceptibly to himself and those near him. And whether in moments of high optimism or pessimism, traces of ambivalence always lingered. About Stalin, with whom he met dozens of times, he remained agnostic. He was inclined to view him in the tradition of autocratic Russian leadership rather than part of an apostolic succession following from Marx, Engels, and Lenin. Stalin's essential character he judged enigmatic.[41] Unfailingly courteous to Roosevelt's envoy and at times disarming, the dictator impressed Harriman with his competence. This was demonstrated by his relocation of Soviet industries beyond the Urals, his detailed knowledge of military matters, and a surprising sensitivity (so said Harriman) to the morale of the civilian population, including the non-Russian minorities. Yet Stalin was the same creature who bullied the Poles, denounced the Anglo-Americans in 1942 and 1943 as craven, and had earlier sentenced millions of his countrymen to concentration camps or firing squads. Three decades after the war, Harriman recorded:

> It is hard for me to reconcile the courtesy and consideration that he showed me personally with the ghastly cruelty of his wholesale liquidations. Others, who did not know him personally, see only the tyrant in Stalin. I saw the other side as well—his high intelligence, the fantastic grasp of detail, his shrewdness and the surprising human sensitivity that he was capable of showing, at least in the war years. I found him better informed than Roosevelt, more realistic than Churchill, in some ways the most effective of the war leaders. At the same time he was, of course, a murderous tyrant. I must confess that for me Stalin remains the most inscrutable and contradictory character I have known—and leave the final judgment to history.[42]

In response to warnings offered by Standley, Harriman answered that he knew the situation in Moscow would be difficult, but Stalin could be handled. The Soviets were "only human." To Roosevelt, even before his nomination had won Senate confirmation, Harriman opined that Stalin desired an understanding with Washington, if only to ensure postwar security and Soviet reconstruction. In the heady days of alliance solidarity following Teheran, Harriman himself supported the idea of providing lend-lease assistance to Moscow for reconstructive purposes. At one point, he counseled that Soviet imports connected to rebuilding would be important for the United States after the war; they would help soften the employment crisis and dislocations bound to follow from reduced defense production. The intransigence of Stalin over Poland and the Baltic republics, his dark suspicions, and instances of uncooperation destroyed what remained in 1944 of Harriman's commitment to unrestricted aid, however. Soviet unwillingness to account for ways in which certain lend-lease items were used—sometimes wastefully, Harriman inferred, or for purposes unrelated to the anti-German war—also quickened his doubts. Earlier U.S. largess had made sense when every means had to be exhausted to ensure Soviet participation in the war. But once the initiative had switched to Allied advantage and it was clear that the Soviets would share in the spoils, Harriman decided they should cooperate more agreeably with the West—a conclusion to which Deane and Kennan had earlier arrived. Lend-lease ought to be calibrated to the fluctuations in Soviet behavior and Anglo–U.S. relations with the USSR placed on a strict quid pro quo basis.

Still, even in late 1945, as the wartime alliance rapidly came apart, he thought that it was desirable and possible for the United States to preserve working relations with Moscow. It was his conviction, given the physical damage and casualties inflicted by Germany, that the "fantastically backward" USSR could not pursue a militarily aggressive policy against America even if Stalin wanted. Harriman actually attributed Soviet bluster to weakness and nervousness about the U.S. monopoly of atomic weaponry. In any case, as he told Dean Acheson (October 1945), if the United States handled its end "reasonably intelligently," the two countries could achieve a modus vivendi.[43]

II

It had been with reasonable intelligence that Harriman made his representations during 1943 to 1945 with Deane and Kennan to the Soviets. He was also careful not to divulge (either overtly or indirectly) any of the temper that occasionally flared between the British and the Americans. The most significant such tempest to involve Harriman followed the Churchill–Stalin meetings of October 1944. He persuaded the prime minister—while massaging his pride—to drop the idea to which he had just gotten Stalin's assent: the division of eastern Europe into Soviet and Anglo-U.S. spheres of influence (Bulgaria and Romania to the Soviets; Greece for the West; Hungary and Yugoslavia to be divided equally). Harriman pointed out that the Americans were not party to the negotiations and could not commit themselves to this summary division of the Balkans. Consequently, neither Churchill nor Stalin ever raised their idea with Roosevelt and at Yalta endorsed instead the Declaration on Liberated Europe, which reaffirmed the Big Three's commitment to principles of democracy in international life. Neither did Harriman betray to the Soviets strongly felt reservations in the embassy about aspects of Roosevelt's wartime policy. Unconditional surrender, for one, was abhorrent to Deane and Kennan. They believed that it encouraged German resistance to greater exertions even though the war's outcome was obvious. On this subject Harriman appears to have been undecided, but the point stands that neither his equivocation nor the dissent of the others was communicated to any Soviet official.[44] As to issues directly touching on Soviet–U.S. relations, Harriman's approach was to Moscow's liking. He was never fawning. He was nonideological and businesslike. Irrespective of whether they agreed with him, Stalin and Molotov seldom doubted where he stood on an issue. As the occasion required, he was also able to bring into play a mix of tact and forthrightness and the confidence that Roosevelt supported him. In the minor offices of his ambassadorship, Harriman also comported himself well. His physical stamina allowed him to survive nocturnal (midnight and beyond) festivities in the Kremlin—often convened to celebrate a Soviet or an Allied battlefield feat. In his deliberate way, Harriman was also alert and adequately prepared whenever called by Stalin for emergency consultation.

The difficulty of coalition politics that vexed Standley's ambassadorship was naturally present in Harriman's. But he was more self-assured in grappling with it. He forcefully answered complaints about the delayed western front with pointed reminders. The Soviets were being willful if they discounted the burden placed on U.S. manpower by the Pacific war, to say nothing of American costs sustained along other fronts: the air war against Germany, campaigns in North Africa and Italy, and the massive production of weaponry, including lend-lease supplies. Regarding lend-lease, Harriman warned Molotov and Anastas Mikoyan, commissar for foreign trade, that U.S. assistance should not be viewed as limitless or automatic. At the minimum, Soviet military intelligence must be forthcoming. Harriman's anxiety that lend-lease items fell victim to carelessness—diesel engines left to rust at Russian docks, a Detroit tire factory transferred to the USSR but left unassembled—and that Soviet appetite for American weapons exceeded battlefield needs was not shared by Hopkins. Still, Harriman's protestations in 1944 to the Soviets about their wasteful habits caused them to pause, as did the Harriman–Hopkins disagreement. They surely wondered what the future would hold should the ailing Hopkins be forced to leave government.

In other areas of Allied coordination, Harriman and Deane prevailed on Stalinist officials to grant (admittedly limited) facilities and information. The most significant concerned their decision to make airbases on Russian and Ukrainian territory available to U.S. bombers operating out of the Mediterranean. The planes were allowed to refuel and reload at bases such as Poltava, striking German targets as they shuttled back and forth. This operation, code-named FRANTIC (October 1943–June 1944), served as a symbol of Soviet–U.S. cooperation and, had it lasted longer, might have caused substantial aerial damage from the east; at the time, the Soviet air force lacked the strategic capability to bomb Germany. But FRANTIC was abruptly ended after a German surprise air raid on Poltava destroyed fifty Flying Fortresses on the ground (while Soviet antiaircraft batteries and Yak interceptors proved worthless). In addition to FRANTIC, Harriman and Deane helped orchestrate a program (short-lived) of intelligence exchange between William Donovan's OSS and the NKVD. And the ambassador personally obtained from Soviet sources, once from Stalin's own lips, reports on the disposition of Tokyo's naval forces and the decline in Japanese morale.[45]

As to the postwar future: Harriman was puzzled that his talks with Soviet leaders about U.S. assistance for reconstruction never got beyond tentative soundings and dissolved into a muddle of misunderstandings. Mikoyan had first raised the issue with the ambassador just before Teheran. Encouraged by Roosevelt, he then pursued the matter, but the Soviets dropped it after a show of enthusiasm. They did not exhibit interest at Yalta or Potsdam, and only belatedly, just before Harriman left Moscow in January 1946, did Stalin ask about the U.S. attitude toward a relief program. Probably the Soviets were conflicted: on the one hand, aid was legitimate, if partial, payment for the disproportionate share of warfare borne by the Red Army. On the other hand, the ambassador's advocacy of accountability for lend-lease supplies bode ill for America's dispensing of peacetime aid. Harriman concluded that the tradition of Soviet suspicion decided the issue—though the temptation to seek U.S. funds in 1945 had been considerable.[46]

He showed himself to particular advantage when, following Roosevelt's death (April 12, 1945), Stalin asked what the Soviets might do to assure Truman of Moscow's cooperative attitude. Harriman answered that Stalin should drop his hitherto stubborn opposition to Molotov's attending the San Francisco Conference (called for late April to found the United Nations). Stalin immediately agreed. No more than a gesture of goodwill, the foreign minister's presence in San Francisco lent the proceedings an additional aura of solemnity.

Harriman's most dramatic success centered on the future orientation of Japan. At midnight on August 10, 1945, just after the bombing of Nagasaki and two days after the entry of Soviet troops into the Far Eastern theater, Molotov summoned him and Clark Kerr to the Kremlin. The minister began by discussing Japan's imminent surrender and the last-ditch effort of hardliners to preserve the emperor's prerogatives. As the conversation progressed, it became clear that the Soviets were in no hurry for the war to end; the Red Army was making rapid advances (170 kilometers, said Molotov) into Manchuria. At this point, the meeting was interrupted by Kennan, who burst in with the latest version—just received by cable—of unconditional surrender that the United States was forcing on Japan. Following their examination of the text, Harriman urged Molotov to subscribe to the newest language of Japanese surrender. At 2:00 A.M., after consultation with "his government" (a euphemism for Stalin), Molotov presented a written statement to the U.S. and British ambassadors that associated the USSR with their position. But this statement also asserted that pending an affirmative reply of surrender from Tokyo, the Allies should reach agreement among themselves "on the candidacy or candidates for representation of the Allied High Command to which the Japanese Emperor and Japanese Government are to be subordinated." The import of this phrase was that the Soviets reserved for themselves influence in approving the men and organization of the occupation regime. Stalin and Molotov evidently had in mind for Japan something resembling the situation in Germany, where the victors shared in the responsibility—and fruits—of administering the country. Harriman responded emphatically, saying that Truman would not allow the USSR to exercise a veto in the selection of the Allied supreme commander, in which connection he mentioned General Douglas MacArthur. Molotov answered that it was possible that two officers could properly be named, in which case Marshal Vasielevsky might share the honors with MacArthur. Harriman exploded. The Soviet idea was "absolutely inadmissible." Nevertheless, said Molotov, the Soviet position was reasonable; the ambassador should transmit its substance to Washington irrespective of whether he approved. Recovering his temper, Harriman replied that the United States had waged a costly war in the Pacific for four years. In doing so, it had also prevented Japan from attacking the vulnerable Soviet Far East. It was therefore just that the Soviets allow the Americans alone to choose the supreme commander. "Mr. Molotov somewhat heatedly [responded]," in the notes of Edward Page, who accompanied Harriman to the Kremlin, "by stating that he did not wish to reply to Mr. Harriman's remarks. For by so doing he would have to make comparison with the European War."[47]

In the end, after further conference with "his government," Molotov withdrew the offending language from the Soviet statement. In doing so, he weakened any future claim that Stalin might make for sharing in the Japanese occupation. But for Harriman, it is likely that the United States would have become ensnared in protracted and acrimonious negotiations with the Kremlin about occupation policy and a Soviet zone.[48] Instead, the cause of an exclusive American position in post-war Japan was advanced and an early Soviet challenge rebuked (though others followed V-J Day).

III

Simultaneous with instances of agreement between the embassy and the Soviets in 1943 to 1945 (e.g., on the modalities of Japanese surrender and occupation), the two also waged sharp conflicts. The aggregate of these constituted a cold war within the larger world war. From it they sprang and upon it they mischievously played. Harriman's task was to confine this dispute to manageable proportions.[49]

The major problems between the mission and its hosts fell into two distinct categories: military-operational and diplomatic-political. The former stemmed from the need to coordinate Allied land and air operations, as Soviet forces from the east and Anglo-U.S. forces from the west converged on Germany. Agreements had to be struck by Deane and implemented by theater commanders to prevent different Allied units from accidentally clashing. As it was, a rash of episodes occurred, including the inadvertent strafing of Red Army soldiers in Yugoslavia by U.S. planes, as well as midair combat and collisions. Unfortunate as they were, these accidents were consistent with the ordinary hazards of war. Nevertheless, they led to bitter recriminations, especially on the Soviet side, which suffered most of the injuries.

The repatriation of prisoners of war was an altogether more delicate matter. Contrary to agreement that Harriman and Deane helped negotiate, Soviet military authorities were, with individual exceptions, unhelpful in locating or assisting the thousands of American POWs who fell to their responsibility as the Red Army entered Poland and Germany. The Soviets let most of the U.S. soldiers fend for themselves, instead of treating their medical needs and providing transportation to authorized points of transit. As part of the POW number straggled into Moscow and the embassy's refuge, having completed treks on foot of hundreds of miles, Harriman and Deane sent impassioned protests to the Defense and Foreign Ministries. They responded by flatly denying that Soviet field commanders were guilty of neglecting or abandoning their U.S. comrades. No less than Stalin declared that former POWs were being cared for, even though conditions of warfare and rapid advance produced inevitable problems. In any event, he charged, the soldiers were in better keeping than Soviet POWs who wound up under American occupation.[50] Owing to Roosevelt's reluctance to press on the POW controversy, Harriman dropped the subject; still, Soviet callousness in this matter was another indication to him that postwar cooperation would be difficult.[51]

As for diplomatic-political matters: in discussing Poland with Molotov and Stalin, Harriman invoked the authority of domestic opinion in the United States and the presumed influence on electoral politics of Polish-American voters. One can only imagine how this appeal struck Stalin. He surely dismissed it as a brand of rhetoric meant to impress the gullible but as unrelated to the real designs of U.S. capitalism. This viewed Poland as an area in which to invest surplus capital and, over the long term, as a point from which to spring aggression against the USSR. In the meantime, Harriman attempted to encourage practical arrangements between the Polish government in London and Moscow. These were entirely frustrated, however. Soviet intransigence on Katyn and sponsorship of the Lublin alternative (composed of figures hostile to Stanislaw Mikolajeczk) demoralized Harriman. As for Katyn itself, Kathleen Harriman and Melby accompanied a Soviet investigating commission to the site of burial. Despite their doubts about the investigation's impartiality, they were reluctant to challenge the Soviet "conclusions" closely. And the ambassador accepted their view that it would be unwise to dispute the findings of America's ally on such an extraordinary subject. He reported in late January 1944, "In all probability the massacre was perpetrated by the Germans."[52]

If there was a distinct turning point in his thinking, it occurred in August and September 1944, when the Soviets made no move to rescue the Polish Home Army as it rose against German occupation in Warsaw. Harriman was staggered by the spectacle of the Red Army, within striking distance of the capital, standing idle as the Polish fighters were slaughtered. And he was offended by the Kremlin's refusal to let Anglo-U.S. planes use Soviet bases as part of a resupply effort to Bor-Komorowski's troops. At this time, Kennan urged that lend-lease aid be discontinued unless or until the Soviets cooperated in the relief of Warsaw. As it was, Harriman's and Deane's pleas that they do something for the underground army—or at least cooperate with the air-bases scheme—were rejected by Stalin. He called the Poles adventurers who were caught in a situation created by their own recklessness. It would be folly for the Red Army to rush its assault on Warsaw before adequate provision had been made for resupply and reinforcement. As to Anglo-U.S. use of Soviet bases, this was out of the question as the planes' safety could not be guaranteed against attacks like the raid on Poltava. This rebuff, signaling Soviet scorn for Anglo-U.S. opinion, killed Harriman's residual hope for a harmonious postwar order.[53]

Harriman and the Presidents

That Roosevelt respected Harriman's counsel in affairs involving the United States with Britain and the USSR is a given of the World War II literature. Present at every meeting among the Big Three, he regularly offered advice and analysis. He helped draft the Declaration on Liberated Europe and had a hand in producing the protocol at Yalta, which acceded to Soviet territorial demands in East Asia (e.g., control over Chinese ports Arthur and Darien) in exchange for Stalin's pledge to enter the anti-Japanese war.

In his reports from Moscow, Harriman laced his optimism—one might call it "official optimism," as that attitude was practically mandated by Hopkins and FDR—about the Grand Alliance with increasingly specific details concerning Soviet ambition. Only a week before Roosevelt died, Harriman cabled him:

> We now have ample proof that the Soviet Government views all matters from the standpoint of their own selfish interests. . . . We must clearly recognize that the Soviet program is the establishment of totalitarianism, ending personal liberty and democracy as we know and respect it. In addition the Soviet Government is attempting to penetrate through the Communist parties supported by it the countries of western Europe with the hope of expanding Soviet influence in the internal and external affairs of these countries.

In another cable, delivered a few days later, Harriman warned that words like *democracy* "have entirely different meanings to the Soviets than to us. . . . Whatever may have been in their minds at Yalta, it now seems that they feel they can force us to acquiesce in their policies."[54] These interpretations of Stalinist policy heightened Roosevelt's anxiety about Soviet intentions. Perhaps, as some scholars contend, the president was rethinking his Soviet policy in April 1945 and would have adopted a tougher line had he lived.[55]

Less widely known than his influence on Roosevelt's evolving views on the USSR are Harriman's doubts concerning the president. However confident he was in FDR's New Deal and areas of wartime leadership, notably lend-lease, he despaired over his handling of east European problems. This bungling did not flow, in Harriman's opinion, from Roosevelt's peculiar blend of Wilsonian idealism and pragmatic streak, which might have created a disjointed policy. Instead, according to Harriman, FDR was simply uninterested in the fate of far-away east Europeans, apart from the indirect role they played in American electoral politics. In Harriman's words, autumn 1944: "[The president] consistently shows very little interest in East European matters except as they affect sentiment in America." During an earlier 1944 visit to Washington, Harriman had already noted that FDR wanted to avoid embroilment in Polish–Soviet matters at any time before the November election and hoped that Stalin and the London Poles might reach satisfactory understanding in the meantime. Even after the election, Roosevelt displayed indifference to these issues, as they seemed to him intractable and less susceptible to U.S. influence than even those in Asia. And when FDR did reluctantly focus his attention on Poland, his ideas struck Harriman as silly. For example, the president suggested that Stalin might allow Lvov to remain a capitalist city within a socialist Ukrainian framework; farmers could sell their produce at urban markets for rubles. Taken aback by this idea, Harriman tried to educate Roosevelt on the reality of Soviet administration: "I [told] him that [Stalin's] government took most of the farm produce and that distribution could not possibly be worked out, aside from all the political difficulties. I carried it as far as I could until he became annoyed that I was unwilling to dream with him." Harriman was also upset by Roosevelt's merry confidence in his ability to arbitrate a Soviet–Polish boundary settlement and his assumption that Stalin would accept his good offices. It was in a sober mood that Harriman wrote after White House meetings: "I do not believe that I have convinced the President of the importance of a vigilant firm policy in dealing with the political aspects in various Eastern European countries. . . . The Department, however, is fully alive to this necessity unless we wish to turn Eastern Europe and Central Europe over to complete Soviet influence if not domination." Yet it was Roosevelt who set the main policy course, and Harriman was shaken when the president told him (May 1944) that he "didn't care whether the countries bordering Russia became communized."[56]

His annoyance with Roosevelt's attitude toward Soviet–east European relations made Harriman discover additional fault in minor matters. In his view, FDR accepted with unseemly alacrity Stalin's invitation to reside in the Soviet diplomatic compound during the Teheran Conference. Acceptance of this offer, made ostensibly to ensure Roosevelt's safety from German assassins said to have infiltrated the city, struck Harriman as the undignified opening in FDR's courtship of Stalin. The same misplaced ardor animated Roosevelt's remarks to Stalin about Britain's presence in the Asian subcontinent and the need to reform India "from the bottom, somewhat on the Soviet line." Harriman also thought Roosevelt ill-advised not to clarify the reasons for his unconditional surrender policy when (again at Teheran) Stalin broached the issue.[57] (Very likely, he was testing the president's resolve to fight Germany and was looking for evidence indicating that Roosevelt might seek a separate deal with Hitler.)

Because he thought Roosevelt had been overly indulgent of Stalin, Harriman was at first heartened when Truman showed himself to be less forgiving. Ironically, however, it soon became apparent to him that his task as ambassador was to pull moderately in the opposite direction. Rather than sound alarms about Soviet policy, he tried in the remainder of his tenure to smooth the jagged rhetoric and actions that marked the end of the anti-German alliance. He thought Truman's famous treatment of Molotov in late April 1945 in connection with laggard implementation of Yalta was overdone. And he was disturbed by the abrupt cancelling of lend-lease shipments to the USSR in May and by its impact on Soviet confidence in Washington. With William Clayton, assistant secretary of state for economic affairs, Harriman persuaded Truman to countermand the order of cancellation. But by then, the propaganda and psychological damage had been done; it appeared that U.S. policy would henceforth try to extract political concessions from the Soviets in Europe by economic pressure.[58]

To quell the distrust beginning to swamp relations between the two countries, Harriman prevailed upon his desperately sick friend, Harry Hopkins, to go to Moscow. There this proven supporter of the Soviet war effort might reassure Stalin of Washington's good faith and find means of steadying the coalition. Once Truman was persuaded of the wisdom in sending Hopkins—a sizable accomplishment in view of the president's doubts about the man and the errand—he made his way to Moscow and held six meetings in May and June with Stalin. These reviewed troubling issues: the future organization of Poland; the fate of Polish guerrilla leaders in Soviet captivity; lend-lease curtailments; the amount and type of German reparations. Questions about China, Korea, and the United Nations were also examined. The talks, conducted in an atmosphere reminiscent of Teheran's cordialness, demonstrated the reluctance of the two governments to push events to the breaking point. Yet the meetings' inconclusiveness also exposed the gulf of conflicting interest and interpretation. Of Poland, Harriman told Truman, just after Hopkins's departure from Moscow:

> I am afraid Stalin does not and never will fully understand our interest in a free Poland as a matter of principle. He is a realist in all of his actions and it is hard for him to appreciate our faith in abstract principles. It is difficult for him to understand why we should want to interfere with Soviet policy in a country like Poland which he considers so important to Russia's security unless we have some ulterior motive.

More telling still of the USSR's new direction, Harriman reported, "[Stalin] aggressively indicated that if we did not wish to deal on a friendly basis with the Soviet Union she was strong enough to look after herself." [59] Nothing that occurred at Potsdam a short time later (July 17–August 2) resolved any of the issues addressed in Hopkins's visit.

Through the remainder of 1945, Harriman was rarely in Moscow, where daily direction of the embassy resided with Kennan. The ambassador became intimately involved with Truman as one of his foreign policy advisers (despite his uneasiness and then antagonism toward the new secretary of state, James Byrnes). Carried by the flood tide of Cold War that eventually swept Washington, Harriman (after a brief stint as envoy to Britain, April–September 1946) held a series of security-related posts under Truman. These included directorship of the Mutual Security Agency, chairmanship of the North Atlantic Commission on Defense Plans, and work on the Marshall Plan. Yet he was never a cold warrior of the extreme ilk. He felt that Soviet leaders were not intent on anything so unfeasible as Europe's military conquest; he remained confident in the wisdom of diplomacy even while not eschewing applications of countervailing force to points of strategic importance (as in Iran, 1946; Berlin, 1948; Korea, 1950).

Truman developed abiding respect for Harriman during the period of his service and in 1956 supported him for the Democratic nomination for president against Adlai Stevenson. Truman argued that his man was uniquely experienced in foreign affairs and qualified to deal with Cold War dilemmas. Eleanor Roosevelt, a Stevenson partisan and the party's grande dame, reminded activists at the nominating convention that Truman had possessed no international background when *he* assumed the mantle of office in 1945.

Cold War Tocsins

Truman's commitment to Cold War in 1946 and the emergence of a consensus that would support policies in subsequent years—Marshall Plan, NATO, Korean intervention—were slower to crystallize than Winston Churchill approved. To the former prime minister, unceremoniously removed from office by voters in July 1945, the wartime coalition was disintegrating while Byrnes and others pursued a policy of conciliation. Fidelity to such a line, Churchill taught, was nonsense in view of Soviet aggression: pressure on Turkey for access through the Black Sea straits, unwillingness to evacuate from the northern sector in Iran, support of Mao's revitalized insurgency in China, and the determination of Soviet agents to assist local communists in countries occupied by the Red Army. In the lugubrious tones of his Iron Curtain speech (March 5, 1946), Churchill warned against Soviet ambition and the necessity of Anglo-American concert:

> If the Western democracies stand together in strict adherence to the principles of the United Nations Charter, their influence for furthering those principles will be immense and no one is likely to molest them. If, however, they become divided or falter in their duty, and if these all-important years are allowed to slip away, then indeed catastrophe may overwhelm us all.[60]

At the time Churchill made these pronouncements, he and those like-minded in the United States had to counter a cascade of appeals for accommodation with the USSR. These were issued by Henry Wallace, supported (inconsistently) by Walter Lippmann, and nourished by popular hopes from the war years that a new world order would emerge—premised on the Four Freedoms and grounded in the realities of Grand Alliance cooperation. As for the official Soviet view, it was expressed in Stalin's speech of February 9, 1946. He declared that contradictions in the imperialist camp (Britain versus America) and the incompatibility of communism and capitalism dictated socialist vigilance and willingness to resist aggression.

As the governments of the wartime coalition fell out nervously, their diplomats played potentially vital roles. They were in a position not only to explain their national attitudes, but also to instruct them. Unluckily for the USSR, its representation in Washington and reporting were mediocre. This condition was not surprising, given the general type of Soviet envoy at the time. His political imagination and initiative had been discouraged for years by purges and by Stalinist shibboleths purporting to explain the capitalist world. In the words of Frank Roberts, Britain's chargé d'affaires in Moscow, the Soviet diplomatic service was composed of frightened people, who dared not "say anything which might cause offense to the Kremlin even if they are themselves able to form an objective view of the countries to which they are posted."[61] Such was the case with Gromyko's successor in Washington, Ambassador Nikolai Novikov. He parroted ideas already tiresomely reiterated by his superiors in Moscow. Without a hint of reflection on how Soviet actions might be interpreted abroad, he told Molotov (September 1946) that capital in America was compelling the country to strive for world supremacy. Its achievement would come at the expense not only of Britain and other imperialist states, but also of Soviet security. He emphasized, too, that the United States was helping to rebuild Germany for sinister purposes. And he warned that continued U.S. monopoly of the atomic bomb and Truman's deployment of military and naval forces in Europe and Asia portended the decision to destroy the USSR as the sole obstacle to Wall Street's global domination.[62]

Belonging to a better category of analysis than Novikov's was the dispatch prepared by Kennan in Moscow in February 1946, the so-called Long Telegram. Written in response to a query originating in the Treasury Department, curious about Soviet reasons for refusing memberships in the International Monetary Fund and World Bank, this report was destined to become a seminal Cold War document. Neither distinguished by literary verve (a result of the telegraphic medium in which it was composed) nor original (when viewed in the full perspective of Kennan's writings), this report catapulted its author from obscurity in the Foreign Service to positions of prominence in Washington. Due to the patronage of Secretary of the Navy James Forrestal, on whom the telegram made a deep impression, Kennan became deputy commandant for foreign affairs at the National War College and then director of the State Department's Policy Planning Staff.[63]

Stripped of its lapses into emotional language, the essence of Kennan's report was to explain Soviet attitude toward the outside world and Stalin's foreign policy. In so doing, Kennan stressed that beneath the ideological pose and fervent rhetoric, the Soviets viewed the world in much the way as their pre-1917 predecessors. This tradition stemmed from instinctive insecurity and a sense of inferiority toward the West. For Stalin and his colleagues, Marxism was a "fig leaf of their moral and intellectual respectability" behind which they justified oppression at home and sought political—not necessarily military—expansion abroad. Kennan added that the Soviet Communist party, though an instrument of Stalinist tyranny, was no longer a source of ideas or stimulation in the USSR. Yet this condition would not prevent Stalin from exploiting foreign communist parties to promote Soviet interests. Through these parties, as well as disparate agencies such as international labor and pan-Slavic organizations, the Soviets would try to weaken the West and hamstring recovery in nonsocialist Europe. To check the challenge posed by this power—inferior to that of the West and not backed by martial aggressiveness comparable to Nazi Germany—Kennan hoped that Truman would educate the public about the quality of Moscow–Washington relations: henceforth, dealings with the Soviets should be placed on a matter-of-fact basis and reciprocity. Meanwhile, the United States should not shrink from providing guidance to a war-weary world; otherwise, the Stalinists would fill the power vacuum in Europe and elsewhere.[64]

The significance of the Long Telegram and of its sponsorship by Forrestal (he distributed copies to members of Truman's cabinet) was that it filled a conceptual gap and amounted to timely analysis. Albeit overstated to arouse Washington from its intellectual lethargy (so judged by Kennan from Moscow), the report contained a plausible interpretation of why the Soviets were not enamored of America's international agenda and were unlikely to cooperate with it. At the time of the telegram's arrival in Washington, nothing approaching a Cold War consensus had formed in Truman's government. Some officials objected strenuously to Kennan's presentation. One was General Lucius Clay, U.S. military governor in Germany, who was enjoying decent relations with his Soviet counterpart. But Kennan's depiction of Kremlin leaders and their world view was embraced by Forrestal and others in Truman's immediate orbit and hastened the hardening of their attitude. Ignoring the subtler side of Kennan's report (that the Soviets were eager to avoid a showdown with the West), Forrestal declared, "We must prepare for war." By the end of 1946, the effect of Kennan's telegram, Churchill's warnings, and Clark Clifford and George Elsey's report on a Soviet threat confirmed Truman's instincts in the need to treat firmly with Stalin.[65]

*   *   *   *

The ultimate question in the immediate aftermath of World War II was whether European society could rescue and reaffirm meaningful standards of civilized conduct. The ceaseless indignation to them, exemplified by Auschwitz, suggested not. Yet reminders of a better past and hints of a hopeful future were even then discernible. In the case of the USSR, where victory against Germany was paid for by the lives of 25 million people, the "mighty Russian word" (Akhmatova's imagery) was still preserved. Its transmittal in a form "free and pure" to future generations was assured, as were the ancient ethical-cultural norms of which it was custodian. As for the practical rewards of Soviet victory, they were palpable in the breadth of Russian army occupation, reaching farther west than at any time since Alexander's troops had marched into Paris following Napoleon's defeat. It was this circumstance and the political realities radiating from it that would dominate the attention of U.S. ambassadors in Moscow for the next several decades.

Any of them who pondered the diplomatic performance in 1941 to 1945 must have been struck by its unevenness. At the level of highest authority stood Roosevelt, whose attitude toward Stalin alternated goodwill with flashes of insight into Soviet totalitarianism. At times, Roosevelt's public comments about Stalin suggested a naïveté worthy of Neville Chamberlain and his views on Hitler. In each case, it appeared that the representative of bourgeois respectability lacked the intellect to fathom the radically ruthless man with whom he dealt. Yet in the case of FDR at least, a shrewd calculus also operated: appeasement during the war of Soviet territorial demands in the Baltics, Poland, and elsewhere was small price to pay for an alliance of expediency, the success of which was promised by the USSR's mammoth military effort.[66]

To a degree, Harriman's ambivalence toward Stalin shadowed that of FDR's, even though he rejected Roosevelt's fanciful ideas about making the Soviet Union into a genuine postwar partner. As for Harriman's ambassadorship in Moscow, it illustrated what a well-organized mission can achieve when taken seriously by Washington. The rapidity of neither modern communication nor modern transportation, as they existed in the 1940s, obviated the need for the refracting medium of the skillful diplomat's style and philosophy, as exemplified by Harriman and Kennan. Under their leadership, the embassy had risen in stature from the bleak Standley period to a place of centrality in interpreting the Soviet Union and devising policy toward it. Yet even as the Truman government began in 1945 and 1946 to formulate its Soviet policy, many of the propositions advanced by Harriman and Kennan about the ambiguous nature of Soviet military power (large army but battered cities and economy) were not closely read by a cabinet unsettled by the actions of NKVD and communist faithful in eastern Europe. Harriman and Kennan (Deane, too) advocated a tactical change of emphasis in contending with the Soviets, not an unrelenting Cold War. So also the Kennan–Harriman emphasis on the USSR as a conventional great state motivated primarily by shifts in the balance of power, not a revolutionary experiment working to overthrow the entire capitalist order, was lost in the gathering din of Cold War hyperbole. The ascendant view in Truman's circle in 1946 was expressed by Clark Clifford, the president's special counsel. He urged that the United States prepare for all contingencies, including a "horrible" war against the Marxist-Leninist USSR. Such a war might erupt with sudden swiftness.[67]

7

Neither War Nor Peace

The Soviet Union confronted daunting tasks of reconstruction during the last years of Stalin. Drought and famine in the Ukraine (1946–1947), the disproportionately high number of old people and youngsters in the labor force, and the numerical imbalance between men and women of child-rearing age (in 1946, 52 million women versus 31 million men) were the most visible signs of national distress. Fought over by German and Soviet armies, expanses of western Russia and the Ukraine were devoid of habitation and agricultural life.[1] Through cajolery and terror, the regime forced its subjects to salvage these areas while reestablishing industrial production and repairing the physical foundations of such devastated cities as Leningrad, Kiev, and Stalingrad. This work was shouldered by a population simultaneously grieving for its war dead and improvising for millions left maimed and inadequately sheltered. Nonetheless, the fortitude of the Soviet nations combined with state necessity to effect a titanic feat in postwar rebuilding. By the mid-1950s, the USSR's principal urban centers, coal and steel processing, and major industries had recovered, though agricultural production continued to lag.

The success of this effort, however partial or unsatisfactory in comparison with that achieved in Western Europe, was all the more remarkable when one considers that the national leadership in 1946 to 1952 was weakened by moral pathologies. It was as though the furies of Mikhail Bulgakov's satanic Moscow (*The Master and Margarita*) had sprung to life to cause new afflictions: the stultifying and xenophobic *Zhdanovshchina,* the triumph of frauds in science such as Trofim Lysenko and ghoulish investigations into brain research and phrenology, vengeful anti-Semitism (claiming even Molotov's wife), the incarceration of hundreds of thousands of returning POWs, the Leningrad affair, the doctors' plot, and preparations (aborted) for another violent party purge in 1953.[2]

In these years, Stalin was the victim of severe infirmities. The Yugoslav communist Milovan Djilas was distraught in his 1948 conference in the Kremlin to see the "conspicuous signs of [Stalin's] senility. No amount of respect and love for his person, which I stubbornly nurtured inside myself, was able to erase that realization from my consciousness."[3] Gluttony, inanity, and a lack of intellectual focus were additional indications to Djilas of his idol's decline. The sight of terror-stricken sycophants surrounding him, competing for his favor and scheming to succeed him, only reinforced Djilas's revulsion. The servility of Stalin's lieutenants equally impressed Ambassador Alan Kirk, who made this observation (1949) after meeting him and the new foreign minister, Andrei Vyshinsky: "[Stalin] certainly dominates the situation here, and Vyshinsky was hopping around like a pea on a hot griddle to do his slightest wish."[4] Thus the ravages of old age, combined with the moral corrosiveness of absolute power and an acute sense of his country's vulnerability, made Stalin and his regime more fearsome and wary than any time in Soviet history.

As for foreign policy: its most distinctive feature during Stalin's last years was its brutality in lands directly subject to Moscow's control, as in Eastern Europe following the 1948 Soviet–Yugoslav split. There the liquidation of people who would not comply with Stalinist dictate proceeded apace with the imposition of Moscow's version of socialism. The new civilization that emerged was not only "stupefying and loathsome" (Czeslaw Milosz's phrase), but also fragile, of dubious long-term value to the USSR.[5] Hungary, Poland, Czechoslovakia, and other countries eventually encompassed by the Warsaw Pact were allied to the USSR in name only and by duress. The second outstanding trait of external policy was its caution in dealing with the United States. Stalin's rhetorical bravado and shrewdness did not outweigh U.S. assets: monopoly on atomic weaponry (lasting to August 1949), possession of superior naval and air power, and command of an unscathed, superproductive economy. Intensifying the overall power imbalance, the Marshall Plan and the founding of NATO helped confine Soviet influence in Europe to the poorer zone. Except for the ill-fated Berlin blockade, Stalin showed no eagerness to challenge the postwar order in Europe or in other regions of U.S. supremacy. In Asia, he lent embarrassingly little support to fraternal parties, lest they entangled the USSR in hopeless conflicts with the US—hence, Soviet coolness to Mao Tse-tung during the final phase of Chinese civil war and later absence from hostilities in Korea.

In 1946 to 1952, neither the United States nor the Soviet Union sustained any effort to resolve the major questions between them: nuclear weaponry, Germany's future, Eastern Europe. These were placed on glacial hold. As an instrument of policy, diplomacy was neglected. Its nadir was reached in October 1952, when after careless words, Ambassador George Kennan was declared persona non grata by Stalin's government.[6] As it was, U.S. envoys in Moscow felt slight encouragement from their hosts (or Truman) to advance the cause of conciliation. Celebrations of Allied victories marked by cannonade, and friendly demonstrations by Soviet citizens in front of the U.S. embassy as on V-E Day, were replaced by official tirades against "nefarious" U.S. diplomats. Daily life in the embassy proceeded in an atmosphere of sullen isolation.

Diplomacy Postponed

The vocational background of Washington's two ambassadors in the late 1940s confirmed the Soviets in their worst fears about U.S. intentions. Like Secretary of State George Marshall, Lieutenant General Walter Bedell Smith and Vice Admiral Alan Kirk had been career officers in the armed services. On one occasion in 1947, in line with the Kremlin's banter about soldiers-turned-diplomats, Molotov asked Marshall whether the ability to goose step was a prerequisite for U.S. envoys—to which he received icy reply.[7]

Commissioned in 1917 and subsequently assigned to combat, intelligence, and staff positions, Smith was an unsentimental soldier. His well-earned reputation was that of a strict officer whose native wit and curiosity offset his lack of university education. He was essentially an autodidact. During World War II, he worked as chief of staff of the Supreme Headquarters Allied Expeditionary Forces (SHAEF). To Eisenhower, Smith was no less than "the general manager of the war," who mastered main issues as well as operational details. Churchill dubbed him "Bulldog" for his tenacity in smoothing out confounding problems of Anglo-U.S. coordination. In the war years and in occupied Germany, Smith also collaborated with Red Army officers on prickly matters (including the repatriation of displaced Soviet citizens) and became acquainted with Vyshinsky and Marshals Zhukov and Sokolovsky. These qualities and experience recommended Smith to Truman and Byrnes. They granted him the unusual courtesy as ambassador of retaining his army commission—partly on the assumption (nowhere verified) that Stalin preferred military men to ordinary diplomats. Eisenhower later remarked that the Soviets got what they deserved in having the rugged Smith forced on them: "It served those bastards right."[8] As for Smith's subordinates in the embassy, even if they did not glow with affection for him, they respected his energetic purpose. Davis Boster, a young political officer in 1947, gave this majority view: "Smith was an authoritarian, hard taskmaster. The discipline was tight and he expected everybody to be super-active in fulfilling duties. He got that. . . . Everybody was conscious that the 'old man' was looking over your shoulder and was not going to tolerate any nonsense."[9]

In his first interview with Stalin and Molotov (April 4, 1946), Smith got straight to the point. After handing them Truman's written invitation to Stalin to visit the United States (rejected on grounds that physicians forbade him long travel), Smith inquired, "What does the Soviet Union want, and how far is Russia going to go?" Mindful of the country's exposed western frontier, he allowed that the Soviets had legitimate security interests. But in elaborating on his question, he stressed that Moscow was taking actions (in Iran and Eastern Europe and through the Italian and French Communist parties) incompatible with continued Allied cooperation. And surely there was no reason to fear the United States, whose benign intentions toward the USSR were implied in the rapidity of demobilization and reduction of forces in Europe. Ways should therefore be found to defuse existing suspicions and to avoid expensive rearmament. To these reassurances, Smith added only one caveat: "If the people of the United States were ever to become convinced that we are faced with a wave of progressive aggression on the part of any powerful nation or group of nations, we would react exactly as we have in the past."[10]

Stalin responded with a recital of his own grievances: Anglo-U.S. duplicity over Iran and unfairness in placing obstacles to Soviet acquisition of oil concessions on favorable terms. Still, he reaffirmed Soviet adherence to the United Nations and the peaceful resolution of international disputes. Denying that his country had designs on the Balkans, he also deplored the tone of U.S. press reports about the USSR, to say nothing of Churchill's recent speech (in Fulton, Missouri), which amounted to an attack on himself. Smith's attempt to respond provoked another round of counterclaims, including Stalin's condemnation of what he called an emergent Anglo-U.S. alliance against the USSR. Words were also traded about Soviet demands on Turkey for a base along the Dardanelles. After two hours of deadlock, the meeting adjourned.[11]

Subsequent conferences with officials were as frustrating to the ambassador as this first. By Molotov, whom he heartily disliked, Smith was once badly used. In May 1948, as the approaching presidential election produced heated debate on foreign policy and Henry Wallace made overtures to Stalin to end the Cold War (by launching "the Century of Peace"), the State Department ordered Smith to instruct Molotov on the bipartisan nature of U.S. diplomacy:[12] come what may, the Soviets ought not to be deceived into wishful thinking by Wallace's support from a minority in the electorate or be confused about America's holding fast on Greece, Turkey, and so forth. At the same time, the Soviets should appreciate the readiness of Truman to participate in comprehensive negotiations to solve East–West issues. Smith conveyed all of this over the course of two separate conversations with Molotov in what were presumably confidential circumstances. Following these talks, however, the Soviet press publicized a distorted version of them. This suggested an American willingness to forsake British, French, and other allies by entering into strictly bilateral negotiations with Moscow. With the unveiling of these "revelations," the Soviets then redoubled their "peace offensive," whose primary goal was to foster suspicion and division among the capitalist powers. Until receiving direct assurances to the contrary from Secretary of State Marshall, Bevin (and the French) was greatly rattled that the Americans had taken initiative without consultation. Smith was naturally embarrassed by this episode and held that it was another evidence, were more needed, of the flexible skill of Soviet propagandists, surpassing in his view the cleverness of Goebbels.[13]

Smith's attempt in August 1948 (synchronized with Britain's chargé d'affaires Frank Roberts and France's ambassador Yves Chataigneau) to resolve the Berlin blockade crisis followed a similar pattern of hopefulness ending in disillusion. Stalin and Molotov seemed receptive at first to producing a practical solution, and as long as the discussions centered on technical issues covering currency reforms in Berlin, Smith was optimistic. The Soviets, though, had ulterior motives in encouraging him: they hoped that conversations with the ambassador would lead to final agreement on Germany's future place in Europe. Above all, they wanted to forestall the centralization of political-economic authority in western Germany and prevent its integration into U.S.-led Europe. But the combination of crude Soviet method against Berlin and the sustainability of the airlift—surprising even to Smith—scuttled the convening of broad German negotiations. The result was that Smith's talks with Stalin and Molotov foundered in late August, breaking down finally over procedural questions concerning the administration of Soviet currency in Berlin. Attempts to revive USSR–Western bargaining at other venue also failed until May 1949, when a round of talks at the foreign-minister level allowed the Soviets to lift the blockade.

Although defeated in his dealings with Soviet officials, Smith was successful in other areas of his responsibility. With the assistance of Foy Kohler, Elbridge Durbrow, and John Paton Davies, Smith provided first-class analyses in support of the U.S. delegates to the 1947 foreign ministers meeting in Moscow. Smith was also a useful accompaniment to Marshall in his stiffer interviews with Soviet officials, just as earlier in Paris (1946) he had assisted Byrnes. All the same, the Moscow conference (March 10–April 24) came apart over Germany and failed to produce agreement on vital matters: reparation payments, German–Austrian peace treaties, and the size of occupation forces in the former Third Reich.

The high level of reportage generated by the embassy during Smith's incumbency was also notable. This ongoing assessment of internal Soviet conditions had a salutary influence on the administration, moderating the more extreme claims then circulating in Washington about Soviet capabilities and goals. Through Kohler primarily, Smith became steeped in the lore of the Marquis de Custine and Neill Brown and their record of observation, which in the late 1940s still seemed relevant. At the same time, Smith was sensible of the damage suffered by the USSR in the recent war and the enormity of reconstruction. Even in the showcase city of Moscow, the disrepair, food shortages (rationing ended in December 1947), and absence of consumer goods were apparent. Flaws in Soviet production (waste, mismanagement, corruption) and the demoralizing impact on factory labor of Stalin's program to refurbish heavy industry were recurrent themes in Smith's reports. As for the country's armed might, Smith held the common misconception that the Red Army was larger than in fact it was: he accepted the inflated estimate of 5 million soldiers. (Adam Ulam calculates that all Soviet armed forces in 1948 numbered fewer than 3 million—probably on the order of 2,874,000 men.)[14] But he also recognized that the Soviet navy, adequate for little more than coastal defense, and the air force, lacking strategic capability, posed a negligible threat to the United States and its allies. Smith concluded that however intent the Soviets were on producing the sinews of modern economy and warfare, several years would elapse before they could reach U.S. levels, let alone surpass them. He predicted that the Americans would enjoy a preponderance of power into the indefinite future. Even if they wanted, the Soviets could not possibly engage in a major war for ten to fifteen years.[15]

Additional debits in the Soviet ledger of power were also obvious. Smith thought that a period of political turmoil (probably violence) would mark the post-Stalinist struggle for succession. As for the broad population, he and his Russian-language officers were impressed by two of its attitudes. First, ordinary Soviet citizens were eager that their country avoid international adventures that might lead to new disasters of war. Contrary to reports in 1947 by some diplomats, such as Laurence Steinhardt in Prague, and by excitable elements in the Western press that "dreams of empire" were animating the Soviets, the embassy stated unequivo-cally, "The great mass of the Russian people wants peace and with it the opportu-nity to repair the ravages of the war and to improve their standard of living." For them, the anti-German struggle had been a nightmare of "deprivation and hard-ship." Another round of violence would exacerbate the hazards of their already precarious existence.[16] The second aspect of Soviet life had to do with the internal detachment of most citizens from the regime's explicit purposes. The population's respect and affection for the Communist party–government apparatus were shal-low. There was little personal identity with or empathy for national leaders—with the exception of Stalin. Instead, it seemed to Smith, most citizens concentrated their energies on living as best they could in stark circumstances while trying to avoid entanglement with authorities. These existential conditions encouraged intensive private life and avocations beyond the reach of officialdom. In sum, the regime was denied access to its subjects' reservoirs of generosity and commit-ment. In the environment of Cold War, this condition had to be counted a liability. Through their outward compliance but inward defiance, the citizenry participated in a silent mutiny.[17]

Not only did Soviet totalitarianism face domestic crises, but the advantages in power presumed to derive from leadership of world communism were illusory. As Smith appreciated, international communism was neither coherent nor monolithic. A rival center to Soviet ideology had already arisen in 1948, following Yugosla-via's expulsion from the Cominform. Tito's successful resistance suggested to Smith that the Soviet zone of influence in Europe would become increasingly unmanageable. For these reasons, he was among the early champions of U.S. trade with and aid to Yugoslavia. He once likened the Soviet wall around Eastern Europe to

> a dike holding in check the churning torrents of the pent-up emotions of [peo-ples], who may know little of real democracy at home but who historically have resisted every kind of foreign rule. The [Yugoslav] breach, like any leak through which angry waters find an outlet, threatens to grow larger with every passing day and, if unmended, eventually to destroy the entire structure of control and inundate the surrounding area.[18]

One measure of the insecurity felt by the Kremlin after Tito's defection was the guardedness with which Foreign Ministry officials treated diplomats from satellite states. To the embassy, it was apparent that these people were regarded with more suspicion than those representing the West.[19]

In the case of Mao's revolution, Smith's understanding benefited from the insight of John Paton Davies. This China-born officer believed that the history of tense relations between the USSR and the Chinese Communist party, to say noth-ing of the historical antipathy between the two nations, would limit their future mutual commitments. Stalin could not view with equanimity the rise of a unified China, neither patrolled by the Soviet army nor subservient to his police agents. The delicate task of the Soviets, Davies held, would be to avoid policies that reinforced Chinese suspicions and inadvertently made China into an Asian Yugo-slavia or Mao into an oriental Tito.[20]

All these considerations touching on the Soviets' economy, politics, and relations with other Communist parties—and the magnitude of U.S. power—persuaded the embassy that Stalin would not pursue a militarily aggressive policy in the foreseeable future. In the confident judgment of Foy Kohler: "We knew that the Soviet Union was not prepared for another war."[21] This view as transmitted was influential with some of the main players in Washington during the late 1940s, notably Kennan (director of the State Department's Policy Planning Staff) and his chief, George Marshall. In March 1948, following the communist coup in Czechoslovakia and days before the Berlin blockade began, Marshall still argued to Defense Secretary James Forrestal that a comparison of Western and Soviet forces did not support the thesis of vast Soviet superiority. Marshall also doubted that Stalin was sure of his own military's strength: "We are not at all certain that the Russians are convinced that the military advantage lies so heavily on their side." And the Joint Chiefs of Staff, even as they devised contingency plans against the USSR, questioned whether Stalin would deliberately start a third world war; accident, rather than calculation, could trigger a Soviet offensive.[22]

However constrained the USSR was militarily, Smith was of a single mind with hard-liners in Washington on one point: as evidenced by the intensity of its anti-U.S. campaign, Moscow absolutely loathed the West and hoped to erode its dominant position. To this end, the Soviets could bring to bear assets of their own. Among them were the energy and determination of the national leadership. Irrespective of their ethical failings, such characters as Molotov, Malenkov, Beria, Kaganovich, Bulganin, and Stalin possessed striking qualities of intelligence and united purpose. These were further buttressed by the discipline and absence of dissent in society created by the police regime. In addition, Smith admitted that communism possessed theoretical appeal—"based on the deepest moral motives" about distributive justice—to people unacquainted with its actual practice. This claim, the recent success of Soviet arms, and the prestige won by communists in the French and Italian resistance movements redounded to Moscow's advantage. Only the most fatuous American could therefore minimize the Soviet threat.[23] As for Stalinist method, here too Smith warned against Western complacency. Through means short of war (duplicity, matériel support of self-styled liberation forces, propaganda, pressure against weak neighboring states), the Soviets intended to harm America and its allies. By a policy of firm containment, which meant for Smith the European Recovery Plan (and NATO), he expected the West to prevail.

The outline of Smith's assessment of Soviet capabilities and policy was shared by his successor, Alan Kirk. But just as there were differences in the two men's brand of leadership (Kirk was relaxed with his subordinates and inspired deeper affection), so they diverged in the shading of their interpretation.[24] Whereas Smith viewed Stalinist ideology as a hybrid, blending elements of Marxism with Russian (and Georgian) intellectual tradition, and as a secondary determinant of policies, Kirk thought otherwise. Although he judged the utopia promised by communism to be a hoax, used by the Kremlin to justify internal repressive practices, he also believed that Marxism-Leninism was key to understanding Soviet diplomacy.

Having little basis on which to form independent judgments, Kirk was influenced in this view by George Morgan. A former professor of philosophy (at Hamilton College and Duke University), he had joined the Foreign Service in 1947. After a period of Russian-language and political studies at the Foreign Service Institute (organized in 1946) and Columbia University, he was assigned to Moscow.[25] According to Morgan (and accepted by Kirk), "Stalin [holds the] conviction that in Leninist-Marxism he has a science of human society and its development in history which makes possible the prediction—and, within limits, the engineering—of the course of history." Morgan reasoned that Stalin would back revolutionary movements in various countries and that his overall policy would be aggressive. But he would from prudence stop short of waging a war for world hegemony.[26] This last proposition dovetailed with Kirk's own calculation: the Soviets would not seek a major fight, for which they were woefully unprepared. Even as the Cold War turned violent in 1950 (Korea), he thought the chance that Stalin would initiate global-scale hostilities was no higher than a ratio of three to two against.[27]

A year earlier, after Soviet scientists detonated their first atomic bomb, Kirk had not been moved to revise the embassy's estimate. Handicapped as it was by a weak economy, the USSR would "not resort to direct military action against the West in the near future and expects and counts on a period of several years of peace." Most likely, Soviet deportment would be marked by blustery self-assurance, but this should not be allowed to cause panic in the West. In this thinking, Kirk was near to Kennan, who also argued that the Soviets would not embark on the risky venture of war simply because they possessed atomic weaponry. And though Andrei Sakharov was inaccessible to Kirk, he would not have been surprised to learn of the scientist's belief at the time: Soviet possession of the bomb was essential to safeguard the country against aggression and as such existed for *purely* defensive reasons.[28] Majority opinion in Truman's government, though, did not share the comparative equanimity of Kennan and Kirk. In late January 1950, the president decided that the United States should produce a hydrogen bomb, a device whose destructive power would be no less than a thousand times greater than the fission weapon.

This acceleration of the arms race gained additional impetus from Mao's founding of the People's Republic of China (October 1949) and declaration that it would side with the USSR in the anti-imperialist contest. With the signing of the Sino-Soviet friendship and mutual defense pact (February 1950), observers felt that the balance of power in East Asia had shifted drastically to American disadvantage. Building on the earlier analyses advanced by John Paton Davies, Kirk's reporting on this subject was considerably more astute, however. He supported that eminently reasonable pre–Korean War policy of Acheson's: by economic blandishments and appeals to Chinese nationalism to woo Mao from exclusive reliance on the USSR. Throughout 1949 and 1950, in fact, Kirk expected the Soviets to encounter problems with their Chinese comrades. In July 1949, for example, he cited evidence showing that the Soviets were intent—no matter if Chinese Marxists objected—on grabbing industrialized Manchuria from China and establishing for themselves positions of privilege in Sinkiang and Inner Mongolia.

Even if a CCP–Soviet settlement over these territories should eventuate, Kirk doubted that Mao would benefit much. Stalin would not be able to fulfill his promise of economic aid, and if he did, the Soviets would exploit all benefits of future modernization for their own purposes, thereby revealing "to Chinese Communists and 'progressives' the true nature of Soviet imperialism." Kirk actually thought that Acheson was overly cautious in not pushing harder for recognition of Communist China. If the Americans failed to act with due speed, he warned, they would dissipate what political leverage they still had on the mainland. One immediate benefit of establishing an embassy would be the inevitable influence and contact between Foreign Service personnel and Maoists. The former could disseminate Western views and underscore the extent of Soviet transgressions in Manchuria.

As for the prolonged Mao–Stalin negotiations in Moscow (December 1949– February 1950), Kirk noted that the Chinese delegation did not indulge its hosts with copious homage and avoided the obsequiousness associated with East European satraps. The niggardliness of Soviet aid to China also struck Kirk as indicative of Soviet postwar poverty and distrust of Mao's long-term reliability. The $300 million in loans hardly compensated for the $2 billion worth of industrial plant and equipment looted by the Soviet army in 1946 in Manchuria. The Sino-Soviet companies established on Chinese territory for the exploitation of mineral resources and air transport were also odious to the Chinese, as was the agreement to allow continued (albeit temporary) Soviet control over ports Darien and Arthur and the Manchurian Railroad. Successful containment of Soviet influence in Asia meant a policy premised on appreciation for the cleavages belying ballyhooed Sino-Soviet solidarity. Paeans to it in the press (and immense paintings commemorating the Mao–Stalin meetings) did not conceal from Kirk the depth of Soviet worry.[29]

The Korean conflict and fighting between Chinese and U.S. troops caused most Americans to lose sight of the tenuousness of Sino-Soviet bonds. Korea also heightened fears of approaching world war. As previously mentioned, this outlook was not shared by people in Embassy Moscow. All the same, Kirk believed that the North Koreans would not have undertaken hostilities without Stalin's enthusiastic direction—a widespread view at the time, but since challenged by scholarship contending that Kim Il Sung had to pry approval and blessings from a skeptical Kremlin.[30] In any event, Kirk's dealings with high Soviet officialdom, never extensive in the first place, came to a dead halt with the outbreak of Korean fighting. When he did meet with figures like Vyshinsky, he had to endure harangues against purported U.S. misdeeds in Korea and the Soviet Far East (where air bases and planes had been accidentally hit). The cumulative impact of these and other episodes took its toll on the ambassador. There crept into his language— already nautically rich—impatient and harsh terms. After Soviet interceptors downed an unarmed U.S. patrol plane over the Baltic, Kirk loosed a torrent of expletives and blasted (in private) the airmen as "tartar fighter pilots." In opposition to those who clung to the idea of comprehensive negotiations, Kirk fumed that it was impossible for Anglo-Americans to find common ground with the "forces of evil."[31] Still, he was circumspect in his public statements, as when he assured readers of *Look* magazine that Russians neither hated Americans nor craved a third world war. Moreover, the United States and its allies must "remain dispassionate and unemotional" in the face of provocative Soviet propaganda and attempts, as in Korea, to undermine Western security. In meetings with Truman, Kirk struck similar themes. And though supportive of overall U.S. policy, including the militarization of containment (per NSC 68), he was less inclined than the president to believe that the Soviets were edging toward another world war. Rather, it seemed to him, they were content to let America deplete its resources in an inconclusive Korean conflict while they husbanded their economic and military strength.[32]

Cold War Moscow

Surpassing the regime of surveillance to which Soviet officials were exposed in London or Washington, life for Westerners in Moscow was grimly constrained. Not only did they lack physical comfort or a varied and healthful diet, but they were inviting targets in the East–West war of espionage.

Beginning with Smith's tenure, Stalin's government promulgated draconian laws, whose effect was to isolate more than ever the foreign community (approximately five hundred people) from contact with the native population. In the opinion of Smith's British colleague, Ambassador Sir David Kelly: "The process of isolating the foreign diplomatic community [was comparable] to the Royal Court in Boccaccio [who] sealed themselves hermetically in the Palace to avoid the plague."[33] The Soviet State Secrets Act made it a capital offense to discuss any subject bearing on national security with a foreigner. This restriction was interpreted in practice to include the most trivial matters. Social contact between Western diplomats and Soviets, including high officials, ceased. Prohibitions on marriages between Soviet citizens and foreigners were also enacted, and exit visas were denied to spouses earlier wed to Westerners. In one case, the Greek ambassador, M. Politis, was prevented from leaving Moscow with his Russian wife. American employees of the embassy, including the translator (and future historian of the USSR) Robert Tucker and his wife, Evgenia, faced similar difficulties and were the subject of lengthy negotiations with the Foreign Office.[34]

Counterespionage in the meantime sought to jam Voice of America broadcasts to the USSR (with varying degrees of success) and was relentless in uncovering Anglo-U.S.-Titoist (and later Zionist) "agents" operating in the Soviet Union. This task gained in psychological momentum as alleged Soviet spies were apprehended in Washington and London and as instances of defection were hailed by the Western press. Celebrated cases included the arrests of Lieutenant Nikolai Redin (in Portland, Oregon) for naval espionage and of Valentine Gubichev, a Soviet member of the United Nations Secretariat—as well as the dramatic 1948 flight of Madame Kosenkina from the Consulate General in New York.[35] With vehemence, *Pravda* protested the "abduction" of Soviet citizens from U.S. city streets and trumpeted indignation when Western "spies" were captured in the middle of their wicked work. Lieutenant Robert Dreher (U.S. Navy), the Associated Press correspondent Robert Magidoff, and the British military attaché General Hilton were among the victims of proletarian vigilance in the late 1940s.[36]

In this period, the embassy suffered two embarrassing desertions. The first involved an army staff sergeant, twenty-one-year-old James McMillin, who worked as a code clerk. He failed to appear at the embassy on the day of his scheduled return to the United States. Instead, he posted letters to Smith and the "Mayor of Moscow." In them, he stated his plans to remain in the USSR, a land more justly governed than any other and in which working people were free. At the time, McMillin was in love with the Soviet wife of another U.S. soldier (already returned home), and she had persuaded him to defect. She was very likely a minor agent of the MVD, which hoped to obtain deciphering information to monitor embassy–State Department cable traffic. Apparently, the damage done was slight. Smith reported that U.S. codes were unassailable, and a clerk of McMillin's type could deliver only those few messages that he had committed to memory.

Less harmful to embassy security but the object of more attention by the Soviet press was the case of Annabelle Bucar. An American citizen of Czech background, she worked as an administrative assistant in the mission's Cultural Information Section. Young and attractive, she had fallen in love with a tenor in the Operetta Theater, Konstantin Lapschin, who had come to the embassy's attention as the suave escort of eligible foreign women.[37] Bucar presumably expected that by renouncing her citizenship and repudiating her connection with the embassy, she would be allowed to marry Lapschin. In any case, she wrote (or at least signed) a widely publicized letter in 1948 to Soviet newspapers, in which she extolled the virtues of the USSR, condemned the cruelties of Western life, and castigated the embassy for its hateful activities: spying, spreading lies through the Russian-language *Amerika* magazine, and operating a sabotage ring. Following this public letter of resignation, the Soviets employed Bucar for a time as a lecturer to factory workers, for whom she contrasted economic slavery in America with the wonders of socialist life.

In 1949, there appeared under Bucar's name a sensational book, *The Truth About American Diplomats*. It sold thousands of copies in the USSR and was translated into foreign languages for international distribution. On the basis of internal evidence, it is plain that Bucar wrote little (if any) of the book, though its personal details (i.e., her giving birth to a baby boy in a Soviet hospital) argued that she had collaborated on the project. It was essentially an unabashed bit of Stalinist fantasy that could have been inspired, if not dictated, only by Soviet authorities.[38] As the willing toadies of financiers, the embassy's officers were accused of helping to devise "plans for the militarization of the [United States], for a fascist domestic regime, for war with the Soviet Union." Epithets described individual members of the mission as "mediocre," "obnoxious," "vicious," "mentality of a stooge," "two-faced." Smith was called a spy-master motivated by an "extreme anti-Soviet attitude." Following the customary genuflections to Stalin's "insight and decision," the book ended with this exclamation: "It is a noteworthy fact that the Soviet Union is young, healthy and vigorous with a capacity for continuous growth, that it is developing, while the United States is confused,

decadent, politically rotten, having fallen into the hands of leaders who are determined to lead the nation to ruin, repeating step for step the mistakes of
Germany."[39]

In a sense, Bucar's book was a harbinger of worse things to come with the
onset of Korean hostilities. Additional travel restrictions were then imposed on
U.S. officials within the USSR, limiting their zone of movement to the Moscow
region (to distances of fifty kilometers and only on certain roads).[40] Soviet cultural
institutions, such as the Lenin State Library, were placed off-limits. Petty obstacles in daily life multiplied, including a number of disadvantageous reevaluations
of the ruble–dollar exchange rate (as applied to resident diplomats). Soviet employees of the embassy became objects of tighter subversion and frame-ups.
Among the many who disappeared in the middle of the night were the chef at
Spaso, the doorman, and the principal gardener. Americans were also made the
villains of radio and newsreel programs, which not only excoriated the United
States for using germ-chemical warfare in Korea, but also accused the diplomats
of smuggling crop-destroying beetles into Soviet agricultural districts. The diplomats also learned from the Soviet press that forced sterilization of penniless people
was increasing in America. And as talks between Moscow and Washington stalled
over lend-lease repayment, the earlier generation of U.S. envoys was accused of
delivering germ-infested food supplies to unsuspecting Soviet citizens in 1941 to
1945. In other words, the U.S. menace, palpable in the very persons posted to
Moscow, justified the actions taken by internal security. Only a strict quarantine
around them prevented the spread of infection, literal and figurative, to the Soviet population.

These accusations led the embassy to conclude that Stalin lacked interest in
maintaining the regular diplomatic channel and would shortly dispense with formal
relations. Kirk's wife, Lydia, wrote home in May 1951: "Moscow tries men's
nerves, as well as their souls." She wondered why more of the Foreign Service
and other personnel did not crack from the strain.[41] As it was, there were officers
who put in for early transfer because of nervous tension or physical ailment. But
the majority performed their duties satisfactorily and took pride in being part of
what they regarded as a first-rate outfit: "the Soviet club." Its special stamp derived from the members' shared experience of hardship and study of Stalinism.[42]
Ironically, given the role of this group in U.S. Cold War policy, it was no more
successful than others in the State Department in defending itself against anticommunist zealotry in the early 1950s.

Under Suspicion

Overweening committees to unmask anti-American activities, self-appointed pro-
tectors of public welfare who ransacked libraries for seditious literature, investigations of Hollywood actors, and professors hounded for alleged communist sympathies have suggested to some writers that there was a symmetry of injustice in
Soviet and U.S. Cold War societies. This is an exaggerated view, equating the
abject terror at the core of late-Stalinism with the shrill but less lethal absurdity

of McCarthyism. Still, the destruction inflicted on American institutions by this phenomenon was considerable.[43] Nowhere was it more extensive than in the apparatus through which the United States conducted its foreign policy. McCarthyism was especially damaging to those Foreign Service officers associated with China policy, such as John Service, Edmund O. Clubb, and John Paton Davies.[44] This last one, the resident East Asian expert in Embassy Moscow from 1945 to 1947, was esteemed by Harriman, Smith, and Kennan. (From Bucar, Davies won this indirect tribute: "He is a master of Eastern intrigue and thinks like a Chinese politician. This, of course, stands him in good stead since there are many parallels between current American diplomacy and reactionary Chinese politics.")[45] In the summer of 1951, Kennan offered a spirited defense of Davies in testimony before Senator Patrick McCarren's subcommittee on internal security. Nonetheless, Davies was forced to leave national service because, so the unsubstantiated charge ran, he had connived to deliver China to Mao and the communists. The injury to Davies (and other results of the anticommunist rampage) actually played a part in General Smith's career in 1953 and 1954, when as undersecretary of state he sought to restore the Foreign Service's morale.[46]

Although attracting less scholarly attention than the fate dealt the China hands, the State Department's Soviet experts suffered equally from the persecution by McCarthy, McCarran, Styles Bridges, William Jenner, and Karl Mundt. From the cohort of World War II and earlier, Charles Thayer and John Melby were victimized and their careers cut short. In the period here reviewed, Davis Boster and Robert Blake, both young language officers, fell (temporarily but not catastrophically) under suspicion.[47]

The perniciousness of the loyalty investigations is well illustrated in the little-known case of Norman Stines, who after two years of commendable work in Moscow was forced to resign from the Foreign Service in 1952. Born in 1914, he had studied journalism at Stanford University and upon graduating was employed for a few years as a sports writer attached to the *Redwood City Tribune*. Yearning for adventure, he then hired on as a purchasing agent for a mining corporation in La Paz, Bolivia. By 1941, he had become the assistant manager of an electric company in that city. With the start of U.S. involvement in the war, he joined the Foreign Service and was stationed first in La Paz and then in Guatemala. He proved competent in both places, though expressing himself crudely about local Jewish refugees from Europe. By 1946, Stines was a vice consul and secretary of the embassy in Guatemala City. He was then transferred to Belgrade, where during 1947 to 1949 he followed the Soviet–Yugoslav controversy. His first contact with communist police and censorship in the Balkans provoked this response: "I have already discovered that I know ALL I WANT to know about Communism. More than that, if I ever meet an American who has a kindly thought about it or even an open mind, I shall let him have it with twenty-one guns loaded. I have become as prejudiced as an old Tory."

Given his aptitude for language and growing interest in East European affairs, Stines was assigned in 1949 to Columbia University for a year of Russian-language and political science study. In Moscow during 1950 to 1952 (as a second and then first secretary and consul), he supervised a demanding drill of political-economic reporting and produced incisive interpretations. His subordinates, by all accounts, found him fair and conscientious. Once the novelty wore off, Stines thought daily life in Moscow irredeemably dreary and frequently became despondent: "It was not a cheerful experience for me." But he worked hard—indeed, he immersed himself in his duties as a means of staving off depression. Stines also got on well enough with his superiors and was devoted to Kirk, whose graciousness he valued. As for his views on the USSR, Stines faulted FDR and Truman for not earlier taking a strong stand against the Soviets; he admired Acheson as a proponent of tough policy. In sum, Stines was a fair example of that breed of men who swelled the ranks of the Foreign Service during and immediately after the war. He was from a moderately well-to-do business family, was decently trained, entertained the standard prejudices, and had vocational experience outside government.[48]

Without warning or explanation, the State Department ordered him in April 1952 to return to Washington. He assumed initially that he was to be reassigned to a new post outside the Soviet Union. In fact, he was under investigation by the department's security division, which questioned his patriotism and resistance to blackmail. By the time Stines left Moscow, the FBI had also been working for months on his case and had called on his friends to determine his reliability. His reaction on learning of the investigation was to dismiss it as "terribly ridiculous." He assumed that his background had been thoroughly examined when he had acquired permanent Foreign Service status in 1945; the results of this original scrutiny would surely save him in 1952.[49]

The case against him was thin, but in that political climate enough to ruin a State Department career. As a Stanford undergraduate in the 1930s, Stines had played with the socialist ideas then fashionable in universities. His political convictions, such as they were in his late adolescence, were of the mild Norman Thomas variety. When his classmate and acquaintance Will Rogers, Jr. (son of the homespun philosopher and cowboy actor) ran for student body president with the endorsement of campus communists, Stines had supported him. Later, while a reporter for the *Redwood City Tribune,* he belonged to the Newspaper Guild, which shifted from the AFL to the CIO—this at a time when the CIO affiliate in the San Francisco Bay area was under increasing communist influence. Still, neither at Stanford nor later did Stines join any communist organizations or advocate their views. Yet it was the charge of his being associated with communism that brought him suddenly back from Moscow.[50]

There were also questions about Stines's sexuality. Despite his having lived for six years with a woman in Central America and subsequent involvements with other women, he remained a bachelor and was uncertain about his preferences. He had mainly unrealized homosexual stirrings and a record of fleeting encounters with a handful of men; these had all occurred years before his joining the Foreign Service (in prep school). Only once as a Foreign Service officer, while still in Guatemala, did he make a furtive but foiled advance toward a man. All the same, he was subjected to a humiliating interrogation in Washington by investigators. He was charged with being schizophrenic, prone to "homosexual panic," and an easy target of communist blackmail. Despite offers of testimonial by colleagues in Moscow, Stines resigned (May 1952) from the Foreign Service. A rather shy man, he had no wish to become a cause célèbre in the manner of Davies or Service. In Stines's words: "I just didn't feel up to a long period of raking over the past, no matter how unjust the charges and their motivation."[51] The government thus lost another veteran analyst at exactly the moment when it could least afford to.

Persona Non Grata

Stines left Embassy Moscow before Kennan arrived in the spring of 1952, but he shared its excitement on learning that this celebrated officer would assume the ambassodorship. Elsewhere too, and to Truman's satisfaction, the announcement of Kennan's appointment was warmly greeted—even as a portent of the Cold War's ending peacefully. Only Radio Moscow struck a discordant chord. Kennan was a spy: "It is not by chance that the State Department appoints as diplomats in Moscow and in the people's democracies shady persons who are usually spies of long standing."[52]

The idea that Kennan's appointment would inaugurate a new era in Soviet–U.S. relations was naive. Still, his was an excellent selection. First, it validated the professional principle as he became the first career diplomat to head the Moscow mission. At the time, he was (with Bohlen) the government's foremost authority on the USSR, was a senior figure in the State Department (counselor), and had served as president of the American Foreign Service Association. In choosing Kennan, Truman endorsed the traditions of reform and organized competence that dated to the 1924 Rogers Act. Additionally, those who applauded the choice of Kennan (the British historian Arnold Toynbee was elated) believed that he was in close touch with Acheson. Despite his absence from Washington from 1950 to 1952 (he had been on sabbatical leave to the Institute for Advanced Study at Princeton), he and Acheson undoubtedly still enjoyed each other's confidence. Finally, Kennan was one of the few ambassadors in his time to have a systematic conception of his calling. It viewed diplomacy as an exercise in amelioration; it eschewed both the narrowly technocratic and utopian temptations to which American practice occasionally fell prey. For him, the task of U.S. policy in 1952 was to strike compromises with Moscow that would allow both countries to carry on— to develop, however they might, their peculiar talents. In the case of the Russians, Kennan had recorded, "[They are] indubitably one of the world's greatest peoples: a talented, responsive people, capable of absorbing and enriching all forms of human experience."[53] By exercising self-restraint and common sense, the Cold War's combatants might yet survive. Before his leaving for Moscow, Kennan wrote to Toynbee this statement of faith in diplomacy:

> The best humanity can hope for . . . is an even and undramatic muddling along on its mysterious and unknowable paths, avoiding all that is abrupt, avoiding the great orgies of violence that acquire their own momentum and get out of hand— continuing, to be sure, to live by competition between political entities, but being

sophisticated and wise about the relationships of power: recognizing and dis-counting superiority of strength . . . rather than putting it suicidally to the test of the sword—imagining the great battles rather than fighting them; seeing to it that armies, if they must be employed at all, are exercised . . . "by temperate and indecisive contests"; remembering at all times that civilization has become a fragile thing that must be kept right-side up and will not stand too much jolting and abuse.[54]

Kennan's eloquent conviction did not dispel those bewilderments that doomed his ambassadorship: the Soviet–U.S. impasse over Korea, divided Europe, and the arms race; the grinding life in Moscow; the loss of public confidence in the State Department as signaled by McCarthy. And contrary to widespread assump-tions at the time, Kennan was not in agreement with Acheson about the thrust of U.S. strategy. To Kennan, the secretary had exaggerated the military problem posed by the USSR. Contra Acheson, he had argued in policy councils against the founding of NATO, disagreed with the mentality of NSC 68, opposed the decision to develop the hydrogen bomb, and believed U.S. actions in Korea were ill-advised (involving the United Nations) and reckless (crossing the thirty-eighth parallel). Notwithstanding his respect for Kennan's mind, Acheson had meanwhile judged that he was out of touch with the power realities of the mid-twentieth century. He once reviled him as a misguided pacifist. In effect, whereas Kennan still thought in 1952 that diplomacy could discover common ground with Stalin (which would lead to limited but useful agreements), Acheson emphasized mili-tary strength as paramount for preventing Soviet aggression and preserving the West. Given their philosophical differences, it was not surprising that Acheson was reserved in his 1952 discussions with Kennan and allowed minimal conversa-tion about the tenets of America's Soviet policy.[55] For his part, Kennan felt distant from the administration and its underlying assumptions. Shortly before going to Moscow, he wrote in his diary: "There [is] no one left in Washington with whom I [can] discuss matters fully, frankly and hopefully against the background of a common outlook and understanding."[56]

Kennan thought his entire career until 1952 was a preparation for the ambassa-dorial office. At the same time, he never entertained illusions about Moscow and was sensitive to the violence of Soviet words against the United States. He ex-pected under these circumstances to reside in Spaso with as much patience as he could muster and to lend himself to whatever negotiations might occur. He reck-oned that for the rest, he would have to steel himself against the disorientation and demoralization that could overcome foreigners in Moscow. The French minister-counselor had committed suicide by hanging not long before Kennan's arrival.[57]

While still in Washington, Kennan paid a courtesy call on the Soviet ambassa-dor, Semenovich Panyushkin, and conferred with Jacob Malik, Moscow's acerbic delegate to the United Nations. Kennan also tried to sound cheerful for the sake of news reporters and their readers. He told them that the Soviets would prefer a reduction of international tensions and a return to more hopeful relations with the West. And he insisted that his conduct as ambassador would be entirely correct; he was unsympathetic to anyone who urged that the embassy be used for subvert-ing Stalinism. Contrary to John Foster Dulles, using inflammatory rhetoric about "liberation" and "rollback," Kennan averred that he opposed interference by one power in the internal affairs of another: "If you go in . . . to unseat a government you place yourself under the moral obligation to have in your pocket something with which to replace it, if you succeed. And I don't think that is a responsibility that I would like to see any of us Americans have for Russia."[58] This and similar statements unfortunately did not allay Stalin's fear that embassies were centers of espionage or that Western diplomats were hell-bent on destroying Soviet security.

Apart from maintaining decorum and seeing to the needs of his staff, Kennan was uncertain of how best to proceed in Moscow. Neither Truman nor Acheson had advised him of an agenda and had not urged him to pursue goals beyond lucid reporting. He did decide not to appear overly eager to arrange a meeting with Stalin, unlike the British ambassador, Sir Alvary Douglas Frederick Gascoigne, who had been kept waiting for months before his request for an audience was granted. Very likely, this departure from standard protocol—politely asking to see the resident potentate—was Kennan's first mistake as ambassador. "God knows," he wrote two decades later, "what impression was produced by it on the aging and semi-mad dictator."[59] Almost certainly, any Soviet leader (not just Stalin) would have been piqued by the discourtesy and implied assertion of superiority when the president's envoy chose not to extend himself.

If he should meet with Stalin or other Politburo members, Kennan was determined that their discussion be private and not used by Soviet spokesmen to score points against the United States (per the Smith–Molotov meetings) or made into an occasion for unrealistic theorizing about future international relations. If called upon, he said that he would be willing to confer with any high Soviet official. But except for one inconsequential conference with Vyshinsky, no such meeting was held, and he was confined to dealing with middle-level functionaries at the Foreign Office.[60]

Kennan's presentation of credentials in May to Nikolai Shvernik, titular head of the the Soviet state, was coolly delivered and glumly received. It served as a reminder to Kennan, who had accompanied Bullitt on his presentation to Kalinin, of the disappointments that had plagued Soviet–U.S. relations since the effervescent days of 1933. Nevertheless, in his prepared remarks, Kennan referred hopefully to Stalin's latest endorsement of peaceful coexistence and stressed that the United States had been acting on this premise ever since the administration of Franklin Roosevelt. He also stated (though it smacked of pro forma) that mutually beneficial political arrangements ought to be forthcoming. Beyond this, Kennan did not venture. Not only was he without precise instructions from his government, but the Soviet reaction to his appointment was unclear. "My reception here," he mused, "has been one hundred percent 'deadpan.' If it reflected any special orders or directives from the top, they could only have been a rigid injunction to avoid anything that might give me a clue to the feelings of the Kremlin." Shvernik's formal statement was unexceptional, and his private words with Kennan were strictly protocolaire. The same held true for Vyshinsky and for other deputy ministers on whom Kennan called. In turn, he was guarded: "If they have kept me guessing, I have kept them guessing in equal measure, which is so far about the only enjoyment I have from this job."[61]

Kennan tried from the beginning to place himself on an unimpeachable footing with the Soviets. For this reason, he hoped to stop his military attachés from conducting their easily detectable intelligence operations. At one point, they mounted a telescopic camera on the roof of the chancery to photograph Soviet war planes as they flew over Red Square during holiday celebrations. From a nearby building, Soviet agents filmed the attachés in the middle of their spying, which caused them to retaliate by photographing the counterintelligence. Such exercises, damned by Kennan as "childish and Boy Scout in nature," reduced the embassy's standing in the diplomatic community—to say nothing of fortifying Stalin in his cynicism about the purpose of the U.S. mission. Kennan was able to curtail these activities, but he was powerless to stop them entirely; the attachés were working independently under orders from their respective service heads. At the time and later, he demanded that all chiefs of mission retain control over (and be advised in advance of) every type of U.S. government activity in lands to which they were posted. Responsibility without authority in Moscow was a recipe for disaster.[62]

Kennan was also perturbed by the adverse impact that U.S. propaganda was having on diplomacy. He had long held that informational programs aimed at politically literate Soviets would help moderate their fear of the West and encourage them in peaceful directions. But he objected to name calling or harping on Soviet backwardness and past misconduct. To Walworth Barbour, director of the department's East European Affairs bureau, he wrote:

> With respect to those things which represent by-products of the internal struggles of the Russian people, which would have been bound to be present in some degree in whatever regime had existed in Russia, and which people have the honesty to overcome by manful and courageous self-criticism, let us observe the discreet silence of the outsider who cannot know all and cannot be expected fully to understand.[63]

Kennan warned that strident propaganda precluded opportunities for diplomatic breakthrough and might derail negotiations in Korea. He recommended that publicists concentrate instead on those features of Soviet activity against which the West had legitimate grievance: lying, self-destructive politics, unwarranted hostility toward the outside world.

When the House Select Committee on the Katyn Forest Massacre completed its investigation in August 1952, Kennan urged that its finding be consigned to the government's archives. Despite his certainty about Soviet culpability, he warned that public dissemination of the committee's report more than a decade after the event would be perceived in Moscow as an escalation in the battle of words. From a diplomatic standpoint, nothing would be gained: "Our concern is less to establish in the eyes of the world our ethical superiority over this [Soviet] system than to find means of living in the same world with it and defending the cause of freedom generally without having to fight a costly and pointless war against it in the coming period."[64] Alas, the ambassador was overruled—rather, ignored—and the committee released its findings to the press with fanfare, which caused an outpouring of Soviet vituperation.

Communist publications accused the United States of using fiendish bacteriological warfare in Korea, torturing POWs, bayoneting pregnant Korean women, and committing other atrocities against peace-loving people. This relentless condemnation caused Kennan to admit to one friend in August: "I find it impossible to adjust comfortably to the incredible volume and hatefulness of lies these people manage to put out about us."[65] Filled with revulsion for the anti-American diatribe, he nonetheless tried to analyze it. He concluded that underlying the cacophony of the hate campaign was a note of real concern about the apathy and latent disaffection of large numbers of Soviet citizens. In other words, the verbal attacks were aimed at rallying popular morale against the day when a direct confrontation with the United States might occur. In any case, he did not think (as was widely held in Washington) that Soviet fulminations were designed to stir support for an aggressive war against Europe or expansion of the one in Asia; other measures needed to prepare for such a conflict were not visible in Moscow.

Bits of the anti-U.S. campaign touched on the ambassador personally. In 1949, there had been published in Moscow, in tandem with Bucar's *Truth About American Diplomats,* another exposé of the U.S. government and its representatives. Ostensibly written by Ralph Parker (formerly of the *New York Times* but by then a Soviet resident married to a Russian), this book, *The Conspiracy Against Peace,* contained a gruesome portrait of Kennan. He was painted as eager for war and despising of the workers and their republic. A few days before Kennan's presentation of credentials, reference was made to Parker's work by a Soviet orator at a Moscow "peace" meeting.[66] This and other evidence persuaded Kennan that people in the highest reaches of the leadership detested him. At one point, Soviet agents even tried to trick him into associating himself with a fantastical conspiracy to assassinate Kremlin leaders. As it was, he chafed under the restrictions of Moscow life: police escort, bugged quarters, prohibitions on even casual contact with citizens. Once a Soviet sentry chased off children who had the temerity of approaching the ambassador's two-year-old son in the garden of Spaso.[67]

As the Soviets were uninterested in diplomacy, Kennan decided that the United States was wasting expense by maintaining an ambassador in Moscow. Better to reduce the embassy staff, withdraw himself, and let the chargé d'affaires direct a minimal mission. "Why the Government wants an ambassador here," he told a friend in August "is difficult for me to fathom."[68] Less than two months later, because of Kennan's indiscretion, Truman was suddenly denied such representation.

The toll on Kennan's equilibrium caused by the Soviet environment was evidenced by his unhappiness with the embassy staff. It numbered talented Foreign Service officers, including Richard Davies, and a future ambassador to the USSR, Malcolm Toon. In the case of these two, Kennan was troubled by their preferring a policy—along the lines of Dulles's rollback—incompatible with his conception of finding compromise with Stalin (Chapter 9). Kennan also complained that he was encumbered by more people than could be usefully employed. Fifty of his subordinates had no productive functions to fill; they cluttered the embassy and made for administrative headaches. Worse still, he imagined that his junior colleagues disdained him. To Bohlen, he confided, "I have been puzzled by the Russian language officers here and their attitude. I cannot for the life of me tell from my contacts with them whether they hate me, despise me, or fear me. I rarely see them unless I specifically summon them, and they rarely comment of their own accord about anything that goes on." He regretted the passing of the good old days of intellectual intensity when with Bohlen and Henderson he would theorize into the late night about the Soviet universe. Not only was that previous spontaneity of interest missing, but where, he wondered, was the respect due to him, who had been personally involved with Soviet–U.S. relations since recognition:

> When I look at the men we have here now and note their deadpan faces and utter lack of readiness to commit themselves, I wonder sometimes whether they do not consider themselves a hundred times wiser than us, their elders, and are not treating me with the same weary correctness which we reserved in our youth for chiefs whom we though were hopelessly behind in their mental processes.[69]

Despite his obtuseness, Joseph Davies had probably detected the contempt swelling in Kennan in 1937. But in 1952, the ambassador was the object of no similar disrespect—quite the contrary. Richard Davies later recollected that he and his colleagues "waited with baited breath and reverence" for Kennan's arrival. According to him, it was Kennan's behavior—not that of his subordinates—that was curious as the months wore on. His habits were that of a recluse: he spent more time at Spaso than at his embassy office; he rarely showed the staff his reports before transmitting them to Washington; he was aloof and uninterested in the opinions of others.[70] In this connection, it is also worth noting that Kennan did not excel in supervising the practical and ceremonial affairs of a large embassy (at the time about a hundred people). He was temperamentally suited for scholarship or research on political matters. Executive responsibility had never been his forte.

Kennan's concentration on duty was further diverted and his discontent aggravated by the plight of colleagues at home whose patriotism was under suspicion. On learning that the issues involving John Paton Davies had still not been resolved in his favor, he was prepared to quit in protest from his ambassadorship and from the Foreign Service. As he told Acheson, his admiration for Davies was based on the latter's intelligence and diligence in both Embassy Moscow and in the Policy Planning Staff; it was absurd to suppose that he had ever done anything against U.S. interests. If Davies should be sacked as a result of McCarren's investigation, Kennan would feel his own judgment had been questioned and his usefulness would be affected. Could the State Department not do more to protect those of its employees who, after years of honorable service, were falling victim to a primitive system of internal investigation? "It [is] a nightmarish thought that this sort of thing can happen to a man by no fault on his part and only by virtue of his effort to do his job as he saw it."[71]

It was against this background—unremitting Soviet hostility, spying and counterspying, distance from his staff, and concern about Davies—that Kennan's signal slip must be understood. While carrying him to a conference in London on NATO issues, his plane stopped briefly at Tempelhof airport in Berlin (September 19, 1952). On the tarmac, in answer to a reporter's question about life in Moscow,

Kennan said that he and his colleagues were treated shamefully by their Soviet hosts. It reminded him, in fact, of when he and other diplomats had been incarcerated for months by the Nazis following Hitler's declaration of war on the United States: "Had the Nazis permitted us to walk the streets [under guard] without having the right to talk to any Germans, that would be exactly how we have to live in Moscow today."[72] This public equating of the USSR with Nazi Germany caused a furor. Given his thoughts about the futility of keeping an ambassador in Moscow and his overall dissatisfaction, it is possible that he hoped (subconsciously) to goad the Soviets into responding as they did. After lambasting him in *Pravda* and *Izvestia,* Stalin's government declared him persona non grata. Under no circumstances would he be allowed to return to Moscow: "[His] anti-Soviet sally leaves no doubt that such a statement could only be made by a person unable to restrain his malevolent hostility to the USSR, who not only desires no improvement in American–Soviet relations, but uses every opportunity to make them worse."[73]

Evidence gleaned by Bohlen in 1955 suggests that Stalin respected Kennan, was amazed at his outburst, and regretted that there was no alternative to demanding his removal. This interpretation, however, must be weighed against other (also inconclusive) evidence indicating the opposite: Stalin and his lieutenants were glad to be rid of a U.S. envoy who assiduously studied Soviet politics and was equipped to follow the forthcoming party congress. Scheduled for October, it featured swift maneuvering between would-be successors to Stalin and his promotion of new favorites against old retainers (Andreyev, Beria, Molotov, and Malenkov). Kennan certainly felt that the party leadership was glad to be rid of him and grateful for his giving them a pretext for dismissal. Still, it would be rash to deny the quality of his insolence from a Soviet standpoint. That he had been on German territory when he lumped the USSR into the same category as Hitlerism stung sensibilities, popular and official. Mikoyan told Bohlen: "That we should be insulted precisely from Berlin was intolerable."[74]

In the years after Moscow, Kennan ruminated on how his ambassadorship had ended. As his memoirs reveal, the episode made him doubt whether he possessed the intellectual and temperamental wherewithal to acquit himself credibly as a diplomat. He was also wounded by Acheson's barb about his inability to muster appropriate taciturnity.[75] It may have even occurred to him that in a narrow sense he had been a greater fiasco than Joseph Davies. Yet Kennan's initial response to the Soviet action was to exonerate himself; he attributed his expulsion to the machinations of Kremlin hardliners. His remorse was minor, reinforcing the point that he was delighted to be clear of Moscow.

It is apparent from his briefings in Washington that Foreign Office personnel had been correct in their dealings with Kennan; they seemed pleased to deal with someone who knew Russian history and culture. Interestingly enough, Kennan did not ascribe blame to Stalin. He thought, instead, that the Generalissimo had been misled by his intelligence-security organs about the nature of the outside world and Kennan's record of activities. This construction seems flimsy, however, and contrary to the fact that Stalin kept his own counsel. He was not easily led astray by his henchmen or secret agents, not even in 1952. More often than not, they were *his* dupes and pawns. Nonetheless, Kennan placed the locus of Soviet hostility to himself squarely within the security organizations: "I could not help but be aware that in the police apparatus there were people animated by the most violent feelings about me."[76] To the degree that this was true, the police doubtless believed along the lines already mentioned: it was undesirable to have Kennan around, when questions of leadership succession and Politburo division were daily becoming manifest.

Back in the United States, Kennan tried to surmount his embarrassment and deflect the criticism that poured in from Western Europe. He emphasized the humorous side. "I came out of Moscow and blew my top," he told State Department officials. He argued that nobody had cause for regret, least of all the Soviets who had wanted from the outset to oust him. As for himself and popular opinion: "I desperately wanted to leave, and succeeded in doing so. The American public was pleased, because its concepts of diplomacy incline generally to the dramatic and defiant rather than the epic and conciliatory."[77] And he considered that ordinary Soviets enjoyed watching their government's display of indignation about remarks that everyone knew were true. He did concede that the Truman administration had reason to be upset because of the jolt to its diplomatic arrangements, but could not afford to upbraid anyone for making an anti-Soviet crack just weeks before the presidential election. Outwardly at least, most people should have been amused.[78]

Unfair though Acheson might have been to him in the past, the secretary had reason to be displeased with Kennan in the autumn of 1952. At a time when he was heavily engaged in finding a solution to the fighting in Korea and hoped to involve the Soviets in producing an armistice, his ambassador had precipitated a needless crisis. To compound matters, Senator William Knowland demanded that the United States break relations with Moscow and send its envoy, Georgi Zaroubin, packing in reprisal for actions against Kennan. Although Acheson squelched this proposal and ignored the subject of the feckless ambassador in conversations with Vyshinsky, the Kennan episode and Acheson's handling of it fitted neatly into the Republican brief: the Democrats were spineless and soft on communism.[79] Thus Kennan's misstep in Berlin created yet another occasion for Truman's (and now Adlai Stevenson's) rivals to heap abuse upon the government and its secretary of state.

In the hiatus between Eisenhower's victory in November 1952 and his inauguration in January, Kennan remained the officially designated ambassador to Moscow. During most of this time, he resided on his farm in East Berlin, Pennsylvania, awaiting his next assignment. It never came. By early spring, it was evident that he would not occupy any niche in the new administration. He was too much of a liability. In Dulles's view, he was a conspicuous remnant from the previous foreign policy, pronounced "immoral" by the secretary. By including him, Dulles ran the risk of antagonizing right-wingers in the Senate and House on whom Eisenhower was dependent for support in domestic and foreign matters. To key Republican senators, Kennan was stigmatized by his association with John Paton Davies. (In December 1952, he was subpoenaed by the Subcommittee for Internal Security of the Senate Judicial Committee and interrogated about his subordinates on the Policy Planning Staff and his own actions as director.) Kennan's meetings with the secretary in March and April 1953 were frosty and Dulles's manipulations to dispense with him obvious. Both John Foster and Allen Dulles raised the possibility of Kennan's joining the CIA, but he rejected it. He was content to leave service "at a time when so much viciousness and falsehood and lack of discrimination seem to mark our public counsels." [80]

*   *   *   *

An ambassador's purpose is threefold. First, he must strive for compromise and common ground with the government to which he is assigned. As such, his art requires the steady application of tact. In the formula of Benjamin Franklin, the successful diplomat possesses "unmovable calmness, . . . a patience that no folly, no provocation, no blunders can shake." Second, as Sir David Kelly was wont to remind his audiences, the normal ambition of an ambassador is to cultivate "the important people and gain their cooperation by discussion and personal influence." Finally, by virtue of his own intellect and broad culture, the ambassador must be able to interpret the significance of local personalities, events, and trends from the myriad reports and contacts available to him.[81] On all these counts, the purpose of US diplomacy in Moscow became unraveled in 1946 to 1952.

In his memoirs, Gromyko was only superficially correct when he identified the reason for Kennan's failure: "He failed to be aware—as any ambassador should—of the borderline between the permissible and impermissible, especially when making remarks about the country to which he was accredited."[82] Rather, Kennan's calamity was the function of a larger failing by both the Soviets and the Americans. On the Soviet side, the country was passing through an intensely introverted phase, the point of which was to repair the war damage and reinstitute a regime of total control that during 1941 to 1945 had perforce been loosened. These aims, and the felt need to keep hidden from outsiders the degree of destruction, made Stalinism hostile to conventional diplomacy. In these circumstances, it was inconceivable that reconciliation could have been advanced by Smith, Kirk, or Kennan. Their gaining cooperation "by discussion and personal influence" with Stalin was ruled out by the morbid suspicion with which he and his coterie viewed the outside world.

On the American side, the reason for diplomatic failure had little to do with the postwar distribution of international power. By all the indices of military and economic strength, the years covered by this chapter constituted a monopolar moment in history. The second fratricide of Europeans in as many decades, the suicidal overextension of Japan, and the leveling war fought on Soviet territory left the United States in possession of most of the world's productive capacity. Irrespective of these advantages, the U.S. government lacked the dignity that should have accompanied its new responsibilities. Neither its recent military triumphs nor the successful Marshall Plan heightened the tone of political discourse in the United States (witness the Truman Doctrine speech), moderated the narrowly partisan debate on foreign policy, or tempered the scrappiness of party competition and electoral politics. At the height of its moral and material standing, the American democracy produced a strain of domestic intolerance whose effect helped unnerve or otherwise damage diplomacy in Moscow. Kennan was as much victimized by McCarthyism as were Davies, Melby, Stines, and Thayer.[83]

As for the main contours of U.S. policy, the evolving concept of containment in 1946 to 1952 (from Kennan's idea to Paul Nitze's NSC 68) represented the latest Western attempt to prevent Russian power from seeping beyond desirable borders. Lord Palmerston's words to the House of Commons in 1860 might easily have been penned by Acheson: "It has always been the practice of the Russian Government to expand its frontiers as rapidly as the apathy or timidity of neighboring states would permit, but usually to halt and frequently to recoil when confronted by determined opposition."[84] As symbol of latter-day Western resolve, the appointment of crusty General Smith and Admiral Kirk served its purpose. The World War II record of the U.S. Army, with which Smith had been associated for three decades, was reminder to Soviet observers of American power. And Kirk stood for that U.S. armed service against which the USSR was only a minor competitor. Both men were also serious watchers of the Soviet scene. During his Moscow tour, Smith became a passable Kremlinologist—admittedly, a pseudoscience based on hunches and spare data but that, given the dearth of better materials, aided Western understanding of the Byzantine side of Soviet politics.[85] Neither Smith nor Kirk, however, was able to make progress on minor issues (such as resuscitating educational-cultural exchanges as had existed in the 1930s) or to inject new life into the successively stalled negotiations on lend-lease, Berlin, and Korea. In this, their failure was no less than Kennan's. Diplomacy had become a principal victim of the Cold War.

III

GREAT POWER RIVALRY

Communism was not defeated by military force, but by life, by the human spirit, by conscience, by the resistance of Being and man to manipulation. It was defeated by a revolt of color, authenticity, history in all its variety and human individuality against imprisonment within a uniform ideology.
                                                    Vaclav Havel, February 1992

8

After Stalin

Radio Moscow announced on March 5, 1953, the death of Joseph Vissarionovich Stalin, lauded in his lifetime as the Guiding Light of Communism, the Genius Leader of Progressive Mankind. This bulletin, broadcast throughout the USSR, was accompanied by funereal music and exhortations to the public to resist panic and despair. There was also official reassurance: the government, composed of his dedicated lieutenants, stood united; the country was ever strong. Thus a nervous new leadership—temporarily led by Beria, Malenkov, Molotov—inaugurated its coming to power and an era of political uncertainty.

Reared on the myth of Stalin's marvelous achievements, citizens throughout the empire wept openly or were stunned by grief into silence. Crowds in Moscow, hoping to glimpse his body as it lay in state, surged past police control, and in the alarm hundreds of people (perhaps two thousand) were trampled to death. At the time, Andrei Sakharov was carried away by the mourning and melancholy thoughts on the universality of death. Although aware of Stalin's responsibility for destroying countless innocent people, he could still write tenderly about him: "I am under the influence of a great man's death. I am thinking of his humanity."[1]

For those in the inner circle, who by luck and pandering had escaped Stalin's vengeance, his passing signified the last phase of the succession struggle, hitherto waged in the sheltering shadow of the master's infallibility. The rise and fall of competing factions in 1953 to 1957, concealed from public view by the ceremony of collective leadership, did not result as previously in the wholesale production of confessions and corpses. Undecided until Khrushchev ousted the "anti-Party group," this contest was marred by only a handful of fatalities. The chief of these, the unlamented Beria, was executed early on (December 1953). Without promising either future life or happiness for Stalin's followers, the Generalissimo's demise nevertheless carried with it a chance of such realization. Foreshadowing the amnesty of millions, Molotov was overjoyed when his wife, Polina Semyonova, was returned to him from Central Asian exile days after Stalin's funeral.[2]

In international policy, Stalin's successors promptly took steps to bolster the USSR's position. Gestures were made toward Mao Tse-tung to consolidate further the Sino-Soviet alliance. Conciliatory moves were taken in the direction of disaffected Tito. Most important, the leadership acted to reduce Cold War tension, but not without anxiety about Washington's exploiting the situation to its advantage.[3] An expression of this forward-looking course was Malenkov's speech (August 8, 1953) to the Supreme Soviet. In it, he underscored the virtues of peaceful coexistence, the desirability of increased Soviet–U.S. trade, and other measures to place East–West relations on a normal basis.[4]

The American response to this demarche was cautious. Whereas the British government, returned to the competence of Churchill and Eden, was eager for an Anglo-U.S. conference in Moscow with the new leaders, Eisenhower warned, "We should not rush things too much and should not permit feeling in our countries for a meeting between heads of states to press us into precipitate initiatives."[5] Notwithstanding ad hoc attempts to mend fences with the USSR (as in Geneva in 1955 and Camp David in 1959), the administration, especially John Foster Dulles, remained lukewarm to the idea that a comprehensive settlement might be negotiated. Consequently, despite the appointment of two envoys who deserve their towering reputations, American diplomacy in Moscow was a sterile exercise. More than in other periods, Soviet–U.S. history during the ambassadorships of Charles Bohlen and Llewellyn Thompson illustrates the unfulfilled potential of Cold War diplomacy. This situation changed for the better, however, with John Kennedy's coming to office and his adroit use of Thompson.

Diplomacy Restrained

I

Senate approval of Bohlen's appointment in 1953 was an ordeal for him and the administration. It also foretold the domestic political limits of that era's diplomacy and demonstrated—not for the last time—Dulles's fear that Bohlen would embarrass or compromise him.[6]

The Senate Committee on Foreign Relations, chaired by Alexander Wiley, held hearings in the first half of March on the nomination. In these, Bohlen was quizzed about the Yalta Conference and his responsibilities as interpreter for FDR and adviser on Soviet affairs. Republican questioning was packed with innuendo about Roosevelt's "sellout" of Eastern Europe and similar nonsense about helping the communists in East Asia. Alger Hiss was also mentioned in the context of twenty years of Democratic "misrule," as was the "passive" and "negative" policy of containment. On all these matters, Bohlen was asked to pass judgment, demonstrating thereby whether he was suitable for public trust. His explanations in support of U.S. wartime policy and testaments on his behalf by such worthies (and Republicans) as former ambassadors Joseph Grew, Norman Armour, and Hugh Gibson persuaded the committee. With the added incentive of Stalin's death and Walter Bedell Smith's urging that everything be done to expedite Bohlen's departure for Moscow, the committee voted unanimously to forward the nomination to the Senate floor. Yet confirmation was not conferred until the end of March, with two Democrats, Pat McCarran and Edwin Johnson, and eleven Republicans, including John Bricker, Barry Goldwater, Styles Bridges, Joseph McCarthy, voting in opposition.

To his detractors, Bohlen was guilty by association with Yalta and other failed foreign policies repudiated by voters in November 1952. McCarthy pronounced him an anathema for his involvement "in the diplomatic intrigues of the New Deal gang." In this conspiracy, he had "called the signals for the betrayal of millions of men and women in Europe and Asia." For the sake of these martyrs, as well as for U.S. security, the nomination should be rejected.[7] Rumors were circulated meanwhile that derogatory material about Bohlen's character and sexual history had been unearthed by the FBI. In spreading this groundless hearsay, the anticommunist sleuth, Assistant Secretary of State for Security Affairs Scott McLeod, played a vile part. The confirmation fight became especially nasty when McCarthy accused Dulles of having whitewashed the FBI's report on Bohlen and preempting McLeod's honest presentation of it. The Wisconsin senator suggested at one point that the nominee take a polygraph test.

The Senate hearings drained Bohlen's composure; he became so frazzled that, in an unguarded moment with Dulles, he offered to withdraw. Yet Eisenhower remained steadfast and spoke publicly in Bohlen's defense. Their association dated to January 1945, when (with Harry Hopkins) Bohlen stopped in Paris on his way to the Yalta Conference. He spent a couple of nights at Eisenhower's headquarters and discussed with him the unfolding military situation. Their acquaintance was renewed in 1951 (again in France), when Eisenhower was supreme commander of NATO and Bohlen was attached to Ambassador David Bruce's staff. They conversed on NATO matters and Soviet–U.S. problems (and played golf). Bohlen was taken by Eisenhower's vigor and—unlike his rambling public speech—found him incisive in private conversation. Although distressed by his unwillingness to tackle McCarthy in public (and puzzled by his failure to defend General Marshall against McCarthy's insults), Bohlen admired the man and felt personally grateful to him: "He was always extremely kind to me." For his part, Eisenhower liked Bohlen and regretted that he had to suffer an inquisitorial exam in the Senate: "[He] was one of the ablest Foreign Service officers I had ever met."[8]

Opposing Eisenhower's magnanimity was Dulles's timidity. He did not want the administration to draw heavily on its limited fund of goodwill among right-wing Republicans, whose future aid would be needed on matters more important than Bohlen. This attitude was reinforced by Dulles's sensitivity to the fate of secretaries of state who had lost congressional and other support (i.e., his predecessor, Dean Acheson, and his own uncle, Robert Lansing). Dulles's earlier backing of Alger Hiss—in 1946 he had endorsed his becoming president of the Carnegie Endowment for International Peace—only intensified his determination to stay clear of questionable characters. Although dutifully testifying for Bohlen in closed and public chambers, Dulles also maintained a discreet distance. The secretary was careful to avoid being photographed with him in March and refused to travel with him to Capitol Hill during the period of their joint testimony. To Eisenhower,

Dulles once intimated that the better part of wisdom would be to retract Bohlen's name—a proposition that annoyed the president and met with dismissal.[9]

In the end, it was Robert Taft's guidance of mainstream Republican senators, Eisenhower's personal prestige, and McCarthy's discrediting antics that secured Bohlen his ambassadorship. Still, nothing better underscored the absence of discrimination in Congress in the McCarthy season than this nomination fight. Taft subsequently let it be known that he would continue to tolerate McCarthy and warned the White House to sponsor "no more Bohlens." In private, the president boiled over the break in Republican party discipline and viewed the eleven renegades as small-minded people who resorted to specious arguments. And though he vowed not to soil the office of the presidency by tangling openly with McCarthy, he decided thereupon to undermine him through subtler means.[10]

At no point during the confirmation proceedings had Dulles considered doing anything but the president's bidding and so garnered votes for Bohlen. Dulles's lack of enthusiasm for him was nevertheless apparent. It accounted partly for the opposition's stubbornness and the later coolness between the secretary and the ambassador. As it was, their previous relations had been strained at times. They had first worked together (clashed might be more accurate) in 1947 as members of George Marshall's delegation during the ill-starred Moscow meetings. One of Bohlen's duties there was to advise local journalists on what had transpired during daily sessions. In a departure from bipartisanship, Dulles also held news conferences and in them gave contrary opinions and embellished (from Bohlen's standpoint) the importance of his own role in dealing with the Soviets. Bohlen was mad enough at Dulles, whom he thought uncommonly ambitious, to complain to Marshall. This protest was unavailing as the forbearing general allowed that the Republican representative had a right to speak with correspondents however he chose. Years later, Bohlen expressed skepticism to Dulles about rollback in Eastern Europe. He begrudged the secretary's unwillingness to employ Kennan in the administration, resented the call for "positive loyalty," and thought Dulles craven for not challenging the intrusive security apparatus in the State Department, exemplified by McLeod's privileged position.[11]

On his side, Dulles did respect Bohlen as a student of Soviet affairs and a senior member of the Foreign Service (he had been counselor of the department, 1947–1949 and 1951–1953). Dulles, too, viewed McLeod with misgivings. When he discovered that he was passing files to McCarthy, he nearly fired him. Not until after McCarthy's eclipse, though, did the secretary muster the courage to curtail McLeod's activities. At the same time, Dulles resented Bohlen's telling the president in April (just before leaving for Moscow) that morale in the Foreign Service had sunk because of the loyalty investigations and McLeod's baleful presence. Perhaps intended as repayment for Bohlen's squawking to Eisenhower, Dulles's parting words to him were gratuitous. Ostensibly in the interest of squelching lingering doubts, Dulles advised him to travel to Moscow with his wife; separate travel arrangements would revive rumors about his sexuality and faithfulness.[12]

Bohlen could have done more in the 1950s to hide his disdain for Dulles, in which feeling he never altered. Even the Yugoslav ambassador in Moscow, Veljko

Mićunović, was aware of Bohlen's antipathy toward the secretary and his conviction that Dulles sought to demean anyone more knowledgeable than himself. The cordial feelings between Eisenhower and Bohlen might also have bothered Dulles, who was quick to spot a threat to his jealously guarded friendship with the president.[13] Although the secretary valued Bohlen's reporting from Moscow and solicited his assessment of post-Stalinist politics, he prevented him at every turn from gaining further in Eisenhower's confidence. Dulles doubtless justified himself with Taft's admonitory statement at the time of Bohlen's nomination: "Our Russian ambassador can't do anything. All he can do is observe and report. He will not influence policy materially"[14] Consequently, Bohlen held nothing like the influential role that he had enjoyed during Truman's time. Once, in April 1956, Sherman Adams inquired whether the cabinet would want to hear from Bohlen on the de-Stalinization campaign, progressing rapidly since Khrushchev's "Secret Speech" at the Twentieth Party Congress. The reply came from Dulles that the cabinet might enjoy such a briefing, but he preferred that Bohlen not speak: "It would build him up too much—he is not working with us."[15]

During his four years in Moscow, Bohlen felt (and indeed was) marginal to the purposes of Dulles. He never replied to the ambassador's advice in 1954 on how to manage the Soviet side of the Chinese–Taiwan offshore-islands conflict. Dulles ignored him at the 1954 conference of foreign ministers in Berlin, except as a translator in talks with Molotov. Nor was Bohlen allowed much part in the Geneva Conference (also 1954) to negotiate a settlement between France and the Vietnamese insurgents. Dulles averred that such participation would ignite fears among conservatives that this New Deal survivor was still playing darkly with U.S. policy. In Geneva in 1955, Bohlen was again left out—though once more he was used to translate, this time for Eisenhower's sentimental conversations with Zhukhov. On one occasion, when in 1956 Bulganin suggested that he and Bohlen organize "heart-to-heart" discussions on vital matters, the ambassador practically begged the State Department to accept him into its deliberations. To act on the proposed talks, he said, "I would have to be much more fully aware than I am at present of our thinking on outstanding questions." In keeping with Dulles's wishes, Bohlen was discouraged from pursuing this or any direct line of communication with Soviet leaders. Pride of place went instead to Eisenhower, who then entered into a publicized but inconsequential correspondence with Bulganin.[16]

Increasingly sophisticated about hierarchies of prestige in Washington, the Soviets did not place importance on courting Bohlen, especially not after Bulganin's approach to him was refused. Even before his arriving in Moscow, Soviet intelligence decided (contradictorily) that Bohlen was an advocate of rollback, a Germanophile, and a supporter of Germany's continued division. Khrushchev certainly never wasted charity on the ambassador. In misplaced pique, he later blamed him for the failure of the Soviet Union and the United States to achieve détente in the 1950s: "He turned out to be a shameless reactionary who supported all the most hateful policies then being conducted by antagonistic forces in the United States. He pulled every dirty trick he thought he could get away with. Rather than improving U.S. relations with us, Bohlen succeeded in freezing them." According to Mićunović, the Soviets were uneasy about Bohlen, but not because of his imagined association with reactionaries. Rather, he knew too much about Soviet politics; they were glad to see him leave when his term expired in 1957 (shades of Kennan).[17] True or not, one point is plain. Pinched between Dulles and Khrushchev, Bohlen was badly situated to enhance Soviet–U.S. relations.

Warily regarded by ministers in the Kremlin and Washington, Bohlen was nonetheless esteemed by his foreign colleagues in Moscow and by his subordinates. In fact, he was very likely more popular with his staff than any ambassador assigned to the Soviet Union. It was not simply that he was a discerning diplomat, the "finest in the American Foreign Service," said David Bruce. He was also devoutly solicitous of his people. He consulted them regularly, included them in numerous social events, and won them with his lively humor and intellect. Robert Martens, a Russian-language officer who lived in Spaso with the Bohlen family, recalled, "[He] had a great easy going personality and a twinkle was usually in his eye. He was easy to talk to, democratic in every way, totally without airs." Similarly, Charles Stefan characterized Bohlen as a "super guy to work for."[18] Moscow-based U.S. journalists were also fond of him, savored his colorful turns of phrase, and welcomed his institution of weekly off-the-record briefings. Enthusiasm for Bohlen in the embassy and press pool was reinforced by the realization that by living in post-Stalinist Moscow one might witness—possibly participate in—changes that would transform the USSR. Hopeful signs in 1953 could be read in the abatement of the hate-America campaign, lifting of several (by no means most) prohibitions applied to travel by diplomats within the USSR, granting of permission to Soviet wives of foreigners to emigrate, suspension of the ambassador's NKVD escort, more open social style among Soviet officials, and cautious but demonstrable demotion of Stalin's standing in the Soviet pantheon of heroes. Bohlen captured much of this brighter mood when in early 1954 he exclaimed to Eisenhower that assignment in Moscow was fascinating for any student of Soviet affairs despite the chronic inconveniences. In 1955, to salute the approaching Geneva meetings and to Bohlen's delight, the entire Politburo attended Fourth of July festivities at Spaso—a previously unthinkable courtesy.[19]

Yet neither the ambassador nor his subordinates mistook the thaw in the Cold War for friendship. They would have agreed with Britain's envoy to Moscow, Sir William Hayter, when this cosufferer of Bohlen's at Soviet entertainments told his superiors: "Anyone who associates closely with the great here needs a strong stomach, metaphorically even more than literally. However pleasant they might be making themselves it [is] impossible not to reflect on the enormities each one of them must have on his conscience." Diplomats were frequently reminded in ways subtle and obvious that Moscow still "wasn't the garden spot of Europe" (Bohlen's quip); most cities by comparison, even divided and bristling Berlin, seemed like Eden. Life for Westerners remained circumscribed; as before, this condition tended to magnify any raspy edges in personal relations among diplomats or in families.

At no time were Bohlen and his family invited to a private Soviet home or allowed contact with local residents of the type usually had in foreign posts. This situation apparently discomfited Mrs. Gromyko, who was drawn to Bohlen's winning wife, Avis, but was dissuaded from befriending her. Neither did all fronts in the East–West war of words fall silent. In May 1954, for example, political cartoonists in *Crocodile* mocked James Forrestal and proposed that a statue of an upside-down figure be erected to his memory with this inscription: "To former Minister of Defense of USA, the active organizer and first victim of war psychosis on the fifth anniversary of his atomic hysterical jump from the window of the 16th floor of the Naval Hospital in Washington. And for the edification of his followers." Bohlen was naturally offended by this cartoon and delivered a curt protest to the Foreign Ministry. More ominously, the new U.S. chancellery under construction in 1953 became infested with listening devices. Forty-three microphones were eventually discovered on floors purported to be most secure. On one occasion, in circumstances similar to when an agent provocateur had sought to entrap Kennan in an anti-Stalin plot, a Soviet citizen stole into the embassy. He claimed that he could put Bohlen in touch with clandestine opposition groups operating in the party, universities, and elsewhere. Over the course of Bohlen's tenure in Moscow, the Soviets expelled seven military attachés and in mid-1953 executed four spies who had allegedly been parachuted into the Ukraine by the United States. Soviet intelligence also tried to compromise at least a dozen mission employees, mostly male clerical staffers. Female agents (dubbed "swallows" by the embassy) were typically used in these gambits, the idea being to ensnare the victims in blackmail and espionage schemes. On learning of any problems, Bohlen quickly organized the departure of wayward individuals; they "were out of the country in twenty-four hours." These sorts of Soviet action reinforced pressures in Washington to expel communist diplomats from America—at a rate, according to Jacob Beam, of one every two months in the mid-1950s. As for the cultural exchanges that Bohlen promoted (epitomized by his hosting of the *Porgy and Bess* cast at a reception for Russian guests), they hardly compensated Soviet artists for their many years of isolation. Oxford scholar Isaiah Berlin recorded this of a 1956 meeting with Boris Pasternak and Anna Akhmatova: "I told [them] all that I could of English, American, French writing: it was like speaking to the victims of shipwreck on a desert island, cut off for decades from civilization—all they heard, they received as new, exciting and delightful." [20]

II

Barred from playing a role in negotiations or profitably offering advice, Bohlen credited his ambassadorship with slight achievement. [21] The exception to this record occurred early in his term and involved breaking a major impediment to improved Soviet–U.S. relations: the Korean War. In mid-May 1953, as armistice talks sputtered in Panmunjom (over the forcible repatriation of North Korean and Chinese POWs), Dulles asked Bohlen on how to approach Molotov. Might means be found to coax the USSR to press the North Korean and Chinese negotiators to be more forthcoming? In line with Bohlen's recommendation that an unofficial approach was more apt to work than one advertised, Dulles instructed him in late May to see the foreign minister. In the ensuing meeting, Bohlen delivered the final Western proposal for an armistice, which contained concessions (again, along the ambassador's advice) on the prisoners question. Implied in the American position was also a warning: if the Panmunjom talks collapsed or continued inconclusively, an intensified war in northeastern Asia would flare up with results detrimental to Soviet interests. In coordination with this Molotov–Bohlen meeting, Eisenhower intimated to the Chinese through Indian intermediaries that the United States might use atomic weapons in Korea. Despite Syngman Rhee's release of communist prisoners from South Korean camps (which almost scuttled the negotiations), an armistice was signed in July. Overall, Dulles seems to have been pleased with Bohlen's performance. But he was also annoyed when a few days after their meeting, news leaked that the U.S. ambassador had met with Molotov with the aim of enlisting him against Moscow's principal Asian allies.[22] This breach of secrecy might explain Dulles's reluctance thereafter to use him in delicate assignments, despite absence of evidence showing the ambassador to blame.

Although lacking satisfactory relations with the Republican State Department, Bohlen was of undoubted usefulness as a political reporter. His premise in 1953 to 1957 was that the USSR intended to avoid war against the militarily superior Western coalition. This view was near to Eisenhower's own judgment, according to which Red Army spokesmen were consistent advocates of caution in the Kremlin.[23] To Bohlen, the Soviet leadership in all its forms—from the original troika, to Bulganin and Khrushchev, to Khrushchev as first among equals—wanted an accommodation with the West: it would reduce the danger arising from prolonged rivalry and establish forms of cooperation. In this interpretation, he was heartened by Malenkov's public assertions (later confirmed by Khrushchev) that nuclear war would destroy every civilization, including advanced socialism. For the sake of progressive humanity, the Soviets also gave sane emphasis to the appropriateness of peaceful (though competitive) coexistence with the West. In private conversation, Zhukov once explained to Bohlen: "The arms race [is] senseless and dangerous and given the development of atomic weapons any new war would be unbelievably destructive."[24]

Bohlen's confidence in Soviet commitment to a modus vivendi was severely tested. Despite the touted "spirit of Geneva," the USSR's withdrawal from its Austrian zone and the Finnish naval base at Porkkala (1955–1956), and the Cominform's dissolution (1956), several events properly concerned U.S. policymakers. Soviet armed forces crushed anticommunist demonstrations in East Berlin in June 1953. An air force B-29 flying in the disputed area off Hokkaido was shot down in November 1954 by Soviet fighter planes, which caused an angry exchange of diplomatic notes. In response to West Germany's rearming and admission to NATO (against which Bohlen argued), the USSR organized the potentially powerful Warsaw Pact. After the failure by Khrushchev to improve relations with Tito in 1956, undone by the invasion of Hungary, Bohlen wondered whether the Soviets might actually invade Yugoslavia.[25]

Regarding the Hungarian revolution (establishment of multiparty politics, withdrawal from the Warsaw Pact, declaration of neutrality) and its suppression by the Soviets, Bohlen was badly used by the communist leadership. In the period between Imre Nagy's organization of a cease-fire and the retreat of Soviet forces from Budapest (late October 1956) and the Red Army's stormy return (early November), Zhukov sought to reassure Bohlen along several lines. These were all misleading. According to Zhukov, the Soviets did not expect to reinforce their troop strength in Hungary; what little fighting had already occurred was sparked by counterrevolutionary violence against socialist soldiers, whose only desire was to protect the achievements of Hungarian Marxism. In any case, the insurgents had no cause to fear Soviet intervention; presumably, the Hungarian proletariat would know how to foil their knavish tricks. Additionally, Bulganin and Khrushchev tried to deceive Bohlen about Soviet aims and paraded their "legally correct" attitude. By his own admission, Bohlen was briefly fooled into thinking that the USSR would withhold military action. But Khrushchev's boasting, mixing truculence and jitters, of Soviet ability to solve any problem in Hungary betrayed him. And Bohlen was able to warn Washington in advance of the invasion, begun on November 4. He also recognized that the West could do little to rescue Hungary, even without the concurrent crisis over Suez and splintering of NATO unity. Protests on Hungary were registered in international forums by U.S. spokesmen, and Bohlen refused, as did other NATO ambassadors, to attend the November 7 celebrations of the Bolshevik revolution.[26]

He was horrified by the repressive actions in Hungary and by Poland's narrow escape from comparable mistreatment months earlier (fortuitously spared by the Gomulka solution). Still, he did not believe that this tide of Soviet reaction signified a return to Stalinist rule in Eastern Europe or in the USSR. Within limits, Gomulka was allowed to experiment with a Polish path to communism, and Nagy's successor, János Kádár, proved to be a more enlightened figure than most of what had preceded him in Marxist Hungary (i.e., Erno Gero). As for domestic Soviet politics, Bohlen felt that the leadership, rigid and severe though it was by Western standards, would not revert to the unchecked practices of high-Stalinism. In the case of Beria's arrest and execution, he did not contend—in contrast to Dulles's wishful thinking—that these events portended internecine conflict among the rulers. Instead, he took seriously the idea that the regime wanted to eradicate Stalinist terror and to prevent a return to one-man rule; in this case, the elimination of Beria served a positive end. Bohlen's view, though correct in the main, caused him to overlook the brittleness of collective leadership. He was therefore slow to appreciate Khrushchev's rise to preeminence and consolidation of personal power. This underestimation of the party chairman also stemmed from Bohlen's scorn for him. He thought Khrushchev "not especially bright" (and boozy) and preferred the more literate Malenkov. Word of Bohlen's opinion, expressed indiscreetly, got back to Khrushchev and helped poison the atmosphere between them.[27]

Set against the history of Soviet recklessness and the barrenness of state ideology (*shablon*), Khrushchev's career in power was essentially a salvaging operation that failed. Neither he nor his successors created a post-Stalinist equilibrium or overcame the legacy of totalitarian chaos. Forced collectivization, purges, and terror had produced a decline in society incapable of responding to the ventilation of reform. Yet as viewed by Bohlen at the time of their introduction, Khrushchev's innovations (especially his tampering with the economy) seemed to augur well for the Soviet nations. From the standpoint of collective morality, his most important contribution, which Bohlen appreciated, was to promote a dual policy: challenging the false party history of Stalin while establishing a semblance of legality and system of norms. In this connection, Bohlen played a role in authenticating Khrushchev's secret speech, that signal effort in 1956 to rehabilitate truth in the Soviet world (and an element necessary to the peaceful coexistence policy).[28] At the same time, Bohlen was aware of the conservative reflexes of the party and police organizations. They would try to stifle Khrushchevian reforms by ignoring them or by resisting them outright. In the ambassador's words: "I realized that any liberalization of a dictatorship is fraught with the dangers of going too far too fast or doing too little too late."[29]

Bohlen did not stay in Moscow long enough to see the fruits of Khrushchev, such as they were—the initially promising but then disastrous virgin-lands scheme, experiments in decentralization, partial lifting of the censorship. Against his will and without meaningful consultation, Bohlen was abruptly removed by Dulles from Moscow in 1957. He was appointed ambassador to the Philippines, a country about which he knew little and in which he had scant interest. From Manila, he nevertheless continued to monitor Soviet events and was fascinated by the maneuvers and countermoves of Khrushchev and his adversaries (Malenkov, Molotov, Kaganovich) that marked the death knell of collective government and the ascendancy of one-man rule. Not until after Dulles's death in 1959 was Bohlen readmitted to the making of America's Soviet policy. Secretary of State Christian Herter called him to Washington and enlisted him as his special assistant on Soviet affairs over the objection of conservative critics. In this capacity, Bohlen served during the hopeful months coinciding with Khrushchev's American tour and those plans (aborted) for a 1960 summit meeting in Paris.[30]

Search for Stability

I

None of his cameo appearances in scholarly monographs on the Cold War has allowed a serious treatment of Llewellyn Thompson or made him vivid in the panorama of twentieth-century U.S. history. Esteemed by his colleagues in the diplomatic corps (in which he served 1929–1969), he begs comparison with his contemporaries: Kennan, Bohlen, and Loy Henderson. In the appreciative words of Undersecretary of State George Ball, Thompson was "the very model of a career ambassador, quick to understand, perceptive, and skillful in framing his observations."[31] Yet he lacked the intellectual intensity of Kennan and the poise of Bohlen. Less captivating and more methodical than they, the soft-spoken Thompson shared traits with Henderson. They came from modest social backgrounds. Both were naturally retiring men. Both were indefatigable workers who put their duty (as they understood it) to the nation above personal considerations. Like Henderson, Thompson never became fully proficient in the Russian language and was not singled out for immersion in things Soviet. He belonged to that second generation (post–Robert Kelley) of Soviet experts hurriedly trained in the early 1940s that, despite its accomplishments, was never as celebrated as the original cadre.

Before the war, Thompson's career was slightly unfocused. Following leave from his family ranch (Baptist, poor) and 1928 graduation from the University of Colorado, his first assignment as a Foreign Service officer was to Ceylon, where he served as a vice-consul in Colombo. From there, he was sent in 1933 to Geneva, where his duties included liaison with the International Labor Organization and its affiliates in the Americas. After a year of study at the U.S. Army War College (during the better part of 1940), Thompson was next sent to Moscow as a second secretary.

It was in the USSR that he first distinguished himself and was awarded the State Department's coveted Medal of Freedom. As Ambassador Laurence Steinhardt and his entourage joined the evacuation to Kuibyshev in 1941, Thompson was left in charge of the embassy building, sundry U.S. properties in Moscow, and a meager staff. "At the risk of capture" (to quote from the official citation), Thompson had volunteered to stay in the capital during the darkest days of German advance and siege. He experienced shelling and deprivation and for his perseverance earned the respect of Muscovites, who were upset with Steinhardt for prematurely fleeing.[32]

Following four years of wartime service in Moscow and then assignment in London, Thompson was recalled to Washington in 1946. In the department, he served successively as chief of East European affairs and deputy assistant secretary of state for European affairs. After two years in Rome (1950–1952) as second in the embassy, Truman selected him to be U.S. high commissioner and ambassador for occupied Austria. During his posting in Vienna, Thompson (and his immense patience) was instrumental in negotiating the accords on Trieste and restoration of Austrian independence.[33]

Despite official appreciation for his work in Vienna (for which he received the U.S. Distinguished Service Award), Thompson decided in late 1955 to retire from the Foreign Service. He had just been offered the presidency of the American Red Cross and, as he explained to Dulles, could expect from this worthwhile office to receive relatively generous remuneration and benefits. These were issues of concern as he contemplated the future of his wife and two young daughters: "In justice to my family I have no alternative but to retire now, which should enable me to save my pension and part of the salary I can earn in other employment." Dulles's response kept Thompson in government service for an additional fifteen years. Assisted by Congress's recent liberalization of retirement benefits, Dulles also appealed to him on other grounds. With unfeigned praise, he told him that his work had been "outstanding." Whereas Dulles doubtless thought of Bohlen and Kennan as hypercritical prima donnas, he was eager to retain Thompson: "I look upon you as one of the few persons that I would be willing to see in any post that the Department has to offer." Within weeks of the threatened retirement, Dulles said that Thompson might soon succeed Bohlen as ambassador to the USSR.[34] When that moment arrived, Bohlen learned of the appointment indirectly and late—circumstances that nearly caused a break in their friendship (saved by Thompson's show of diffidence).[35]

Dulles's mistreatment of Kennan and Bohlen, as well as their dissent from the main line of U.S. policy in the 1950s, explains their severe judgment of him—moderated decades later in Kennan's case by the findings of historians working on the Eisenhower era.[36] By contrast, and again like Henderson, Thompson went along with the Eisenhower–Dulles regime, suppressing qualms about the security apparatus in the State Department. He always enjoyed its confidence as a result. Thompson also respected Dulles, whom he thought compelling, at least in private settings. There he displayed to Thompson's satisfaction a depth of mind and personal warmth lacking in his public appearances. But at no time was Thompson an insider, and he faulted Dulles for being sluggish in not realizing earlier the profundity of change in post-Stalinist Moscow. By the end of Eisenhower's second term, Thompson also felt himself to be unappreciated by the administration. Frustrated in his attempts to advise the president closely and to encourage Soviet–U.S. rapprochement, Thompson looked hopefully in 1961 to the incoming Democrats.[37]

II

What distinguished Thompson's ambassadorship from that of his predecessors was the quality of intimacy he achieved with Soviet officials, specifically Khrushchev.[38] Unimpeded by the fatuousness that had marred relations between Joseph Davies and Stalin, the Khrushchev–Thompson link was based on forthright recognition of the chasm in difference between Soviet and U.S. societies and the fact that another war would produce incalculable damage.

The woodenness of Soviet–U.S. gatherings in Moscow was largely displaced in Thompson's years, as Khrushchev and he sought each other—a circumstance approved by Eisenhower. Their families enjoyed weekend retreats together at Khrushchev's dacha, formerly site of Stalin's grim bacchanalia. These unprecedented occasions mixed business with pleasure. Hikes in the countryside, chirping children, boat outings, and discussions of household matters competed with debates over the merits of socialism versus capitalism or reviews of matters of state. Years later, Khrushchev's son Sergei recalled,

> The main thing I remember today is the mood of those weekends. I don't remember what the discussions were about, but I still have a clear image of nice people strolling with Father around the dacha grounds. . . . [I]t seem[ed] as if two friendly families were getting together, rather than representatives of two great powers whose relations left a lot to be desired.[39]

The families also exchanged gifts, such as the ingenious English toasting cups presented by Mrs. Thompson; their design reduced the amount of liquor to be gulped. They even exchanged confidences, as when Mrs. Khrushchev spoke wearily of her husband's fluctuating moods: "He's either way up here or way down there." And the premier confessed to Thompson that the obligatory round of heavy dinners and frequent toasts wore him out. Khrushchev even allowed the ambassadress to tease him, as when she suggested that he go incognito—wearing a beard—to the United States in 1959, thereby saving the natives from upset. When on Khrushchev's U.S. tour (accompanied by the Thompsons) the mayor of Los Angeles spoke stridently about communism and the USSR—causing Khrushchev to throw one of his tantrums—Mrs. Thompson burst into tears, so deep was her stake in the success of personal diplomacy.[40]

Neither these family excursions nor the friendly meetings between Thompson and Khrushchev alleviated the hardship for Americans living in Moscow, however. The city remained a hardship post testing the mettle of any diplomat, novice or veteran. Eleanor Roosevelt, who visited the USSR in 1957 and encountered difficulties routinely faced by embassy personnel, later declared, "I think I should die if I had to live in Soviet Russia." Substandard and crowded housing was a source of unending complaint by Thompson's subordinates. This problem was aggravated by the arrival of an administrative officer, Idar Rimestad, who had a knack for affronting mission members and restricting further the spartan pleasures of their Soviet life. He forbade the weekend use by families of embassy cars (until then a time-honored practice), grudgingly made arrangements for apartment repairs, and was niggardly in his rationing of tickets to local opera and ballet productions. The diplomats meanwhile chafed under the rule of travel restrictions (one-third of the USSR was still closed to travel by foreigners—and so remained to the end). They lived in dread of winding up in an unhygienic hospital or falling prey to Soviet medicine. They were still forced to import heaps of fresh fruit, vegetables, and meats to ensure minimally healthful diets. Moreover, the organs of revolutionary vigilance did not rest, not even in the days of Khrushchev's rousing American visit and myriad references to the "spirit of Camp David." Listening devices were as ubiquitous as before and continually unearthed in the diplomats' residences and offices; the working assumption was that every room was bugged. When Thompson had something confidential to discuss with a colleague, he would (in the accustomed fashion) exchange written notes in lieu of conversation. Under these circumstances, discipline within the embassy was not relaxed by Thompson; as with Bohlen, lapses were infrequent. Meanwhile, Soviet authorities discouraged contact between embassy officials and Muscovites. In Robert Martens's recollection: "People were scared to death. You didn't want to ever have a second meeting with anybody because they very likely would be put away as a result." To underscore their policy, the Soviets declared John Baker, a second secretary in the embassy, persona non grata in May 1958. His unpardonable sin had been to befriend Soviet students he had met during lectures at Moscow State University. Thompson protested this Soviet action, insisting that his man was not desirous of corrupting Soviet youth for American ends. What happened to the youngsters contacted by Baker was never discovered by the embassy. In any event, Thompson's declaration of Baker's innocence was rejected. As with the Kennan incident six years earlier, there was an uproar in Congress, one of whose members (Representative Feighan) proposed that Ambassador Mikhail Menshikov be expelled. This action was not taken, although a smaller fry in the Soviet embassy was ordered to leave Washington.[41]

Notwithstanding these vexations, the Thompson–Khrushchev tie constituted a breakthrough. It helped ensure for the first time since Harriman a usable channel of communication in Moscow between the two governments. Confident of his standing with Khrushchev, Thompson did not hesitate when appropriate to be blunt. He told him that the use of Soviet or East German forces in Berlin would be met by strenuous Western military countermoves. He spoke strongly against the detention of U-2 pilot Gary Powers (intercepted May 1, 1960) and U.S. plane crews earlier gone missing over Soviet airspace; he argued that Moscow's support of communist insurgents in Laos and the Congo bode ill for the USSR–U.S. future. In turn, Khrushchev was candid with Thompson, as when he expressed dismay for Eisenhower's bungling of the U-2 affair or worried aloud that Soviet–U.S. relations would deteriorate if Richard Nixon should be elected president in 1960 (Thompson argued reassuringly to the contrary). But never did the tone of these Khrushchev–Thompson talks become ad hominem or belligerent. They were conducted with personal regard of a kind entirely absent in previous years.[42]

An advantage of his standing with Khrushchev was that it quickened Thompson's knowledge of Soviet political personalities and augmented the quality of his interpretive reporting. He recognized in 1957, earlier than Bohlen would have, that Khrushchev's preeminent position made a sham of the collective leadership idea. He was, in Thompson's phrase, "conspicuously in the driver's seat" after his humbling of the antiparty cabal and Zhukov's removal from the Presidium. By November 1957, with Malenkov in eastern Kazakhstan managing a hydroelectric plant, Molotov exiled to Outer Mongolia as ambassador, Kaganovich directing a cement plant east of the Urals, and Zhukov stripped of his duties as defense minister, few obstructions remained to Khrushchev's becoming a "one-man dictatorship." Yet, reported Thompson, Khrushchev was not invulnerable to a palace coup, especially if his economic reforms went awry. As it was, Khrushchev represented the best promise to develop Soviet material life. Although not exactly a bulwark against police activities, he was disinclined to return his country to Stalinism. A "fanatic communist," quick-tempered, and sensitive to slights, he was to Thompson a better negotiating partner for the United States than any of the unrepentant Stalinists hoping to replace him. Khrushchev's faith in Soviet productive capacity, his notion that Marxism-Leninism by its example would win converts throughout the Third World, and his prophesies that communism would overwhelm the West by nonviolence made for an "exceedingly complex character." However, it was one with whom Americans could deal. Hence Thompson's preference for Soviet–U.S. meetings at all levels, including between the president and premier, where understanding could progress.[43]

The keenness of Thompson's analyses of the Soviet position on Germany, international communism, and the prospects for peace were also attributable to his access to the voluble Khrushchev (their talks sometimes running three or four hours). When Khrushchev's 1958 ultimatum on Berlin (threatening to relinquish to East German authority all communication lines to the city if the Western powers failed to demilitarize West Berlin) caused a crisis, Thompson did not conclude that another war was imminent. He realized from the outset that Berlin mattered only secondarily to the Soviets. Rather, the country of which it was the traditional capital was of transcendent importance as Khrushchev calculated Soviet security requirements. The essential issue was that he wanted an unambiguous East–West agreement on Germany and its role in Europe. To this end, he was willing to stir a scare over access to Berlin if it led (however circuitously) to a German solution. This meant for the USSR that a future, unified Germany must not align itself with

NATO. Behind Khrushchev's proposals at the time on an East–West withdrawal from the heart of Europe was this obstinacy, stated to Thompson: 250 years should pass before the two parts of Germany were permitted to reunite. In addition, concern over the stability of Walter Ulbricht's regime and other Warsaw Pact clients was animating Khrushchev. The presence of Western spies and propagandists in Berlin, the flow of East Europeans to its refuge, and the invidious comparison between the city's two sectors were unsetting. Beginning in Berlin, the entire socialist commonwealth might unravel. Thompson cabled in 1961 to Dean Rusk (who as the new secretary of state inherited the American side of the Berlin matter): "Soviet Union interested in stabilization their western frontier and Communist regimes in Eastern Europe, particularly East Germany which probably most vulnerable. Soviets also deeply concerned with German military potential." To manage the Berlin imbroglio, he urged Eisenhower (and then Kennedy) to adopt a firm line of negotiation but never to abandon hope of a diplomatic settlement. Thompson's contribution to this settlement during a number of desultory talks with Gromyko was minor. But his ongoing assessment of Soviet motives was astute, and his brief on the need for tenacious diplomacy sensible and read as such in Washington.[44]

When it came to the study of Soviet relations with other communist countries, Thompson's reportage was at its best, though he tended to overstate the influence of Marxist ideology as a determinant of foreign policy. Of Castro's revolution, he felt that the Soviets were at first indifferent. But they soon recognized Cuba as a strategic asset nestled near the U.S. mainland and fragile states in the Americas. In addition to this opportunistic approach to Cuba, said Thompson, the Soviets became sentimentally attached to the revolutionaries as they treaded the socialist path first opened in 1917.[45]

Thompson was a particularly close student of the emergent Sino-Soviet dispute. Despite the incredulity of some in Washington who were mesmerized by the idea of monolithic communism (notably Walter Robertson, assistant secretary for East Asian affairs), Thompson inveighed that the communist alliance was being rent asunder along ideological, economic, and security lines. Based on his conversations with Khrushchev and on intelligence sources, it became plain to him that the Kremlin had several worries: the desire of China to acquire nuclear weaponry, its pretensions to world communist leadership, its insatiable hunger for Soviet economic-technical assistance, and its attempts to involve the USSR in contests of will against the United States on behalf of Chinese irredentism (i.e., the offshore islands, Taiwan). Thompson wrote in 1960 that "while Soviet and Chinese may succeed in plastering over cracks in their relations, they will probably not succeed in actually resolving their differences and in long run I believe these will tend to grow more acute." Even though Thompson refrained from predicting when a total Sino-Soviet break would occur, he was convinced that it would happen and that American policy could reap advantages. It was simply erroneous to think, like Robertson, that Sino-Soviet disagreements were crafty inventions meant to mislead Western policymakers.[46] Just what influence Thompson had on Eisenhower's and Dulles's perception of the fraying communist coalition is impossible to say. They never responded, at least as far as documents show, directly to his reports on the subject. His words, filtered through White House and State Department offices, were probably read and reinforced the administration's predisposition: when possible, the United States should press China militarily, economically, and diplomatically, thereby causing Mao to make unacceptable demands of Moscow.[47]

As for the Soviet–U.S. security relationship, Thompson was again a source of insight into Khrushchev's thinking. He agreed with Dulles that the premier's boasts about Soviet rocket superiority in the late 1950s and loose talk about the number of nuclear-tipped missiles needed to destroy London or Paris were unnerving. Yet he was inclined to view such talk as bravado and as a measure (if crudely stated) of Soviet resolve to avoid future war—not as an indication of aggressive intentions. Thus at the time of *Sputnik,* he admitted that achievements in Soviet science (and by extension in military technology) would fuel Khrushchev's braggadocio and might encourage him to adopt a more assertive foreign policy. But Thompson was equally affected by periodic lectures addressed to himself and other resident diplomats, whose theme was that Americans knew nothing of the heartbreak of modern warfare. The Soviets, according to standard theme, had no illusions and were determined to prevent a recurrence of violence on the scale of 1914 or 1939. In this spirit, Zhukov, for one, tried to impress on Thompson the imperative of declaring a halt to the Cold War. Alexei Kosygin, a rising political star in the late 1950s, talked wistfully to him of curtailing arms spending and of concentrating resources on raising the living standards in America and Russia.[48] Khrushchev himself occasionally expressed anxiety to Thompson about the wastefulness and dangers inherent in the nuclear arms race. All these USSR protestations caused him to think that the United States and the USSR could usefully expand their negotiations agenda. "I continue to believe," he wrote in the autumn of 1957, "that for internal reasons Khrushchev genuinely desires to reach a détente covering a considerable period of time."[49] Thompson subsequently had high hopes for the May 1960 Eisenhower–Khrushchev meeting in Paris, in whose planning he was involved. And he would have seconded this private avowal of Eisenhower's to a critic of the summit conference:

> My feeling is that the world is headed toward an arms race of such magnitude as can culminate only in unbearable burdens on our peoples at best, or general war at worst. No efforts should be spared to find some way out of this grim prospect. Face to face talks with Mr. Khrushchev, while I expect very little from them, represent nearly the only course left now to this end. Such action does not involve approval of Mr. Khrushchev himself or his methods, nor does it, to my mind, represent any act of appeasement whatsoever.[50]

Khrushchev's indignation in Paris over the U-2 episode and cancellations of the summit and Eisenhower's scheduled visit to the USSR disconcerted Thompson: a rare opportunity to ease tensions was misplayed by both sides. He later ruminated that the U-2 issue had provided a pretext for Khrushchev's wrecking the summit; the Soviets had already decided that agreements on Berlin, Germany, and arms control would not be forthcoming in the first round of negotiations and not before the U.S. elections decided a new president. The Soviets could not be sure that pledges made by Eisenhower in exchange for Moscow's concessions would be honored by the next administration. Thompson also speculated that the Soviets felt compelled to repair the damage in the communist world resulting from the rift with China "before facing [the] West in show-down negotiations."[51]

In the months following the Paris debacle, he watched with apprehension as the USSR took measures and issued declarations that incensed Western governments: walking out in June from the ten-nation disarmament meeting, shooting down a U.S. reconnaissance plane over international waters in the Barents Sea in July, threatening to extend a unilateral guardianship over Austria and signing a peace treaty with East Germany, publicly wondering whether to send Red Army units to the Congo to maintain its independence from American and UN imperialists, charging that the Monroe Doctrine was dead, asserting that the USSR might support Cuba with missiles if the United States began operating against Castro. Yet Thompson, the perennial optimist, was not persuaded that these actions and threats implied an incurably hard Soviet policy. That would come at the expense of things still valued by Moscow—from binding agreements on Germany and arms control to anticipated benefits derived from cultural-economic exchanges with the West. Should Khrushchev go too far in a Cold War direction, he might be replaced by his party colleagues, said Thompson. The premier's inability to break the impasse with the West or to raise the agricultural economy to sustainable high rates of production meant that he could become a liability. In June 1960, Thompson revised his estimation of Khrushchev's remaining time in office from four or five years to one or two.[52]

Adviser in Camelot

A Democrat and an admirer of Kennedy, Thompson made little secret of his enthusiasm for the 1960 electoral results. And he was pleased to stay on in Moscow through the first eighteen months after inauguration.[53] This period covered the Bay of Pigs invasion (April 1961), an operation about which he was uninformed and against which his natural caution might have warned. This period also counted Kennedy's tongue-tied performance in Vienna with Khrushchev in June 1961. Thompson had originally urged Kennedy to meet his Soviet counterpart, expecting the president would then better understand Khrushchev and with him could break the ice in bilateral relations that had congealed toward the end of the Eisenhower administration. In subsequent years, Kennedy could not resist chiding Thompson: "[The president] several times teased me about having recommended the Vienna meeting, saying that it had not gone very well, but he always ended up by admitting that it had been useful to him to get to know Khrushchev at firsthand."[54]

The continuing crisis over Berlin, culminating with the erection of the wall (August 1961), and the resumption by both sides of atmospheric nuclear testing were additional complications during Thompson's ambassadorship. If any one label might be applied to him during these events, it would be that of pragmatic idealist. This oxymoron (though inelegant) captures Thompson's faith in the efficacy of the diplomatic art to settle questions between the rival powers—for which reason, he was studiously attentive and available to Khrushchev. At the same time, Thompson taught that the United States ought not retreat from its strategic and moral positions, however blatant Soviet provocation. As part of his campaign in 1961 to tutor the new administration, the ambassador cabled Dean Rusk:

> I am sure we would err if we should treat Communist threat at this time *as being primarily of military nature. I believe Soviet leadership has* long ago correctly appraised meaning [of] atomic military power. They recognized major war [is] no longer acceptable means [of] achieving their objectives. We shall, of course, have to keep our *powder* dry and have plenty of it, for obvious reasons. (Thompson's italics)

To deal with a nonmilitary but potentially lethal Soviet challenge, Thompson personally advised Kennedy along these lines: the United States must take steps to ensure that the Western system worked well and that its member states remained united; the country should also place itself constructively on the side of emergent nations and anticolonialism and demonstrate by deeds that the future belonged to the West, not to the USSR.[55]

As for his relations with Kennedy, they were superior to those with Eisenhower. He had respected Thompson but from afar; he never consulted the ambassador closely and inadvertently neglected him. Kennedy knew better how to employ and reward Thompson, who for all his self-effacement also possessed healthy pride. They met a number of times, including at the outset of Kennedy's term with other Soviet veterans: Harriman, Kennan, and Bohlen. This meeting was marked by Kennedy's listening and canvassing of opinion, which generated a consensus along Thompson's views. Bohlen afterward spoke for himself and Thompson when he pronounced ecstatically, "I never heard of a President who wanted to know so much." To his wife, Jane, Thompson declared that such an inquisitive president was "too good to be true." When the time was appropriate, Kennedy also discussed with him the choice of his successor in Moscow. One possible candidate was the attorney general, Robert Kennedy, whom the Soviets especially wanted. Presumably, he would have ensured access to the president, thereby circumventing the State Department (supposed bastion against Soviet–U.S. détente). Neither the president nor Thompson was receptive to this formula; in the end, Kennedy picked Thompson's (and the Foreign Service's) favorite for the embassy, Foy Kohler.[56]

On returning to Washington in the summer of 1962, Thompson worked under Dean Rusk as his adviser on Soviet affairs. In that capacity, he played a supporting part in composing Kennedy's June 1963 American University speech, which identified ways of ending the Cold War: "History teaches us that enmities between nations, as between individuals, do not last forever." He was more prominently involved in helping to negotiate the limited test-ban treaty in 1963, though the major task was undertaken by Harriman.

Thompson's most important work derived from his membership in that body of presidential advisers chosen to conduct the U.S. side of the 1962 Cuban missile crisis (October 16–28), the Executive Committee of the National Security Council (ExCom). As the only member of the ExCom with direct experience of the Soviet

Union, he proved invaluable. In their distinctive ways, fellow ExCom associates Robert Kennedy, Dean Rusk, and Defense Secretary Robert McNamara credited Thompson's understanding of Khrushchev as unmatched—though he, like Bohlen, had mistakenly believed the Soviets would not dare to place nuclear warheads on Cuban-based missiles. In keeping with his general viewpoint, Thompson's line during the crisis was that the missiles could be removed by means short of war.[57]

In the ExCom's grueling sessions (from which he was briefly excused to attend his mother's funeral), Thompson was closely questioned about Khrushchev's motives, probable state of mind, immunity to coup d'état, and likely response to one or another type of U.S. action. In addition, Thompson was used to draft Kennedy's letters to Khrushchev and to decipher the deeper meaning of the premier's messages to the president. In this connection, it was Thompson's idea (not Robert Kennedy's, as legend holds) to respond to Khrushchev's first letter, which contained a basis for resolving the crisis, and to ignore the second, more emotional one. Thompson also argued on behalf of the naval blockade (euphemistically labeled quarantine) and against the rasher proposals of aerial bombardment or amphibious invasion. And he accurately predicted that the Soviets would try to run a ship through the blockade to test U.S. resolve, but would back down if they were made to know that Washington was not bluffing. A so-called surgical strike or military landing, he warned Kennedy, would dangerously escalate the crisis and might cause Khrushchev to respond impulsively—by launching military action against West Berlin or U.S. missile sites in Turkey. From thence, nuclear war would be but a small step. Above all, counseled Thompson, Khrushchev must have time to reflect on his actions and not be driven to desperate measures. On a matter bearing on the Soviets' sensitivity to legalistic matters, it was Thompson who forced the ExCom's concentration on obtaining approval for U.S. actions by the Organization of American States. Abram Chayes, the State Department's legal counsel in 1962, subsequently observed, "Having to consider the legal position carefully contributed . . . to the wisdom of our choices." Finally, on the advice of Thompson and after intensive coaching by him, Robert Kennedy was used to approach Soviet ambassador Anatoly Dobrynin. Kennedy's message was that either the Soviets removed the missiles from Cuba or the Americans would; but this ultimatum was tempered with the assurance—at Thompson's urging—that the Americans were eager to avoid a military conflict. Thompson actually recommended the attorney general for this errand to satisfy the Kremlin's conspiratorial view of U.S. politics and on the assumption that Dobrynin would pay more attention to him than to any person shy of the president. Thus on varied and critical aspects of the Cuban episode, Thompson's judgment had an effect: he left a mark on America's Soviet policy at the moment of gravest peril. Rusk and McNamara honored him as the "unsung hero" of the missile crisis.[58]

*   *   *   *

Soviet history after Stalin was shaped by unsteady adjustment to the unfathomable dictator's career. Patchy reform alternated with and struggled against reaction. This contest between rival conceptions of the Soviet future helped focus the attention of diplomats in Moscow for more than three decades. Ultimately, Soviet socialism was not rescued by Stalin's successors but overthrown because they lacked the audacity of their predecessors, who mimicked the moral language of generosity and promise of earthly paradise while blighting the human landscape. The eventual collapse of Soviet power in 1991 was thus brought about by a continuing crisis of confidence within the political class, exemplified in the first instance by Khrushchev's erratic career. A creature and critic of Stalin, he neither fully knew nor assimilated his generation's ordeal of totalitarianism. Yet in the decade after 1953, Khrushchev's experience of Stalin was the main source of Soviet political imagination; it served as an antidote to the extravagance of utopian promise and blurred the mounting evidences of national failure.

Containment policy in the Eisenhower–Kennedy era played a decidedly inferior role in these fateful events. Still, U.S. policy had an influence—albeit not in the way assumed by its exuberant apologists, who declared at the end of the Cold War that the United States had won it by perseverance and God's grace.[59] Prosaic professional diplomacy with its hard-earned knowledge, personified by Thompson, had contributed hugely to averting a war in 1962 from which there would have been no recovery. This achievement was all the more striking in light of diplomacy's being undervalued in American culture and subjected to active assault in the early 1950s.

Primitive thought during the Cold War was not the exclusive province of the McCarthy wing of the Republican party. The Wisconsin senator and his cronies were vivid examples of it, nevertheless. Although they failed to destroy Bohlen, it was not for want of trying. The leading student of Soviet affairs in the government's employ (his competitor for this title, Kennan, was by then a private scholar ensconced in Princeton) arrived in Moscow upset by his congressional trial. His British colleague, Ambassador Alvary Gascoigne, reported to Churchill:

> Bohlen seem[s] to me to have been rather shaken up by the horrible attacks which were made upon him by certain members of the United States Senate. I really do not know what will happen to the American Foreign Service if McCarthy and [company] are allowed to continue their despicable manoeuvres against officials who are only trying to show loyalty to the Government that employs them. It is, of course, a great pity from our own point of view that this is happening to the American diplomats; I fear that we may not get the same good type and excellent quality of person to deal with in the future as we have in the past.[60]

This concern of foreign sympathizers like Gascoigne was shared by many figures in U.S. government, including Thompson, who in 1953 worried that diplomats were becoming economical with the truth to avoid the censure of McCarthy and the suspicion of McLeod. This condition would surely lead, critics said, to "a frame of mind [that] feared to report the truth just the way Russian diplomats feared to tell the truth to the Kremlin," with resultant injuries to understanding and intelligent policy.[61]

Thompson's survival instincts meant that his criticisms of Dulles's State Department were as surreptitiously voiced as his Democratic party preferences. Consequently, though organized competence within the government apparatus was damaged in the 1950s, it survived through Thompson and was vindicated in the 1962 Cuban missile crisis. Assignments to the Soviet Union, personal acquaintance with its rulers, and study of its history enabled Thompson while on the ExCom to make (in Robert Kennedy's tribute) predictions about Khrushchev's behavior that were "uncannily accurate" and to deliver recommendations that "were surpassed by none." In this way, Thompson's Soviet career refuted the seductive but false thesis that mass communication and rapid transportation had rendered ambassadorial diplomacy obsolete. Rather, as Bohlen contended in his 1972 eulogy at Thompson's funeral, "the quiet continuous contacts and the confidential discussions which are the essence of diplomacy prepare the way for the public agreements. It was here that Thompson excelled." To this affirmation, Bohlen could have added—as Robert McNamara did—that in difficult matters involving a major country, it is necessary that the president have available and listen to pertinent area experts. As the former defense secretary rued in 1989: "Look at the mess our nation got into in the Iran-Contra affair, and in Vietnam. The [Reagan] administration had absolutely no understanding of Iran, and we [Kennedy–Johnson] had little more of Indochina because we had eliminated all of the Chinese specialists during the McCarthy era." Might the functional equivalent of a Thompson have intervened to avert or otherwise moderate these moments of colossal misjudgment?[62]

9

Controlled Rivalry

The future is an unknown country, admittedly. Yet the recent past is only slightly less mysterious. Its rough shape can be apprehended, but its distinctive texture is obscure, to say nothing of the framework of meaning to which it might plausibly belong. Absence of perspective and the stealthy intervention of partisanship make hazardous the writing of contemporary history, defined here as since the Cuban missile crisis. From the standpoint of traditionalists, contemporary history, with its mélange of anecdotes and deceptive familiarity, lacks respectability. Added to these problems is another equally insuperable to the production of sturdy interpretation: the inaccessibility of most primary materials. Given the unripened quality of historical data and heavy reliance on conjecture, claims of judgment are thus (usually) more tentative in evaluating the events of one's own time than those distant. Narrative in this case relies on the vocabulary of qualification. To paraphrase Paul Valéry's aphorism, scholarship here is not finished. It is abandoned.

Each subsection in this chapter corresponds to what future historians will regard as identifiable moments in Soviet–U.S. affairs, deserving of separate and full treatment. However impressionistic and synoptic the following, it nevertheless shows that the pattern underlying the history of diplomats in Moscow during the pre-Brezhnev era continued afterward. On both sides of the Brezhnev divide, America's Soviet policy benefited when the embassy was in competent hands. Conversely, it suffered when the mission was sacrificed to political expediency or ignored by Washington or its assets otherwise squandered.

Toward Détente

Relations between the two powers improved markedly, if briefly, after the Cuban emergency. Not a year had elapsed before both sides and the British negotiated the Limited Nuclear Test Ban Treaty (August 1963) and established a crisis communications link, the Hot Line. Thereafter, the two governments signed (January 1967) with sixty additional others a treaty curtailing the use of outer space for military purposes. They later approved a nuclear nonproliferation treaty.

President Lyndon Johnson met with Premier Alexei Kosygin at Glassboro State College (New Jersey) in June 1967 to discuss issues of mutual concern: the Six-Day War, Vietnam, and controls on nuclear weaponry. Despite Johnson's effort to accent the positive ("great progress in reducing misunderstanding"), Glassboro failed to advance the cause of détente. By mid-1967, it was hostage to America's Vietnam adventure and Soviet support of Ho Chi Minh. Anxiety in Moscow about Mao's China—in the paroxysm of Cultural Revolution—and recognition that Soviet and American interests might converge there did not offset the felt obligation to assist fraternal Vietnamese communists in their war against imperialism. Prohibitions on cultural expression in the USSR following Khrushchev's 1964 "retirement," the 1968 Warsaw Pact invasion of Czechoslovakia, and enunciation of the Brezhnev doctrine underscored further the difference in Soviet and U.S. viewpoints.

During this period, when promise faded into failure, the United States was represented in Moscow by a journeyman diplomat, Foy Kohler, and (on an ill-advised second tour) by Llewllyn Thompson. Each in his way sought to preserve and expand the area of confidence between the rival powers. In this, they were overwhelmed by the intractability of problems separating the two nations and creeping skepticism in Washington about the utility of ambassadorial diplomacy.

By neither temperament nor background did Kohler fit into the Kennedy schema. It encouraged the use of diplomats who exhibited that brand of élan prized by the president. As Undersecretary of State Chester Bowles expressed it, the administration was determined to recruit "a new breed of envoy."[1] In this connection, the distinguished historian of Japan, Edwin O. Reishchauer, was sent to Tokyo. Harvard economist John Kenneth Galbraith went to New Delhi. Highly visible veteran diplomats of stature were also employed. Bohlen was sent to Paris, Kennan to Belgrade, and David Bruce to London. Not only did Kohler fall outside this best-and-brightest category, but he seemed to insiders to embody the traits of the State Department as it emerged from Eisenhower's custodianship: uncreative, slow, hidebound. Robert Kennedy, who was caustic on the subject of the State Department's competence, thought Kohler precisely the type of mediocrity unable to accomplish anything significant. Besides, he gave the attorney general "the creeps." Harriman campaigned against Kohler's appointment on the grounds that he was comprehensively unimaginative. It was only out of deference to the Foreign Service's explicit desire, and on the supposition that a noncareer man in Moscow would be savaged by professionals in the embassy, that President Kennedy approved Kohler.[2]

He had joined the Foreign Service shortly after completing studies at Ohio State University in 1931. His early career saw assignments in southeastern Europe (Romania, Yugoslavia, Greece) and the Middle East (Egypt). During the closing stage of World War II, he served as assistant chief in the department's Division of Near Eastern Affairs. Following additional experience in Greece and London and study at the National War College (1946), he was made first secretary (then counselor) of the embassy in Moscow under Walter Bedell Smith.

In the Soviet Union, Kohler and his scholarly minded wife, Phyllis Penn, became enamored with the writings of the Marquis de Custine. Phyllis Kohler edited and published an abridged edition of these in 1951 with the hope of illustrating similarities between the *ancien régime* and Stalinism.[3] Meanwhile, husband and wife, who had previously experienced Greece under Nazi occupation, managed to survive Moscow, with its alarms and the pressure of living in isolation. To his longtime friend and mentor, Loy Henderson, Kohler allowed in 1948: "The German occupation of Greece, which gave me ulcers some years ago, was nothing in comparison [to life in Moscow]. Nevertheless, a spell of it is well worthwhile if only because no one would ever believe it who didn't see it with his own eyes."[4] After Moscow, Kohler was named chief of the International Broadcasting Division of the Voice of America (VOA), at the time a recently organized innovation in the propaganda war. From there, Kohler was shifted in 1952 to the State Department's Policy Planning Staff, directed by Paul Nitze.

To this point, Kohler's career had depended on his skeptical mind and laconic discretion. These qualities displaced his small-Ohio-town (Oakwood) parochialism and had secured his reputation in the Foreign Service for conscientiousness.[5] With each success, however, came additional pressure, which he relieved by drink. His career was nearly ruined in December 1952, when he and his wife caused a traffic accident after attending a dinner party in Arlington, Virginia. They were subsequently arrested for drunkenness and unruly behavior. At the hospital where Kohler was treated for copious bleeding of the head, his wife (suffering concussion) became hysterical, slapped a nurse, and was strapped down on a hospital litter without sedative. She cursed her medical tormentors and police interrogators and accused them all of behaving in a manner worthy of the Soviets. Aggravating matters, Kohler had in his possession classified documents (concerning North Africa) that were not permitted off the premises of the State Department building.

Inquiries by the tabloid press and official investigators followed. Kohler had to confess his carelessness and dispel suspicions about the reasons for having confidential papers on his person. He explained that he was taking them (all of an ordinary nature) home for closer study; neither he nor his wife was a communist or sympathetic to Soviet totalitarianism. On the contrary, he pleaded, they were "active fighters against these evils." Refusing to resign under fire, Kohler pressed his case for leniency into the Eisenhower period. Not only did some congressional critics and editorial writers demand his resignation, but Scott McLeod expected it. The crisis climaxed in March 1953, just as Bohlen was taking his bruising test in the Senate. Only the intervention of his former boss, Walter Bedell Smith (then undersecretary of state), saved Kohler from being fired. He was reprimanded, though, and exiled to professional purgatory in the embassy at Ankara. After a period of probation and good conduct, he was allowed back to Washington, and in 1958 Dulles named him deputy assistant secretary for European affairs. His last job in the Eisenhower government involved Germany; in 1961, he headed the president's task force on Berlin.[6]

The effect of the Arlington incident on Kohler was twofold. First, it quickened his caution, reinforced already by the habits of mind fostered in the Foreign Service. It was against the resultant colorlessness in him that Harriman so vehemently objected in 1962. Second, Arlington heightened Kohler's sensitivity to the real and imagined slights of senior officers. Reticent rather than confident, he seems to have been defensive about his standing in the Soviet field, where his linguistic and other expertise shone less brightly than that of Kennan, Bohlen, or Thompson. It was hurt pride and jealousy that once caused him to damn Kennan as a poor diplomat, "more emotional than 'realistic,' self-centered and intellectually arrogant to the Nth degree." A symptom of Kohler's touchiness was that he required ministrations of reassurance—not flattery exactly, but testimonials that cumulatively drew the sting from his 1952 misstep. His counselor for political affairs in Moscow, Malcolm Toon (himself once victimized by Kennan), hit the right chord when he told Kohler in 1977: "It is high time to set to rest the claim that [Kennan] knows more about the Soviets than any living American. I would place you far above George in this respect."[7]

Except for coordinating Richard Nixon's whirlwind visit to the USSR in 1959, Kohler had not spent time in the Soviet Union since his tour with Smith. What encouraged him most on returning to Moscow in 1962 was the extent of improvement since Stalin. People were friendlier, better fed, more stylishly dressed. Jazz concerts, readings of daring poetry, and exhibitions of abstract painting were popular, despite proscriptions on much modern art. Lesser citizens and officials were also obviously less afraid. As Kohler told an audience at the National War College:

> The contrast in [Soviet] society as I saw it in the years just after the war, in Stalin's day, and now is really like night and day in terms of the use of police power and the fear people feel. At the time when we were there before literally anyone who had any standing whatsoever kept a bag packed ready for that two-o'clock-in-the-morning knock on the door. That fear is gone.

Still, he recognized that desirable change did not constitute metamorphosis. Basic restrictions were still in place: society was controlled and hobbled by a backward economy. The embassy also remained a target of suspicion and espionage. Just days after he presented his credentials, the Soviets gave Kohler his first persona non grata case. The assistant naval attaché, Commander Raymond Smith, was implicated by the police in spying. Before Kohler's term expired, he was to confront twelve additional cases that resulted in the expulsion of Foreign Service and uniformed officers (typically in retaliation for diplomats expelled from Washington or the Soviet UN delegation in New York). There was also the squalid KGB campaign to recruit embassy personnel for intelligence purposes through sexual blackmail. As for Soviet leaders, Kohler agreed that from a humanitarian standpoint Khrushchev represented a quantum leap over Stalin. But from the perspective of U.S. security, Kohler thought he was more worrisome than his dreaded predecessor. He was likelier to play for high stakes abroad to promote the ideology he professed.[8]

Had Khrushchev during his Cuban gamble been in direct touch with Llewellyn Thompson, for whom his admiration never faltered, he might have acted more cautiously. As it was, the premier was barely acquainted with Thompson's successor. What little Khrushchev knew of him, he disliked. There was, in short, no personal understanding that might have helped Kohler to exercise a restraining influence during the critical October weeks. Unsurprisingly, Kohler's role in the emergency was overshadowed by that played by the ExCom, Khrushchev, and the Soviet ambassador in Washington, Anatoly Dobrynin.[9]

Kohler's first audience with Khrushchev occurred on October 16, the very day that Kennedy learned the Soviets were installing in Cuba ballistic missiles capable of delivering nuclear warheads to the U.S. mainland. In their conversations, the premier was sweet reasonableness on Cuban matters. The Americans need not worry that the USSR would place offensive weapons on the island. Would they kindly desist from harassing with spy planes Soviet merchant ships conducting peaceable trade with Cuba? As for the Cuban port that the Soviets were helping to build, its function was to support the local fishing industry. Contrary to reports from troublemakers opposed to ending the Cold War, this port had no sinister purpose. In this same amiable fashion, Khrushchev and the ambassador also discussed Berlin, the premier's forthcoming trip to New York (to address the UN), and lesser matters such as the need to expand the scope of cultural exchanges. Only on the topic of Jupiter missiles based in Turkey, about which Kohler had not been briefed, did Khrushchev betray testiness. After the interview, Kohler cabled Rusk that his host had been forthcoming on the main topics and otherwise agreeable.[10]

During the missile crisis, as a show of optimism that it would end favorably, Kohler honored his prearranged schedule. It included courtesy calls on ambassadors (from Ceylon, Sudan, Austria, Greece, Iran) and on Soviet officials with whom he discussed prospects for reinvigorated exchange programs.[11] Although not taken into confidence by either his own government or Moscow, Kohler was additionally useful in transmitting urgent messages between the Kremlin and the White House. He was supremely efficient, both in responding to summonses from the Foreign Ministry to send Khrushchev's letters to Kennedy and in conveying U.S. texts to the Soviets.

As the officer responsible for the well-being of U.S. citizens in Moscow, Kohler had their children assemble in the safety of Spaso House while in the neighborhood of the embassy demonstrators threw rocks, jeered, and shouted "Hands off Cuba!" In this fracas, orchestrated by party agitators, the ambassador's limousine was dented, and a few windows in the chancery were smashed. That was, however, all that resident Americans suffered during the crisis, apart from the imposition of a stricter ban on travel to outlying provinces. Nothing like a war scare permeated the embassy, where the assumption held that the Cuban matter was difficult but unlikely to end in hostilities. At the time, in fact, most Americans in Moscow had not the faintest idea of how near the nations were to war. Rebecca Matlock, whose husband was then a junior officer in the consular section, recounted, "We didn't know until afterwards about those planes sitting on the runway waiting to take off for Cuba and all the preparation for the possibility of war." Moreover, as people in the embassy later concurred, Americans in Moscow were never at serious risk from mobs. A majority of the participants had been pressed into service and were not hostile toward Americans, who remained popular, as they had been for years, with the average Soviet.[12] Even as demonstrators went through the prescribed taunts and chants, they showed apathy for Castro, a factor that Kohler surmised influenced Khrushchev's decision to withdraw the missiles. The citizenry's unease with Khrushchev's impetuousness was also apparent to the ambassador, who gave this testimony:

> On this given Saturday I had a call to pay on the Persian Ambassador so I set out from the Embassy around twelve o'clock in one of those great big government limousines with a big flag flying, and I had gone a block and a half down the street when lo and behold there came about a thousand Russians marching along with signs and obviously headed for the Embassy. They saw me and I saw them and they kind of waved and smiled; they did not have anything against me or the flag; they were just doing what they were told to which was to march to a point about a kilometer away. Then after I left the Persian Embassy they called me and said, "Do not come back because we really have a flock of them here now. Go home." So I started off again and this time I ran into another group of these poor factory workers being marched in for miles from factories outside, and this time I went with them and rode along beside them for quite a long ways. The same thing was true. It could not have been friendlier. There was no mistaking, though, on the part of those who realized, how serious the crisis had been and the following week I [received] endless expressions of relief. . . . It was very obvious that the Russian people had no stomach for an adventure that [would] involve them in a war about Cuba.

Having stared into the "abyss" (Kohler's term) and recoiled from it, the Soviets resolved after Cuba to make progress on issues dividing them from Washington. This attitude made possible a spurt of agreements on limited cooperation: exchanging information on weather, space, and atomic energy—and signing the treaty banning above-ground testing of nuclear weapons.[13]

In this season of improved relations, as well as during the subsequent chill coinciding with Brezhnev's and Kosygin's coup, Kohler was an energetic proponent of cultural exchanges and Soviet–U.S. economic relations. His reasoning here was grounded in unblinking realism. As he understood it, the ultimate objective of the Kennedy and Johnson administrations was to encourage changes in the Soviet Union that would result in a less antagonistic country. The United States, whenever possible, should therefore shape public discourse in the USSR about policy choices. In other words, Americans might help fashion the direction of communist evolution.

Exchange programs in Kohler's time encompassed travel and consultation between Soviet and U.S. scientists, writers, educators, doctors, artists, students, and musicians. (American tourists to the USSR numbered about twenty thousand per year by 1965; only a hundred or so Soviets traveled the other way.)[14] Prominent among these people on the U.S. side were Robert Frost, Irving Stone, musicologist Nicholas Slonimsky, biographer James MacGregor Burns, geographer Chauncy Harris, and physicist Norman Ramsey. They reported that their audiences were not only interested in their specialized subjects, but also unabashedly curious about all things American. These events, complemented by the lifting of restrictions on *Amerika* magazine and reduced jamming of VOA broadcasts, meant that an alternative interpretation of the world was available to Soviet citizens. Kohler predicted that the ignorance that afflicted many should diminish. Better knowledge of the West, coinciding with the emergence of disaffected youth in the USSR, would breed discontent incompatible with Soviet pretensions. In a nation where most people were bored by the desiccated ideology invoked at the Twenty-Third Party Congress (1966), where serious history could not be written, and where (said official post-1964 interpretation) the regime had been led by a tyrant and then a fool, the hunger for truth was voracious. For this situation, claimed Kohler, the United States could take partial credit:

> I have to say that this ferment has been greatly stimulated by our exchange programs. . . . [They] have built up a pool of thousands and thousands and thousands of very chosen Soviet elite in every field you can imagine who have contacts with the West, who have absorbed ideas from the West. These influences are reflected in what they do, what they write, what they publish, and what they teach.

To intensify this trend, the ambassador also maintained contact with members (approved and not) of the intelligentsia.[15]

Kohler's understanding of U.S. economic advantage and its implications for strategy was equally shrewd and accounts for his support of the 1966 East–West trade relations act. He held that trade policy ought not inhibit Soviet economic growth, but should channel its course. Such a policy would exploit the desire of those Soviets who, like Khrushchev, wanted to improve the consumer and agricultural sectors. Crop failures in the mid-1960s and the slow pace of reforms meant the economy was susceptible to outside manipulations. As case in point, Kohler hoped the United States would seize on the Soviet agricultural campaign, with its emphasis on building a robust fertilizer industry:

> If I could sell them a hundred chemical fertilizer factories tomorrow, I would do it and I think I would even give them up to five years credit on them. Why? We would thus influence the allocation of their very limited resources. It would be bound to come out of other fields that from our point of view are less desirable for the investment of their funds and their efforts. For every dollar they paid for fertilizer plants, they would incur maybe three dollars in local construction out of limited budget resources. They would have to divert personnel to it. They would have to create an educational program so that their people would learn how to use fertilizers to make crops grow. They would have to create a distribution system for those fertilizers.

In line with this point, Kohler also applauded the deal struck with Moscow by the Italian automobile company Fiat. He predicted that this decision would cost the Soviets about $800 million for the production of nearly half a million cars by 1970:

> This is the use of Western trading power to force diversion of resources into the consumer sector. And eventually this has to come out of the only places it can come out, which is military and space programs. For every dollar they spend for this type of equipment they are going to have to spend a couple dollars for the

buildings and the Russian components. Then they are going to get into some of these problems that we have in the west; they are going to have to have roads, garages, motels, filling stations.

On still another occasion, Kohler argued against allowing the Soviets to buy U.S. pipe over nineteen inches in diameter, intended for a line from the USSR to East Germany. Through it, oil would be sent for processing in East Germany's petrochemical plants, thereby making that country's economy even more dependent on the USSR. Although the Soviets could certainly produce the necessary pipe, the expenditure of time and energy would cost them dearly. Regarding the cost of the arms race, Kohler was also prescient. His thinking on this subject actually anticipated those policymakers who in the 1980s thought an accelerated arms race would break the Soviets. It was evident to him that the communist economy, less than half the size of the American, could not afford to keep up with U.S. military spending *and* sustain a decent level of living. "Someday," he mused, "something will have to give." During his Moscow tour, rumors of food riots in the south and the lengthening line of bread lines in Russian cities were closely monitored by Western embassies.[16]

For these shortages and other crises (the product of "hare brain schemes," said his successors), Khrushchev was removed from office in 1964. Thereafter, Kohler and British ambassador Humphrey Trevelyan attested, the USSR became a decidedly duller place, run by people determined to stifle experimentation.[17] And as Soviet–U.S. relations declined with expanding American involvement in Vietnam, life in the embassy reverted to the gloom of earlier years. While the Soviet press depicted Johnson and McNamara as warmongers who murdered Vietnamese civilians, "spontaneous" demonstrations by workers were staged in front of the embassy. Denunciation of U.S. war crimes by Soviet speakers during national holidays and social events became so vociferous that Kohler stopped attending them. The charge was also revived that the embassy was a nest of spies and wreckers, the worst of whom was the ambassador himself. A new twist was added when Norris Garnett, a black attaché, was expelled because he had "incited" African students to forsake their university studies in Moscow, depart for the West, and then issue anti-Soviet defamations. In fact, there was a CIA presence in the embassy by the 1960s. But it was not responsible for anything like the creativity attributed to Garnett. Its work concentrated on analyzing agricultural output and differed not at all from reporting conducted by the Foreign Service. The CIA's exotic activities included bugging the limousines of high-ranking Soviet officials. Apart from bilge about their private lives, these dubious feats produced no significant knowledge about the USSR.[18]

The last two years of Kohler's term amounted to a holding action against the day when circumstances might permit improved relations. In the meantime, he tried to preserve what remained from earlier years of cooperation.[19]

To help break the Soviet–U.S. logjam, President Johnson assigned Llewellyn Thompson in late 1966 to another tour in Moscow. He expected that Thompson (then serving as ambassador-at-large) could find ways to improve matters, especially regarding arms control and Vietnam. Editorial writers in the *New York*

Times and *Washington Post* were pleased about Thompson's reappointment. James Reston expressed a common view when he observed, "[He] must be the only American official who has not been blamed by the Soviets for all the crimes of the human race."[20]

Thompson was not elated about returning to the USSR. His health was poor, for one thing; he suffered from ulcers that sapped his energy. Additionally, he did not know Khrushchev's successors and feared that he could not cultivate them. He doubted, too, that he could advance an agenda in Moscow as long as the United States and the USSR were at odds on Southeast Asia. Only LBJ's insistent appeal overcame Thompson's better judgment.[21]

The ambassador's misgivings were confirmed. During his two-year assignment, he was mostly bored, was often sick, and felt that he was wasting time—with the exception of his interpreting the jangled Moscow mood during the 1967 Middle East war. In the opinion of his deputy chief of mission, Emory Swank, Thompson was depressed in the USSR—a condition that might have accounted for his aloofness from his staff. In contrast to the days of Khrushchev, he lacked entrée to the Kremlin, which anyway was dominated by an impassive Brezhnev crowd. As for the Soviets, they evidently respected Thompson as an advocate of détente. Yet because of Vietnam (then Czechoslovakia) they chose to be cool and failed to capitalize on his presence. He was foiled in the conduct of even secondary issues, such as concluding with the Soviets a convention to reduce incidents at sea between the two countries' warships (which played dangerous games of stalking and tag). Continuing demonstrations in front of the chancery against U.S. "imperialism" in Vietnam and support for Israeli "aggression" did not help Thompson's mood either.[22]

He nevertheless tried to advance arms control talks. His potentially important colloquies here with Dobrynin, aimed at launching high-level negotiations, met with indifference and ultimately failure. Soviet officials were also obdurate in dealing with him on the North Korean seizure of the intelligence ship *Pueblo* in January 1968. The Foreign Office told him that under no circumstances would it assist in obtaining the release of the ship or its crew, which had intruded within twelve miles of the North Korean coast. (The ship was freed after the United States apologized in December 1968.) Besides, said officials, the Americans needed a lesson given their "criminal" attitude toward taking hostages—by which they meant helping Stalin's daughter, Svetlana Aliluyeva, when she defected in April 1967 to the U.S. embassy in New Delhi. Soviet spying aimed at diplomats in Moscow and stalling on authorization for a new U.S. compound further drained Thompson. As for Vietnam, he made no headway in causing the Soviets to press their Ho in a conciliatory direction.[23]

The denouement was the Warsaw Pact invasion of Czechoslovakia in August 1968. Like other Soviet watchers, Thompson speculated on whether Brezhnev would act militarily to squash Alexander Dubček's regime. In any case, Thompson thought that Brezhnev could not long tolerate the Czech version of humane socialism; its example threw into vivid relief the multiple defects of the Soviet system. Moscow would have to destroy it. Still, Thompson was unable to guess either the timing or the method of repression. He was on holiday outside the

USSR when the invasion occurred. It fell to Swank to abstain (in adherence to NATO policy) from contacts with the Foreign Ministry and to suspend bilateral programs. Normal contact was resumed within a few months. By then (January 1969), Thompson's assignment to Moscow had mercifully ended.[24]

Perils of Kissinger

External policy in Nixon's presidency was dominated by that species of intellectual who revels in the exercise of power, a creature not so rare as the popular mind assumes. For Professor Henry Kissinger, scholarly playfulness of thought had to adjust to the imperatives of power at home and abroad. The actual encounter in 1969 to 1976 between his philosophical assumptions and political realities produced a dizzying performance. It was applauded by admirers, lambasted by critics, and envied by former colleagues, who (Kissinger chided) believed that policy would have advanced properly were they in charge. His disdain for bureaucracies as bastions of ineptitude that mangle creativity caused him to bypass the State Department in favor of select advisers. They backed his virtuoso performances in the Middle East, in Paris negotiations on Vietnam, in Moscow, and in Peking. His preference for working unencumbered combined easily with that dark angel in Richard Nixon's nature: abiding distrust and obsession with secrecy. The result was that Nixon and Kissinger ran foreign policy as though it were a two-man conspiracy.[25]

During the years when Kissinger was national security adviser, he campaigned to run international affairs from the White House. He successfully undercut the secretary of state, William Rogers, as the chief diplomatic officer. On assuming the secretaryship (September 1973–January 1977), Kissinger ignored the State Department, thereby accelerating its demotion as the main agency for conducting foreign policy. Consequently, its part in Kissinger's détente strategy—juggling inducement and penalty to encourage moderate Soviet behavior—was insignificant. The U.S. side of strategic arms negotiations (and 1972 agreements on ABM and SALT I), of economic and cultural-technical cooperation, and of attempts to codify the superpower relationship was handled by a jealous cognoscente. William Dyess, who directed State's Soviet desk at the time, plaintively recalled, "I was the Soviet desk officer, but I was not. The Soviet desk officer was Henry Kissinger because he decided what was going to be done."[26]

Kissinger's neglect of the foreign-policy apparatus produced atrophy and demoralization in the Moscow mission. During a hopeful moment in Soviet–U.S. history, with its profusion of bilateral agreements, the embassy was reduced to a piddling role.

Jacob Beam deserved better than the part in which he was cast in 1969 to 1973. He was more than just an old-school diplomat of the sort dismissed by Kissinger. An accomplished professional, his knowledge of central and Eastern Europe had been acquired in Nazi Germany (1934–1940), Yugoslavia (1951–1952), Poland (as ambassador, 1957–1961), and Czechoslovakia (as ambassador, 1966–1969). During those months between Kennan's abruptly canceled tour in

1952 and Bohlen's arrival in Moscow, Beam served as chargé d'affaires ad interim—the embassy's senior officer. It was he who first reported the tremulousness coming from the Kremlin in the days immediately following Stalin's death. At this time, one anguished comrade whispered to Beam that the mistakes of the past should be forgotten; both sides should start anew to build a safer world. It was at Beam's initiative, in defiance of small-minded orders from Washington, that the embassy lowered the flag to half-mast, a gesture to Stalin's mourners whose march led by the mission complex. Bohlen thought Beam's political reporting astute; he hoped to retain him in Moscow, an idea squelched by Dulles's assigning Beam to the Policy Planning Staff.[27]

Nixon's reason for selecting Beam in 1969 is not entirely clear. Perhaps, as he later suggested, Nixon chose him because of their acquaintanceship, dating to the vice president's visit to Warsaw in 1959 and reinforced during Nixon's trip to Prague in 1967. As it was, Beam's confirmation by the Senate was not entirely smooth. In February 1969, Senator Strom Thurmond criticized his governance of Embassy Warsaw, which had been plagued by security and espionage scandals. These had led to the early retirement of some staff members, the return of compromised Marine guards, and the construction of an embassy building so peppered with listening devices that part of it had to be demolished. Also in 1968, newspaper articles alleged that Beam had maintained an illicit liaison with a female agent of the Polish Communist Central Committee and had sent classified documents to her. In the event, an examination by security investigators cleared him of all suspicion. Throughout this unpleasantness, Nixon remained by his man—a fact that explains Beam's loyalty to the president, even after Watergate.[28]

The ambassador harbored no similar feelings for Kissinger, however. His memoirs, otherwise low key, bristle with resentment at the professor who dominated international policy. Beam records his several astonishments. After a conference with Kissinger, he learned that the logic of confidentiality meant keeping Secretary of State Rogers uninformed about the meeting's substance (drafting a letter to Kosygin). On another occasion, Kissinger wanted the head of the Soviet desk removed from a meeting because he did not know him. Another Kissinger shortcoming, Beam charged, was his slowness in recognizing the value of initiatives that sprang from outside his charmed circle (as when Willy Brandt undertook *Ostpolitik,* later capitalized on by the administration). Kissinger's arrogance and use of smear also repelled Beam. He concluded that Kissinger's intellectual gifts did not compensate for his character defects, but fed his appetite for power.[29]

Whatever the merit of Beam's critique, it was not disinterested. He fared poorly under Kissinger. He felt the embarrassment, then the infuriation, of exclusion, while Dobrynin in Washington enjoyed Kissinger's confidence—becoming his preferred "back channel" to the Kremlin. Kissinger's shabby treatment of Beam was amply illustrated in April 1972. Still only the national security adviser, Kissinger arrived in Moscow on Air Force One with a party of aides (and Dobrynin) in circumstances of utmost secrecy. During their four days of meetings with Brezhnev, in preparation for the May summit conference, Beam was left unenlightened about their being in the capital. Not until all substantive matters—including the Basic Principles of Soviet–U.S. Relations—had been discussed and agreements reached did Kissinger reveal his presence in Moscow and brief the ambassador (with additional injunctions against informing Rogers). This protocol fiasco not only symbolized Rogers's and Beam's irrelevance, but also effectively made them objects of an intrigue in which the USSR and Nixon conspired against professional U.S. diplomacy. The Soviets saw that Kissinger had wanted to humble the embassy for reasons of his own and thus were disinclined to treat with it. Thereafter, Beam's access to the top leadership practically ceased.[30]

Instead of resigning (as his friends suggested), Beam soldiered on in the desolation of tertiary issues. Although present at the 1972 Nixon–Brezhnev meeting, he was marginal to discussion of such core questions as strategic arms control and force reductions in Europe, or even economic matters (including the resolution of ancient lend-lease disputes). Rather, Beam functioned as a messenger carrying letters to Brezhnev and Kosygin on the Vietnam War, Sino-Soviet dispute, and Arab–Israeli conflict. But even as a messenger, Beam's position was untenable: he was left unaware of the specificity and reasoning behind U.S. policies. For example, when he made representations to the Foreign Ministry about U.S. intentions during the 1970 Jordanian civil crisis, Kissinger told him nothing about Sixth Fleet deployments in the eastern Mediterranean—lest, presumably, he act as an unauthorized "back channel" to Rogers.[31]

Concentration on unexceptional matters in Beam's case meant overseeing embassy security, which even during the headiest days of détente remained a KGB target.[32] He also made inquiries concerning the rumored detention of U.S. naval and army personnel (from the Korean War) in Soviet prisons. He lodged complaints against the USSR's denunciation of the Southeast Asian war and registered anger that Moscow—hopeful partner in détente—was not doing more to press Hanoi to compromise. Later, as the issue of human rights assumed importance, Beam worked in step with "quiet diplomacy" to ameliorate the plight of Soviet Jews, Volga Germans, and dissidents. In practice, when this effort interfered with détente, the embassy withheld asylum from families and individuals who had sheltered there and returned them to the mercies of local police officials. Beam also did what he could to deflect Soviet criticisms of the treatment meted to Angela Davis and other martyrs moldering in U.S. jails. And he assured Foreign Ministry officials that violent attacks by the Jewish Defense League on the Soviet UN mission were felonious under U.S. law.[33]

Whether America's Soviet policy would have been better conceived or executed had Beam been consulted is impossible (as of this writing) to answer. The declassification of documents might reveal a mind that penetrated deeply into Soviet politics and international relations. Perhaps he argued powerfully against Kissinger's insistence on distance between the U.S. government and Alexander Solzhenitsyn. What is now available in the public domain suggests, however, that this dutiful officer lacked the temperament to challenge Kissinger or his strategy to entangle the USSR in an economic-political dependency. Nor is there evidence to argue enough originality on Beam's part to have given Nixon reason to pause. Still, the reporting by Beam and his staff was entirely sound on Soviet matters: simmering national feeling in the trans-Caucasus; anti-African sentiment among Muscovites; disquiet about possible Sino-U.S. rapprochement; the government's inability to ensure adequate quantities of wheat. Beam was also perfectly right to contend that communist ideology was not a source of inspiration, though it remained a sanction to enforce conformity.[34] Moreover, from the perspective of this writing, it is fair to credit Beam's prophetic statement written in 1978—a time when Western observers were nervous about an assertive USSR, unrestrained by the mesh of fading détente: "National differences and complaints will soon create major problems for the Soviet Union. . . . nationality problems may be among the stresses and strains which [will] accompany forthcoming change."[35]

After Beam's resignation in 1973, the embassy went for more than a year (until Walter Stoessel's arrival in March 1974) without an ambassador. Détente, as conceived by Nixon and Kissinger, could proceed satisfactorily without ambassadorial ornaments. The embassy filed routine reports and acted as a bit player. This at a time when the Soviet and U.S. governments held the second détente summit (Washington, 1973) with an eye to widening areas of agreement—and coped with the challenges posed by the 1973 Yom Kippur War and Jackson–Vanik legislation (tying U.S. credits and granting of most-favored-nation status to Soviet emigration policy). During this season of neglect, the mission was led by an able Foreign Service officer, Adolph ("Spike") Dubs. As chargé, he ran an orderly embassy and won Kissinger's praise for efficiency but earned not a word for imagination.[36]

Given Kissinger's treatment of the mission and of Beam, Stoessel required assurance that his assignment would be worthwhile, from both the personal and the national standpoint. Kissinger complied. He spoke about his respect for Stoessel; he preferred him over all other candidates; his own mode of operation was going to change in ways favorable to the embassy. On this last point, Kissinger elaborated at length. Thenceforth, he would rely less on Dobrynin and would encourage Gromyko to work closely with Stoessel. Kissinger would also keep the ambassador fully informed, consult him on a regular basis, and include him in meetings concerning superpower relations. The massaging worked. Despite misgivings, Stoessel resigned his position as assistant secretary of state for European affairs and accepted Moscow.[37]

Although not noted for loyalty to his subordinates (whom he spied on with wiretaps), Kissinger genuinely respected Stoessel. In his memoirs he paid this tribute: "I considered him one of the very best Foreign Service Officers—expert, thoughtful, disciplined." In this evaluation, Kissinger shared majority State Department opinion. It prized Stoessel as a man not only possessing good judgment, but also immensely sensitive to the needs of both subordinates and superiors ("a team player"). Born in 1920 and educated at Stanford, Columbia University's Russian Institute, and Harvard's Center for International Affairs (where he first met Kissinger), he was a close student of Soviet and European politics. His postings had included Moscow in the late 1940s, France, and Germany; direction of the department's Soviet desk; participation in high-level East–West meetings; and minister-counselor in Moscow during Kohler's ambassadorship. In 1968 to 1972, Stoessel was assigned to Warsaw as envoy. There he was used to communicate to the resident Chinese communists that Kissinger and Nixon sought relations with Peking. For his performance in this operation, Stoessel was rewarded with Kis-

Nikita Khrushchev and Llewellyn Thompson.
(Courtesy of Jane Thompson)

Charles Bohlen.
(Library of Congress)

Foy Kohler and Lyndon Johnson.
(Library of Congress)

Richard Nixon, Jacob Beam, and Henry Kissinger.
(Library of Congress)

Walter Stoessel and Leonid Brezhnev.
(Courtesy of Mary Ann Stoessel)

Anatoly Dobrynin, Cyrus Vance, Andrei Gromyko, and Malcolm Toon.
(Library of Congress)

Jimmy Carter and Thomas Watson, Jr.
(Jimmy Carter Library)

Arthur Hartman and Andrei Kozyrev, foreign minister of the Russian Republic.
(Courtesy of Arthur Hartman)

Jack Matlock, Brent Scowcroft, John Sununu, and Mikhail Gorbachev.
(Courtesy of Jack Matlock)

Robert Strauss.
(Library of Congress)

singer's confidence and made assistant secretary for European affairs. Fluent in Russian and French (with passing knowledge of Spanish, German, and Polish), he was likened by the *New York Times* to Hollywood's model of the diplomat: attractive, self-possessed, sophisticated.[38]

If any serious charge can be attached to Stoessel, it would concern those contradictory qualities of mind that have always been valued in the State Department: the ability to think creatively about international problems while obeying national policy. That these qualities are not easily harmonized was evident in Stoessel. As his reports from Moscow in 1974 to 1976 make clear, he was perceptive about the Soviet Union and in sympathy with America's détente policy. A few years later, however, as deputy secretary of state in President Reagan's first administration, he expressed hard-line views on these same subjects. He was also critical of people to whom he had earlier looked for support in his approval of détente (for example, George Kennan, who in the 1980s was upset over the state of Soviet–U.S. relations). This shift in Stoessel's attitude was partly attributable to the need of the functionary to support the dominant policy line, irrespective of private judgment. The change was also related to his ability to grasp several sides to any issue (for example, the nature of Soviet power). Thus there was in Stoessel's makeup something of the self-protective mechanism of the chameleon and an ability to justify to himself changes of heart. Without being aware of it, he subtly adjusted his thinking to blend with the changing intellectual environment in Washington. At its worst, this flexibility of mind meant that he wavered at times and was neither clearly for nor clearly against any particular policy. To his successor in Moscow, Malcolm Toon, Stoessel was for all his decency simply too nice, too neutral, too irresolute to deal effectively with the Kremlin (or Kissinger).[39]

Yet it was precisely his sensitivity for people and atmosphere that enabled Stoessel to write dispatches from Moscow richly depicting Soviet life: the misery of dissidents lost between their hatred for the communist system and their fantastic notions about Western wealth and compassion; the swelling of national pride in the non-Russian republics; the anxiety of musicians (from rock stars to Rostropovich) who feared the renewal of restrictions on their art and travel; the pride of mid-level managers in meeting (or exceeding) their quotas for production in an economy racked by corruption; the hopefulness of leaders, who still thought they could properly feed and shelter their subjects; the resentment in the Foreign Ministry at those outsiders ("crazy" George Meany, "irresponsible" Henry Jackson) who presumed to preach to the USSR about its ethical deficiencies.[40]

Stoessel portrayed to Washington a country in which the process of change was, in Nadezhda Mandelstam's phrase, "spectacularly slow." Still, moral and material progress, if not entirely steady, had been tangible since 1953. Despite widespread cynicism about the official ideology and a sense of inferiority vis-à-vis the West, society also retained traits of previous Russian culture: patience, toughness, patriotism. As for the non-Russian nationalities, Stoessel was as alert as Beam to their resentment of Moscow; the empire was in danger (eventually) of spinning apart. Until then, Stoessel advised, the inefficient Soviet economy (without meaningful reforms in sight) would lumber along. Not yet on the verge of collapse, its future promised little for manufacturers, workers, or consumers (except the military). Its perennial weakness in agricultural production was likely to worsen and cause greater dependence on foreign grain imports. Increased Soviet involvement in the world economy (*interdependence* was the catchword of the day, and Stoessel used it liberally) was bound to tame the militarily powerful USSR over time, thereby enhancing Western security.[41]

As for Brezhnev's intentions toward the West, Stoessel disputed the thesis that détente was a cover for aggression. He held that Soviet leaders had *never* intended to conquer the United States. Instead, their fear of U.S. retaliatory power reinforced their caution whenever contemplating military actions. The Soviets would probably continue to push opportunistically in areas of minor importance (in the Third World) to outflank China and the United States, thereby accruing advantage in the global balance of power. As for the inevitable replacement by younger men of the Soviet gerontocracy, Stoessel thought that this, too, was compatible with Western security. Brezhnev's successors would be less afflicted by neurotic inferiority toward the West and therefore less inclined to assert Soviet superiority on every occasion. Responsible American statecraft ought to plan accordingly: devise means to induce future leaders to bring the USSR into the world mainstream. In addition, the United States should not despair at instances of Soviet outlandishness, but be patient and self-controlled. The Soviet–U.S. contest would surely end on terms favorable to the West, as it enjoyed a preponderance in the vital categories of wealth, cohesion, military strength, and morale.[42]

Apart from his producing literate reporting, available evidence indicates little about Stoessel's status in making policy. He appears not to have been used so extensively as Kissinger had promised. Yet he was treated more reasonably than the deserted Beam. Stoessel played a part in negotiating the 1973 threshold test ban and the sale of U.S. grain to the USSR. He was on hand for the November 1974 Ford–Brezhnev summit (which concentrated on SALT II matters) at Vladivostok and talks between U.S. and Soviet delegations in Helsinki. Twice he met (September 1975, October 1976) with President Ford and Kissinger in the White House; on the first occasion, Gromyko and Dobrynin also attended.[43] Stoessel accompanied Russell Train of the Environmental Protection Agency during his visit with Nikolai Podgorny and other Soviets with putative interest in ecology. Unfortunately, the substance of Stoessel's contribution in these meetings cannot yet be determined.[44]

One point is clear. As the Watergate scandal weakened and then destroyed Nixon's presidency, Stoessel played a major role in interpreting the event for the Soviets. To them, Watergate appeared to represent the success of détente's foes. Brezhnev told Stoessel of his admiration for the embattled president and hoped that he would survive. In the meantime, Soviet doubts grew about Nixon's bargaining position and ability to deliver his side of détente. The ambassador tried patiently to explain the peculiarities of the U.S. Constitution and impeachment procedures. On the subject of Gerald Ford, he tried to reassure his listeners that Nixon's successor was committed to arms control, better economic relations, sundry forms of technical cooperation, and all the other symbols and substance of détente. Despite Stoessel's efforts to bolster the Soviets' confidence in Ford, Nixon's departure from the scene coincided with (though it did not cause) the souring of détente. From their standpoint, the Americans had used the "smoke-screen" of détente to freeze the USSR out of Middle Eastern diplomacy, to destroy a Marxist regime in Chile, and to abet playing the so-called China card. In the United States, popular and congressional support for détente was also eroding. The USSR was accused of misdeeds in the 1973 Yom Kippur War. Soviet sponsorship of Cubans in Angola and maneuvering for advantage elsewhere in Africa (Somalia, Ethiopia), Brezhnev's failure to restrain North Vietnam in 1975 as it smashed the south, charges of cheating and bad faith over SALT, and the undeniable reality of Soviet strategic power and a modernizing Red Navy all contributed to disillusionment. In the 1976 presidential campaign, détente had fallen into such disrepute with the electorate that Gerald Ford avoided using the word. For people in the embassy, this darkening situation meant increases in surveillance and attempts to interfere with their lives. One episode involved Marshall Brement, Stoessel's political counselor. While on leave outside the USSR, he was forbidden by the Foreign Ministry to return to Moscow—in retaliation for Washington's preventing a KGB officer to rejoin the Soviet mission at the United Nations.[45]

End of Détente

As feeling in the United States swung from interest in détente to customary suspicion of the USSR, Jimmy Carter was elected president. By the time he left office, despite his commitment to arms control (better yet, to disarmament), SALT II was nowhere near ratification. SALT III had been indefinitely postponed. Détente was buried by an avalanche of events and revelations: turmoil in Poland, Soviet brigade in Cuba, invasion of Afghanistan, MX missile, wheat embargo, Olympic Games boycott. Critics such as Eugene Rostow and Paul Nitze, founders of the Committee on the Present Danger, and senators such as Patrick Moynihan and Henry Jackson felt vindicated. And in 1980 the Americans elected as president Ronald Reagan, who for years had attacked détente as a misconceived policy from which only the Soviets benefited. From amid these circumstances, ambassadors in Moscow salvaged little.

Malcolm Toon was not temperamentally close to the president or Secretary of State Cyrus Vance. Whereas they instinctively sought compromise, Toon was recalcitrant. Regarding the USSR, he was also skeptical about the desirability or feasibility of full-scale détente. A carryover from the Ford administration, he was among the most senior of Soviet hands at the time of Carter's inauguration. This son of Scottish immigrants had joined the diplomatic corps shortly after World War II, in which he had skippered a PT boat in the South Pacific. In common with the experience of other specialists on the USSR, his preambassadorial career counted assignments in Eastern Europe as well as in Moscow. These included Warsaw, Budapest, Prague (as ambassador, 1969–1971), and Belgrade (as ambassador, 1971–1975). By 1976, he had also served in London, Rome, and Tel Aviv (as ambassador, 1975–1976) and in the State Department on regional desk.

Toon's first assignment to "that benighted capital," as he dubbed Moscow, was in 1951 to 1952. This posting was disappointing, almost fatal to his career.

The problem was that Ambassador Kennan did not care for him as a personality (cocksure) or as a diplomat. Specifically, Kennan was incensed by an essay—"After Containment, What?"—that Toon and Richard Davies had written in 1952. Its thesis challenged Kennan's conception of policy as defective; it was too defensive, surrendered initiative to the enemy, and failed to use the West's economic-military advantage. In place of containment and its inability to bring "liberation to the enslaved peoples," the United States should pursue a plan to detach the East European states from the Soviet grip. Through subversion, psychological warfare, and open force if necessary (under UN auspices), the West could regain for the free world the German Democratic Republic, Czechoslovakia, and Poland. This breakthrough in areas on the USSR's periphery should lead to the collapse of Stalinist power:

> Properly conceived and implemented, a policy of detachment in Eastern Europe could work with the speed of a chain reaction. The successful detachment of a part of the periphery of Stalin's empire would undoubtedly have serious repercussions at the center and throughout the Soviet Union. Much of Stalin's power derives from the success of his imperialist policy. A major defeat within the empire would strike a telling blow at his hold over the Soviet peoples. It might well be the stimulus from without which, as we know from history, is the prerequisite of the collapse of great empires.[46]

Toon and Davies had submitted their article to a competition sponsored by the *Foreign Service Journal* before they learned of Kennan's appointment to Moscow. To him, their proposed policy was as provocative of World War III as anything then being touted by Dulles. Besides, it was outrageous that diplomats in Moscow, who should be working to find common ground with their hosts, were in reality devising far-fetched plans to destroy them. Toon later recounted, "I may have been brash, but I wasn't stupid. I certainly would never have written this paper if I had known [Kennan] was going to be our ambassador." As luck had it, this essay came to his attention just before he assumed his responsibilities—during the last days, in fact, of his Washington briefing. Kennan's reaction was to "get the scorpions off the premises" (Toon's phrase). He immediately set in motion the machinery to have them transferred before their terms expired. In this, he got his way; ironically, they did not leave until after Kennan's ignominious removal from Moscow. Years later, Kennan apologized to Toon for his harsh treatment, which included writing a damaging fitness report that resulted in Toon's demotion (from FSO-4 to FSO-5) and a succession of minor consular assignments. These injuries nearly caused Toon to quite the Foreign Service. For years afterward, he nursed a grudge against his former chief, replaced gradually by cautious friendship.[47]

Toon's second posting to Moscow during Kohler's incumbency was routine. As political counselor, he worked beside the ambassador and they became friends. As Soviet condemnation of U.S. policy in Southeast Asia grew more strident, Kohler tended to despair for the future. At one point, in response to rash remarks by Kosygin, Kohler declared that war between the superpowers might break out.

Toon did not share such an excitable view; he succeeded in balancing Kohler's gloomier conclusions and reportage.[48]

The circumstances of Toon's ambassadorial assignment in Moscow were tortured. Kissinger had hoped to replace Beam with him in 1973 and had floated this idea among Soviet leaders. The reply came back, through Dobrynin, that Toon was unacceptable; insistence on his appointment would be read as indicating Nixon's lack of seriousness in détente. Kremlin reasoning here was not difficult to fathom. Toon had never been reserved in expressing his feeling for the Soviet system, which he regarded as inefficient and cruel: "The Soviets don't like me, and I don't like them." Kissinger, who approved of Toon for his intelligence, subsequently gave way to Soviet preference and selected the milder Stoessel.[49]

In 1976, while détente was fraying, Kissinger tried again to have Toon delivered to Moscow. President Ford announced his selection in September. The Soviets stalled for three months. They finally accepted him after Kissinger (on Toon's urging) told Dobrynin that unless his man was received, Dobrynin himself would have to leave Washington. Relations between the two states would thenceforth proceed without benefit of ambassadorial representation. Dobrynin, then in his twenty-fourth year as envoy, was regarded as an authority in Moscow on the Americans. Reluctantly, the Politburo agreed to Kissinger's terms. "The interesting part of this story," Toon later reflected, "is that the Soviets, who hated me, were prepared to pay the price of having me come to Moscow as ambassador in order to keep Dobrynin in Washington."[50]

By the time this issue had been resolved by Kissinger, the November elections had decided the next president. The Soviets probably expected Carter to relieve them of the obligation of receiving Toon by appointing someone else. In any case, eager not to prejudice relations with the Democratic administration, they did not complain against him. He therefore went to Moscow on an interim basis. His status was not actually reconfirmed until after Carter examined a number of alternative candidates for ambassador, in which connection Sargeant Shriver's name was mentioned. The result was that in the first months of 1977, Toon operated in limbo. He performed the business of ambassador, but had little contact with Washington and was thought by most observers slated for early replacement. As it was, a number of Carter's counselors advised against saddling foreign policy with Toon. Harriman, for one, recommended the appointment of a prominent businessman to send a positive signal to Brezhnev. It was Jody Powell, the president's press secretary, who proved decisive. He warned that if Toon should be let go, it would appear that Carter was soft on the Soviets. The president's national security adviser, Zbigniew Brzezinski, very likely also had a hand in keeping Toon in Moscow. In their attitude toward the Soviets, these two had much in common, as shown in Toon's original meeting with White House officials.[51]

In his first meeting (June 1977) with Carter, alone in the Oval Office for forty-five minutes, Toon received two nasty blows. First, he learned that Carter and Brezhnev were engaged in direct correspondence, the substance of which he knew nothing. Second, and more perturbing, the president had "rather strange ideas about the Soviet Union." According to Toon, Carter had determined on the basis

of Brezhnev's letters that the two leaders were developing strong personal bonds
and pursing identical objectives: peace and international stability. "[Carter] was
talking this way about a guy whose hands were dripping with blood," Toon later
blurted. After his meeting with the president, a livid ambassador marched down
the corridor to see Brzezinski, whom he had known for years. He announced that
the security adviser had "a big job" to do: telling the president about the political
facts of life—to which assertion Brzezinski agreed.[52]

As Brzezinski understood it, Carter's human-rights policy could be used as a
weapon in the Soviet case. William Odom, Brzezinski's military assistant, explained it this way: "Human rights was a brilliant policy. . . . Why shouldn't we
stand up and cry out against the oppression of human rights in the Soviet Union.
. . . It was a very pragmatic tactic to really beat up morally on the Soviets."[53]
Unluckily for Toon, this Brzezinski–Odom approach to human rights conflicted
with Carter's orders to improve relations with the USSR and save what remained
of détente. Carter himself neither sorted through the implications of his human-
rights diplomacy nor appreciated its likely impact on Soviet leaders, who were
understandably sensitive about this area of national life. Notwithstanding his sympathy for Brzezinski's and Odom's hard attitude toward the USSR, Toon was
caught in the middle of this conceptual and policy muddle.

His first assignment was to present a letter of support from Carter to Andrei
Sakharov, at the time labeled public-enemy-number-one by Moscow. Toon realized that if he delivered it or had direct dealings with the dissident scientist, he
would be finished as ambassador. And the president's policy of repairing relations
with the Soviet regime would be damaged. Toon explained to his staff at the time:
"The administration claim[s] that it want[s] a good working relationship with the
Brezhnev administration, but this [is] precisely the wrong way to go about it." He
therefore suggested to Carter that he use subtler means of reaching Sakharov with
his message of support. The reply came back (from Brzezinski) that all angles had
been considered. He should proceed with his instructions. Still, determined not to
wreck his mission at the outset, Toon ducked his orders. Instead of going in
person, he had the letter to Sakharov presented by one of the embassy's junior
officers. This ruse to protect ambassadorial standing failed, however. The day
after Sakharov got his letter, Deputy Foreign Minister Georgi Kornienko called
Toon to his office. He said that if the ambassador dealt with Sakharov, he should
not expect again to meet with ranking Soviet officials. Toon responded that he did
not need guidance on how to run mission affairs. All the same, he thereafter
avoided contact with Sakharov, a man for whom, incidentally, he had deep respect. After the appointment of his successor in 1979, Toon met (during his last
day in Moscow) with Sakharov for hours.[54]

Not only was Toon in his official capacity reluctant to see Sakharov, but he
was also anxious that his subordinates keep a polite distance from him. In November 1977, when it could have delivered by official pouch letters from Sakharov to
George Meany of the AFL-CIO and to the German editors of *Kontinent Quarterly,*
the embassy declined. To have helped might have sparked a new round of dispute
on human rights at exactly the time when progress was being made on SALT II.
On other occasions and for similar reasons of preserving détente, Toon forbade

the embassy from becoming a support center for dissidents or refusniks. For example, after tolerating their camping in the chancery for two months, Toon told the Vashchenko and Chmykhalov families—would-be Pentecostal emigrants—to vacate American premises. One of his subordinates reportedly told these survivors of Soviet prisons and antireligious persecution: "The embassy cannot help you and this is not a hotel. We gave you all the necessary things you needed while you were here, but now you must leave, with God." Similarly, Toon was slow to argue to Soviet authorities the cause of Alexander Slepak, a dissident to whom candidate Carter had sent a personal telegram during the 1976 campaign. In the final analysis, in Toon's view, Carter's high-minded generalities about human rights came at the expense of specific agreements with the Soviet regime—a regime, however odious, with which the United States had to live.[55]

Toon's skepticism about Carter's approach to the Soviets (and to himself) was reinforced by the administration's arms control initiative of March 1977. As part of the president's attempt to go beyond Nixon's version of SALT II, Vance took to Moscow a set of poorly conceived proposals. They were so slanted to U.S. advantage that they virtually guaranteed Soviet refusal. In essence, the idea was to place tighter restraints on existing and future Soviet ICBMs and MIRVs. To Georgi Arbatov, head of the USA-Canada Institute, the proposal reinforced suspicions in Moscow that Carter was insincere about arms control. As for Toon, he was not consulted by Vance about the proposals, but was shown them only after their adoption by Carter. This neglect was unfortunate because the ambassador had a solid background in arms control issues: in 1958 as adviser to the U.S. test ban treaty delegation in Geneva and in 1960 as part of the U.S. disarmament delegation. When Vance did ask for Toon's opinion, the ambassador predicted that the Soviets would reject the proposals. After they did, Toon's credibility went up slightly among Carter's advisers. But for the most part, they failed to use him in SALT. Ignoring him in an area of his competence contributed to Toon's sense that he was not getting through to Carter and led him to resign in 1979.[56]

The Soviets themselves tolerated Toon and allowed him modest access. Foreign Minister Gromyko, with whom he often met, admired his crispness of mind and negotiating skills. He also saw the mentally tired and physically ailing Brezhnev, who lacked focus and seemed confused. Other officials with whom Toon talked included the well-informed Minister of Culture, Pyotr Demichev, and assorted deputy ministers of the Defense and Foreign Ministries. As for Washington's continued reliance on Dobrynin for transmitting ideas to the Kremlin, Toon thought this was dangerous: "I have always felt that if you are speaking to a government which doesn't have a really good understanding as to your political process, which is true of Moscow . . . then you are far better off if you speak through your ambassador to make sure that your point of view gets across without any embellishment or distortion." Of ordinary citizens whom Toon was able to greet, his attitude corresponded with that of earlier diplomats: he liked their qualities of mind, but was less forgiving of slovenly work habits instilled during decades of communist rule. On racism in the USSR, Toon once expressed himself publicly (in connection with the mistreatment of African students), which caused outcries in *Pravda*.[57]

Toon was disappointed with his Moscow career. He originally thought he had a chance of helping return bilateral relations to what he termed "a safe and reliable keel." By this, he meant addressing the Kremlin through the embassy and skillfully using its expert officers. The attempt by Nixon, Kissinger, and Carter to establish close links with the Soviet leadership was misplaced, he thought; it obscured the divergence between Soviet and U.S. interests that could not be bridged by personal ties. (Carter did somewhat better on this score than his predecessor, Toon believed.) In any case, he hoped at the minimum to repair damage to the mission inflicted during the Kissinger era. He reported to Kohler in December 1977: "I have made a yeoman effort since my arrival here to restore the Embassy to its former position of preeminence and while I have had some some success I am frank to admit that we have a long way to go. We must still live in the disastrous wake of Jake Beam's stewardship and to lesser extent, Walt Stoessel." But to Toon's chagrin, Vance continued Kissinger's practice of making Dobrynin his main channel to the Kremlin. Vance used him almost exclusively on SALT II matters, leaving Toon to seethe.[58]

As for the mission's daily life, Toon of necessity ran a strict organization and kept a protective watch on his staff. Cultural exchanges still existed, with their attendant glow of goodwill, though none rivaled for spectacle the 1975 docking of *Apollo* and *Soyuz* spacecraft. All the same, Moscow remained for U.S. diplomats a place of danger. When part of the chancery was devastated by fire (1977), Toon delayed giving Soviet firemen access to the building so that embassy personnel could first protect or remove classified documents and equipment. Despite these precautions, KGB officers infiltrated security areas, compromising embassy integrity. Sometimes Soviet antics could be amusing, as when a female Russian assistant in the embassy's cultural section (assumed by many to be a KGB colonel) was caught with her ear to the keyhole, listening to conversation in the adjoining room. Less amusing was the increased incidence of blood irregularities among the mission's professional and custodial staffs (also among their families, particularly children). This problem, originally detected in the early 1970s, probably resulted from the Soviets beaming microwaves at the embassy's sensitive sections. Concern about birth defects by pregnant women, a mysterious outbreak of appendicitis, and cases of cancer caused morale to plummet. A number of people asked for early transfer from Moscow. The purpose of the microwaves, none injurious to human health (according to Soviet medical literature), was unclear. Even in 1992, Toon could only guess. Perhaps the microwaves were meant to damage the health of his staff; perhaps (and more likely) they triggered microphones planted in the embassy; perhaps they were part of a shielding mechanism to interrupt the transmission to the embassy of plants scattered in Moscow. Whatever the Soviet motive, the effect was unnerving and yet another reason why Toon was content to leave.[59]

His replacement, Thomas Watson, formerly head of the IBM Corporation, was the type of ambassador that Toon disliked. Although he believed Watson well meaning, he felt his successor lacked the background necessary to represent U.S. interests. The prerequisites were Russian-language competence, prior exposure to the weirdness of Soviet life, knowledge of the nation's history, and toughness.

This last quality meant for Toon that only "a mean SOB," like himself or Kis-singer, could get anywhere with the Kremlin. The Foreign Service's Soviet experts had been the source of envoys for more than twenty-five years. There was no reason in Toon's opinion, which he broadcast, to break with this tradition in 1979: "In those sensitive posts where it is terribly important for us to try to know exactly what is going on, we ought to have a real professional. I think, frankly, we made a mistake by sending Watson to Moscow."[60]

Toon's assessment of Watson was echoed in Senate chambers and elsewhere at the time of his nomination. At one point, to help tutor him, Frederick Starr of the Woodrow Wilson Center in Washington assembled a number of nongovernmental specialists on the USSR. One of them, a respected historian (and a liberal in sympathy with Carter), later confessed that Watson displayed "not the slightest idea of anything" related to the country of his assignment. His "ignorance was unbelievable," and the attempt to instruct him had a "surreal air." Apparently, the existence of the Sino-Soviet rift was news to him. During the same period, stories circulated suggesting that Watson's memory was faulty and his health uncertain. This first criticism was unfair, but the second concern was not unfounded. In 1970, at the age of fifty-six, he had suffered a massive heart attack. Although he subsequently returned to an active life, the illness and triple-bypass surgery caused him to resign as director of IBM. In Moscow, his tour was interrupted four weeks after his arrival, when he returned to the United States for a gall bladder operation and recuperation.[61]

To this indictment, more charges may be added. Watson was without any foreign language except for a halting command of rudimentary French and Russian. His intellectual interests were circumscribed and never went appreciably beyond his pampered career in prep school and playboy life at Brown University. His ideas about society were permeated with the sloganeering of corporate culture, fostered by his domineering father, who exalted the ideal of the resourceful salesman elected to the One Hundred Percent Club. Denizen of a world belonging to Sinclair Lewis (*Babbit*), Watson was arguably the least qualified person to represent the United States in Russia since Wilson's appointments: George Marye and David Francis.[62]

Still, a fair assessment must take into account the other side of Watson's experience and character, both of which carried the Senate in 1979. Although Carter did not know him well, his selection was meant as a signal to the Soviets: their political cooperation with the United States could pave the way for exchanges of high-level technology (the computers produced by IBM). In addition, Watson was personally close to two cabinet officers, Vance and Secretary of Defense Harold Brown. They had previously served under him on IBM's board of directors. He was also on good terms with Harriman, an éminence grise of the Democratic party who supported the nominee early on. It should also be noted that Watson was not a stranger to politics. He was a lifelong Democrat (though not a party operator of the Joseph Davies variety), and he had completed responsible work in Washington. In 1977, Carter had named him chairman of the General Advisory Committee on Arms Control and Disarmament (GAC), on the strength of Vance's and Brown's recommendation. The charge of this blue-ribbon commission was to provide the president with independent views on nuclear strategy and development. Most GAC members during the period of Watson's chairmanship—including McGeorge Bundy, Brent Scowcroft, Lane Kirkland, Wolfgang Panofsky—hoped to find ways of reducing the level of weapons amassed by the superpowers. In this capacity, GAC sat in judgment of the MX-missile and neutron-bomb proposals. And it urged both Soviet and U.S. heads of state to involve themselves directly in arms control negotiations. Worried at the outset that he was unequipped to master the complexities of arms control, Watson performed well during his two-year stint—winning the president's gratitude for his advice on SALT II and the knotty problem of verification.[63]

Watson was also not without Soviet experience. He had first visited Moscow (1937) after graduating from Brown. Like many of his generation, he was intensely curious about the USSR and wondered if it possessed answers to economic-political questions plaguing the West. He was quickly disabused of this idea, partly on the basis of conversations with the embassy's second secretary, George Kennan. During World War II, as an officer in the army air corps, Watson again visited the Soviet Union and flew over extensive areas of it. He was attached to the staff of Major General Follett Bradley, who organized lend-lease shipment of eight thousand transport and combat planes over the Alaska–Siberia ferry route (Alsib). In Moscow during 1942, Watson not only met Winston Churchill at an Anglo-U.S. reception, but also made the acquaintance of Llewellyn Thompson (who became a friend) and Soviet citizens, many of whom he became fond. He was moved by the Muscovites' grit, tried to help them in various ways, and retained admiration afterward for their heroism: "Turning back Hitler's invasion was one of the great triumphs of Soviet history, and I was proud to have witnessed it and to a small degree participated." Still, he was not oblivious to the bitterness aroused among lend-lease personnel by Soviet officials who accused Alsib of being perverted (spying on Soviet territory) and needlessly complicated its operation. After the war, Watson returned to the USSR as a businessman and was able to turn to good account his earlier part as an Allied soldier. As ambassador, he hoped to draw again on that goodwill reserved for Westerners who had experienced anything of the nation's wartime suffering.[64]

Apart from the normal ambition of producing sound interpretation, Watson's goals for his mission were twofold. First, the former GAC chairman wanted to promote arms control, thereby lessening that source of insecurity that had led him (in the 1960s) to build a bomb shelter for his family and to sponsor the Family Shelter Loan Program for IBM employees. Second, he hoped to correct the imbalance that existed between the treatment of the ambassador in Moscow and that given Dobrynin in Washington. Americans should enjoy access to the top leadership comparable to what presidents accorded the resilient Dobrynin. With the signing of SALT II (summer 1979), Watson and Carter agreed that the Soviets might be more generous in this regard.[65]

On the personal side, Watson had to overcome the reluctance of his wife, Olive, who worried that Moscow would exact a heavy penalty on her husband's health. Moreover (again from her perspective), the long distance and separation from their children and grandchildren would be painful. Yet Watson's appeals about the rewards of public service and his hope that he would add materially to arms control convinced her. The prospect of staying in elegant Spaso House for a couple of years also made palatable the idea of living in Moscow—that "odd place," Olive Watson once observed, where downcast citizens swilled vodka to obliterate themselves. As for his diplomatic inexperience, Watson took comfort in the example of Harriman, that premier example of the businessman turned successful ambassador. A fan of Llewellyn Thompson, he also hoped to emulate him by establishing bonds with Soviet leaders sufficient to redeem détente. His idea was in fact to hold conversations with every member of the Politburo. However desirable this acquaintance with the elite, it would be difficult to obtain in the opinion of Mark Garrison, the embassy's deputy chief of mission.[66]

Garrison was (along with Robert German, the political counselor) a crucial counterpoint to Watson. Not only did he provide on-the-job training in the intricacies of diplomatic life, but he was also Watson's instructor on things Soviet. Garrison belonged to that category of specialist who knew the USSR from firsthand experience (through stints with Beam and Toon) and possessed serviceable Russian. Garrison and Watson eventually became friends, and in their postdiplomatic careers collaborated in the founding of an institute (at Brown University) funded by Watson, for the study of U.S. policy and security. Garrison became the first director of its center for foreign-policy development. Unflappable and concise, he got on reasonably from the outset with Watson, whom he respected for his "ability to command the attention of Carter and Vance." Although he tried to woo his skeptical staff with praise and encouragement, the sort he previously applied at IBM, Watson was also changeable. As such, he was the victim of his residual volatility (slackened but not eliminated by the effect of his heart attack) and self-doubt, underscored by the disparity in knowledge between himself and his Foreign Service subordinates. Matters here came to a crisis with the Soviet invasion of Afghanistan, which occurred less than two months after Watson presented his credentials to Vice President V. V. Kuznetsov.[67]

The embassy was as unprepared for the invasion as the broader U.S. intelligence community (distracted by the ongoing Iranian revolution and kidnapping of diplomats in Teheran). Watson was especially at a loss. To his Canadian colleague, Ambassador Robert Ford, he confessed that he was unfit for coping with the emergency. The truthfulness of this sad admission was also apparent to Watson's staff, as it worked frantically—and independently of him—to interpret Soviet actions. Long hours and the situation's urgency placed an additional strain on everyone. In this setting, resentful of being outpaced by his underlings, Watson lost his temper. In his candid memoirs, he recalled embassy life in the first days after the Soviets invaded:

> I was a novice, and not a young man, and Garrison and German and the rest of the staff were working on pure adrenaline, exchanging telexes with Washington so fast that I couldn't keep up. I said, "Look, you guys know all about this, but I'm the fellow who is really responsible here, so if you don't mind I'd like to follow along." But they kept hurrying ahead until I got mad. I told Garrison, "I don't know whether I'm going to be able to get along with you in this embassy."

Garrison responded that whether he and Watson could get along was inconsequential; in a more relaxed atmosphere, they could sort out their personal feelings. Until then, the urgent task was to do what they could for their country. Instead of relieving Garrison, as he was sorely tempted, Watson recovered his composure and presided over the composition of a detailed analysis of the invasion ("a serious and unacceptable change in Soviet policy") that was forwarded to Vance. Watson later said that without Garrison he would have dissolved in panic.[68]

The ambassador's dealings with the Foreign Office were rough in December 1979. Instead of meeting with him, Gromyko initially detailed a deputy minister, Maltsev (christened Minister No by Watson), to explain the invasion. The interview was miserable, with Maltsev alternately taciturn and openly rude. He reiterated the Soviet line: the Red Army had intervened at the request of Amin to suppress a bestial insurrection; the Americans should avoid entanglement in matters intimately involving the USSR and one of its neighbors; basically, the issues concerned the domestic life of Afghanistan. When at last permitted to meet with Gromyko, Watson was treated to a rare display of the minister's choler. In this interview, Watson expressed incredulity that Amin's assassination and replacement by Babrak Karmal (who arrived in Kabul on a Soviet plane in synchronization with the invasion) were part of events purely internal to Afghanistan. Leaping from his chair, pushing toward Watson, the minister shouted that he and the United States were deceived. The self-righteous President Carter and potential sanctions did not represent absolute justice or the judgment of God! A startled ambassador thereupon discontinued the discussion. After reassurance from Gromyko that his outburst was not personally intended, Watson left the audience, mumbling that the Cold War had resumed.[69]

Unlike previous occasions when Soviet force was used abroad (Hungary, 1956; Czechoslovakia, 1968), the violation of Afghanistan caused the U.S. government to recall its ambassador from Moscow. This action indicated extreme disapprobation, as the Soviets for the first time had employed massive violence in a zone outside the Warsaw Pact area. Watson's recall (early January 1980) also enabled Carter to receive directly from him the embassy's recommendation. The consensus was that U.S. options were limited. On the one hand, Washington should exclude actions that risked military confrontation with the USSR: "This wasn't a drop-the-bomb situation, or one in which we'd send in troops." On the other hand, the Soviets had to understand that their move was viewed as constituting a radical departure in communist foreign policy. Therefore, American measures had to pinch, in which case selective economic embargo (grain, high-technology items) and boycott of the 1980 Moscow Olympics made sense. These proposed steps were conveyed by Watson during meetings with Carter and the cabinet. They were adopted, along with other penalties, including reduction of Soviet fishing in U.S. waters, postponement of the Soviet consulate's opening in New York, and elimination of exchanges (art exhibitions, scholars, students). The president also issued a dire warning in his 1980 State of the Union Address: a Red Army attempt to gain control of the Persian Gulf would trigger a U.S. response that would use any means, including military, to drive the Soviets out (the Carter Doctrine). Finally, he withdrew ratification of the SALT II treaty from consideration by the Senate, though both countries still honored (most of) its provisions.[70]

Meanwhile, Embassy Moscow monitored the expanding Soviet war in Afghanistan and sought to understand its purpose. Unlike many in Washington, Garrison did not believe that the incursion was part of a larger design to capture the Persian Gulf oil fields. After all, the country was a mountainous cul-de-sac. Rather, he thought KGB chief Yuri Andropov, Defense Minister Dimitri Ustinov, and Gromyko (Brezhnev being too ill to exercise real power) had hoped that a quick intervention would stabilize the situation for Kabul's Marxists. (Garrison later speculated that Amin's assassination had been an accident.) War against Afghanistan's Muslim rebels may also have been designed to preempt the spread of Islamic revival into Soviet Central Asia. In any case, said Garrison, irrespective of its precise goals, the invasion was a crude attempt to reaffirm the Brezhnev Doctrine and extend it beyond Eastern Europe to south Asia.[71]

As for Watson, the war ruined his ambassadorship. He who had hoped to advance détente and arms control wound up "slowing down relationships." Following his January meetings with Carter, he returned to a sullen Moscow in which social contact had ceased between Soviet officials and U.S. diplomats. The conduct of business, which centered on ways of saving SALT II, was uncompromisingly glum—punctuated by demonstrations of anger. Watson's private talks with Gromyko were icy; the minister resisted attempts to break the impasse. Watson concluded that he could achieve nothing and waited for his tour to end. Discussion within the Foreign Service and among congressional Republicans, to the effect that circumstances now required a professional diplomat, made Watson even more morose. To boost embassy morale (and his own), he organized a new round of dances, lectures on Russian culture and history, and visits by celebrities (Bob Hope, Lowell Thomas). Watson and his wife also traveled to unrestricted sites—Leningrad, Baku, and Yalta—determined on "showing the American flag." In Moscow, he revived his enthusiasm for amateur photography, roaming city streets to record scenes of daily life.

None of this nervous activity outweighed Watson's disappointment with a futile assignment: "It gnawed at me that I was so much less effective at this job than I had been at the GAC." His last months in the Soviet Union were marked by melancholy (and regret when Vance resigned as secretary of state in April). Reagan's landslide victory in the November 1980 election dejected Watson further as he contemplated the Soviet–U.S. future: "[His ideas] are not only unrealistic but would be a disaster for the United States if they were ever implemented."[72]

* * * *

In the two decades following the first ambassadorship of Thompson, U.S. diplomacy fared badly (though the level of political reporting remained high). His splendid performance should have marked the start of a confident period of professionalism in Moscow. Instead of flourishing, it was undermined. First, as U.S. involvement in Vietnam and Soviet support of Ho Chi Minh intensified, neither the competent Kohler nor Thompson was able to promote a program of negotiations. Professional diplomacy was next deflated in the Nixon–Kissinger era. The president scorned its practitioners. Characteristically, after discussing (1969) with Bohlen and Thompson the difficulty of maintaining a triangular Sino-Soviet-U.S. relationship, Nixon fired a torrent of abuse about the "incorrigible softheadedness" of the Foreign Service. Albeit less blunt on this matter, Kissinger basically agreed. Foreign observers and Soviets alike were puzzled by the administration's dismissal of Embassy Moscow. Canada's Robert Ford wrote this epitaph in 1989 for the Beam and Stoessel ambassadorships: "It was at the time, and still is, a mystery shrouded in the complex personalities of Nixon and Kissinger why affairs were conducted in such a way that the enemy seemed to be the professional American diplomats rather than the Kremlin."[73] As for diplomacy during the Carter period: it was ably handled by Toon, but he also lacked the president's support. Although his successor, Watson, enjoyed higher favor, he lacked the intellectual bearing to provide leadership in the embassy. No less than Toon, he was unable to halt the superpower relationship from disintegrating.

Cumulatively, these failures argue against the pretensions of professional diplomacy. When Soviet–U.S. relations did achieve breakthrough, it owed little to the ambassadors in Moscow. The big picture of détente, tactical maneuvering, and major interpretations were all conceived in Washington by a dynamic, if imperious, duo. Additionally, when Soviet–U.S. affairs turned downward, the professional diplomat proved no more effective than the overwhelmed Watson in reversing a dangerous trajectory. At the same time, the notion took hold in the popular mind that summitry, the transatlantic telephone, electronic intelligence, and jet aircraft had forever displaced the envoy on the scene. Mediocre imagination and ineptitude were other defects said to handicap diplomats, who rarely transcended their timid selves. This view was expressed pithily by Agatha Christie in 1970 (*Passenger to Frankfurt*): "In these days of tangled foreign relations, safety, especially if one were to reach ambassadorial rank, was preferable to brilliance."

Yet none of the above obviates the earlier record of success compiled by diplomats in Moscow. Nor does it follow that disregard for the embassy by the executive branch added to the quality of America's post-1962 Soviet policy. As the record of the last ambassadors in communist Moscow demonstrates (1981–1991), professional diplomacy and incisive interpretation were critical to making sense of the crumbling USSR. Spy vehicles orbiting in space may have been useful for tracking deployments of Soviet weaponry and adherence to treaties. Periodic summits may have helped cement ties between national leaders and fostered confidence. But none of these was suitable substitute for those specialists in place, who scanned the failing pulse of Soviet power. Their study of it—and its radiations in the social, economic, and political life of the country—resulted in sound policy recommendations. They, in turn, eased the intellectual transition in Washington as the world lurched away from the verities of a bipolar schema to things novel.

10

Collapse and the Art of Diplomacy

The history of the decline and fall of the Soviet empire will one day produce its own Edward Gibbon. This second historian might (reasonably) be convinced by this observation from his predecessor: "There is nothing more contrary to nature than the attempt to hold in obedience distant provinces." George Kennan certainly approved of Gibbon's insight, especially as it anchored his ideas about containing the USSR.[1]

Broader interpretations will place the Soviet empire in the context of European disorder since 1789 and its varieties of brutality. The essential problem arose from the European decision to break with traditional metaphysical moorings. Idolatry of state power resulted. The intellectual and spiritual aridity of this situation ultimately caused the Soviet edifice to collapse. Moreover, as a second Gibbon might prefer to emphasize, the vengeful national idea that had already scattered into oblivion those empires that the USSR most closely resembled could be stayed only temporarily. The ramshackle, multiethnic, multireligous Habsburg and Ottoman empires vanished at precisely the moment when Lenin secured for Bolshevism the czarist patrimony of diverse lands and peoples. The subsequent arrangement was makeshift. It depended for decades on police power and vague promises of a bright future, but eventually imploded. The empire that John Quincy Adams had first visited broke into its national component parts during the ambassadorship of Jack Matlock. His successor, Robert Strauss, arrived in a Moscow that was no longer communist or the heart of a confident imperium. In this connection, Gibbon's words also resonate: "The decline was the natural and inevitable effect of immoderate greatness. . . . The causes of destruction multiplied with the extent of conquest."[2]

Collapse

Matlock was preceded in Moscow by an accomplished diplomat, Arthur Hartman, whose first four years as ambassador coincided with one of the drearier periods in Soviet–U.S. history. Inwardly, the core of Soviet power was being eroded by a

dismal economy. Impending political turmoil was manifest in the crises of gerontocracy as three infirm Soviet leaders (each past seventy) died within years of
one another: Leonid Brezhnev (1982), Yuri Andropov (1984), and Konstantin
Chernenko (1985).

Outwardly, however, the USSR was strong and more assertive than at any
time since Khrushchev's 1962 Cuban adventure. In the early 1980s, the Soviets
fielded an army of 100,000 soldiers in Afghanistan. Aiming to make that nation
into a compliant satellite, the Red Army pursued its objective with uncommon
ferocity, transforming the little country into a killing field.[3] The stretch of Soviet
power in Europe was again made plain to the Poles, when in December 1981 the
Solidarity trade union was banned and General Wojciech Jaruzelski imposed martial law. In Central America, the lengthening shadow of Soviet power was remarked by the Reagan administration, edgy lest its client in El Salvador fall to
insurgents backed by Castro and Nicaragua's Sandanista regime. The 1983 shooting down of a Korean airliner (KAL 007) as it strayed into Soviet airspace, the
boycotting of the 1984 Los Angeles Olympics, and continuing sponsorship of
Cuban troops in Angola and Ethiopia reinforced the impression of Soviet viru-
lence. Introduction of weapons systems such as the Backfire bomber and SS-20
intermediate-range ballistic missile was also heeded by NATO planners.

On the U.S. side, President Reagan endorsed an extravagant space-based missile defense system in 1983, the Strategic Defense Initiative (SDI). Despite widespread protests at home and abroad, the United States emplaced Pershing II missiles that year in Western Europe, thereby enhancing NATO's modernization and
countering the earlier Soviet deployment of SS-20s. Clandestine U.S. support for
the mujaheddin in Afghanistan (i.e., hand-held Stinger missiles) was increased.
The president meantime abandoned the traditional diplomatic vernacular. While
Soviet statements about him kept pace in their vitriol, Reagan revived Cold War
imagery, castigating the USSR as the "focus of evil in the modern world."

Hartman doubted whether he should accept the offer of Moscow in view of
the administration's withering rhetoric. On the one hand, he viewed Soviet political culture as primitive, symbolized by goose-stepping soldiers in the Kremlin and
the public display of Lenin's mummified corpse. Nor did he doubt that the regime
could act cruelly. At the time of the downing of KAL 007 and the death of its
270 passengers, he asserted, "The Soviets have a stinking system. We should not
be surprised at what they are capable of." Yet, on the other hand, Reagan's ideological posturing worried him; it seemed to preclude serious business between the
superpowers (arms control, principally). Hartman wondered whether he would
preside over an embassy that seldom spoke with its hosts. Only on receiving
assurances from Secretary of State Alexander Haig that the substance of Reagan's
Soviet policy would be mainly nonideological ("pragmatic") was Hartman molli-
fied. At the same time, very importantly, he was in basic agreement with the
government's key point: the need to buttress U.S. strategic and NATO weaponry
as precondition for future negotiations with the Soviets. (Incidentally, Hartman's
approval of these improvements did not mean that he supported SDI. He characterized it as a "kooky" idea.)[4]

On still another score, Hartman had reservations. As a Foreign Service officer, he embraced the code of professionalism. Although his career to date had included work on arms control and meetings with Soviet officials, his area of competence was Western Europe, specifically France. In his specialization, he had enjoyed an enviable career. His assignments included work on the Marshall Plan in Paris, postings to London and Brussels, the assistant secretaryship for European affairs under Kissinger, and ambassadorship to France. In all of these, he showed himself fully effective. He had little direct knowledge of the Soviet Union, however, and did not know Russian. He would normally have opposed the appointment of anyone with similar disabilities. Yet he was given to understand that if he refused Moscow, the assignment would go to a nonprofessional. The possibility of another Watson bothered him enough to seek the advice of Soviet hands. Kohler and Kennan, among others, urged him to accept the post, adding that the cause of professionalism would not suffer unduly.[5]

In preparing for Moscow, Hartman was introduced by Kennan to Custine's treatise on Russia and the memoirs of Lady Londonderry, who had accompanied her husband to St. Petersburg after Napoleon's defeat. These nineteenth-century works, with their testaments to Russian suspicions, taught Hartman useful lessons about Soviet society. In 1987, he observed: "[The Soviets] fear foreigners. They fear foreign contact and even with all the glasnost that Gorbachev talks about, he's basically dealing with four-hundred years of a closed society, of a feeling that they are at the mercy of foreigners, that they are weaker than foreigners, that they are inferior in many ways." (Once in Moscow, Hartman's education was intensified by his professional staff. It included Warren Zimmerman, deputy chief of mission and later ambassador to Yugoslavia, and roughly sixty Foreign Service officers. The expertise of the substantive officers ranged over the spectrum of Soviet life: domestic politics, the economy, party organization, defense policy.)[6]

Finally, Secretary Haig, whom Hartman had known for years, convinced him that he would enjoy the administration's confidence and play a role in making its Soviet policy. Regular consultation, inclusion in top-level meetings, and direct access to the secretary of state were all promised—and fulfilled in Haig's and (later) George Shultz's terms. Even though Reagan tended to disparage professional diplomacy ("the striped pants types at State"), Haig and Shultz made certain that when on leave in Washington, Hartman briefed the president. How much Reagan assimilated in these encounters was never clear to the ambassador, who thought the meetings were "exotic." Still, he appreciated Haig's and Shultz's solicitude as they routinely sought his appraisal of the Soviet scene and of arms control issues. Their attempts to end the embassy's isolation and to raise the ambassadorial office's standing with the Kremlin also earned Hartman's gratitude.[7]

His relations with Soviet officialdom were never more than correct. The ailments of old age and deaths among the leaders circumscribed Hartman's early career in Moscow. Brezhnev struck him as "a kind of sad figure," without adequate mental or other capacity. As it was, Hartman was present at the state services for Brezhnev, Andropov, and Chernenko. After each of them, he conferred with other members of the U.S. funeral delegation (Vice President George Bush, Shultz) to assess Soviet prospects and implications for Western policy. Like Bush, Hartman viewed Andropov as abrasive and formidable. Chernenko, by contrast, was obviously no more than a transitional figure. His lackluster career and impaired health meant that he would never exercise meaningful leadership. As for Mikhail Gorbachev, Hartman was wary. Despite his agenda of desirable reforms, he remained for Hartman a confirmed ideologue whose attempts to refurbish the national economy would produce a stronger communist adversary. At both the 1985 (Geneva) and 1986 (Reykjavik) summit meetings, Hartman was among those anxious onlookers who feared that Reagan might be duped by the steely-eyed Soviet into making concessions detrimental to U.S. security. Confusion over what Reagan said at Reykjavik, followed by Shultz's attempt to dispel the impression that the president had agreed to eliminate all nuclear weapons, was case in point for Hartman.[8]

The ambassador's conversations with Foreign Ministry figures varied in tone. In the early period, his talks with Gromyko were unfruitful on KAL 007, Central America, Afghanistan, and arms control. Gradually, though, the atmosphere between the two men improved. It seems that Hartman played a positive part in the thaw that began in January 1984, as both Reagan and Andropov departed from the severity of earlier remarks to resuscitate bilateral talks. This trend, accelerated by Eduard Shevardnadze's coming to office in 1985, resulted in improving the Hot Line between Washington and Moscow, lifting the 1980 ban on Soviet fishing in U.S. waters, signing trade agreements, and reinstating commercial flights (halted in 1978) between the two countries. While negotiators in Geneva from East and West made slow headway on the arcana of strategic and other arms control, the Soviets signaled Hartman that they wanted to end the war in Afghanistan and curtail involvement with Central American Marxists.[9]

As the hard edge of Soviet–U.S. rivalry softened, relations between the embassy and official Moscow brightened. In line with his predecessors, Hartman believed an important task of the mission was to penetrate the veil of Soviet ignorance and prejudice about the United States. He was therefore critical of Carter's reduction of cultural exchanges following the Afghan invasion: "We tend to forget that there is a purpose of being in Moscow and that is to *have* contact and not to cut ourselves off from contact." As intellectual life became more relaxed under Gorbachev, Hartman tried to make the embassy and Spaso House into magnets for Soviet artists, journalists, scientists, and musicians. At official and informal functions, they met with their Western counterparts, whom Hartman imported. Other U.S. purposes were also advanced on these occasions. Diplomats gauged the reactions of thoughtful Soviets to events in their country (the 1986 nuclear disaster at Chernobyl, for example), rather than sifting through distortions of them in *Izvestia* and *Pravda*. In this spirit of friendlier contact, the ambassador and his wife also traveled extensively, making trips to Siberia, Central Asia, and the Caucasus.[10]

Hartman knew that greater openness on his part could create problems for embassy security. All the same, he emphasized the positive side, even to the point of being exceeding calm about KGB listening devices implanted in and around the chancery. Ninety percent of what he said (he once told a startled Shultz), he wanted the Soviets to hear.[11] Their attempts to embarrass Foreign Service officers and nonofficial Americans in Moscow were another matter, however. These became so relentless that Hartman warned the Foreign Ministry that two Soviets in the United States might properly be deported for every American mistreated in the USSR. During his ambassadorship, numerous correspondents and diplomats were either detained or expelled, usually in retaliation for action against Soviet nationals in Washington and New York. Charges of spying were leveled against Andrew Nagorski of *Newsweek* (1982) and Nicholas Daniloff of *U.S. News & World Report* (1986). This second episode—much publicized at the time—almost derailed the Reagan–Gorbachev meeting in Reykjavik, but ended with Daniloff's return to America via Embassy Moscow. The final arrangement allowed that charges would not be pressed against him. And Gennadi Zakharov, under indictment by a federal grand jury on counts of espionage, was permitted to plead nolo contendere. Permission was granted Zakharov to leave the U.S. on condition that two Soviet political prisoners be allowed to come to America. In a strict sense, Zakharov was not exchanged for Daniloff, but for Yuri Orlov and another dissident.[12] Diplomats expelled by the Soviets numbered nine and included Michael Sellers, second secretary in the embassy's political division. Soviet harassment also claimed a Marine guard at the U.S. consulate in Leningrad, who was beaten up by plainclothes policemen. Typewriters at the embassy, purportedly bugged by the KGB in the late 1970s, resulted in investigations in the early 1980s. In August 1985, the State Department accused Soviet agents of using nitrophenylpentadienal, a white powdery substance (possibly a carcinogenic), to track U.S. officials in Moscow.[13]

Diplomatic life was further buffeted in October 1986, when Gorbachev's government announced that all 260 Soviet employees of the embassy (and consulate in Leningrad) were to be withdrawn. The explanation for this action is even now unclear. It seems to have been taken only after the Kremlin had learned of U.S. plans to phase out Soviet workers who held sensitive positions in the embassy—such as switchboard operators and motor-pool drivers. The idea was to replace these people with Americans. Hartman himself was unhappy with this plan and had argued against it. He feared that an addition to the complement of U.S. citizens in Moscow would increase the chances for subversion. He told Shultz that he already had his hands full watching over various Americans. His young bachelor Marines, for example, not only lapsed into indiscipline and rowdiness, but had to be pulled "out of beds all over Moscow." He would have liked to replace them with married and retired noncommissioned officers or police officers (along the lines of British practice.) Nonetheless, on State Department orders, he devised a two-stage scheme that was under way when all Soviet help was removed. (The catalyst for Moscow's action was related to an expulsion of officials from the United States at the time of Daniloff's arrest.) Thereafter, the embassy's professional staff had to cope with the quirks of Soviet plumbing, stand in feet-killing lines to buy provisions, and acquire on-the-job training in car mechanics, building repair, and yard maintenance. Alas, the Americans lost the battle of custodial care. By the time Hartman left Moscow in 1987, the embassy building had become dilapidated and a firetrap: "Stacks of old newspapers clogged corridors, wastebaskets were unemptied, light fixtures shone a dirty yellow, and extension cords snaked around the floor."[14]

Managerial problems in the embassy were underscored by two revelations on the security side. First, it was discovered that the half-finished new chancery was riddled with Soviet listening devices; it could not readily be made secure. Work on the building was halted in August 1985, by which time $22 million had been invested. Specialists argued that it ought to be razed or abandoned. In his capacity as head of an investigating panel on embassy security, James Schlesinger recommended (June 1987) that the building's top three floors should be demolished. The Soviets, meanwhile, pleaded innocent. Not until December 1991 did KGB head Vadim Bakatin volunteer to Ambassador Robert Strauss that the USSR had bugged the embassy. He gave Strauss details on how this was done and samples of the devices installed. Bakatin suggested hopefully that this cooperation would enable the United States to remove the offending instruments, thus saving money on future construction.[15]

The second embarrassment during Hartman's tenure occurred in early 1987, when it was reported that Marine guards at the embassy had formed romantic attachments to Soviet women employed by the KGB. Sergeant Clayton Lonetree confessed to having passed classified information to one such intimate friend. Another Marine, Corporal Arnold Bracy, claimed to having let Soviets search "burn bags" for classified documents. Nocturnal entertainments at the embassy were said to have allowed Soviet women additional access (on thirty occasions) to "secure" areas. Subsequent investigations of the scandal found that the embassy had not been nearly so compromised as originally feared. Bracy later repudiated his statement, and all charges against him were dropped. The Naval Investigative Service found that Lonetree *had* provided information to the Soviets, for which he was given a twenty-five-year sentence at Fort Leavenworth. But neither he nor Bracy had given any Soviet free run of the embassy. In the judgments of Shultz and Hartman, the KGB had not penetrated to a significant degree. In large measure, they later insinuated (the preponderance of evidence supports them), the episode had been blown out of proportion by "security zealots." Still, at the time when this story surfaced, Washington was swept by frenzy over what was alleged to have been the "worst intelligence fiasco" since Pearl Harbor. Vice President Bush excoriated Hartman for the embassy's problems—a factor in his decision to retire in 1987. Upon their return from Moscow, Dan Mica and Olympia Snowe, ranking members of the House Foreign Affairs Subcommittee on International Operations, declared that the embassy had been irreparably harmed. To fix the damage, William Brown, a Russian-speaking Foreign Service officer (at the time ambassador to Thailand), was sent to Moscow with instructions to scrutinize matters and make recommendations. To Shultz's chagrin, Brown (and the CIA) urged that State Department employees be subject to lie-detector tests, a reckless idea that the secretary squelched. Brown also supported the notion of hiring civilian guards. In the event, all of the Lonetree–Bracy cohort were rotated out of Moscow; their replacements drawn from a tightly screened Marine elite.[16]

Soviet–U.S. relations took a dramatic turn for the better in 1987. Shultz went to Moscow that April and made tangible progress with Gorbachev and Shevardnadze—despite obstacles to maintaining secure lines within the embassy and between it and Washington. (The State Department had an especially equipped van loaded with communications equipment flown to Moscow. It was then located in an area that could be protected from electronic eavesdropping.) They discussed possible agreement on intermediate-range nuclear forces (INF); an accord to share information on unmanned space probes was also signed. At the end of the year, Gorbachev and Reagan signed a treaty in Washington providing for the demolition of 2,600 Soviet and American INF missiles and for verification inspections of each country's installations. Talks were also held on Soviet withdrawal from Afghanistan and a far-ranging treaty on the reduction of strategic weapons. Emblematic of it all, the Soviet chief of staff, Marshal Sergei Akhromeyev, was honored as a guest at the Pentagon.[17]

Mindful of the embassy's security mishaps and guided by directives from Washington, Jack Matlock ran a strict organization. Hartman feared that his successor would virtually lock up the mission. This concern turned out to be exaggerated, however. Vigorous outreach was a staple of Matlock's from the outset. Spaso House was never closed to Soviet politicians or to dissident artists and refusniks. Under Matlock it became, in fact, an intellectual salon, with Russian being the primary language. A brilliant moment occurred in 1990, when Spaso hosted maestro Mstislav Rostropovich on his return to the USSR after a sixteen-year exile. This was a political as much as a musical celebration, symbolizing the end of the Cold War.[18]

Yet security problems persisted, and KGB provocateurs still prowled. A near disaster occurred in March 1991, when part of the chancery was damaged by fire. The attic of the twelve-story building was consumed by flame, the roof was destroyed, and water damage left the code room unusable. Soviet firemen had responded quickly to the blaze and fought it—with antiquated equipment—for more than six hours. In this time, as many as four KGB officers, garbed as firemen, also entered what they thought were secure areas of the embassy (trailed by U.S. Seabees in fire suits). Luckily for American intelligence, zones of the embassy housing CIA operations were not discovered by the agents; material endangering people who assisted Western intelligence never went missing. Matlock later recalled:

> The KGB did not know where in the building our most secure facilities were. During the fire in 1977, they had been able to pinpoint the location of the code room and the Defense Attaché's secure facility. . . . This time, they went right to the old locations, and our Seabees watched with amusement as they rummaged through stacks of newspapers and unclassified press tickers.

Even so, the Bush administration was alarmed that "these [KGB] guys were able to wander around the building for an extended period of time." The personal effects of embassy officers were rifled, and a carpet woven by Matlock's wife,

Rebecca, was stolen from the office. Inconsequential communication equipment—cassette recordings of unclassified press briefings—also disappeared.[19]

Candid and demanding, Matlock struck some of his staff as pushy. He was not universally loved and by his own admission drove his subordinates hard. "I can be rather curt," he explained in 1987, "if people don't get out and learn the language and sit and complain about the job." At the same time, he was less reliant on his staff than Hartman in interpreting the USSR. Indeed, he was the most scholarly inclined ambassador in Moscow since Kennan. And his intuitive understanding of Soviet news reporting and official pronouncements rivaled Bohlen's. In the words of one State Department admirer, Matlock had "a finger-tip feel of Soviet reality." Like Bohlen and Kennan, he was also a diligent student of Stalin's career and had mastered the Russian language. As a freshman at Duke University (class of 1950), he read Dostoevsky and was thereafter an avid student of Russian culture—later translating for publication not only Soviet political tracts, but also the poetry of Andrei Voznesensky. He subsequently took graduate work at Columbia University and taught Russian language and literature at Dartmouth (1953–1956). He joined the Foreign Service in 1956, surmounting qualms that a career in it might be rocky in McCarthy's wake. Matlock's non-Soviet assignments included Austria, Germany, Ghana, Zanzibar, and Tanzania. In his African posts, totaling eight years, he studied Soviet initiatives and influence. He concluded that communist activity on the continent amounted to an inoculation, not an infection: Moscow's aid representatives were wholly inept. They were too obviously glad to have escaped the restrictions of Soviet life. Their attitudes of arrogance and condescension grated on the sensibility of liberated peoples, plenty resentful of European swagger.[20]

Matlock's first assignment to Moscow (1961–1963) was under Thompson and Kohler. Serving in the consular section, his most memorable case involved a repatriation loan for a disaffected American and a visa for his Russian wife. The man, who had acted erratically in his interview, was Lee Harvey Oswald. During the same Soviet tour, Rebecca Matlock underwent the harrowing experience of giving birth to their son, Joseph, in a Moscow hospital. As for political life, Matlock was encouraged by Khrushchev's reforms—though their later repeal made him skeptical about the permanence of Gorbachev's. Matlock also served as the department's Soviet desk officer from 1971 to 1974, was minister-counselor and then deputy chief of mission during Stoessel's and Toon's incumbencies, and was chargé d'affaires ad interim in 1981 pending Hartman's appointment. After his ambassadorship to Czechoslovakia (1981–1983), from where he also advised the National Security Council (NSC) on Soviet matters, Matlock returned to Washington. On the recommendations of Richard Burt and Mark Palmer, Shultz made him director of the NSC's European and Soviet affairs, in effect replacing his friend Richard Pipes (whose ideological stance and opposition to summitry irritated Shultz). Matlock was esteemed at the NSC, where he evaluated those changes brought about by Gorbachev. He also devised the administration's strategy for negotiating with the USSR. It embraced a four-part agenda: reducing arms, ending Soviet–U.S. military competition in the Third World, promoting protection of human rights, and eliminating the Iron Curtain (euphemistically called "improving" the "working relationship"). Matlock held that these areas of negotiation were interrelated and that progress in one depended on progress in all. "Soviet internal behavior," he maintained, "would have to change as well as its external behavior if normal relations were to develop between us." A U.S. policy of pressure would encourage, though not trigger, Soviet liberalization at home and abroad. In Reagan's and Shultz's opinion, Matlock's work was superior. He was the clear choice in 1987 to represent the United States in Moscow.[21]

In this office, Matlock warned Shevardnadze of Reagan's impatience with continued Cuban aid to the Sandinistas—to which the minister replied that the main problem in Central America was Washington's inflexible policy. When in January 1991, "Black Beret" riot control troops from the Interior Ministry seized Communist party headquarters in breakaway Lithuania, Matlock snapped that these actions would undermine upcoming East–West negotiations. The killing of fifteen people in Vilnius (January 13, "Bloody Sunday") caused him to denounce the event and declare that officials responsible for the outrage should be punished. Otherwise, he told Alexander Bessmertnykh (Shevardnadze's successor) the summit meeting scheduled for later in the year would be canceled and assistance to the economy withheld. Against these protests, Gorbachev responded that Soviet law must be everywhere respected, even in the restive Baltic republics. Surely, the Americans could appreciate how compromised his position vis-à-vis hard-liners would be if he appeared to let foreigners dictate internal policy. Expressions of USSR. concern over Armenian–Azerbaijani violence and suffering in Nagorno-Karabakh had earlier elicited Foreign Ministry protests to Matlock. On still other occasions, retrograde Soviet elements charged the United States with trying to subvert the Soviet Union. The CIA, said KGB chief Vladimir Kryuchkov, was as busy as ever in trying to disrupt the motherland's tranquility. The news program *Vremya* charged the AFL-CIO with helping to finance striking coal miners and offering legal assistance incompatible with Soviet sovereignty. Even Gorbachev, annoyed with what he saw as State Department preaching on human rights, suggested that America had lots to learn about the humane treatment of minorities. Matlock would be well advised to seek recommendations from the Central Committee on how to improve the lives of American blacks and Indians. These attempts to rouse popular suspicions or to use the United States as a scapegoat for Soviet troubles met with the ambassador's objections, some of which he publicly broadcast.[22]

While conveying the character of U.S. concerns, Matlock did the government's other important bidding: helping to maintain Gorbachev in power as the best alternative against Soviet hard-liners. A dramatic instance of this support occurred in June 1991. On the basis of information from Gavril Popov, liberal mayor of Moscow, Matlock warned Gorbachev of a possible coup attempt against him. It purportedly featured resurgent conservatives: Dimitri Yazov, Vladimir Kryuchkov, and Prime Minister Valentin Pavlov. This time, the alarm turned out to be premature—but six weeks later, the same group led a junta to seize power. Bemused by U.S. anxiety over his political health, Gorbachev was nevertheless grateful to Matlock (and President Bush) for his solicitude and uttered words to this effect: "Thanks, but don't worry. I'll take care of it tomorrow, as you will see." Matlock was keenly aware, as Soviet power loosened in Eastern Europe, that the United States would harm its own cause if it overplayed rhetoric about winning the Cold War. The need for magnanimity was not lost on Bush either. In his 1989 visit to Poland and Hungary (to strengthen economic ties with both countries), he was careful to avoid needling words about Moscow's retrenchment. After the dissolution of Soviet power, Matlock elaborated on the idea that Western self-congratulation would demoralize emergent democracy:

> If Russians are told incessantly by outsiders that Russia is a failure because communism went bankrupt and the Soviet empire collapsed, that Russia no longer counts as a player on the world scene because the West no longer considers it a military or ideological threat, that Russia is in fact incapable of developing true democracy because the necessary genes are lacking from its cultural DNA, then it will doubtless be more difficult for responsible Russian leaders to bring their country through its current time of troubles with political and economic freedom intact.[23]

Matlock's relations with Kremlin leaders surpassed for intimacy those established between Llewellyn Thompson and Khrushchev. He was admired by the Soviets for his fluency in Russian (and other languages) and lucidity on politics and history. He knew every member of the Politburo and most of the leadership in the union republics besides. He was able early to establish contact with Shevardnadze, who became increasingly forthcoming. He listened to the ambassador and eschewed the Gromyko tradition of confrontation. Shevardnadze was also the first Soviet leader to suggest to Matlock that the empire might splinter along its ethnic fault lines. Matlock also met frequently with Gorbachev. They discussed the domestic affairs of the USSR with a comprehensiveness hitherto unknown in Soviet–U.S. history. Gorbachev's belated renunciation of communism and conversion to democracy moved Matlock, and he admired him as a master politician. But, like Hartman before, Matlock was never enamored of him and counseled caution. Boris Yeltsin, by contrast, made an unambiguous impression on the ambassador, who thought him a reformer of greater substance than most U.S. officials perceived in the late 1980s. They first met in August 1987, by which time Yeltsin had made his reputation as a critic of slow-paced reforms. A few months after this meeting, Yeltsin was dismissed as the Moscow party chief. Throughout Yeltsin's banishment from power, Matlock stayed in touch with him, becoming finally quite friendly. The ambassador found him particularly clearheaded on the inferior living conditions suffered by ordinary people; it was appalling that Gorbachev should deny to himself the counsel of an astute person at a time when the party was disconnected to common folk. Instead, Gorbachev was foolishly staking his personal prestige on the humbling of Yeltsin, for which the party secretary ultimately paid.[24]

Crowded with change in Soviet international policy, the years 1988 to 1991 produced unsurpassed arms control accords with the United States, withdrawal from Afghanistan, the disbanding of COMECON and the Warsaw Pact, the end of communist regimes in Eastern Europe, and the reunification of Germany. For his part in ending Soviet–U.S. rivalry and tensions in Europe, Gorbachev received the Nobel Peace Prize in October 1990. To Matlock, none of this progress sprang from newly minted Soviet altruism, however. Rather, it resulted from an ongoing crisis within the USSR, which Gorbachev was hard pressed to cure. His primary aim was to consolidate Soviet socialism, overextended by foreign misadventures in the 1970s. A breathing spell was necessary. Once productivity and resilience had been restored, reported Matlock, the USSR could resume its competition with the West. Yet achievement of the primary goal was unlikely. As the ambassador later reflected, "If [Gorbachev] made the sort of changes that would make the Soviet Union productive, it would become less a threat, and if he didn't make the changes, then the economy would continue its decline." In the meantime, the embassy followed events with these questions uppermost. Would Gorbachev adopt more radical policies if his initial efforts failed? Could most of the rest of the leadership be counted upon? Could Gorbachev insulate himself from removal by a cabal in the Central Committee? Could he weaken the Communist party's monopoly on political power? Might he break from the party if it proved hostile to reform and to becoming an engine of change? Would accumulated frustrations cause Gorbachev to give up on reforms and to concentrate on preserving his personal power? These issues animated the fateful political maneuvering of 1988 to 1991 and were evaluated constantly by the embassy as events unfolded.[25]

Matlock understood that Gorbachev's reforms were "mind-boggling." Glasnost, perestroika, and new thinking (*novoe myshlenie*) reflected the leadership's intention to drag the country into the realms of normality and modern economy. Nevertheless, he thought reactionaries in the party and state apparatus might yet regroup. If so, they would replace Gorbachev or, minimally, force him in a conservative direction. In short, the liberal swing in politics, culture, and economy was reversible—at least up until 1991. Even if not repealed, the reforms would take years to work. Economic restructuring and the decentralization of decision making would not produce desirable effects for at least two decades, Matlock predicted in 1988: "Maybe if perestroika is wildly successful in twenty or twenty-five years there will be enough of a free market there for Soviet membership [in GATT and other international economic agencies] to be relevant." Until then, Americans should understand that profits in the socialist market would remain modest and grow slowly. Meanwhile, the country was bound to pass through crises, the most troubling of which were caused by the centrifugal forces of nationalism.[26]

Although ambivalent about the reasons driving Gorbachev's attempt to overhaul the USSR, Matlock believed that success of the reforms was in the U.S. interest: "I think we would be better off with a more productive Soviet system in which more of the economic production would go to satisfy the needs of the people and less to satisfy a military machine which could be used for aggressive purposes." But at no time did he argue that the United States should identify itself closely with Gorbachev's political or personal fate. First of all, he realized that Gorbachev's popularity at home was steadily waning. Increased food prices and scarcities demoralized ordinary citizens, while the shedding of empire in Eastern Europe raised questions in military and diplomatic quarters about national prestige. The great innovator might be scrapped by a wrathful class composed of the disaffected and recently dispossessed. In addition, Matlock held that the United States lacked the intellectual wherewithal to involve itself deeply in the affairs of a country so profoundly alien as the Soviet Union. Varieties of aid made sense to him insofar as they were well used on the receiving end, a determination that few Americans could competently make. Good intentions might result in wasting U.S. resources on Soviet problems beyond the ken of those in the Kremlin—never mind that of bureaucrats in Washington. In these circumstances, Americans should avoid euphoria about changes occurring in the USSR, encourage those compatible with Western interests, and cultivate strength as it provided the most reliable basis for negotiating with the Soviets.[27]

Matlock's guarded optimism was apparent in Reagan's circumspect dealings with Gorbachev and attitude toward arms control, epitomized by the refrain "trust but verify." This mix of skepticism and endorsement was also evident in the early Bush government. However, whereas Matlock had enjoyed complete confidence of the Reagan people, his relations with George Bush and Secretary of State James Baker were less satisfactory—at least at first. By the time they came to office, he was an identifiable advocate of improved Soviet–U.S. economic relations (as a way of encouraging liberalism in the USSR) and of regularly scheduled summit meetings ("normal diplomacy at the highest level"). Bush and National Security Adviser Brent Scowcroft did not want to be hurried into either of these. At the same time, administration mavens were saying that Matlock should be replaced; he had been sullied by the "softheadedness" of late Reagan, who had warmed too much to the seductive Gorbachev. Matlock was retained, however, for his value as an expert and as a signal of continuity with previous policy. After his three-year tour ended in 1990, he was urged to reenlist.[28]

After weathering the transition from Reagan to Bush, Matlock's next difficulty with Washington arose over differences in interpreting Soviet politics, specifically the duel between Gorbachev and Yeltsin. The ambassador appreciated earlier than the White House that Gorbachev's influence was ebbing. Yeltsin's growing stature, by contrast, was confirmed in his election in May 1990 to the presidency of the Russian Federation. Running on a platform of economic and political sovereignty for Russia, he defeated Gorbachev's own candidate, Alexander Vlasov. Given the changing order of power in Soviet politics and the weakening of centralization in favor of the republics, Bush ought to seek an understanding with Yeltsin, Matlock advised. This idea did not mean that Yeltsin should receive favorable treatment over Gorbachev. But he should be dealt with as though he were a leading member of the loyal opposition in a European democracy. Channels of communication should be kept open to both Yeltsin and Gorbachev. Matlock therefore supported Yeltsin's request in 1991 to meet with senior officials in Washington. Neither Bush nor Scowcroft was eager to treat with Yeltsin, however. His 1989 American tour, including a brief meeting at the White House, had made a bad impression. Not only had stories in *Pravda* accused him of heavy drinking and excessive shopping, but Scowcroft had found him inexcusably boorish. More important, Bush did not want to undermine Gorbachev or the patently tenuous union of republics. He might be replaced by characters whose world view and ambitions were unpleasant to contemplate. Total disappearance of central authority in the

Soviet Union would also call into doubt the validity of arms control agreements (i.e., the reductions in START, signed in July 1991) and raise questions about command and control. In the longer term, the collapse of central power might produce anarchy and despoiling war on territories of the former USSR—hence Bush's warning (summer 1991) in Kiev against "suicidal nationalism." Although sensitive to these issues, Matlock argued that political realities were rapidly changing and that democracy stood a better chance of surviving in the several republics than in any imaginable framework of Soviet power. Thus prudence and higher moral purpose lay with Yeltsin. In step with many Russians, not least of all Yeltsin and Solzhenitsyn, Matlock argued that Russia was as much a victim of Soviet misrule and imperialism as any other republic: "Russia was colonized and exploited [like] the other nations subject to that empire." Russia would also have to pass through the trauma of decolonization—the relative ease or difficulty of which had implications for Western well-being.[29]

Matlock did not win his argument. Bush preferred to deal with Gorbachev until the end of his political career following the coup attempt (August 18–21, 1991) by Vice President Gennadi Yanayev (figurehead) and the Committee for the State of Emergency (prominently, Kryuchkov, Pavlov, Yazov, and Pugo). To Matlock, this unflinching commitment to Gorbachev was one more indication of Bush's reflex to personalize foreign policy, while ignoring underlying political forces. The resultant hesitation could be costly, as when the United States had earlier reacted tardily to Gorbachev's retreat from Stanislav Shatalin's five-hundred-day economic-reform plan. In any case, the putsch's failure, subsequent declarations of independence by the Soviet republics, and Yeltsin's ascendancy in Russian politics vindicated Matlock's interpretation. His successor in Moscow, Robert Strauss, originally selected as a show of support for Gorbachev, wound up dealing exclusively with Yeltsin and a new Russia. In this role, he turned out to be a perky advocate for Russia, recommending aid, debt relief, and investment. Only by such means, he said, would orderly liberty and economic stability have a chance. Initially skeptical of the wisdom in Strauss's appointment (he was a Democratic party power-broker), Matlock was subsequently pleased as the Texan adopted the view that toddling Russian democracy required U.S. encouragement. By the end of 1992, Russia had been granted MFN status, and Congress had passed the Freedom Support Act, which allocated $1.4 billion of aid to Russia and other former Soviet republics. More generous assistance, including multilateral packages, was later forthcoming. Just days before leaving office in January 1993, Bush signed START II with Yeltsin, limiting Russia to 3,000 nuclear warheads and the United States to 3,500.[30]

Matlock, incidentally, was critical of Bush's approach to strategic and conventional arms control. In his view, the administration could have signed a START treaty with the USSR in 1989. The two sides could also have reached agreement on conventional forces in Europe that year (rather than 1990). According to him, the basic difficulty was that Bush and Scowcroft were infuriatingly slow to see that the Cold War was finished. Additionally, Bush, whose relations with the right wing of the Republican party were uneasy, lacked Reagan's leeway in making agreements with the Soviets. Hoping to retain conservative support, he did not want to appear overly eager to strike a security accord with the traditional enemy. Thus START was delayed. Problems subsequently arose that could have been avoided had it gone into effect earlier, when the Soviet Union was still unified. A single political entity could have enforced START's provisions. Instead, despite promises of compliance by the successor regimes to the USSR, the United States had to deal with unexpected complexity: governments holding nuclear weapons in Belarus, Ukraine, and Kazakhstan demanded new considerations.[31]

The Art of Diplomacy

Bush's appointment of Strauss in 1991 was not everywhere praised. The *New York Times* did herald him as "an inspired choice" because of his bargaining skills, political acumen, and friendship with Baker and Bush. And those monitoring human rights in the USSR were encouraged by the sending of a seventy-two-year-old Jew to Moscow. Yet he was unfamiliar with Russian and Soviet history and lacked background in foreign policy. Moreover, before Bush broached the subject, Strauss had never desired to lead a diplomatic mission. His earthy language, braggadocio, and career as a fixer (begging comparison with Clark Clifford) also caused a buzz. One commentator, Andrew Rosenthal, wrote that Strauss's Texas humor and deportment made "him a brass band in the chamber-music world of diplomats and Sovietologists."[32] To the scholar Walter Laqueur, dispatching Strauss raised anew "the philosophical question of what ambassadors are good for these days." He opined that in an era when foreign ministers can cover several countries in a day, assisted by instantaneous communication, vital business was transacted directly between capitals. He guessed that Strauss and his embassy would likely play a passive role, as the main action between the two countries occurred elsewhere. In Moscow itself, there was disbelief over the appointment. Many Soviet officials and Foreign Service officers later converted to Strauss. In the meantime, Matlock had to defend him. He argued that Strauss's access to Bush and connections to business and Congress assured him of an influence in policymaking; these made up for other inexperience. Nor did Matlock, contrary to what some observers thought, deliberately snub Strauss. As best he could, he briefed his successor and wished him well.[33]

Strauss's record in Moscow was satisfactory, especially for a novice in diplomacy. Doubters in the embassy appreciated his receptivity to ideas, especially on the need to mobilize Western aid to relieve Russia's failing economy. His Trojan efforts in this cause—as inflation roared and critics agitated against sending money down a "rat hole"—won him respect from Foreign Service officers and Russians alike, not least of whom was Yeltsin. Strauss formed a working relationship with the Russian president, whose bluster and Siberian directness were compatible with his own Texas style. They became chummy enough for Yeltsin to seek (and receive) pointers from the ambassador on how best to approach the U.S. Congress for aid. Strauss was also a quick learner and attentive to his staff—above all, his knowledgeable deputy, James Collins. This veteran diplomat had been in charge of the embassy when the coup began, Matlock having just returned to the United

States. Collins was the first U.S. official to confer with Yeltsin in the emergency, and it was he who assured Bush of Yeltsin's steady defiance of the plotters. Strauss's visibility during the coup attempt was also noteworthy. At that time, the embassy complex was almost completely inaccessible. Across the street from the Russian parliament (White House), secured by Yeltsin and his followers, the embassy had been engulfed by barricades erected against possible attack. Arriving in Moscow on the last day of the coup, with tanks blocking the main roads, Strauss insisted on being taken to the chancery. His armored Cadillac maneuvered through miles of military vehicles and the maze of defenses protecting the White House. He immediately got in touch with Dobrynin, who said wistfully that the coup might fizzle. A few days later, after Gorbachev had been released by his disgraced captors, an enormous public funeral was held in Moscow's Manezh Square for the three young men killed during the violence. After elbowing his way through the crowd, Strauss reached the flatbed truck on which Gorbachev was standing. The president, by then an unsure figure, helped the ambassador onto the impromptu platform. To the ecstatic response of 400,000 people, Strauss quoted Patrick Henry: "Give me liberty or give me death." He added with flourish that the men had not died in vain and that liberty would now prosper in Russia. Bush, who had flatly condemned the coup (as opposed to French president François Mitterrand's waffling), was as delighted by Strauss's performance as were the cheering Muscovites. In the confusing weeks that followed, as power was transferred from Gorbachev to Yeltsin and from the union to the stampeding republics, Strauss urged the administration to be scrupulously correct. When Scowcroft, for example, publicly intimated that Yeltsin had an instinct for the demagogic and unhealthy ambitions, Strauss fired back, "This Yeltsin-bashing is really stupid!" Nobody was helped by it, certainly not Gorbachev, whose fading position was beyond redemption.[34]

There was another side to the ledger of Strauss's ambassadorship, however. It was not simply that he was less conversant with or absorbed by Russia than Matlock. Indeed, in fairness, Strauss had never pretended to be comparably engaged, either intellectually or professionally. Still, a result of this lack of immersion was that he held back. Matlock had visited all fifteen Soviet republics (and half the autonomous ones) to address assemblies. He had made Spaso House into a center of Soviet–U.S. dialogue. Strauss, however, was less concerned with seeing Russia or coming to terms with its vibrancy. Sensitive people felt the indifference as Spaso's cavernous rooms less frequently hosted intellectual soirees. Some grumbled that delegations of crass businessmen would entirely displace Russian artists and scientists. Moreover, whereas Matlock considered Embassy Moscow to be the most vital mission in the world at a critical juncture in history, Strauss never had similar enthusiasm. He disliked diplomatic protocol, was put off by Russian inefficiency, and damned incessant KGB surveillance. More significantly, he felt cut off in Moscow from the world that most mattered to him: Democratic party politics, national power, Washington news and gossip. As the 1992 presidential campaign got under way, Strauss's restlessness became a widely discussed topic in Moscow's foreign community.[35] He found solace in his daily faxes from home and nightly phone calls to pals in Texas and Washington. All the same, he was chafing and made clear his pleasure at leaving Moscow, just weeks after his Democrats and Bill Clinton won the White House.[36]

The juxtaposition of Matlock's and Strauss's Moscow careers poses anew a persistent question: Is diplomacy better served by career officers, instead of by nonprofessionals from the donor or political classes? Against the latter group stands Strauss's lapses into inattentiveness brought on by his preoccupations. If one adds to this the unhappy experience of Watson in Moscow, then the case against amateurs in the contemporary era is substantially reinforced. But the case for professional diplomacy was not helped by Matlock's prediction—just before he returned to America—in August 1991: a coup against Gorbachev would not be mounted because potential plotters were inhibited by a modicum of good sense. The risk of starting a civil war acted as a deterrent, he told reporters.[37] This misjudgment was another illustration of a phenomenon intriguing to Laqueur: intellectuals tend to be mistaken as often as the rest of humanity, albeit on a higher plane of sophistication.[38]

The answer to the question of professional versus amateur remains equivocal in the broader perspective of U.S. policy toward the USSR. From 1933 onward, the United States was represented in Moscow by some extremely able people who came from outside the Foreign Service. Of them, Harriman was the most estimable. It would be misleading, however, to overlook the soundness of Steinhardt, Smith, or Kirk. The good performances of these four must be taken into account by those critics who would emphasize the perils of amateurism—Bullitt's misplaced hopes, Davies's curious duplicity, Standley's comprehensive discouragement.

The record compiled by professional diplomacy never produced disasters, though Kennan's misstep in 1952 was embarrassing. The tenures of Bohlen, Kohler, Beam, Stoessel, Toon, and Hartman included rough episodes, however. These mainly stemmed from Soviet antipathy and the embassy's neglect by and conceptual distance from Washington. Only the cases of Thompson (the first time) and Matlock can easily be made compelling for the Foreign Service's own. Even so, the conditions determinant of ambassadorial success—here meaning the mediation of Soviet–U.S. estrangement—lay beyond the reach of any envoy to influence, professional diplomat or no. Harriman, Thompson, and Matlock all enjoyed support by Washington and the serious attention of Soviet leadership. Only when these prerequisites were satisfied were the ambassadors able to further understanding between the two powers, thereby advancing U.S. purpose.[39]

Ambassadors in Russia, in its imperial and Soviet incarnations, have mirrored the general evolution of U.S. diplomacy. Republican in form, democratic in temperament, unapologetically commercial, the United States never had an established patrician class trained to reliable public service. The bumpkin aristocracy of the Old South did not make up the deficiency, try though it did (in which connection the mischief of Cassius Marcellus Clay is illustrative). In lieu of the traditional class for envoys, administrations in the nineteenth century depended on party men and successful entrepreneurs. They had to compete after World War I with the products of civil service reform (exemplified by the 1924 Rogers Act), which encouraged a mentality emphasizing merit and professionalism. This contest of privilege and private access against demonstrated competence in the diplomatic corps was not clearly decided during Soviet–U.S. history—neither philosophically nor practically. Matters were also complicated because a career officer was never strictly, in the sense of a personal or political commitment, the president's man. "Any new president," Dean Rusk once commented, "comes in with a certain arms-length attitude toward the Foreign Service." Resentment among career diplomats has also been understandable, as when Kennan wrote querulously in 1977:

> The American political establishment has a long-standing, almost traditional aversion to professionalism in diplomacy. The principle on which it proceeds is that experience in any other conceivable walk of professional life—the law, business, journalism, you name it—would obviously be a better qualification for senior responsibility in the diplomatic field than experience in the Foreign Service itself.

This complaint notwithstanding, there was a preference among policymakers after World War II to choose career diplomats for Moscow. The idea was that the United States should be represented by the best qualified person irrespective of vocation, which usually meant someone from the Foreign Service.[40]

As preceding chapters have documented, even when led by an accomplished professional, Embassy Moscow was not assured of playing a useful role in America's Soviet policy. During the Cold War, the embassy functioned in several ways on the frontline: as "eyes and ears" of the United States, an actor in the devising of strategy, a conveyer to the Kremlin of attitude and position. But in these roles, the mission was not routinely assisted by Washington—symbolized by the shabbiness of working conditions in the chancery in the 1980s. Still, the diplomats in Moscow did not fail in the ultimate sense: hot war never broke out. As such, the goal of their profession, the importance of which has added dimension in the nuclear age, was achieved. They alone were not responsible for this outcome, but their contribution to it as mediators of Soviet–U.S. antagonism is undeniable, witness Llewllyn Thompson.[41]

In its other aims, too, the embassy enjoyed success. Although it felt much like a fortress under siege and its inmates were denied the relative freedom to mix and travel enjoyed by U.S. journalists and visiting students, the embassy's interpretative reporting was high.[42] Its political section (as opposed to its cultural and consular components) always included people who possessed a strong academic understanding of the USSR and had the requisite language skills. Regularly in touch with journalists, from whom they learned and with whom they formed a community, the political officers also relied on diverse sources—from the exotic, to official news media, to intuition based on daily exposure to Soviet life. Their sensitivity to the divergence between external rhetoric and internal Soviet reality made the political officers in Moscow the most admired group in the Foreign Service. The respect of peers and the esprit de corps forged by shared experience in a harsh environment enabled the Soviet hands to survive seasonal neglect by Washington. Finally, the embassy, especially the ambassador, was at least theoretically positioned to represent the United States to the Soviet peoples (not just to the regime).

Even though this objective was frustrated during most of Soviet history, it periodically was achieved with benefits to U.S. policy (as when Standley's grousing brought forth official admission that lend-lease was helping in the war against Hitler). Decades later, Matlock established rapport with the public, becoming a celebrity through frequent television and lecturing appearances. His obvious interest in things Soviet and his willingness to engage publicly a variety of subjects (American life, Russian literature, Iraq's invasion of Kuwait) helped lower suspicions of the United States inculcated over decades by propaganda. In this way, he helped make it safer for Gorbachev to move toward the United States. Matlock's addresses (fully or in part in their own tongue) to Ukrainian, Baltic, and other minority audiences also reassured them, subliminally if in no other way. After all, it was a senior U.S. official who by his presence acknowledged these peoples as different from the Russians, as deserving of regard.[43]

*   *   *   *

A historic commonality exists among all diplomats as practitioners of a pragmatic art. Thus to study the ambassadors in communist Moscow is more than an examination of a discrete aspect of U.S. Cold War policy. It is to consider the broad question of diplomacy and international relations within a specific context. Like diplomats always and everywhere, the ambassadors in Moscow wanted access to the host government, dialogue with it, and freedom of movement as well as inviolability of themselves and their mission. All these were circumscribed, supporting the point that in the USSR envoys did not serve so much as endured, did not conduct diplomacy so much as waged it.[44] In this, their experience differed not at all from other countries' representatives to the Soviet Union and diverged in degree but not in kind from that of their forerunners in St. Petersburg. At the same time, like others before them, the imaginations of twentieth-century ambassadors were quickened by encounters with the land and people. Kennan was drawn to Russia's preindustrial quality, Bohlen to its piteousness and eminence, Thompson to its intimacy, Matlock to its classical literature. Yet as witnesses to the phenomenon of Soviet totalitarianism, the ambassadors also belonged to a smaller fraternity. Its responsibility was to explain to Western governments—and citizens—the USSR's singularity. Lord Strang (with the British embassy, 1930–1933) spoke for this fraternity when he testified:

> No one who has served in Moscow can ever be quite the same person again.
> . . . The pattern of life in the Soviet Union would be incredible if it did not
> exist. Only those who have watched its processes as they unfold before their eyes
> can realize how incredible it may appear to be, and yet they can testify that it
> exists. Those who have had this experience may be pardoned if they think that,
> among themselves, they can speak a language and carry thoughts which no one
> who has not shared that experience can fully understand.[45]

Soviet power corresponded with the era of European crisis that began with World War I and ended with communism's failure on the continent in 1991. On the ideological plane, the three-way contest of fascism versus communism versus representative democracy exhausted itself. In the economic sphere, capitalism (from its unfettered variant to social democracy) succeeded rhetorically and substantively. In the domain of power politics, the competition for influence in central and Eastern Europe ended on terms favoring Germany and compromising Russia. Since the vanquishment of fascism and communism and the USSR's breakup, a new contest has erupted, no less fateful than previous ones. It pits Europe of the community—conceptualized by Robert Schuman and Jean Monnet—against virulent nationalism. For Russia, Ukraine, and other successor states to the Soviet Union, there are parallel dilemmas here. Will they exercise prudence and imagination, allowing themselves to benefit from association within a broad framework, as in the Commonwealth of Independent States (CIS)? That body is now anemic. But in time and with applications of political imagination, it could become a worthwhile entity—or in its perverted form a vehicle for Russian imperial reassertion. Might the states of the defunct Soviet Union succumb to those tribal passions that have ruined former Yugoslavia and produced mayhem in the Caucasus and Central Asia? How will the former European provinces of the Soviet Union, with their feeble economies and precarious democratic institutions, be accommodated by the rest of the continent? On all these questions hang the prosperity and peace of Europe and much of the rest of the world, including the United States. These issues, organically linked to the end of the Cold War, also reaffirm the wisdom of the Florentine diplomat. Machiavelli taught nearly five centuries ago: "Nor let any state ever believe that it can always adopt safe policies, rather let it think that they will all be uncertain; for this is what we find to be in the order of things: that we never try to escape one difficulty without running into another."[46]

As the record of ambassadors in Soviet Moscow confirms, diplomacy has no epiphanies. Its world is not occupied by angels and devils, but by imperfect, frightened people trying to preserve their security and that of their children. Giving way as it must to compromise in the arid zone of estrangement, diplomacy after the Cold War perforce still belongs to the politics of amelioration—not to heroism in the grand manner. Meticulous study of the other (be it Russia or Ukraine, to say nothing of Japan or the Middle East and elsewhere) continues to have its place, without which the formation of intelligent U.S. policy is unsustainable. Realism still requires the patient cultivation of foreign leaders and peoples by Americans attuned to others' history and ambitions. Finally, as America's Soviet policy has shown, success in diplomacy requires taking the long view of both problems and solutions. Some areas encompassed by the former Soviet Union (in Central Asia, for example) might well fall victim to anarchy or despotism or both. Other areas (like the Baltic republics) will probably evolve in ways less antipathetic to the United States. Populous, potentially affluent, and armed with nuclear weapons, Russia and Ukraine will matter most to the United States and its allies in future years. Perhaps patterns of thought and behavior ingrained over centuries of autocratic rule (and intensified by the experience of 1917–1991) will be displaced in Russia and Ukraine by ones congenial to the United States. In any case, it is certain that neither country will quickly become a paragon of Western liberalism; the Pandora's box of the post–Cold War has spewed forth new maledictions of jingoism and anti-Semitism (in the figure of Vladimir Zhironovsky, for example). As in earlier decades, U.S. ambassadors will likely become involved, willingly and not, in the cause of religious and civil rights on those territories. Apart from again having to deflect charges of meddling and sermonizing, the diplomats will best be aided in their arguments by the example of a just United States. Composed in 1946, these words of Kennan's endure: "Every courageous and incisive measure to solve internal problems of our own society, to improve self-confidence, discipline, morale and community of spirit of our own people, is a diplomatic victory . . . worth a thousand diplomatic notes and joint communiqués."[47]

Two further lessons for the future of U.S. diplomacy can be drawn from its experience in the Soviet Union. First, there is no ready formula for success. Coups, invasions, provocations, and other turmoil are recurrent phenomena in the lives of nations. Sibyls, not fallible diplomats, can perfectly predict the initiation and finale of such events. The ambassador's obligation, then, is to stay abreast of the main political currents running through the country of residency. Knowing the direction of their flow, not their ultimate destination, is the envoy's responsibility. Kohler was exactly right for his time and since when he declared, "Modern diplomacy is . . . a continuing and exhausting study of whole societies and of their inter-relationships. It requires a knowledge of the history and culture, of the political, economic, technological and social forces at work in the society . . . and of the effect they will have on relations between that society and other[s]." Matlock's misreading (that an anti-Gorbachev coup would not take place) in August 1991 is thus less important than his discernment of the deep causes and consequences of Soviet dissolution. He may have overestimated the good sense of Yanayev, Kryuchkov, Yazov, and the rest of their company. Surprised though he was by the coup, Matlock correctly predicted its failure: Russia was not ready for civil war; the army was unprepared to launch combat against civilians.[48]

The second consideration is that diplomacy will continue to reflect the peculiar blend of U.S. political habits and institutions. The embassy's history in St. Petersburg and Moscow amply illustrates national defects and virtues. Ignorance of larger political realities abetted failure in the cases of Francis Dana, George Marye, David Francis, and Thomas Watson. Casualness of approach and the vicissitudes of domestic politics explain John Randolph, Cassius Clay, Simon Cameron, and Joseph Davies. Yet attempts to transcend America's populist and intellectually indolent self have produced felicitous results. This reality was evident before communist Moscow in the persons of John Quincy Adams, Neill Brown, Andrew White, and George Meyer—thereafter in the Foreign Service's cadre of Soviet experts and several ambassadors since 1933. In the post–Cold War world, menaced by ethnic conflicts, riven by widening gaps between rich and poor, burdened by nuclear weapons, and confronted by environmental degradation, it is plain that the United States cannot afford to neglect the quality of its major ambassadorships—or let their occupants fend for themselves in the world's more discouraging capitals.

The vast sterility of the Cold War obscured the fact that the sovereign state is inadequate for dealing with many contemporary emergencies: population explosion, the north–south cleft, AIDS, cultural clashes. The supposedly self-reliant state and present international system may, indeed, be obsolete and on their way to extinction—arguably, to be superseded by multinational companies, permeable borders, and regional units such as the European Union. Yet the modern state is tenacious of life and liable to inhabit any of the brave new worlds posited by theorists (Paul Kennedy to Samuel Huntington).[49] The functional need of the ambassadorial office will not soon vanish in any event. The history of Embassy Moscow alternates as a cautionary tale and an example of what is required to avoid disaster.

NOTES

Introduction

1. Hans Morgenthau and Kenneth Thompson, *Politics Among Nations: The Struggle for Power and Peace* (New York, 1985), p. 594.

2. In addition to Paul Hollander's *Political Pilgrims: Travels of Western Intellectuals to the Soviet Union, China, and Cuba, 1928–1978* (New York, 1981) and Hugh De Santis's *The Diplomacy of Silence: The American Foreign Service, the Soviet Union, and the Cold War, 1933–1947* (Chicago, 1980), any reader would benefit from the following: Martin Weil, *A Pretty Good Club: The Founding Fathers of the U.S. Foreign Service* (New York, 1978); Peter Filene, *American Views of Russia* (Homewood, Ill., 1968); Benson Grayson, ed., *The American Image of Russia, 1917–1977* (New York, 1978); Daniel Yergin, *Shattered Peace: The Origins of the Cold War and the National Security State* (Boston, 1977); Daniel Harrington, "Kennan, Bohlen, and the Riga Axioms," *Diplomatic History* (Fall 1978); Thomas Maddux, "American Diplomats and the Soviet Experiment: The View from the Moscow Embassy, 1934–1939," *South Atlantic Quarterly* (Autumn 1975); Frederic Popas, "Creating a Hard Line Toward Russia: The Training of State Department Experts, 1927–1937," *Diplomatic History* (Summer 1984). Henry Kissinger's *Diplomacy* (New York, 1994) is a meditation on statecraft as condicted at the highest level of executive responsibility; his book barely touches on nonambassadorial diplomacy.

There is a fine book on German diplomats in the USSR by Wilhelm Joost, *Botschafter bei den roten Zaren: Die deutschen Missionchefs in Moskau, 1918 bis 1941, nach geheimakten und personlichen Aufzeichnungen* (Vienna, 1967).

3. Harold Nicolson, *Diplomacy* (London, 1963), pp. 39–40.

4. Morgenthau and Thompson, *Politics Among Nations,* p. 150. The full text from Neill Brown can be found in Despatches from U.S. Ministers to Russia, 1808–1906, Microfilm 10-3-9, M 35, Roll 15, National Archives (hereafter NA); C. M. Ingersoll, "My First Years in Russia, 1847–1848," pt. 1, diary entries for June 7 and August 9, 1847, and "My Visit to Moscow in the Month of May 1849," Ingersoll Papers, Boston University.

5. For a detailed account of early U.S. encounters with the Soviet government, see David McFadden, *Alternative Paths: Soviets and Americans, 1917–1920* (New York, 1993).

6. Jack Matlock, "Changes in Our World and in Our Profession," *Newsletter of American Association for the Advancement of Slavic Studies,* November 1990, p. 1.

Chapter 1

1. George Kennan, *Soviet-American Relations, 1917–1920,* vol. 1: *Russia Leaves the War* (New York, 1956, 1967), pp. 3–4.

2. Unless otherwise noted, all dates in this and subsequent chapters will be given in the Western (Gregorian) calendar.

3. See "Proceedings of the Continental Congress, 1780," in Nina Bashkina et al., eds., *The United States and Russia: The Beginnings of Relations, 1765–1815* (Washington, D.C., n.d.), p. 33.

4. For more about Sayre and his activities in St. Petersburg, see John Alden, *Stephen Sayre: American Revolutionary Adventurer* (Baton Rouge, 1983), pp. 123–136. A French version of wartime diplomacy—and it is highly partisan—is P. Fauchille's *La Diplomatie française et la Ligue des Neutres de 1780* (Paris, 1893).

5. Consult the following for Francis Dana and his tour in Russia: W. P. Cresson, *Francis Dana: A Puritan Diplomat at the Court of Catherine the Great* (New York, 1930); Max Laserson, *The American Impact on Russia, 1784–1917* (New York, 1962); Thomas Bailey, *America Faces Russia: Russian–American Relations from Early Times to Our Day* (Gloucester, Mass., 1964); Samuel Bemis, *John Quincy Adams and the Foundations of American Foreign Policy* (New York, 1949); Nikolai Bolkhovitinov, *Stanovlenie Russko–Amerikanskikh otnoshenii, 1775–1815* (Moscow, 1966); John Hildt, *Early Diplomatic Negotiations of the United States with Russia* (Baltimore, 1906); David Griffiths, "Nikita Panin, Russian Diplomacy, and the American Revolution," *William and Mary Quarterly,* July 1970.

6. France had been humbled by British seapower during the Seven Years War (1756–1763) and expelled from Canada. French claims to India were dashed by Britain with the capture of Pondicherry in 1761.

7. Bashkina, ed., *United States and Russia,* p. 33.

8. Catherine read the *Journey* and wrote ten pages of scathing commentary. According to her private secretary, Catherine believed that Radishchev "was a rebel, worse than Pugachev."

9. David Griffiths, "American Commercial Diplomacy in Russia, 1780–1783," *William and Mary Quarterly,* July 1970, p. 406. For an absorbing treatment of Harris, see Isabel de Madariaga's *Britain, Russia, and the Armed Neutrality: Sir James Harris's Mission to St. Petersburg During the American Revolution* (New Haven, 1962).

10. Until 1893, all United States missions were represented at the highest level by a minister plenipotentiary or an envoy extraordinary and minister plenipotentiary. Adams was minister plenipotentiary in Russia. The first American to hold the rank of envoy extraordinary and minister plenipotentiary in St. Petersburg was William Pickney (1816–1818). The first to hold the rank of ambassador was Ethan Hitchcock, who served in St. Petersburg from 1897 to 1899.

The consular service, charged with promoting U.S. trade interests and protecting citizens abroad, functioned independently of the diplomatic corps. Not until Congress's passage of the Rogers Act (1924) were the consular and diplomatic services merged into a new entity, the Foreign Service. More on this issue appears in Chapter 4.

11. Grimm's prediction anticipated Tocqueville's more famous statement: the United States and Russia were "marked by the will of Heaven to sway the destinies of half the globe" (Eugene Anschel, ed., *The American Image of Russia, 1775–1917* [New York, 1974], p. 25).

12. See, for example, John Stoessinger's useful but somewhat misleading account of early U.S.–Russian relations and perceptions in his *Nations in Darkness: China, Russia, and America* (New York, 1978), pp. 103–106, 116–117.

13. Jones's career in Russia ended ignominiously. He was accused of raping a young woman and was forced to leave the country. After the scandal, Catherine concluded that Jones was "a wrongheaded fellow." See John Alexander, *Catherine the Great: Life and Legend* (New York, 1989), p. 29; Samuel Eliot Morison, *John Paul Jones: A Sailor's Biography* (Boston, 1959).

14. John Quincy Adams to Abigail Adams, 1783, in Bashkina, ed., *United States and Russia*, p. 210.

15. Frank Golder, *Guide to Materials for American History in Russian Archives* (Washington, D.C., 1917), p. 20.

16. William A. Williams, *American–Russian Relations, 1781–1947* (New York, 1952), p. 6; Thomas Jefferson to William Duane, 1807, in Bashkina, ed., *United States and Russia*, pp. 478–479.

17. John Quincy Adams to Abigail Adams, 1810, in Bashkina ed., *United States and Russia*, pp. 639–640.

18. John Spear Smith to Senator Samuel Smith, 1810, in ibid, p. 666.

19. Deposition of Christian Rodde, December 1814, in ibid, p. 1098; Alfred Crosby, *America, Russia, Hemp, and Napoleon: American Trade with Russia and the Baltic, 1783–1812* (Columbus, 1965), pp. 276–279. In 1821, Adams gave a deposition damaging to Harris. Nevertheless, Harris was able to continue his government career. He was the American chargé d' affaires in France when James Buchanan met him in 1833. Buchanan wrote in his diary that Harris was "a man sufficiently civil and ceremonious, but a mannerist. . . . He has been so long in Europe as to have lost much of his American feelings, if he ever possessed them in a strong degree. Not unskillful as a diplomatist. He is remembered kindly in Russia" (*Mission to Russia: 1831–1833* [New York, 1908, 1970], p. 386). It appears that Alexander I would have been pleased to see Harris elevated from consul to American minister in St. Petersburg. See Golder, *Guide*, p. 93.

20. Bemis, *John Quincy Adams*, pp. 170–171.

21. John Quincy Adams to James Monroe, 1813, in Bashkina, ed., *United States and Russia*, pp. 920–921.

22. Charles Francis Adams, ed., *The Diary of John Quincy Adams, 1794–1845*, vol. 2: *Russian Memoirs* (Philadelphia, 1874; New York, 1970), p. 424.

23. Bemis, *John Quincy Adams*, p. 178; John Quincy Adams to Abigail Adams, 1812, in Bashkina, ed., *United States and Russia*, pp. 896–897.

24. Levett Harris to Ivan Weydemeyer, 1815, in Bashkina, ed., *United States and Russia*, p. 1105.

25. Andrei Dashkov to Nikolai Rumiantsev, 1814, in ibid., pp. 1089–1093. Dashkov was unpopular with his hosts, and the Russian Ministry of Foreign Affairs scolded him for his complaining about conditions in the United States. See Golder, *Guide*, pp. 25–26.

26. Churchill exclaimed in 1946, "From Stettin in the Baltic to Trieste in the Adriatic an iron curtain has descended across the continent. Behind that line lie all the capitals of the ancient states of central and eastern Europe. All these famous cities and the populations around them lie in what I must call the Soviet sphere." For Marx, see J. A. Doerig, ed., *Marx Versus Russia* (New York, 1962), p. 12.

27. J. A. Doerig, Introduction and Afterword to Doerig, ed., *Marx Versus Russia*.

28. Ibid, p. 46.

29. It is certain that Custine was familiar with Tocqueville's seminal work on the

United States, the first volume of which was published in 1836. On this point, see George Kennan, *The Marquis de Custine and His Russia in 1839* (Princeton, 1971), pp. 18–23.

30. Walter Bedell Smith, Introduction to Phyllis Kohler, ed., *Journey for Our Time* (Chicago, 1951), p. 8.

31. "In Russia," Custine said, "the government interferes with every thing and vivifies nothing. In that immense empire, the people, if not tranquil, are mute; death hovers over all heads, and strikes capriciously whom it pleases: man there has two coffins, the cradle and the tomb. The Russian mothers ought to weep the birth more than the death of their children" (*Empire of the Czar: A Journey Through Eternal Russia* [Paris, 1843; New York 1989], p. 16).

32. Ibid., p. 594.

33. Ibid., p. 619.

34. Kennan, *Marquis de Custine*, p. vii; Viktor Erofeev, "Neither Salvation Nor Sausage," *New York Review of Books*, June 14, 1990, p. 25.

35. Kennan, *Marquis de Custine*, p. 111.

36. C. M. Ingersoll, "My First Year in Russia, 1847–1848," pt. 2, diary entry for August 30, Ingersoll Papers, Boston University.

37. Harold Bergquist, "Russian–American Relations, 1820–1830: The Diplomacy of Henry Middleton, American Minister at St. Petersburg" (Ph.D diss., Boston University, 1970).

38. Marc Raeff, "An American View of the Decembrist Revolt," *Journal of Modern History* 25 (1953): 290. Also see N. Bolkhovitinov, "Dekabristy i Amerika," *Voprosy istorii*, no. 4 (1974); Anschel, ed., *American Image of Russia*, pp. 87–89.

39. George Ticknor Curtis, *Life of James Buchanan*, (New York, 1883), vol. 1, p. 187.

40. Ibid., p. 171; Buchanan, *Mission to Russia*, pp. 229–230, 313.

41. John Belohlavek, *George Mifflin Dallas: Jacksonian Patrician* (University Park, Pa., 1977), p. 75.

42. George Dallas, *Dairy of George Mifflin Dallas While United States Minister to Russia, 1837–1839* (New York, 1892, 1970), p. 45.

43. Anschel, ed., *American Image of Russia*, p. 103.

44. Neill Brown, no. 2, August 16, 1850, and no. 26, January 27, 1853, in Despatches from U.S. Ministers to Russia, 1808–1906, Microfilm 10-3-9, M 35, Roll 15, NA.

45. Curtis, *Life of James Buchanan*, p. 146.

46. Motley's diplomatic career did not end with his Russian tour. During the Civil War, he was U.S. minister to Austria and in 1869 to 1870 was minister to Great Britain. His reputation continues to rest on his scholarship on Dutch history. Andrew Dickson White returned to St. Petersburg as minister from 1892 to 1894. More on White in Chapter 2.

47. Brown, no. 20, May 27, 1852, NA.

48. Norman Saul, *Distant Friends: The United States and Russia, 1763–1867* (Lawrence, Kans., 1991), pp. 53, 63, 87; John Lewis Gaddis, *Russia, the Soviet Union, and the United States: An Interpretive History* (New York, 1978), p. 12.

49. Belohlavek, *George Mifflin Dallas*, p. 74.

50. Henry Adams observed that Randolph's performance in Russia "was worthy of the satire of Juvenal, [it] still stands as the most flagrant bit of jobbery in the annals of the United States government" (*John Randolph* [Boston, 1910], p. 294). For additional anecdotes on the drunken Arthur Bagby and the linguistically maladroit Charles Todd, see Saul, *Distant Friends*, pp. 168–169.

51. George William Curtis, ed., *The Correspondence of John Lothrop Motley* (New York, 1889), vol. 1, p. 81.

52. Belohlavek, *George Mifflin Dallas,* p. 64.

53. In 1819, Alexander invited the United States to join the Holy Alliance. This invitation was rejected as being incompatible with republican principles.

54. For a detailed treatment of U.S.–Russian relations in 1820 to 1830 see Bergquist, "Russian–American Relations." For Soviet treatments of Russian concern about 'he Monroe Doctrine, see N. Bolkhovitinov, *Doktrina Monro* (Moscow, 1959), and the relevant section in S. B. Okun, *Rossiisko-Amerikanskaia Kompaniia* (Moscow, 1939).

55. Bailey, *America Faces Russia,* p. 65; Alexandre Tarsaidze, *Czars and Presidents* (New York, 1958), pp. 119–124; Golder, *Guide,* p. 63.

56. Williams, *American–Russian Relations, 1781–1947,* p. 19.

57. Tarsaidze, *Czars and Presidents,* pp. 155–156.

58. Brown, no. 15, January 28, 1852, NA.

59. Anschel, ed., *American Image of Russia,* p. 103. Not all Americans were persuaded that future Russian–U.S. relations would remain harmonious. Shortly after leaving the presidency, Andrew Jackson declared, "The next great war we have will be with Russia. . . . a growing absolute monarchy and a thriving democratic government are naturally antagonistic. It is easy to find pretexts for war; our vicinity to her North-western Pacific possessions will suffice" (quoted in Saul, *Distant Friends,* p. 163).

60. Curtis, ed., *Correspondence of John Lothrop Motley,* vol. 1, p. 96.

61. Thomas Seymour did explore parts of Russia after relinquishing his post in St. Petersburg. He visited Kazan, Saratov, Astrakhan and the Caspian Sea. See Saul, *Distant Friends,* p. 241.

62. Brown, no. 26, January 27, 1853, NA; Saul, *Distant Friends,* p. 113.

63. For a fine study of Pickens, see John Edmund, *Francis W. Pickens and the Politics of Destruction* (Chapel Hill, N.C., 1986).

64. Thanks to the efforts of Angus Ward (assigned to the embassy shortly after Soviet–U.S. relations were established in 1933), many of the records of nineteenth- and early-twentieth-century American diplomats were recovered for the State Department and National Archives. See Harold Langley, "Hunt for American Archives in the Soviet Union," *American Archivist,* April 1966, pp. 265–275.

65. George Kennan, "The War Problem in the Soviet Union," p. 1, March 1935, Box 1, Kennan Papers, Princeton University; George Kennan to author, October 24, 1989; *Foreign Relations of the United States* [hereinafter referred to as *FRUS*], *The Soviet Union, 1933–1939,* pp. 289–291.

66. Walter Bedell Smith, *My Three Years in Moscow* (Philadelphia, 1950), pp. 13, 32, 46, 85, 111, 131, 157, 280, 304; Hans Morgenthau and Kenneth Thompson, *Politics Among Nations: The Struggle for Power and Peace* (New York, 1985), p. 150.

67. In his capacity as historian, Kennan asserted that Custine's observations of Nicholas's Russia were probably the most incisive ones ever made about Stalin's reign and were useful in understanding Brezhnev's USSR. See Kennan, *Marquis de Custine,* pp. viii, 124; Kohler, ed., *Journey for Our Time,* pp. 3–5; Smith, Introduction, pp. 7–20.

68. Kennan, *Marquis de Custine,* p. 89.

69. Ibid., p. 94.

70. Brown, no. 15, January 28, 1852, NA. In his X article, Kennan insisted that "the issue of Soviet-American relations is in essence a test of the over-all worth of the United States as a nation among nations." Earlier in the Long Telegram, he stated, "If we cannot abandon fatalism and indifference in face of deficiencies in our own society, Moscow will

profit" (X, "The Sources of Soviet Conduct," *Foreign Affairs*, July 1947, pp. 566–582; *FRUS, 1946*, vol. 6, p. 708).

Chapter 2

1. Chancellor of the Exchequer William Gladstone declared in a speech at Newcastle, "Jefferson Davis and other leaders of the South have made an army; they are making, it appears, a navy; and they have made what is more than either, they have made a nation" (quoted in James McPherson, *Ordeal By Fire: The Civil War and Reconstruction* [New York, 1982], p. 301).

2. After the war, Jefferson Davis wrote, "Had [the European] powers promptly admitted our right to be treated as all other independent nations, none can doubt that the moral effect of such action would have been to dispel the pretension under which the United States persisted in their efforts to accomplish our subjugation" (*The Rise and Fall of the Confederate Government* [New York, 1881, 1958], vol. 2, p. 370).

3. Useful books on Civil War diplomacy and international relations include D. P. Crook, *The North, the South, and the Powers, 1861–1865* (New York, 1974); B. B. Sideman and L. Friedman, eds., *Europe Looks at the Civil War* (New York, 1960); D. Jordan and E. J. Pratt, *Europe and the American Civil War* (Boston, 1931); Jay Monaghan, *Diplomat in Carpet Slippers: Abraham Lincoln Deals with Foreign Affairs* (Indianapolis, 1945); James Callahan, *The Diplomatic History of the Southern Confederacy* (Baltimore, 1901); Frank Lawrence Owsley, *King Cotton Diplomacy* (Chicago, 1959).

4. Sideman and Friedman, eds., *Europe Looks at the Civil War*, p. 20; Alexandre Tarsaidze, *Czars and Presidents* (New York, 1958), p. 182.

5. Jordan and Pratt, *Europe and the American Civil War*, p. 201. Holmes had earlier captured the sentiment of Northerners when he wrote a panegyric to Russian–U.S. friendship that included these two stanzas:

> When darkness bid the stormy skies
> In war's long winter night,
> One ray still cheered our straining eyes,
> The far-off Northern light.
>
> A nation's love in tears and smiles
> We bear across the sea;
> O Neva of the hundred isles,
> We moor our hearts in thee!

This poem is quoted in full in Joseph Loubat, *Gustavus Fox's Mission to Russia in 1866* (New York, 1873, 1970), p. 181.

6. See Howard Kushner, "The Russian Fleet and the American Civil War: Another View," *The Historian*, August 1972; William Nagengast, "The Visit of the Russian Fleet to the United States: Were Americans Deceived?" *Russian Review* (January 1949); Frank Golder, "The Russian Fleet and the American Civil War," *American Historical Review*, July 1915; E. A. Adamov, "Russia and the United States at the Time of the Civil War," *Journal of American History* (1930).

7. Sideman and Friedman, eds., *Europe Looks at the Civil War*, p. 245.

8. For more on Russian attitudes toward the Civil War, see relevant sections in ibid.; Nikolai Sivachev and Nikolai Yakovlev, *Russia and the United States: U.S.–Soviet Relations from the Soviet Point of View* (Chicago, 1979); Max Laserson, *The American Impact on Russia, 1784–1917* (New York, 1950, 1962); Frank Golder, "The American Civil War Through the Eyes of a Russian Diplomat," *American Historical Review* 26 (1921); M. Malin, "K istorii russko-amerikanskikh otnoshenii vo vremia grazhdanskoi voiny v SShA,"

Krasny Arkhiv 94 (1939). Popular Russian and official attitude toward black slavery is reviewed in Allison Blakely, *Russia and the Negro: Blacks in Russian History and Thought* (Washington, D.C., 1986). The radical writer Nicholas Chernyshevsky condemned slavery in the South and believed that the freeing of blacks was a symbolic blow against Russian feudalism.

9. Jordan and Pratt, *Europe and the American Civil War,* pp. 14–15.

10. Cassius Marcellus Clay, *The Life of Cassius Marcellus Clay* (Cincinnati, 1886), pp. 294–295; Albert Perry, "Cassius Clay's Glimpse into the Future," *Russian Review,* April 1943; p. 64.

11. Clay, *Life,* pp. 302, 312, 462.

12. U.S. Congress, *Papers Relating to Foreign Affairs,* 38th Cong., 2nd sess. (Washington, D.C., 1865), pt. 3, p. 288.

13. See Albert Woldman, *Lincoln and the Russians* (Cleveland, 1952), chap. 1.

14. Ibid., pp. 155, 161; James Robertson, *A Kentuckian at the Court of the Tsars: The Ministry of Cassius Marcellus Clay* (Berea, Ky., 1935), pp. 81, 145; Monaghan, *Diplomat in Carpet Slippers,* p. 344; Clay, *Life,* p. 335; *Papers Relating to Foreign Affairs,* pt. 3, pp. 255–266, 287, 295; U.S. Congress, *Papers Relating to Foreign Affairs,* 38th Cong., 1st sess. (Washington, D.C., 1864), pt. 2, pp. 797, 799; U.S. Congress, *Papers Relating to Foreign Affairs,* 39th Cong., 1st sess. (Washington, D.C., 1866), pt. 2, pp. 364, 385.

15. Bergh's response to the cruelty inflicted on horses in St. Petersburg begs comparison with that of Friedrich Nietzche. In 1889, already in precarious psychological condition, Nietzche was walking along a street in Turin when he saw a cabman furiously flog his horse. Nietzche threw his arms around the neck of the animal and collapsed in tears onto the ground. He was a broken man and never recovered his emotional balance.

One last word about Bergh: he was also a developer and popularizer of the clay pigeon and recommended this device as an alternative to the shooting of live birds. For his efforts to abolish bird hunting, angry sportsmen made threats on his life.

16. Clay once reported to Seward, "Much of the good feeling existing towards this legation is owing to the character and merits of Mr. Curtin, who has learned the Russian language and speaks it fluently . . . to the delight of all Russia. He is a great acquisition to this legation and deserves well of the country" (U.S. Congress, *Papers Relating to Foreign Affairs,* 39th Cong., 2nd sess. [Washington, D.C., 1867], pt. 1, p. 392).

17. See Joseph Schafer, ed., *Memoirs of Jeremiah Curtin* (Madison, 1940), vol. 2, chap. 8; Clay, *Life,* p. 410; Perry, "Cassius Clay's Glimpse into the Future," pp. 62–63.

18. For a fuller account of Clay, see H. Edward Richardson, *Cassius Marcellus Clay: Firebrand of Freedom* (Lexington, Ky., 1976).

19. See Erwin Stanley, *Simon Cameron, Lincoln's Secretary of War: A Political Biography* (Philadelphia, 1966), chap. 6.

20. Marie Hansen-Taylor and Horace Scudder, eds., *Life and Letters of Bayard Taylor* (Boston, 1885), vol. 1, pp. 408–409; *Papers Relating to Foreign Affairs,* 38th Cong., 1st sess., pt. 2, pp. 785–787.

21. *Papers Relating to Foreign Affairs,* 38th Cong., 1st sess., pt. 2, pp. 763–785.

22. Richmond Beatty, *Bayard Taylor: Laureate of the Gilded Age* (Norman, Okla., 1936), pp. 226–227; Hansen-Taylor and Scudder, eds., *Life and Letters,* p. 407; Clay, *Life,* p. 328.

23. Woldman, *Lincoln and the Russians,* pp. 41–42, 262.

24. Joint Resolution no. 37, *Statutes at Large of the United States* (Washington, D.C., 1923), vol. 14, p. 355.

25. For Clay's account of Fox's visit, see *Life,* pp. 409–412. There he makes the boast, nowhere else substantiated, that he originated the idea of America's sending a high-

ranking delegation to Alexander after the assassination attempt. Also consult Loubat, *Fox's Mission to Russia.*

26. Robertson, *Kentuckian at the Court of the Tsars,* p. 235.

27. The following are useful in reviewing the U.S. purchase of Alaska: T. M. Batueva, "Prokhozhdenie dogovora o pokupke Aliaski v Kongresse SShA v 1867–1868 gg," *Novaia i noveishaia istoriia,* no. 4 (1971); Glyndon Van Deusen, *William Henry Seward* (New York, 1967); F. W. Seward, *Seward at Washington as Senator and Secretary of State* (New York, 1891); Howard Kushner, *Conflict on the Northwest Coast: American–Russian Rivalry in the Pacific Northwest, 1790–1867* (Westport, Conn., 1975); Hector Chevigny, *Russian America: The Great Alaskan Venture, 1741–1867* (New York, 1965). An excellent documentary history of Russian activities in the New World is Basil Dimytryshyn, ed., *The Russian American Colonies, 1798–1867* (Portland, Ore., 1989).

28. For details of Clay and the Perkins claim, Robertson, *Kentuckian at the Court of the Tsars,* chap. 12.

29. See Clay, *Life,* pp. 336, 441; Mark Twain, *The Innocents Abroad* (New York, 1869, 1967), p. 262; Anschel, ed., *American Image of Russia,* pp. 128–129, 157–159.

30. Soon after the grand duke left the United States, Alexander removed Catacazy from his Washington post. He was ordered to Paris, where he made more trouble for his government. Catacazy's version of his career in the United States is his *Un Incident diplomatique* (Paris, 1872).

31. Titian Coffey, "Curtin as Minister to Russia," in William Egle, ed., *The Life and Times of Andrew Gregg Curtin* (Philadelphia, 1896), p. 430.

32. *FRUS, 1870,* p. 234. Schuyler became a published authority on Russian and Near Eastern matters. He wrote a biography of Peter the Great, a travelogue based on his experiences in Russian Turkistan, and an account of Turkish atrocities in Bulgaria. This last work (1876) helped to inflame Russian feeling that led to the 1877/1878 war against Turkey, fought ostensibly on behalf of Slavdom and Christian Orthodoxy.

33. See Harnett Thomas Kane's (with Victor Leclerc) colorful, albeit untrustworthy, *The Scandalous Mrs. Blackford* (New York, 1951). Under the name Fanny Lear, Blackford published her own account, *Le Roman d'une Américaine en Russie* (Paris, 1875).

34. See *FRUS, 1872,* pp. 487–492; *FRUS, 1874,* p. 837; *FRUS, 1875,* p. 1062. *A Compilation of the Messages and Papers of the Presidents* (New York, 1897–1922), vol. 9, p. 4162.

35. *FRUS, 1874,* pp. 807–808.

36. Edward Bradley, *George Henry Boker* (Philadelphia, 1927), p. 308.

37. *FRUS, 1878,* pp. 758–760; *FRUS, 1879,* pp. 918–919.

38. Alexander seems not to have been too distraught at the empress's death. Within six weeks of her demise, he celebrated a morganatic marriage with his mistress of long standing.

39. John Foster, *Diplomatic Memoirs* (Boston, 1909), vol. 1, p. 199.

40. *FRUS, 1881,* p. 1020.

41. For more on Pobedonostsev, see Robert Byrnes, *Pobedonostsev: His Life and Thought* (Bloomington, 1968). His philosophic-political treatise was translated into English in 1898 as *Reflections of a Russian Statesman.* The quotation is taken from the section dealing with new democracy. See Murray Polner's English-language edition (Ann Arbor, 1965).

Alexander Blok gave this testimony in his "Revenge":

In those mute and distant years
A dull gloom filled all hearts.
Pobedonostsev had unfurled

His owlish wings over Russia.
There was neither day nor night,
Only the shadow of giant wings.

42. For more on Foster, see Michael Devine's *John W. Foster* (Athens, Ohio, 1981).

43. Foster, *Diplomatic Memoirs,* vol. 1, pp. 200, 204, 215.

44. In addition to the Russian subsections in *FRUS, 1880,* and *FRUS, 1881,* see Cyrus Adler and Aaron Margalith, *With Firmness in the Right: American Diplomatic Action Affecting Jews, 1840–1945* (New York, 1946), pp. 179–192.

45. Adler and Margalith, *With Firmness in the Right,* p. 178.

46. Ibid., p. 212.

47. Ibid., p. 215; *FRUS, 1891,* p. 739.

48. George Brandes, *Impressions of Russia,* ed. Richard Pipes (New York, 1889, 1966), p. 6.

49. Frederick Travis, *George Kennan and the American–Russian Relationship, 1865–1924* (Athens, Ohio, 1990), p. 178. Travis's book is invaluable for any student of late-nineteenth-century U.S.–Russian relations. For more on Kennan, see his *Siberia and the Exile System* (New York, 1891), and also of interest are Russian commentaries: D. A. Kolesnichenko, "Dzhordzh Kennan i tsarskaia okhranka," *Prometei,* no. 7 (1969); E. I. Melamed, *Dzhordzh Kennan protiv tsarizma* (Moscow, 1981).

50. George Kennan to Andrew Dickson White, March 22, 1896, Box 118, Kennan Papers (elder), Library of Congress.

51. Pierre Botkine, "A Voice for Russia," *Century Magazine,* February 1893, p. 613.

52. *FRUS, 1890,* p. 700; Travis, *George Kennan,* pp. 172–173.

53. Glenn Altschular, *Andrew D. White—Educator, Historian, Diplomat* (Ithaca, 1979), p. 32; Andrew Dickson White, *Autobiography* (New York, 1904), vol. 1, pp. 461, 468, 475.

54. Andrew Dickson White, *Autobiography* (New York, 1905), vol. 2, pp. 6–7, 27, 29, 72.

55. Ibid., pp. 72–100.

56. Ibid., pp. 55–71.

57. Ibid., pp. 51–52; *FRUS, 1894,* p. 535.

58. Adler and Margalith, *With Firmness in the Right,* p. 468.

59. *FRUS, 1893,* p. 539; White, *Autobiography,* vol. 2, pp. 9–10. A fine analysis of the famine and the czarist response is in Richard Robbins, "The Russian Famine of 1891–1892 and the Relief Policy of the Imperial Government" (Ph.D. diss., Columbia University, 1970). As many as 275,000 people died from the famine. The most famous victim of the cholera was Peter Tchaikovsky (1840–1893).

60. Bailey, *America Faces Russia,* p. 125; White, *Autobiography,* vol. 2, pp. 9, 31.

61. *FRUS, 1894,* p. 560.

62. *FRUS, 1895,* pt. 2, p. 1125; *FRUS, 1899,* pp. 594–599. For a comparative review of Russian and European economic development in the second half of the nineteenth century, see A.J.P. Taylor, Introduction to *The Struggle for Mastery in Europe, 1848–1918* (London, 1954, 1971).

63. M. A. DeWolf Howe, *George von Lengerke Meyer: His Life and Public Services* (New York, 1920), p. 329. For a scholarly assessment of the toll inflicted by terrorists, see Anna Geifman, *Thou Shalt Kill: Revolutionary Terrorism in Russia, 1894–1917* (Princeton, 1993).

64. Philip Ernest Schoenberg, "The American Reaction to the Kishinev Pogrom of 1903," *American Jewish Historical Quarterly,* March 1974; pp. 262–262.

65. *FRUS, 1906,* pt. 2, pp. 1296–1297, 1311; *FRUS, 1905,* pp. 779, 831.

66. *FRUS, 1911*, pp. 695–699; Adler and Margalith, *With Firmness in the Right*, pp. 285–291.

67. *FRUS, 1911*, pp. 696–698.

68. Charles Wilson to Secretary of State, March 14, 1914, *Confidential U.S. Diplomatic Post Records, 1914–1941*, pt. 1, Reel 1.

69. Kennan to White, March 22, 1896.

70. Howe, *Meyer*, p. 111.

71. For a fascinating eyewitness account by an American naval officer of the 1904/1905 war at sea, consult Richard A. von Doenhoff, ed., *The McCully Report: The Russo-Japanese War, 1904–1905* (Annapolis, 1906, 1977).

72. For more about U.S.–Russian rivalry in the Far East, the Russo-Japanese War, and American mediation, see the following: Tyler Dennett, *Roosevelt and the Russo-Japanese War* (Gloucester, Mass., 1925, 1959); Edward Zabriskie, *American–Russian Rivalry in the Far East, 1895–1914* (Philadelphia, 1946); John White, *The Diplomacy of the Russo-Japanese War* (Princeton, 1964); Charles Neu, *An Uncertain Friendship: Theodore Roosevelt and Japan, 1906–1912* (Cambridge, Mass., 1967). Parts of the following should also be consulted: Arthur Thompson and Robert Hart, *The Uncertain Crusade: America and the Russian Revolution of 1905* (Amherst, 1970); Michael Hunt, *Frontier Defense and the Open Door* (New Haven, 1973); Pauline Tomkins, *American–Russian Rivalry in the Far East* (New York, 1949); Lev Zubok, *Ekspansionistkaia politika SShA v nachale XX-ogo veka* (Moscow, 1969); Theodore Roosevelt, *An Autobiography* (New York, 1913); Abraham Yarmolinsky, ed., *The Memoirs of Count Witte* (New York, 1967); Baron R. R. Rosen, *Forty Years of Diplomacy*, vol. 1 (London, 1922).

73. Howe, *Meyer*, pp. 157–162.

74. Roosevelt, *Autobiography*, p. 293.

75. See Dennett, *Roosevelt and the Russo-Japanese War*, pp. 290–294. Dennett claims that Meyer's reports contained meager information about the revolution. Dennett adds that as a rule, "An embassy has always been an extremely poor place from which to study a revolution."

76. Howe, *Meyer*, pp. 144–146, 153, 157, 174, 198, 241; Meyer to Secretary of State Root, July 18, 1906, in Despatches from U.S. Ministers to Russia, Microfilm 10-3-9, M 35, Roll 66, NA.

77. Howe, *Meyer*, pp. 174, 176, 178–179, 236, 240, 297; Meyer to Root, December 26, 1905, Roll 63, NA.

78. Howe, *Meyer*, pp. 305, 308, 511.

79. Ibid., pp. 198, 304; Foster, *Diplomatic Memoirs*, vol. 1, pp. 207–208; John Foster, *Diplomatic Memoirs* (Boston, 1909), vol. 2, p. 152; Altshuler, *White*, pp. 273–274.

80. Lewis Leonard, *The Life of Alphonso Taft* (New York, 1920), p. 186; Andrew Dickson White, *A History of the Warfare of Science with Theology in Christendom*, 2 vols. (New York, 1896).

81. Foster, *Diplomatic Memoirs*, vol. 1, pp. 213–214; White, *Autobiography*, vol. 2, pp. 355–372; Howe, *Meyer*, pp. 220–221; *Register of the Department of State* (Washington, D.C., 1905), p. 21; Rachel West, *The Department of State on the Eve of the First World War* (Athens, Ga., 1978), p. 4.

82. Henry Mattox has argued that amateur U.S. diplomacy performed well—at least in the 1890s—and compares it favorably with the German foreign service of that decade. See his *Twilight of Amateur Diplomacy: The American Foreign Service and Its Senior Officers in the 1890s* (Kent, Ohio, 1989).

83. West, *Department of State*, p. 106.

Chapter 3

1. Statistics for Russia in World War I vary greatly. The numbers cited here are from R. E. Dupuy and T. N. Dupuy, eds., *The Encyclopedia of Military History* (New York, 1986), p. 990.

2. See Durnovo's memorandum in Frank Golder, ed., *Documents of Russian History, 1914–1917* (New York, 1927), pp. 3–23.

3. *FRUS, 1915, Supplement,* p. 59; George Marye, *Nearing the End in Imperial Russia* (London, 1928), p. 349.

4. Marye, *Nearing the End,* pp. 37–38, 103–107, 226, 367; *FRUS, 1915, Supplement,* pp. 59–61. Sazonov did not mention Marye in his memoirs, *Fateful Years, 1909–1916* (London, 1928).

5. Rasputin was assassinated in December 1916 by conspirators who included a member of the Imperial family. They had hoped that their belated action would save the Romanov dynasty.

6. Marye, *Nearing the End,* pp. 139–140, 306, 392, 444–450; Sir George Buchanan, *My Mission to Russia and Other Diplomatic Memoires* (London, 1923), vol. 2, p. 46. Nicholas's statement fits perfectly with this anecdote from Bertolt Brecht and his encounter with the East German government. In 1953, after labor unrest and rioting in East Berlin, the authorities said they were disappointed in the citizens' misconduct. Brecht suggested that the government elect itself a new people.

7. Three useful but by no means compatible reviews of Wilson and U.S. policy before the 1917 intervention are in Edward Buehrig, *Woodrow Wilson and the Balance of Power* (Bloomington, 1955); Arthur Link, *Wilson and the Struggle for Neutrality, 1914–1915* (Princeton, 1960); Ernest May, *The World War and American Isolation, 1914–1917* (Cambridge, Mass., 1966).

8. Charles Wilson to Secretary of State, May 14, 1915, *Confidential U.S. Diplomatic Post Records, 1914–1941,* pt. 1, Reel 3.

9. Arthur Link, ed., *The Papers of Woodrow Wilson,* (Princeton, 1966–   ), vol. 36, pp. 125–126.

10. Marye, *Nearing the End,* pp. 218, 433.

11. Link, ed., *Papers of Wilson,* vol. 29, p. 373; vol. 31, p. 469; vol. 33, p. 511; vol. 35, pp. 358, 526; Marye, *Nearing the End,* p. 460.

12. Maurice Paleologue, *An Ambassador's Memoirs,* 6th ed. (New York, n.d.,) vol. 2, pp. 110–111; vol. 3, pp. 19–20; Jamie Cockfield, ed., *Dollars and Diplomacy: Ambassador David Rowland Francis and the Fall of Tsarism, 1916–1917* (Durham, N.C., 1981), p. 17.

13. Charles Wilson to Secretary of State, January 16, 1914, *Confidential U.S. Diplomatic Post Records, 1914–1941,* pt. 1, Reel 1; Marye, *Nearing the End,* pp. 459–479.

14. *FRUS, The Lansing Papers,* vol. 2, p. 310; Cockfield, ed., *Dollars and Diplomacy,* p. 57.

15. Jordan was repelled by the violence of the Bolshevik Revolution and elated when time came for him and Francis to return to the United States. Jordan compared the United States to "heaven." From a Bolshevik perspective, this son of slaves and servant to a member of the ruling class was deficient in understanding his true interest.

Jordan's letters appear in Mrs. Clinton Bliss, "Philip Jordan's Letters from Russia, 1917–1919," *Bulletin of the Missouri Historical Society,* January 1958; pp. 139–166. Also see Jamie Cockfield, "Philip Jordan and the October Revolution, 1917," *History Today,* April 1978.

16. See Paul Harper, ed., *The Russia I Believe In: The Memoirs of Samuel N. Harper,*

1902–1941 (Chicago, 1945), pp. 91–95. Apparently, Francis also had a taste for smut. See Earl Packer's recollection of Francis in Foy Kohler and Mose Harvey, eds., *The Soviet Union: Yesterday, Today, Tomorrow* (Miami, 1975), pp. 157–163.

17. Harper, ed., *Russia I Believe In*, pp. 92–93. Francis told Secretary of State Lansing that deCram was "a loyal Russian, hates Germany and is very desirous to serve the Allies, especially America" (Francis to Lansing, June 20, 1918, in *Russia in Transition: The Diplomatic Papers of David Francis, U.S. Ambassador to Russia, 1916–1918*, (Reel 10 [hereafter *Francis Papers*]).

18. State Department telegram, 861.00/451-1/2, NA. See Francis's letters to "Dear Madame," March 27, 1918, April 18, 1918; to Edward Weyde, May 3, 1918; and to Robert Imbrie, May 25, 1918, Reel 9, *Francis Papers*.

In late November 1918, deCram reported that she was without money or employment, did not know of her husband's fate, and was physically weak, but at least her sons were alive. See to Francis [from illegible], November 27, 1918, Reel 11, *Francis Papers*.

19. George Kennan, *Russia Leaves the War* (Princeton, 1956; New York, 1967), pp. 38–41. Kennan's *Russia Leaves the War* and its companion volume, *The Decision to Intervene* (Princeton, 1958; New York, 1967), remain indispensable studies of Russian–U.S. relations in 1917 to 1920.

20. Cockfield, ed., *Dollars and Diplomacy*, pp. 41, 50–51; Paleologue, *Ambassador's Memoirs*, vol. 3, pp. 19–20.

21. Cockfield, ed., *Dollars and Diplomacy*, pp. 12, 33.

22. Ibid., p. 78; *FRUS, Lansing Papers*, p. 312.

23. Francis to Secretary of State, n.d., *Confidential U.S. Diplomatic Post Records 1914–1941*, Reel 3, pt. 1; Cockfield, ed., *Dollars and Diplomacy*, pp. 29, 44; Link, ed., *Papers of Wilson*, vol. 38, p. 69; Francis, *Russia from the American Embassy*, pp. 34, 57.

24. See Francis to Ambassador William Sharp, June 17, 1918, about the personal affairs and unhappiness of Livingston Phelps, second secretary to the embassy, Reel 10, *Francis Papers;* Cockfield, ed., *Dollars and Diplomacy*, p. 71.

25. Unless the reader be misled: Francis and the other ambassadors in attendance at the session when Miliukov made his attack on Sturmer left (at the request of the government) before its unleashing; they then attended a meeting of the State Council, the conservative upper chamber of the national legislature, whose members upheld the principles of church and czar.

In Russia, Francis lost much of his body weight. He also suffered bladder and prostate difficulties that were treated in London by surgery (late 1918). He bore these ailments with considerable courage. See Francis to "Dear Perry," August 26 and October 7, 1918, Reel 10, and to "Dear Jane," October 25, 1918, Reel 11, *Francis Papers*.

26. *FRUS, Lansing Papers*, vol. 2, p. 319.

27. As a scholar, Wilson did at least once (1901) express critical views in public print ("When a Man Comes to Himself") about the Russian autocracy. Ambassador Bakhmetev was concerned in 1915 about the possible effects of this writing on U.S. opinion and was assured by the president that his view of Russia had since then improved. See ibid., pp. 307–308. For the full text of Wilson's message to Congress, see Link, ed., *Papers of Wilson*, vol. 41, pp. 519–527.

28. The Cadet leader Miliukov was the Provisional Government's original minister of foreign affairs, and the Octoberist Alexander Gurchkov was minister of war and navy.

29. Francis thought the events of March constituted "the most amazing revolution" (*FRUS, 1918, Russia*, vol. 1, p. 5).

30. Francis, *Russia from the American Embassy*, pp. 94–95, 163.

31. Order Number 1 stipulated that officers were entitled to command only during field

operations; otherwise, military units would be run by democratic committees and free elections. Acceptance of this idea accelerated the already advanced breakdown of troop discipline.

32. The commission included a military and a naval officer: Major General Scott and Rear Admiral Glennon. Also included were industrialists and financiers: Cyrus McCormick, Charles Crane, and Samuel Bertron. The YMCA was represented by John Mott. American workers were represented by the conservative socialist Charles Russell and James Duncan, vice president of the American Federation of Labor.

33. Trotsky, president of the Petrograd soviet (as of September 1917), had no patience for either Gompers or the leaders of American socialism. Of those he encountered in New York, he made this observation: "They think that Wilson was infinitely more authoritative than Marx. And, properly speaking, they are simply variants of 'Babbitt,' who supplements his commercial activities with dull Sunday meditations on the future of humanity. These people live in small national clans, in which the solidarity of ideas usually serves as a screen for business connections" (*My Life* [New York, 1970], p. 274).

34. For an analysis of the multiple inadequacies of U.S. aid in summer 1917 to Russia, see Kennan, *Russia Leaves the War,* pp. 19–23. Also useful are Alton Ingram, "The Root Mission to Russia, 1917" (Ph.D. diss., Louisiana State University, 1970), and sections of Paul Miliukov, *Rossiia na perelome,* vol. 1 (Paris, 1927).

35. *FRUS, 1918, Russia,* vol. 1, pp. 220–221.

36. Frequent ministerial turnovers in the Provisional Government alarmed Francis. The resignation of some men (Guchkov, for example) whom he thought "excellent," greatly discouraged him. See ibid., pp. 52–53.

37. R. H. Lockhart, *British Agent* (New York, 1933), p. 279.

38. Francis, *Russia from the American Embassy,* p. 141; *FRUS, 1919, Russia,* p. 27. Francis told Maddin Summers (March 27, 1918), "Trotsky who is amenable to flattery, is vain, loves to be conspicuous, plays to the galleries and is I understand now dressing like a gentleman" (Reel 9, *Francis Papers*).

39. For a defense of the Lvov–Kerensky regime, see Robert Browder and Alexander Kerensky, eds., *The Russian Provisional Government, 1917,* 3 vols. (Stanford, 1961).

40. See Louise Bryant's account of her stay in the "greatest and youngest of democracies" in *Six Red Months in Russia* (Philadelphia, 1918; London, 1982). John Reed's *Ten Days That Shook the World* (New York, 1987) is still an exciting book to read. The quotation is from p. 188. In a letter to his son Perry, Francis wrote on November 26, 1917, "I never knew of a place where human life is as cheap as it is now in Russia" (*Russia from the American Embassy,* p. 188).

41. In addition to Lockhart's *British Agent,* see William Hard's *Raymond Robins' Own Story* (New York, 1920); Jacques Sadoul, *Notes sur la Revolution Bolchevique* (Paris, 1920).

42. Richard Pipes, *A History of the Russian Revolution* (New York, 1990), p. 589.

43. *FRUS, 1918, Russia,* vol. 1, pp. 322–323.

44. Ibid., p. 321. For more about this tangled affair, see Andrew Kalpaschnikoff, *A Prisoner of Trotsky's* (Garden City, N.Y., 1920), with Forward by Ambassador Francis; Edgar Sisson, *One Hundred Red Days: A Personal Chronicle of the Bolshevik Revolution* (New Haven, 1931), chap. 10; Kennan, *Russia Leaves the War,* chap. 10.

In his *Prisoner of Trotsky's,* Kalpaschnikoff gave this witness: "The Bolsheviki carried the trade mark of disorder and were precise and definite in their desire to murder and destroy. . . . These leaders, though often basing everything on immoral and criminal desires, succeeded very easily in taking into their hands the whole of Russia because they represented the autocracy of the mob" (p. xviii).

45. Bliss, "Philip Jordan's Letters," p. 147.

46. On March 27, 1918, Francis wrote, "I believed the Bolshevik leaders to be German agents and to be in the receipt of money from Germany" (Reel 9, *Francis Papers*).

47. Francis, *Russia from the American Embassy*, p. 218.

48. The German-dictated Treaty of Brest-Litovsk was severe. In addition to the territories surrendered in European Russia, the Bolsheviks also made territorial concessions to Turkey. More than 60 million people were wrested from Moscow's control, along with 75 percent of its iron industries and coal fields. More than a quarter of the arable land was lost, and Russia had to pay a huge indemnity. See John Wheeler-Bennett, *The Forgotten Peace: Brest-Litovsk, March 1918* (New York, 1939), and *The Treaty of Brest-Litovsk and Germany's Eastern Policy* (Oxford, 1940).

49. *FRUS, 1918, Russia*, vol. 1, p. 399.

50. Francis, *Russia from the American Embassy*, p. 232.

51. Lockhart, *British Agent*, p. 278.

52. The killing of the czar, his wife, and his son and daughters was symbol and substance of the civil war. Both sides identified children and families as legitimate targets of devastation. Not until the Gorbachev period did any Soviet publication question the validity of executing Nicholas and his family. See P. Cherkasov, *Novyi Mir* 7 (1988).

53. See Richard Ullman's excellent *Anglo-Soviet Relations, 1917–1921: Intervention and the War* (Princeton, 1961), pp. 245–248; Francis, *Russia from the American Embassy*, chap. 18; John Long, "American Intervention in Russia: The North Russian Expedition, 1918–1919," *Diplomatic History* (Winter 1982).

54. Francis was unhappy about leaving Russia and looked forward to returning after his health improved. If nothing else, he yearned to be witness to Bolshevik ruin. As he told a colleague: "I hope to remain here [in Russia] as long or long enough to see justice meted out—may all, the oppressed and the oppressor, get what they deserve" (Francis to Basil Miles, April 8, 1918, Reel 9; Francis, address to the American Soldiers in Northern Russia, November 5, 1918, Reel 11, *Francis Papers*).

55. Summers viewed Robbins as a would-be usurper of his position in Moscow. See Summers's letters to Francis, April 11, 1918, May 1, 1918, Reel 11, *Francis Papers*. In the second letter, he exploded, "I am especially disgusted with the situation as I feel that the attitude of Robins here has decidedly undermined the work of the Embassy, the Consular Service and all other institutions, and I firmly believe that it is time that some action should be taken to have the thing stopped."

56. Francis, *Russia from the American Embassy*, p. 335. Francis was not certain of the number of Allied troops necessary for implementing his idea. The numbers he presented to Wilson were once as high as 200,000 and as low as 100,000. See Link, ed., *Papers of Wilson*, vol. 55, pp. 234–235.

57. Scholarly literature on the intervention is large. Some of the best works are James Morley, *The Japanese Thrust into Siberia* (New York, 1957); Betty Miller Unterberger, *America's Siberian Expedition, 1918–1920* (Durham, N.C., 1956), and *The United States, Revolutionary Russia, and the Rise of Czechoslovakia* (Chapel Hill, N.C., 1989); Richard Ullman, *Anglo-Soviet Relations, 1917–1921*, 3 vols. (Princeton, 1961–1972); George Kennan, *The Decision to Intervene* (Princeton, 1958); John Silverlight, *The Victors' Dilemma: Allied Intervention in the Russian Civil War* (New York, 1970). Soviet scholarship from the Stalinist era is represented by A. I. Melchin, *Amerikanskaia interventsiia v 1918–1920 gg* (Moscow, 1951), and the practically unreadable A. Berezkin, *SShA Aktivnyi organizator i uchastnik voennoi interventsii protiv Sovetskoi Rossii 1918–1920 gg* (Moscow, 1952). Scholarship from the pre-Stalinist period is more interesting—for example, I. Subbotovsky, *Soiuzniki, Russkie reaktsionery i interventsiia: kratkii obzor* (Leningrad, 1926).

58. William Bullitt was also eloquent in a plea to Colonel House against U.S. interven-

tion in Russia. He warned him in June 1918: "How shall we stand before the common people of the world if we join hands with the upper classes of Russia? Have they ever cared much for the things we care about? I *know* that an invasion of Siberia is as wrong strategically and politically, as it is wrong morally" (Bullitt to House, June 24, 1918, Bullitt Papers, Yale University).

59. C. K. Cumming and Walter Pettit, eds., *Russian-American Relations, March 1917–March 1920* (New York, 1920), pp. 298–303; Chicherin to Mr. Poole, July 4, 1918, Reel 10, *Francis Papers*.

60. *FRUS, 1918, Russia,* vol. 2, pp. 477–484; V. I. Lenin, *Collected Works* (Moscow, 1946), vol. 29, p. 487; Colonel Bugbee, "Letters from Siberia," pp. 8–9, Bugbee Papers, Hoover Institution.

The civil war's ferocity is vividly conveyed in Peter Kenez, *Civil War in South Russia,* 2 vols. (Berkeley, 1971, 1977). Fighting, hunger, disease, and terrorism caused the deaths of 7 to 10 million Russian civilians and soldiers in 1917 to 1921.

61. Consult George Kennan, "The Sisson Documents," *Journal of Modern History,* June 1956.

62. James Libbey asserts that Francis "stood higher than most as a man eminently qualified for the post [of ambassador to Russia] in 1916" *Alexander Gumberg and Soviet–American Relations, 1917–1933* ([Lexington, Ky., 1977], p. 2).

63. See the following: Link, ed., *Papers of Wilson,* vol. 45, pp. 216–219, 243; vol. 48, pp. 265, 276; vol. 51, p. 178; vol. 54, p. 260; *Congressional Record,* 65th Cong., 3rd sess., pp. 18876–18881; William Bullitt, *The Bullitt Mission to Russia* (New York, 1919); Will Brownell and Richard Billings, *Close to Greatness: A Biography of William C. Bullitt* (New York, 1987), pp. 67, 108–109; John Thompson, *Russia, Bolshevism, and the Versailles Peace* (Princeton, 1966); Arno Mayer, *Politics and Diplomacy: Containment and Counterrevolution at Versailles, 1918–1919* (New York, 1967).

Francis, who was described by one member of the French diplomatic mission as "disastrous," did not formally relinquish his ambassadorship until March 1921. See Comte Louis de Robien, *The Diary of a Diplomat in Russia, 1917–1918* (New York, 1967), p. 292.

64. Robins was embarrassed by Bolshevik statements that he was scheduled to replace Francis, and he tried to reassure the ambassador on this score. Robins to Francis, April 26, 1918, Reel 9, *Francis Papers*.

65. Robins to Francis, April 1, 1918, Reel 9, *Francis Papers*.

66. Link, ed., *Papers of Wilson,* vol. 48. pp. 141–143; Edgar Sisson, *One Hundred Red Days,* p. 30.

67. Link, ed., *Papers of Wilson,* vol. 36, p. 402.

68. Bullitt believed that Wilson should have organized a high-level group "to consist of the Departments and Boards [operationally concerned with Russia] with a Chairman in whom the President could have complete confidence. The Chairman of this Board would not be subservient to any Department. He would deal personally with the President. It would be his business to gather all the information in regard to Russia received by any Department and to plan our Russian policy—political, commercial, military" (Bullitt to Colonel House, May 20, 1918 and September 20, 1918, Bullitt Papers).

69. Bullitt and the Bolsheviks struck an agreement that might have provided the basis for further Russian–Western negotiations. The agreement called for various measures, including an end to all military operations in Russia, a lifting of the Allied blockade and resumption of trade relations, an exchange of official representatives, the granting of amnesty for Russians who fought against the Red Army, the removal of Allied forces from Russia, and acceptance by the revolutionaries of debts incurred by the czarist empire. See Orville Bullitt, ed., *For the President, Personal and Secret: Correspondence Between*

Franklin D. Roosevelt and William C. Bullitt (Boston, 1972), pp. 5–6; Bullitt, *Bullitt Mission to Russia,* p. 40.

70. For a first-rate treatment of Wilson and his ideas, see Thomas Knock, *To End All Wars: Woodrow Wilson and the Quest for a New World Order* (New York, 1993).

Chapter 4

1. In "Lessons of the New Economic Policy: Thinking Aloud at the CPSU CC Plenum," *Isvestia,* March 10, 1989, V. Sitotkin records these words of Lenin's in late 1923:

> Of course we have failed. We thought we could create a new communist society at the wave of a magic wand. But this will take decades, generations. So that the party does not lose heart, faith, and its will for struggle, we must depict the return to an exchange economy . . . as a temporary deviation. But we ourselves must be clearly aware that the attempt has failed and that it is impossible to change suddenly people's outlook and the habits they have acquired over the ages. We can try to drive the population into the new system by force, but the question would still be whether we would retain power in this all-Russian slaughter house.

2. The Soviet failure to create an economically advanced society is poignantly conveyed in Stephen Kotkin, *Steeltown, USSR: Soviet Society in the Gorbachev Era* (Berkeley, 1991).

3. Clarence Starr, "Russian Story," p. 6, Box 6, Starr Papers, Hoover Institution. Also see John Scott's last chapter, "What Makes Russia Tick," in his *Behind the Urals: An American Worker in Russia's City of Steel* (Bloomington, 1989).

4. On this point, see Eugene Lyons, "To Tell or Not to Tell," *Harper's,* June 1935; Paul Hollander, *Political Pilgrims: Travels of Western Intellectuals to the Soviet Union, China, and Cuba, 1928–1978* (New York, 1981), p. 110.

5. In *Stalin's Apologist: Walter Duranty, The New York Times's Man in Moscow* (New York, 1990), S. J. Taylor emphasizes Duranty's personal ambition to explain his career in the Soviet Union. Whitman Bassow probes for psychological reasons in understanding Duranty and connects them to his physical deformity and unattractive appearance in *The Moscow Correspondents: Reporting on Russia from the Revolution to Glasnost* (New York, 1988).

6. Bertrand Russell, *Autobiography, 1914–1944* (Boston, 1968), pp. 141–143. See Eugene Lyons, *Assignment in Utopia* (New York, 1937), and Zara Witkin's unpublished book manuscript in Box 1, Witkin Papers, Hoover Institution. Michael Gleb of Franklin and Marshall College is scheduled to publish Witkin's fascinating volume with University of California Press.

7. Walter Arnold Rukeyser, "I Work for Russia: How the Worker Lives," *The Nation,* June 3, 1931, p. 607.

8. See Benjamin Weissman, *Herbert Hoover and Famine Relief to Soviet Russia, 1921–1923* (Stanford, 1974), and Bertrand Patenaude's forthcoming study of the ARA. The ARA in Russia wanted to alleviate the plight of people in rural areas but was not oblivious to the political implications of doing so. Frank Golder, an ARA veteran, wrote thus about his leaving Russia: "As I stood on the Destroyer looking over Odessa, tears almost came into my eyes at the thought of the misery and suffering endured by those big hearted and fine people and I felt so sorry for them. That, no doubt, is the feeling of every ARA man when he leaves Russia. Yet there is nothing more that we can do. We are leaving and that is right. We have done a monumental piece of work, for in addition to feeding the hungry we have started forces at work which are bound to have results" (Golder to Christian Herter, May 8, 1923, Box 42, Golder Papers).

9. The Hoover Institution possesses the papers of the Provisional Government's embassy in Washington. At Hoover, see Russia. Posol' stvo (United States), Records, 1897–1947.

10. In the words of the American commissioner in Riga, "It is entirely possible, or even probable, that some time in the indefinite future these so-called states may once again become on integral part of Russia" (*FRUS, 1922,* vol. 2, p. 871).

11. My characterizations of Coleman, Macgowan, and Lehrs are drawn from "The Legation at Riga," "Memoirs," vol. 2 (unpublished section), pp. 337–342, Henderson Papers, Hoover Institution. Also see Natalie Grant, "The Russian Section, a Window on the Soviet Union," *Diplomatic History* (Winter 1978).

In Riga (1922–1929), Hugh Martin played an intelligence role and was in touch with the secret services of various countries; these supplied him with reports of uneven quality about Soviet Russia. A former subordinate of David Francis's in Petrograd, Earl Packer also served in Riga's Russian section during 1922 to 1924.

12. See the seventy-five reels (taken from National Archives, Record Group 84) of the Foreign Service Posts of the State Department for the Soviet Union, 1919–1933. They are available as *Russia and the Soviet Union: Internal and External Affairs, 1914–1941,* pt. 2. For Soviet–U.S. relations, see Reels 16 and 18 of Section A and Reels 12, 13, 16, 17, 18, 22, 23, 24, 27, 30, 31, 34, 36, and 39 of Section B.

13. There is a sizable literature on the history of the Foreign Service. The following studies contain sections on the Rogers Act and other pre–World War II reforms: Hugh De Santis, *The Diplomacy of Silence: The American Foreign Service, the Soviet Union, and the Cold War, 1933–1947* (Chicago, 1979); Waldo Heinrichs, *American Ambassador: Joseph Grew and the Development of the United States Diplomatic Tradition* (New York, 1966); Warren Ilchman, *Professional Diplomacy in the United States, 1779–1939* (Chicago, 1961); Robert Schulzinger, *The Making of the Diplomatic Mind: The Training, Outlook, and Style of United States Foreign Service Officers, 1908–1931* (Middletown, Conn., 1975); Martin Weil, *A Pretty Good Club: The Founding Fathers of the U.S. Foreign Service* (New York, 1978). A complement to the above is Teddy James Uldricks, "The Development of the Soviet Diplomatic Corps, 1917–1930" (Ph.D. diss., Indiana University, 1972).

14. Foy Kohler and Mose Harvey, eds., *The Soviet Union: Yesterday, Today, Tomorrow* (Miami, 1975), pp. 164–165. Also see Frederic Propas, "Creating a Hard Line Toward Russia: The Training of State Department Soviet Experts, 1927–1937," *Diplomatic History* (Summer 1984); Thomas Maddux, "American Diplomats and the Soviet Experiment: The View from the Moscow Embassy, 1934–1939," *South Atlantic Quarterly* (Autumn 1975).

15. George Baer, ed., *A Question of Trust: The Origins of U.S.–Soviet Diplomatic Relations: The Memoirs of Loy W. Henderson* (Stanford, 1986), pp. 164–166.

16. Ibid, p. 189.

17. For a judicious study of Henderson's public career and intellectual life, see H. W. Brands, *Inside the Cold War: Loy Henderson and the Rise of the American Empire, 1918–1961* (New York, 1991). I wrote a review of this book for *International History Review,* May 1992.

18. George Kennan, *Memoirs: 1925–1950* (Boston, 1967), pp. 29–30.

19. George Kennan, Manuscript—Part I, p. 2, File 1933–1938, Box 25, Kennan Papers, Princeton University.

20. Charles Bohlen, *Witness to History, 1929–1969* (New York, 1973), p. 10.

21. See Daniel Yergin, *Shattered Peace: The Origins of the Cold War and the National Security State* (Boston, 1977), chaps. 1 and 2; Weil, *Pretty Good Club,* pp. 50–56.

22. For more about the significance of Riga and points raised against Yergin and Weil,

see Bohlen, *Witness to History,* pp. 12, 176; Baer, ed., *Question of Trust,* pp. xxii, 264; David Mayers, *George Kennan and the Dilemmas of U.S. Foreign Policy* (New York, 1988), pp. 25–26; Daniel Harrington, "Kennan, Bohlen, and the Riga Axioms," *Diplomatic History* (Fall 1978); Kennan to Bohlen, p. 2, January 26, 1945, Box 3, Bohlen Papers, Library of Congress.

23. Taylor, *Stalin's Apologist,* p. 184.

24. For more on Stalin's effort to achieve rapprochement with Germany in the early 1930s, see Robert Tucker, *Stalin in Power: The Revolution from Above, 1928–1941* (New York, 1990), pp. 223–237.

25. See the following for assessments of the 1933 Roosevelt–Litvinov negotiations: Robert Browder, *The Origins of Soviet–American Diplomacy* (Princeton, 1953); Thomas Maddux, *Years of Estrangement: American Relations with the Soviet Union, 1933–1942* (Tallahassee, Fla., 1980); *Dokumenty vneshnei politiki SSSR* 26, pp. 609–610, 658–659; Donald Bishop, *The Roosevelt–Litvinov Agreements* (Syracuse, N.Y., 1965); Edward Bennett, *Recognition of Russia* (Waltham, Mass., 1970); *FRUS, 1933–1939, Soviet Union,* pp. 21–22, 43–46.

26. Anglo-Soviet relations were broken in May 1927 and did not resume until December 1929.

27. *FRUS, Soviet Union, 1933–1939,* p. 7.

28. Ibid., pp. 6–11.

29. Ibid., pp. 14–17. Also see R. Walton Moore to Secretary of State, November 4, 1933, Box 18, Moore Papers, Franklin D. Roosevelt Library. Useful material pertaining to the American side of Soviet–U.S. negotiations in 1933 is found in Box 18 of this collection.

30. Mayers, *George Kennan and the Dilemmas,* p. 26.

31. Tucker, *Stalin in Power,* p. 195. Roosevelt to Litvinov, November 16, 1933, cited in Browder, *Origins of Soviet–American Diplomacy,* p. 228.

32. See Kelley to Mr. President, September 21, 1933, p. 3, Kelley Papers, Georgetown University; Commission on the Ukraine Famine, *Investigation of the Ukrainian Famine, 1932–1933, Report to Congress* (Washington, D.C., 1988), pp. 151–184.

33. Tucker, *Stalin in Power,* pp. 189, 191. The numbers are from Robert Conquest, *The Harvest of Sorrow: Soviet Collectivization and the Terror-Famine* (New York, 1986), p. 306. His analysis of the famine's casualties is the most definitive. It should be noted that scholarly estimates of the numbers of fatalities range from between 3 and 4 million to between 7 and 10 million. For a review of this scholarship, see Tucker, *Stalin in Power,* p. 195.

34. A. Enoukidze to Max Huber, December 26, 1933 (attached to letter from John Barton Payne to Franklin Roosevelt), January 22, 1934, Box 2, 1934–1935, Official File, Roosevelt Papers, Franklin D. Roosevelt Library.

35. The phrase comes from Stanley Hoffmann's *Duties Beyond Borders: On the Limits and Possibilities of Ethical International Politics* (Syracuse, N.Y., 1981).

36. Bennett, *Recognition of Russia,* p. 104.

37. Not until Gorbachev was there anything like a candid discussion among Soviet scholars and journalists about collectivization and the famine. Some of the earliest and best began to appear in late 1987/early 1988 in *Literaturnaia Gazeta.*

38. The phrase "why did the heavens not darken" is from Arno Mayer, *Why Did The Heavens Not Darken? The "Final Solution" in History* (New York, 1989).

39. Peter Kenez, "Years of Terror," *New Leader,* December 10–24, 1990, p. 23; Kenez, Review of Robert Conquest's *Harvest of Sorrow, Society,* no. 1 (1988).

40. Commission on Ukraine Famine, *Investigation of the Ukrainian Famine,* p. 163.

Also see the following: Robert Kelley to Reverend Nicholas Kopachuk, January 5, 1934, and E. L. Packer to Dr. Luke Myshuha, November 6, 1934, File Soviet Precedent IX.A.1, The Ukraine, Box 28, Records of the Division of Eastern European Affairs, 1917–1941, RG 59, NA.

41. A number of my friends and colleagues disagree with my assessment of Roosevelt's recognition of Moscow in 1933. After seeing this chapter, Peter Kenez wrote me (March 5, 1991), "I continue to think that you are on thin ground arguing on the one hand that U.S. policy should not have a 'moralistic strain' and on the other that in the matter of recognition in 1933 it should have had. What would have been a better time to recognize, one wonders? 1936? 1937? 1938?"

My imperfect solution—of waiting somewhat longer to recognize the USSR or at least discussing with its representative the conditions of life in the countryside—is not the equivalent of endorsing the moralistic strain. By ignoring the famine issue entirely as the administration did in negotiations with Litvinov, the American side allowed the United States to become implicated with Soviet policy.

42. Taylor, *Stalin's Apologist,* p. 185. Duranty thought that as many as 10 million people had died in 1932 and 1933 from lack of food in the USSR. See Kenneth Bourne and D. C. Watt, eds., *British Documents on Foreign Affairs: Reports and Papers from the Foreign Office,* vol. 2: *The Soviet Union,* (Frederick, Md., 1983), p. 271.

43. In his letter to Senator David Walsh, urging Kelley's promotion to assistant secretary, Constantine McGuire observed that Kelley did not belong to the "white-spat brigade;" this included patricians such as Sumner Welles, who won the appointment. After reciting Kelley's accomplishments (linguistic and otherwise), McGuire concluded, "As you can well imagine, the gentry who run the State Department have had him around because they had to have some one qualified to do what he does—not because of his race, religion, or social background" (McGuire to Walsh, January 25, 1933, Kelley Papers).

44. T. Michael Ruddy, *The Cautious Diplomat: Charles E. Bohlen and the Soviet Union, 1929–1969* (Kent, Ohio, 1986), p. 3.

45. As part of an administrative reorganization of the State Department in 1937, Kelley's Division of East European Affairs was liquidated and its functions were incorporated into the new Division of European Affairs. Kelley was sent to serve in the embassy in Turkey. These actions indicated, at least to Kennan and Bohlen, the administration's hostility to the intellectual and political orientation of Kelley's program. This interpretation, however strongly held by its proponents, was exaggerated and did not take into account the department's program of economy and overall reduction at the time. Insensitivity, clumsiness, and stupidity were behind Kelley's being badly used—but not the sinister motives detected by his younger champions. See Kennan's comments in *Memoirs: 1925–1950,* pp. 83–85.

Chapter 5

1. See the following: Hannah Arendt, *The Origins of Totalitarianism* (New York, 1951); Carl Friedrich and Zbigniew Brzezinski, *Dictatorship and Autocracy* (Cambridge, Mass., 1957); William Kornhauser, *The Politics of Mass Society* (Glencoe, Ill., 1959); Leonard Schapiro, ed., *Political Opposition in One-Party States* (London, 1972); J. L. Talmon, *The Origins of Totalitarian Democracy* (New York, 1960); Robert Tucker, "Towards a Comparative Politics of Movement Regimes," *American Political Science Review,* June 1961.

2. See Will Brownell and Richard Billings, *So Close to Greatness: A Biography of William C. Bullitt* (New York, 1987); Orville Bullitt, ed., *For the President "Personal and*

Secret" : Correspondence Between Franklin D. Roosevelt and William C. Bullitt (Boston, 1972); Beatrice Farnsworth, *William C. Bullitt and the Soviet Union* (Bloomington, 1967).

3. See Joseph Davies, *Mission to Moscow* (New York, 1941); Andrei Gromyko, *Memoirs* (New York, 1989), p. 30.

4. Steinhardt's correspondence from the USSR from September 1940 to November 1941 has been lost. For details, see his papers and reading guide at the Library of Congress.

5. Boris Pasternak, *Doctor Zhivago* (New York, 1981), p. 506. The tale of a nonfictional female victim of Stalin's is chronicled in Anna Larina's autobiography, *This I Cannot Forget: The Memoirs of Nikolai Bukharin's Widow* (New York, 1993).

6. See Philip Kerr to Undersecretary of Foreign Office, July 11, 1919, and press release (in which Bullitt's reports of conversation with Lloyd George are called "tissue of lies"), Kerr Papers, Scottish Record Office.

7. Farnsworth, *Bullitt and the Soviet Union,* pp. 107–108; Eugene Lyons, *Assignment in Utopia* (New York, 1937), p. 564; Louis Fischer, *Men and Politics* (New York, 1941), p. 303.

8. See Bullitt to Colonel House, May 20, 1918 and September 20, 1918, Bullitt Papers, Yale University. In the first letter, he revealed, "I wish I could see Russia with as single an eye as Reed. I am unable to wind through the welter of conflicting reports about the Bolsheviki to anything like solid conviction." His own bewilderment in this area he thought was shared by many people in government service; therefore, experts on the Soviet republic were needed.

9. Charles Bohlen, *Witness to History, 1929–1969* (New York, 1973), pp. 16–17.

10. See sections in ibid; George Kennan, *Memoirs: 1925–1950* (Boston, 1967); George Baer, ed., *A Question of Trust: The Origins of U.S.–Soviet Diplomatic Relations: The Memoirs of Loy Henderson* (Stanford, 1986); File I.F.3 Official American Personnel in USSR, Records of the Division of Eastern European Affairs, 1917–1941, RG 59, NA.

11. Bullitt to Mr. President, May 18, 1934, Box 50, President's Secretary's File, Roosevelt Papers, Franklin D. Roosevelt Library. Rebecca Matlock is writing a history of Spaso House and the diplomats who lived there. The working title of her book is "Spaso House, Backdrop to History."

12. *FRUS, Soviet Union, 1933–1939,* p. 60.

13. Bullitt, ed., *For the President,* p. 73; Department of State, For the Press, January 8, 1934, Box 18, Moore Papers, Franklin D. Roosevelt Library.

14. Bullitt to Moore, May 14, 1934, Box 3, Moore Papers. In this letter, Bullitt also expressed doubts about the suitability of most American women in Moscow. He wrote, "I am inclined to believe that it will be impossible for American women to be happy with this town unless they are of an exceptional intellectual type. There is absolutely nothing for a woman to do here. The Russians will not invite American women to their houses for the simple reason that the women bore them." Also see Bullitt to Colonel House, July 2, 1934, Bullitt Papers, Yale University; Kennan, *Memoirs: 1925–1950,* p. 69.

15. White and Bullitt were involved in a near-fatal accident in June 1934 as they approached Leningrad. Bullitt's explanation is in Box 18, June 29, 1934, Moore Papers. Partial text is in Bullitt, ed., *For the President:*

> We were just at the edge of a hummocky marsh cut across by deep ditches. [White] had to land between the ditches, on a tiny patch of marshy land, with only a hundred feet of altitude in which to maneuver. He did a quick side-slip, straightened the plane out and brought her down with somewhat of a thud necessarily in the marsh. The landing speed of the plane is about sixty miles an hour and we had the good fortune to roll a short distance before the wheels got definitely caught in the marsh and we went over. The Soviet officials who were

waiting to receive me got a magnificent scare, as I doubtless should have had I been on the ground and not in the plane. They came racing across the marsh, falling on their noses, to pick out the dead man, but by the time they arrived we had loosed our belts and climbed out and received them as if we were quite in the habit of landing upside down. (pp. 90–91)

16. Bohlen, *Witness to History*, pp. 23–24; Bullitt, ed., *For the President*, p. 93. For an account of the Soviet–American venture in polo, see Charles Thayer, *Bears in the Caviar* (Philadelphia, 1950), pp. 115–129.

17. Kennan, *Memoirs: 1925–1950*, p. 60; Baer, ed., *Question of Trust*, p. 294; Bohlen, *Witness to History*, p. 26.

18. Bullitt to R. Walton Moore, June 14, 1934, Box 3, Moore Papers; Bullitt to Robert Kelley, June 20, 1934, Kelley Papers, Georgetown University.

19. Moore to Bullitt, June 18, 1934, Box 3, Moore Papers.

20. Bullitt to Mr. President, September 8, 1934, Box 50, President's Secretary's File, Roosevelt Papers; Bullitt to Moore, September 8, 1934, Box 3, Moore Papers.

21. See M. Litvinov, *Vneshniaia politika SSSR* (Moscow, 1937); Jonathan Haslam, *The Soviet Union and the Search for Collective Security, 1933–1939* (New York, 1984); Jiri Hochman, *The Soviet Union and the Failure of Collective Security, 1934–1938* (Ithaca, 1984).

22. Bullitt to Moore, March 29, 1934, Box 3, Moore Papers; George Kennan, *Soviet Foreign Policy, 1917–1941* (Princeton, 1960), p. 81; Bullitt to Moore, June 21, 1935, Box 3, Moore Papers.

23. Bullitt, ed., *For the President*, p. 6; Donald Day, "Claim Bullitt Is Buying Soviet Rubles Abroad," *Chicago Tribune*, April 21, 1934; Bullitt to Moore, July 13, 1934, Box 3, Moore Papers.

24. Hanson was an unhappy man. In late 1934, he committed suicide. See Baer, ed., *Question of Trust*, p. 330.

25. Bullitt to Mr. President, August 3, 1935, Box 50, President's Secretary's File, Roosevelt Papers.

26. Bullitt to Mr. President, July 15, 1935, Box 50, President's Secretary's File, Roosevelt Papers; *FRUS, Soviet Union, 1933–1939*, pp. 225, 244–248.

27. In *Another Life: The House on the Embankment*, trans. Michael Glenny (New York, 1976), Yuri Trifonov wrote of the 1930s: "There was also fear—utterly despicable, blind, formless, like a creature born in a dark cellar—fear of making a false move, fear of defying . . . what? Nobody knew. And that fear was embedded deeply, under dense layers."

For a plausible reconstruction of the Kirov affair, see Robert Conquest, *Stalin and the Kirov Murder* (New York, 1989).

28. Bullitt to R. Walton Moore, March 30, 1936, Box 3, Moore Papers. Also see Bullitt to Moore, April 27, 1935, Box 3, Moore Papers. In this second letter, Bullitt wrote, "The fear [is] only natural as almost anyone who has had contact with foreigners in Russia during the past year is being sent to Siberia. For example every single acquaintance of the Japanese language students in Leningrad has been exiled."

29. Farnsworth, *Bullitt and the Soviet Union*, p. 141; "Elbridge Durbrow: He Was There—50 Years Ago," *State* August–September 1983, pp. 31–33.

30. See Kennan, *Memoirs, 1925–1950*, pp. 79–81; Baer, ed., *Question of Trust*, pp. 405–410; Bohlen, *Witness to History*, pp. 15–16.

31. Bullitt to R. Walton Moore, April 25, 1935, Box 3, Moore Papers. Also see Bullitt to Moore, September 22, 1934, and May 11, 1935, Box 3, Moore Papers. Author's interview with Hermann Eilts, April 24, 1991.

32. Bullitt to R. Walton Moore, October 26, 1935, Box 3, Moore Papers.

33. Bullitt to Mr. President, March 4, 1936, Box 50, President's Secretary's File, Roosevelt Papers.

34. Bullitt to R. Walton Moore, November 24, 1936, Box 3, Moore Papers. Also see Bullitt's message to the secretary of state, April 20, 1936, *FRUS: Soviet Union, 1933–1939*, pp. 291–296. Most of this message was composed by Kennan and contained his themes. The message ended with this classically Kennan injunction:

> We should be as steady in our attitude as the Soviet Union is fickle. We should take what we can get when the atmosphere is favorable and do our best to hold on to it when the wind blows the other way. We should remain unimpressed in the face of expansive professions of friendliness and unperturbed in the face of slights and underhand opposition. We should make the weight of our influence felt steadily over a long period of time in the directions which best suit our interests. We should never threaten. We should act and allow the Bolsheviks to draw their own conclusions as to the cause of our acts.
>
> Above all, we should guard the reputation of Americans for businesslike efficiency, sincerity, and straightforwardness. . . . There is no weapon at once so disarming and effective in relations with the communists as sheer honesty.

35. *FRUS, Soviet Union, 1933–1939*, p. 303.

36. Ibid., p. 300.

37. Ibid., pp. 301–303.

38. Bohlen, *Witness to History*, p. 51; Thayer, *Bears in the Cavier*, p. 166.

39. Davies, *Mission to Moscow*, p. 280.

40. For a good account of the film version of Davies's book, see David Culbert, ed., *Mission to Moscow* (Madison, 1980). Davies wanted Frederic March to play the leading role; instead, the honor went to the handsome Walter Huston, who, unlike Davies, was not bald.

41. The following is a sample of Davies's many critics: Robert Williams, *Russian Art and American Money, 1900–1940* (Cambridge, Mass., 1980), p. 260; Bohlen, *Witness to History*, pp. 44, 56; Kennan, *Memoirs: 1925–1950*, pp. 82–84; Paul Hollander, *Political Pilgrims: Travels of Western Intellectuals to the Soviet Union, China, and Cuba, 1928–1978* (New York, 1981), p. 130; Robert Tucker, *Stalin in Power: The Revolution from Above, 1928–1941* (New York, 1990), pp. 408, 503; Farnsworth, *Bullitt and the Soviet Union*, pp. 174–175; Richard Ullman, "The Davies Mission and United States–Soviet Relations, 1937–1941," *World Politics*, January 1957; Robert Conquest, *The Great Terror: Stalin's Purges of the Thirties* (New York, 1973), p. 673.

I accept the Bohlen–Kennan view of Davies in my *George Kennan and the Dilemmas of U.S. Foreign Policy* (New York, 1988), pp. 43–44. In an interview with the author, November 10, 1987, Kennan again expressed uncompromising views on Davies.

42. Robert Coulondre, *De Staline à Hitler: Souvenirs de deux ambassades, 1936–1939* (Paris, 1950) p. 112; Baer, ed., *Question of Trust*, pp. 410–423.

A few historians (for example, Elizabeth Kimball Maclean and Daniel Yergin) cautiously endorse Davies in their publications. Foster Rhea Dulles, writing in 1944, was enthusiastic. See Elizabeth Kimball Maclean, "Joseph E. Davies and Soviet–American Relations, 1941–1943," *Diplomatic History* (Winter 1980); Daniel Yergin, *Shattered Peace: The Origins of the Cold War and the National Security State* (Boston, 1977); Foster Rhea Dulles, *The Road to Teheran: The Story of Russia and America, 1781–1943* (Princeton, 1944).

John Lewis Gaddis has written a judicious résumé of Davies's activity in Moscow, but he neither blames nor praises the ambassador. See his *Russia, The Soviet Union, and the United States: An Interpretive History* (New York, 1978), pp. 132–135.

43. Diary, January 2, 1937, Box 3, Davies Papers, Library of Congress. Compare the

passage with the much milder version in *Mission to Moscow* (p. 6), in which no mention is made of the Soviets possibly attacking U.S. territory.

44. Kennan, *Memoirs: 1925–1950*, p. 83.

45. Diary, June 28, 1937, Box 5, Davies Papers.

46. Kennan to Thayer, May 22, 1935, Thayer Papers, Harry S. Truman Library; Gromyko, *Memoirs*, pp. 27–30; Joseph O'Connor, "Laurence A. Steinhardt and American Policy Toward the Soviet Union, 1939–1941" (Ph.D. diss., University of Virginia, 1968), pp. 18–19, n. 6. Davies, Speech of Farewell, June 9, 1938, Box 123, Davies Papers; Kenneth Bourne and D. C. Watt, eds., *British Documents on Foreign Affairs: Reports and Papers from the Foreign Office*, vol. 14: *The Soviet Union*, (Frederick, Md., 1983), pp. 367–368.

47. Robert Kelley to Mr. Carr, February 23, 1937, Kelley Papers; Davies to Bullitt, February 2, 1937, Box 3, Davies Papers; Davies to Cordell Hull, November 12, 1937, Box 6, Davies Papers; Diary entry, May 4, 1938, Box 7, Davies Papers; Davies to E. K., March 17, 1938, Box 7, Davies Papers; Davies to Kelley, February 10, 1937, Box 3, Davies Papers.

48. For a discussion of Davies's frequent (and often dishonest) editing of his letters, see Thomas Maddux, *Years of Estrangement: American Relations with the Soviet Union, 1933–1941* (Tallahassee, Fla., 1980), p. 182, n. 9.

49. Journal, January 26, 1937, Box 3; Diary, July 8, 1937, Box 5; Litvinov on the Defendants, March 4, 1934, Box 7; Journal, February 1, 1937, Box 5; Diary, March 2, 1938, Box 7; Davies to Dearest Bijou, March 6, 1938, Box 7; Davies to Roosevelt, February 4, 1937, Box 3; Davies to Dearest Bijou, June 30, 1937, Box 5; Davies to Colonel House, January 27, 1937, Box 3, Davies Papers.

50. Davies, *Mission to Moscow*, pp. 302–303; Diary, January 22, 1937, Box 3, Davies Papers; Diary, July 5, 1937, Box 5, Davies Papers; Davies to Marvin McIntyre, October 6, 1937, Box 1911–1924, Official File, Roosevelt Papers; Davies to Pat Harrison, February 18, 1937, Box 3, Davies Papers; Davies to Birney Baruch, October 25, 1937, Box 6, Davies Papers; Diary, May 21, 1938, Box 8, Davies Papers; Davies to Joseph Tumulty, April 22, 1938, Box 7, Davies Papers; Davies to Marvin McIntyre, March 15, 1937, Box 4, Davies Papers.

51. Davies to Dear Chief, January 18, 1939, Box 3584–3617, Official File, Roosevelt Papers.

52. Davies was a vulgarian, and he did not hesitate to use words such as *nigger*. See, for example, his discussion with the British ambassador in Diary, March 30, 1938, Box 7, Davies Papers.

53. Keith Eagles, "Ambassador Joseph E. Davies and America–Soviet Relations, 1937–1941" (Ph.D. diss., University of Washington, 1966), pp. 178–190; Maddux, *Years of Estrangement*, pp. 96–97. The following are in the Davies Papers: Journal, February 19, 1937, Box 4; Davies to Sumner Welles, June 28, 1937, Box 5; Davies to Key Pittman, June 29, 1937, Box 5; Davies to Marvin McIntyre, June 10, 1937, Box 5; Diary, March 30, 1938, Box 7; Davies to Sumner Welles, March 1, 1938, Box 7; Davies to Steve Early, March 9, 1937, Box 4.

54. Davies, *Mission to Moscow*, pp. 255–256; Arnold Offner, *American Appeasement: United States Foreign Policy and Germany, 1933–1938* (Cambridge, Mass., 1969), p. 214.

55. Kennan, Manuscript—Part I (n.d., probably written in 1938 or 1939), pp. 5–12, Box 25, Kennan Papers, Princeton University.

56. Bohlen, *Witness to History*, p. 56.

57. Kirk to Secretary of State, 760F.62/614, August 20, 1938, Box 22, President's Secretary's File, Roosevelt Papers; also see in the same box, Kirk to Secretary, 760F.62/853, September 16, 1938.

58. Both Herwarth and German ambassador Count Werner von der Schulenburg belonged to the aristocratic opposition to the Nazis. Schulenburg was killed by them following the aborted 1944 attempt on Hitler's life. Herwarth survived the war and became the Federal Republic's first ambassador to Great Britain. For Herwarth's version of his contacts with Bohlen, see his *Against Two Evils: Memoirs of a Diplomat-Soldier During the Third Reich* (London, 1981), pp. 154–167.

Recent Russian versions of German–Soviet relations from Hitler's rise to power to the nonaggression pact include I. F. Maximychev, *Diplomatiia mira protiv diplomatii voiny: Ocherk Sovetsko-Germanskikh diplomaticheskikh otnoshenii v. 1933–1939* (Moscow, 1981); A. Orlov an C. Tushkeich, "Pact 1939 goda: Alternativy ne Bylo," *Literaturnaia Gazeta*, October 26, 1988; D. Volkogonov, "Nakanune Voiny," *Pravda*, June 20, 1988; V. Sipols, "Za neskol'ko mesiatsev do 23-ogo Avgusta 1939 goda," *Mezhdunarodnaia Zhizn*, May 1989.

59. For attempts by Soviet agents to purchase U.S. naval ships, see the sections in *FRUS, Soviet Union, 1933–1939*. The phrase "of a low dishonest decade" is from W. H. Auden in his "September 1, 1939."

60. Cordell Hull, *The Memoirs of Cordell Hull* (New York, 1948), vol. 1, pp. 603–604.

61. Steinhardt to Sumner Welles, January 11, 1940, Box 78, Steinhardt Papers, Library of Congress.

62. Steinhardt to Willis Thornton, March 8, 1940, Box 79; Steinhardt to Calvin Brown, February 1, 1940, Box 78; Steinhardt to Hinkie, June 6, 1940, Box 79, Steinhardt Papers.

63. Steinhardt to Hageman Hilty, August 25, 1939, Box 78, Steinhardt Papers; Steinhardt to Carl Trygger, March 26, 1940, Box 79, Steinhardt Papers.

64. The following letters in the Steinhardt Papers show Steinhardt's enthusiasm for his staff in Moscow: Steinhardt to Henderson, December 23, 1939, Box 78; Steinhardt to Henderson, August 11, 1939, Box 78; Steinhardt to Henderson, undated, Box 78; Steinhardt to M. A. Thompson, December 1, 1941, Box 79. Steinhardt's feelings were generally reciprocated. See, for example, Baer, ed., *Question of Trust*, pp. 520–522; Willis Armstrong interview, October 20, 1987, p. 4, Foreign Affairs Oral History Project, Georgetown University.

Bohlen was not a fan of Steinhardt's. In *Witness to History* (pp. 88–89), Bohlen criticized him for being overly ambitious and egotistical. Neither was British ambassador Sir Stafford Cripps favorably disposed to him. Cripps wrote his daughter in 1940: "I didn't care for the American Ambassador, a typical bumptious USA business-lawyer type. I wouldn't trust him very much" (quoted in Gabriel Gorodetsky, *Stafford Cripps' Mission to Moscow, 1940–1942* [Cambridge, 1984], p. 47).

65. Steinhardt to Henderson, January 29, 1940, Box 78; Steinhardt to George Spiegelberg, June 20, 1940, Box 79, Steinhardt Papers.

66. In November, the *City of Flint* was allowed to leave Murmansk, and it sailed to Norway. The authorities there interned the German crew and released the Americans. See Bohlen, *Witness to History*, p. 96; Maddux, *Years of Estrangement*, pp. 112, 197; relevant section in *FRUS, Soviet Union, 1933–1939*.

67. Steinhardt to Henderson, December 13, 1939, and December 23, 1939, Box 78, Steinhardt Papers.

68. O'Connor, "Steinhardt and American Policy," p. 122.

69. Steinhardt to Henderson, September 28, 1939, October 20, 1939, January 29, 1940, Box 78, Steinhardt Papers.

70. Steinhardt to Frank Walker, February 1, 1940, Box 78, Steinhardt Papers.

71. Ibid.

72. Steinhardt to Rudolf Schoenfeld, December 9, 1939, Box 78, Steinhardt Papers; Steinhardt to Arthur Schoenfeld, March 1, 1940, Box 79, Steinhardt Papers; Steinhardt to Henderson, March 2, 1940, Box 79, Steinhardt Papers; Thurston to Secretary of State, August 27, 1940, Box 23, President's Secretary's File, Roosevelt Papers; Steinhardt to Secretary of State, September 22, 1940, Box 23, President's Secretary's File, Roosevelt Papers.

73. Steinhardt's cables to Secretary of State, April 12, 1941, and June 12, 1941, Box 23, President's Secretary's File, Roosevelt Papers; O'Connor, "Steinhardt and American Policy," pp. 133, 135, 167–168.

74. Steinhardt to Secretary of State, March 24, 1941, Box 96, Steinhardt Papers.

75. *FRUS, 1941,* vol. 1, pp. 712–714; Maddux, *Years of Estrangement,* p. 140.

76. *FRUS, 1941,* vol. 1, pp. 176–177, 886–887; Whitman Bassow, *The Moscow Correspondents* (New York, 1988), p. 102; O'Connor, "Steinhardt and American Policy," p. 166; Ivan Yeaton, unpublished memoirs, chap. 3, Yeaton Papers, Hoover Institution.

77. *FRUS, 1941,* pp. 836–843, 852–853; W. Averell Harriman and Elie Abel, *Special Envoy to Churchill and Stalin, 1941–1946* (New York, 1975), pp. 84–85, 93, 95–96, 106–107, 213–214; Rudy Abramson, *The Life of W. Averell Harriman, 1891–1986* (New York, 1992), p. 294.

78. Steinhardt to Rudolph Schoenfeld, December 2, 1941, Box 79, Steinhardt Papers.

79. Benson Lee Grayson, ed., *The American Image of Russia, 1917–1977* (New York, 1978), pp. 150–152.

80. E.M.W.'s Memorandum for the President, May 18, 1944, Box 49, President's Secretary's File, Roosevelt Papers.

81. Joseph Davies, Journal, March 26, 1937, Box 4, Davies Papers. The original Latin phrase concerning diplomats is "Legatus est vir bonus peregre missus ad mentiendum Respublicae causa." See Hermann Eilts, "Diplomacy—Contemporary Practice," in Elmer Plischke, ed., *Modern Diplomacy: The Art and the Artisans* (Washington, D.C., 1979), p. 3.

82. Quoted in Warren Kimball's excellent *The Juggler: Franklin Roosevelt as Wartime Statesman* (Princeton, 1991), p. 7.

83. Joseph Davies, Diary, July 17, 1945, Box 18, Davies Papers.

84. Steinhardt to Henderson, December 13, 1939, Box 78, Steinhardt Papers.

Chapter 6

1. See Winston Churchill, *The Grand Alliance* (Boston, 1950), and John Deane, *The Strange Alliance: The Story of Our Efforts at Wartime Cooperation with Russia* (New York, 1947); Adam Ulam, *Expansion and Coexistence: Soviet Foreign Policy, 1917–1973* (New York, 1974), p. 178.

2. For an example of Soviet scholarship on World War II, see *Istoriia Velikoi Otchestvennoi Voiny Sovetskogo Soiuza* (Moscow, 1960).

3. Alexander Werth, *Russia at War, 1941–1945* (New York, 1964), p. xiv.

4. Ulam, *Expansion and Coexistence,* p. 330. In the estimation of General Walter Bedell Smith, "Lend-Lease was a very valuable supplement, but Soviet industry did the main job" (*My Three Years in Moscow* [Philadelphia, 1949], p. 134).

5. See Vojtech Mastny's *Russia's Road to the Cold War* (New York, 1979); John Erickson in *The Road to Stalingrad* (London, 1975) uses the phrase "atavistic savagery" (p. viii).

6. William Standley and Arthur Ageton, *Admiral Ambassador to Russia* (Chicago, 1955), p. 15.

7. Robert Sherwood, *Roosevelt and Hopkins: An Intimate History* (New York, 1948), p. 561.

8. W. Averell Harriman and Elie Abel, *Special Envoy to Churchill and Stalin, 1941–1946* (New York, 1975), p. 214.

9. Standley and Ageton, *Admiral Ambassador*, p. 126; FO 371, N1432/100/38; Andrei Gromyko, *Memoirs* (New York, 1989), p. 145. In one undated document, the admiral wrote, "I felt then and I feel now that Thurston was a little chagrined at the fact that he had not been given the post as our representative in Moscow when Mr. Steinhardt left" (Russia Memos, 4-25-1942 to 3-13-1943, Standley Papers, University of Southern California [hereafter USC]).

10. Standley and Ageton, *Admiral Ambassador*, p. 148; Kemp Tolley, *Caviar and Commissars: The Experience of a U.S. Naval Officer in Stalin's Russia* (Annapolis, 1983), p. 52; George Herring, *Aid to Russia, 1941 to 1946: Strategy, Diplomacy, the Origins of the Cold War* (New York, 1973), p. 83.

11. For accounts of Standley's first meeting with Stalin, see Standley and Ageton, *Admiral Ambassador*, pp. 151–158, and *FRUS, 1942*, vol. 3, pp. 545–548. During this meeting, the two men also discussed a possible Alaska–Siberia air route to facilitate U.S. conveyance of lend-lease aid to the USSR, the delivery of Soviet raw resources to the United States, and developments along the eastern front.

12. For details of Standley's plan, see *FRUS, 1942*, vol. 3, pp. 446–447.

13. The worst submarine and torpedo bomber attacks on Western convoys by Germany occurred in summer 1942. For a detailed account of one such raid, see David Irving, *The Destruction of Convoy PQ. 17* (New York, 1968).

14. Memorandum of Conversation between Standley and Lozovski, September 9, 1942; Telegram from State Department to American Embassy, Kuibyshev, August 19, 1942; Memorandum of Conversation between Standley and Molotov, July 3, 1942, Russian Memos, 4-25-1942 to 3-13-1943, Standley Papers, USC.

15. *FRUS, 1942*, vol. 3, p. 606.

16. Tolley, *Caviar and Commissars*, p. 196.

17. *FRUS, 1942*, vol. 3, p. 598.

18. Edward Bennett, *Franklin D. Roosevelt and the Search for Victory: American–Soviet Relations, 1939–1945* (Wilmington, 1990), p. 79; John Lewis Gaddis, *The United States and the Origins of the Cold War, 1941–1947* (New York, 1972), pp. 74–75; Standley and Ageton, *Admiral Ambassador*, pp. 473, 498.

19. Memorandum of Conversation between Standley and Molotov, August 21, 1942; Memorandum of Conversation between Standley and Vyshinsky, July 25, 1942, Russian Memos, 4-25-1942 to 3-13-1943, Standley Papers, USC.

20. Standley and Ageton, *Admiral Ambassador*, pp. 201–203, 247, 252, 453, 474.

21. *FRUS, 1942*, vol. 3, pp. 618–624; Harriman and Abel, *Special Envoy*, pp. 149–167; Standley and Ageton, *Admiral Ambassador*, pp. 208, 265–294.

22. *FRUS, 1942*, vol. 3, pp. 637–650.

23. Standley and Ageton, *Admiral Ambassador*, p. 341.

24. Ibid., p. 333.

25. Quentin Reynolds, "Diplomat on the Spot," *Collier's*, July 24, 1943.

26. Abraham Schenck to Mr. President, March 10, 1943, Box 4, 740, Official File, Roosevelt Papers, Franklin D. Roosevelt Library; Diary entry, March 9, 1943, Box 12, Davies Papers, Library of Congress; Sherwood, *Roosevelt and Hopkins*, pp. 705–706; Harriman and Abel, *Special Envoy*, p. 198; Memorandum of Conversation between Standley and Clark Kerr, March 13, 1943, Standley Papers, USC. Also see Ivan Maisky, *Memoirs of a Soviet Ambassador* (New York, 1968).

27. Conversations of Admiral Standley, November 5, 1942, Russian Memos, 4-25-1942 to 3-13-1943, Standley Papers, USC.

28. Standley and Ageton, *Admiral Ambassador,* p. 363. Author's conversation with Thomas Julian (of National Defense University) at the June 1991 meeting of the Society of Historians of American Foreign Relations, Washington, D.C.

29. Memo Pl, March 1943, Box 12; Memorandum by Loy Henderson, April 28, 1943, Box 13; Davies to Dearest Marjorie, May 23, 1943, Box 13, Davies Papers.

30. Davies to Dearest Marjorie, May 23, 1943, Box 13, Davies Papers; Standley and Ageton, *Admiral Ambassador,* pp. 370–372.

31. Joseph Davies visit, May 19–29, 1943, Standley Papers, USC; Rudy Abramson, *The Life of W. Averell Harriman, 1891–1986* (New York, 1992), p. 148.

32. Address to the Russian War Relief rally, Boston, Mass., June 25, 1944, Box 6, Standley Papers, Library of Congress. Also see Standley's optimistic "Stalin and World Unity," *Collier's,* June 30, 1945.

33. *FRUS, 1943,* vol. 3, p. 541.

34. Martin Kitchen, *British Policy Towards the Soviet Union During the Second World War* (New York, 1986), p. 135.

35. The best account of Harriman's career is Abramson, *Life of W. Averell Harriman.*

36. George Kennan, *Memoirs: 1925–1950* (Boston, 1967), pp. 233–234.

37. Charles Bohlen, *Witness to History, 1929–1969* (New York, 1973), p. 127; John Melby interview, June 16, 1989, pp. 18–19, Foreign Affairs Oral History Project, Georgetown University; Robert Newman, *The Cold War Romance of Lillian Hellman and John Melby* (Chapel Hill, N.C., 1989), p. 27; Deane, *Strange Alliance,* pp. 3, 10–11. For a critical review of Harriman's public career and his ambassadorship (for being soft on the USSR), see Jacob Heilbrunn, "The Playboy of the Western World," *New Republic,* July 27, 1992.

38. Strobe Talbott, ed., *Khrushchev Remembers: The Last Testament* (New York, 1974), pp. 396–397, 431–434; Gromyko, *Memoirs,* pp. 145–147.

39. Memorandum on Embassy Staff Moscow, December 1, 1943; Harriman to Harry Hopkins, January 20, 1944, Box 171, Harriman Papers, Library of Congress.

40. Kathleen Harriman's letters from Moscow to friends and family and Meiklejohn's two-volume diary from the war are invaluable sources of information on the life and policies of the embassy. Kathleen Harriman's letters are scattered throughout the W. Averell Harriman Papers; the Meiklejohn diary is in Box 211 of the Harriman Papers. Bohlen once described Harriman's relations with junior officers as "feudal." To Charles Thayer, Bohlen wrote, "[Harriman] will give [his subordinates] complete support if they will give him in return their complete loyalty" (Bohlen to Thayer, December 10, 1958, Correspondence File, Box 1, Thayer Papers) Harry S. Truman Library. Evidently, there was also some resentment felt by Foreign Service officers for Kathleen Harriman, who not only enjoyed easy access to the ambassador, but allegedly organized an "alternative chancery" in Spaso House. See Richard Davies interview, Foreign Affairs Oral History Project.

41. Harriman and Abel, *Special Envoy,* p. 406.

42. Ibid., pp. 535–536.

43. Ibid., pp. 218–219, 508; Standley and Ageton, *Admiral Ambassador,* p. 490; *FRUS, 1943,* vol. 3, p. 581; Harriman to Secretary Hull, February 14, 1944, Box 171, Harriman Papers; Harriman to Harry Hopkins, January 7, 1944, Box 157, Hopkins Papers, Franklin D. Roosevelt Library; Minutes, Secretary's Staff Committee, April 21, 1945, Box 178, Harriman Papers; Harriman, "Soviet–American Relations," July 6, 1945, Box 180, Harriman Papers; Ambassador's Staff Conference, October 10, 1945, Box 183, Harriman Papers; Harriman to Acheson, October 12, 1945, Box 183, Harriman Papers.

44. Deane, *Strange Alliance*, p. 162; David Mayers, *George Kennan and the Dilemmas of U.S. Foreign Policy* (New York, 1988), pp. 80–84; Mastny, *Russia's Road to the Cold War*, p. 145.

45. Harriman, Memorandum of Meeting at Spaso House, October 19, 1943, Box 170, Harriman Papers; Harriman to Hull, January 9, 1944 (?), Box 171, Harriman Papers; Harriman and Abel, *Special Envoy*, pp. 298, 308–310; Deane, *Strange Alliance*, pp. 107–125; Abramson, *Life of W. Averell Harriman*, p. 360.

46. United States ambassador to the USSR, December 1, 1943, Box 1, Official File, Roosevelt Papers; Harriman and Abel, *Special Envoy*, pp. 252–253, 533–534.

47. Edward Page, Memorandum of Conversation in the Kremlin, August 10, 1945, Box 181, Harriman Papers; Harriman and Abel, *Special Envoy*, pp. 498–501.

48. Harriman and Abel, *Special Envoy*, p. 501.

49. Ibid., p. 224; Deane, *Strange Alliance*, pp. 241–242.

50. Deane, *Strange Alliance*, pp. 182–201; *New York Times*, June 13, 1992.

51. Harriman and Abel, *Special Envoy*, p. 422.

52. Harriman to Secretary of State, January 25, 1944; Kathleen Harriman's report on Katyn, February 23, 1944; John Melby's report on Katyn, February 23, 1944, Box 187, Harriman Papers. Also see Allen Paul, *Katyn: The Untold Story of Stalin's Polish Massacre* (New York, 1991).

53. Kennan, *Memoirs: 1925–1950*, pp. 210–211; Harriman and Abel, *Special Envoy*, pp. 335–365; Harriman to Harry Hopkins, September 10, 1944, Box 157, Hopkins Papers. Also see Diane Clemens, "Averell Harriman, John Deane, the Joint Chiefs of Staff, and the 'Reversal of Cooperation' with the Soviet Union in April 1945," *International History Review*, May 1992. Clemens's criticism of Harriman is the opposite of Heilbrun's. She charges Harriman with virtually starting the Cold War.

54. *FRUS, 1945*, vol. 5, pp. 817–824.

55. See John Gaddis's discussion in *Russia, the Soviet Union, and the United States: An Interpretative History* (New York, 1978), p. 167.

56. Harriman and Abel, *Special Envoy*, pp. 311, 366, 369–370; Harriman, Memorandum of Conversations with FDR, pp. 8–9, October 21–November 19, 1944, Box 175, Harriman Papers.

57. Harriman and Abel, *Special Envoy*, pp. 264, 266, 269.

58. Ibid., pp. 454, 460.

59. Harriman to Truman, June 8, 1945, Box 180, Harriman Papers.

60. Churchill's Iron Curtain speech, in Benson Lee Grayson, ed., *The American Image of Russia, 1917–1977* (New York, 1978), pp. 176–179.

61. Frank Roberts to Ernest Bevin, March 17, 1946, in Kenneth Jensen, ed., *Origins of the Cold War: The Novikov, Kennan, and Roberts "Long Telegrams" of 1946* (Washington, D.C., 1991), p. 49. Also see Sean Greenwood, "Frank Roberts and the 'Other' Long Telegram: The View from the British Embassy in Moscow, March 1946," *Journal of Contemporary History*, January 1990.

62. Novikov to Molotov, September 27, 1946, in Jensen, ed., *Origins of the Cold War*, pp. 3–16. Also see John Lewis Gaddis, et al., "The Soviet Side of the Cold War: A Symposium," *Diplomatic History* (Fall 1991); it contains an illuminating discussion of Novikov's report (especially the remarks by Kennan, Viktor Mal'kov, and Steven Merritt Miner). Novikov's lack of independent judgment is confirmed in his memoir, *Vospominaniia Diplomata: Zapiski, 1938–1947* (Moscow, 1989), pp. 352–353.

63. Mayers, *George Kennan and the Dilemmas*, pp. 99–101; Kennan was assisted in the final draft of the Long Telegram by the embassy's military attaché, Brigadier General

Frank Roberts (not to be confused with the British chargé). See Roberts, Memorandum to all Officers, June 7, 1946, Box 1, Roberts Papers, Harry S. Truman Library.

64. *FRUS, 1946,* vol. 6, pp. 696–709.

65. Clark Clifford with Richard Holbrooke, *Counsel to the President: A Memoir* (New York, 1991), p. 110; Mayers, *George Kennan and the Dilemmas,* p. 100; Melvyn Leffler, *A Preponderance of Power* (Stanford, 1992), pp. 100–140.

66. See Charles Maier, ed., *The Cold War in Europe: Era of a Divided Continent* (New York, 1991), p. 55. He has a thoughtful discussion on the political and ethical significance of the Grand Alliance.

67. Thomas Etzold and John Gaddis, eds., *Containment: Documents on American Policy and Strategy, 1945–1950* (New York, 1978), pp. 64–71.

Chapter 7

1. These figures should be viewed as approximations. They are from Isaac Deutscher, *Stalin: A Political Biography* (New York, 1966), p. 575. According to Roy and Zhores Medvedev, the war left 15 million widows and more than 20 million people incapacitated. See the Medvedevs' *Khrushchev: The Years in Power* (New York, 1978), p. 154. Soviet agricultural production in 1945 was 40 percent below its 1940 level. See *Narodnoe khoziaistvo v SSSR v 1964* (Moscow, 1965), p. 246.

2. Bulgakov's novel, *The Master and Margarita,* was begun in 1928 and finished (more or less) in 1940, the year of his death.

The quality of Soviet cultural life during 1946 to 1953 is illustrated by this account in *Pravda* February 26, 1949, of a writers' attack against "anti-patriotic" literary critics:

> Step by step the Soviet writers uncovered the pernicious activities and dastardly methods of the cosmopolitan [read Jewish] doubledealers and their lickspittles. Like worms the anti-patriots gnawed at the healthy organism of our literature and art. Theses insolent pygmies, reptiles of criticism, imagine themselves to be 'supermen,' headmen of Soviet literature and art. But in the test they proved to be beggarly slaves, fawning before the anti-popular, corrupt bourgeois culture of the West, before everything foreign just because it is foreign. They spit upon the great Russian art.

3. Milovan Djilas, *Conversations with Stalin* (New York, 1962), pp. 151–153.

4. Kirk to Acheson, August 23, 1949, 711.61/8-2349, RG 59, NA.

5. Czeslaw Milosz, *The Captive Mind* (New York, 1981), p. xiii.

6. The section in this chapter dealing with Kennan is partly drawn from David Mayers, *George Kennan and the Dilemmas of U.S. Foreign Policy* (New York, 1988), chap. 9.

7. Charles Bohlen, *Witness to History, 1929–1969* (New York, 1973), p. 269. Some of Truman's domestic critics were concerned about the number of former military officers in the diplomatic corps and State Department. Eisenhower was also sensitive to the issue of soldiers in government. For this reason, he decided against making Walter Bedell Smith the White House chief of staff. See Robert Donovan, *The Presidency of Harry S. Truman, 1945–1948: Conflict and Crisis* (New York, 1977), p. 143; H. W. Brands, Jr., *Cold Warriors: Eisenhower's Generation and American Foreign Policy* (New York, 1988), p. 75.

8. *Current Biography, 1953,* pp. 579–582; Forrest Pogue, *George C. Marshall: Statesman, 1949–1959* (New York, 1987), p. 28; Walter Bedell Smith, *My Three Years in Moscow* (Philadelphia, 1950), pp. 14, 17, 22–23, 26; Brands, *Cold Warriors,* p. 72.

9. Davis Boster interview, p. 3, Foreign Affairs Oral History Project, Georgetown University.

10. *FRUS, 1946,* vol. 6, pp. 732–733; Smith, *My Three Years,* pp. 37, 46–47.

11. *FRUS, 1946*, vol. 6, pp. 734–736.

12. See the Stalin and Wallace letters as reprinted in the *New York Herald Tribune*, May 17, 1948.

13. Smith, *My Three Years*, p. 167; *FRUS, 1948*, vol. 4, pp. 845–864.

14. Adam Ulam, *Expansion and Coexistence: Soviet Foreign Policy, 1917–1973* (New York, 1974), p. 404.

15. Smith stated, "The United States is still stronger than the Soviet Union. If Stalin lives, and carries out his objectives, it is probable that during the next five to ten years the economic position of the Soviet Union will advance relatively more rapidly than that of the United States. But the Soviet Union will not, in my opinion, overtake the United States during this period" (*My Three Years*, p. 320). See also Melvyn Leffler, *A Preponderance of Power* (Stanford, 1992), p. 149.

16. Smith, *My Three Years*, p. 82; *FRUS, 1948*, vol. 4, p. 804.

17. Smith, *My Three Years*, p. 279.

18. Ibid., pp. 189–191, 203, 205–206, 321; *FRUS, 1949*, vol. 5, pp. 854–987.

19. Smith, *My Three Years*, pp. 207–208.

20. *FRUS, 1949*, vol. 5, pp. 559–561.

21. Ibid., pp. 603–609; Talk by Foy Kohler, April 20, 1950, Box 14, Durbrow Papers, Hoover Institution; Brands, *Cold Warriors*, p. 75.

22. Marshall, Memorandum for Forrestal, March 23, 1948, 711.61/3-2348, NA. For a comprehensive review of JCS plans and analysis, see Steven Ross and David Rosenberg, eds., *America's Plans for War Against the Soviet Union, 1945–1950*, 15 vols. (New York).

23. Smith, *My Three Years*, pp. 80, 169, 325, 330, 333; *FRUS, 1949*, vol. 5, pp. 596–597.

24. Kirk's career (U.S. Naval Academy, class of 1909) culminated in his command of naval forces in the June 1944 invasion of France. In March 1946, he was transferred to the retired list and appointed ambassador to Belgium, where he remained until his assignment to Moscow. Kirk's only pre-1949 visit to Russia occurred in 1911, when he briefly visited St. Petersburg. Alan Kirk interview, p. 29, Oral History Project, Columbia University.

25. Martin Mayer, *The Diplomats* (New York, 1983), p. 172.

26. George Morgan [Historicus, pseud.], "Stalin on Revolution," *Foreign Affairs*, January 1949, pp. 177, 213; Lydia Kirk, *Postmarked Moscow* (New York, 1952) p. 59; George Morgan interview, pp. 3–5, Foreign Affairs Oral History Project.

27. *FRUS, 1950*, vol. 4, p. 1278; Leffler, *Preponderance of Power*, p. 369.

28. *FRUS, 1949*, vol. 5, pp. 603, 658–659, 664, 678–681; Andrei Sakharov, *Memoirs* (New York, 1990), pp. 97, 164.

29. *FRUS, 1949*, vol. 9, pp. 107, 963; *FRUS, 1950*, vol. 4, p. 1174; U.S. embassy in Moscow to Acheson, April 19, 1949, 893.00/4-1949, RG 59, NA; also see David Mayers, *Cracking the Monolith: U.S. Policy Against the Sino-Soviet Alliance, 1949–1955* (Baton Rouge, 1986), chaps. 1–3.

30. *FRUS, 1950*, vol. 4, p. 1243. See Robert Simmons, *The Strained Alliance* (New York, 1975), and Sergei Goncharov, John Lewis, and Xue Litai, *Uncertain Partners: Stalin, Mao, and the Korean War* (Stanford, 1993), an excellent book in which the authors demonstrate that Kim Il Sung had to persuade his Soviet and Chinese comrades of the wisdom and feasibility of invading South Korea.

31. *FRUS, 1950*, vol.4, pp. 1111, 1145.

32. W. H. Lawrence, "Assignment to Moscow, Toughest of Posts," *New York Times Magazine*, June 12, 1949; Kirk interview, "The People in Russia," *Look*, April 22, 1952; "Cold War Requires Cool Heads, Says Admiral Kirk," Box 8, Bohlen Records, NA; Meeting with the President, February 4, 1952, 611.61/2-452, RG 59, NA; Visit with the Presi-

dent, October 26, 1951, 611.61/10-2651, RG 59, NA; *FRUS, 1950,* vol. 4, pp. 1276–1278; *FRUS, 1951,* vol. 4, pp. 1524–1525; Address by Kirk to the Alfred Smith Memorial Dinner, October 18, 1951, Alan Kirk File (883), Official File, Truman Papers, Harry S. Truman Library.

33. David Kelly, *The Ruling Few or the Human Background to Diplomacy* (London, 1953), p. 374.

34. Smith, *My Three Years,* pp. 103–104; *FRUS, 1946,* vol. 6, pp. 808–809; Robert Tucker to author, January 27, 1992.

35. *FRUS, 1946,* vol. 6, pp. 737–742, 768; *FRUS, 1948,* vol. 4, 1038–1039; *FRUS, 1949,* vol. 5, pp. 776–805; Smith, *My Three Years,* p. 180.

36. Leslie Stevens, *Russian Assignment* (Boston, 1953), pp. 206–210, 404–405; Whitman Bassow, *The Moscow Correspondents: Reporting on Russia from the Revolution to Glasnost* (New York, 1988), p. 188; Smith, *My Three Years,* pp. 185–186.

37. My spelling of the tenor's surname comes from Smith, *My Three Years,* p. 186. It would be more accurate to render the name as Lapshin—or less likely, Lapshchin.

38. *FRUS, 1949,* vol. 5, pp. 581–583; Stevens, *Russian Assignment,* pp. 105, 264; Smith, *My Three Years,* pp. 186–187; George Kennan to author, February 1, 1990; Kohler to General Smith, March 1, 1949, Box 5, Kohler Papers, University of Toledo.

39. Annabelle Bucar, *The Truth About American Diplomats* (Moscow, 1949), pp. 26, 65, 175.

40. Kirk Address to Alfred Smith Dinner, p. 3, October 18, 1951, Alan Kirk File (883), Official File, Truman Papers.

41. Kirk, *Postmarked Moscow,* p. 251; Talk by Foy Kohler, April 20, 1950, Box 14, Durbrow Papers.

42. Boster interview, p. 4, Foreign Affairs Oral History Project.

43. In a letter to his sister Avis (Bohlen's wife), Thayer wrote when McCarthy was ill and reports were circulating about Khrushchev's being morose, "Do you suppose there is any connection between Khrushchev's sadness and Joe McCarthy's serious illness?" (Thayer to Avis Bohlen, May 2, 1957, Correspondence File, Box 1, Thayer Papers, Harry S. Truman Library).

44. For more on McCarthyism and the fate of China hands, see the following: Richard Freeland, *The Truman Doctrine and the Origins of McCarthyism* (New York, 1974); Robert Griffith and Athan Theoharis, eds., *The Specter: Original Essays on the Cold War and the Origins of McCarthyism* (New York, 1974); Paul Lauren, ed., *The China Hands' Legacy: Ethics and Diplomacy* (Boulder, 1987); Lewis Purifoy, *Harry Truman's China Policy* (New York, 1976); Richard Rovere, *Senator Joe McCarthy* (New York, 1960); Ellen Schrecker, *No Ivory Tower: McCarthyism and the Universities* (New York, 1986); Walter Goodman, *The Committee: The Extraordinary Career of the House Committee on Un-American Activities* (London, 1964).

45. Bucar, *Truth About American Diplomats,* pp. 52–56; W. Averell Harriman and Elie Abel, *Special Envoy to Churchill and Stalin, 1941–1946* (New York, 1975), pp. 522; Smith, *My Three Years,* p. 88; George Kennan, *Memoirs: 1925–1950* (Boston, 1967), p. 239.

46. Brands, *Cold Warriors,* p. 76.

47. See Robert Blake interview, December 29, 1988, p. 7, Foreign Affairs Oral History Project; Boster interview, p. 7, Foreign Affairs Oral History Project.

48. See the following in the Stines Papers, Hoover Institution: Stines to his father, December 15, 1947, Box 2; Stines to Dearest Marie, May 24, 1939, Box 1; Stines to Dearest Mother, July 25, 1950, Box 2; Stines to Dearest Mother and Father, September 4, 1950, Box 2; Stines to Mother and Dad, October 17, 1950, Box 2; Stines to Dearest

Mother, December 8, 1950, Box 2; Stines to Dear Vi, December 10, 1950, Box 1; Stines to Dearest Mother, March 3, 1951, Box 2; Stines to Dearest Mother, July 17, 1951, Box 2; Stines to Dearest Mother, August 9, 1951, Box 2; Stines to Dearest Mother, October 9, 1951, Box 2; Stines to Dearest Mother, April 15, 1952, Box 3; Stines to Dearest Mother, May 1, 1952, Box 3. Author's interview with Malcolm Toon, October 26, 1992.

49. Robert Smith to Dear Hagel (?), March 12, 1952, Box 1, Stines Papers.

50. Stines to Dearest Mother, May 1, 1952, Box 3, Stines Papers.

51. Ibid.; Stines to Dearest Mother, May 11, 1952, Box 3, Stines Papers. Author's interview with Charles Stefan, former Foreign Service Officer and colleague (in Belgrade) of Stines, June 21, 1992.

52. Stines to his mother, January 5, 1952, Box 2, Stines Papers; *FRUS, 1951,* vol. 4, p. 1673; *FRUS, 1952–1954,* vol. 8, p. 962; United Press report, December 9, 1951.

53. George Kennan, *Sketches from a Life* (New York, 1989), p. 107.

54. Kennan to Arnold Toynbee, April 7, 1952, File 1952, Box 29, Kennan Papers, Princeton University.

55. David McLellan, *Dean Acheson* (New York, 1976), p. 176; Mayers, *George Kennan and the Dilemmas,* p. 160; George Kennan, *Memoirs: 1950–1963* (New York, 1972), p. 107.

56. Kennan, *Memoirs: 1950–1963,* p. 111.

57. Ibid., p. 106; Stevens, *Russian Assignment,* pp. 352–353.

58. Transcript of Kennan's Press Conference, April 1, 1952, File 1-C-28, Box 18, Kennan Papers.

59. Kennan, *Memoirs: 1950–1963,* p. 122.

60. Kennan's Draft of Line to Be Taken with Soviet Leaders, May 1952, File 1-D-20, Box 24, Kennan Papers; *FRUS, 1952–1954,* vol. 8, pp. 1011–1013; Richard Davies interview, Foreign Affairs Oral History Project.

61. Kennan to H. Freeman Mathews, May 16, 1952, File 1952, Box 29, Kennan Papers.

62. *FRUS, 1952–1952,* vol. 8, pp. 1004–1010; Kennan, *Memoirs: 1950–1963,* p. 136; Kennan, Outline of Advice, December 1952, File 1-D-27, Box 24, Kennan Papers.

63. Kennan to Walworth Barbour, August 1, 1952, File 1952, Box 29, Kennan Papers.

64. Kennan to H. Freeman Mathews, August 8, 1952, File 1952, Box 29, Kennan Papers.

65. Kennan to Lewis Douglas, August 12, 1952, File 1952, Box 29, Kennan Papers.

66. Kennan, *Memoirs: 1925–1950,* pp. 242–246, and *Memoirs: 1950–1963,* pp. 151–152.

67. Kennan, *Memoirs: 1950–1963,* pp. 157–158.

68. Kennan to Bernard Gufler, August 12, 1953, File 1952, Box 29, Kennan Papers.

69. Kennan to Bohlen, August 21, 1952, File 1952, Box 29, Kennan Papers.

70. Frank Rounds, Jr., interview, September 21, 1962, Oral History Project; Davies interview, Foreign Affairs Oral History Project.

71. Kennan to Acheson, July 1952, File 1952, Box 29, Kennan Papers. This letter was unsent, but it is a fair indication of Kennan's intentions at the time.

72. Kennan to author, October 8, 1985; Kennan, *Memoirs: 1950–1963,* pp. 159.

73. *Pravda,* September 26, 1952.

74. Charles Bohlen's letter and recommendation to Livingston Merchant, August 23, 1955, Box 36, Bohlen Papers.

75. Kennan, *Memoirs: 1950–1963,* p. 166; Dean Acheson, *Present at the Creation* (New York, 1969), p. 697.

76. Kennan, Transcript of Remarks to the Research and Analysis Division of the State Department, January 22, 1953, File 1-D-28, Box 24, Kennan Papers.

77. Kennan, Address to State Department Personnel, late November 1952, File 1-D-26, Box 24, Kennan Papers.

78. Ibid.

79. Acheson, *Present at the Creation,* p. 697.

80. Kennan to C. Burlington, March 25, 1953, File 1953, Box 29, Kennan Papers.

81. Smith, *My Three Years,* p. 224; Kelly, *Ruling Few,* p. 374; Lord Strang, "Sir David Kelly, An Outstanding Envoy," *The Times,* March 29, 1959.

82. Gromyko, *Memoirs,* p. 303.

83. In a consoling letter to Thayer, Kennan wrote, "However one looks at it, one must concede that the practices of Government in our country have developed in recent years in such a way as to make it dubious whether anyone with a certain degree of imagination and sensitivity and individuality can remain in the ranks of its servants without great discomfort for both parties" (Kennan to Thayer, April 9, 1953, Correspondence File, Box 3, Thayer Papers).

84. Kelly, *Ruling Few,* p. 394; for an analysis of the evolution of containment policy, see John Gaddis, *The Strategies of Containment: A Critical Appraisal of Postwar American National Security Policy* (New York, 1982).

85. Neither Kennan nor Bohlen was much impressed by the method or findings of Kremlinology. See Davies interview, Foreign Affairs Oral History Project.

Chapter 8

1. Andrei Sakharov, *Memoirs* (New York, 1990), p. 164. Sakharov's response to Stalin's dying is partly explained by Bohlen's observation in March 1953: "Although it is true, of course, that millions of Russians may be rejoicing over Stalin's death, it is also true that millions are weeping. It is a traditional Russian reaction to cry for the death of the Czar, regardless of what kind of ruler he may have been. Stalin, like his Czarist predecessors, has been given a special place in the minds of the Russian people as the all-wise and kindly 'father' whose ministers are responsible for the evil deeds of the rulers" (*FRUS, 1952–1954,* vol. 8, pp. 1100–1102).

2. Andrei Gromyko, *Memoirs* (New York, 1989), pp. 377–378. The charges against Beria are documented in D. M. Stickle, *The Beria Affair* (Commack, N.Y., 1992). Also see Amy Knight's *Beria: Stalin's First Lieutenant* (Princeton, 1993). Knight argues that Beria backed reforms—going beyond Khrushchev's—to buttress the sagging Soviet polity and economy. He was nevertheless loathed by his colleagues, who feared him and were eager to defeat his personal ambition.

3. Soviet concern that the Americans would try to exploit Stalin's death in the satellite areas and in the USSR was well founded. For an example of American thinking in the months after Stalin's death, see Dulles's remarks as recorded in Minutes of Cabinet meeting, July 10, 1953, Whitman File, Cabinet, Box 2, Eisenhower Library.

4. *Soviet News,* August 15, 1953.

5. Peter Boyle, ed., *The Churchill–Eisenhower Correspondence, 1953–1955* (Chapel Hill, N.C., 1990), p. 49.

6. Dulles's telephone conversation with Bohlen, March 16, 1953, White House Memoranda Series, Box 8, Dulles Papers, Eisenhower Library.

7. Joseph McCarthy speech, pp. 12–13, March 25, 1953, White House Memorandum Series, Box 8, Dulles Papers, Eisenhower Library.

8. Dwight Eisenhower, *Mandate for Change, 1953–1956* (Garden City, N.Y., 1963), p. 212; C. L. Sulzberger, *A Long Row of Candles* (Toronto, 1969), p. 637. Charles Bohlen interview, p. 5, Oral History Project, Columbia University.

9. *FRUS, 1952–1954,* vol. 8, p. 1130.

10. Herbert Parmet, *Eisenhower and the American Crusades* (New York, 1972), p. 246; Robert Ferrell, ed., *The Eisenhower Diaries* (New York, 1981), p. 234. For accounts of the Senate's handling of the Bohlen matter, see Charles Bohlen, *Witness to History, 1929–1969* (New York, 1973), pp. 309–336; T. Michael Ruddy, *The Cautious Diplomat: Charles Bohlen and the Soviet Union, 1929–1969* (Kent, Ohio, 1986), pp. 109–124; U.S. Congress, Senate, Committee on Foreign Relations, *The Nomination of Charles Bohlen to Be United States Ambassador to the Union of Soviet Socialist Republics*, 83rd Cong. 1st sess., *Congressional Record*, 1953.

11. Dulles was reluctant to bring Kennan into the State Department because he feared adverse reaction by congressional conservatives. See *FRUS, 1952–1954*, vol. 8, p. 1180.

12. Leonard Mosley, *Dulles: A Biography of Eleanor, Allen, and John Foster and Their Family Network* (New York, 1978), pp. 193–194; *FRUS, 1952–1954*, vol. 8, p. 1139; Bohlen, *Witness to History*, pp. 335–336; Robert Blake interview, Foreign Affairs Oral History Project, Georgetown University, p. 7; Bohlen interview, p. 22, Oral History Project; Dulles to McLeod, March 20, 1953, White House Memoranda Series, Box 8, Dulles Papers, Eisenhower Library.

13. Author's conversation with Bohlen's son-in-law, Professor David Calleo, during conference ("The Realist Tradition in U.S. Foreign Policy") at Bard College, October 18 to 20, 1991; Veljko Mićunović, *Moscow Diary* (Garden City, N.Y., 1980), p. 213; Ronald Pruessen, "John Foster Dulles and the Predicaments of Power," in Richard Immerman, ed., *John Foster Dulles and the Diplomacy of the Cold War* (Princeton, 1990), p. 22; Eisenhower to Bohlen, February 6, 1954, Box 36, Bohlen Papers; Sulzberger, *Long Row of Candles*, p. 958.

14. Bohlen, *Witness to History*, p. 322.

15. *FRUS, 1955–1957*, vol. 24, p. 93.

16. Bohlen, *Witness to History*, pp. 362, 365, 381, 386. Bohlen to State Department, March 7, 1956, 611.61/3-756, RG 59, NA; Dulles to Undersecretary of State, May 17, 1954, JFD Chronological Series, Box 7, Dulles Papers, Eisenhower Library.

17. Strobe Talbott, ed., *Khrushchev Remembers: The Last Testament* (New York, 1974), p. 360; Mićunović, *Moscow Diary*, p. 227; Vladislav Zubok, "Soviet Intelligence and the Cold War: The 'Small' Committee on Information, 1952–1953," Cold War International History Project, Woodrow Wilson International Center for Scholars, December 1992. Zubok cites *B.N. Ponomarevu—Spravka o Charlze Bolene*, March 25, 1953, pp. 192–197; *Dopolnitel'nie svedeniia o Bolene*, March 25, 1953, p. 204; *Molotovu V.M.—Spravka na Bolene*, pp. 221–226, all in KOI, vol. 14.

18. Mićunović, *Moscow Diary*, p. 227; Frank Roberts to Sir W. Strang, April 9, 1953, FO 371 106532, and Sir William Hayter to J. G. Ward, February 17, 1956, FO 371 122797, Public Records Office (PRO), Kew; Bohlen, *Witness to History*, p. 347; Sulzberger, *Long Row of Candles*, p. 987; Emory Swank interview, pp. 12–13, Foreign Affairs Oral History Project; Robert Martens's letter to author, February 6, 1992; author's interview with Charles Stefan, June 21, 1992; Jacob Beam, *Multiple Exposure: An American Ambassador's Unique Perspective on East–West Issues* (New York, 1978), pp. 36–37.

19. *FRUS, 1952–1954*, vol. 8, p. 1226; Whitman Bassow, *The Moscow Correspondents* (New York, 1988), p. 284; Swank interview, pp. 13–14, Foreign Affairs Oral History Project. To her brother, Charles Thayer, Avis Bohlen reported that her husband was still in 1957 exhilarated by his work in Moscow: "Chip eats it all up!" (Avis Bohlen to Thayer, January 19, 1957, Box 1, Thayer Papers, Harry S. Truman Library).

20. Sir William Hayter, Report of December 22, 1956, FO 371 129139, PRO; Isaiah Berlin, *Personal Impressions* (New York, 1981), p. 187; Bohlen, *Witness to History*, pp. 342–346; *FRUS, 1955–1957*, vol. 24, pp. 256–257; *FRUS, 1952–1954*, vol. 8, pp. 1186–

1187; Beam, *Multiple Exposure,* p. 57; Bohlen to James Byrnes, February 26, 1953, Box 29, Bohlen Papers; Bohlen to Secretary of State, May 28, 1954, and June 10, 1954, 611.61/5-2854 and 611.61/6-1054, RG 59, NA; Martens to author; Swank interview, Foreign Affairs Oral History Project.

21. Bohlen, *Witness to History,* pp. 444–445.

22. Ibid., pp. 349–352; Ruddy, *Cautious Diplomat,* p. 129.

23. *FRUS, 1955–1957,* vol. 24, p. 24; Daniel Yergin, *Shattered Peace: The Origins of the Cold War and the National Security State* (Boston, 1977), p. 402.

24. Bohlen to Secretary of State, June 10, 1955, 611.61/6-1055, RG 59, NA.

I have found nothing in the Bohlen papers (or elsewhere) that sheds light on whether the embassy was aware of the extent of damage done by nuclear tests to the health of thousands of Soviet soldiers and civilians in 1954. For details on unearthed reports from Soviet Defense Ministry archives, see *New York Times,* November 7, 1993.

25. Mićunović, *Moscow Diary,* p. 184.

26. Bohlen, *Witness to History,* pp. 405–424; *FRUS, 1955–1957,* vol. 25, pp. 335–338, 348, 394.

27. Bohlen, *Witness to History,* p. 370; *FRUS, 1952–1954,* vol. 8, pp. 1155, 1260; Michael Beschloss, *The Crisis Years: Kennedy and Khrushchev, 1960–1963* (New York, 1991), p. 50; Bohlen to Ambassador Hayter, July 25, 1957, Box 36, Bohlen Papers; Mićunović, *Moscow Diary,* pp. 49–50. Khrushchev erroneously believed that Bohlen thought of him as a drunkard. In fact, the ambassador thought Bulganin guiltier on this score, though he allowed that Khrushchev could hold his own. See Bohlen to Thayer, July 9, 1959, Correspondence File, Box 1, Thayer Papers.

28. *FRUS, 1955–1957,* vol. 24, pp. 111–113.

29. Bohlen, *Witness to History,* p. 405.

30. Bohlen's ouster by Dulles from Embassy Moscow is recounted in ibid., pp. 441–445. Eisenhower to Bohlen, July 16, 1959; Bohlen to Eisenhower, July 29, 1959, Whitman File, Administration, Box 7, Eisenhower Library.

31. As were Bohlen and Kennan, Thompson was born in 1904. Michael Beschloss alone among historians has provided a sustained assessment of Thompson. See Beschloss's excellent *Crisis Years.* Also see George Ball, "JFK's Big Moment," *New York Review of Books* February 13, 1992, p. 18.

32. C. L. Sulzberger nicely captured Thompson's activities in Moscow in his wartime journal. See *Long Row of Candles,* pp. 181–182.

33. For Thompson's role in the Trieste matter, see *FRUS, 1952–1954,* vol. 8, pp. 239–589, and Llewellyn Thompson interview, Oral History Project. As an example of the scholarly neglect of Thompson, see Audrey Cronin, *Great Power Politics and the Struggle over Austria, 1945–1955* (Ithaca, 1986). In what is otherwise a fine book, Thompson is not mentioned.

34. Thompson to Dulles, August 12, 1955; Dulles to Thompson, September 1, 1955; Thompson to Dulles, September 15, 1955; Dulles to Thompson, September 26, 1955; Dulles, Memorandum of Conversation with Thompson, October 12, 1955; General Correspondence and Memoranda Series, Box 3, Dulles Papers, Eisenhower Library.

35. See Bohlen, *Witness to History,* pp. 441–442, and "A Model for Diplomats," *New York Times,* February 10, 1972.

36. See Richard Immerman, ed., *John Foster Dulles and the Diplomacy of the Cold War* (Princeton, 1990), pp. 263–283.

37. Eisenhower, *Mandate for Change,* p. 416; *FRUS, 1958–1960,* vol. 2, p. 317; Thompson interview, pp. 20, 25–27, Dulles Oral History, Princeton University; Beschloss, *Crisis Years,* pp. 36–37.

38. In the words of Davis Boster (Thompson's lieutenant in the embassy), "He proba-

bly thought that the success of his mission would depend on the development of that special relationship" (Boster interview, p. 19, Foreign Affairs Oral History Project).

39. Sergei Khrushchev, *Khrushchev on Khrushchev: An Inside Account of the Man and His Era* (Boston, 1990), p. 196.

40. Ibid., p. 264; Talbott, ed., *Khrushchev Remembers: The Last Testament*, p. 388; Beschloss, *Crisis Years,* pp. 49–54; Thompson to Secretary of State, November 13, 1959, White House, Office of the Staff, International Series, Box 16, Eisenhower Library.

41. Benson Grayson, ed., *The American Image of Russia, 1917–1977* (New York, 1977), p. 238; FO 371 135415, May 23, 1958, PRO; Memorandum for Senator Fulbright, April 9, 1959, RG 59, NA; Memorandum for the President, January 25, 1960, White House, Office of the Staff, International Series, Box 16, Eisenhower Library; Kozlov Visit, June 26, 1959, White House, Confidential, Subject Series, Box 64, Eisenhower Library; Idar Rimestad, Hans Tuch, Richard Funkhouser, and Robert Martens interviews, Foreign Affairs Oral History Project.

42. Beschloss, *Crisis Years,* pp. 35, 180; Thompson to Secretary of State, September 8, 1960, White House, Office of the Staff, International Series, Box 15, Eisenhower Library; Thompson to Secretary of State, September 9, 1960, Whitman File, International Series, Box 49, Eisenhower Library.

43. *FRUS, 1955–1957,* vol. 24, pp. 154, 178–180; Thompson to Secretary of State, September 8, 1960, Whitman File, Dulles–Herter Series, Box 11, Eisenhower Library; Thompson to Secretary of State, August 8, 1959, 611.61/8-859, RG 59, NA; Thompson, "Current Strains Within the Soviet System," January 29, 1960, Box 125A, President's Office Files, Kennedy Library.

44. Thompson to Secretary of State, February 4, 1961, Box 125A, President's Office File, Kennedy Library; Thompson, Conversation with Khrushchev, June 25, 1959, Concerning Germany and Berlin, 611.81/6-2959, RG 59, NA; Thompson to Secretary of State, June 26, 1959, 611.61/6-2559, RG 59, NA; Thompson to Secretary of State, January 1, 1960, Whitman File, Box 49, International Series, Eisenhower Library; Beschloss, *Crisis Years,* pp. 175, 244, 365–366; Thomas Schoenbaum, *Waging Peace and War: Dean Rusk in the Truman, Kennedy, and Johnson Years* (New York, 1988), pp. 338, 352.

45. Beschloss, *Crisis Years,* pp. 98, 129.

46. Sir Frank Roberts, Annual Report on the Soviet Union for 1960, FO 371 159534, PRO; Thompson to Secretary of State, November 13, 1959, RG 59, NA; Walter Robertson to Acting Secretary of State, July 18, 1958, RG 59, NA; Foy Kohler to Secretary of State, September 10, 1958, 611.61/9-1058, RG 59, NA; Thompson to Secretary of State, October 14, 1960, and November 28, 1960, White House, Office of the Staff, Box 15, International Series, Eisenhower Library; Thompson to Secretary of State, September 11, 1960, Whitman File, Box 11, Dulles–Herter Series, Eisenhower Library.

47. See David Mayers, *Cracking the Monolith: U.S. Policy Against the Sino-Soviet Alliance, 1949–1955* (Baton Rouge, 1986), chaps. 4, 5.

48. Thompson to Secretary of State, August 12, 1958, 611.61/8-1258, RG 59, NA; Thompson to Secretary of State, December 23, 1957, 611.61/12-2357, RG 59, NA; *FRUS, 1955–1957,* vol. 24, pp. 185–186.

49. Thompson to Secretary of State, November 8, 1957, 611.61/11-857, RG 59, NA; Memorandum of Conversation between Ambassadors Kroll and Thompson in Moscow, February 21, 1959, 611.61/2-2159, RG 59, NA; Thompson to Secretary of State, May 4, 1959, 611.61/5-459, RG 59, NA.

50. Eisenhower to Cola Parker, August 22, 1959, Whitman File, DDE Diaries, Box 44, Eisenhower Library.

51. Thompson also briefly entertained the idea that the Soviets had walked out because

they had achieved a breakthrough in weapons technology; in this case, they would delay negotiations until such time that they had acquired a position of absolute superiority.

Thompson to Secretary of State, July 28, 1960, and October 7, 1960, White House, Office of the Staff, Box 15, International Series; Thompson to Secretary of State, June 6, 1960, Whitman, Box 10, Dulles–Herter Papers, Eisenhower Library.

52. Thompson to Secretary of State, June 4, 1960, Whitman File, Box 10, Dulles–Herter Papers, Eisenhower Library.

53. Beschloss, *Crisis Years,* pp. 36, 66–67.

54. Llewellyn Thompson interview, pp. 2–4, Kennedy Library.

55. Thompson to Secretary of State, February 2, 1961 (including corrected p. 2 of section 2); McGeorge Bundy, Notes on Discussion of the Thinking of the Soviet Leadership, Cabinet Room, February 11, 1961, President's Office Files, Box 125A, Kennedy Library.

56. Thompson interview, p. 4, Kennedy Library; Beschloss, *Crisis Years,* pp. 68–70, 408, 673.

57. James Blight and David Welch, *On the Brink: Americans and Soviets Reexamine the Cuban Missile Crisis* (New York, 1989), pp. 51, 179–180; Robert Kennedy, *Thirteen Days: A Memoir of the Cuban Missile Crisis* (New York, 1969). Raymond Garthoff has acknowledged Thompson's importance, but he has also characterized his analysis during the crisis as "rather oblique and guarded" (Blight and Welch, *On the Brink,* p. 54).

58. Blight and Welch, *On the Brink,* pp. 44–45, 53, 179–180, 214, 282, 383; Raymond Garthoff, "The Havana Conference on the Cuban Missile Crisis," *Cold War International History Project Bulletin:* (Spring 1992) 2–4; Beschloss, *Crisis Years,* pp. 453, 482, 520; Thompson interview, pp. 9–12, 49, Kennedy Library. Also worth consulting is Robert Smith Thompson's *The Missiles of October: The Declassified Story of John F. Kennedy and the Cuban Missile Crisis* (New York, 1992).

59. See, for example, George Bush's State of the Union Address, *New York Times,* January 29, 1992.

60. Sir Alvary Gascoigne to P. Mason, April 17, 1953, FO 371 106532, PRO.

61. Sulzberger, *Long Row of Candles,* pp. 874–875.

62. Bohlen, "Model for Diplomats"; Kennedy, *Thirteen Days;* Blight and Welch, *On the Brink,* p. 282.

Chapter 9

1. Chester Bowles, *Promises to Keep: My Years in Public Life, 1941–1969* (New York, 1971), p. 371.

2. Ibid., p. 368; Rudy Abramson, *The Life of W. Averell Harriman, 1891–1986* (New York, 1992), p. 592; Michael Beschloss, *The Crisis Years: Kennedy and Khrushchev, 1960–1963* (New York, 1991), pp. 408, 578; Arthur Hartman interview, p. 44, Foreign Affairs Oral History Project, Georgetown University.

3. See Phyllis Kohler, ed., *Journey for Our Time* (Chicago, 1951).

4. Kohler to Loy Henderson, March 5, 1948, Box 3, Kohler Papers, University of Toledo. Also see Kohler to Gordon Merriam, March 8, 1948, Box 4, and Kohler to General Walter Bedell Smith, March 1, 1949, Box 5, Kohler Papers.

5. My characterization of Kohler is based on Beschloss's sketch of him in *Crisis Years,* pp. 577–580; an interview with Hermann Eilts on July 23, 1992; and the Davis Boster and Richard Funkhouser interviews, Foreign Affairs Oral History Project.

6. For documentation on the Arlington incident, see Boxes 15 and 16, Kohler Papers. Also useful are Kohler's interview for the John Foster Dulles Oral History Project, Princeton University. Beschloss mentions the episode in *Crisis Years,* p. 578.

7. Kohler to Henry (Stanford?), April 27, 1989, Box 80, and Malcolm Toon to Kohler, December 3, 1977, Box 81, Kohler Papers.

8. In Kohler Papers, see Kohler's lecture to the National War College (hereafter NWC), "Trends and Prospects of U.S.–Soviet Relations," January 25, 1967, p. 10, Box 8. And see his NWC "Lecture of Opportunity," September 18, 1963, Box 8; Mrs. Kohler to Dear Folks, September 29, 1962, Box 3; Kohler to Elbridge Durbrow, October 9, 1962, Box 2; Washington Talking Paper, January 1963, Box 4; American Officials Stationed at the United States Embassy In Moscow Who Have Been Expelled Since January 1, 1946, Box 16. Also see pp. 7–8 of Kohler's interview for the Dulles Oral History Project for his comparison of Stalin and Khrushchev.

During Kohler's ambassadorship, Frederick Barghoorn, a Yale political scientist, was temporarily detained (1963) by Soviet authorities.

9. Kohler's remarks on the Cuban crisis in the film *Ambassadors Emeriti* (Alfred P. Sloan Foundation, 1984); Beschloss, *Crisis Years,* p. 496.

10. Beschloss, *Crisis Years,* pp. 8–9; Reminder Notes—Khrushchev Interview—October 16, 1962, and Kohler-Khrushchev, October 16, 1962, Box 15, Kohler Papers.

11. See Call on Kharlamov, October 24, 1962, Diary of October 23–25, 1962, Box 77, and Your Call on Romanovsky, October 19, 1962, Box 2, Kohler Papers.

12. On leaving his post as economic officer of the Moscow embassy in 1958, Bill Turpin had observed, "There is probably no other country in the world where Americans are more popular with the average citizen" (George Winters to Phyllis Kohler, October 22, 1958, Box 78, Kohler Papers; author's interview with Jack Matlock, May 28, 1993; Foreign Service Spouse Oral History, with Rebecca Matlock, p. 10).

13. Kohler, "Lecture of Opportunity," pp. 14–16, 18; Richard Funkhouser interview, p. 8, Foreign Affairs Oral History Project; Kohler, "Trends and Prospects of U.S.–Soviet Relations," p. 18.

14. Victor Franzusoff interview with Kohler, 1966, Box 8, Kohler Papers.

15. Kohler to William Tyler, June 11, 1963, Box 5, Kohler Papers; Kohler, "Trends and Prospects of U.S.–Soviet Relations," pp. 11–13; Department of State press release of Kohler's remarks upon signing (February 22, 1964) the Agreement on Exchanges with the USSR in 1964–1965; William Dyess interview, p. 23, Foreign Affairs Oral History Project.

16. Kohler, "Trends and Prospects of U.S.–Soviet Relations," p. 9, and "Lecture of Opportunity," pp. 4, 8–9, in Q and A section; FDK/Gromyko, February 25, 1963, Box 18, Kohler Papers; Foy Kohler, *Understanding the Russians: A Citizen's Primer* (New York, 1970), p. xviii; Humphrey Trevelyan, *Worlds Apart: China 1953–1955; Soviet Union, 1962–1965* (London, 1971), p. 215.

17. Humphrey Trevelyan, *Public and Private* (London, 1980), pp. 51–59; Kohler's remarks in *Ambassadors Emeriti.*

18. Trevelyan, *Worlds Apart,* p. 217; *Nedelia* May 23–29, 1965; Kohler to Charles Bohlen, August 23, 1965, Box 1, Kohler Papers; Richard Funkhouser interview, p. 7, Foreign Affairs Oral History Project; Beschloss, *Crisis Years,* p. 579.

19. Kohler, "Trends and Prospects," p. 18.

20. "Better Relations with Moscow," *New York Times,* October 7, 1966; "Good Appointments," *Washington Post,* October 7, 1966; *Congressional Record,* pp. 24699–249700, October 7, 1966.

21. Lyndon Johnson, *The Vantage Point: Perspectives of the Presidency, 1963–1969* (New York, 1971), p. 475; press conference of Llewellyn Thompson, p. 2, June 13, 1967, and Thompson to Secretary of State, April 19, 1967, Johnson Library.

22. Emory Swank interview, p. 19, and Davis Boster interview, p. 19, Foreign Affairs

Oral History Project; Charles Bohlen, *Witness to History, 1929–1969* (New York, 1973), p. 526; Robert A. D. Ford, *Our Man in Moscow: A Diplomat's Reflections on the Soviet Union* (Toronto, 1989), pp. 257, 261.

23. Johnson, *Vantage Point,* pp. 479–480, 490, 535; Dobrynin–Thompson Conversations, February 17, 1966–September 6, 1968, vol. 2, Box 227, and USSR-Hidden Microphones in Moscow Embassy, Box 9, National Security File, Johnson Library.

24. Emory Swank interview, pp. 19–20 Foreign Affairs Oral History Project. On the Prague Spring, see Karen Dawisha, *The Kremlin and the Prague Spring* (Berkeley, 1984); Jiri Valenta, *The Soviet Invasion of Czechoslovakia, 1968: Anatomy of a Decision* (Baltimore, 1979).

25. Theodore Draper, "Little Heinz and Big Henry," *New York Times Book Review,* September 6, 1992, p. 18. Among the many works containing criticism of Kissinger, see Walter Isaacson, *Kissinger: A Biography* (New York, 1992); Robert Schulzinger, *Henry Kissinger: Doctor of Diplomacy* (New York, 1989); Seymour Hersh, *The Price of Power: Kissinger in the Nixon White House* (New York, 1983). None of Kissinger's apologists have done better then he in defending his record. See his two-volume memoir: *White House Years* (Boston, 1979) and *Years of Upheaval* (Boston, 1982).

26. William Dyess interview, p. 36, Foreign Affairs Oral History Project.

27. Jacob Beam, *Multiple Exposure: An American Ambassador's Unique Perspective on East–West Issues* (New York, 1978), pp. 31–33; Whitman Bassow, *The Moscow Correspondents: Reporting on Russia from the Revolution to Glasnost* (New York, 1988), p. 145; Bohlen, *Witness to History,* p. 338.

28. Beam, *Multiple Exposure,* p. 213; Strom Thurmond to Mr. President, February 3, 1969, White House Special Files, President's Office File, Box 1, Nixon Presidential Materials Project, NA; Harry Fleming, Memorandum for the President, February 18, 1969, White House Central Files, Foreign Relations, Box 26, Nixon Presidential Materials Project.

29. Beam, *Multiple Exposure,* pp. 218, 227, 253, 265–266.

30. Ibid., pp. 263–264, 272; Raymond Gartoff, *Détente and Confrontation: American–Soviet Relations from Nixon to Reagan* (Washington, D.C., 1985), p. 94; Kissinger, *White House Years,* p. 1153; Ford, *Our Man in Moscow,* p. 269; Michael Wygant interview, p. 16, Foreign Affairs Oral History Project; author's interview with Charles Stefan, June 21, 1992.

31. Kissinger, *White House Years,* pp. 173, 617; Richard Nixon, *The Memoirs of Richard Nixon* (New York, 1978), p. 478; Beam, *Multiple Exposure,* pp. 215–217.

Malcolm Toon was among those people who urged Beam to resign after Kissinger's mistreatment of him. He decided to stay on, largely to spare Nixon any embarrassment. Author's interview with Malcolm Toon, October 26, 1992.

32. Marshall Brement and David Nalle interviews, Foreign Affairs Oral History Project; Beam, *Multiple Exposure,* p. 227.

33. Roland Elliot to Theodore Grevers, April 5, 1974, White House Central Files, Countries, Box 78, Nixon Presidential Materials Project; R. T. Curran to Peter Rodman, December 9, 1970, and Press Briefing Paper regarding Rigerman case; Secretary of State to U.S. embassy, Moscow, January 1, 1971, White House Central Files, Countries, Box 71, Nixon Presidential Materials Project.

34. Beam, *Multiple Exposure,* pp. 240–243, 258, 283, 294.

35. Ibid., pp. 244–245.

36. Kissinger, *Years of Upheaval,* p. 559. While ambassador to Afghanistan in 1979 (February), Dubs was taken hostage by guerrillas, who demanded the release of pro-

Chinese Tadzhik fighters. In the assault mounted by Afghan police against the kidnappers, Dubs was killed. Soviet advisers to the police played an ambiguous role.

37. Walter Stoessel, memorandum, November 26, 1973, Stoessel Papers (not yet cataloged), Georgetown University.

38. Kissinger, *White House Years*, p. 188; *New York Times,* January 21, 1970; Eugene Boster interview, p. 21, Foreign Affairs Oral History Project; author's interview with Jack Matlock, May 28, 1993.

39. In Stoessel Papers, see Walter Stoessel's "Final Report from Moscow on the State of the USSR and U.S.–Soviet Relations, September 9, 1976; Alexander Haig to President Reagan, May 26, 1982; Walter Stoessel, Meeting of Former U.S. Ambassadors to the Soviet Union, May 18, 1981; author's interview with Malcolm Toon, October 26, 1992.

40. The following documents, all in the Stoessel Papers, represent a sample of the subjects covered by Stoessel in his reports. Ambassador Stoessel's Visit to Tbilisi (n.d.); Overall Evaluation of Ambassador's Visit (to Armenia, n.d.); Stoessel, Memorandum on Rostropovich's Plans, March 22, 1974; Memorandum for the Record, Conversation with [name deleted], May 6, 1976; Protocol Visit to *Pravda* by Ambassador Stoessel, December 12, 1974; A Soviet Deputy's Work, June 17, 1974; Conversation with I. T. Grishin, May 29, 1974; Conversation with Arbatov, April 20, 1974; Podgorny's Comments About Visit of Senator Jackson, March 7, 1974; Further Comments by Brezhnev, March 12, 1974.

41. Stoessel, Final Report from Moscow, pp. 1–12. This is an excellent paper. Its conclusions have stood the test of time.

42. Ibid.

43. See entries in President Ford's Diary, September 18, 1975, and October 18, 1976, Ford Library; Memorandum of Conversation, December 12, 1974, Stoessel Papers.

44. Stoessel, Final Report from Moscow.

45. Kissinger, *Years of Upheaval,* p. 1153; Ford, *Our Man in Moscow,* p. 269; Nixon, *Memoirs,* p. 1026; Garthoff, *Détente and Confrontation,* p. 424; in Stoessel Papers: Memorandums of Arbatov on President Ford, August 31, 1974; Meeting between Averell Harriman and Brezhnev, June 4, 1974; Stoessel's Call on the President, February 7, 1974; Marshall Brement interview, pp. 10–11, Foreign Affairs Oral History Project.

46. Malcolm Toon and Richard Davies, "After Containment, What?" (permission to read and cite this fourteen-page essay by courtesy of Malcolm Toon); the essay and cover letter to the *Foreign Service Journal* (March 25, 1952) remain in Toon's possession.

47. Malcolm Toon interview, pp. 44–46, Foreign Affairs Oral History Project; author's interview with Toon, October 26, 1992.

48. Author's interview with Toon.

49. Ibid.; Malcolm Toon, "The Soviet Union and Eastern Europe in a World in Change," in Kenneth Thompson, ed., *The Presidency and a World in Change* (Lanham, Md., 1991), pp. 99, 114; Kissinger, *White House Years,* p. 141.

50. Toon, "Soviet Union and Eastern Europe," pp. 114–115; author's interview with Toon; Toon interview, Foreign Affairs Oral History Project.

51. Ford, *Our Man in Moscow,* p. 302; Garthoff, *Détente and Confrontation,* p. 575; Toon, "Soviet Union and Eastern Europe," pp. 114–116.

52. Toon interview, Foreign Affairs Oral History Project; Toon, "Soviet Union and Eastern Europe," p. 116; author's interview with Toon.

53. Miller Center Oral History "Brzezinski" with Madeline Albright, William Odom, and Leslie Denend, p. 49, Carter Library.

54. Toon, "Soviet Union and Eastern Europe," pp. 117–118.

55. *International Herald Tribune,* November 8, 1977. Leonard Sussman to Brzezinski,

November 11, 1977, and Brzezinski to Leonard Sussman, November 30, 1977; Jim Switzer and Ben Young to Mr. President, September 12, 1978; Vashchenko and Chmykhalov Families to President Carter, August 27, 1978; Augustina Vashchenko to Jim Switzer and Ben Young, August 28, 1978, Subject File, Box FO-12, White House Central Files, Carter Library. Memorandum for the President from Stewart Eizenstat, July 7, 1978, White House Central Files, Countries CO57, Carter Library. *Ambassadors Emeriti.*

56. Garthoff, *Détente and Confrontation*, pp. 566, 801–827; Gaddis Smith, *Morality, Reason, and Power* (New York, 1986), pp. 45, 77; Toon interview, pp. 37–38, Foreign Affairs Oral History Project; Toon, "Soviet Union and Eastern Europe," p. 117.

57. Kohler to Cyrus Vance, March 7, 1977, Box 81, Kohler Papers; Toon interview, pp. 38–39, 49, Foreign Affairs Oral History Project; Memorandum for Zbigniew Brzezinski, May 3, 1979, White House Central files, Subject File, Box FO-12, Carter Library; author's interview with Toon.

58. Toon interview, pp. 51–52, Foreign Affairs Oral History Project; Toon to Kohler, December 3, 1977, Kohler Papers.

59. Memorandum for Robert Lipshutz from Joyce Starr, January 6, 1978, Staff Offices, Counsel Lipshutz, Box 44, Carter Library; interview with Willis Sutter, p. 28, Foreign Affairs Oral History Project; Marshall Brement interview, pp. 30–31, Foreign Affairs Oral History Project; Senator Robert Dole to Mr. President, March 9, 1977, White House Central File, Countries CO57, Carter Library; author's interview with Toon; Fact Sheet 1975A (on radiation problem, n.d.), Stoessel Papers; Mark Garrison to author, April 27, 1993; *New York Times,* March 29, 1991.

60. Author's interview with Toon; Toon interview, pp. 47–48, Foreign Affairs Oral History Project; Barry Rubin, *Secrets of State: The State Department and the Struggle over U.S. Foreign Policy* (New York, 1987), pp. 135–136, 183.

61. Author's interview with historian, who prefers that his or her name not be used, November 9, 1992; Thomas Watson, Jr., with Peter Petre, *Father, Son, and Co.: My Life at IBM and Beyond* (New York, 1991), pp. xii, 450; Watson to Mr. President, December 12, 1979, White House Central File, Subject File, Box FO-12, Carter Library.

62. In his April 27, 1993, letter to me, Mark Garrison argued that my portrait of Watson is unfair:

> From the time I first met him in 1979, he was and is intellectually engaged on key U.S. public policy issues, domestic and foreign. True, his engagement tended to focus on forests rather than trees, and was aimed at identifying the true nature of a problem and the underlying national interest, then finding a solution. He has an inquiring mind, always looking for creative solutions and often himself offering creative ideas in order to stimulate others' thinking. His service as chair of the GAC illustrates his ability to mobilize citizens with good common sense in trying to force officialdom to think straight about nuclear weapons in general and the MX in particular. As for his being the 'least qualified' for the post, I suggest taking into account the reason for his appointment: to send to Moscow a person qualified, by virtue of his stature and ease in high-level dealings, to open a dialogue with the aging Soviet leadership, following successful conclusion of SALT II, that could move U.S.–Soviet relations to a totally new level. Not unlike the appointment of Harriman during an earlier period of hope and good relations.

After Watson's death (at the age of seventy-nine), Cyrus Vance referred to him as "a splendid ambassador to the Soviet Union" (*New York Times,* December 30, 1993).

63. Smith, *Morality, Reason, and Power,* p. 45. Watson, *Father, Son, and Co.,* pp.

439–440, 444, 447. Brzoezinski to Watson, August 8, 1979; Carter to Watson, May 31, 1979, and Carter to Watson, May 9, 1979, White House Central File, Name File, Carter Library.

64. Watson, *Father, Son, and Co.*, pp. 60–61, 108–110, 440, 452.

65. Ibid., pp. 440, 448–449, 452–451; Watson to Brzezinski, December 12, 1979, White House Central File, Name File, Carter Library.

66. *Ambassadors Emeriti;* Watson, *Father, Son, and Co.*, pp. 448–449, 453–458; Garrison to author.

67. Watson, *Father, Son, and Co.*, p. 456; Garrison to author.

68. Watson, *Father, Son, and Co.*, pp. 359–360, 478; Ford, *Our Man in Moscow,* p. 320; author's interview with Mark Garrison, November 13, 1992.

69. Watson, *Father, Son, and Co.*, pp. 458–461.

70. Ibid., p. 461; Ford, *Our Man in Moscow,* p. 320; Jimmy Carter, *Keeping Faith: Memoirs of a President* (Toronto, 1982), pp. 431–596; author's interview with Garrison.

71. Garrison to author.

72. Author's interview with Garrison; Thomas Watson, Jr., to author, July 22, 1992; Watson, *Father, Son, and Co.*, pp. 462–465; Watson to Mr. President (handwritten), May 10, 1980, and Watson to Mr. President, September 15, 1980, White House Central File, Subject File, Box FO-12, Carter Library.

73. Kissinger, *White House Years,* pp. 189–190, Ford, *Our Man in Moscow,* p. 269. If actions mean more than words, there is something disingenuous about Kissinger's dedicating his *Diplomacy* (New York, 1994) to the men and women of the Foreign Service.

Chapter 10

1. George Kennan, *Memoirs: 1925–1950* (Boston, 1967), p. 130; David Mayers, *George Kennan and the Dilemmas of U.S. Foreign Policy* (New York, 1988), pp. 83–85. David Remnick, a *Washington Post* correspondent in Moscow during 1988 to 1991, has written an absorbing account of the final years of the USSR: *Lenin's Tomb: The Last Days of the Soviet Empire* (New York, 1993).

2. Peter Witonski, ed., *Gibbon for Moderns* (New Rochelle, N.Y., 1974), p. 38.

3. Henry Bradsher, *Afghanistan and the Soviet Union* (Durham, N.C., 1985), p. vii.

4. Arthur Hartman interview, Foreign Affairs Oral History Project, Georgetown University; author's interview with Hartman, February 5, 1993; George Shultz, *Turmoil and Triumph: My Years as Secretary of State* (New York, 1993), p. 364.

5. Hartman interview, Foreign Affairs Oral History Project.

6. Ibid.; author's interview with Hartman. Foreign Service officers not involved in political and economic reporting would include fiscal specialists, consular officers, and those in commercial, cultural, and press relations.

7. Author's interview with Hartman; author's interview with George Shultz, December 21, 1990; Ronald Reagan, *An American Life* (New York, 1990), p. 560; Shultz, *Turmoil and Triumph,* p. 122.

8. Michael Beschloss and Strobe Talbott, *At the Highest Levels: The Inside Story of the End of the Cold War* (New York, 1993), p. 6; author's interview with Hartman; Reagan, *American Life,* pp. 614–615.

9. Alexander Dallin, *Black Box: KAL 007 and the Superpowers* (Berkeley, 1985), p. 3; author's interview with Hartman; Shultz, *Turmoil and Triumph,* p. 870; Murray Sayle, "Closing the File on Flight 007," *New Yorker,* December 13, 1993.

10. Author's interview with Hartman; Hartman interview, Foreign Affairs Oral History Project.

11. Shultz, *Turmoil and Triumph,* p. 588; author's interview with Hartman.

12. Nicholas Daniloff's ordeal is recounted in his lively *Two Lives, One Russia* (Boston, 1988); Whitman Bassow, *The Moscow Correspondents: Reporting on Russia from the Revolution to Glasnost* (New York, 1988), p. 360; Jack Matlock to author, August 9, 1993.

13. *Foreign Affairs Chronology, 1978–1989* (New York, 1990), pp. 135, 166, 194, 228–229, 264, 266–267; Matlock to author, August 9, 1993.

14. Shultz, *Turmoil and Triumph,* pp. 536, 879–880; author's interview with Hartman; Hartman interview, Foreign Affairs Oral History Project.

Matlock's explanation of events concerning Soviet locals at the embassy is compatible with the compressed one I have provided (itself drawn primarily from Shultz and Hartman). In his August 9, 1993, letter to the author he wrote:

> To summarize a *very* complex sequence of events, when the Soviets continued to hold Daniloff despite Reagan's personal assurance to Gorbachev that he was not an intelligence officer, we required the USSR to remove 25 officials, suspected intelligence officers, from their United Nations mission, and made it clear that no visas would be issued for replacements. At the same time we privately warned the Soviets that any retaliation against our embassy in Moscow (which, of course, was not a counterpart of their UN mission) would not be tolerated. We also specifically warned them that, in the event of retaliation against our embassy, we would require them to reduce their embassy to a size comparable to ours. (Theirs was over twice as large.)
>
> In fact, following the Reykjavik summit, the Soviets retaliated against our embassy in Moscow and we did what we had warned: a ceiling was placed on the Soviet embassy of (if memory serves) 217 employees. This required them to remove 55 of their "diplomats." In doing so, we recognized that the Soviets would probably retaliate by removing the Soviet employees, but we set the ceiling high enough to bring Americans to Moscow to do these functions. The Soviets then responded to our action with the order to our Soviet employees to cease working in Moscow and Leningrad.

15. *New York Times,* January 27, 1989; March 15, 1989; October 6, 1991; December 14, 1991.

16. Author's interviews with Hartman and Shultz; Shultz, *Turmoil and Triumph,* pp. 879–900. Also see Ronald Kessler, *Moscow Station: How the KGB Penetrated the American Embassy* (New York, 1989); Susan Bloch, "Our Man in Moscow," *Duke—A Magazine for Alumni and Friends,* July–August 1987, p. 4.

17. In his letter to the author, Matlock gave this appraisal of the security problems that had dogged the embassy during Hartman's time:

> [They] received tremendous public attention at the time and presented us with significant political, public relations and management worries. However, they were totally secondary to what was really going on in the U.S.–Soviet relationship, and—with the hindsight of history—ultimately trivial. It is yet to be demonstrated that these various alleged "security lapses" at Embassy Moscow endangered a single life or put the U.S. at a negotiating disadvantage on any issue. The truly damaging spy cases (Howard, the Walker family and others) all occurred in the United States. But it was our bad luck that comparatively minor incidents (Lonetree) and some predictable developments (bugging of the new embassy, which we had anticipated and which we knew how to counter) occurred just after these more serious espionage cases were brought to light. They were used by circles—particularly in Congress—who had axes to grind: a desire to deprive the Soviets of the embassy site allocated them; a desire to demonstrate that Embassy Moscow and the State Department were more lax in security than the CIA, Navy and NSA (all of whom, it turned out, had unwittingly harbored

real spies). Embassy Moscow became a totally undeserved scapegoat, and unfortunately, since these incidents occurred on or came to light during Hartman's watch, he was quite unfairly charged with responsibility.

18. Author's interview with Hartman; *New York Times,* February 14, 1990; Matlock to author, August 9, 1993. On the one hand, Matlock did not want to hamper legitimate contact between embassy personnel and Soviet citizens. On the other, he required strict accountability: "Besides protecting our officers from provocations, [new regulations] also offered some protection to innocent Soviet citizens, who otherwise would be brought under intense pressure by the KGB if they were seeing officials from the American embassy. If they never saw the American alone in private premises, they had a perfect excuse to resist KGB attempts to force them to 'set up' their American contact."

19. *New York Times,* March 29, 1991; May 1, 1991; Marie Brenner, "Mr. Ambassador! Bob Strauss Comes Home," *New Yorker,* December 28, 1992–January 4, 1993, p. 151; author's interview with Jack Matlock, May 28, 1993; Matlock to author, August 9, 1993.

20. Author's interview with Captain Sergei Alexis Yonov, U.S. naval attaché at Embassy Moscow (August 1990–August 1992), October 20, 1992; Yonov's letter to author, July 17, 1993; author's interview with Shultz; author's interview with Matlock; Lawrence Elliot, "Our Man in Moscow," *Reader's Digest,* April 1991, p. 131; *Charlotte Observer,* April 5, 1987; Jack Matlock, "Literature and Politics: The Impact of Fyodor Dostoevsky," *Political Science Reviewer* (Fall 1979).

As of this writing, Matlock is working on two books. One, tentatively titled "Autopsy of an Empire," examines the collapse of the Soviet Union. The other analyzes the making of Reagan's Soviet policy. Matlock has also compiled and edited an index to Stalin's writings.

21. Shultz, *Turmoil and Triumph,* p. 275; author's interview with Matlock; interview with Rebecca Matlock by Foreign Service Spouse Oral History, pp. 6, 8–9; Matlock to author, August 9, 1993; Jack Matlock, "Prospects for U.S.–Soviet Relations," Marshall Visitor Address, International House, New York, April 13, 1989, p. 4; Elliott, "Our Man in Moscow," p. 130.

22. Beschloss and Talbott, *At the Highest Levels,* pp. 60, 299–301, 312, 320–321; *New York Times,* November 20, 1989; March 22, 1991; Shultz, *Turmoil and Triumph,* p. 895.

23. Beschloss and Talbott, *At the Highest Levels,* pp. 85–86, 395–399; Jack Matlock, "To the Editor," *Foreign Affairs* (1992–1993): 206; Matlock to author, August 9, 1993.

24. Author's interview with Matlock; Matlock to author, August 9, 1993.

25. Author's interview with Yonov; Jack Matlock, "U.S.–Soviet Relations: A View From Moscow," *Occasional Papers Series,* Institute for Soviet and East European Studies, University of Miami (Miami, 1989), vol. 2, pp. 5, 14. Matlock to author, August 9, 1993.

26. Matlock, "U.S.–Soviet Relations," pp. 3–4, 8, 11–12.

27. Ibid., pp. 9, 16; Beschloss and Talbott, *At the Highest Levels,* pp. 229–230.

28. Author's interview with Shultz; author's interview with Matlock; Beschloss and Talbott, *At the Highest Levels,* pp. 31–.34.

29. *Pravda,* September 18, 1989; Beschloss and Talbott, *At the Highest Levels,* 347–350, 359, 361; Matlock, "To the Editor," p. 206; author's interview with Matlock.

30. Brenner, "Mr. Ambassador!" pp. 152–153; author's interview with Matlock; *New York Times,* November 19, 1991; June 18, 1992; July 12, 1992; November 7, 1992; November 15, 1992.

31. Author's interview with Matlock.

32. *New York Times,* June 5, 1991; December 15, 1991.

33. *New York Times,* June 14, 1991; author's interview with Matlock; author's interview with Yonov; Brenner, "Mr. Ambassador!" p. 152.

34. Brenner, "Mr. Ambassador!" pp. 152–153; Beschloss and Talbott, *At the Highest Levels,* pp. 426, 436, 444–445; author's interview with Yonov; author's interview with Matlock.

35. Some pundits theorized that Bush had made Strauss ambassador to Moscow in order to deprive the Democrats of his services in 1992.

36. Brenner, "Mr. Ambassador!" pp. 153–156; author's interview with Matlock.

37. I am possibly unfair in my characterization of Matlock's remarks in August 1991. In his letter to the author, he explained his version of events in fascinating detail:

> What I said, when asked by the press in August 1991, whether I thought a coup would be successful, was that there were people who would like to carry one out, but I doubted that they would succeed. Therefore, I assumed that those who might be tempted probably would decide not to try.
>
> It was possibly a mistake to say anything that sounded like a prediction since it was bound to be simplified and thus distorted by the press, but I had a purpose in putting it as I did. . . . Press reporting of what I said, however, would not have misled policymaking officials in Washington, who were familiar with the embassy's reporting. Our reporting to Washington was vastly more detailed and nuanced; after all, we knew about the Popov warning . . . and knew other facts about pressures on Gorbachev to declare a state of emergency. He had been close to it in January, but partly under pressure from us, had refrained. However, since the plotters had failed in June and—I thought—could not count on the Army if people came out to protest, they would probably continue, for a time at least, to connive behind the scenes without an overt move.
>
> However, I could not, as American Ambassador, explain all this at a press conference, and if I had predicted a coup, this would have been all over the papers and—incredible as it may seem—might even have been read as a green light from the United States to the plotters. Saying that I thought they had sense enough to refrain from an attempt to seize power would potentially have the opposite effect. (Though I had no illusion that it would weigh heavily in their calculations!) Nevertheless, the point is that one must not assess public statements by officials as if they were mere expressions of opinion by journalists or scholars. Though I would insist that public officials never be dishonest, at the same time they must carefully weigh the effects their words can have on events themselves. Sometimes it is just not appropriate to say in public all the things one would in reports to one's government.

38. Author's interview with Matlock; *New York Times,* June 14, 1991.

39. Matlock made this shrewd observation in his letter to the author: "Diplomacy is something that must be practiced with one's own government as much as with foreign governments and this is something that professionals are more likely to forget than non-professionals, who usually owe the job to connections at home rather than to their expertise."

40. Dean Rusk, Oral History Interview, no. 1, pp. 33–36, Johnson Library; author's interview with Shultz. For an example of this presumption, see Clare Booth Luce, "The Ambassadorial Issue: Professional or Amateurs?" *Foreign Affairs,* October 1957, p. 114; George Kennan, *The Cloud of Danger: Current Realities of American Foreign Policy* (Boston, 1977), p. 224.

41. For a sustained analysis of diplomacy's mediation of estrangement in international life, see James Der Derian, *On Diplomacy* (Oxford, 1987).

42. The relationship between U.S. journalists and diplomats in communist Moscow was important, but is too big a subject to have treated extensively in this book. According

to Matlock, in his Soviet experience the diplomats enjoyed significant advantages over the news reporters. In his letter to author, he stated:

> There were exceptions in both groups, but most of the time our embassy political officers traveled more than journalists (closed area rules were the same for both groups but we had more people than any individual news bureau) and had more contacts in Moscow than all but an exceptional two or three journalists. The diplomats learned from journalists, indeed, but the journalists almost certainly learned more from them. I recall a reporter from the old New York *Herald Tribune* in the early 1960s who would not write a story on internal Soviet affairs without consulting us in the political section. We all did a lot of backgrounding, and the ambassador normally met with the press at least twice a month.

43. Peter Kenez to author, May 14, 1993; Kennan, *Cloud of Danger,* p. 225; author's interview with Matlock; copies of Matlock's speeches to Soviet diplomatic academy, January 12, 1989, to tank academy, February 24, 1989, and April 29, 1988, in author's possession, courtesy of Matlock; author's conversations in Leningrad and Moscow, 1988 and 1990; Lawrence, "Our Man in Moscow," p. 131.

44. Matlock has provided this moving and useful qualification to my comments on the condition of U.S. diplomats in Moscow. In his letter to the author he wrote:

> You are very accurate when . . . you describe their desires and conclude that all were "circumscribed"—*if* you exclude the embassy's activity from about 1989, maybe even 1988. During the last few years of the Soviet Union's existence we had access, substantial though not complete, freedom to travel, an intensive and broadening dialogue. We felt the target of KGB surveillance still, as—I suspect—Soviet diplomats in Washington were aware that the FBI was interested in them, but our interaction with the people grew by what seemed quantum leaps. We were operating basically as a normal embassy (though one hard pressed with overwork) in a country which was neither an ally nor implacably hostile, but was changing before our eyes in ways we previously could only have dreamed of. Our colleagues at home seemed to hang on every word we reported, even when they did not always agree with our assessments. Those of us who were equipped for the task (endurance of past conditions helped) not only served, but enjoyed it. It was the most exhilarating experience of my life, and I believe that was true of many of my colleagues.

45. Michael Palliser, "Diplomacy Today," in Hedley Bull and Adam Watson, eds., *The Expansion of International Society* (Oxford, 1984), p. 374; William Strang, *Home and Abroad* (Westport, Conn., 1956, 1983), p. 60; James Pacy to author, December 8, 1992.

46. Niccolò Machiavelli, *The Prince,* ed. and trans. Mark Musa (New York, 1964), p. 191.

47. *FRUS, 1946,* vol. 6, p. 708.

48. Cited in Elmer Plischke, ed., *Modern Diplomacy: The Art and the Artisans* (Washington, D.C., 1979), p. 1.

In his letter to the author, Matlock also said this about his August 1991 remarks regarding a possible coup attempt: "I would maintain that my comments were essentially correct, even though they did not predict the specific event which occurred. After all, what people were really asking was not whether some group or another would try to take power and fail, but whether Gorbachev's removal by a successful coup was imminent. My analysis was fully adequate for policymaking. One reacts one way if a coup is destined to succeed and another if it is likely to fail. If I had predicted a successful coup (privately or publicly) then my analysis would really have been incorrect."

49. See Paul Kennedy, *Preparing for the Twenty-First Century* (New York, 1993); Samuel Huntington "The Clash of Civilizations?" *Foreign Affairs* (Summer 1993).

BIBLIOGRAPHY

Archival and Manuscripts Collections

Bohlen, Charles. Papers. Library of Congress.

Bohlen, Charles. Records. National Archives.

Bugbee, Fred William. Papers. Hoover Institution.

Bullitt, William C. Papers. Franklin D. Roosevelt Library.

Bullitt, William C. Papers. Yale University.

Carter Library, Jimmy. Collections; Oral Histories.

Clay, Cassius M. Papers. Library of Congress.

Columbia University. Oral Histories.

Confidential U.S. Diplomatic Post Records, Russia: From Czar to Commissars, 1914–1918. Frederick, Md. Microfilm collection.

Davies, Joseph. Papers. Library of Congress.

Despatches from U.S. Ministers to Russia, 1808–1906, Microfilm 10-3-9. National Archives.

Diplomatic Instructions of the Department of State, 1802–1906, Russia, January 2, 1833–December 27, 1864, Microfilm 10-1-5. National Archives.

Dulles, John Foster. Papers. Princeton University.

Durbrow, Elbridge. Papers. Hoover Institution.

Eisenhower Library, Dwight D. White House, Office of the Staff, International Series; Dulles Papers, General Correspondence and Memoranda Series; Whitman, Dulles-Herter; Whitman, Cabinet; White House. Confidential, Subject Series; DDE Diaries; Oral Histories.

Ford Library, Gerald. Collections.

Foster, John. Papers. Library of Congress.

Georgetown University. Foreign Affairs Oral History Project, Oral Histories.

Golder, Frank. Papers.

Harriman, W. Averell. Papers. Library of Congress.

Henderson, Loy. Papers. Hoover Institution.

Herter, Christian. Papers. Dwight D. Eisenhower Library.

Hopkins, Harry. Papers. Franklin D. Roosevelt Library.

Hunt, William Henry. Papers. Library of Congress.

Ingersoll, Ralph. Papers. Boston University.

Johnson Library, Lyndon B. National Security File; Collections; Oral Histories.

Kelley, Robert. Papers. Georgetown University.

Kennan, George (elder). Papers. Library of Congress.

Kennan, George (younger). Papers. Princeton University.

Kennedy Library, John F. President's Office File; Oral Histories.

Kerr, Philip. Scottish Record Office, Edinburgh.

Kirk, Alan. Official File. Harry S. Truman Library.

Kirk, Alan. Papers. Library of Congress.

Kohler, Foy. Papers. University of Toledo.

Lyons, Eugene. Papers. Hoover Institution.

Marshall, George. Papers. George Marshall Library.

Meyer, George von. L. Papers. Library of Congress.

Moore, R. Walton. Papers. Franklin D. Roosevelt Library.

Nixon Presidential Materials Project. Collections. National Archives.

Pickens, Francis. Papers. Library of Congress.

Public Record Office. Collections. Kew, London.

Records of the Division of Eastern European Affairs, 1917–1941, RG 59. National Archives.

Roberts, Frank. Papers. Harry S. Truman Library.

Roosevelt Library, Franklin D. Official File; President's Personal File; President's Secretary's File; Map Room File.

Russia and the Soviet Union: Internal and External Affairs, 1914–1941. Frederick, Md. Microfilm collection.

Russia in Transition: The Diplomatic Papers of David Rowland Francis, U.S. Ambassador to Russia, 1916–1918. Frederick, Md. Microfilm collection.

Russia. Posol' stvo (United States), Records, 1897–1947. Hoover Instution.

Standley, William. Papers. Library of Congress.

Standley, William. Papers. University of Southern California.

Starr, Clarence. Papers. Hoover Institution.

Steinhardt, Laurence. Papers. Library of Congress.

Stines, Norman. Papers. Hoover Institution.

Stoessel, Walter. Papers. Georgetown University.

Thayer, Charles. Papers. Harry S. Truman Library.

Todd, Charles. Papers. Library of Congress.

Truman Library, Harry S. Oral Histories. Truman Papers.

Witkin, Zara. Papers. Hoover Institution.

Wolfe, Bertram. Papers. Hoover Institution.

Yeaton, Ivan. Papers. Hoover Institution.

Interviews and/or Correspondence

Calleo, Professor David.

Connor, Professor Walter.

Conquest, Professor Robert.

Eilts, Ambassador Hermann.

Garrison, Foreign Service Officer Mark.

Golovenchenko, Dr. Alexei.

Hartman, Ambassador Arthur.

Kenez, Professor Peter.

Kennan, Ambassador George.
Kennedy, Foreign Service Officer Charles Stuart.
Khrushchev, Mr. Sergei.
Lyne, Ambassador Steven.
Martens, Foreign Service Officer Robert.
Matlock, Ambassador Jack.
Shultz, Secretary of State George.
Stanton, Foreign Service Officer William.
Stefan, Foreign Service Officer Charles.
Stoessel, Mrs. Mary Ann (Walter).
Thompson, Mrs. Jane (Llewllyn).
Toon, Ambassador Malcolm.
Tucker, Professor Robert.
Watson, Ambassador Thomas.
Yargin, Dr. Andrei.
Yonov, Captain (USN) Sergei.

Selected Books and Unpublished Manuscripts of Related Interest

Abramson, Rudy. *The Life of W. Averell Harriman, 1891–1986*. New York, 1992.
Acheson, Dean. *Present at the Creation*. New York, 1969.
Adams, Charles Francis, ed. *The Memoirs of John Quincy Adams*. Vol. 2. Philadelphia, 1874.
Adams, Henry. *John Randolph*. Boston, 1910.
Adler, Cyrus, and Aaron Margalith. *With Firmness in the Right*. New York, 1946.
Alden, John. *Stephen Sayre: American Revolutionary Adventurer*. Baton Rouge, 1983.
Alexander, John. *Catherine the Great: Life and Legend*. New York, 1989.
Altschuler, Glenn. *Andrew D. White—Educator, Historian, Diplomat*. Ithaca, 1979.
Ambrose, Stephen. *Eisenhower: The President*. New York, 1984.
Anschel, Eugene, ed. *The American Image of Russia, 1775–1917*. New York, 1974.
Arendt, Hannah. *The Origins of Totalitarianism*. New York, 1951.
Aucaigne, Felix. *L'Alliance russo-américaine*. Paris, 1863.
Babey, Anna Mary. *Americans in Russia, 1776–1917: A Study of the American Travelers in Russia*. New York, 1938.
Baer, George, ed., *A Question of Trust: The Origins of U.S.–Soviet Diplomatic Relations: The Memoirs of Loy W. Henderson*. Stanford, 1986.
Bailey, Thomas. *America Faces Russia: Russian–American Relations from Early Times to Our Day*. Gloucester, Mass., 1964.
Baker, Roy. *Woodrow Wilson: Life and Letters*. Vols. 5 and 6. Garden City, N.Y., 1935, 1940.
Balfour, John. *Not Too Correct an Aureole: The Recollections of a Diplomat*. Salisbury, 1983.
Bashkina, Nina, et al., eds. *The United States and Russia: The Beginnings of Relations, 1765–1815*. Washington, D.C., n.d.
Bassow, Whitman. *The Moscow Correspondents: Reporting on Russia from the Revolution to Glasnost*. New York, 1988.
Beam, Jacob. *Multiple Exposure: An American Ambassador's Unique Perspective on East–West Issues*. New York, 1978.
Beitzell, Robert. *The Uneasy Alliance: America, Britain, and Russia, 1941–1943*. New York, 1972.

Belohlavek, John. *George Mifflin Dallas: Jacksonian Patrician*. University Park, Pa., 1977.

Bemis, Samuel. *John Quincy Adams and the Foundations of American Foreign Policy*. New York, 1973.

Bengquist, Harold. "Russian–American Relations, 1820–1830: The Diplomacy of Henry Middleton, American Minister at St. Petersburg." Ph.D. diss., Boston University, 1970.

Bennett, Edward. *Franklin Roosevelt and the Search for Security in American–Soviet Relations, 1939–1945*. Wilmington, 1990.

Bennett, Edward. *Recognition of Russia: An American Foreign Policy Dilemma*. Waltham, Mass., 1970.

Berlin, Isaiah. *Personal Impressions*. New York, 1980.

Beschloss, Michael. *The Crisis Years: Kennedy and Khrushchev, 1960–1963*. New York, 1991.

Beschloss, Michael, and Strobe Talbott. *At the Highest Levels: The Inside Story of the End of the Cold War*. Boston, 1993.

Blakely, Allison. *Russia and the Negro: Blacks in Russian History and Thought*. Washington, D.C., 1986.

Bland, Larry. "W. Averell Harriman: Businessman and Diplomat, 1891–1945." Ph.D. diss., University of Wisconsin, 1972.

Bohlen, Charles. *Witness to History, 1929–1969*. New York, 1973.

Bolkhovitinov, Nikolai. *The Beginnings of Russian–American Relations, 1775–1815*. Cambridge, Mass., 1975.

Bolkhovitinov, Nikolai. *Doctrina Monro*. Moscow, 1959.

Bordin, Ruth. *Andrew Dickson White: Teacher of History*. Ann Arbor, 1958.

Bourne, Kenneth, and D. C. Watt, eds. *British Documents on Foreign Affairs: Reports and Papers from the Foreign Office*. Frederick, Md., 1983.

Bowles, Chester. *Promises to Keep: My Years in Public Service, 1941–1969*. New York, 1971.

Boyle, Peter, ed. *The Churchill–Eisenhower Correspondence, 1953–1955*. Chapel Hill, N.C., 1990.

Bradley, Edward. *George Henry Boker: Poet and Patriot*. Philadelphia, 1927.

Bradley, John. *Allied Intervention in Russia*. London, 1968.

Bradsher, Henry. *Afghanistan and the Soviet Union*. Durham, N.C., 1985.

Brands, George. *Impressions of Russia*. Edited by Richard Pipes. 1889; New York, 1966.

Brands, H. W. *Cold Warriors: Eisenhower's Generation and American Foreign Policy*. New York, 1988.

Brands, H. W. *Inside the Cold War: Loy Henderson and the Rise of the American Empire*. New York, 1991.

Brownell, W., and R. N. Billings. *So Close to Greatness: A Biography of William C. Bullitt*. New York, 1987.

Bryant, Louise. *Six Red Months in Russia*. London, 1982.

Brzezinski, Zbigniew. *Power and Principle*. New York, 1983.

Bucar, Annabelle. *The Truth About American Diplomats*. Moscow, 1949.

Buchanan, George. *My Mission to Russia*. 2 vols. Boston, 1923.

Buchanan, James. *Mission to Russia: 1831–1833. His Speeches, State Papers, and Private Correspondence*. New York, 1970.

Buehrig, Edward. *Woodrow Wilson and the Balance of Power*. Bloomington, 1955.

Bull, Hedley, and Adam Watson, eds. *The Expansion of International Society.* Oxford, 1984.

Bullard, Arthur. *The Russian Pendulum: Autocracy-Democracy-Bolshevism.* New York, 1919.

Bullitt, Orville, ed. *For the President Personal and Secret: Correspondence Between Franklin D. Roosevelt and William C. Bullitt.* Boston, 1972.

Bullitt, William. *The Bullitt Mission to Russia.* New York, 1919.

Byrnes, James. *All in One Lifetime.* New York, 1958.

Byrnes, Robert. *Pobedonostsev: His Life and Thought.* Bloomington, 1968.

Carter, Jimmy. *Keeping Faith.* New York, 1982.

Chevigny, Hector. *Russian America: The Great Alaskan Venture, 1741–1867.* New York, 1965.

Chicherin, George. *Two Years of Foreign Policy: The Relations of the RSFSR with Foreign Nations, from November 7, 1917 to November 7, 1919.* New York, 1920.

Churchill, Winston. *The Grand Alliance.* Boston, 1950.

Clements, Kendrick. *James Byrnes and the Origins of the Cold War.* Durham, N.C., 1982.

Clifford, Clark, with Richard Holbrooke. *Counsel to the President: A Memoir.* New York, 1991.

Cockfield, Jamie, ed. *Dollars and Diplomacy: Ambassador David Rowland Francis and the Fall of Tsarism, 1916–1917.* Durham, N.C., 1981.

Commission on the Ukranian Famine. *Investigation of the Ukranian Famine, 1932–1933, Report to Congress.* Washington, D.C., 1988.

Conquest, Robert. *The Great Terror: Stalin's Purge of the Thirties.* New York, 1973.

Conquest, Robert. *The Harvest of Sorrow: Soviet Collectivization and the Terror-Famine.* New York, 1986.

Conquest, Robert. *Stalin and the Kirov Murder.* New York, 1989.

Coulondre, Robert. *De Stalin à Hitler: Souvenirs de deux ambassades, 1936–1939.* Paris, 1950.

Craig, Gordon, and Felix Gilbert, eds. *The Diplomats, 1919–1939.* Princeton, 1953.

Cresson, W. P. *Francis Dana: A Puritan Diplomat at the Court of Catherine the Great.* New York, 1930.

Cronin, Audrey. *Great Power Politics and the Struggle over Austria.* Ithaca, 1986.

Crook, D. P. *The North, the South, and the Powers, 1861–1865.* New York, 1974.

Crosby, Alfred. *America, Russia, Hemp, and Napoleon: American Trade with Russia and the Baltic, 1783–1812.* Columbus, 1965.

Crowl, James. *Angels in Stalin's Paradise: Western Reporters in Soviet Russia, 1917–1937. A Case Study of Louis Fischer and Walter Duranty.* Washington, D.C., 1982.

Culbet, David, ed. *Mission to Moscow.* Madison, 1980.

Curtin, Jeremiah. *Memoirs of Jeremiah Curtin.* Madison, 1940.

Curtis, George Ticknor. *Life of James Buchanan.* New York, 1883.

Curtis, George William, ed. *The Correspondence of John Lothrop Motley.* Vol. 1. New York, 1889.

Custine, Marquis de. *Empire of the Czar.* New York, 1989.

Dallas, Susan, ed. *Diary of George Mifflin Dallas While United States Minister to Russia, 1837 to 1839.* 1892; New York, 1970.

Dallek, Robert. *Franklin D. Roosevelt and American Foreign Policy, 1932–1945.* New York, 1979.

Dallin, Alexander. *Black Box: KAL 007 and the Superpowers.* Berkeley, 1985.

Daniloff, Nicholas. *Two Lives, One Russia.* Boston, 1988.

Davies, Joseph. *Mission to Moscow.* New York, 1941.

Davis, Jefferson. *The Rise and Fall of the Confederate Government.* 1881; New York, 1958.

Dawisha, Karen. *The Kremlin and the Prague Spring.* Berkeley, 1984.

Deane, John. *The Strange Alliance: The Story of Our Efforts at Wartime Cooperation with Russia.* New York, 1947.

Degras, J. *The Communist International, 1919–1943.* New York, 1956.

Dennett, Tyler. *Roosevelt and the Russo-Japanese War.* Gloucester, Mass., 1959.

Der Derian, James. *On Diplomacy: A Genealogy of Western Estrangement.* Oxford, 1987.

De Santis, Hugh. *The Diplomacy of Silence: The American Foreign Service, the Soviet Union, and the Cold War, 1933–1947.* Chicago, 1980.

Deutscher, Isaac. *Stalin: A Political Biography.* New York, 1966.

Devine, Michael. *John W. Foster.* Athens, Ohio, 1981.

Djilas, Milovan. *Conversations with Stalin.* New York, 1962.

Dmytryshyn, Basil, ed. *The Russian American Colonies, 1798–1867.* Portland, Ore., 1989.

Doerig, J. A. *Marx Versus Russia.* New York, 1962.

Donovan, Robert. *The Presidency of Harry S. Truman, 1945–1948: Conflict and Crisis.* New York, 1977.

Dubie, Alain. *Frank Golder: An Adventure of a Historian in Quest of Russian History.* Boulder, Colo., 1989.

Dulles, Foster Rhea. *The Road to Teheran: The Story of Russia and America, 1781–1943.* Princeton, 1944.

Eagles, Keith. "Ambassador Joseph E. Davies and American-Soviet Relations, 1937–1941." Ph.D. diss., University of Washington, 1966.

Edmonds, Robin. *The Big Three: Churchill, Roosevelt and Stalin in Peace and War.* New York, 1991.

Edmunds, John. *Francis W. Pickens and the Politics of Destruction.* Chapel Hill, N.C., 1986.

Egle, William, ed. *Life and Times of Andrew Gregg Curtin.* Philadelphia, 1896.

Eisenhower, D. D. *Mandate for Change.* Garden City, N.Y., 1963.

Eisenhower, D. D. *Waging Peace.* Garden City, N.Y., 1965.

Ericson, John. *The Road to Berlin.* Boulder, Colo., 1983.

Ericson, John. *The Road to Stalingrad.* Boulder, Colo., 1984.

Erwin, Stanley. *Simon Cameron, Lincoln's Secretary of War: A Political Biography.* Philadelphia, 1966.

Evans, Eli. *Judah P. Benjamin: The Jewish Confederate.* New York, 1988.

Evans, Oliver. *George Henry Boker.* Boston, 1984.

Farnsworth, Beatrice. *William C. Bullitt and the Soviet Union.* Bloomington, 1967.

Fauchille, P. *La Diplomatie française et la Ligue des Neutres de 1780.* Paris, 1893.

Ferrell, Robert. *The Eisenhower Diaries.* New York, 1981.

Filene, Peter. *Americans and the Soviet Experiment, 1917–1933.* Cambridge, Mass., 1967.

Fiskcher, Louis. *Men and Politics.* New York, 1941.

Ford, Robert A. D. *Our Man in Moscow: A Diplomat's Relections on the Soviet Union.* Toronto, 1989.

Foster, John. *Diplomatic Memoirs* 2 vols. Boston, 1909.

Francis, David. *Russia from the American Embassy, April 1916–November 1918.* New York, 1922.

Friedrich, Carl, and Zbigniew Brzezinski. *Totalitarian Dictatorship and Autocracy.* Cambridge, Mass., 1957.

Gaddis, John Lewis. *Russia, the Soviet Union, and the United States: An Interpretative History.* New York, 1978.

Gaddis, John Lewis. *Strategies of Containment: A Critical Appraisal of Postwar American National Security Policy.* New York, 1982.

Gaddis, John Lewis. *The United States and the Origins of the Cold War, 1941–1947.* New York, 1972.

Gartoff, Raymond. *Détente and Confrontation: American–Soviet Relations from Nixon to Reagan.* Washington, D.C., 1985.

Geifman, Anna. *Thou Shalt Kill: Revolutionary Terrorism in Russia, 1894–1917.* Princeton, 1993.

Gleason, Abbott, *Young Russia: The Genesis of Russian Radicalism in the 1860s.* New York, 1980.

Golder, Frank. *Guide to Materials for American History in Russian Archives.* Washington, D.C., 1917.

Golder, Frank, ed. *Documents of Russian History, 1914–1917.* New York, 1927.

Goncharov, S., J. Lewis, and X. Litai. *Uncertain Partners: Stalin, Mao, and the Korean War.* Stanford, 1993.

Gorodetsky, Gabriel. *Stafford Cripps Mission to Moscow, 1940–1942.* London, 1984.

Grayson, Benson Lee, ed. *The American Image of Russia, 1917–1977.* New York, 1978.

Griffin, Gilderoy. *Memoir of Colonel Chas. S. Todd.* Philadelphia, 1873.

Grimsted, Patricia Kennedy. *The Foreign Ministers of Alexander I: Political Attitudes and the Conduct of Russian Diplomacy, 1802–1825.* Berkeley, 1969.

Gromyko, Andrei. *Memoirs.* New York, 1989.

Gurko, V. I. *Features and Figures of the Past: Government and Opinion in the Reign of Nicholas II.* Edited by Sterling, Wallace. Stanford, 1939.

Gwynn, Stephen, ed. *The Letters and Friendships of Sir Cecil Spring Rice.* London, 1929.

Haig, Alexander. *Caveat: Realism, Reagan, and Foreign Policy.* New York, 1984.

Hanson, Betty Crump. "American Diplomatic Reporting from the Soviet Union, 1934–1941." Ph.D. diss., Columbia University, 1966.

Hard, William. *Raymond Robins' Own Story.* New York, 1920.

Harlow, Giles, and George Maerz, eds. *Measures Short of War: The George F. Kennan Lectures at the National War College, 1946–1947.* Washington, D.C., 1991.

Harper, Paul, ed. *The Russia I Believe In: The Memoir of Samuel N. Harper, 1902–1941.* Chicago, 1945.

Harriman, W. Averell, and Elie Abel. *Special Envoy to Churchill and Stalin, 1941–1946.* New York, 1975.

Haslam, Jonathan. *The Soviet Union and the Search for Collective Security, 1933–1939.* New York, 1984.

Hasty, O. P., and S. Fusso, eds. *America Through Russian Eyes, 1874–1926.* New Haven, 1988.

Hayter, William. *The Kremlin and the Embassy.* London, 1966.

Heinrichs, Waldo. *American Ambassador: Joseph C. Grew and the Development of the United States Diplomatic Tradition.* New York, 1986.

Herring, George. *Aid to Russia, 1941–1946: Strategy, Diplomacy, and the Origins of the Cold War.* New York, 1973.

Hersh, Seymour. *The Price of Power: Kissinger in the Nixon White House.* New York, 1983.

Herwarth, Johnnie von. *Against Two Evils: Memoirs of a Diplomat-Soldier During the Third Reich.* London, 1981.

Higler, Gustav, and Alfred Meyer. *The Incompatible Allies: A Memoir-History of German–Soviet Relations*. New York, 1953.

Hildt, John. *Early Diplomatic Negotiations of the United States with Russia*. Baltimore, 1906.

Hochman, Jiri. *The Soviet Union and the Failure of Collective Security, 1934–1938*. Ithaca, 1984.

Hoffmann, Stanley. *Duties Beyond Borders: On the Limits and Possibilities of Ethical International Politics*. Syracuse, N.Y., 1981.

Hollander, Paul. *Political Pilgrims: Travels of Western Intellectuals to the Soviet Union, China, and Cuba, 1928–1978*. New York, 1981.

Holmes, Oliver Wendell. *John Lothrop Motley: A Memoir*. Boston, 1879.

Horton, R. G. *The Life and Public Service of James Buchanan*. Port Washington, N.Y., 1971.

Howe, M. A. Dewolfe. *George von Lengerke Meyer: His Life and Public Services*. New York, 1920.

Hull, Cordell. *The Memoirs of Cordell Hull*. 2 vols. New York, 1948.

Hunt, Michael. *Frontier Defense and the Open Door: Manchuria in Chinese–American Relations, 1895–1911*. New Haven, 1973.

Ilchman, Frederick. *Professional Diplomacy in the United States, 1779–1939*. Chicago, 1974.

Immerman, Richard, ed. *John Foster Dulles and the Diplomacy of the Cold War*. Princeton, 1990.

Ingram, Alton. "The Root Mission to Russia, 1917." Ph.D. diss., Louisiana State University, 1970.

Irving, David. *The Destruction of Convoy PQ 17*. New York, 1968.

Isaacson, Walter. *Kissinger: A Biography*. New York, 1992.

Isaacson, Walter, and Evan Thomas. *The Wise Men: Six Friends and the World They Made*. New York, 1986.

Jacobs, Travis Beal. *America and the Winter War, 1939–1940*. New York, 1980.

Jensen, Kenneth, ed. *Origins of the Cold War: The Novikov, Kennan, and Roberts "Long Telegrams" of 1946*. Washington, D.C., 1991.

Johnson, Lyndon. *The Vantage Point: Perspectives of the Presidency, 1963–1969*. New York, 1971.

Jones, Robert. *The Roads to Russia: United States Lend-Lease to the Soviet Union*. Norman, Okla., 1969.

Joost, Wilhelm. *Botschafter bei den roten Zaren: Die deutschen Missionchefs in Moskau, 1918 bis 1941 nach geheimakten und personlichen Aufzeichnungen*. Vienna, 1967.

Jordan, D., and E. Pratt. *Europe and the American Civil War*. New York, 1969.

Kalpaschnikoff, Andrew. *A Prisoner of Trotsky's*. Garden City, N.Y., 1920.

Kane, Harnett Thomas, with Victor Leclerc. *The Scandalous Mrs. Blackford*. New York, 1951.

Kelly, David. *The Ruling Few, or the Human Background to Diplomacy*. London, 1952.

Kenez, Peter. *Civil War in South Russia, 1919–1920*. Berkeley, 1977.

Kennan, George. *The Cloud of Danger: Current Realities of American Foreign Policy*. Boston, 1977.

Kennan, George. *The Marquis de Custine and His Russia in 1839*. Princeton, 1971.

Kennan, George. *Memoirs: 1925–1950*. Boston, 1967.

Kennan, George. *Memoirs: 1950–1963*. New York, 1983.

Kennan, George. *Sketches from A Life*. New York, 1989.

Kennan, George. *Soviet–American Relations, 1917–1920*. Vol. 1: *Russia Leaves the War*. Princeton, 1956.

Kennan, George. *Soviet–American Relations, 1917–1920*. Vol. 2: *The Decision to Intervene*. Princeton, 1958.

Kennan, George. *Soviet Foreign Policy, 1917–1941*. Princeton, 1960.

Kennan, George [elder]. *Siberia and the Exile System*. 2 vols. 1891; Chicago, 1958.

Kennedy, Paul. *Preparing for the Twenty-First Century*. New York, 1993.

Kennedy, Robert. *Thirteen Days: A Memoir of the Cuban Missile Crisis*. New York, 1969.

Kessler, Ronald. *Moscow Station: How the KGB Penetrated the American Embassy*. New York, 1989.

Khrushchev, Sergei. *Khrushchev on Khrushchev: An Inside Account of the Man and Era*. Boston, 1990.

Killen, Linda. *The Russian Bureau: A Case Study in Wilsonian Diplomacy*. Lexington, Ky., 1983.

Kimball, Warren. *The Juggler: Franklin Roosevelt as Wartime Statesman*. Princeton, 1991.

Kimball, Warren. *The Most Unsordid Act: Lend-Lease, 1939–1941*. Baltimore, 1969.

Kirk, Lydia. *Postmarked Moscow*. New York, 1952.

Kirk, Russell. *Randolph of Roanoke: A Study in Conservative Thought*. Chicago, 1951.

Kissinger, Henry. *Diplomacy*. New York, 1994.

Kissinger, Henry. *White House Years*. Boston, 1979.

Kissinger, Henry. *Years of Upheaval*. Boston, 1982.

Kitchen, Martin. *British Policy Toward the Soviet Union During the Second World War*. London, 1986.

Knight, Amy. *Beria: Stalin's First Lieutenant*. Princeton, 1993.

Knock, Thomas. *To End All Wars: Woodrow Wilson and the Quest for a New World Order*. New York, 1993.

Knox, Alfred. *With the Russian Army*. 1921; New York, 1971.

Kofsky, Frank. *Harry S. Truman and the War Scare of 1948: A Successful Campaign to Deceive the Nation*. New York, 1993.

Kohler, Foy. *Understanding the Russians: A Citizen's Primer*. New York, 1970.

Kohler, Foy, and Mose Harvey, eds. *The Soviet Union: Yesterday, Today, Tomorrow*. Miami, 1975.

Kohler, Phyllis, ed. *Journey for Our Time*. Chicago, 1951.

Kornhauser, William. *The Politics of Mass Society*. Glencoe, Ill., 1959.

Kotkin, Stephen. *Steeltown, USSR: Soviet Society in the Gorbachev Era*. Berkeley, 1991.

Kushner, Howard. *Conflict on the Northwest Coast: American–Russian Rivalry in the Pacific Northwest, 1790–1867*. Westport, Conn., 1975.

Larina, Anna. *This I Cannot Forget: The Memoirs of Nikolai Bukharin's Widow*. New York, 1993.

Lasch, Christopher. *The American Liberals and the Russian Revolution*. New York, 1962.

Laserson, Max. *The American Impact on Russia, 1784–1914*. New York, 1962.

Lauren, Paul, ed. *The China Hands' Legacy: Ethics and Diplomacy*. Boulder, Colo., 1987.

Lear, Fanny [Hattie Blackford]. *Le Roman d'une Américaine en Russie*. Paris, 1875.

Lederer, Ivo, ed. *Russian Foreign Policy*. New Haven, 1962.

Leffler, Melvyn. *A Preponderance of Power: National Security, the Truman Administration, and the Cold War*. Stanford, 1992.

Levin, Gordon. *Woodrow Wilson and World Politics*. New York, 1968.

Lewis, Leonard. *Life of Alphonso Taft*. New York, 1920.

Libbey, James. *Alexander Gumberg and Soviet–American Relations, 1917–1933*. Lexington, Ky., 1977.

Link, Arthur. *Wilson and the Struggle for Neutrality, 1914–1915.* Princeton, 1960.

Link, Arthur, ed. *The Papers of Woodrow Wilson.* Princeton, 1966–

Litvinov, M. *Vneshniaia politika SSSR.* Moscow, 1937.

Lockhart, R. H. Bruce. *British Agent.* New York, 1933.

Loubat, Joseph. *Gustavus Fox's Mission to Russia, 1866.* 1873; New York, 1970.

Lyons, Eugene. *Assignment in Utopia.* New York, 1937.

Madariaga, Isabel de. *Britain, Russia, and the Armed Neutrality of 1780: Sir James Harris's Mission to St. Petersburg During the American Revolution.* New Haven, 1962.

Maddux, Thomas. *Years of Estrangement: American Relations with the Soviet Union, 1933–1941.* Tallahassee, Fla., 1980.

Maier, Charles, ed. *The Cold War in Europe: Era of a Divided Continent.* New York, 1991.

Maisky, Ivan. *Memoirs of a Soviet Ambassador: The War, 1939–1943.* London, 1967.

Manning, Clarence. *Russian Influence on Early America.* New York, 1953.

Marye, George Thomas. *Nearing the End in Imperial Russia.* Philadelphia, 1929.

Mastny, Vojtech. *Russia's Road to the Cold War.* New York, 1979.

Mattox, Henry. *Twilight of Amateur Diplomacy: The American Foreign Service and Its Senior Officers in the 1890s.* Kent, Ohio, 1989.

Maximychev, I. F. *Diplomatiia mira protiv diplomatii voiny: Ocherk Sovetsko-Germanskikh diplomaticheskikh otnoshenii v. 1933–1939.* Moscow, 1981.

May, Ernest. *The World War and American Isolationism, 1914–1917.* Cambridge, Mass., 1966.

Mayer, Arno. *Politics and Diplomacy of Peacemaking: Containment and Counterrevolution at Versailles, 1918–1919.* New York, 1967.

Mayer, Arno. *Why Did the Heavens Not Darken? The "Final Solution" in History.* New York, 1989.

Mayer, Martin. *The Diplomats.* New York, 1983.

Mayers, David. *Cracking the Monolith: U.S. Policy Against the Sino-Soviet Alliance, 1949–1955.* Baton Rouge, 1986.

Mayers, David. *George Kennan and the Dilemmas of U.S. Foreign Policy.* New York, 1988.

Mazour, Anatole. *The First Russian Revolution, 1825.* Stanford, 1937.

McFadden, David. *Alternative Paths: Soviets and Americans, 1917–1920.* New York, 1993.

McLellan, David. *Dean Acheson.* New York, 1976.

Medvedev, Roy and Zhores Medvedev. *Khrushchev: The Years in Power.* New York, 1978.

Melamed, E. I. *Dzhordzh Kennan protiv tsarizma.* Moscow, 1981.

Melanson, Richard, and David Mayers. *Reevaluating Eisenhower: American Foreign Policy in the 1950s.* Urbana, Ill., 1987.

Mićunović, Veljko. *Moscow Diary.* Garden City, N.Y., 1980.

Miliukov, Paul. *Rossiia na perelome.* 2 vols. Paris, 1927.

Millis, Walter, ed. *The Forrestal Diaries.* New York, 1951.

Milosz, Czeslaw. *The Captive Mind.* New York, 1981.

Miner, Stephen. *Between Churchill and Stalin: The Soviet Union, Great Britain, and the Origins of the Grand Alliance.* Chapel Hill, N.C., 1988.

Moens, Alexander. *Foreign Policy Under Carter.* Boulder, Colo., 1990.

Molotov, V. M. *Sto sorok besed s Molotovym: Iz F. Chueva.* Moscow, 1991.

Monaghan, Jay. *Diplomat in Carpet Slippers: Abraham Lincoln Deals with Foreign Affairs.* Indianapolis, 1945.

Morgenthau, Hans, and Kenneth Thompson. *Politics Among Nations: The Struggle for Power and Peace*. New York, 1985.

Morison, Samuel Eliot. *John Paul Jones: A Sailor's Biography*. Boston, 1959.

Morley, James. *The Japanese Threat to Siberia, 1918*. New York, 1957.

Nagengast, William. *Russia Through American Eyes, 1781–1863*. Fort Knox, Ky., n.d.

Neu, Charles. *An Uncertain Friendship: Theodore Roosevelt and Japan, 1906–1912*. Cambridge, Mass., 1967.

Newman, Robert. *The Cold War Romance of Lillian Hellman and John Melby*. Chapel Hill, N.C., 1989.

Nicolson, Harold. *Diplomacy*. London, 1963.

Nitze, Paul. *Tension Between Opposites: Reflections on the Practice and Theory of Politics*. New York, 1993.

Nixon, Richard. *Memoirs*. New York, 1978.

Noulens, Joseph. *Mon Ambassade en Russie Sovietique, 1917–1919*. 2 vols. Paris, 1933.

Novikov, Nikolai. *Vospominaniia diplomata: Zapiski, 1937–1947*. Moscow, 1989.

O'Connor, Joseph Edward. "Lawrence A. Steinhardt and American Policy Toward the Soviet Union, 1939–1941." Ph.D. diss., University of Virginia, 1968.

Oeste, George. *John Randolph Clay: America's First Career Diplomat*. Philadelphia, 1966.

Offner, Arnold. *American Appeasement: United States Foreign Policy and Germany, 1933–1938*. Cambridge, Mass., 1969.

Okun, S. B. *Rossiisko-Amerikanskaia Kompaniia*. Leningrad, 1939.

Owsley, Frank. *King Cotton Diplomacy*. Chicago, 1959.

Paleologue, Maurice. *An Ambassador's Memoirs*. 6th ed. 3 vols. New York, n.d.

Paul, Allen. *Katyn: The Untold Story of Stalin's Polish Massacre*. New York, 1991.

Pipes, Richard. *The Russian Revolution*. New York, 1990.

Plischke, Elmer, ed. *Modern Diplomacy: The Art and the Artisans*. Washington, D.C., 1979.

Pogue, Forrest. *George C. Marshall: Statesman, 1945–1959*. New York, 1987.

Putnam, Peter. *Seven Britons in Imperial Russia, 1698–1812*. Princeton, 1952.

Raeff, Marc. *The Decembrist Movement*. Englewood Cliffs, N.J., 1966.

Reagan, Ronald. *An American Life*. New York, 1990.

Reed, John. *Ten Days That Shook the World*. New York, 1987.

Remnick, David. *Lenin's Tomb: The Last Days of the Soviet Empire*. New York, 1993.

Richardson, H. Edward. *Cassius Marcellus Clay: Firebrand of Freedom*. Lexington, Ky., 1976.

Robbins, Richard. "The Russian Famine of 1891–1892 and the Relief Policy of the Imperial Government." Ph.D. diss., Columbia University, 1973.

Robertson, James. *A Kentuckian at the Court of the Tsar: The Ministry of Cassius Marcellus Clay*. Berea., 1976.

Robien, Louis de. *The Diary of a Diplomat in Russia, 1917–1918*. New York, 1967.

Roosevelt, Elliot, ed. *FDR: His Personal Letters, 1926–1945*. 2 vols. New York, 1950.

Roosevelt, Theodore. *Autobiography*. New York, 1958.

Rosen, R. R. *Forty Years of Diplomacy*. 2 vols. London, 1922.

Rowny, Edward. *It Takes One to Tango*. Washington, D.C., 1992.

Rubin, Barry. *Secrets of State: The State Department and the Struggle over U.S. Foreign Policy*. New York, 1987.

Ruddy, Michael. *The Cautious Diplomat: Charles E. Bohlen and the Soviet Union, 1929–1969*. Kent, Ohio, 1986.

Sadoul, Jacques. *Notes sur la Révolution Bolchevique*. Paris, 1920.

Sakharov, Andrei. *Memoirs*. New York, 1990.

Saul, Norman. *Distant Friends: The Evolution of United States–Russian Relations, 1763–1867*. Lawrence, Kans., 1991.

Sazanov, Serge. *Fateful Years, 1909–1916*. London, 1928.

Schafer, Joseph, ed. *Memoirs of Jeremiah Curtin*. Vol. 2. Madison, 1940.

Schecter, Jerrold, ed. *Khrushchev Remembers: The Glasnost Tapes*. Boston, 1991.

Schoenbaum, Thomas. *Waging Peace and War: Dean Rusk in the Truman, Kennedy, and Johnson Years*. New York, 1988.

Schrecker, Ellen. *No Ivory Tower: McCarthyism and the Universities*. New York, 1986.

Schulzinger, Robert. *Henry Kissinger: Doctor of Diplomacy*. New York, 1989.

Schulzinger, Robert. *The Making of the Diplomatic Mind: The Training, Outlook, and Style of United States Foreign Service Officers, 1908–1931*. Middletown, Conn., 1975.

Scott, John. *Behind the Urals: An American Worker in Russia's City of Steel*. Bloomington, 1989.

Seward, Frederick. *Seward at Washington as Senator and Secretary of State*. New York, 1891.

Seymour, Charles. *The Intimate Papers of Colonel House*. 2 vols. Boston, 1926.

Shapiro, Leonard, ed. *Political Opposition in One-Party States*. London, 1972.

Sherwood, Robert. *Roosevelt and Hopkins: An Intimate History*. New York, 1948.

Shultz, George. *Turmoil and Triumph: My Years as Secretary of State*. New York, 1993.

Sideman, B. B., and L. Friedman, eds. *Europe Looks at the Civil War*. New York, 1960.

Sipolis, Vilnis. *The Road to Great Victory: Soviet Diplomacy, 1941–1945*. Moscow, 1984.

Sisson, Edgar. *One Hundred Red Days: A Personal Chronicle of the Bolshevik Revolution*. New Haven, 1931.

Sivachev, N., and R. Yakovlev. *Russia and the United States: U.S.–Soviet Relations from the Soviet Point of View*. Chicago, 1979.

Smith, Gaddis. *American Diplomacy During the Second World War*. New York, 1985.

Smith, Gaddis. *Morality, Reason, and Power*. New York, 1986.

Smith, Walter Bedell. *My Three Years in Moscow*. Philadelphia, 1950.

Standley, William, and Arthur Ageton. *Admiral Ambassador to Russia*. Chicago, 1955.

Stevens, Leslie. *Russian Assignment*. Boston, 1953.

Stickle, D. M. *The Beria Affair*. Commack, N.Y., 1992.

Stimson, Henry, and McGeorge Bundy. *On Active Service in Peace and War*. New York, 1947.

Stoessinger, John. *Nations in Darkness: China, Russia, and America*. New York, 1978.

Strang, William. *Home and Abroad*. Westport, Conn., 1983.

Straus, Oscar. *Under Four Administrations*. Boston, 1922.

Sulzberger, C. L. *A Long Row of Candles*. Toronto, 1969.

Talbott, Strobe, ed. *Khrushchev Remembers*. Boston, 1970.

Talbott, Strobe, ed. *Khrushchev Remembers: The Last Testament*. New York, 1974.

Tarsaidze, Alexandre. *Czars and Presidents: The Story of a Forgotten Friendship*. New York, 1958.

Taubman, William. *Stalin's American Policy: From Entente to Détente to Cold War*. New York, 1982.

Taubman, William, ed. *Khrushchev on Khrushchev: An Inside Account of the Man and His Era*. Boston, 1990.

Taylor, Marie, and Horace Scudder, eds. *Bayard Taylor: Life and Letters*. Boston, 1884.

Taylor, S. J. *Stalin's Apologist: Walter Duranty, The New York Times's Man in Moscow*. New York, 1990.

Thayer, Charles. *Bears in the Caviar*. Philadelphia, 1951.

Thayer, Charles. *Diplomat.* New York, 1959.

Thomas, Benjamin Platt. *Russo-American Relations, 1815–1867.* Baltimore, 1930.

Thompson, Arthur, and Robert Hart. *The Uncertain Crusade: America and the Russian Revolution of 1905.* Amherst, 1970.

Thompson, John. *Russia, Bolshevism, and the Versailles Peace.* Princeton, 1966.

Thompson, Kenneth, ed. *The Presidency and a World in Change.* Lanham, Md., 1991.

Thompson, Robert Smith. *The Missiles of October: The Declassified Story of John F. Kennedy and the Cuban Missile Crisis.* New York, 1992.

Tolley, Kemp. *Caviar and Commissars: The Experience of a U.S. Naval Officer in Stalin's Russia.* Annapolis, 1983.

Tomkins, Pauline. *American–Russian Relations in the Far East.* New York, 1949.

Travis, Frederick. *George Kennan and the American–Russian Relationship, 1865–1924.* Athens, Ohio, 1989.

Trevelyan, Humphrey. *Public and Private.* London, 1980.

Trevelyan, Humphrey. *Worlds Apart: China, 1953–1955, Soviet Union, 1962–1965.* London, 1971.

Trotsky, Leon. *My Life.* New York, 1970.

Tucker, Robert. *Stalin in Power: The Revolution from Above, 1928–1941.* New York, 1990.

Ulam, Adam. *Expansion and Coexistence: Soviet Foreign Policy, 1917–1973.* New York, 1974.

Ulam, Adam. *Stalin: The Man and His Era.* New York, 1973.

Uldricks, Teddy James. "The Development of the Soviet Diplomatic Corps." Ph.D. diss., Indiana University, 1972.

Ullman, Richard. *Anglo-Soviet Relations, 1917–1921.* 3 vols. Princeton, 1961–1972.

United States Department of State. *Foreign Relations of the United States.* Washington, D.C., series.

United States. Department of State. *Principal Officers of the Department of State and United States Chiefs of Mission, 1778–1988.* Washington, D.C., 1988.

Unterberger, Betty. *American Intervention in the Russian Civil War.* Lexington, Mass., 1969.

Unterberger, Betty. *America's Siberian Expedition, 1918–1920: A Study of National Policy.* Durham, N.C., 1956.

Unterberger, Betty. *The United States, Revolutionary Russia, and the Rise of Czechoslovakia.* Chapel Hill, N.C., 1989.

Valenta, Jiri. *The Soviet Invasion of Czechoslovakia, 1968: Anatomy of a Decision.* Baltimore, 1979.

Vance, Cyrus. *Hard Choices.* New York, 1983.

Van Deusen, Glyndon. *William Henry Seward.* New York, 1967.

Volkgonov, Dimitri. *Stalin: Triumph and Tragedy.* Edited and translated by Harold Shukman. New York, 1991.

Watson, Thomas, with Peter Petre. *Father, Son, and Company: My Life at IBM and Beyond.* New York, 1990.

Weil, Martin. *A Pretty Good Club: The Founding Fathers of the U.S. Foreign Service.* New York, 1978.

Weinberg, Steven. *Armand Hammer: The Untold Story.* Boston, 1989.

Weissman, Benjamin. *Herbert Hoover and Famine Relief to Soviet Russia, 1921–1923.* Stanford, 1974.

Welles, Sumner. *Seven Decisions That Shaped History.* New York, 1950.

Welles, Sumner. *The Time for Decision.* New York, 1944.

Werth, Alexander. *Russia at War, 1941–1945*. New York, 1964.

West, Rachael. *The Department of State on the Eve of the First World War*. Athens, Ga., 1978.

White, Andrew Dickson. *Autobiography*. 2 vols. New York, 1905.

White, Andrew Dickson. *A History of the Warfare of Science with Theology in Christendom*. 2 vols. New York, 1896.

White, Andrew Dickson. *Seven Great Statesmen in the Warfare of Humanity with Unreason*. New York, 1910.

White, John. *The Diplomacy of the Russo-Japanese War*. Princeton, 1964.

Williams, Robert. *Russian Art and American Money, 1900–1940*. Cambridge, Mass., 1980.

Williams, William A. *American–Russian Relations, 1781–1947*. New York, 1952.

Woldman, Albert. *Lincoln and the Russians*. Cleveland, 1952.

Wright, C. Ben. "George F. Kennan, Scholar-Diplomat: 1926–1946." Ph.D. diss., University of Wisconsin, 1972.

Yarmolinsky, Abraham, ed. *The Memoirs of Count Witte*. New York, 1967.

Yergin, Daniel. *Shattered Peace: The Origins of the Cold War and the National Security State*. Boston, 1977.

Zabriskie, Edward. *American–Russian Rivalry in the Far East: A Study in Diplomacy and Power Politics, 1895–1914*. Philadelphia, 1946.

Zetlin, Mikhail. *The Decembrists*. New York, 1958.

Zubok, Lev. *Ekspansionistkaia politika SShA v nachale XX-ogo veka*. Moscow, 1969.

Selected Journal Articles of Related Interest

Adamov, E. A. "Russia and the United States at the Time of the Civil War." *Journal of Modern History*. no. 2 (1930).

Ball, George. "JFK's Big Moment," *New York Review of Books*. February 13, 1992.

Blinn, Harold. "Seward and the Polish Rebellion of 1806," *American Historical Review* July 1940.

Bliss, Mrs. Clinton A. "Philip Jordan's Letters from Russia, 1917–1919." *Missouri Historical Society* January 1958.

Bolkhovitinov, Nikolai. "Dekabristy i Amerika." *Voprosy istorii*, no. 4 (1974).

Botkine, Pierre. "A Voice for Russia," *Century Magazine*, February 1893.

Brenner, Marie. "Mr. Ambassador! Bob Strauss Comes Home," *New Yorker*, December 28, 1992–January 4, 1992.

Clemens, Diane. "Averell Harriman, John Deane, the Joint Chiefs of Staff, and the 'Reversal of Cooperation' with the Soviet Union in April 1945," *International History Review* (May 1992).

Cockfield, Jamie. "Philip Jordan and the October Revolution, 1917." *History Today*, April 1978.

Draper, Theodore. "Little Heinz and Big Henry." *New York Times Book Review*, September 6, 1992.

Elliot, Lawrence. "Our Man in Moscow." *Reader's Digest*, April 1991.

Gaddis, John Lewis, et al. "The Soviet Side of the Cold War: A Symposium." *Diplomatic History* (Fall 1991).

Golder, Frank. "The American Civil War Through the Eyes of a Russian Diplomat." *American Historical Review* 26 (1921).

Golder, Frank. "The Purchase of Alaska," *American Historical Review* 25 (1920).

Golder, Frank. "Russian–American Relations During the Crimean War." *American Historical Review* 31 (1926).

Golder, Frank. "The Russian Fleet and the Civil War." *American Historical Review*, January 1915.

Golder, Frank. "The Russian Offer of Mediation in the War of 1812." *Political Science Quarterly*, October 1916.

Grant, Natalie. "The Russian Section, a Window on the Soviet Union." *Diplomatic History* (Winter 1978).

Greenwood, Sean. "Frank Roberts and the 'Other' Long Telegram: The View from the British Embassy in Moscow, March 1946." *Journal of Contemporary History*, January 1990.

Griffiths, David. "American Commercial Diplomacy in Russia, 1780–1783." *William and Mary Quarterly*, July 1970.

Griffiths, David. "Nikia Panin, Russian Diplomacy, and the American Revolution." *Slavic Review*, March 1969.

Harrington, Daniel. "Kennan, Bohlen, and the Riga Axioms." *Diplomatic History* (Fall 1978).

Heilbrunn, Jacob. "The Playboy of the Western World." *New Republic,* July 27, 1992.

Huntington, Samuel. "The Clash of Civilizations?" *Foreign Affairs* (Summer 1993).

Kenez, Peter. "Years of Terror." *New Leader,* December 10–24, 1990.

Kennan, George. "The Sisson Documents." *Journal of Modern History*, June 1956.

Kennan, George [X., pseud.]. "The Sources of Soviet Conduct." *Foreign Affairs*, July 1947.

Kirk, Alan. "The People in Russia." *Look,* April 22, 1952.

Kolesnichenko, D. A. "Dzhordzh Kennan i tsarskaia okhranka." *Prometei*, no. 7 (1969).

Kushner, Howard. "The Russian Fleet and the American Civil War: Another View." *The Historian* August 1972.

Langley, Harold. "Hunt for American Archives in the Soviet Union." *American Archivist*, April 1966.

Laqueur, Walter, ed. "The Western Image of the Soviet Union, 1917–1962," *Survey* (April 1962).

Lawrence, W. H. "Assignment to Moscow, Toughest of Posts," *New York Times Magazine*, June 12, 1949.

Long, John. "American Intervention in Russia: The North Russia Expedition, 1918–1919." *Diplomatic History* (Winter 1982).

Luce, Clare Booth. "The Ambassadorial Issue: Professional or Amateurs." *Foreign Affairs*, October 1957.

Lyons, Eugene. "To Tell or Not To Tell." *Harper's,* June 1935.

Maclean, Elizabeth Kimball. "Joseph E. Davies and Soviet–American Relations, 1941–1943." *Diplomatic History* (Winter 1980).

Maddox, Robert James. "Woodrow Wilson, the Russian Embassy, and Siberian Intervention." *Pacific Historical Review,* November 1967.

Maddux, Thomas. "American Diplomats and the Soviet Experiment: The View from the Moscow Embassy, 1914–1939." *South Atlantic Quarterly* (Autumn 1975).

Mastny, Vojtech. "The Cassandra in the Foreign Commissariat: Maxim Litvinov and the Cold War," *Foreign Affairs* (January 1976).

Matlock, Jack. "Changes in Our World and in Our Profession." *Newsletter of American Association for the Advancement of Slavic Studies,* November 1990.

Matlock, Jack. "Literature and Politics: The Impact of Fyodor Dostoevsky." *Political Science Reviewer* (Fall 1989).

Matlock, Jack. "Prospect for U.S.–Soviet Relations." Marshall Visitor Address, International House, New York, 1989.

Matlock, Jack. "U.S.–Soviet Relations: A View from Moscow." *Occasional Papers,* Ser. 2 no. 5. Graduate School of International Studies, University of Miami, August 1989.

Matlock, Jack. "U.S.–Soviet Relations: Status and Prospects." *Studia Diplomatica* 39 (1986).

Morgan, George [Historicus, pseud.]. "Stalin on Revolution." *Foreign Affairs,* January 1949.

Nagengast, William. "Moscow, the Stalingrad of 1812: America's Reaction Toward Napoleon's Retreat From Russia." *Russian Review* 8 (1949).

Nagengast, William. "The Visit of the Russian Fleet to the United States: Were Americans Deceived?" *Russian Review,* January 1949.

Orlov, A., and C. Tushkeich. "Pact 1939 goda: Alternativy ne Bylo." *Literaturnaia Gazeta,* October 26, 1988.

Parry, Albert. "Cassius Clay's Glimpse into the Future: Lincoln's Envoy to St. Petersburg Bade the Two Nations Meet in East Asia," *Russian Review,* April 1943.

Phillips, Hugh. "Mission to America: Maksim Litvinov in the United States, 1941–1943." *Diplomatic History* (Summer 1988).

Propas, Frederic. "Creating a Hard Line Toward Russia: The Training of the State Department Soviet Experts, 1927–1937." *Diplomatic History* (Summer 1984).

Raeff, Marc. "An American View of the Decembrist Revolt." *Journal of Modern History* 25 (1953).

Reynolds, Quentin. "Diplomat on the Spot." *Collier's,* July 24, 1943.

Rukeyeser, Walter Arnold. "I Work for Russia: How the Worker Lives." *The Nation,* June 3, 1931.

Sayle, Murray. "Closing the File on Flight 007." *New Yorker,* December 13, 1993.

Schoenberg, Philip. "The American Reaction to the Kishinev Pogrom of 1903." *American Jewish Historical Quarterly* (March 1974).

Sipols, V. "Za neskol'ko mesiatsev do 23-ogo Avgusta 1939 goda." *Mezhdunarodnaia Zhizn,* May 1989.

Standley, William. "Stalin and World Unity." *Collier's,* June 30, 1945.

Tolstaya, Tatyana. "In Cannibalistic Times." *New York Review of Books,* April 11, 1991.

Tucker, Robert. "Towards a Comparative Politics of Movement Regimes." *American Political Science Review,* June 1961.

Ullmann, Richard. "The Davies Mission and United States–Soviet Relations, 1937–1941." *World Politics,* January 1957.

Zubok, V. "Soviet Intelligence and the Cold War: The 'Small' Committee of Information, 1952–1953." Cold War International History Project, Woodrow Wilson Center for Scholars, December 1992.

INDEX

ABM Treaty, 221
Acheson, Dean, 4, 152, 171–172, 177–180, 183–185, 193
Adams, Charles Francis, 36, 39, 42, 66
Adams, John, 12, 14
Adams, John Quincy, 6, 13, 16–18, 20–23, 27, 32–33, 53, 66, 239, 258
  approval of Napoleon's defeat, 20
  relations with Russian officialdom, 19
  skillful diplomacy, 28–29
  understanding of things Russian, 19
Adams, Sherman, 195
Afghanistan, Soviet invasion of, 4, 227, 235–236, 240, 242
Akhmatova, Anna, 134, 162, 197
Akhromeyev, Sergei, 245
Alabama (Confederate ship), 36, 46
Alaska, 16
  sale of, 35, 44–46, 68
Alexander I, 18–22, 25, 28, 162
Alexander II, 36–37, 43–44, 46–47, 54, 57
  assassination attempts on, 48–49
  government's attitude toward U.S. Civil War, 36–39
Alexander III, 50, 56
Alexandra (empress), 61, 74–75
Alexis (grand duke), 47
Algiers, 16
Aliluyeva, Svetlana, 220
Allied Control Commission for Italy, 143
Ambassadorial diplomacy, 3–4
  contrasted with high diplomacy, 4
  durability of, 5
  poor reputation of, 4–5, 28
Ambassador, The (James), vii
American Communist party, 115, 123

American Federation of Labor, 78, 101
American Historical Association, 53
American Red Cross, 78, 87, 99, 201
American Relief Administration, 85, 97, 104
  aims of Russian campaign, 96
Amerika (magazine), 174
Amicus, 30
Amin, Hafizullah, 236
Andreychin, George, 112
Andreyev, Andrei, 184
Andropov, Yuri, 237, 240, 242
Anglo-Japanese accord (1902), 60
Anglo-Soviet treaty (1942), 136
Angola, 227, 240
Antietam, 36, 42
Apollo–Soyuz mission, 232
Appomattox, 38
Arbatov, Georgi, 231
Arendt, Hannah, 108
Argentina, 71
Armour, Norman, 192
Arms race, 33, 179
Atlantic Charter, 126
Atomic bomb
  first Soviet detonation, 171
  U.S. monopoly, 152, 160, 165
Auchwitz, 106, 162
Austerlitz, battle of, 20
Austria, 17, 23, 69, 124, 207, 246
Autobiography (White), 55

Babbit (Lewis), 233
Backfire bomber, 240
Bakatin, Vadim, 244, 250, 252
Baker, John, 203
Bakhmetev, George, 71

Bakunin, M., 48
Ball, George, 200
Baltic republics, 129, 151, 162, 257
    nonaggression pacts with USSR, 114
Bancroft, George, 66
Banks, N. P., 45
Barbour, Walworth, 181
Battle of Russia (film), 137
Bay of Pigs invasion, 207
Beam, Jacob, 197, 223–226, 229, 232, 235,
    238, 254
    career and background of, 221–222
Beaverbrook, Lord, 132, 140, 149
Belarus, 252
Belgium, 129
Belinisky, V., 31
Benckendorf, Alexander, 24
Benjamin, Judah, 42
Bennington College, 150
Bergh, Henry, 40–41
Beria, Lavrenti, 170, 184, 191
    arrest and execution, 199
Berkman, Alexander, 80
Berlin
    blockade and airlift, 7, 165, 167–168
    Conference (1878), 3
    crisis (1948), 159
    Wall, 207
Berlin, Isaiah, 197
Bessmertnykh, Alexander, 247
Bethmann-Hollweg, Theobald von, 69–70
Bevin, Ernest, 167
Biddle, Anthony, 126
Biely, Andrei, 11–12
Big Three, 7
Bismarck, Otto von, 3, 41, 43, 47
Blackford, Hattie, 47–48
Blaine, James, 51
Blake, Robert, 176
Blum, Leon, 115
Bobrinski, Count, 59
Bodisco, Alexander, 29
Bogrov, Dimitri, 57
Bohlen, Avis, 197
Bohlen, Charles, 3, 6–7, 10, 32, 98–99, 101,
    107, 109, 112, 114, 116, 121, 124–126,
    150, 178, 182–184, 201, 203–204, 208,
    210–211, 213–215, 238, 246, 254, 256
    ambassadorial tenure, 195–200
    appointment hearings, 192–194
    criticism of Joseph Davies, 119
    on death of Stalin, 293n.1
    education and background, 10
    influence of Soviet terror on, 118
    meeting with Molotov, 197–198
    view of Harriman, 151
Boker, George, 49
BOLERO (World War II), 144
Bolivia, 176
Booth, John Wilkes, 43
Borah, William, 101

Bor-Komorowski (general), 137, 156
Borodino, battle of, 18
Boster, Davis, 166, 176
Botkine, Pierre, 52–53
Bowles, Chester, 213
Bracy, Arnold, 244
Bradley, Follett (major general), 234
Brandes, George, 52
Brandt, Willy, 222
Braun (priest), 144
Brecht, Bertolt, 271n.6
Breckinridge, Clifton, 56
Brement, Marshall, 227
Brest-Litovsk negotiations, 80–82
Brezhnev, Leonid, 64, 222–223, 226–227,
    229–231, 237, 240–242
Brezhnev Doctrine, 237
Bricker, John, 193
Bridges, Styles, 176, 193
"Bronze Horseman" (Pushkin), 11–12
Browder, Earl, 115
Brown, Harold, 233
Brown, Neill, 6, 26, 29–34, 168, 258
Brown, William, 244
Brown University, 233–235
Bruce, David, 193, 196, 213
Brusilov, Alexis (general), 74, 76
Bryan, William Jennings, 68, 71, 97
Bryant, Louise, 79, 86
Brzezinski, Zbigniew, 108, 229
Bucar, Annabelle, 174, 176
Buchanan, Sir Andrew, 41
Buchanan, Sir George, 68, 70
Buchanan, James, 25–29, 31–32
Budenny, Semyen, 110
Bugbee, Fred (colonel), 85
Bukharin, N., 93, 109, 112, 118–119
Bulgakov, Mikhail, 164
Bulganin, Nikolai, 170, 195, 198–199
Bullard, Arthur, 87
Bullitt, William, 3, 7, 12, 32–33, 86, 101–102,
    103, 108–110, 112–113, 116–118, 120,
    125, 134–135, 180, 254
    airplane accident involving, 280n.15
    anti-Jewish remarks, 113
    assessment of embassy staff, 117
    collaboration with Kelley in selecting embassy
        staff, 110
    critical view of USSR, 117
    ebullience of, 133
    introduction of polo and baseball to USSR,
        112
    meeting with Stalin, 111
    1919 secret mission and agreement with
        Soviets, 88, 275n.69
    plot in embassy against, alleged, 114–115
    reaction to 1935 Comintern meeting, 115–
        116
    reason for his selection as ambassador, 110
Bull Run, battles of, 38, 42
Bundy, McGeorge, 234

Burns, James MacGregor, 217
Burns, James (major general), 133, 140, 146–147
Burt, Richard, 246
Bush, George, 242, 244, 247–248, 251–253
Butler, Hugh, 145
Byrnes, James, 159–160, 166, 168

Cadets (Russia), 63
Cambodia, 106
Cameron, Simon, 35, 39, 66, 258
    exiled to St. Petersburg, 41
Campbell, George Washington, 27
Canada, 35–36
    U.S. invasion of, 18, 21
Carlsbad Program, 124
Carnegie Endowment for International Peace, 193
Carter, Jimmy, 7, 227, 229–233, 235–237
Carter Doctrine, 236
Casablanca Conference (1943), 144
Cassini, Count, 61–62
Casterlereagh, Viscount Robert Stewart, 21
Castro, Fidel, 205, 217, 240
Catacazy, Constantine, 46–48
Cathcart, Lord, 19
Catholic Church (USSR), persecution of, 97
Catherine the Great, 11, 13, 15, 22
    attitude toward U.S. War of Independence, 14
    "Mother of Independence," 17
Central America, 29
Central Intelligence Agency, 219, 244, 247
    presence in Embassy Moscow, 219
Century Magazine, 52
Cessarskaya, Emma, 95
Ceylon, 200
Chaadaev, Peter, 23
Chaikovsky, Nicholas, 83
Chamberlain, Neville, 162
Chamberlin, William Henry, 94
Chataigneau, Yves, 167
Chayes, Abram, 209
Chekhov, Anton, 112
Chernenko, Konstantin, 240, 242
Chernobyl, 242
Chicago, Great Fire of, 47
Chicherin, Georgi, 83, 85, 96
Chile, 227
Chilston, Viscount, 123
China, 61, 63, 102, 108, 115, 124, 138, 159–160, 171, 226
China hands, 176
Chmykhalov family, 231
Churchill, Winston, 3, 83, 137–140, 149, 159, 166, 192, 210, 234
    iron curtain speech, 23, 160, 167
    meeting with Stalin
        August 1942, 144
        October 1944, 152
CIA. See Central Intelligence Agency
City of Flint (U.S. ship) affair, 127

Civil War (Russian), foreign intervention in, 83–84, 96
Civil War (U.S.), 32, 35–43, 53, 68, 88
Clark Kerr, Archibald, 142, 146, 149, 154
Clausewitz, Karl von, 67
Clay, Cassius Marcellus, 35, 39–42, 44–45, 53, 65–66, 88, 254, 258
    expertise on Russia, 46
    preministerial career, 39
    view of Polish-Russian conflict, 40
Clay, Green, 40
Clay, Henry, 25, 39
Clay, Lucius, 161
Clayton, William, 158
Cleveland, Grover, 71
Clifford, Clark, 162–163, 252
Clinton, Bill, 254
Clubb, Edmund O., 176
Cody, Buffalo Bill, 47
Cold War, vii, 3–5, 7, 23, 33, 64, 139, 161, 163, 169, 171, 187, 208, 216, 236, 255, 258
Cole, Felix, 84–85
Coleman, Frederic, 97
Collectivization (USSR), 6
Collins, James, 252–253
Columbia University, 171, 176, 224, 246
COMECON, 248
Cominform, 169, 198
Comintern, 98, 101, 103, 105, 137, 147
    meddling in U.S. labor organizations, 96
    Seventh Congress Meeting, 115
Commercial treaties
    Russian-U.S. (1832), 29, 56, 64, 106
    Soviet-U.S. (1938), 125
Commonwealth of Independent States, 257
Confederacy (C.S.A.), 35–37, 39–40, 42
Congo, 204, 207
Conquest, Robert, 106
Conspiracy Against Peace (Parker), 182
Constantine (grand duke), 44
Constituent Assembly, 81
Containment, 33, 170, 172, 192
Continental Congress, 11–14, 16
Continental System, 18, 20
Coolidge, Calvin, 96
Cornell University, 27, 53
Coulondre, Robert, 119, 123
Crane, Charles, 66
Creel, George, 87
Crimean War, 35, 37–38, 45, 53, 98
    defects of Russian army, 30
    U.S. attitude toward Russia, 29–30
Cripps, Sir Stafford, 129–130
Crocodile (magazine), 197
Crosley, Walter (captain), 86
Cross, Samuel, 107
Cuba, 29, 205, 207. See also Bay of Pigs
    missile crisis, 4, 208–209, 211, 217
Curtin, Andrew, 47
Curtin, Jeremiah, 41

Curzon line, 130
Custine, Astolphe Louis Léonor, Marquis de,
    22, 25–26, 30–31, 54, 168, 214
  compared with Kennan (younger), 33
  compared with Tocqueville, 23
  critique of Russia, 23–24
  influence on twentieth-century U.S. diplo-
    mats, 32–33
Czechoslovakia, 114, 165, 170
  coup (1948), 7
  crisis with Germany (1938), 124
  invasion by Warsaw Pact, 213, 220

Dallas, George, 25–27, 30–31
Dana, Francis, 11–12, 14–15, 18, 32, 37, 258
  personality and background, 13
Daniloff, Nicholas, 243
Dashkov, Andrei, 21–22
Davies, John Paton, 168, 176, 178, 183, 185,
    187
  on Sino-Soviet relations, 169, 171–172
Davies, Joseph, 3–4, 7, 120, 124–125, 134–
    135, 140, 146, 149, 183–184, 202, 233,
    254, 258
  assessment of Soviet power, 122
  assessment of Stalin, 147
  on the balance of power, 123
  goals in Moscow, 119
  Machiavellian instinct of, 133
  Mission to Moscow, 109, 118–119, 121–122,
    137, 147–148
  and the purges, 118–119, 121
  respect for Foreign Service staff, 121
Davis, Richard, 182–183, 228
Davis, Angela, 223
Davis, Jefferson, 43
D-Day, 138
Deane, John, 150, 152–153, 155–156, 162
Decembrists, 16, 25, 31
Declaration on Liberated Europe, 152, 154
deCram, Matilda, 72, 74, 78, 80, 86
Decree on Peace, 80
De Gaulle, Charles, 144
Demichev, Pyotr, 231
Democracy in America (Tocqueville), 23
Denmark, 20, 129
De Santis, Hugh, 4
Détente, 7, 100, 208, 212–213, 221, 223–227,
    229–230, 235, 238
Diamandi, Count Constantine, 81–83
Diplomacy of Silence, The (De Santis), 4
Djilas, Milovan, 164–165
Dnieper–Liman campaign (June 1788), 16
Dobrynin, Anatoly, 209, 216, 220, 222, 224,
    226, 229, 231, 234, 253
Doctor Zhivago (Pasternak), 110
Dombrovine, Hadimir, 49
Donovan, William, 153
Dostoevsky, Feodor, 31, 246
Dreher, Robert, 173
Dreiser, Theodore, 94, 134

Dubček, Alexander, 220
Dubs, Adolph, 224
Duke University, 171, 246
Dulles, Allen, 186
Dulles, John Foster, 7, 185–186, 192–199, 202,
    228
  appreciation of Llewellyn Thompson, 201
  views on liberation and rollback, 179–180
Dungan (congressman), 56
Duranty, Walter, 94, 101, 107, 109, 120
Durbrow, Elbridge, 110, 168
Durnovo, Peter, 68
Dyess, William, 221
Dzerzhinsky, Felix, 93

East European Affairs, Division of (State Depart-
    ment), 98–99
  liquidation of, 279n.45
East Germany, 207, 219
Ecole Nationale des Langues Orientales Vi-
    vantes, 100
Eddy, Spencer, 58
Eden, Anthony, 192
Egypt, 213
Eisenhower, Dwight D., 7, 166, 192–196, 198,
    205, 207–208
El Salvador, 240
Elsey, George, 162
Emancipation Proclamation, 37
Embassy Moscow (U.S.)
  CIA presence, 219
  fire
    1977, 232
    1991, 245
  security problems, 120, 173–175, 181, 203,
    223, 232, 243–246, 253, 303N.17,
    304n.18
  withdrawal of Soviet employees, 243–244,
    303n.14
Emerson, Ralph Waldo, 54
Engels, Friedrich, 151
Enoukidze, A., 104
Estonia, 97
Ethiopia, 227, 240
Eulogius (bishop), 59
European Union, 258
Evart, William, 51
Everett, Edward, 26

Fairbanks, Jr., Douglas, 142
Falconet, Etienne, 15
Famine
  in Russia
    1891–1892, 55
    1921–1923, 85, 93, 96, 106
  in the Ukraine
    1931–1933, 104, 106
    1946–1947, 164
Faymonville, Philip, 110, 146–148, 150
Federalists, 21
Feighan (congressman), 203

Ferdinand, Archduke Francis, 67
Finland, 57, 128–131
  war with USSR, 127, 133
Fischer, Louis, 94
Five-Year Plan
  first, 93
  second, 117
Ford, Gerald, 226, 229
Ford, Robert, 235, 238
Foreign Service (U.S.), reform of, 98, 178, 254
Foreign Service Journal, 228
Forrestal, James, 161–162, 170, 197
Fort Sumter, 32, 43
Foster, John, 35, 49–51, 64–65
Foster, William, 115
Fourteen Points, 88–89
Fourth International Prison Congress (1890), 53
Fox, Gustavus, 44
France, 19, 21, 23–24, 28, 36, 39, 47, 68. 80,
  83, 99, 102, 114, 117, 123–124, 129–130,
  135–136, 138, 224
  attitude toward U.S. Civil War, 36
  Franco-Prussian War, 47
  revolution, 17, 25, 63
Francis, David, 4, 67, 71–72, 76–83, 85–89,
  141, 233, 258
  anti-Bolshevik views, 84
  attitude toward Jewry, 73, 80
  compared with Marye, 74–75
  contemporaries' assessment, 86
  meeting with Lenin, 81
  preambassadorial career, 71
  work on behalf of German and Austrian
  POWs, 73–74
Franklin, Benjamin, 12, 14, 16, 186
FRANTIC (World War II), 153
Friedland, battle of, 20
Friedrich, Carl, 108
Frost, Robert, 217

Galbraith, John Kenneth, 213
Garnett, Norris, 219
Garrison, Mark, 235–237, 301n.62
Gascoigne, Sir A. D. F., 180, 210
Geneva Conference (1955), 195
George III, 13–14
Georgetown University, 101
German, Robert, 235
Germany, 26, 47, 83, 99, 102–103, 105, 108–
  109, 115–116, 121, 131–135, 138, 140,
  155, 158, 161, 162, 166, 168, 175, 184,
  214, 224, 246, 248, 257. *See also* East
  Germany, West Germany
  crisis with Czechoslavia (1938), 124
  invasion of USSR, 136–137
  Khrushchev's view of, 204–206
  nonaggression pact with USSR, 7, 123–125,
  129–130, 148
  World War I, 67–71, 77, 79
Gero, Erno, 199
Gettysburg, 43

Ghana, 246
Gibbon, Edward, 239
Gibson, Hugh, 192
Giers, Nicholas de, 51
Gilmore, Eddie, 148
glasnost, 241, 249
Globe (newspaper), 29
Goebbels, Joseph, 167
Gogol, Nikolai, 31
Goldman, Emma, 80
Goldschmidt, Sir Julian, 54
Goldwater, Barry, 193
Gompers, Samuel, 78
Gomulka solution, 199
Gorbachev, Mikhail, vii, 7, 241–242, 245–251,
  253–254, 256
Gorchakov, Alexander, 37–38, 40, 42–44, 46,
  77
  talks with Baynard Taylor, 42
GPU (State Political Administration), 126
Grand Alliance, 4, 7, 100, 121, 135, 157, 160
  character of, 136–139
Grant, Ulysses, 46–47
Great Britain, 13, 21, 24, 27–29, 38–39, 44,
  68, 80, 83, 99, 102, 123–124, 131, 137,
  140
  Anglo-Soviet treaty (1942), 136
  attitude toward U.S. Civil War, 36
Great Patriotic War, cult of, 136
Greece, 129, 167, 213–214
Greeley, Horace, 45
Gresham, W. Q., 55
Grew, Joseph, 66, 192
Grimm, Baron Friedrich von, 16
Gromyko, Andrei, 120, 140, 150, 186, 205,
  224, 226, 231, 236–237, 242
Gromyko, Mrs. Andrei, 197
Guatemala, 176–177
Gubichev, Valentine, 173
Guild, Curtis, 58–59
Gumberg, Alexander, 81
Gumilev, Nicholas, 94
Gwin, William, 30
GYMNAST (World War II), 144

Habsburg Empire, 69, 239
Haig, Alexander, 240–241
Hamilton College, 171
Hammer, Armand, 95
Hammer, Julius, 95
Hanson, George, 110, 114–115, 117
Harding, Warren, 96–97
Harper, Samuel, 72, 104, 107
Harriman, Kathleen, 150, 156
Harriman, W. Averell, 3–4, 95, 139–140, 149,
  152, 159, 162–163, 176, 203, 208, 213,
  215, 229, 233, 235, 254
  attitude toward Standley, 144–145
  meeting with Stalin (1941), 132
  relations and disagreement with FDR, 156–
  158

Harriman, W. Averell (*Continued*)
    relations with and judgment of Stalin, 151
    Soviet perception of, 150, 153
    on surrender of Japan, 154–155
Harris, Chauncy, 217
Harris, Sir James, 13–15
Harris, Levett, 17
    questionable conduct of, 19–20
Harrison, Benjamin, 51, 53
Hartman, Arthur, 240, 242–244
    embassy security problems during tenure,
        303n.17
    pre-Moscow career, 241
Harvard Law School, 124
Harvard University, 16, 60, 98–99, 107, 224
Hay, John, 60, 66
Hayter, William, 196
Henderson, Loy, 98, 101, 107, 109–110, 112,
        114, 116, 119–120, 125–126, 131, 183
    compared with Thompson, 200, 202
    early experience and background, 99
    evaluation of Zinoviev–Kamenev trial, 117–
        118
    friendship with Kohler, 214
Henlein, Konrad, 124
Henry, Patrick, 253
Herter, Christian, 200
Herwarth, Hans von, 125
Herzen, Alexander, 24
Heyking (colonel), 49
High diplomacy, 3, 5
Hilton (general), 174
Hiss, Alger, 192–193
*History of the Warfare of Science with Theology
    in Christendom* (White), 64
Hitler, Adolf, 102, 106, 114, 116, 123–124,
        130, 132, 135, 140, 148, 158, 162
Ho Chi Minh, 213, 237
Hoffman, Wickham, 49
Hoffmann, Stanley, 105
Hollander, Paul, 4
Holmes, Oliver Wendell, 37
Holy Alliance, 22, 28
Hone, Philip, 28
Hoover, Herbert, 85, 96
Hope, Bob, 237
Hopkins, Harry, 140, 157, 193
    disagreement with Harriman on lend-lease,
        153
    meeting with Stalin
        1941, 132
        1945, 158–159
Hot Line, 213, 242
House, Colonel Edward, 69–70, 77, 84, 87–88
Hughes, Charles, 97
Hull, Cordell, 102–105, 121, 123, 125, 127–
        128, 130–131, 140, 143, 147, 149
Human rights, 64, 223, 230, 246
Hungary, 23, 165, 248
    1956 revolution, 198–199
Hunt, William, 51, 64

Huntington, Samuel, 259
Huntington, Samuel (president of Continental
        Congress), 13, 15
Hydrogen bomb, 171

Ignatiev, Count Nicholas, 50
Imperial Academy of Science, 14, 19
Ingersoll, C. M., 6, 24, 27, 31
Iran, 160, 166–167
    crisis (1946), 159
Iran-Contra affair, 211
Iraq, 256
Iron curtain speech (Churchill), 23, 160, 167
Isolationist policy (U.S.), 7
Italy, 105
Izvestia, 102, 184, 242

Jackson, Andrew, 25, 28–29
Jackson, Henry, 223, 227
Jackson, Stonewall, 42
Jackson–Vanik amendment, 224
James, Henry, vii
Japan, 64, 97, 103, 105, 111, 113, 115, 123–
        124, 131, 133, 138, 186, 257
    alliance with Russia (1916), 7
    Anglo-Japanese accord (1902), 60
    surrender of, 154–155
    war with Russia, 35, 60–63
Jaruzelski, Wojciech, 240
Jay, John, 12
Jeannette (U.S. ship), rescue of, 51
Jefferson, Thomas, 16, 18
Jenner, William, 176
Jewell, Marshall, 47–48
Jewish Defense League, 223
Jews
    discrimination of U.S. Jews in Russia, 48, 50
    German genocide of, 106
    refugees from Russia in U.S., 51, 55
    Russian, 6, 48, 58–59, 64, 69, 73, 80, 113
Johnson, Andrew, 45
Johnson, Edwin, 193
Johnson, Lyndon, 213, 219
Joint Chiefs of Staff, 170
Jones, Gareth, 104
Jones, John Paul, 16–17
Jordan, Philip, 72, 80
Journal de St. Petersburg, 42
Journey from St. Petersburg to Moscow (Rad-
        ishchev), 15
Judson, William (general), 79–81, 86, 88

Kadar, Janos, 199
Kaganovich, Lazar, 170, 200, 204
Kaledin (general), 80
Kalinin, Mikhail, 111, 121, 124, 180
Kalpashnikov affair, 80
Kamenev, Leo, 93, 109, 117–118
Kandinsky, Wassily, 94
Kant, Immanuel, 54
Karakozov, Dimitri, 43

Karmal, Babrak, 236
Katyn massacre, 137, 148, 156, 181
Kazakhstan, 252
Kelley, Sir David, 173, 186
Kelley, Robert, 104, 106–107, 110, 120
  education and background, 98–99
  reservations about recognizing USSR, 102–103
Kenez, Peter, 106
Kennan, George (elder), 52–53, 55, 59–60
Kennan, George (younger), 3–4, 6, 12, 32–33,
    98, 101, 107, 109–110, 112, 114, 116–
    117, 120, 122, 124, 134, 139, 150, 152,
    154, 156, 159, 163, 165, 170–171, 176,
    180, 182, 185–187, 196–197, 200–201,
    210, 213, 215, 225, 234, 239, 241, 246,
    254–256, 258
  conflict with Toon, 228
  criticism of Davies, 119
  evaluation of Harriman, 149
  influence of Soviet terror on, 118
  objection to U.S. intelligence operations in
    Moscow, 181
  persona non grata in USSR, 183–184
  pre-Soviet career, 99–100
  theory of diplomacy, 178–179
  writing and impact of Long Telegram, 161–162
  X article, 34
Kennedy, John F., 192, 205, 207, 209, 213,
    216
  American University speech, 208
Kennedy, Joseph, 125
Kennedy, Paul, 259
Kennedy, Robert, 208–209, 211, 213
Kerensky, Alexander, 76–79, 86–87
  government's debt, 113
KGB (Committee of State Security), 223, 227,
    232, 244–245, 253
Khrushchev, Nikita, 7, 191, 196, 199–200,
    202–204, 206–208, 216, 219, 248
  de-Stalinization campaign, 195
  Kohler's assessment, 215
Khrushchev, Mrs. Nikita, 202
Khrushchev, Sergei, 202
Kim Il Sung, 172
Kirk, Alan, 165–166, 172–173, 177, 186–187,
    254
  on Soviet Marxism, 170–171
Kirk, Alexander, 121, 125
  on Soviet attitude toward German–Czech
    crisis, 124
Kirk, Lydia, 175
Kirkland, Lane, 234
Kirov, Sergei, 116–118
Kissinger, Henry, 7, 223, 225–226, 229, 232–
    234, 238, 241
  criticism by Beam of, 222
  modus operandi, 221–222
Knowland, William, 185
Knox, Philander, 58–59

Kohler, Foy, 168, 208, 213, 216, 232, 237,
    241, 246, 254, 258
  Arlington incident, 214–215
  compared with Kennan, Bohlen, and
    Thompson, 215
  on East–West economic relations, 218–219
  on Soviet attitude toward world war, 170
  on usefulness of exchange programs, 217–218
Kolchak, Alexander, 84
Komissarov, Osip, 43–44
Kontinent Quarterly, 230
Korea, 60, 63, 159
Korean Airlines (KAL) flight 007, 240, 242
Korean War, 4, 7, 159, 165, 171–173, 175,
    179, 181–182, 187, 197
  POWs, 223
Kornienko, Georgi, 230
Kornilov, Lavr (general), 76, 86
Kosciuszko, Thaddeus, 17
Kosenkina, Madame, 173
Kossuth, Lajos, 29–30
Kosygin, Alexei, 206, 213, 222–223, 228
Krabbe, (admiral), 37
Kremlinology, 187
Kryuchkov, Vladimir, 247, 258
Kuhlmann, Richard von, 82
Kuibyshev, 131, 141
Kulaks, struggle against, 101
Kuniholm, Bertel, 110, 114, 117
Kuwait, 256
Kuznetsov, V. V., 235

LaGuardia, Fiorello, 86
Lamar, L. Q. C., 37, 42
Lansing, Robert, 74, 77–78, 87–88, 193
Laos, 204
Lapschin, Konstantin, 174
Laqueur, Walter, 252, 254
Laski, Harold, 94
Latvia, 97
Lauriston, Count, 20
League of Armed Neutrality, 13
League of Nations, 88–89, 114
Ledyard, John, 17
Lee, Robert E., 36
Lehrs, John, 97–98, 100
Lend-lease, 132, 134, 143, 147, 151–154, 157–
    159, 187, 256
  delays in delivery of, 142, 144
  repayment of, 175
  Soviet ingratitude for, 145–146
  value of, 138
Lend-Lease Administration, 133, 146
Lenin, V. I., vii, 76, 78, 80–82, 86, 88–89,
    93, 96, 112, 151, 239
  lessons of New Economic Policy, 276n.1
  thesis on inevitable conflict, 85
Leningrad, siege of, 133
Leningrad Symphony (Shostakovich), 136
Limited Test Ben Treaty, 212, 217
Lincoln, Abraham, 34, 37–41, 43, 88

Lindley, Francis, 82
Lippmann, Walter, 160
Lisiansky, Yuri, 16
Literary life in USSR (1946–1953), 289n.2
Lithuania, 97, 247
Litvinov, Maxim, 96, 102, 104, 106, 111, 113–115, 120–121, 125, 148
Liverpool, Lord, 21
Livingston, Edward, 29
Lockhart, R. H., 78–79, 83
Lomonosov, Mikhail, 14
Londonderry, Lady, memoirs of, 241
London Disarmament Conference (1935), 139
London *Times*, 39
Lonetree, Clayton, 244
Long Telegram, 34, 139, 161, 162
Look (magazine), 173
Loris-Melikov, Mikhail, 49–50, 57
Los Angeles Olympics (1984), 240
Lothrop, George, 53, 65
Louis XVI, 62
Lozovsky, Solomon, 141
Lusitania (British ship), 70
Luxembourg, 129
Lvov, George, 76
Lyons, Eugene, 94
Lysenko, Trofim, 164

MacArthur, Douglas, 154
McCarran, Patrick, 176, 193
McCarthy, Joseph, 17, 193–194
McCarthyism, 175–176, 187, 210–211, 246
McCormack, John, 127
McCormack, Robert, 66
Macgowan, David, 97–100
Machiavelli, Niccolò, 257
McLeod, Scott, 193–194, 211, 214
McMillin, James, 174
McNamara, Robert, 209, 211, 219
Madison, James, 18, 21
Magidoff, Robert, 174
Maisky, Ivan, 148
Malenkov, Georgi, 170, 184, 191–192, 198, 199–200, 204
Malik, Jacob, 179
Maltsev, Viktor, 236
Manchuria, 60, 102, 154, 171–172
Mandelstam, Nadezhda, 225
Mandelstam, Osip, 94
Manhattan Project, 138
Mann, Dudley, 36
Mao Tse-tung, 160, 165, 192, 206
Marcy, William, 30
Marshall, George, 150, 165–168, 170, 193
Marshall Plan, 159, 186
Martens, Robert, 196, 203
Marx, Karl, 24–25, 30, 150–151
    criticism of Russia and Nicolas I, 22–23
Marye, George, 66–68, 71, 73–74, 85–86, 89, 233, 258
    early career and background, 70

work on behalf of German and Austrian POWs, 69
Mason, James, 36
Master and Margarita (Bulgakov), 164
Matlock, Jack, 3–4, 7, 239–240, 245–246, 248–254, 256, 258
    background, 246
    on life in Embassy Moscow (1988–1991), 306n.44
    on possible coup in Moscow (August 1991), 305n.37, 306n.48
    on relationship between U.S. diplomats and journalists in USSR, 305n.42
    on security problems at U.S. embassy during Hartman's tenure, 303n.17
    on withdrawal of Soviet employees from U.S. embassy, 303n.14
Matlock, Joseph, 247
Matlock, Rebecca, 216, 246
Maximilian (archduke), 36
Mayakovsky, Vladimir, 94
Mazzini, Giuseppe, 30
Meany, George, 225, 230
Meiklejohn, Robert, 150
Melby, John, 150, 156, 176, 187
Menshikov, Mikhail, 202
Mexico, 35–36, 102, 105
Meyer, George von Lengerke, 35, 50, 61–65, 128, 258
Mezentsev (general), 49
Mezhlauk, Valery, 121
Miantonomoh (U.S. ship), 44
Mica, Dan, 244
Michella, Joseph, 146, 148
Mićunović, Veljko, 195–196
Middleton, Henry, 26, 28, 31–32
    background and attitudes, 24
    disagreement with Marx and Custine, 25
    objection to Decembrists, 25, 31
Mikolajeczk, Stanislaw, 156
Mikoyan, Anastas, 153, 184
Miliukov, Paul, 75, 77
Milosz, Czeslaw, 165
Mirbach, Count, 83
Mission to Moscow (Davies), 109, 118–119, 121–122, 137, 147–148
Mitterand, François, 253
Molotov, Vyacheslav, 137, 141–144, 148, 152–153, 156, 158, 160, 166, 168, 170, 184, 195, 200
    exile in Outer Mongolia, 204
    meeting with Bohlen, 197–198
    on surrender of Japan, 154–155
    talks with Smith, 167
Monitor (Union ship), 43
Monnet, Jean, 257
Monroe, James, 20, 24, 28, 66
Monroe Doctrine, 28, 207
Montesquieu, C. L. de, 15
Moore, R. Walton, 102–103, 105, 108, 112–113

Moralistic tradition (U.S. foreign policy), 105
Morgan, George, 171
Morgenthau, Hans, 32
Morgenthau, Henry, 102
Moscow Olympics (1980), 236
Moscow State University, 203
Moskovskii Sbornik (Pobedonostsev), 50
Motley, John Lothrop, 26, 31
Moynihan, Patrick, 227
Muggeridge, Malcolm, 104
Mundt, Karl, 176
Muraviev (foreign minister), 60
Muraviev, Nikita, 25
Mussolini, Benito, 124
MX missile, 227, 234

Nagasaki, atomic bombing of, 154
Nagorski, Andrew, 243
Nagy, Imre, 198–199
Napoleon I, 18, 20–21, 162
Napoleon III, 36–37, 44
Narodnaia Volia, 48–49, 64
Nation, 95
National Security Council
    Executive Committee, 208, 216
    NSC 68, 173, 179
National War College, 161, 214–215
NATO. *See* North Atlantic Treaty Organization
Nechaev, Serge, 48
Nelidov, A. I., 62
Nesselrode, Karl von, 28–29
Netherlands, 129
Neutrality Act (1935), 116
New Economic Policy (USSR), 93, 276n.1
New Moscow (painting, Pimenov), 109, 134
New York Herald, 46
New York Magazine, 16
New York Times, 107, 252
Neymann, A. F., 121
Nicholas (grand duke), 47
Nicholas I, 11, 22–29, 53, 68
    empire compared with Stalin's, 32
Nicholas II, 55–56, 57, 59–63, 71, 74
    abdication, 76
    execution, 83
Nicolson, Harold, 5
Nitze, Paul, 187, 214, 227
Nixon, Richard, 204, 221–224, 232, 238
NKVD (Commissarat of Internal Affairs), 141,
    153, 162, 196
Nonaggression pact (1939), 7, 123–125, 129–
    130, 148
North Atlantic Treaty Organization, 159, 165,
    170, 179, 193, 198, 205
North Star (film), 137
Norway, 130
Noulens, Joseph, 79, 81
Novikov, Nikolai, 160
NSC 68, 173, 179
Nye, Gerald, 114

October Manifesto, 63
"Ode to Freedom" (Radishchev), 15
Odom, William, 230
Office of Strategic Services, 153
Offshore islands crisis, 195
OGPU (Unified State Political Administration),
    116
Ohio State University, 213
Open Door Notes, 60
Operation Barbarosa, 131
Oregon Territory, 29
Orlov, Yuri, 243
Orr, James, 64
Orthodox Church (USSR), persecution of, 97
OSS. *See* Office of Strategic Services
Osteuropa Institute, 107
Oswald, Lee Harvey, 246
Ottoman Empire, 14, 239
Oumansky, Constantine, 113, 128, 131

Page, Edward, 143, 148, 155
Pahlen, Count Feodor, 18, 21
Paine, Thomas, 16
Paleologue, Maurice, 70, 73, 79
Palmer, A. M. (attorney general), 96
Palmer, Mark, 246
Palmerston, Lord (prime minister), 36–37,
    187
Panin, Nikita, 14
Panofsky, Wolfgang, 234
Panyushkin, Semenovich, 179
Paris Conference (1960), 206
Parker, Ralph, 182
Parsons, Herbert, 58
Passenger to Frankfurt (Christie), 238
Pasternak, Boris, 11–12, 197
Paul I, 22
Paulus, Friedrich (field marshal), 138
Pavlov, Valentin, 247
Pearl Harbor, 136
Penn, Phyllis, 214
Perestroika, 249
Perkins, Benjamin, 45–46
Perovskaya, Sophia, 64
Pershing II missile, 240
Pestel, Paul, 25
Peterhoff (British ship) episode, 36
Peter the Great, 11, 17, 26
Philippines, 200
Philips, William, 102
Philosophical Letters (Chaadaev), 23–24
Pickens, Francis, 32
Pierce, Franklin, 29–30
Pimenov, Yuri, 109–110
Pindell, Henry, 66, 71
Pinkos, Henry, 50–51
Pipes, Richard, 246
Pittman, Key, 70, 123
Plehve, Viacheslav, 57
Pobedonostsev, Constantine, 50, 54, 57
Podgorny, Nikolai, 226

Pogroms, 35, 50–51
  at Kishnev (1903), 57
Pokrovsky, Nicholas, 75
Poland, 17, 23, 29, 46, 66, 102, 104, 114, 151,
  155–159, 162, 165, 227, 248
  insurrection (1863), 37–38, 43
  invasion by USSR (1939), 126–127
Policy Planning Staff (State Department), 161,
  183–184, 214
Political dissidents (Russia), 6, 35, 52–53, 62–
  63
Political Pilgrims (Hollander), 4
Politics Among Nations (Morgenthau), 32
Politis, M., 173
Polk, Frank, 73
Pol Pot, 106
Popov (admiral), 37
Popov, Gavril, 247
Post, Marjorie Merriweather, 109
Potemkin, Gregory, 14
Potsdam Conference (1945), 134, 137, 153
Powell, Jody, 229
Powers, Gary, 204
Pravda, 81, 102, 147, 184, 242, 250
Princeton University, 98
Prinkipo Conference, 85
Propaganda war against U.S. by USSR, 181–
  182
Protocols of the Elders of Zion, 58
Protopopov, A. D., 74
Provisional Government, 59, 67, 76–79
Prussia, 17, 23
  Franco-Prussian War, 47
Pueblo (U.S. ship) episode, 220
Pugachev, Emelian, 14
Pugo, Boris, 251
Purges (USSR), 6, 109–110, 118–119, 121,
  123, 164
Pushkin, Alexander, 11, 31
Pyatakov, Gregory, 109, 120

Radek, Karl, 83, 109, 112, 115, 120
Radishchev, Alexander, 15, 22
Ramsey, Norman, 217
Randolph, John, 27–28, 32, 66, 258
Rapallo agreement, 85, 97
Rasputin, Gregory, 68, 75
Rathenau, Walter, 97
Reagan, Ronald, 227, 240–242, 245, 251
Recognition of USSR (U.S.), 101–103, 105
Red Army, 123, 131, 149, 154–156
  achievements, 137
  countries occupied by, 160
  estimates of size (1948), 168
Redin, Nikolai, 173
Redwood City Tribune, 176–177
Reed, John, 67, 79, 86, 110
Reishchauer, Edwin, 213
Relations, U.S.–Russian, established (1809), 18
Repin, Ilya, 50
"Requiem" (Akhmatova), 134

Reston, James, 220
Retch (newspaper), 59
"Revenge" (Blok), 268n.41
Revolutionary War (U.S.), 12–14
Revolution of 1848, 30
Reykjavik Conference, 243
Reynolds, Quentin, 148
Ribbentrop, Joachim von, 137
Riga listening post, 6, 96–101
Rimestad, Idar, 203
Roberts, Frank, 160, 167 .
Robertson, Walter, 205
Robeson, Paul, 94
Robins, Raymond, 6, 67, 78, 81–84, 87, 100–
  101
Rodzyanko, Michael, 77
Rogers, Will, Jr., 177
Rogers, William, 221–223
Rogers Act (1924), 98, 178, 254
Rolland, Romain, 95
Rollback, 194
Romania, 81, 104, 114, 129, 213
Romanov dynasty, 22, 35, 56
Rome–Berlin Axis, 124
Romm, Vladimir, 121
Roosevelt, Eleanor, 159, 203
Roosevelt, Franklin D., 6–7, 100, 104, 106–
  108, 110–111, 115–117, 122–126, 132–
  137, 139, 141, 143–153, 155, 162, 177,
  180, 192
  death, Soviet response, 154
  moral embargo against USSR, 127–128, 130
  reasons for recognizing USSR, 101–102,
  105
  relations with Harriman, 156–158
  Soviet policy, criticized, 119
  and State Department, 140
  unconditional surrender policy, 138
Roosevelt, Theodore, 58–59, 61–62, 88
  attitude toward Nicholas II, 60
Root, Elihu, 77–78
Rosengolts, Arkady, 121
Rosenthal, Andrew, 252
Rostow, Eugene, 227
Rostropovich, Mstislav, 225, 245
Rothschild, Lord, 54
Rukeyser, Walter Arnold, 95
Rumiantsev, Nikolai, 18–19, 21–22
Rusk, Dean, 205, 208–209, 216, 255
Russell, Bertrand, 94
Russell (foreign secretary, U.K.), 36
Russell, Richard, 145
Russia in 1839 (Custine), 23–24
Russian-American Company in Alaska, 28
Russian Revolution (1905), 60–63
Russiia Viedomosti (newspaper), 59
Russo-Japanese War, 35, 60–63
Rykov, Alexis, 93, 109

Sacco, Nicola, trial and execution of, 96
Sadoul, Jacques, 79

Saint Petersburg
  depictions of, 11–12, 26
  society, contrasted with Washington, D.C.,
    18–19
Saint Petersburg legation (U.S.)
  inadequate salaries at, 28, 65
  increased appreciation of America at, 32
  isolation of, 26
  strain of life at, 27
Sakharov, Andrei, 171, 191, 230
SALT I, 221
SALT II, 226–227, 230–232, 234, 236–237
SALT III, 227
San Francisco Conference (1945), 154
Sayre, Stephen, 14
Sazanov, Sergei, 58–59, 68, 73, 75
Schapiro, Leonard, 108
Schiff, Jacob, 56
Schlesinger, James, 244
Schleswig-Holstein crisis, 43
Schneck, Abraham, 146
Schuman, Robert, 257
Schuyler, Eugene, 47–49
Scott, John, 95
Scowcroft, Brent, 234, 250–251, 253–254
Semyonova, Polina, 191
Service, John, 176
Seward, William, 37–38, 40, 43, 45–46
  on selection of ambassadors, 65
Seymour, Thomas, 30, 53
Shatalin, Stanislaw, 251
Shattered Peace (Yergin), 100
Shaw, George Bernard, 94
Shevardnadze, Eduard, 242, 245, 247–248
Short, William, 18
Shriver, Sargeant, 229
Shultz, George, 241–245
Shvernik, Nikolai, 180
Siberia and the Exile System (Kennan, elder), 52
Simon, Sir John, 116
Sino-Soviet alliance, 7
Sino-Soviet dispute, 205–206, 223
Sisson, Edgar, 72, 86–87
Six-Day War, 213
SLEDGEHAMMER (World War II), 144
Slepak, Alexander, 231
Slidell, John, 36
Slonimsky, Nicholas, 217
Smith, Al, 149
Smith, Emory, 53
Smith, John Spear, 19
Smith, Raymond, 215
Smith, Walter Bedell, 32–33, 168–169, 174,
    176, 186–188, 192, 214, 254
  preambassadorial career, 166
  talk with Stalin (1946), 166–167
Snowe, Olympia, 244
Socialist justice, promise of, vii
Society for the Prevention of Cruelty to Ani-
    mals, 41
Sokolovsky (marshal), 166

Solzhenitsyn, Alexander, 52, 223, 251
Somalia, 227
Song of Russia (film), 137
Soviet Union, collapse of, 4, 239
Spain, 124
Spaso House, 111, 116, 120, 140, 175, 179,
    183, 196, 216, 235, 242, 245, 253–254,
    256
  invaded by secret microphones, 128
  strained life in, 182
Speransky, Count Mikhail, 19
Sportsman's Sketches (Turgenev), 37
Sputnik, 206
Stalin, Joseph, vii, 7, 12, 74, 93, 100, 103–
    105, 109, 111, 113–114, 118–119, 124–
    125, 127–134, 141–142, 144–145, 147–
    153, 155–156, 158–159, 161–162, 164,
    168–172, 175, 179–182, 184, 186, 200,
    202, 209, 215
  attempts to work with Third Reich, 102
  cult of, 191
  death of, 7, 191–192, 293n.1
  deification of, in civic religion, 108
  diplomatic channel with U.S., minor role of,
    116
  1946 speech on need for socialist vigilance,
    160
Stalingrad, Soviet victory at 137–138
Stamm (lieutenant), 148
Standley, William, 143, 148–153, 162
  meeting with Stalin, 141–142
  preambassadorial career, 139–140
  on Soviet ingratitude for lend-lease, 145–146
Stanford University, 176–177, 224
Starr, Frederick, 233
START, 251–252
State Secrets Act (USSR), 173
Stefan, Charles, 196
Steiger, Boris, 112
Steinhardt, Laurence, 108–109, 124, 126, 129,
    131, 133–135, 168, 201, 254
  attitude toward Soviet invasion of Finland,
    127–128
  marginalization of and resignation, 132
  on 1939 nonaggression pact, 129–130
  preambassadorial career, 125
  on probable Red Army defeat by Germany,
    131
Stevens, John, 78
Stevens, Thaddeus, 45
Stevenson, Adlai, 159, 185
Stines, Norman, 176, 187
  case against, 177–178
Stinger missile, 240
Stoeckl, Baron Edouard de, 37–38, 43–45
Stoessel, Walter, 229, 232, 238, 254
  career and background, 224–225
  political reporting, 225–226
Stolypin, Peter, 57, 63
Stone, Irving, 217
Stowe, Harriet Beecher, 37

Strang, Lord, 256
Strategic Defense Initiative, 240
Straus, Oscar, 56
Strauss, Robert, 239, 251–253
Sturmer, Boris, 75
Suez crisis (1956), 199
Summers, Maddin, 79, 84, 97, 100
Sumner, Charles, 38, 45
Suvorov, Alexander, 16
Swank, Emory, 220–221
Sweden, 14
Synagman Rhee, 198

Taft, Alphonso, 64, 66
Taft, Robert, 194–195
Taft, William, 58, 62
Taiwan, 205
Talmon, J. L., 108
Tannenberg, battle of, 66
Tanzania, 246
Taylor, Bayard, 41–43
Teheran Conference (1943), 137–138, 144, 147, 151, 153, 158
Thayer, Charles, 112, 117–118, 126, 176
Third International. 88. See also Comintern
Thomas, Lowell, 237
Thomas, Norman, 177
Thompson, Jane, 202–204, 208
Thompson, Llewellyn, 3–4, 7, 126, 192, 205–207, 210–211, 213, 215, 234–235, 237–238, 246, 248, 254–256
    background, 200–201
    intimacy with Khrushchev, 202–203
    role in Cuban missile crisis, 208–209
    second tour (1966), 219–221
Thompson, William Boyce, 87
Thurmond, Strom, 222
Thurston, Walter, 126, 140
Tito, Josip (marshal), 169, 192, 198
Tkachev, Peter, 48
"To a Friend" (Pasternak), 94
Tocqueville, Alexis de, 23
Todd, Charles, 26, 31
Tolstoy, Count Dimitri, 48
Tolstoy, Leo, 31, 50, 54, 65
Toon, Malcolm, 182, 215, 225, 229–233, 235, 238, 254
    background and career, 227–228, 231
Totalitarianism, 108, 134, 162, 169, 214, 256
Toynbee, Arnold, 178
Train, Russell, 226
Treaty of Brest-Litovsk (1918), 83, 143
Treaty of Ghent (1814), 21
Treaty of Paris (1783), 16
Treaty of Tilsit (1807), 18
Treaty of Vienna (1815), 21
Tree, Lambert, 53
Trent (British ship) episode, 36
Trepov, Alexander, 75
Trepov, Feodor, 49

Trevelyan, Humphrey, 219
Tripartite Pact (1940), 130
Trotsky, Leon, 78–80, 82, 86, 93, 100, 118, 136, 149
Troyanovsky, Alexander, 111, 123
Truman, Harry, 134, 154, 158–159, 161–162, 165–167, 173, 178, 180, 182, 185, 201
    decision to produce hydrogen bomb, 171
Truman Doctrine, 186
Truth About American Diplomats (Bucar), 174, 182
Tuck, S. Pickney, 97
Tucker, Evgenia, 173
Tucker, Robert, 104, 173
Tukhachevsky, Mikhail (marshal), 109
Turchin, John (colonel), 37
Turgenev, Ivan, 31, 37
Turkey, 14, 16, 23, 130, 133, 160, 167, 209
    Jupiter missiles based in, 216
    treaty with U.S. (1830), 29
Twain, Mark, 46, 52
Twenty-Third Party Congress, 218

Ukraine, 252, 257
Ulam, Adam, 168
Ulbricht, Walter, 205
Uncle Tom's Cabin (Stowe), 37
Unconditional surrender policy, 138, 143, 152, 158
Union of American Hebrew Congregations, 51
Union (U.S.), 35, 42
United Nations, 139, 154, 159, 167, 179
University of Chicago, 72, 107
University of Colorado, 201
University of Michigan, 26, 53
University of Paris, 98
Ustinov, Dmitri, 237
U-2 episode, 204, 206

Valéry, Paul, 212
Van Buren, Martin, 28
Vance, Cyrus, 227, 231–233, 235–237
Vandenberg, Arthur, 127
Vanzetti, Bartolomeo, trial and execution of, 96
Vashchenko family, 231
Vasielevsky (marshal), 154
Verac, Marquis de, 13
Versailles peace, 3
Vicence, Duc de, 20
Vietnam War, 33, 211, 213, 219–220, 223
Vlasov, Alexander, 250
Vlasov, Andrei (general), 137
"Voice for Russia" (Botkine), 52
Voice of America, 173, 214
Vologda, 82–83, 141
Voltaire, 15
Voroshilov, Clement, 110, 113
Voznesensky, Andrei, 246
Vyshinsky, Andrei, 141, 165–166, 172, 185
    meeting with Kennan, 180

"Wait for Me" (Simonov), 136
Wallace, Henry, 160, 167
Walsh, Edmund (priest), 101
Walsh, Robert, 17
War and Peace (Tolstoy), 141
War Communism, 93
Ward, Angus, 110, 126
War of 1812, 18
Warsaw Pact, 165, 198, 248
    invasion of Czechoslovakia, 213, 220
Washington and Lee University, 97
Washington University, 71
Watergate, influence on Soviet perceptions of détente, 226
Watson, Olive, 234–235
Watson, Thomas, 4, 232–238, 241, 258
    preambassadorial career, 233–234
Webb, Beatrice, 94
Webb, Sidney, 94
Welles, Gideon, 38
Welles, Sumner, 123, 125, 127, 130–131, 146
Wells, H. G., 94
West Germany, 198
White, Andrew Dickson, 26, 35, 53–57, 59, 64, 258
    view of Russian civilization, 65
White, Thomas, 110, 112
Wilcyznski, Marx, 50–51
Wiley, Alexander, 192
Wiley, Johyn, 110, 114, 117
Wilhelm II, 61, 69
Willkie, Wendell, 148
    meeting with Stalin, 144–145
Wilson, Charles, 69–70
Wilson, Hugh, 123
Wilson, Woodrow, 4, 66, 68, 70–71, 73, 77, 83–84, 86–87, 105, 114, 138
    Fourteen Points, 88–89
    1916 offer to mediate European war, 74
    poor understanding of Russia, 76
Winant, John, 149
"Wind of War, The" (Akmatova), 136
Winship, North, 86
Witkin, Zara, 95

Witte, Sergei, 56–57
World War, Soviet attitude toward, 206
World War I, 5–6, 11, 86, 88, 139, 254, 256.
    See also specific sujects
    Russian aims, 67
    Russian casualties, 67
World War II, 4–5, 7, 88, 121, 134, 138, 166, 213, 255. *See also specific subjects*
    American POWs in Soviet custody, 155
    second front, 134, 143–145
    Soviet casualties, 162
    Soviet interpretation of, 136–137
Wotton, Sir Henry, 133–134

X article, 34

Yale University, 98, 124
Yalta Conference (1945), 100–101, 137–138, 152–153, 156–158, 192–193
Yanayev, Gennadi, 251, 258
Yasnya Polyana, 112
Yazov, Dimitri, 247, 258
Yeaton, Ivan (major), 131
Yegorov, Alexander (marshal), 111
Yeltsin, Boris, 248, 250–253
    rivalry with Gorbachev, 250
Yergin, Daniel, 100
Yom Kippur War, 224, 227
Yugoslavia, 129–130, 136, 155, 198, 213, 257
    split with USSR, 165, 176

Zakharov, Gennadi, 243
Zanzibar, 246
Zaroubin, Georgi, 185
Zasulich, Vera, 49
Zhdanovshchina, 164
Zheleznyakov, A. G., 81
Zhironovsky, Vladimir, 257
Zhukov, Georgi (marshal), 166, 195, 198–199, 206
    removal from Presidium, 204
Zimmerman, Warren, 241
Zimmermann telegram, 75
Zinoviev, Gregory, 82, 93, 109, 117–118